MW00799702

THE MINT
ON CARSON STREET

A TRIBUTE TO THE CARSON CITY MINT &
A GUIDE TO A COMPLETE SET OF "CC" COINS

By Rusty Goe

Acknowledgments

Sources and credits for pictures and quotes have been cited in captions or footnotes.

Special acknowledgements go to:

Jim Richards for offering his layout artist services in the early stages of the project to show us what the finished work might actually look like; Hal V. Dunn for being generous in sharing his postcards and other Carson City memorabilia; Gordon Harris for tracking down a picture for the section on Norman Biltz; Jack Haddock for checking in every once in awhile and providing some 19th century newspapers from Nevada; John F. Nash for sharing information about his stepfather Norman H. Biltz; Jane Colvard at the American Numismatic Association library for help checking out reference material upon request; Deanna LaBonge at the Nevada Historical Library in Carson City for being a friendly librarian during the early stages of this project; Bob Nylen at the Nevada State Museum for ordering pictures we requested; and various members of the staff at Southgate Coins and Collectibles for clerical assistance.

Final layout and typography was performed by Jennifer Meers, who also served as proofreader, copy-editor, and graphic design consultant.

No one deserves more credit than my wife Marie Goe; for running the ship at Southgate Coins throughout the duration of this lengthy project and for enduring months of my absence from home life. She is much more than a wife to me, for which I am very grateful.

ON THE COVER

A street scene in front of the Carson City Mint looking north to the V&T Railroad depot, circa 1890s. (*Courtesy Nevada State Museum • Stagecoach art courtesy Wells Fargo*)

© 2003 by Rusty Goe and Southgate Coins and Collectibles.
Second Printing © 2004

All rights reserved, including duplication of any kind or storage in electronic or visual retrieval systems. Permission is granted for use of brief excerpts from this book in printed reviews, magazine articles, and coin catalogues, provided credit is given to the author and the title of the work. Written permission is required for other uses of the information or illustrations in books or in electronic or other media.

ISBN-0-9746169-1-5

Published by

SOUTHGATE COINS AND COLLECTIBLES
P.O. Box 17068
Reno, NV 89511

The Mint on Carson Street

Table of Contents

Introduction

Miners panning

$20 Gold Pieces will be as plentiful as blackberries.
                                    - Abraham Curry. Carson City, NV 1867

Coins will soon be rattling out like peas out of a hopper.
                                    - Carson Daily Appeal, 1866

During the years the Carson City Mint was open for business, rumors circulated about clandestine operations involving skimming, producing illegal coins, bribery of employees, and forgeries of accounting records. Investigations were ongoing and deliberations constantly ensued in Washington D.C. about whether to shut the facility down, or allow it to remain open, oftentimes on a suspensatory basis.

When the mint at Carson City, Nevada was under construction, allegations were filed against the building contractor, who was also recognized as the town's founder. He was charged with, among other things, being unpatriotic and for publicly criticizing the President of the United States. To counter such accusations, the *Father of the Carson City Mint* sent testimonials in his honor from Nevada's Governor and both U.S. Senators to Treasury officials. And for good measure, he publicly promised to send the first $20 gold piece minted on opening day to the President.

From the day the Carson City Mint opened, demands that it be closed were lodged by bureaucrats in Washington. Only a cunning and winsome speech by a golden-tongued orator from Nevada's legislature saved the local mint from extinction just three months into its inaugural year.

Underlying this serial drama of real-life events was the backdrop of the prodigious Comstock Lode that defined an era. Within three years of the Carson Mint's commencement, the nation was embroiled in a political battle over monetary standards. Congress passed an act demonetizing standard silver dollars, creating a line of demarcation unparalleled since the Civil War.

Nevada's own political leaders and mining industry barons vacillated between self-serving interests and loyalty to the state, which in time weakened Nevada's economic base and threatened its statehood.

Two of America's most controversial coin denominations were introduced during the duration of the Carson City Mint's service. One of the dates minted of the short-lived 20-cent denomination, 1876-CC, became a recognized rarity amongst coin collectors within 15 years after being struck.

Explorer, frontiersman, Kit Carson. *(Dictionary of American Portraits, Dover Publications)*

More than a century after the Carson City Mint released its final coin, every collector and many non-collectors have become familiar with the silver dollars with the two "C"s. Yet, despite this acquaintance with the mint's coins, very little is known about what went on behind the scenes while the coins were being produced. Hundreds of obscure facts have been hidden in time, as have many of the individual biographies from a roster of interesting personalities.

Though the "CC" coins are known worldwide and certain aspects of this mint's history have been re-told countless times, still it is as if modern collectors were looking through a dusky window revealing nothing but a blurred reflection of all that happened when examining this fascinating theme. Much is known at face level, but little below the surface about arguably the most popular mint in the coin collecting world.

A VERY EXPENSIVE DIME

On May 22, 1996, a dime struck by employees at the Carson City Mint in 1873 sold for $550,000 at an auction in New York City. There had been 12,400 of these dimes coined, certainly a low mintage figure, but not consistent with the price it sold for. In comparison, another 10-cent piece minted in 1894 at San Francisco was one of only 24 pieces minted, a small number to be sure. This 1894-S dime had been a recognized "celebrity" coin for 100 years. There are nine known examples,

Typical gunslinger of the old West. (*Photo courtesy The Nevada Historical Society*)

and one of them sold on the same night as the 1873-CC *Without Arrows* dime for $451,000! But why does a coin with a mintage of 12,400 sell for $550,000? The laws that rule coin collecting provide an answer for every seemingly baffling experience (most of them anyway). In the case of the 1873-CC *Without Arrows* dime, although 12,400 were minted, only one specimen survives today. Theories abound attempting to explain how this happened, but if you think it has to do with lost or melted coins, you are probably right on target. In the early years of the 21st century this illustrious dime will trade hands for $1 million.

Carson City has a history of puzzling and unpredictable happenings. Everything associated with it is very intriguing, in contrast to everyday life which can be boring enough. Enthusiasts who collect Carson City coins usually receive more enjoyment than they anticipate; certainly the collector who paid $550,000 for the 1873-CC *Without Arrows* dime did. Think about it. The first person who owned this dime paid 10 cents for it. According to Q. David Bowers, after the coin had served as an assay specimen, "a numismatist – quite possibly a member of the Mint staff asked for the coin for face value."[1]

Most reports agree that the coin was retained at the Mint in Philadelphia and through a series of exchanges and negotiations, eventually came into the possession of William H. Woodin, who later served in FDR's cabinet as Secretary of the Treasury. This coin had three subsequent owners prior to November 1950, at which time it was purchased by Louis E. Eliasberg, Sr. for the reported sum of $4,000, completing his world famous collection.

GROWING POPULARITY

In the 80 years immediately following the first mintage of coins at Carson City (1870-1950), only two issues from that mint were counted among the more celebrated coins produced at a U.S. mint since the Mint's founding in 1792: the 1876-CC 20-cent piece, with an estimated surviving population of fewer than 20 pieces is one example; the 1873-CC *Without Arrows* quarter, with only three specimens known, could hold its own in top 25 lists with ease. When Louis Eliasberg bought the 1873-CC *Without Arrows* dime, the collecting community realized that it was time to place it in the number one position on the list of rarities from the Carson City Mint.

Through the second half of the 20th century, coins from the Carson City Mint soared to the top of want lists, with many dates becoming highly regarded. From the 1980s on, it was not uncommon for the rarest "CC" coins to sell for six figures. In 1975, an 1873-CC *Without Arrows* quarter from the *James A. Stack Collection* sold for $80,000 plus the buyer's fee, nearly reaching the six-figure level. Thirty years earlier, in the auction Abe Kosoff titled *The World's Greatest Collection,* a similar Uncirculated specimen sold for $750, a lot of money in 1945. And for comparison, in that same auction, an 1876-CC 20-cent piece sold for $1,500, a 1794 Choice Uncirculated silver dollar brought $2,000, the first year of issue 1795 $10 gold piece in Gem Uncirculated sold for $190 and, after fierce bidding, a Gem Uncirculated MCMVII (1907) $20 gold High Relief went to a winning bidder for $130. Just a few years earlier, in 1941, a Choice Uncirculated 1804 silver dollar, the *King of Coins,* had sold for $4,250. Shifting back to the previously mentioned 1975 *James Stack*

[1] Bowers and Merena, *The Louis E. Eliasberg, Sr. Collection,* April 1996.

sale, a 1901-S Gem Uncirculated Barber quarter sold for $5,500, and a choice prooflike 1796 quarter found a new home for a strong winning bid of $9,000, both considered major rarities, yet overshadowed by the 1873-CC *Without Arrows* quarter.

THE EXCITING 1970S

In addition to the *James Stack* sale, the 1970s are also remembered for the GSA *Black Box* Carson City silver dollars sold by the U.S. government through the mail. Collectors began scouring coin shows looking for coins with the "CC" mintmark and a common bourse floor question was "Hey, you got any "CC's?" Ads in coin trade papers were scanned from front to back by collectors looking for "CC" coins. Collectors' attention was also focused on Nevada when in 1974, long time Reno resident LaVere Redfield died and over 400,000 silver dollars were discovered in the appraisal of his estate. While most locals were more interested in the land Redfield owned, within a few years his silver dollars made headlines in collector publications. After a series of negotiations with the Redfield estate, A-Mark Corp. in California purchased the massive hoard and commissioned the Paramount Coin Company in Ohio to market the silver dollars, which included Carson City coins as well as those from other mints. Regardless, the promotions made it known that the silver dollars had come from Nevada and this was perfect for marketing purposes.

Sales of GSA "Black Box" "CC" silver dollars thrived during this period. Nevada had been called the "Silver State" for decades and was becoming known for silver dollars. After all, the casinos in the state had used silver dollars on their tables and in slot machines for years. It was very popular for tourists to bring a few of the silver dollars back home as souvenirs and gifts. When the book opened on the story of this fascinating, freewheeling and fun loving state, the desire to own coins from its State mint in Carson City grew stronger and stronger. Read on and you will learn many exciting facts and be introduced to an assortment of captivating people.

A VARIETY OF COLLECTING OPPORTUNITIES

A dime, a 20-cent piece, a quarter, a half dollar, three different types of silver dollars, and $5, $10, and $20 gold pieces comprise a set of the coin denominations produced at the Carson City Mint. From this group, the dime, quarter, half dollar, and one of the silver dollars bear the Seated Liberty design. And the 20-cent piece resembles the Seated Liberty coins on the obverse, but has an eagle similar to that of the trade dollar on the reverse and features plain edges instead of reeded. The trade dollar is unique in appearance, as is the easily recognizable Morgan silver dollar. Rounding out this set, the three gold coin issues are all of the Coronet Liberty Head style.

The story behind the Carson City Silver Dollars

The Carson City Mint in Nevada produced only 13 years of the silver dollar designed by George T. Morgan. Known as the Morgan dollars, they all bear the unique "CC" mint mark — the only mint to use more than one letter on its coins. The Carson City Mint was closed in 1893 and no coins have been minted there since that year.

All coins stored there were shipped to other mints and Federal Reserve Banks throughout the Country. But, with the large number of silver dollars in circulation at the time and the growing popularity of one dollar bills, there was no demand for the silver "cartwheels" produced at Carson City.

In the early 1900s the demands for silver to support the war effort resulted in massive coin melts. The stored CC dollars were thought to have been lost in the melts. However, in 1964, when silver was no longer used in coinage or for the redemption of silver certificates, the General Accounting Office made an audit of the Treasury's silver dollars and discovered nearly three million uncirculated silver dollars from the long-closed Carson City Mint.

Under Public Law 91-607, Congress authorized the General Services Administration (GSA) to sell the last of the Government's holdings of 90% silver dollars. The law requires GSA to adhere to the sale plan approved by the Joint Commission on the Coinage in disposing of the 2.9 million Carson City Silver Dollars. The commission considered many different proposals for selling the coins and decided on the present method as the most equitable way of making these coins available to the American public. The Silver Dollars must be sold by public mail bid with a pre-established minimum price set near their numismatic value. The proceeds from these sales will be returned to the General Fund of the U.S. Treasury for the benefit of the American public.

Prior to the sale beginning, a representative sampling of the total Carson City Silver Dollar holdings was examined by a team of numismatic experts. In addition to the team's finding that the vast majority of the coins were in excellent condition, a large number of errors, varieties and types were found. It has been the GSA's policy throughout the sale to award all coins, regardless of any unusual aspects of individual coins which might enhance their value, on a completely random basis. The packaging has been performed in such a way that, at the time of bid awards, no one knows any characteristics of the coin in a package other than the year. In the case of the Mixed CC's, even the year is unknown.

This is your opportunity to acquire a true legacy from the days of America's great silver mining era.

General Services Administration
Arthur F. Sampson, Administrator

Typical silver mining scene, late 1880s.

THE CARSON CITY SILVER DOLLARS THE LAST OF A LEGACY

Portion of the brochure from the GSA sales of "CC" silver dollars in the 1970s. (*Author's personal collection*)

ABRAHAM CURRY

On October 21, 1873, Abe Curry died in the city he founded, Carson City, Nevada. He was 58 ½ years old and had suffered a stroke several days earlier. The city of Carson was in mourning and locals staged an elaborate funeral. Telegrams and letters poured in from all over the country. President Grant sent his condolences, the Director of the U.S. Mint at Philadelphia sent his respects, and Senators and Congressmen expressed their sympathies. The story was carried as front-page news in papers from Colorado to California. In respect to its founder, the Carson City Mint closed for a day in spite of backlogs in coin production.

Abraham Curry's legacy and the influence he wielded to a certain degree extended into many peoples' lives and to events in the history of the United States. For coin collectors throughout the past 125 years, Curry's accomplishments have been a catalyst for the passionate pursuit of coins with the "CC" mintmark.

"CC" and "C" mintmarks.

Abraham Curry came to northern Nevada in 1858, and together with a group of several men purchased the Mormon settlement at Eagle Valley on the land that would become historic Carson City (a town that could have easily been named Curry City). Curry endeavored fearlessly to give the new city respectability and as good fortune would have it, gold and silver were discovered 15 miles to the east in Virginia City, Gold Hill and Silver City.

Curry worked hard to have a mint established near the town site, and finally in 1863 during the Civil War, the U.S. Treasury authorized a branch mint to be built. On January 8, 1870 the Carson City Mint opened and was ready for production. In the western states where the coins were distributed, people found it strange that there were two letters for the mintmark. But the "C" mintmark had already been used from 1838 to 1861 at Charlotte, North Carolina. In later years, this "CC" mintmark would add to the fascination of the coinage from this mint.

1873: AN IMPORTANT YEAR

In October of 1873, the United States was experiencing severe economic conditions, especially in the East. This caused the value of silver to decline and created a ripple effect that flowed to the mining states of the West.

Many remedies were suggested to avert substantial losses and a collapse of the economy. One such solution was to redeem the estimated $46 million in circulating fractional paper money for silver coins, creating a demand for silver, thus causing silver prices to rise. Naturally, Nevada was 100% behind this plan, and a dying Abe Curry was one of the plan's staunchest supporters.

It was also in 1873 that the first trade dollars were minted, another story in itself; but the circumstances surrounding the introduction of the new trade dollar greatly affected the State of Nevada.

THE ATTRACTIONS OF CARSON CITY COINAGE

From all of this emerged the coinage that has become the most popular, as a whole, of all of the coins ever minted in the United States. That is a big statement and some may argue that individual coins like the 1804 dollar, 1913 Liberty Head nickel, 1933 Saint-Gaudens $20, or series such as Early American coppers or California Fractional gold outshine Carson City coinage. Still, the "CC" coins encompass many of the qualities that make coin collecting exciting and enjoyable to a mass audience.

First, there is the legend, myth, history, art and romance that draw people into coin collecting. Without a doubt, the Old West theme is a very popular genre, and western movies, western TV series, and western novels elicit more interest and enthusiasm than those of practically any other theme. And the fact that "CC" coins were minted in a city that birthed the legend of the *Bonanza/Ponderosa* era have excited large segments of the population. It is one thing to imagine a cowboy slapping a silver dollar or a $10 gold piece made in Philadelphia on the bar of a saloon. It is quite another thing to imagine this happening in the same city where the coin was minted. Perhaps it is safe to speculate that if coins had been minted in Dodge City, Kansas or Tombstone, Arizona they would generate the same enthusiasm as Carson City coins do. It is providence, however, that allowed this small town at the foot of the Sierra, not far from Lake Tahoe, the largest alpine lake in America, to represent, through its coinage, the Old West saga that is incredibly popular not only in the United States, but worldwide. It is little wonder that when the GSA "CC" silver dollars were sold, one of the advertising slogans was *"The Coins Jesse James Never Got."*

Lake's Crossing on the Truckee River in 1868. Within a year the name would be changed to Reno.

Secondly, the Carson City Mint shares with Charlotte and Dahlonega the distinction of having produced coins during a brief 23 year period, offering collectors a limited number of dates and coins, but a diverse choice of sets to work on. And this diversity of possible collections is the third enticement Carson City coins offer to collectors. There is the ever popular "CC" Morgan dollar set consisting of 13 dates (14 if the 1900-O/CC is included). Next might be a type set of all the different denominations that were minted at Carson City, which consists of the dime, 20-cent piece, quarter dollar, half dollar, Seated Liberty dollar, trade dollar, Morgan dollar and the $5, $10 and $20 gold pieces. There is also the complete set of every date and denomination minted at Carson City comprising 111 pieces. As of this writing only Louis Eliasberg is noted for having successfully completed this task, which will be showcased in a later chapter, as will the sets of two other collectors who came close, one with 109 pieces and the other with 110. Of course there are many variations of these collecting choices, such as just the silver coins, a complete set of $5 gold pieces, or a set of trade dollars. It all becomes clear that Carson City coinage offers the collector many choices, all challenging, exciting and rewarding.

Classic rarities from the Carson City Mint are a fourth attraction, with dates like the 1876-CC 20-cent piece, 1873-CC *Without Arrows* quarter and the premiere 1873-CC *Without Arrows* dime of which there is only one known. And, unlike some other celebrated rarities such as the 1804 dollar, 1913 Liberty nickel and the $4 gold Stellas, all coins from the Carson City Mint were produced for circulation.

Like most legends, the mystique of the Carson City Mint, because of its location, its association with the old west and its short life span, will be permanently etched, like snapshot photos of movie stars who died in their prime, in the minds and imaginations of collectors as long as there are *Red Books*.

THE AUTHOR'S GOAL

The goal of this book is to provide readers with a brief profile of the life and times of the Carson City Mint and in the process describe the coins produced there. Whether you are a beginning coin collector or a seasoned dealer specializing in "CC" coins, hopefully you will be absorbed from beginning to end. If you are new to coin collecting, perhaps you will develop a curiosity for coins with the "CC" mintmark and learn things about this hobby that will make your collecting days more rewarding. If you have collected coins for many years, and already have a passion for "CC" coins, hopefully you will discover something about the subject you did not know before and find in this book a reminder of why you appreciate coins from this small city in Nevada.

Through the pages of this book, readers will be given a brief summary of the founding of Carson City and the circumstances surrounding how and why a mint was established there. Central to the study are the 111 coins of different date and denomination combinations that were coined at the Carson City Mint. Accordingly, each one will be described, some briefly and some in depth. Also featured are some of the personalities who collected Carson City coins. One such person is Louis E. Eliasberg, Sr., the only collector who owned all 111 varieties at the same time. There is a brief sketch of Eliasberg the collector, with a list of 16 of the key "CC" coins from his collection. Another featured collector is Norman H. Biltz, who played a prominent role in Nevada's emergence from being a sparsely populated mining community to becoming a popular state in which major businesses came to establish national and regional headquarters. Biltz remained behind the scenes during his 45 plus years in Ne-

Main Street, Reno, in 1870.

vada, and several decades after he died in 1973, his collection of 109 of the 111 coins minted at Carson City was put on permanent display at the mint which now serves as the Nevada State Museum. A third collection, which we will call the *Battle Born Collection* was assembled by a native Nevadan and consists of 110 of the 111 possible coins from the Carson City Mint. Early collector interest in the Carson City series will also be discussed, focusing on the period between 1880 and 1950.

You will read personal experiences of collectors pursuing their beloved "CC" coins. A chapter entitled *Collecting Opportunities* explores the many options for building sets of "CC" coins. A comprehensive set of appendices including population figures, price histories, and aggregate market totals, can be found in the back of the book.

It has not been the author's intent to be simply a *compiler of data,* but to also give

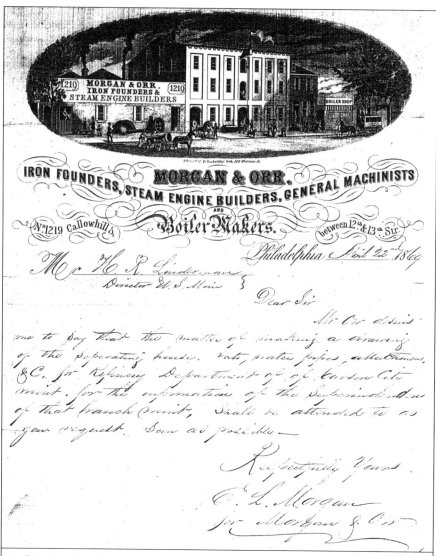

April 22, 1869 letter from C.L. Morgan of Morgan & Orr to H.R. Linderman concerning a request for refinery department equipment at the Carson City Mint. This company made coin presses as well. (*Courtesy Nevada State Museum*)

a personal slant to the information contained in this volume. In writing this guide, the author has made deliberate selections of the people, places, events and special coins that are featured. Undoubtedly, there will be some things left out that you, the reader, will feel should have been included. Hopefully this book will serve as a catalyst to launch you into further study. When the doors of this subject are opened, it becomes clear how expansive a study it can be.

Ironically, there is a city in Michigan also named Carson City. It is doubtful, however, that when this name is mentioned, those that hear it, (other than locals in the Michigan city) think of anyplace other than Carson City, Nevada. The overwhelming popularity of Carson City coins is not exaggerated, they have a universal appeal.

This mint in the Comstock region of northern Nevada could have been located in Virginia City, Gold Hill, Silver City, or Reno. Imagine if you can, mintmarks such as "VC," "GH," "SC," or simply "R." But destiny determined that the mintmark would be "CC" and coins with this impression on their surface have become prime numismatic treasures.

FORMAT OF THE BOOK

Chapters one through five serve as an introduction to the background, related historical events, operations, and ultimate closure and sale of the Carson City Mint. Each of these chapters, though following a chronological timeline, consists of a series of essays or short articles, rather than a continuous narrative. By adopting this style the author has attempted to present in condensed form a wider variety of facts, statistics, political activities, biographical profiles, and anecdotes interrelated both to the Carson City Mint and the years in which it existed. Specific coins of interest from the years covered in each chapter are highlighted, often by synthesizing events occurring well into the 20th century. Readers will be transported back and forth in time and hopefully not get too lost in the time travel.

Chapters six and seven are devoted to a complete set of silver and gold coins from the Carson City Mint. Gold coins from the mint have been studied, examined and so thoroughly described in Doug Winter's book *Gold Coins of the Carson City Mint* that, although included in this guide, are subordinate to the silver coins in terms of attention focused.

Besides statistical data, a *Reflections* section provides pertinent information (sometimes anecdotes) about every coin produced at the Carson City Mint. Any values or population data are as of the year of publication, 2003. It is important to keep in mind that these figures are volatile and subject to change.

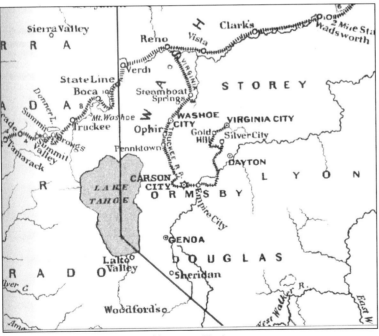

Nevada's Bonanza Territory

THERE'S JUST SOMETHING ABOUT IT...

In certain ways the Carson City Mint can be compared to Saratoga Racetrack in New York. It is not the biggest, not the fanciest, and obviously not all of the classic *performers* have come from there. And like Saratoga, Carson City is certainly not one of the largest communities in the country. But the history and ambience of both places elicit great enjoyment and emotion. Every August, horse race fans flock to Saratoga Racetrack for a brief racing season and those fortunate enough to be there are taken back in time. As a bonus, the Horse Racing Hall of Fame is there, capturing the most memorable moments in horse racing history.

In September of each year, there is a coin show held at the old Carson City Mint building, now home to the Nevada State Museum. In terms of size, it is one of the smallest coin shows in the country, with fewer than 35 dealer tables set up inside, and an auxiliary section outdoors under a tent.

People come from all over the country to attend this two-day event. It is not because the coins on display are any more special than those displayed at larger coin shows. But the show's location at this most popular former U.S. Mint creates a memorable experience for all the attendees. To add to the allure, the dealer tables are set up in the very rooms in which the Carson City Mint conducted business more than 120 years ago. One of the old original coin presses is on display, as are many of the unique artifacts from the Comstock era. One of the highlights of a visit is viewing one of the most memorable and complete sets of "CC" coins ever assembled. Purchasing a coin with the "CC" mintmark while attending this show is thrilling. You are actually purchasing it in the place where it all began.

It is the sincere desire of the author of this book that you will enjoy timeless memories for every moment you spend studying and examining the subject of the Carson City Mint and its coins through these pages. This is in many ways an enthusiast's guide – Enjoy!

CHAPTER ONE

The Birth of a Legend (1870-1873)

Ponderosa Map

Mint marks in their progressive issue at New Orleans, Dahlonega, Charlotte, San Francisco, and Carson City, show the direction of our country's growth and its development of mineral wealth.

- Augustus G. Heaton,
A Treatise On the Coinage of the United States Branch Mints, 1893.

COINAGE RECORD • UNITED STATES MINT AT CARSON CITY, NEVADA

YEAR	DIMES	QUARTERS	HALF DOLLARS	TRADE DOLLARS	DOLLARS	HALF EAGLES	EAGLES	DOUBLE EAGLES	NUMBER OF PIECES	TOTAL $
1870		3,340	54,617		12,462	7,675	5,908	3,789	92,791	$215,090.50
1871	20,100	10,890	139,950		1,376	20,770	7,185	14,687	214,958	545,523.50
1872	24,000	9,100	272,000		3,150	16,980	5,500	29,650	360,380	876,725.00
1873	31,191	16,462	337,060	124,500	2,300	7,416	4,543	22,410	545,882	833,275.60

CARSON CITY'S EARLY DAYS

Abraham Curry was 43 years old when he arrived in the Eagle Valley area of northern Nevada. He had left his wife and five daughters in Cleveland, Ohio, to seek his fortune in the mines of California. He wanted his family to be able to live comfortably and he was willing to sacrifice being separated from them for a season to achieve this goal. Curry brought his 18-year-old son, Charles, on the journey, and during their stay in California, Curry met three men who seemed to share his spirit for adventure. Today, you can drive through modern Carson City and come upon streets or subdivisions named after Benjamin F. Green, Frank M. Proctor, John J. Musser, and Abraham Van Santvoord Curry.

When Abraham Curry arrived in Nevada he was in pursuit of a suitable location to build a general merchandise store. After his first attempt to negotiate with a landowner near the old Mormon site of Genoa, Nevada failed, Curry told his friends that he would build his own city.

Shortly thereafter, Curry and his partners hired a surveyor to examine a ranch that was for sale. Despite the surveyor's advice that the partnership find a new site, Curry and his three partners purchased nearly 1,000 acres of land, and immediately began plotting out what became known as Carson City. In 1858, with foresight and rugged individualism, Curry built a town square and proclaimed that it would one day be the site of a Capitol building. Not incidentally, this was six years before Nevada was even considered for statehood, and in fact, at the time, Nevada was only a district in the Utah Territory.

Abe Curry, a tireless builder and early civic leader.
(Courtesy Nevada State Museum)

Curry and the settlers in the new town site of Carson City survived a severe winter between 1858 and 1859, experiencing a loss of livestock, life threatening food shortages, and threadbare shelters. Then as winter turned to spring in 1859, word of potentially rich mineral deposits nearby sent local fortune seekers scurrying in all directions. Other events were taking shape as well, setting the stage for expansion as well as disaster in the decade to come.

Indian wars and the death of town leader Major William M. Ormsby in the first years of Carson City's settlement added to the hardship being experienced by the locals. In pioneer-like determination, the new city forged ahead, thanks in great part to Curry's resoluteness and leadership. Within no time, Curry's vision began to unfold and troublesome times turned to recreation and levity.

One of Curry's first contracting endeavors was a civic building he used for dances and other public events.

Wherever Curry went, whiskey followed, being one of his favorite gifts to distribute to his friends. Outdoor activities were very much a part of the locals' recreational life, with the first horse race being held early in 1859. Picnics, barbecues and games were also enjoyed on a regular basis.

Who would have guessed that 12 years later, this site would be the capital of the State of Nevada and the proud home of a branch mint of the United States. These are the roots from which came the most desirable series of coins ever sought by collectors. Curry would have savored the favorable attention focused on the coins minted in the building that stood on the land he had staked out for this purpose.

Two of the four original founders of Carson City. At left, Frank M. Proctor who served on the Constitutional Convention in 1864. At right, John J. Musser, who became a district attorney in 1863. (*Photos courtesy Nevada State Museum*)

ABE CURRY, MAN ON A MISSION

Being at the right place at the right time, gives resourceful people the opportunity they need to rise from the rank and file of the rest of humanity. In 1859, silver was discovered in an area called Gold Canyon, approximately 14 miles from Carson City. Curry took a shot and staked a claim on one of the highest ledges of the Comstock Lode. As if orchestrated by a script, Curry merged his claim with the one staked by the town butcher, Alva Gould, and presto!, the Gould and Curry Mine was unveiled to the world. Always ready to turn the page and see what would come next, Curry sold his interest in the Gould and Curry Mine six months later for $2,000 and used the money to move his family from Cleveland to Carson City. Alva Gould sold his position in the mine too. Combined, Gould and Curry received less than $5,000 for a mine that would eventually produce over $16 million in bullion.

Finally reunited with his wife and daughters, Curry was invigorated and set his face like flint as a man with a mission. There was hardly anything around Carson City that he did not have some interest or influence in. He was always buying real estate. He built a hotel (which later became the state prison), an engine house for the local fire

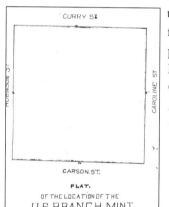

Land contract for purchase of site from the Jobs and Mr. Riddle, and the original land plat for the mint site. (*Courtesy Nevada State Museum*)

department, and a roundhouse for the Virginia & Truckee Railroad. The quantity of gold and silver bullion coming out of the local mines was overwhelming, and discussions about having a mint and assay office in the area began in the early 1860s. The sentiment of those most involved was: If a local mint could be established, the bullion would remain in Nevada. Curry and other local citizens were relentless in their campaign for Carson City to become the capital of the new Territory of Nevada and for the city to have its own mint.

Curry was emotionally bound to Carson City and his commitment was undying. He said that forsaking Carson City would be like forsaking his children. Once it was established that Carson City would be Nevada's capital, Curry resolutely lobbied Washington D.C. to have a mint built there.

Other than giving his life, a man cannot show greater commitment than by opening his wallet – Curry offered both. He was zealous during the building phase of the mint project, and often fronted money for payroll and materials. This was an inequitable affair, as so often Curry's reimbursements would be unfairly delayed by Washington, while at the same time, local creditors harassed him for past due bills. Yet still, Curry kept to the task at hand.

Curry was also hindered by the constant clamoring of agitators attempting to defame him. For instance, J.F. Morse, superintendent and special agent writing from San Francisco on March 27, 1869, investigating appropriations and delays at the Carson City Mint, informed A.B. Mullett, Supervising Architect in Washington, D.C. that he had spoken with *Col'* Curry on several occasions, and was assured that the mint building would be completed by January 1869. Since it was already March 1869 and there were further foreseeable delays, Morse had no choice to give the project an extension. Apparently, Morse was not impressed with Curry and reported that the project was running over budget. In his concluding remarks to Mullett, Morse cast doubts on the future success of what he described as a "very costly edifice… Whether its operations as a mint will ever be of any local advantage is a question about which there is much difference of opinion, even in Carson City."[1] Morse continued, "While on my way from Washington to that place, the prospective advantages of this mint were frequently discussed in my hearing. The impression left on my mind was that even its local benefits would be of very limited extent, but the question of its vitality, being entirely without the sphere

of my official action was kept out of view in my communication to the Department."[2] Then Morse snidely remarked how lucky the locals should consider themselves to be, "…the expenditure of three or four hundred thousand dollars on this institution ought to convince the distant people of Nevada that the government is not unmindful of their welfare."[3]

Another of Curry's nemeses was John Cradlebaugh, ex Union officer, and in 1865 and 1866, the Chairman of the Administration Union in Carson City. Evidently, Cradlebaugh had aspirations of his own to be put in charge of the new mint being constructed. He carried around a letter, perhaps prepared by himself stating, "John Cradlebaugh, Carson City Nevada; Will you accept the Superintendence of the Branch Mint at Carson City." Space was then left for two signature blocks, one for Cradlebaugh, and the other for Secretary of the Treasury, Hugh McCulloch.

In a vicious smear campaign against Curry, Cradlebaugh sent letters to Secretary McCulloch and President Andrew Johnson requesting the removal of Abraham Curry from his position of Superintendent of the construction of the Carson Mint. Cradlebaugh accused Curry of being "one of the most vindictive and bitter opponents of the Administration in the State."[4] Furthermore, Cradlebaugh informed the Secretary of the Treasury that Curry "does not hesitate and has frequently denounced the President upon the street as a traitor…"[5] In Cradlebaugh's letter to President Johnson he spoke in more specific terms concerning Curry's offense, informing the President that Curry "has spared no occasion to use the most vile language of Your Excellency and boastingly declares with an oath prefixed that no supporter of the Administration shall have a days work on the Mint."[6]

In his own defense, Curry sent letters to Washington refuting Cradlebaugh's accusations, and in fact, pointing a judgmental finger right back at him, complaining that, "…John Cradlebaugh…[has] tried in every possible way to vex and irritate me in order to draw from me an unguarded expression that [he] might make use of it at

[1] Letter from J.F. Morse to A.B. Mullett, March 27, 1869.
[2] Ibid.
[3] Ibid.
[4] Letter from John Cradlebaugh to Secretary McCulloch, June 17, 1865.
[5] Ibid.
[6] Letter from John Cradlebaugh to President Andrew Johnson, July 3, 1866.

Abe Curry's letter defending himself against Cradlebaugh's accusations in 1866. (*Courtesy Nevada State Museum*)

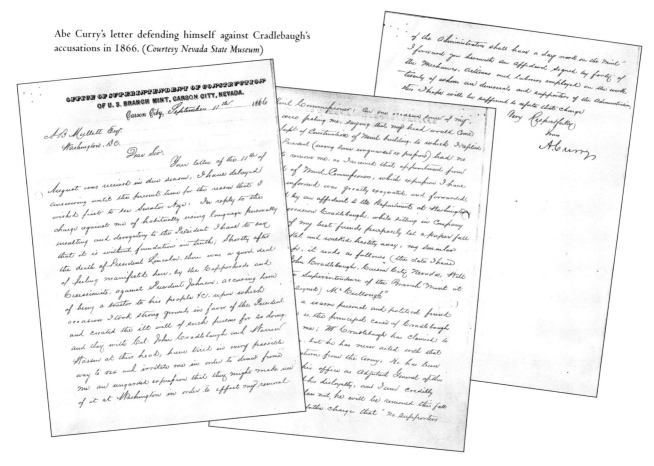

Washington in order to effect my removal as Mint Commissioner."[1] Appealing to those in Washington to consider the tarnished reputation of his accuser he charges that Cradlebaugh "has claimed to be a Union man, but he never acted with that party since his return from the Army."[2] And being regarded as an egregious administrator, Cradlebaugh "has been requested to resign his office as Adjutant General of this State on account of his disloyalty, and I am credibly informed that if he does not, he will be removed this Fall."[3] As for the purported statement Curry made about not allowing anyone belonging to the party of the current Administration to work at the Mint, he attached a page of signatures of his construction crew, 20 of whom were members of President Johnson's party.

Curry's letters, supported by the endorsements of Nevada Senators Nye and Stewart proved to be more than sufficient to clear his name and allow him to proceed with the construction of the mint.

Less than two weeks after Curry's hassle with Cradlebaugh the city was ready to celebrate the grand ceremony of the laying of the cornerstone for the mint. On September 24, 1866, a brass band led by a parade of the Masonic Order driving carriages filled with politicians and local dignitaries traveled up Carson Street and stopped in front of the construction site. Curry fired his cannon and items were placed in the cornerstone including coins donated by the Curry family (No "CC"s of course).

A long list of names made up the various committees in charge of the celebration, with one name conspicuously omitted, John Cradlebaugh. There were, however, four future Carson City Mint Superintendents on the list of names: Sam C. Wright, James Crawford, H.F. Rice, and of course, Abe Curry.

Curry was at his best when it came to celebrations and especially with grand balls and dances. He, along with committee members arranged a ball later in the evening at the Carson Pavilion complete with a tasty supper, plenty of music, and lots of beverages. Locals danced and partied nigh until midnight. And then the next day, a Tuesday, it was back to work.

Throughout the construction of the mint, Curry kept in close touch with officials at the Treasury and political leaders in Washington. Several times he actually trav-

---

[1] Letter from Abraham Curry to A.B. Mullett, September 11, 1866.
[2] Ibid.
[3] Ibid.

eled to the nation's capital lobbying for appropriations and further support for his project. On one visit in 1868, he ran into journalist Mark Twain with whom he was acquainted from Twain's days at the *Territorial Enterprise* in Virginia City, and frequent stays at his brother Orion Clemens' home in Carson City. By this time Twain had long been departed from Nevada, but was still sending articles back to the *Enterprise*. In one article written after seeing Curry in Washington, Twain poked fun at his old friend, writing that "I think Curry is the best dressed man in Washington, [and] he also has a superb set of false teeth, but he has to carry them in his pocket most of the time, because he can't swear good when he has them in."[1] Twain surmises that Curry is in Washington because, "he wants to get another appropriation to put another layer of stone on that Mint, I guess. I expect I had better find out… and keep an eye on him… he will be wanting to run this Government next."[2]

Back in Carson City, Curry continued in his duties as Superintendent of construction. As completion grew near, he was proud as could be, and would often invite friends, local dignitaries and reporters inside to view the progress. In November of 1868, a reporter from the *Daily Appeal* shared his first hand account of a visit: "Thanksgiving Day…was the first time we ever took a look inside the Mint. We are not good at architectural descriptions…but we will just say, in general terms, that the Carson Branch Mint is by long odds the most thoroughly and substantial built structure on the Pacific Coast."[3] Apparently Abe Curry, feeling a sense of relief that Ulysses S. Grant would soon be replacing Andrew Johnson as President, told his guest reporter that as soon as Grant was in the White House and the Carson Mint is open, "he means to send the first double eagle that is coined there to President Grant…"[4]

Despite Curry's unbridled optimism, he was plagued by growing pessimism filtering out of Washington. For example, in January of 1869, the month Curry had promised mint construction would be completed, instead of support coming from the Treasury Department he read Secretary Hugh McCulloch's negative report to Congress predicting that the mint in Carson would be a losing proposition, "It seems probable therefore…that the business of the branch mint at that place will not greatly exceed [$1 million] and that the expense of conducting the establishment will be greatly in excess of its receipts."[5] Abraham Curry was ready to prove McCulloch wrong, but first he needed to get the Carson City Mint completed and more importantly, opened.

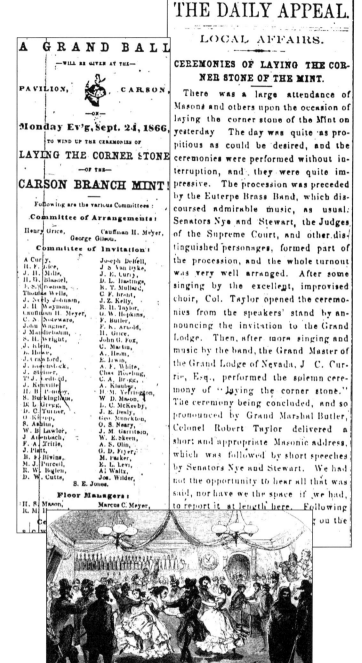

THE CARSON MINT CORNERSTONE CELEBRATION

The laying of the cornerstone for the Carson Mint on September 24, 1866, was cause for great celebration, including a Grand Ball which may have resembled this lively event in a dance hall. Also shown is an article regarding the laying of the cornerstone of the new mint as reported in the *Daily Appeal*.

---

[1] Article, Mark Twain reporting to the *Territorial Enterprise*, January, 1868.
[2] Ibid.
[3] *Carson Daily Appeal*, November 28, 1868.
[4] Ibid.
[5] Documents from Third Session of the 40th Congress, Report by Secretary of the Treasury Hugh McCulloch, January 1869.

By the end of the 1860s, the nation was slowly moving out of hard economic times caused by the Civil War. Cities around the Comstock Lode in Nevada had faired much better than other areas because of the money that poured out of the mines, and Abe Curry had almost achieved his goal of providing a comfortable living for his family. His story however, reads like a tragic epic. With all his success and fulfillment came heartbreak. His son Charles had died in 1863 at the age of 27 and Curry never fully recovered from this tragedy. In 1867, Curry was unable to pay his creditors and filed for bankruptcy. Notices appeared on the front page of the four-page Carson *Daily Appeal* and greatly embarrassed *Old Abe*, but Curry persevered and recovered. He could have become the wealthiest man in Nevada, as he was in a position many times to make great fortunes. He was so much at the center of everything in the developing regions of the Comstock Lode and Carson City that he had more opportunities than 100 men would have had in their lifetimes. But, those who knew him said he seemed to live only for the present and did not save his money for the future. He would reap considerable profit on an investment and turn around and spend all the money, or invest in another venture.

But when the Carson City Mint opened in January 1870, Curry was permanently enshrined in the annals of numismatics as the father of the most glorious series of coins ever minted in the United States. Curry had the mint dressed up like a wedding bride on opening day. He spared no expense, and was a stickler for detail. Bricks for the chimney were of the finest quality, and Curry made sure that the furnace bricks and mortar were from the leading supplier in England. Landscaping crews adorned the grounds with a manicured lawn, surrounded by trees, shrubs, and fresh flowers. It was an impressive sight as it stood in the corner lot, not blocked by any other structures. Standing at a distance, locals could see the mountains in the background and nearly the entire valley in all directions. Use your imagination to picture what must have been running through the minds of the citizens of Carson City when those first Seated Liberty silver dollars rolled off the die press in February of 1870. Read this tribute published in the *Carson Daily Appeal* on February 20, 1870:

Deserved Tribute – A deserved tribute to Col. Curry. The prettiest, neatest, and most appropriate among "pocket pieces" for a "Washoeite" to carry, is one of the beautiful and acceptable silver dollars, first coined at the United States Branch Mint at Carson. They are an emblematic, condensed history in themselves, being composed of the staple product, the very foundation of the country itself, dug from the depths of the Comstock Ledge – "Washoe silver," favored throughout the world. Yes, and coined by old Abe Curry, one of the original owners of the ledge, being a locator of the famous Gould and Curry mine, and now Superintendent of the Mint. He is the first to coin in this State the precious metal of which he was one of the first discoverers. Even should the Mint be abolished or turned into a pest house or distillery to-morrow, Col. Curry has a right to brag over what he has achieved, although his indomitable perseverance and forced success has not made him rich. Honor to whom honor is due.

An 1871 Gold Hill *Daily News* article reported "Abraham Curry built more, worked harder, and did more for Carson City than any other man." Those living at the time would probably have considered Major William Ormsby a co-founder of the city of Carson, Nevada and Curry himself—out of respect—would probably have wanted to share the credit. But Ormsby died in 1860, two years after the city was founded. Curry is more responsible than any

Major William M. Ormsby arrived in the Carson City area in 1857. He was killed on the battlefield in 1860 during the Pyramid Lake wars with the Indians. (*Courtesy Nevada State Museum*)

other man for the world having "CC" coins, and that is why it is easy for the collector to proclaim that *Abe's the man!*

Legend has it that someone unfamiliar with mintmarks, asked Curry what the "CC" stood for on the back of a silver dollar. Supposedly Curry beamed with a sly grin and told the person "It stands for compliments of Curry, naturally."

CONGRESSMAN FITCH DEFENDS NEVADA'S MINT

The stage was set for the Carson City Mint to write its own chapter in history, and the opening of this institution was a crucial step forward at this time in the history of the United States. Since the start of the Civil War, the only two mints officially operating were at Philadelphia and San Francisco, causing depletion in the coinage supply. Mints at Charlotte, Dahlonega and New Orleans had closed when seized by the Confederacy, and of those three, only the New Orleans Mint would resume operations, although not until 1879.

The Treasury Department's experience with the branch mint in San Francisco caused them to be concerned and suspicious when considering establishing another branch mint *out west*. An investigation had been conducted in the late 1860s at the San Francisco Mint about a significant loss of gold. The accounting practices were audited in a 19th-century version of the Enron case. Consequently, the Treasury was reluctant to authorize the new mint at Carson City.

In addition there seemed to always be petty individuals ready to spoil the party. In 1870, the same year the Carson City Mint opened, certain constituencies represented by coactive members of Congress proposed an amendment to close the Carson City Mint. In defense of keeping it open, a certain Mr. Thomas Fitch, Congressman from Nevada gave a heroic speech on the floor of the House of Representatives. He began by praising the new mint and applauding the efforts of those who built it. This is an excerpt from his opening remarks as reported in the *Carson Daily Appeal*, March 1, 1870:

Thomas Fitch, Congressman from Nevada, 1870. When Fitch was the editor of the *Occidental* newspaper in Virginia City, Mark Twain described him as "a felicitous skirmisher with a pen."

The mint is at last completed, the machinery in place, the officers appointed, the institution ready for the transaction of business. But a few days since the announcement was made that the first money had been coined at this branch mint. The supervising architect of the Treasury, after a personal examination, pronounced the Carson branch mint to be one of the most faithfully and economically constructed public buildings in the country. The Director of the Philadelphia Mint, in his last annual report, speaking of the Carson branch mint says:

"Under the supervision of skilled and experienced men, with an honest, energetic administration of its affairs, this branch may fully meet the expectations of its friends and greatly promote the general prosperity of that interesting portion of our country."

Then Mr. Fitch, with sarcasm in his delivery, continued:

Sir, the people of that "interesting portion of our country" will be filled with astonishment and dismay when they shall learn of the remarkable act of retrogressive policy with regard to this mint recommended by the Committee on Appropriations. Behold, in the place of an appropriation

of $91,800, in accordance with the estimates of the Department, to carry on this mint during the ensuing fiscal year, it is provided, first, that two watchmen shall have $2,000 to take care of the building, and then, in violation of usage, at least by legislation in the body of an appropriation bill, it is provided that the act establishing a branch mint at Carson City shall be replaced. Sir, if this mint is to be thus destroyed in its infancy, I ask, why was it ever begotten and brought forth? If it shall be thus slain the interesting people of the "interesting portion of our country" may well exclaim:

Since you so very soon were done for, I wonder what you were begun for.

He slashed his verbal saber through the thin armor of deceitfulness when he alluded to outside influence:

The Government has expended over three hundred thousand dollars on this branch mint, and it is now ready for the transaction of business. The first money has already been coined in it, and yet it is here proposed to strike it from existence and to put an end to it, or at the most to make an appropriation of $2,000 for two watchmen to take care of the building. I fear the Committee on Appropriations have listened to interested advisers. I fear that interested influences have been busy to prejudice the judgment of the committee. Possibly there be those not privileged to a voice within this Hall, who in the opinion of the committee are more able to judge of the peculiar requirements of Nevada, and more willing to admit and encourage all necessary restrictions upon public expenditures within her limits, than I myself.

Now it was time for him to unload both barrels and demolish all arguments:

I am not here to guess who it is that has struck in the dark so swiftly and so surely at the Carson mint. It is enough that I present upon this floor, with all the candor I owe to the subject and with that sentiment of deep concern I feel for my distant people, an earnest protest against this measure of destruction recommended by the Committee on Appropriations. Why, sir, the Comstock ledge, which produces every year about twelve million dollars' worth of silver and gold bullion, is within fifteen miles of railroad of this branch mint which it is now proposed to abolish. The Pine Grove mining region, producing a considerable quantity of gold, is about sixty miles southeast of it. Rich gold vaines [*sic*] have been discovered at Mono, one hundred miles south, and the Central Pacific railroad, which passes through rich mining districts, runs but about twenty-five miles north of this place.

From these facts it will be seen that the prospect of this branch mint for business is as fair as that of any other branch mint in the country, while its facilities for doing business in the shape of improved machinery and competent officers are equal to those of any in the country.

It was a slam-dunk. The spokesman for the *mint-busters* withdrew the portion of the amendment to close the Carson City Mint. That section was changed to read:

Branch mint, Carson City; For salaries of superintendent, assayer, melter and refiner, chief coiner, assistant assayer, assistant melter and refiner, assistant chief coiner, and clerks, $20,200.

For wages of workmen and adjusters, $54,000. For chemicals, charcoal, and wood, incidental and miscellaneous expenses, $17,600.

Mr. Fitch closed by comparing the paltry appropriations for Carson City to other government expenditures:

The $91,800 estimated for by the Department is as necessary an expenditure for Nevada as is the $2,000,000 which will be required to finish the new post office at Boston, or the $4,000,000 which will be required to complete a similar building for New York. It is very much more necessary than the millions of dollars which will be voted here to send a mixed assortment of Quakers and blankets, saw-mills and schoolbooks to vicious and unappreciative savages.

The bill passed the Senate and it was settled, the mint at Carson City would remain; it would receive the funding necessary to keep it operating smoothly. In hindsight, it is interesting to muse over what it would have meant to future coin collectors and the demand for Carson City coins if this facility had only minted coins in those first two months of 1870.

As a final note about Mr. Tom Fitch, when the Republicans failed to nominate him for Congress one year, he stood up, addressing the crowd and proclaimed, "Gentlemen, from the bottom of my heart I can now sym-

Thomas Fitch's speech before Congress in support of the Carson City Mint, as reported in the March 1, 1870 *Carson Daily Appeal*.

pathize with Lazarus [in the Bible], for I too have been 'licked' by dogs." He was obviously a gifted and witty orator.

Despite Nevada's vast emptiness, it was still a small society. The common people of Nevada, came down from their mining towns, came down from the mountains, and came in from the grazing ranches, to witness a spectacle bigger than life.

Ranch hands, sheepherders, miners, cowboys, store-owners, saloonkeepers, prostitutes, reporters, schoolteachers, blacksmiths, the native Indians, the gamblers and thieves, and all other citizens, transients, and passersby, would have memories of the **Birth Of A Legend**!

It was time for Nevada to show the rest of the country what it was made of. The city fathers of Carson, Nevada dressed their new mint up in regal splendor. Abe Curry and the rest of the locals were proud to have an official U.S. Mint on their main street. Salt Lake City did not have one. Neither did Sacramento, nor Portland, nor Helena, nor any of the other major cities in the western states except San Francisco. Now Nevada could proclaim that it was *going to be somebody*.

NEVADA IN THE 1860S

Through the decade of the 1860s, the area known as the Comstock had behaved like a young unbridled heir to a family fortune. The wealth from the mines opened the doors to lavish spending and passionate living. Virginia City became a must-see destination stop for adventurous Americans, as well as international travelers. The *Territorial Enterprise* newspaper chronicled the exciting (and sometimes mythical) events happening in the boomtowns at the base of the Sierra Nevada Mountains. Soon to become famous reporters Dan DeQuille and Mark Twain fas-

Dan DeQuille (William Wright), reporter for the *Territorial Enterprise*.

Crowd in front of the Ormsby House in 1863. (*Courtesy Nevada State Museum*)

cinated readers with local news stories. There was world class entertainment, fine food, elegant homes with custom-made furnishings, tailored clothing, cures for baldness, elegant jewelry, chinchilla and cassimere suits, imported cigars, fully stocked hardware stores, imported glassware and china, and many of the other *indulgences of the senses, regardless of the cost* that were symbolic of a sophisticated metropolitan region. An advertisement in the Carson *Daily Appeal* by the Ormsby House expressed the local philosophy of what life is all about:

> The Ormsby House has been thoroughly refitted throughout and put in complete order for the comfort and pleasure of all who may please to give him a call.
>
> Tables will at all times be supplied with all the substantials as well as the luxuries that the market affords. No pains will be spared to please guests and every attention will be paid to their respective wants at all times.
>
> The BAR is well stocked with Fine Liquors, Wines, &c.
>
> Attached to the House is a BILLIARD ROOM containing Three Tables of the latest improved styles, with good cues, balls and fine light.

Comstockers and residents of Carson Valley would soon have their own railroad. But first, they had their own mint. What a treasure. Life could not have been better. It was a self-contained habitat that provided everything necessary for life, liberty, and the pursuit of happiness.

STATEHOOD AND PROGRESS

When Curry founded the city of Carson in 1858, the region was known as Carson County in the Utah Territory. On October 31, 1864 Nevada officially became the 36th state in the union, in spite of the fact that the total population was only 21,000; it is not known whether this total included the large Indian population consisting primarily of Shoshones, Paiutes, and Washoes.

No one was keeping exact records at the time because it was expedient that the proclamation for Nevada's Statehood be signed by President Abraham Lincoln before the November 1864 presidential election. In one of the quickest maneuvers in the political history of the United States, Governor James W. Nye sent by telegram the entire draft of the Nevada Constitution (over 6,500 words) to Washington D.C. on Oct 17, 1864, and President Lincoln signed the proclamation less than a week before the national election. Obviously, the sudden wealth generated from the mines of Nevada caught the attention of a nation in turmoil. President Lincoln also realized what an advantage it would be to him to have Nevada's vote to help pass the Thirteenth Amendment. For a lesson in how swiftly government can act if the incentive exists, you need only review the timeline of events that resulted in Nevada's Statehood, the authorizing of a Mint, and the actual minting of coins.

In 1860, Nevada's population was 6,857 people, a figure which made it difficult to attain even territorial status. By 1870, Nevada had become a state, boasted of respectable cities and had a mint! When Superintendent Abe Curry officially opened the mint in Carson City on January 8, 1870, Nevada had arrived. Dies were sent from Philadelphia and then a very exciting event occurred, a total of 2,303 of the first Seated Liberty silver dollars ever minted with double letters for a mintmark were delivered in February. The two C's used for the mintmark looked very distinctive and speaking the mintmark letters out loud had a certain ring to it. As was customary, examples of the new coins were given to officials and dignitaries, and the first silver dollar minted at Carson City in February 1870 was presented to President Ulysses S. Grant. Another was presented to the Governor of Nevada, Henry G. Blasdel.

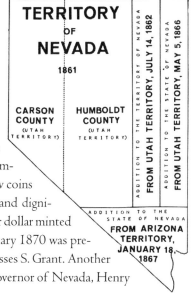

In retrospect, those first "CC" silver dollars added a new dimension to coin collecting. All of the other coins minted in the United States are very important to numismatics, but deep down, many collectors dream about, lust over, and covet "CC" coins.

Telegram sent to Secretary
Seward by Governor Nye on
behalf of Nevada's statehood,
October 1864.

Office U. S. Military Telegraph
WAR DEPARTMENT.

The following Telegram received at Washington 12 RM. Oct- 18 1864.

2) From Carson City Nev Ter Oct- 17 1864.

W H Seward
    Constitution of Nevada Conforming
to Enabling Act of Congress adopted
by vote of people at recent
election by over nine thousand
majority. The vote & copy
of Constitution I have
forwarded with proper certificate
to Prest. Two copies sent previously
out have probably miscarried.
Of utmost importance that he
immediately issue proclamation admitting
Nevada as a state. Have
this done at once. Answer
when done.
    Jas W Nye Govr

declare and proclaim that the said State
of Nevada is admitted into the Union on
an equal footing with the original States.

    In witness whereof, I have hereunto
set my hand, and caused the seal of the
United States to be affixed.

    Done at the City of Washington
this Thirty-first day of October,
in the year of our Lord one
thousand eight hundred
and sixty-four, and of the
Independence of the
United States the
Eighty-ninth.

                Abraham Lincoln

By the President:

    William H Seward
    Secretary of State.

Oct 31, 1864

The President of the United States of America

A Proclamation:

    Whereas the Congress of the United States
passed an Act which was approved on the 21st
day of March, last, entitled, "An Act to enable
the people of Nevada to form a Constitution and
State Government, and for the admission of such
State into the Union on an equal footing with
the original States;"

    And whereas, the said Constitution and
State Government have been formed pursuant
to the conditions prescribed by the fifth section
of the Act of Congress aforesaid, and the
certificate required by the said act, and also
a copy of the Constitution and ordinances have
been submitted to the President of the United
States;

    Now, therefore, be it known that I, Abraham
Lincoln, President of the United States, in
accordance with the duty imposed upon me by
the Act of Congress aforesaid, do, hereby,

Copy of original proclamation of Nevada's statehood, October 31, 1864.

SOLD FOR $170,000!

Now for a moment, skip ahead to 1997...There are a few people still bidding when the price reaches $100,000. You could hear several people in the audience whispering how crazy anybody would be who would pay that much for an 1870-CC Seated Liberty quarter in Choice Uncirculated condition. At least 20 people had been prepared to pay $50,000 to $75,000. One shrewd dealer had assured his customer that it was a cinch; he'd be able to buy it for him for no more than $65,000 (so much for that theory). Members of the crowd sat in astonishment as they watched the bidding rise higher and higher. Finally there were just two bidders. Then, Dave Bowers, the auctioneer, called out "$160,000, do I hear $170,000? There's $170,000 in the back to my left, do I hear $180,000?"

At that point, the discouraged underbidder, already exceeding his limit by $25,000 to $30,000, dropped out. "Sold for $170,000." There was applause. The auctioneer took a drink of water and a deep breath and murmured something like "my, my." Added to the winning bid of $170,000 was a $17,000 buyers fee, bringing the total to $187,000. This was the *Louis E. Eliasberg, Sr. Collection* sale, held in New York City in April 1997, 127 years after the first quarter was struck at the Carson City Mint.

A total of 8,340 1870-CC quarters had been coined in that first year of the mint's operation. It is not known for sure, but it is estimated that approximately 98% of the quarters had remained in the mint's vault awaiting further instruction from the main Mint at Philadelphia. Apparently, half dollars, silver dollars and $5, $10, and $20 gold pieces were the denominations most distributed at the time. So, the quarters sat stacked in canvas bags with only a few escaping as mint workers exchanged 25 cents of their own money for a new quarter. Residents of Carson City, Nevada bought some of the new quarters to have as souvenirs and good luck pieces and officials in town were given examples as gifts. If local commercial needs had required it, quantities would have been released yet there is no record of this occurring. If the entire mintage had been distributed, surely there would be more examples extant today. As is customary, a small quantity of the new quarters was sent via security transit to the Assay Commission in Philadelphia to be tested for weights, fineness, and measures. In a later chapter you will learn what happened to the remainder of this first year's mintage of quarters.

The scene at the *Eliasberg* sale was overwhelming. During this same auction, mega rarities like the 1804 silver dollar and the 1884 and 1885 Proof trade dollars would be sold, all approaching or exceeding the one million dollar mark. But the 1870-CC quarter was special. It was the first Uncirculated example of this date to sell in 23 years, the last being described as "brilliant uncirculated, some proof-like surfaces, one of the finest known," in a Stack's auction in 1974.[1] The winning bid in 1974 had been $5,250. As of the writing of this book, this specimen has not been certified by any of the grading services. On the other hand, the *Eliasberg* specimen was later graded MS-64 at NGC and is thus far the only certified Uncirculated example of this date. There was no precedent for the price it would bring, but the winning bidder understood the significance of the coin and would have paid $250,000 or more to own it. Two more Carson City quarters came up for bid a few minutes later at the auction, and would complete the purchase of a threesome of legendary coins that nearly overshadowed the celebrity coins in the sale, certainly grabbing the spotlight and shining it brightly on Carson City coinage.

The *Eliasberg* 1870-CC quarter.
(*Courtesy Bowers and Merena*)

The Carson City Mint, pictured shortly after its opening in 1870. (*Courtesy Nevada Historical Society*)

[1] Stack's, *H. Philip Spier Sale*, March 8, 1974.

ABE CURRY RESIGNS

Meanwhile, back to 1870 and a shocking development. Almost without warning, Abe Curry turned in his resignation as Mint Superintendent in September. Only his family, a small group of staff workers, and a few close confidants had known of Curry's intentions. His reason for giving up the post he had worked so hard to earn was to fulfill his ambition, to become first the state's Lieutenant Governor, and then possibly the Governor.

With less than two months to campaign, Curry relied heavily upon his reputation as the founder of the State's capital city, not to mention all the other contributions he had made. But his bid ended within a week of his entering the race when he lost his party's nomination to J.S. Slingerland at the Republican Convention in Elko on September 14, 1870.

In his earlier years in Carson City, Curry had served as a Councilman and in the Nevada House of Representatives. But this was before he sacrificed everything to get the mint built. Though most of his neighbors in Carson City admired him, he had never been accepted into the State's political power machine, and these were the men who pulled the strings, deciding who would be placed in office. Curry could have been a part of this group, but he was a maverick who refused to be led by the reins.

1870-CC Liberty Seated silver dollar.

So now, within the course of two weeks, Curry who was 55, found himself out of a job and no longer in the Lieutenant Governor's race.

His friend Henry F. Rice who had served with him on the original Mint Commission replaced him as Superintendent. Curry would always be a welcome guest at the mint, yet he would never again serve in an official capacity. Only he knew of all that had gone on behind closed doors during the time he served as Mint Superintendent. Years later, rumors would circulate about the special privileges Curry afforded himself while supervising the Carson Mint, yet if he had in fact received any benefits he certainly left none of them behind.

A story is told of Sir Isaac Newton who at one time held the office of the Master of the Mint in London. Newton supposedly told his friends that one of the bo-nuses of his position was that he was allowed to keep a percentage of all that he coined.

If any person in America would have been keen to benefit from such a practice it would have been Abe Curry. For him, the Carson Mint was his sole domain. He could have been like a business owner who dips into the till from time to time, although if that had been the case, it begs the question; why did he give it up? Beneath it all, and casting all spurious innuendos aside, Curry's legacy in Nevada is too praiseworthy for him to be labeled a thief.

THE FIRST YEAR'S SIX DENOMINATIONS

The dies for the 1870 quarters had arrived in Carson City on New Year's Eve of 1869. However, it was not until April 20, 1870 that the first 3,540 quarters were produced. There would be two more scant deliveries of these future numismatic rarities in 1870, one in May, and the last in August. Half dollars, on the other hand, were minted in greater quantity, 54,617 pieces, although still just a fraction of the quantities produced at the Philadelphia and San Francisco mints. As mentioned, the Seated Liberty silver dollars were the first coins of any type minted in 1870 at Carson City, 12,462 in all. On March 1, 1870 the first 400 $5 Liberty gold pieces were minted. Next in the production line were the $10 Liberty gold pieces. Breen reports that the first 1,332 Liberty double eagles were minted on March 10, 1870.[1] All told, 92,087 combined pieces from the six denominations bearing the new "CC" mintmark were introduced to the world in the first year of operation. Face value amounted to $214,738.50, certainly not enough to make much of an impression on the rest of the country. But the local citizens of Carson City, Nevada were mighty proud.

More details and data about the first year of issue coins may be found in Chapter 6, *The Silver Coins*, and Chapter 7, *The Gold Coins*.

[1] Walter Breen, *Complete Encyclopedia of U.S. and Colonial Coins.*

A winter scene typical of the Carson valley in the 1870s to 1880s.

❧ 1871 ❧

1870 had been a successful first year of operation for the new mint in Carson City. Now it was time to introduce the dime to its assortment of coin denominations. Breen states that 6,400 dimes were minted in February 1871 and the total mintage for the year was 20,100 pieces.[1] An interesting yet unrelated event also occurred in 1871 when the first professional baseball association was organized in March. Originally named the National Association of Professional Baseball Players, it would one day evolve into the National and American Leagues. Just as no one in 1871 could have predicted that 130 years later the value of certain coins would exceed $100,000 (even reaching $7 million+), no one alive at that time would have believed that the salaries of professional baseball players would eventually exceed $10 million. Inflation works wonders for a country's economic system.

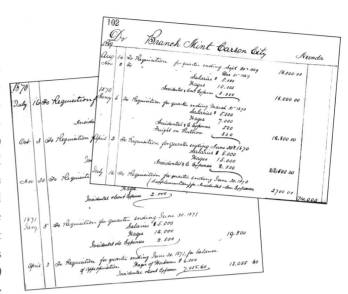

Ledger sheet of expenses at the Carson Mint for part of 1870 and 1871.

MINTAGES REMAIN LOW IN SECOND YEAR

As is obvious from the skimpy mintage figures, Carson City dimes were not necessary for the region's coinage supply. In fact, when reviewing the mintage figures for dimes struck at the Carson City Mint in 1871, 1872, 1873 (both varieties), and 1874, as compared to dimes minted at Philadelphia and San Francisco, the Carson City dimes represent between $1/2$% to $1 1/2$% of all dimes coined. In other words, there was a combined mintage of 11,395,660 dimes from Philadelphia and San Francisco as compared with just 97,588 from the Nevada mint. Carson City coins were destined to become very scarce.

What is the reason for the low mintages? In truth, Philadelphia should have either authorized a substantial quantity of "CC" dimes, or simply halted production altogether. Since no one is alive who was there at the time, and no records have been discovered which could shed light on the original plan, today's collectors are left to speculate. Realistically it does not matter except for two things: how many of those 97,588 "CC" dimes were released into circulation, and how many of the ones kept in reserve were melted? Surviving population figures suggest that 90% or more were kept in reserve and later melted. There are approximately $8/10$ of 1% (that is .008) of the original 97,588 dimes from the Carson City Mint from the years 1871 to 1874 known to sur-

vive today. Dimes minted at the Philadelphia and San Francisco mints between 1860 and 1874 have lower survival rates. Collectively, there were approximately 175 million dimes minted at these two mints during this period and estimated surviving population totals reveal that only $3/100$ of 1% of the dimes exist today. Some of the San Francisco dimes from the 1860s have a survival rate of $8/1000$ of 1%. Records reveal that the United States melted nearly as many coins as it minted and the Coinage Act of 1873 and decisions made in subsequent years made short work of most of the silver coins that had been minted up till then.

Coin collectors are the beneficiaries of these low mintages. For, if there were not any

Portion of instructions on how to operate the mint at Carson City.

truly rare coins, hobbyists would soon lose interest. Fads prove to be short term and collectibles available in mass quantities present no challenge. After the first 50 cases of modern baseball cards, the thrill is gone. Newspapers report about auction sales of John Lennon glasses, or Marilyn Monroe dresses, or Jacqueline Kennedy Onassis tableware, where winning bidders are paying $10,000, $50,000 or even $100,000 for the privilege of owning a piece of a celebrity's history, because these items are rare. They also are emblematic of a time or an era that needs to be preserved because of its significance in a culture's memories. Coins are wonderful examples of this very thing. Numerous numismatic authors from Q. David Bowers to Lee F. Hewitt have written of "holding history in your hands" and how coins represent the art, culture, and the ideas of a nation. If a person does not collect coins, then what do they collect: bottle caps, cars, cookbooks, butterflies, postcards, stamps, watches, musical instruments? Carson City coins have provided thousands of people with incentives to pursue a rewarding pastime.

LEGAL TENDER ACT

In October of 1871, the original draft of Lincoln's Emancipation Proclamation was lost when the Chicago Historical Society building was destroyed in the devastating fire that almost burned that city to the ground. More than 17,000 buildings were destroyed and the estimated damages were $200 million. The heroic fortitude of the people of Chicago resulted in a relatively short recovery time. Also in 1871, the Supreme Court overturned a ruling from 1870 declaring the Legal Tender Act to be unconstitutional. Many citizens of the United States believed that Congress did not have the right to authorize the issuance of paper money that would be unlawful for people to accept as payment.

Gold and silver were the unanimous choices for use in commerce in the western states, and there was more of it coming from the ground around Carson City than at any other place and time in history.

CARSON CITY GETS A CAPITOL BUILDING

Also in 1871, Abe Curry's second greatest wish came true. In a ceremony reminiscent of the one staged in 1866 for the mint building, the cornerstone for the state Capitol was laid on June 9, 1870. A sturdy brass box had been constructed to hold the memorial articles that were buried in the cornerstone. Included with the items deposited were copies of local newspapers, the State constitution, an Enabling Act to organize Nevada's statehood, a history of the new V&T Railroad, bylaws of various lodges and fire companies, a detailed, "History of the Untied States Branch Mint at Carson to date, showing that $130,000 has thus far been coined...,"[1] and for good measure, Uncirculated examples of the 1870-CC quarter, half dollar, and silver dollar. As reported in an earlier edition of the *Daily Appeal*: "This box is a model of neatness, ... made at Bittner & Co.'s by George S. Hadley. It is a piece of very creditable work indeed. Upon the lid is splendidly engraved the following inscription: 'Corner Stone, Capitol Building, of the State of Nevada, June 9th, A.D. 1870...' "[2] Also inscribed on the lid was a list of 11 men who were instrumental in the Capitol Building project, chief among them being local contractor Peter Cavanaugh who supervised the construc-

> CORNER STONE RECEPTACLE BOX.—The Gold Hill News has the following description of the box which has been made as a receptacle of the memorials which are to be placed in the corner stone of the Capitol:
>
> This box is substantially made of solid brass, and weighs fourteen pounds. It is 12 inches long, 10 inches wide and 10 inches deep, and filled with black velvet, being intended to receive and preserve all the various documents and other articles to be deposited within the corner stone day after to-morrow, at the great celebration. This box is a model of neatness, and was made at Bittner & Co.'s by George S. Hadley. It is a piece of very creditable work indeed. Upon the lid is splendidly engraved the following inscription: "Corner Stone, Capitol Building, of the State of Nevada, laid by the Grand Lodge of Free and Accepted Masons of the State of Nevada, June 9th, A. D. 1870. Joseph Gosling, architect. Peter Cavanaugh, contractor. J. C. Hazlett, F. Stadtmuller, J. H. Sturtevant, Wm. H. Corbett, J. R. Johnson, John Klein, J. H. Mills, Capitol Building Commissioners. Presented by Eugene Bittner & Co., Gold Hill. George S. Hadley, mechanic. Thomas Kent, engraver, Virginia City."
>
> If there is time in which to do it we hope that "John Klein" be changed to Jacob Klein, for that is that Commissioner's name.

Article about the cornerstone box for the Capital building from the June 8, 1870 *Carson Daily Appeal*. (*Courtesy Leonard Augsburger*)

An 1870-CC quarter and silver dollar from the Carson City Capitol Building cornerstone. Both are in Uncirculated condition. An 1870-CC half dollar was also deposited during the cornerstone ceremony. (*Courtesy Nevada State Museum*)

---

[1] *Carson Daily Appeal*, June 12, 1870, courtesy of Leonard Augsburger.
[2] *Carson Daily Appeal*, June 8, 1870, courtesy of Leonard Augsburger.

tion. In subsequent years, Cavanaugh would construct many of the notable buildings in the capital city.

Construction was completed on schedule and with a population of less than 2,500, Carson City now boasted a Capitol building. At a cost of nearly $175,000 the magnificent structure stood on the opposite side of Carson Street five blocks south of the mint. Decorated with the finest furnishings and equipped with crystal glass and rich marble floors, the legislators were gleeful when holding their first session in the building in January of 1871. A brilliant silver cupola would later beam the message to the nation that this was indeed the *Silver State*.

SKIPPING AHEAD 126 YEARS
Another Carson City Rarity
Crosses the Block

There is something about a well-attended rare coin auction that excites the senses. The action is swift. Between 120 and 150 lots are sold per hour, 20 to 30 seconds per lot. Bidders must be on their toes. All bidding strategies must be decided in advance. There is little time to alter your course during the auction. Some attendees get caught up in what is referred to as *auction fever*, causing a bidder to far exceed his maximum bid. If you have set a limit of $2,000 for a certain lot in the auction and then as fast as lightning, the bid reaches $2,000, sometimes it is hard to put that paddle down. Think quickly. Okay, $2,100. Now it's $2,200. Fast. Okay, $2,300. Where are these other bidders coming from!?!? (It seems like your bidder number is being batted back and forth like a ping pong ball.) Now it's $2,400. Then $2,500. You shoot the paddle up one more time, $2,600, and hold your breath, going once, going twice. You are silently screaming at the auctioneer to hurry up and bang the gavel down. Finally, he calls SOLD! For $2,600 to

CORNER STONE MEMORIALS.—We don't much relish the notion of being obliged to copy from our cotemporaries the list of articles deposited in the corner stone But Grand Secretary Van Bokkelen having gone off with it and given it to the Gold Hill News, and we wishing to keep a record of the matter reproduce it from that paper :

A copy of the proceedings of the Grand Lodge of Free and Accepted Masons of Nevada, from organization to date ; the name of the I. O. O. F. and Good Templars ; the Declaration of Independence ; the Constitution of the United States as amended till date ; Organic Act of the Territory of Nevada ; Enabling Act to organize the State ; Constitution of the State ; Act creating the Board of State Capitol Commissioners ; a full set of the State and a full set of the Nevada Territorial laws ; By-laws of the various fire companies, of the Odd Fellows, Masons and other societies ; a copy of each newspaper now published in this State ; a list of the names of the officers and a history of the Virginia and Truckee Railroad ; a history of the United States Branch Mint at Carson to date (showing that $130,000 has thus far been coined), and a great number of parchment scrolls recording all sorts of facts. It also contains a silver bar from Birdsall & Co.'s reduction works, Dayton, worth $6 70 ; a bar from the Dunderberg mine, worth $6 ; one silver dollar, one silver half dollar and one quarter of a dollar of a dollar of Carson coinage, date 1870 ; a coin of the year 1836 ; a silver medal upon which is inscribed the history of the Lodge of Good Templars of Dayton,

Article from the June 12, 1870 issue of the *Carson Daily Appeal*, regarding laying the cornerstone for the Capitol building, which was finished in 1871.

The *Eliasberg* 1871-CC quarter.
(Courtesy Bowers and Merena)

bidder number 369. You feel a rush and before you even realize what you have done, the next lot is already open for bidding. Auctions move fast and can be very exciting. Combining these observations with an auction featuring a once in a lifetime collection, you have the formula for a very thrilling experience.

In the previously mentioned *Eliasberg Collection* auction on April 6, 1997, lot 1497 comes up for bidding. There were 10,890 quarters minted in Carson City in 1871, and in the 130 plus years since, only three Uncirculated specimens have surfaced. In the *Encyclopedia of U.S. Seated Liberty Quarters*, Larry Briggs estimates that there are 31 to 75 surviving in all grades. Combined population reports from the major grading services list a total of fewer than 20 certified in all grades. Probably more than half of the uncertified Carson City quarters are pitted, corroded and in other ways, of very low quality. Lot number 1497 was an 1871-CC quarter described as "Landmark, in Gem Mint State."

The cataloguer wrote, "It is one of the great rarities in the Liberty Seated series. Even worn specimens are very difficult to find."[1] As the catalogue description continues further tribute is paid, "Here is one of the most remarkable coins in the present offering, a legendary piece which will be forever remembered . . ."[2]

At this point in the auction the winning bidder for the historic *Eliasberg* 1870-CC quarter had only been given a few minutes to savor his conquest, when he realized he was involved again in spirited bidding competition for the 1871-CC. Records showed that the highest reported price paid for an 1871-

[1] Bowers and Merena, *The Louis E. Eliasberg, Sr. Collection*, April 6, 1997.
[2] Ibid.

CC quarter up till that time was $28,600 in 1988 at the *Norweb* sale, also an Uncirculated coin, eventually graded MS-64 by PCGS. No one knew how much the *Eliasberg* specimen would bring, but the buyer of the 1870-CC quarter was not to be denied. Within 30 seconds, he had only one other competitor and quickly, it was over and the price realized was $150,000 plus a $15,000 buyer's fee. The winning bidder's final competitor, in a desperate attempt, had exceeded his pre-auction limit by nearly $50,000. But this underbidder had already won the 1876-CC 20-cent piece previously offered in the sale, although he had lost the 1870-CC quarter just a few minutes earlier to the same enthusiast who had just won the 1871-CC quarter. It was obvious that Gem Mint State Carson City coins were bringing big premiums this night.

MANAGEMENT SHIFT AT THE MINT

Switching back to the 19th century, H.F. Rice, a local Wells Fargo agent, had replaced Abraham Curry as Mint Superintendent at the end of 1870 and was ready to take the mint at Carson City to the next level. Rice had been on the original Mint Commission with Abe Curry and had thrown the second shovel full of dirt at the ground breaking ceremony in July of 1866.

In 1871 the total number of coins minted increased to 214,958, which was more than double the first year's total of 92,791. As stated earlier, dimes made their debut in 1871 with a total mintage of 20,100. Denominations that realized significant increases were: half dollars (from 54,617 to 139,950), $5 gold pieces (from 7,675 to 20,770), and $20 double eagles (from 3,789 to 14,687). The Seated Liberty silver dollar was the only denomination that decreased in mintage, dropping from a total of 12,462 in 1870 to 1,376 in 1871. Elsewhere in the country, the fate of the Seated Liberty dollar was being decided by political powers devising corrupt plans that would enable insiders to benefit from new silver laws. Germany was demonetizing silver (removing its legal tender status) in 1871. This would cause silver prices to plummet within a few years, requiring Nevada's political bosses to preserve the value of the "Big Bonanza" flowing from the Comstock Lode. But at the Carson City Mint in 1871, there was one objective: produce coins and put Nevada on the map in as grand a style as possible. Always supportive, the local newspaper, the Carson *Daily Appeal* covered the *happenings and events* at the mint on a daily basis, on a par with how local newspapers around the country in modern times cover the activities of their sports teams.

Further details and data about the second year issue coins may be found in Chapter 6, *The Silver Coins* and Chapter 7, *The Gold Coins.*

> ### Reno Tailor's Prototype for Levi 501 Jeans
>
> You also might find it interesting to note that during this same time in 1871, Jacob Davis, a local tailor on Virginia Street in Reno, was responding to the challenge of providing heavy-duty work pants for the hundreds of mining workers employed in the Comstock re-gion. His denim, copper-riveted, heavy-duty men's pants were replicated by the Levi-Strauss Company of San Francisco, and given the brand name of Levi 501 jeans. Davis eventually moved to San Francisco when he was hired by Levi-Strauss to oversee the production of their jeans. News of Davis' success was followed by Reno, Carson City, and Virginia City reporters, and was another source of pride-by-association for northern Nevada residents. The silver dollars produced at Carson City would find their way into the pockets of many a man's Levi jeans.

Wells Fargo check from Nevada Territorial Governor James W. Nye to Wells Fargo agent H.F. Rice written on December 13, 1861. This was only nine months after Nevada was granted territorial status. Henry F. Rice would become the second mint superintendent at the Carson City Mint. Troubled by a scandalous life, Rice reportedly committed suicide in Stockton, California in November, 1877.

1872

CARSON CITY MINT RECEIVES A SUCCESSFUL REPORT CARD

At the end of 1872, the *Carson Daily Appeal* ran a story that would cause local citizens to fluff out their feathers with pride. An article entitled "The Mint and the Carson Branch," reviewed the Philadelphia Mint's assessment of affairs at the two-year-old mint. It read:

> We have just examined with attention and interest the report of the Director of the Mint at Philadelphia.
>
> We regret that our brief space does not allow us to indulge in the pleasure of publishing enough of the report of the Director of the United States Mint to show fully the creditable working of the Branch Mint in Carson. The Director, in his report to the secretary of the Treasury, says: 'This Branch Mint has been most successful in its operations during the past year.'

The article concluded on a positive note:

> The remarks of the Director on the Carson Mint, close with the full approval of all the changes and measures of improvement that Superintendent Rice recommended; and with the expression of the fullest confidence in the future of the Branch Mint under the energetic and painstaking superintendency of the present manager.

Production totals increased by nearly 70% in 1872 from 214,958 coins to 360,380 coins, the bulk of this attributed to an increase in half dollars, rising by some 132,000 pieces. In fact, half dollars were the most plentiful of all coins produced during the first four years of operations at the Carson City Mint, partially due to the denomination's desirability for export purposes. Additionally, half dollars were more versatile in commercial trade in the Pacific state region where paper currency was not generally accepted. Totals for silver coinage production during the years 1870 to 1874 at Carson City reveal how lopsided the aggregate totals were between dimes, quarters, halves and regular issue silver dollars. There were 86,108 dimes, 44,792 quarters (58,542 if Breen's figures are used), and 19,288 dollars minted. In comparison, there were 862,627 half dollars produced. For the sake of accuracy, it must also be noted that there were 1,497,700 silver trade dollars minted through 1874, although they were designed specifically for export.

President Ulysses S. Grant served two terms from 1869 through 1877. (*Dictionary of American Portraits, Dover Publications*)

TWAIN'S ROUGHING IT PUBLISHED

In other news from around the nation, 1872 was a presidential election year in which Ulysses S. Grant defeated Horace Greeley. Susan B. Anthony (who would be controversially linked to the design of the most unpopular coin in U.S. history) tested the 14th Amendment during this election when she led a group of women who attempted to vote, and was arrested. It would not be until August 26, 1920, 48 years later, that the 19th amendment became law, ratifying women's right to vote. Nevada women however, won the right to vote in 1914. Mark Twain's book, *Roughing It* (subtitled *A Record of Several Years of "Vagabondizing" in the West*), was also published in 1872 and became a best seller, symbolizing in so many ways the attraction people have for the Old West. Virginia City was the Las Vegas of its era and Twain described the rough and tumble exploits that so many people experienced there. The Nevada miners, saloon keepers, barmaids, thieves, livery and stable men, stagecoach drivers, and everyone and everything else brought together by the enormous supply of precious metals coming out of the ground stirred readers' imaginations.

In August 1861, Twain (Samuel Clemens) had traveled by stagecoach from Missouri to Carson, Nevada with his brother Orion Clemens, the new Secretary of the Nevada Territory. In September of 1862, Twain was employed as a reporter at the *Territorial Enterprise* in Virginia City covering the 2nd territorial legislature in Carson City in November of 1862. Although Mark Twain had left the land of the Comstock six years before the mint opened in Carson City, his writings have been influential in describing and glamorizing the heart of what makes the coins from that mint so endearing. One of Twain's tales in *Roughing It* concerns an incident that alludes to the high cost of living in that area during those times:

Mark Twain's *Roughing It* was published in 1872.

> Then I handed him a silver five cent piece, with the benevolent air of a person who is conferring wealth and blessedness upon poverty and suffering. The yellow-jacket took

it with what I judged to be suppressed emotion, and laid it reverently down in the middle of his broad hand. Then he began to contemplate it, much as a philosopher contemplates a gnat's ear in the ample field of his microscope. Several mountaineers, teamsters, stage drivers, etc., drew near and dropped into the tableau and fell to surveying the money with that attractive indifference to formality which is noticeable in the hardy pioneer. Presently the yellow jacket handed the half dime back to me and told me I ought to keep my money in my pocket-book instead of in my soul, and then I wouldn't get it cramped and shriveled up so!

BACKGROUND OF THE DESIGNS
USED FOR CARSON CITY COINAGE

Now for a little background information: a trio of designers was responsible for the Seated Liberty design, used for dimes, quarters, halves, and the first of the three silver dollar issues produced by the Carson City Mint. These three men were Christian Gobrecht, Titan Peale, and Thomas Sully, who, following the directive of Mint Director Dr. Robert Patterson, used England's Seated Britannia copper coin as a model, which displayed Lady Britannia holding a shafted trident.

Accordingly, the new U.S. coin design would display Lady Liberty holding a staff with a cap hanging on it. This cap on a pole is referred to as a *pileus* (Latin for felt cap), and was given to slaves as a sign that they had been granted their freedom. In respect to the new coin design it symbolized the United States becoming a free nation. Some government officials were opposed to using such a symbol, insisting, as Thomas Jefferson once had, that the United States of America was not made up of *emancipated slaves.*

Designers Peale and Sully were the artists and Gobrecht was the engraver. Robert Ball Hughes eventually made slight modifications to the portrait of the seated Ms. Liberty. The reverse of the coin displays a version of a heraldic eagle, which was designed from similar models, created by Robert Scot and William Kneass.

There were slight modifications made to the original design through the years, chiefly the addition of *arrows* and *arrows and rays* near the date. When the Carson City Mint began minting coins for the first time in 1870, the Seated Liberty design had gone through all of its design changes, except for the *arrows* which were added in 1873 to signify the increase in the silver content mandated by the Coinage Act of that year.

William Barber's obverse design used for the 20-cent piece was very similar to the Seated Liberty series. Barber's reverse design displayed the same eagle clutching arrows and branches found on his trade dollar and, unlike the trade dollar, lacked the motto *In God We Trust.* Also lacking was the country's motto, *E Pluribus Unum*, which curiously enough did appear on the trade dollar.

1872-CC QUARTER A BARGAIN AT $99,000

Flipping the channel forward 125 years, into the late 20th century, representatives from most of the major coin companies in the United States were in attendance. Reporters from the two most widely circulated weekly coin newspapers were there. The local press from New York City was covering the event. At the front podium were auctioneer Q. David Bowers and assistant auctioneer John Babalis. The auction company's co-partner Ray Merena, auction coordinator and media liaison Christine Karstedt, and several of the company's staff were keeping track of bidding activity. In the crowded hotel ballroom were seated

Some precursors to the Liberty Seated design: left to right, Great Britain's Lady Britannia as shown on a British copper, a portrait of Thomas Sully's daughter, and a Seated Liberty sketch by Christian Gobrecht.

collectors and coin dealers from every economic level and age group. The attire was a cross sampling of suits and ties, casual business clothes, and leisurely slovenliness. Occasions like the *Eliasberg* auction in April 1997 are almost as rare as the coins that were being sold. There are many rare coin and paper money auctions held every year, many of them featuring headline making consignments. But sales like that of the *Eliasberg Collection* rank at the top of the list of all auctions held in a century. Some participants in such an event feel privileged to buy any item offered, just to have a memento of the occasion. Prices realized ranged from $33 for a British token, to $1,815,000 for a silver dollar. One company purchased 10% of the total $22,982,061 sold. There were some people in attendance who only wanted to watch. Some dealers formed temporary partnerships and pooled their money making purchases they would eventually sell and split the profits (or in some cases the losses). All things considered, auctions like these are very exciting.

The *Eliasberg* 1872-CC quarter. (*Courtesy Bowers and Merena*)

The winning bidder of the 1870-CC and 1871-CC Seated Liberty quarters was poised and confident when the bidding for the 1872-CC quarter began. He was well aware that the combined price paid for the 1870-CC and the 1871-CC quarters was $352,000, approximately $100,000 less than what he had budgeted to pay for the two coins. His maximum bid for the 1872-CC quarter was $200,000, so he had plenty of cushion, and in the back of his mind knew that acquiring the coin would be like a walk in the park. Bidding soon reached $50,000 and finally at $90,000, all competing bidders dropped out. Sold, $90,000. With the 10% buyer's fee, the price realized was $99,000.

Three of the rarest, most superb quality, extremely desirable coins minted at Carson City were in the possession of a single owner again; three coins that belong together and should never be broken up. Seeing them side by side arouses the senses. Though the 1873-CC *Without Arrows* dime may be the premier coin from the Carson City Mint, the 1870, 1871, 1872-CC quarters, as a set, rank a close second, in the author's opinion. In an issue of

Coin World, several weeks after the April 1997 *Eliasberg* sale, "Trends" reporter Keith Zaner listed a selection of coins that sold in the auction that in his opinion sold for less than they deserved to. Among the coins on his list were the 1796 Bust quarter MS-66 ($176,000), 1876-CC 20-cent piece MS-65 ($148,500), 1827/3 Restrike Bust quarter Proof-65 ($77,000), and the threesome of Carson City quarters, 1870-CC MS-64 ($187,000), 1871-CC MS-65 ($165,000), and 1872-CC MS-66 ($99,000). Zaner made an interesting comment, "Even though the Carson City Seated Liberty quarter dollars brought six-figure results, their true rarity should have put their value above the $200,000 (for each) level." Over $22 million in rare coins and collectibles sold in that auction. Yet *Coin World's* staff reporter focused in on those three Carson City quarters because they sold for less than they should have, an observation that was only possible to make after the sale. Beforehand, there was no precedent established for how much coins like these should sell for in comparison to other rarities. It became clear, after the May 1996 *Eliasberg* sale, in which the 1873-CC *Without Arrows* dime sold for $550,000, and the April 1997 sale in which many of the scarce, high quality "CC" coins sold for record prices, that the coin market genuinely respected the round metallic remnants from the branch mint in Nevada.

Men from Engine House #2 posing in front of the United States Land Office in Carson City. (*Courtesy Nevada State Museum*)

MINTAGES FOR 1872

Production totals increased by over 65% in 1872 at the Carson City Mint, the most significant increase was again for half dollars, whose mintage rose from 139,950 the year before, to 272,000. Gold double eagle totals rose 200%, increasing to 29,650. Official coinage records from the U.S. Mint report that there were 9,100 quarters minted in 1872, a figure used in coin collecting publications such as the *Red Book* (*A Guide Book of United States Coins*) for the first 100 years after this coin was minted. There was a difference of opinion however between numismatic researchers during the last two decades of the 20th century, continuing into this new century, about what the actual mintage total was. As stated in the Bowers and Merena Eliasberg auction catalog from April 1997, "Until 1977 it was thought that the 1872-CC (quarter) had a mintage of only 9,100 pieces . . . However, exploration in the National Archives turned up previously unknown coinages."

Abe Curry in his fireman's suit during a better time in his life.

Documentation from those early years at the Carson City Mint is rather obscure. It is possible that portions of the mintages reported for 1872 overlapped with those of 1873. For example, coinage records indicate that there were 4,000 1872 quarters produced on December 31, 1872. Coincidentally, 4,000 is the same total for the 1873-CC *Without Arrows* quarters, which by necessity would have had to have been coined in the first six weeks of 1873, as the coinage act of 1873 was passed on February 12, 1873, increasing the amount of silver used in dimes, quarters, and half dollars, causing production on these denominations to cease until after April 1873. It seems more likely, however, that the 4,000 quarters reported as being coined on December 31, 1872 would have been the ones dated 1873. Something else to consider is that the quantity of quarters minted in 1870, 1871, and 1872 appeared to be consistent: 8,340; 10,890; and 9,100 (if the original figures are used), and it makes no sense for the mintage to suddenly have increased to 22,850 in 1872. Today's survival rate for the 1872-CC quarter leans toward the mintage figure being slightly higher than those for the 1870-CC and 1871-CC quarters, however, it is entirely possible that if an adjustment must be made from the historically accepted 9,100 total, a more accurate figure might be 14,850 to 18,850. Regardless, the 1872-CC ranks in the top five in rarity ratings for Carson City Seated Liberty quarters, and until more corroborative evidence is discovered it may be prudent to use the Treasury's mintage figure of 9,100.

Further details and data about Carson City coinage from the year 1872 may be found in Chapter 6, *The Silver Coins*, and Chapter 7, *The Gold Coins*.

❀ 1873 ❀

A knowledge of the coinage of the different branch mints gives to many usually considered common dates great rarity if certain mint marks are upon them.

- Augustus G. Heaton, *A Treatise On the Coinage of the United States Branch Mints*, 1893.

Abe Curry in his mid 50s. (*Courtesy Nevada Historical Society*)

A PIVOTAL YEAR

If there was a pivotal year in the history of the Carson City Mint it would have to be 1873. For one, the last Seated Liberty silver dollars were issued in 1873. Correspondingly, the first trade dollars were issued in that year. Of greatest consequence, the Coinage Act was passed and with the advent of the Mint Act that passed into legislation on February 12, 1873, the Treasury Department attempted to convert the coinage system of the United States to a metric scale. Dimes would weigh 2 ½ grams, quarters 6 ¼ grams, and half dollars 12 ½ grams. This system would then be compatible with money in Europe.[1]

In compliance with the Coinage Act, the weight of silver coins was increased by a slight amount, resulting in a modified *With Arrows* design on the dimes, quarters and halves. It also caused the melting of millions of the lighter weight silver coins struck at all mints prior to March of 1873 after April of that year. This especially affected surviving quantities of Carson City dimes and quarters minted from 1870 to 1873.

THE DEATH OF ABRAHAM CURRY

By far, the most significant event to occur in 1873, as far as citizens of Carson City were concerned, was the death of Abraham Curry on October 19 of that year. This article from the October 22, 1873 edition of the *Territorial Enterprise* illustrates what the local folk thought of their city's founder:

The Carson Appeal of October 21 has the following concerning the death and burial of Colonel Abe Curry: At 4 o'clock on Sunday morning, October 19, after lying paralytic in his bed for about forty-four hours, Colonel Abraham Curry departed this life. He died calmly and painlessly, and in the midst of his family and friends. He paid the price of living a life which never knew ill health by thus passing away suddenly and unwarned. From the time of his receiving the fatal stroke he never spoke nor opened his eyes. Yesterday he was followed to the grave, and his funeral was the most numerously attended of any we have ever seen here. On Sunday the remains were taken in charge by the brethren of Carson Lodge No. 1 F. and A. M., and removed from his residence to their hall, from whence the cortege proceeded to the grave. The procession, which was led by a brass band

playing appropriate music, was composed of the immediate family of the deceased, his late associates and the later employees in the Mint, the Masonic brethren, the Odd Fellows of Carson and visiting brethren, the Improved Order of Red Men, (a large delegation from Virginia and Gold Hill being among the number) the three Carson Engine Companies, and fifty vehicles of all sorts (other than the four mourners carriages). This made a procession well on to a mile in length. In the procession were many distinguished citizens and State and Federal officers. A notable feature of the procession was two wagons filled with Chinese.

The Colonel had many friends amongst these peculiar people. And there is a touching incident to be related concerning the little daughter of Dr. Ah Kee who attends the public school here. Curry in the kindness of his heart had presented this little child with several dresses made in American fashion – had given her one, in fact, only the day before he was taken down. When this little girl heard her benefactor was dead she begged to be allowed to see him; and so she came to visit his remains—"to let him see her new dress," she said – and when she saw how still and changed he was she fell to crying as if her heart would break. At the grave the ceremonies were very impressive. First the ritual of the Red Men was read by the Sachem of one of the Storey county Lodges, and then the prayer by Jonas Seely, Chaplain; then the ritual of the Odd Fellows by Thomas Wells, N.G., and a prayer by Rev. James Woods, Chaplain; then the Masonic ritual and prayer by ex Mayor Currie of Virginia City, Past Grand Master. During the day the Mint and all the State and county offices, Wells Fargo & Co.'s express and bank, and nearly all the business houses and saloons were closed, and the streets were filled with silent spectators.

Without question, this was the largest event of any kind ever held in Carson City up till that time, surpassing by a large margin the cornerstone ceremonies from years past.

A familiar figure at the funeral was William "Billy" Lynch, a former servant of Abraham Lincoln, and one of Abraham Curry's most loyal employees. After Lincoln's

---

[1] Neil Carothers, *Fractional Money*.

assassination, Lynch "continued in the employ of Andrew Johnson until 1868. At that time…Curry, director of the U.S. Mint at Carson City, was in Washington on business.

Abe Curry befriended Billy Lynch during a visit to Washington, D.C., and brought him to Carson City where he worked as porter at the Carson City Mint. (*Courtesy Daun Bohall Collection*)

While there he met Lynch and offered to take him to Nevada. President Johnson told Lynch that the west "was a rough country, but the latter was eager for adventure and accepted Mr. Curry's offer."[1]

During the last leg of Curry and Lynch's trip back to Carson City they rode in a stagecoach driven by one of the more colorful characters of the day, Hank Monk. Some of Lynch's early memories of Carson City were that it "was nothing but a mudhole then, you couldn't cross the main street without rubber boots. [And] we used to hunt rabbits where the Capitol is now."[2] He also recalled that, "Saloons were plenty… and men rode their horses right up to the bar…Mr. Johnson was right, it was a 'rough country'."

Curry assigned Lynch to the duties of porter and all around handyman when the new mint opened, positions Lynch held long after Curry was gone. Lynch held Curry in the highest honor, always having fond recollections of what a "grand man" Curry was. In Lynch's words, "Old Abe was a good man. He always saw to it that I had a job."[3]

A COMPLETE 1873-CC COIN SET

Skipping ahead to April of 1997, collector Waldo Bolen finally accomplished his goal of acquiring one example of each coin minted at the Carson City Mint in 1873, when he was the winning bidder for the *Eliasberg* 1873-CC *Without Arrows* quarter. Bolen also purchased the 1873-CC *With Arrows* quarter at the same sale. In May 1996, Bolen had purchased the legendary 1873-CC *Without Arrows* dime from the second of three *Eliasberg* sales.

(The first *Eliasberg* sale was held in October of 1982). This excerpt, from Heritage's auction catalog of April 1999, describes Bolen's adventure:

Unique 1873-CC *Without Arrows* dime. (*Courtesy Bowers and Merena*)

The coin remained in the Eliasberg Collection until sold by Bowers in May, 1996 for $550,000. The buyer from the Eliasberg Sale was noted collector Waldo Bolen. Bolen had already spent years assembling a collection of dimes—a complete set of every dime produced by the U.S. Mint, except for the unique 1873-CC *No Arrows*. He then sold his dimes at auction. When the 1873-CC finally came on the market, he purchased it, just for the pleasure of knowing that he had owned every U.S. dime. Bolen became so enamored of the issue that he decided to build a complete 11-piece 1873-CC set around the lynch pin *No Arrows* dime.

It took Bolen one year to complete the 11 piece set, his 48th year as a coin collector. Always ready to begin his next new challenge, Bolen sold this wonderful set just two years later.

What does the collector do when the set is finally completed? Maybe the set is upgraded, maybe a new set is begun, or, as in Bolen's case, the collection is sold. The

---

[1] *Nevada State Journal*, February 22, 1927.
[2] Ibid.
[3] Ibid, also *With Curry's Compliments*, Doris Cerveri.

THE WALDO BOLEN 1873-CC COLLECTION

DENOMINATION	GRADE	LOT#	PRICE REALIZED
No Arrows Dime	MS 64 PCGS	5928	$632,500.00
Arrows Dime	MS 64 PCGS	5927	71,875.00
No Arrows Quarter	MS 62 PCGS	5926	106,375.00
Arrows Quarter	MS 63 PCGS	5925	66,125.00
No Arrows Half Dollar	MS 66 PCGS	5924	69,000.00
Arrows Half Dollar	MS 63 NGC	5923	13,225.00
Seated Dollar	AU 58 NGC	5922	41,400.00
Trade Dollar	MS 63 PCGS	5921	17,825.00
Half Eagle ($5)	XF 40 PCGS	5920	7,762.50
Eagle ($10)	XF 45 NGC	5919	9,487.50
Double Eagle ($20)	MS 60 PCGS	5918	20,700.00

enjoyment and reward come from assembling the set, though the thrill of accomplishment may be fleeting, or it may last a lifetime. Like Q. David Bowers says, "Getting there is half the fun."

MR. 1873

Continuing on the subject of interest in 1873 coinage, collector Harry X Boosel had such a passion for coins from 1873, that he became known as *Mr. 1873*. This quote, from the collection of papers later compiled into a small book titled *Mr. 1873*, reveals a glimpse into Mr. Boosel's passion:

> The next revealing document is the report itself, which is also dated April 16, 1873 from the Carson City Mint. This document is indeed a treasure. It shows that there were 4,000 quarters minted at the Carson City Mint in 1873 **without arrows**, 12,400 dimes of 1873 for Carson City **without arrows** and 122,500 Carson City halves of 1873 **without arrows**. It is an easy thing to merely subtract these figures from the figures known all these years for the total coinage for the year 1873 and here is what we get:

	1873 WITHOUT ARROWS	1873 WITH ARROWS	1873 TOTAL
Dimes	12,400	18,791	31,191
Quarters	4,000	12,462	16,462
Halves	122,500	214,560	337,060

The figures arrived at above have been verified by other existing documents which gave the actual totals by date for the Carson City Mint for the remaining part of the year 1873 as indicated previously when mentioning the Test Coins. All figures quoted are correct and proven.

Another interesting item is the fact that five (5) dimes of the year 1873 from Carson City **without arrows** were sent to Philadelphia for Assay. Only one is known to exist today, and that came from the Philadelphia Mint – so it is easy to surmise its origin. No doubt those remaining at Carson City were remelted after April 1, 1873, as they could not legally be issued after that date, being lighter in weight than the Coinage Act of 1873 required.

1873-CC *Without Arrows* quarter. (*Author's personal collection*)

STATEMENT OF COINS RETAINED FOR ASSAY DURING THE MONTHS OF JANUARY, FEBRUARY AND MARCH 1873

GOLD

DATE 1873	NO. OF DELIVERY	NO. OF PIECES	DENOMINATION	VALUE OF DELIVERY	*TOTAL MINTED
February 12, 1873	1	1	Double Eagle	$20,000	1,000
March 31, 1873	2	1	Double Eagle	20,000	1,000

SILVER

DATE 1873	NO. OF DELIVERY	NO. OF PIECES	DENOMINATION	VALUE OF DELIVERY	*TOTAL MINTED
January 18, 1873	1	1	Dollar	$1,000	1,000
January 18, 1873	1	9	Half Dollars	11,000	22,000
January 18, 1873	1	2	Quarter Dollars	1,000	4,000
March 3, 1873	2	1	Dollar	1,300	1,300
March 3, 1873	2	16	Half Dollars	20,000	40,000
March 3, 1873	2	5	Dimes	1,240	12,400
March 12, 1873	3	7	Half Dollars	8,000	16,000
March 27, 1873	4	12	Half Dollars	15,000	30,000
March 31, 1873	5	6	Half Dollars	7,250	14,500

H. F. Rice Superintendent.

COMMEMORATING CURRY

Switching back to the inexhaustible subject of Abraham Curry, a brief word about his ex partners may be of interest. Curry's original team of Proctor, Musser and Green went their separate ways within a few years after arriving in the new territory. Records show that Proctor and Musser gave up their interest in the foursome's Warm Springs Hotel, and Green accepted 25 pounds of butter for his 1/4 share. Green became a jeweler and gunsmith and eventually moved back to California. Musser practiced law, and Proctor was a partner in various businesses with other men in Carson City and eventually lived in Elko, Nevada, Montana and Washington where he died an old man. John Musser had died in 1871 at the young age of 41 in Carson City.

A common thread that wove through Curry's life concerned his business dealings. By 1863, the Gould and Curry Mine that *Old Abe* and Alva Gould had sold their interests in, was producing millions of dollars in bullion and at one time was the largest mine on the Comstock. Curry knew what he had given up. Nevertheless he forged onward, with seemingly no thought of his past mistakes. Doris Cerveri in her book *With Curry's Compliments, the Story of Abraham Curry*, writes:

Throughout his business career Curry made thousands of dollars, enjoyed the best food and liquor, smoked the best cigars and provided handsomely for his family. He could have been one of the richest men in Nevada. If he thought of the future at all, it was probably only in relation to what he hoped Carson City would become. There is no indication that he made plans for security in his old age or provided for his wife's future welfare. There was always tomorrow. As his obituary stated, Curry made considerable money but never saved any of it. Mary [his wife] discovered, when a decree setting aside his estate to her was filed, that after a lifetime of work he left nothing except nine lots in Block 39 of the Proctor and Green subdivision in Carson City and the home he had built several years earlier.

Elvira [Curry's daughter], who earlier had worked at the mint as an adjuster, moved in with her mother and for several years the two of them took in roomers and boarders. Times were always hard for the women Curry left behind, as their lack of money remained a serious problem. Mary suffered a stroke which left her paralyzed for over a year before her death in 1912.

Mrs. Curry's obituary in the July 29, 1912 issue of the Carson Appeal stated that she was the oldest woman residing in that section of Nevada. According to the article, she died in her sleep, July 29, at the age of 94 years, eight months.

Collectors of Carson City coins today can be grateful to Curry for his efforts to have a mint established, and might find this article from the Carson Daily Appeal dated July 14, 1891 very interesting and perhaps unbelievable:

Not a stone or monument of any kind, character or description marks the spot where the late Abe Curry is buried at Carson. Col. Curry did more for Carson in his lifetime than any other 50 men have accomplished. To him Carson was very largely indebted for the mint; for the help given him by late Senator James Nye, he was able to build that monument that adorns Carson Street. He built the courthouse, state prison, Warm Springs Hotel, now a part of the state's property, the Curry Engine House and numerous other buildings of lesser note. He was one of the very few progressive citizens that pulled that town out of the mud in 1864-65. One would think the least the city could do would be to erect a stone to his memory if it were nothing more than a plain, white slab.

Cerveri continues

It wasn't until 1964 that a large stone was brought from the Sierra by Nevada Highway Department personnel. It was cut in half, engraved by Tan Boone of Sonora, and put in place over Curry's grave after its location was verified by Ellinor Robinson Raffetto, Curry's great-great-granddaughter.

Possibly, the U.S. Mint could honor Abraham Curry with a commemorative coin at some point in the future, perhaps on a replica of an 1870-CC Seated Liberty silver dollar, or if nothing else, at least a postage stamp. The government has honored people like Abner Doubleday for inventing our national pastime of baseball (Of questionable accuracy, by the way). Would Carson City exist without Abe Curry? Would there have been a mint there? There is no way to decide for sure. It is the author's opinion that there would definitely be a void in coin collecting without "CC" coins. Northern Nevada supported the westward expansion of the United States. It is fitting that coins bearing the mintmark of one of its most important cities have been left as *snapshots in time* for us to study and enjoy. A little soapboxing? Perhaps. But, this book would not be in your hands if not for the author's love and passion for coins from the Carson City Mint.

HOME MEANS NEVADA

WRITTEN & MUSIC BY BERTHA RAFFETTO

Way out in the land of the setting sun,
Where the wind blows wild and free,
There's a lovely spot, just the only one
That means home sweet home to me.
If you follow the old Kit Carson trail,
Until desert meets the hills,
Oh you certainly will agree with me,
It's the place of a thousand thrills.

Whenever the sun at the close of day,
Colors all the western sky,
Oh my heart returns to the desert grey
And the mountains tow'ring high.
Where the moon beams play in shadowed glen,
With the spotted fawn and doe,
All the live long night until morning light,
Is the loveliest place I know.

Home means Nevada
Home means the hills,
Home means the sage and the pine.
Out by the Truckee, silvery rills,
Out where the sun always shines,
Here is the land which I love the best,
Fairer than all I can see.
Deep in the heart of the golden west
Home means Nevada to me.

Home means Nevada
Home means the hills,
Home means the sage and the pine.
Out by the Truckee, silvery rills,
Out where the sun always shines,
Here is the land which I love the best,
Fairer than all I can see.
Deep in the heart of the golden west
Home means Nevada to me.

The official song of the State of Nevada, authored by Abe Curry's great-granddaughter Bertha Raffetto, describes the sentiments of many of the thousands of people, past and present, who have discovered all that Nevada has to offer. *Home Means Nevada* was adopted in 1935 as Nevada's official state song.

THE PANIC OF 1873

While the Carson City Mint was engaged in coin production in September of 1873, the leading brokerage firm, Jay Cooke & Company, failed to meet its obligations to its clients. As a result, millions of dollars were lost. Unfortunately, this was just the tip of the iceberg of the devastating effects the Panic of 1873 would have on the economy of the United States, as post Civil War inflation put a strain on bank reserves. Jay Cooke & Company had sold government bonds to aid the North's war efforts and then parlayed the profits from bond sales into railroad investments. This led to the company's financial disaster.

President Ulysses S. Grant's tight money policy was unpopular, however he stood firm, even after Congress passed a bailout which would have increased the money supply. Grant vetoed the bill the following year; and it is debatable whether this inflationary measure would have prevented the failure of thousands of businesses through the 1870s, which resulted in record unemployment. After enduring a terrible depression for five years, most of the nation began experiencing a long awaited recovery. Arguments raged during those five years over which monetary system was the best. Some advocated national bank notes backed by gold, while others promoted the elasticity of greenbacks. Out West hard money ruled, and silver advocates warned of the dangers of demonetized silver coins. Their answer was a bimetallic monetary system that maintained silver at par with gold. Much of the public then, as is so often the case, was unaware of what big government was doing behind the scenes. In the face of panics, depressions and hyper-inflationary periods, the only thing that enables the populace to survive is grit and perseverance. If the citizens of the United States were able to trust the politicians who were elected to lead them, they could be confident, knowing that their best interests were being looked out for. But who could have known in 1873 that certain high ranking officials were planning to profit from the hard times most people were suffering through? It was apparently more important to these officials to manipulate the silver market and nearly ruin the currency system, than it was to stop interfering with the currency, gold and silver ratios.

As a result of a decrease in the value of silver, which caused the face value of coins to rise in comparison to their metal weight, massive quantities of coins eventually began appearing in commercial exchanges. It was indeed puzzling for most people to figure out when the silver in a coin was worth more than the coin itself, or when the face value of paper money was worth more than the gold it was linked to, or when silver coins should be used to buy gold, or vice versa. How was the average citizen supposed to know? It was indeed very confusing. An article in the October 29, 1873 issue of the *New York Times* reveals how confusing this can be:

> The low price of silver has brought a large amount of it into circulation. Silver dimes, half-dimes, quarters, half-dollars, and even dollars, are given out as change for currency over bar and restaurant counters with the utmost nonchalance by the attendants. The coin is generally fresh from the Mint, and it is examined critically and with curiosity by many who have never seen an American coin before.

Strange as it seems, many people in the East had forgotten what silver coins looked like! Out in the West it was a different story. The citizens knew what silver and gold coins looked like and in many instances, would not even accept paper money. Paradoxically, within three years, the country would be saturated with silver coins.

Consider these totals from the Carson City Mint alone. From 1870 to 1873 a total of 923,710 combined silver dimes, quarters and half dollars had been minted. Yet, from 1874 to 1877 Carson City produced 34,488,107 combined silver dimes, quarters and halves, 37 times as many subsidiary silver coins minted through the mid-1870s as were produced between 1870 and 1873. The chart below shows the comparisons between the two four year divisions during the first eight years of coin production at Carson City.

COINAGE RECORD
UNITED STATES MINT AT CARSON CITY, NEVADA

YEAR	DIMES	20 CENTS	QUARTERS	HALF DOLLARS	TOTALS
1870			8,340	54,617	62,957
1871	20,100		10,890	139,950	170,940
1872	24,000		9,100	272,000	305,100
1873	31,191		16,462	337,060	384,713
TOTAL	75,291		44,792	803,627	923,710
1874	10,817			59,000	69,817
1875	4,645,000	133,290	140,000	1,008,000	5,926,290
1876	8,270,000	10,000	4,944,000	1,956,000	15,180,000
1877	7,700,000		4,192,000	1,420,000	13,312,000
TOTAL	20,625,817	143,290	9,276,000	4,443,000	34,488,107

$$\frac{34,488,107}{923,710} = 37.34$$

As mentioned, a large percentage of pre-1874 silver coins would eventually be melted. This and other changes that the monetary system of the United States experienced in its search to achieve equilibrium provide many opportunities for coin collectors.

FULL MINT STATUS FOR CARSON CITY

H.R. Linderman, representing self serving pseudo silver supporters, managed to get a bill passed into legislation which provided for a 420 grain, 90% fine silver *commercial* dollar, and thus the trade dollar was introduced in 1873. In the next chapter more information will be provided about the trade dollar, but suffice it to say, it seemed to Linderman and his constituents like the best solution to revive the price of silver.

This same legislation, which introduced the trade dollar, also elevated the status of the branch mints to the level of U.S. Mints. Abe Curry lived long enough to proudly hear that the facility he was so instrumental in bringing into existence, was officially named the *United States Mint at Carson*. In 1873 the superintendent at the Carson Mint, H.F. Rice, earned a salary of $3,000 per year, and the assayer, melter and refiner were each paid $2,500 a year. Among other duties, the superintendent was required to render daily, monthly, quarterly and annual reports to the Director of the Mint in Philadelphia. These reports provided the following information:

- Daily receipts
- Payments and balances
- Annual, quarterly, and monthly deposits
- Production of coins minted
- Balances, assets, liabilities
- Records of assay coins reserved for annual assay
- Coins and bullion on hand
- Cost of operations and losses

For most of the years it was in service, superintendents at the Carson City Mint provided accurate reports, though at times, which will be discussed later, there were embarrassing exceptions.

JOHN PERCIVAL JONES

Another important figure in Nevada's history that was active during this time period was John Percival Jones, elected Senator in 1873 and serving the State in that of-

Inside the Nevada State Treasurer's Office.

fice until 1903. Jones had moved to California in 1850 to join in the Gold Rush. He tried his hand at mining, but his diplomatic prowess led him into public life and he eventually became a California State Senator. A failed run for Lieutenant Governor in 1867 left him broke and seemingly without a backup plan, so he decided to move to the East Coast. Before he left, he was offered and accepted the position of superintendent of the Kentuck mine in Gold Hill, Nevada. The following year, 1868, Jones became superintendent of the Crown Point mine in Gold Hill, and within two years, he was a millionaire. During his three decades in office he would play a major role in the silver issue. This article, which appeared in the *Carson Appeal* on November 25, 1873, provides a glimpse into the influence newly elected Senator Jones was being relied on to wield in Washington D.C.:

As we are informed by the papers of last evening, Governor Pollock and Arthur Orr, Mint machinist, under convoy of Senator Jones, will arrive here to-day. Their object is the inspection of the Mint with a view to such improvements and enlargements there as may be practicable. Much is to be hoped for from this visit.

The article continues by linking Jones' silver interests to his role as a senator.

These visitors are men whose recommendations in Mint matters go a long way with the Washington authorities, and Senator Jones being one of the most prominent silver miners in the United States and therefore very largely interested in all matters looking to the enhancement of facilities for the refining and coining of the precious metals, of course he and they will work harmoniously and with a view to enlarging the capacities of the Mint, and for such widening of the scope of the coinage laws as is needed by our mining interests.

Consequently, the significance of the silver coinage issue is stressed:

The restoration of the finances of the country to a coin basis being one of the larger and more immediately obvious questions with which Congress will have to deal, and our Senator, understanding that branch of the subject which has to do with the production and handling of the bullion and it being a commercial necessity here in Nevada that the Mint should coin silver half and quarter dollars it is not at all impossible that the said laws may be so amended as to set the mint at work doing this much needed service.

Invariably, the citizens of Carson City always felt a need to look out for themselves.

> With increased requirements of course, an increase of room will be needed; and so there will have to be more employees and more money to pay them with. These matters constitute the legislation most important in the eyes of the citizens of Carson, and so there is much to be hoped for from this visit to-day.

At this time, most of the nation was struggling to survive the effects of the dawning depression, but the residents in the western section of northern Nevada were busy with further development of their region. And then the discovery in early spring of 1873 of the great silver strike forever known as the *Big Bonanza* changed the course of history. While the rest of the country faltered under a depreciated currency standard, California and Nevada were on a precious metals standard.

BRIEF REVIEW OF THE FIRST DIMES AND QUARTERS MINTED IN 1873 AT CARSON CITY

At the Carson City Mint in early 1873, certain dimes and quarters were coined that future generations of coin collectors would hold in the highest esteem. It was business as usual in January of 1873 when 4,000 standard quarters *Without Arrows* were struck. Numismatists have debated since 1977 whether there were 4,000 quarters with the date 1872 minted on New Years Eve 1872, or whether the 4,000 quarters were, in fact, the 1873 dated pieces reportedly struck in January of 1873. But official Treasury Department records have maintained that no quarters were struck in December of 1872. After all, was there such a need for 4,000 quarters that mint workers would have rushed to coin them on the last day of 1872 making sure the quarters bore the 1872 date? And this, in spite of the fact that the 1873 obverse dies had already been delivered to the mint in December. It seems a stretch to believe that the Superintendent would have minted two sets of 4,000 quarters each with different dates within a period of 18 days; especially since there was not that much of a need for quarters in the first place. Records at the Carson City Mint were sketchy at times and leave room for variation, but as

The Eliasberg 1873-CC *With Arrows* quarter. (*Courtesy Bowers and Merena*)

a rule, collectors have been less concerned with how things happened and more concerned with the final outcome. It does not really matter, for instance, when or how many 1873-CC *Without Arrows* quarters were minted, because today there are only five surviving specimens known.

Likewise, the 1873 *Without Arrows* dimes were minted in Carson City in small quantities; official records reporting that 12,400 "CC" dimes were minted on February 5, 1873. Then on February 12, 1873, the Mint Act was passed making these dimes obsolete, legislation that would go into effect on April 1, 1873. Consequently, the fate of silver dimes, quarters and halves minted before February 12, 1873 was sealed.

WHY SO FEW CARSON CITY SILVER COINS?

Miners were mining, bankers were banking, mint employees were minting, and yet, the quantities of "CC" silver coins in circulation were shrinking. Since the Carson City Mint had opened in 1870, mintages of silver dimes and quarters had been kept at a minimum through 1873.

Is there an explanation? These quotes from Walter Breen's *Complete Encyclopedia of U.S. and Colonial Coins*, although not citing any references, attempt to explain the reason.

> From Breen's section on Seated Liberty dimes:

> Official orders deliberately limited the Carson City Mint's output for political reasons, and this limitation in turn, was intended to provide an official excuse for abolition!

> And from the chapter on Seated Liberty quarters:

> CC-Mint [silver] coins from 1870-73 are of great rarity in all grades, because issues were deliberately kept limited for political reasons by official policy emanating from the Philadelphia Mint — which limitation was in turned urged as reason for abolishing the Carson City Branch!

> Then again from the Seated Liberty halves section:

> Whereas the Carson City emissions were deliberately limited by official orders for political reasons, which limited output, was there after adduced as justifying a campaign to abolish that branch!

In lieu of supporting documents, Breen's comments serve as nothing more than mere speculation, yet they may provide some insight as to what took place behind the scenes.

In Heaton's *Treatise on Mint Marks* in 1893, the author expounds on what gives collectible coins value. Heaton states the obvious, "The value of a coin depends upon its rarity." He further informs the reader that the rarity of mintmarked coins is the result of a "known small coinage" (mintage total). But then Heaton adds an interesting side note, predating Breen's similar comments by more than 90 years, "what is practically the same [as a small mintage total], though not as evident, [is] a partial issue only of the amount coined [original mintage total]." Obviously, by 1893, it had become known to collectors that not all of the coins produced at the various mints were being released into circulation.

SUPERINTENDENT'S PLEA FOR INCREASED COINAGE AT CARSON MINT

By 1873 the silver mines on the Comstock were generating mass quantities of the white metal. Independent miners preferred to trade silver bullion for minted coins. Congress had put an end to this practice with the passage of the Coinage Act. Miners were forced to sell their silver at a discount to brokers, or exchange it for trade dollars. Newly appointed Carson City Mint Superintendent Frank D. Hetrich, who replaced H.F. Rice after Rice resigned amidst controversy, wrote a letter of appeal to the Director of the Mint in Philadelphia on behalf of the silver miners in the Comstock region.

The permission to coin this Bullion into Silver Coin would be of much assistance to the Mine owners in the development of the Mines, and a sensible relief to the mining population which they employ.

I have several applications within the past month from such persons, some within the last week. Some of whom have even taken the returns for their Bullion in Trade Dollars to circulate as coin at par for the partial relief it will give them in their business. These parties look to the Mint for a relief from the corner in which they are placed and are very much disappointed when they are told that they cannot get their Bullion converted into coins.

If I could be authorized to coin even $50,000 subsidiary Silver Coin per month it would be a great relief to the mining interests of these new districts. Besides this, there are numbers of individual miners working independent claims on the Comstock who, in their small way, produce lots of Bullion worth $250 - $1,000. If they cannot get this Bullion coined they are obliged to part with it to the Brokers and Bankers at a large discount, and even these buyers wish to convert it into coin when purchased.

Hetrich attempted to word his request in as non-threatening a way as possible, so as not to make it too burdensome for the Mint Director.

As to any depreciation of Silver values arising from all the Silver Coin which would be issued by this Mint, were it left without any restrictions, I do not think any apprehension need be entertained, as all that would be coined, beyond what would immediately go into the interior for use of local trade, would not be of sufficient amount to produce the slightest effect upon the market.

In this place the supply of Silver Coin is so that Bankers and business men have a scant supply for their ordinary business.

Carson City, looking north from the top of the Capitol building. The Mint is on the left approximately 10 buildings toward the mountains. (*Courtesy Nevada State Museum*).

Hetrich then gets specific in his request,

> For these considerations I would suggest the propriety of my being authorized to coin half dollars, quarters dollars, and dimes, not exceeding One Hundred Thousand Dollars per month; the bullion from which this coinage is made to be paid for in Silver Coins.

Unfortunately, his plea fell on deaf ears, and the only silver coins authorized to be minted in the last quarter of 1873, besides trade dollars, were $1,280 face value in half dollars, *With Arrows* (2,560 pieces).

COLLECTING CARSON CITY COINS FROM 1873

To recap, there is only one 1873-CC *Without Arrows* dime known to exist, and the 1873-CC *Without Arrows* quarter is the rarest regular issue Seated Liberty quarter. As of 1991 the only three specimens known of this date and variety were from the *Eliasberg, Norweb* and *James A. Stack* collections, all of these being in Uncirculated condition. In the final decade of the 20th century, two more 1873-CC *Without Arrows* quarters were discovered, both in circulated condition, bringing the total extant to five. Rumors of a sixth specimen in AU condition began to spread in the early years of the 21st century.

Varieties of the 1873-CC dimes and quarters bearing the arrows on either side of the date are also extremely scarce. These arrows of course, signified that the weight of the silver in the new coins had been increased as a provision of the Mint Act passed on February 12, 1873. Production on the *With Arrows* coins commenced midway through 1873. As a point of reference, the difference in the weight of the coins could probably only be determined in a laboratory, since it was infinitesimal. After a stint in circulation, any differences in the weights of *Without Arrows* and *With Arrows* coins would have been undetectable due to wear.

For collectors, these varieties have provided the challenge of obtaining an example of both for a type set. The terms *Without Arrows* and *With Arrows* are significant as they relate to coins from all mints, but they take on a much more special meaning in the Carson City series. As of the writing of this book, there are only two Uncirculated examples known of the 1873-CC *With Arrows* dime and two of the 1873-CC *With Arrows* quarter, with fewer than 25 examples of each in all grades. Louis E. Eliasberg, who owned the only known example of the 1873-CC *Without*

Arrows dime as part of his complete U.S. coin collection, managed only an example graded VG-8 to fill his slot for the 1873-CC *With Arrows* dime.

In addition to the rarest Seated Liberty dime and quarter being produced at the Carson City Mint in 1873, the rarest Seated Liberty silver dollar with the "CC" mintmark bears the 1873 date. A total of 2,300 were minted, with a large percentage most likely melted within the first year of issue. Although there were greater numbers of half dollars minted at Carson City in 1873, large quantities were also subsequently melted. As with the dimes and quarters of 1873, the halves feature the *Without Arrows* and *With Arrows* varieties, the surviving *Without Arrows* specimens being extremely rare in higher grades. Additionally, the controversial trade dollar made its debut in 1873.

There are eight distinct types of 1873 silver coins from the Carson City Mint. In addition to these silver coins, there were three denominations of gold coins, the $5, $10 and $20 all featuring the Liberty Head design. Mintages of the two smaller denomination gold coins were kept at a minimum, as all parties concerned awaited the verdict on the silver-gold-currency issue. Once again the $20 double eagles had the highest mintage of the three gold denominations, although its output dropped from 29,650 the year before, to 22,410 in 1873.

It had been an eventful first four years at the Carson City Mint by the end of 1873. Locals mourned the loss of the man responsible for this prestigious facility being located in their serene community. Now that it was there, practically no one would ever speak the name of this town again without thinking of the mint that gave it an identity.

You can read more about the mintages and other interesting statistics about the coins from 1873 in Chapter 6, *The Silver Coins*, and Chapter 7, *The Gold Coins*.

CHAPTER TWO

The Trade Dollar Era (1874-1878)

Mint marks in their amount of issue in varied years at different points offer the monetary pulse of our country to the student of finance.

- Augustus G. Heaton
A Treatise On the Coinage of the United States Branch Mints, 1893.

COINAGE RECORD • UNITED STATES MINT AT CARSON CITY, NEVADA

YEAR	DIMES	20-CENT PIECES	QUARTERS	HALF DOLLARS	TRADE DOLLARS	DOLLARS	HALF EAGLES	EAGLES	DOUBLE EAGLES	NUMBER OF PIECES	TOTAL $
1874	10,817			59,000	1,373,200		21,198	16,767	115,085	1,596,067	$3,979,141.70
1875	4,645,000	133,290	140,000	1,008,000	1,573,700		11,828	7,715	111,151	7,630,684	4,963,168.00
1876	8,270,000	10,000	4,944,000	1,956,000	509,000		6,887	4,696	138,441	15,839,024	6,402,215.00
1877	7,700,000		4,192,000	1,420,000	534,000		8,680	3,332	42,565	13,900,577	3,990,020.00

EIGHTEEN SEVENTY-FOUR was a transitional year for coinage produced at the Carson City Mint. Whereas in 1873, the mint could boast of having minted 11 different denomination/variety combinations, 1874 would have claims only to six.

FINANCIAL CONCERNS IN 1874

The United States, as usual, was facing economic challenges and the panic of 1873 continued to cause growing financial concerns, especially for farmers who were deep in debt from the reconstruction period following the Civil War. Peter Cooper, a New York industrialist was nominated by the Greenback Party as its candidate for the presidency at their 1874 convention. Formed in the early 1870s, the Greenback Party sought to inflate the currency held by so many indebted farmers and businessmen. There were actually three different monetary units used in

REPORT OF THE DIRECTOR OF THE MINT.					65

F.—Statement of Subsidiary and Trade-dollar coinage at the Mints of the United States under the coinage act of 1873, during the fiscal year ending June 30, 1873.

Mints.	Trade-dollars.	Half-dollars.	Quarter-dollars.	Dimes.	Total.
United States mint, Philadelphia	....	$398,000	$83,000	$96,400	$577,400
United States mint, San Francisco	....	16,000	8,000	10,000	34,000
United States mint, Carson City	....	53,000		875	54,590
Total	....	467,000	91,875	107,115	665,990

Coinage record for all three mints from July 1, 1872 through June 30, 1873. Notice the skimpy number of dimes and quarters produced at the Carson Mint during that 12 month period: 7,150 dimes and 3,500 quarters. From the *Annual Report of the Director of the Mint*, for 1873. All totals are face value amounts.

commerce at this time; silver, gold and paper money. Bullion and currency traders made money through arbitrage. But the mass population grew weary of being paid in one form of money, only to experience a loss in buying power when attempting to pay for something else. Greenbacks were not on a par with silver and gold in 1874, as purchases requiring \$10 in silver or gold coin might require \$11 or \$12 in paper money and *Greenbackers* wanted to reverse this.

The Treasury Department made plans to retire all fractional paper money in circulation, approximately \$30 million at the time. Using silver coins as specie payment (trading paper for metal) would result in profits to the Treasury's account. A serious repercussion to this would be a coin shortage, created if the silver coins paid out in exchange for paper money were hoarded or exported aboard. By the middle to late 1870s this coin shortage was not only alleviated, it was reversed, and in turn this caused a glut of silver coinage in circulation and made it very lucrative to exchange silver coins for paper money. The ultimate goal of Congressional authorities was to establish a currency system requiring greenbacks, or other notes to be on a par with gold or silver regardless of the actual bullion value.

A Brief Glimpse into Trade Dollars

A new monetary unit called the trade dollar was introduced in 1873, which would be produced at the Carson City Mint from 1873 through 1878. The very first trade dollars in U.S. history were minted at the Philadelphia Mint on July 11, 1873, and 12 days later, the first trade dollars with the "CC" mintmark appeared, 2,580 issued to locals who had deposited silver bullion. The *Coinage Act of 1873* stated:

> The silver coins of the United States shall be a trade dollar; a half dollar, or fifty-cent piece; a quarter dollar, or twenty-five cent piece; a dime, or ten cent piece; and the weight of the trade dollar shall be 420 grains troy; the weight of the half dollar shall be 12 1/2 grams, the quarter-dollar and the dime shall be, respectively, one-half and one-fifth of the weight of said half-dollar; and said coins shall be a legal tender at their nominal value for any amount not exceeding five dollars in any one payment.

Trade dollars contained 378 grains of fine silver. This was an increase of 6.75 grains above the Seated Liberty silver dollars, which were discontinued after 1873. A troy ounce is equal to 420 grains and the increase of 6.75 grains based on a silver bullion price of \$1.29 per ounce amounted to approximately two cents. At the time, the ratio in silver content between the old standard silver dollar and the minor silver coins was uniform. Silver dollars

ANNUAL REPORT

OF THE

DIRECTOR OF THE MINT

TO THE

SECRETARY OF THE

FOR

THE FISCAL YEAR ENDING JU

WASHINGTON:
GOVERNMENT PRINTING OFFICE.
1873.

99 REPORT OF THE DIRECTOR OF THE MINT.

H.—*Standards of United States coins.*

Denomination.	Value.	Act of April 2, 1792		Act of July 28, 1834		Act of Jan., 1837.		Act of Mar. 3, 1849		Act of Mar. 3, 1851		Act of Mar. 3, 1853		Coinage act, 1873—Feb. 12, 1873.	
		Weight.	Fineness.	Weight.	Fineness.	Weight.	Fineness.	Weight.	Fineness.	Weight.	Fineness	Weight.	Fineness.	Weight.	Fineness
GOLD.		*Grains.*		*Grains.*		*Grains.*		*Grains.*		*Grains.*		*Grains.*			
Double-Eagle	\$20 00							516	900					516	900
Eagle	10 00	270	$916\frac{2}{3}$	258	899.225	258	900	258	900					258	900
Half-Eagle	5 00	135	$916\frac{2}{3}$	129	899.225	129	900	129	900					129	900
Quarter-Eagle	2 50	67.5	$916\frac{2}{3}$	64.5	899.225	64.5	900	$64\frac{1}{2}$	900					64.5	900
Three dollar	3 00											77.4	900	77.4	900
Dollar	1 00							25.8-10	900					25.8	900
SILVER.															
Dollar	1 00	416	892.4			412.5	900							420	900
Half-dollar	50	208	892.4			$206\frac{1}{4}$	900					192	900	$12\frac{1}{2}$ grams, or 192.9 grains	900
Quarter-dollar	25	104	892.4			$103\frac{1}{8}$	900					96	900	$6\frac{1}{4}$ grams, or 96.45 grains	900
Dime	10	41.6	892.4			$41\frac{1}{4}$	900					38.4	900	$2\frac{1}{2}$ grams, or 38.58 grains	900
Half-dime	5	20.8	892.4			$20\frac{5}{8}$	900					19.2	900		
Three-cent	3									$12\frac{3}{8}$	*750	11.52	900		

*$\frac{3}{4}$ silver, $\frac{1}{4}$ copper.

MINOR COINS.

Copper cents, authorized by act of April 2, 1792.
Copper half-cents, authorized by same act. Discontinued under act of February 24, 1857.
Nickel cent, authorized by act of February 21, 1857; weight, 72 grains; composed of 88 per cent. copper, 12 per cent. nickel.
Bronze two-cent, authorized by act of April 22, 1864; weight, 96 grains; composed of 95 per cent. copper, 5 per cent. tin and zinc.
Bronze one-cent, authorized by act of April 22, 1864; weight, 48 grains; composed of 95 per cent. copper, 5 per cent. tin and zinc.
Nickel three-cent, authorized by act of March 3, 1865; weight, 30 grains; composed of 75 per cent. copper, 25 per cent. nickel.
Nickel five-cent, authorized by act of May 16, 1866; weight, $77\frac{16}{100}$ grains; composed of 75 per cent. copper, 25 per cent. nickel.

Cover page of the 1873 *Annual Report of the Director of the Mint.* These volumes were packed with information and statistics, including the standard weights and fineness of U.S. coins from 1792 through the changes made because of the Coinage Act of 1873.

contained 371.25 grains of fine silver, dimes contained one-tenth of that, and quarters and halves, one-quarter, and one-half of that, respectively. On the other hand, the trade dollar bore no relationship to the minor silver coinage. Although the initial purpose of the coin was not clear, it became apparent that trade dollars were not intended for domestic use, but instead, were meant for shipment to the Orient.

The monetary system of the United States has always been a work in progress, having been set in motion by the nation's founding fathers. Succeeding generations have subverted the system, and changed the laws as often as a politician changes his campaign promises. Trade dollars, for example, were eventually denied legal tender status in 1876 when the price of silver declined.

Nearly 36 million examples of this controversial denomination were coined at U.S. mints, with slightly more than 4.2 million trade dollars produced at the Carson City Mint from 1873 through 1878. In the first year of production, 124,500 were issued with the "CC" mintmark, but by 1874 that number had increased more than tenfold.

The fascinating story of the trade dollar is told in several other studious reference works on the subject. You are encouraged to examine *The Crime of 1873* by Robert Van Ryzin, *Fractional Money* by Neil Carothers, *The United States Trade Dollar* by John Willem and *Silver Dollars and Trade Dollars of the United States* by Q. David Bowers.

FARMERS, RANCHERS, AND INFLATED CURRENCY

Revolutionary advancements in agriculture and industry proliferated during the trade dollar era. One such occurred when Joseph Glidden invented barbed wire, which changed the face of cattle ranching in the United States. In 1874 approximately five tons of barbed wire was produced. By the end of the decade over 40,000 tons of the innovative fencing was being manufactured per year.

In addition to the challenges farmers and ranchers faced growing their crops and tending their herds, they were confronted with the volatile monetary system in the

Trade dollar in Uncirculated condition.

United States. It was discouraging to receive payment for their products and labor in paper money, only to discover that their cash was discounted 10% to 20%, depending on who they were trading with, and what part of the country it was in.

The Greenback Party's plan was to exert pressure on the government to lower the value of silver, by causing a rise in the gold value of greenbacks. Then the government could purchase silver at a discount with inflated greenbacks. Silver coinage could then be produced and exchanged into general circulation resulting in a tidy profit to Treasury coffers. Ranchers, farmers, bankers and other businessmen, whose assets were assessed in greenbacks, would realize increases in their net worth, at least on paper.

Greenbacks were not the issue in the western United States, especially Colorado, California, Nevada, Oregon, Washington, Idaho, Montana, and Utah, as paper money was not used to the degree that it was east of the Rockies. The mineral wealth of this region provided more economic stability, at least to those linked to the mining of it.

The government's plan teetered on a delicate thread. If unsuccessful, the inflated value of greenbacks would plunge, forcing the Treasury to buy bullion silver at prices greater than the value of the coins produced from it. At that point, the public would gladly exchange all forms of currency, including fractional notes, for silver coins which could then be sold into the bullion markets at a profit. Bullion dealers would then melt the coins and sell the silver back to the Treasury, resulting in a merry-go-round, which would ultimately lead to a shortage of currency and subsidiary silver coins in circulation.

LITTLE MINT INCREASES OUTPUT AND GETS A NEW SUPERINTENDENT

Meanwhile, the Carson City Mint was on a pace to increase the face value output of its coins by nearly 500%, the bulk of it coming from trade dollars and $20 gold pieces.

To facilitate the increased output, the superintendent at the Carson City Mint, Frank D. Hetrich, supervised construction improvements. New equipment, along

Letter from Carson City Mint Superintendent Frank D. Hetrich to the Treasury Department requesting appropriations for improvements due to a substantial increase in business. Hetrich informs his superiors that if expansion needs are not met, one of the Carson Mint's biggest customers might withdraw his deposits which would result in a loss of $400,000 per month.

March 1874 letter from Director of the Mint H.R. Linderman informing Treasury official A.B. Mullett that Carson City's request for appropriations had been denied. Linderman concludes by predicting that when the bullion is exhausted from the Comstock mines, the Carson Mint's days will be numbered. (Courtesy Nevada State Museum)

with two new furnaces, doubled the mint's production capacity. In August 1874 Superintendent Hetrich, who had held his position for a little more than a year, resigned. James Crawford assumed the superintendent's position and served longer than any superintendent in the Carson City Mint's history (1874 to 1885). Born in Hardinsburg Kentucky in 1835, Crawford responded to the lure of the gold rush in California in 1852, and nine years later, at the age of 26, moved to the Comstock region, settling in Lyon County, Nevada.

Crawford achieved success in the mining industry and went on to become an Assemblyman in the Nevada State legislature, serving from 1866 through 1873. His appointment to the position of Mint Superintendent at Carson City met with the hearty approval of his many friends and constituents in the Carson Valley.

James Crawford worked tirelessly to earn the Carson Mint respectability, and was rewarded with much needed appropriations during his stint. Throughout his career as Mint Superintendent, Crawford received many accolades from authorities in Washington D.C. and Philadelphia.

Carson City, and the state at large needed leaders like Crawford, because even after Nevada became a state in 1864, residents of the *Silver State* felt like unwanted stepchildren, as many Easterners were of the opinion that its statehood was gained through *back door entry*. When the mint in Carson City was declared the *United States Mint at Carson City, Nevada*, ending its branch mint status, the most prominent newspaper in the Comstock area, the *Territorial Enterprise*, wrote:

> The little mint at Carson is about all that the government ever granted to Nevada. Surely, it is not too much to ask of the government that this [mint] be perfected.

The newspaper concluded by pointing out that more gold and silver was coming out of Nevada's mines than all other mines in the country combined. And the country would most assuredly benefit from this massive quantity of bullion. However, Nevada would not be granted full acceptance and legitimacy until the 1990s, when media sources seemed to be tripping over themselves to herald Nevada as "The fastest growing state" in the country. By the 1990s it was popular for *decent* people and *legitimate* companies to move there.

COLLECTING CARSON CITY COINS OF 1874

Collectors know that there are no "CC" Mint Seated Liberty quarters from the year 1874. Although there is no explanation for this, when you look at "CC" quarter

mintages from 1870 to 1873, it becomes apparent that the U.S. Mint was not depending on Carson City to provide significant quantities of this denomination to the country's money supply. The absence of 1874-CC *Arrows* quarters puts great demand on the 1873-CC *Arrows* quarter to fill the space for this variety in a type set of Carson City coins. Perhaps mint employees were tempted to produce a few 1874-CC quarters, but there are no records of dies being sent, and certainly, the appearance of one such coin would quickly be judged a counterfeit.

Dimes minted at the Carson City Mint in 1874 had the lowest mintage of all "CC" Mint dimes, and are extremely rare. As of the publication of this book (2003), only four Uncirculated specimens are listed in the NGC and PCGS census and population data, with two listings being for the same coin. Half dollar production dropped to 59,000, its lowest level since the Carson Mint opened in 1870.

Gold coin mintages at Carson City increased significantly in 1874. The number of $5 gold half eagles struck nearly tripled from the previous year, $10 eagle mintage multiplied nearly fourfold, and, as mentioned earlier, the $20 double eagle mintage increased 500% from 1873 totals.

More information about the coins from 1874 can be found in Chapter 6, *The Silver Coins*, and Chapter 7, *The Gold Coins*.

SILVER ASSAY COINS
FROM THE
Mint of the United States.
AT
CARSON,
For the Calendar Year 1874

18	NUMBER OF PIECES					VALUE		STANDARD WT
Months	Dollars	Half Dollars	Quarter Dollars	Dimes	Half Dimes	Dolls.	Cts.	Ounces
January,	1	9	2			6	00	
February,	–	–						
March,	1	41	–	5		22	80	
April,		8				4	00	
May,								
June,		40	2	3		20	80	
July,	9	11	3	12		18	45	
August,	3	27				16	50	
September,	4	10				9	00	
October,	19	2				20	00	
November,	8	.				8	00	
December,	24					24	00	
TOTALS,	69	148	7	20		146	75	
	69	140	REMARKS	22		146 75		
						59		
						77 75		

List of silver coins sent from the Carson Mint to Philadelphia to be inspected by the Assay Commission during the calendar year of 1874. When the face value of the coins was totalled, the 69 trade dollars were subtracted for some reason. It is also curious that seven quarters are included, although no quarters were minted at Carson City in 1874. (*National Archives*)

❧ 1875 ❧

SO MUCH SILVER, SO MANY COINS

The U.S. Mint purchased more than $9 million of silver bullion during 1875 and Treasury silver purchases reached $15 million the following year. The government's actions sustained the *Bonanza* period in the Comstock Lode region and were comparable to the subsidies paid to farmers of grain to protect them from bankruptcy. There is no doubt that silver mining interests influenced Congressmen; to be sure, there was much collusion in this area, resulting in generous payoffs for elected officials. The silver was being purchased at approximately 13% to 15% over market value, an inflated price to begin with, because without government support, silver prices would probably have dropped more than 25%.

Carson City Mint Superintendent, James Crawford, contacted officials at the Philadelphia Mint in a vigorous campaign to obtain much needed government appropriations to enable his mint to keep pace with higher levels of production. The number of coins minted at Carson City in 1875 would increase almost fivefold from the previous year's total.

Silver coins accounted for the majority of the production increases. In 1875, there were 4,645,000 silver dimes minted compared to only 10,817 the previous year. As mentioned, there were no quarters minted at Carson City in 1874; in 1875 there were 140,000. Half dollar production increased from 59,000 in 1874 to 1,008,000 and trade dollars reached their peak mintage in 1875, but it was only a 13¹/₂% increase from the previous year.

If the Treasury Department, the Mint, silver miners, and *connected* politicians had things their way, the silver coinage system of the United States would have conformed to the weight and fineness of the trade dollar. This quote from the *Annual Report of the Director of the Mint* from 1875 states it clearly.

> If our coinage system consisted of a 10c, 20c, 25c, 50c and Trade Dollar, all with relative measurements, it would be good for the country's overseas trade, as well as for the silver miners of this country, who depend on a steady demand for the precious metal to maintain their profits.

Gold coin production at the Carson City Mint remained steady in this year dominated by silver coinage, decreasing to slightly less than $2.4 million face value, only $277,127 less than 1874's output. Lower quantities of gold half eagles and eagles accounted for the drop, explaining why these two denominations dated 1875 are so much scarcer than the 1875-CC double eagle.

The constant roar of milling operations around Virginia City gave ample evidence of the magnitude of

Panoramic view of Virginia City in 1878. Production from the mines had reached peak levels and would begin to taper off in 1879. In its time, this was one of the most prosperous cities in the history of the United States.

silver ore being extracted from the depths of the mountainous region. An observer once pointed out that $3 million per month was being added to the wealth of the United States from the ore being mined on the Comstock.

SHORT BITS, LONG BITS AND ODD BITS

A *bit* in terms of the coinage of the United States referred to 12 $^1/_2$ cents, equal to the Spanish *real*. There were eight reals to a dollar. The antiquated term *piece of eight*, referred to one real, or one bit; two bits, obviously was twenty-five cents, or a quarter. Merchant tokens from the 19th century often had a value of 12 $^1/_2$ cents. It seems trivial in today's culture to think of customers and merchants worrying over a few cents, but in those times, it was necessary to pinch pennies.

There were very few minor coins in circulation in the Pacific states. If a merchant priced an item at 15 cents, the customers could safely pay a quarter and receive a dime in change. But, if the item was priced at 10 cents, the change for a quarter rendered might only be ten cents, depending on whether there were any half dimes or newly introduced nickel five-cent pieces in the cash register. There was also a severe shortage of one-cent coins, especially in the Western states. Merchants would price items at 12 $^1/_2$ cents, and pay out one of their store's merchant tokens with 12 $^1/_2$ cents face as change for a quarter. Dimes were nicknamed *short bits* since they were only 80% of the value of a full bit.

This paragraph from Robert Louis Stevenson's *Across the Plains*, provides us with a slice of the commercial side of life in the last quarter of the 19th century.

In the Pacific States they have made a bolder push for complexity, and settle their affairs by a coin that no longer exists – the BIT, or old Mexican real. The supposed value of the bit is twelve and a half cents, eight to a dollar. When it comes to two bits, the quarter-dollar stands for the required amount. But how about an odd bit? The nearest coin to it is a dime, which is, short by a fifth. That, then, is called a SHORT bit. If you have one, you lay it triumphantly down, and save two and a half cents. But if you have not, and lay down a quarter, the bar-keeper or shopman calmly tenders you a dime by way of change; and thus you have paid what is called a LONG BIT, and lost two and a half cents, or even, by comparison with a short bit, five cents. In country places all over the Pacific coast, nothing lower than a bit is ever asked or taken, which vastly increases the cost of life; as

even for a glass of beer you must pay fivepence or sevenpence-halfpenny, as the case may be. You would say that this system of mutual robbery was as broad as it was long … A quarter is only worth two bits, a short and a long. Whenever you have a quarter, go to the post-office and buy five cents worth of postage-stamps; you will receive in change two dimes, that is, two short bits. You can go and have your two glasses of beer all the same; and you have made yourself a present of five cents worth of postage-stamps into the bargain.

THE 20-CENT PIECE MAKES ITS DEBUT

A new denomination was introduced by the Treasury Department in 1875. The 20-cent piece or double *short bit* was intended to alleviate the quandary over coinage exchange. Merchandise priced at 10 cents could be paid for with a 20-cent piece with a return of a dime to the patron. Of course, where there's a will, there's a way. If people feel justified in cheating others, no conversion of the monetary system will prevent it.

Twenty-cent piece introduced in 1875, this piece minted in San Francisco. The motto "IN GOD WE TRUST" was left off. (*Courtesy American Numismatic Rarities*)

Nevada Senator John Percival Jones (mentioned in a previous chapter) introduced the bill to authorize the silver 20-cent piece in 1874. Jones, a silver miner, was a champion of the silver supporters, a fearless proponent of the trade dollar, and saw an opportunity to create even more demand for silver. After all, the more silver coins the government produced, the more silver would be purchased from the mining companies.

President Grant signed the bill authorizing the 20-cent piece in March of 1875. The first "CC" examples were minted on June 1, 1875. Added to the other silver coins minted at Carson City in 1875, the new 20-cent pieces brought the silver coinage total to 7,499,990, over five times the total of 1,443,017 from 1874.

CARSON MINT SHARES IN SILVER COIN STOCKPILE

A review of the progression of mintage totals from the first year of 1870 through 1875 reveals how the work load at the Carson City Mint presented a challenge for those responsible for its operation. This is especially true, considering that there had been no agenda, no prognostication given to mint employees, to prepare them for what was to come.

Superintendent Crawford knew that if the Carson City Mint was going to handle the pressure of these rapidly increasing production levels, he was going to need help from the Treasury Department. There was a need for more employees, as well as an expansion of the facilities, and additional equipment. A second coin press was purchased, but further appropriations would have to wait until the following year.

Back in 1860, with the Comstock in its infancy, the estimated market value of the mines was $4 million. Fifteen years later, in 1875, this value was estimated to be $300 million, and was beginning to reach peak levels before evolving into volatile boom/bust cycles. For the time being, the silver mines continued to yield abundant loads of bullion, but success, of course, depended on a continuous demand for it.

The new Specie Payment Act, introduced by Senator John Sherman, passed into law in January 1875, calling for larger quantities of silver dimes, quarters and half dollars to be issued, in order to redeem fractional paper money that had been introduced at the beginning of the Civil War. This act was supposed to be the perfect solution to guarantee mining companies a steady outlet for their silver, and correspondingly, prevent future coin shortages. In unison with the increased production levels at the Carson City Mint, both San Francisco and Philadelphia were ordered to mint greater and greater quantities of coins. Even with the massive increases in coinage production, there were large surpluses of silver from the ore flowing out of the Comstock mines. The silver coins sat in mint vaults, continuing to accumulate in quantities far in excess of the country's need. Ironically, less than five years earlier, there had been a severe shortage of coins in circulation.

TOTAL NUMBER OF PIECES MINTED AT CARSON CITY	
Silver And Gold Coins	
YEAR	QUANTITY
1870	92,791
1871	214,958
1872	360,380
1873	545,882
1874	1,596,067
1875	7,630,684

DEATH OF WILLIAM C. RALSTON

A name often mentioned in discussions about California's impact on the State of Nevada is William C. Ralston, majority owner of the Bank of California in San Francisco, and controlling partner in many businesses around Virginia City and the Comstock region at the time the Carson City Mint was established. Contemporaries of Ralston were William Sharon, John Percival Jones, John W. Mackay, James C. Fair, William S. O'Brien, James C. Flood, D.O. Mills, E.J. *Lucky* Baldwin, and H.R. Linderman. It would be easy to make a case that these men were responsible in part for the amount of coins produced at Carson City. It is a historical fact that enormous wealth was created through their efforts; they also had incredible influence on Nevada's economy, and it was no secret how much political weight they possessed.

Concerning the California/Nevada connection, there was always a mutual interdependence between Nevada and California. California capital management, California workers, and California customers helped build the Comstock. Although California's influence greatly benefited the commercial, industrial and population growth in Nevada, it has been said that the *Golden State* took more than its share in return. Water and mineral resources, once abundantly available in Nevada, would become the source of raging power struggles carrying forward into the last half of the 20th century. In the end, Nevada would often have the distinction of being *California's Colony.*

Original coin press number 1 at the Carson City Mint. This 12-ton workhorse was used to produce every coin at the mint from 1870 until a second press arrived in 1875.

Unfortunately, because of improprieties caused by greed, some Californians such as Ralston were not able to enjoy their fleeting success. In a position of almost total unaccountability, Ralston knew how to cook the books in the bank's accounting ledgers. More than a century later, infamous companies such as Enron and Worldcom would follow a similar path (on a much grander scale of course). Ralston met his fate on August 27, 1875, just one day after his bank collapsed in the midst of a run by worried depositors, when he died a mysterious death off the shores of San Francisco heading toward Alcatraz Island.

Shortly after Ralston's death, the Bank of California would be reorganized and eventually earn part-time Nevadans like William Sharon much wealth and prestige. Sharon also managed to buy a seat in the United States Senate in 1875, representing Nevada, although he lived most of the time in California when he was not in Washington D.C.

DISASTROUS FIRE OF 1875

Citizens living in the Comstock region showed their resiliency time and time again. Corrupt bankers could not destroy them. Dishonest politicians, while they made it very difficult at times, only caused the Nevadans to roll up their sleeves and stand their ground. Natural disasters were tragic, but eventually, with a determined fortitude, the areas that were left in ruins would be rebuilt.

Sketch of the V&T Railroad.

One of the most devastating disasters to ever occur in the Comstock region left over 10% of the population of Virginia City homeless. The fire of 1875 was started on October 26, when an oil lamp was knocked over at Kate Shea's boarding house. The flames were blazing before *Crazy Kate* (as she was called) could call for help, and within a short period of time, the fire swept through the neighborhood. There had been drought like conditions in Virginia City, and the wind was blowing hard. By midday, the citizens had the fire under control, but not before nearly half of the town had been destroyed. An earlier fire in 1869, concentrated in three mines, killed 37 men. On both of these occasions, the citizens rebuilt and forged ahead. The resolve of the human spirit often restores whatever disaster or man destroys.

ALLEGATIONS OF IMPROPRIETY

The following year in March 1876, there were allegations concerning skimming at the Carson Mint and lightweight trade dollars being struck. These deficient trade dollars were blamed in part on their having been severely damaged in the Virginia City fire. Mint Director Linderman and the Treasury Department accepted this explanation and charges were dropped. At the same time, a gang of men in the mining region had stolen thousands of dollars of silver from the company they worked for in 1875, but this, of course, was not a reflection on the mint in Carson City, although any acts of this nature sent waves of suspicion back to Washington D.C., concerning Nevada's credibility.

Superintendent Crawford closed out 1875 defending his mint to the end. He answered the charges that the 1875-CC trade dollars were lighter in weight than standards required, by detailing the security measures employed to ensure quality control. Groups of 1,000 coins would be turned over to the officer in charge, who subsequently selected several random pieces, which were in turn weighed and checked for quality; if any one was found to be below standard, the entire 1,000 coin lot would be melted. This report satisfied authorities, thus bringing the case to a close.

THE KENTUCKY DERBY AND DWIGHT L. MOODY

Elsewhere in 1875, two major events occurred that would prove to be prominent in divergent fields of human interest. Horse racing and Christian revival meetings generally attract different crowds and both have played central roles in their respective societal niches throughout the history of the United States. On May 17, 1875, the first Kentucky Derby was run at Churchill Downs. As of the publication date of this book, there have been 129 runnings of this famous horse race.

Also in 1875, Dwight L. Moody began holding revival meetings in the East. Moody would gain much respect during his ministry, and his youth work influenced such organizations as the YMCA and YWCA. There is a Bible Institute and church named after Moody in Chicago.

Many interesting events were due to take place the following year, but Carsonites could look back proudly on the first six years of operations at the Mint on Carson Street.

More information about the silver and gold coins from 1875 may be found in Chapter 6, *The Silver Coins*, and Chapter 7, *The Gold Coins*.

1876

PETER COOPER AND THE 1876 ELECTION

The depression that began in 1873 continued to plague the United States as the calendar turned to 1876. The Grant administration suffered through one crisis after another and the President's opposition continually blamed everything on him and his Republican Party. As in every generation, political scandals were surfacing on a regular basis, and 1876 would be a red-letter year for them. The Greenback Party, the so-called *soft money* advocates, held their inaugural presidential convention in Indianapolis in 1876 and Peter Cooper was nominated as the party's presidential candidate.

Through 1874, it had been illegal for the Treasury to mint silver coins for the purpose of redeeming paper money, although paper money was issued to redeem silver coins. The Treasury could use paper money to buy silver bullion for the purpose of minting silver coins, and then exchange the coins to redeem fractional paper money. Finally, in January 1875 the Specie Payment Act became law, which legalized the production of silver coins for the purpose of redeeming paper money. As long as the value of the silver in the coins was on par with the value of the paper money, this system worked. But, if paper money became worth less than the silver, the owner of the silver coins would exchange them for gold, or gold backed currency.

By 1876, the Specie Payment Act threatened to thwart the Greenback Party's strategy by lowering the inflationary rates of currency. Although the Greenbacks staged a vigorous campaign, Cooper only received 1% of the popular vote in the national election, as Rutherford B. Hayes, the Republican candidate, beat out Samuel Tilden to become the 19th President of the United States. This was the first presidential election in the history of the United States to have the results disputed. Democratic candidate Samuel J. Tilden had received 184 electoral votes; Republican Hayes had received 166 with 19 electoral votes undecided. These disputed votes were those from Florida, Louisiana, South Carolina, and Oregon. At the time, the three southern states were still under carpetbag rule which cast doubts on their credibility by Northern politicians. Oregon at the time had only one vote and was

of less consequence. The election dispute was not settled until March 2 of the following year (1877) when a committee's decision awarded the 19 votes to Rutherford B. Hayes.

Although Peter Cooper was unsuccessful in his presidential bid, he will always be remembered for the Union he established. This Union served as a free college for students who might otherwise have been unable to afford a formal education. It is interesting to note that five notable coin designers benefited from the opportunity to attend Cooper's Union College in New York City. Coin collectors and numismatists have long admired the coins designed by Augustus Saint Gaudens, ($20 gold piece and $10 Indian gold piece), John Flanagan (Washington quarter), Adolph A. Weinman (Mercury dime and Walking Liberty half dollar), Victor David Brenner (Lincoln cent), and Antonio DeFrancisci (Peace dollar), all of whom attended Cooper's Union College.

WILLIAM BARBER'S 20-CENT DESIGN

William Barber, who had become Mint engraver in 1869, learned his skills in England. He later immigrated to the United States, and at the age of 58, became an assistant to Mint Engraver James Longacre. Longacre had achieved success with his designs of the Coronet Liberty gold $1 and $20 coins, as well as the Indian cent, copper two-cent, silver and nickel three-cent pieces and the Shield nickel five-cent pieces.

Barber had submitted several designs for the newly authorized 20-cent piece in 1874 and 1875. One of the designs displayed a sculptured head of Miss Liberty on the obverse with *LIBERTY* inscribed in her coronet with

Wells Fargo stagecoach in front of the St. Charles Hotel in Carson City. Names of passengers were listed in the *Carson Daily Appeal* every day. (*Courtesy Nevada State Museum*)

hair pulled tightly back, held by a ribbon. The reverse featured a heraldic shield with *20* in large font incusely engraved in the center. The top periphery boldly spelled out *UNITED STATES OF AMERICA*, with the word *CENTS* at the bottom beneath the shield. Some people were of the opinion that the portrait of Miss Liberty resembled England's Queen Victoria. This design might have received a more favorable reception by the public as it in no way resembled the Seated Liberty quarters already in circulation and would be less likely to be confused with them. The Treasury's position, however, was that the country's coinage should be uniform in appearance. As a result, the 20-cent pieces closely resembled the contemporary quarters and caused confusion among patrons and store owners. The one concession that the Treasury did allow, was a plain edge on the 20-cent pieces, instead of the more common reeded edges. Breen suggests that the plain edge was "a favor to the illiterate," while Mint officials claimed the plain edge was to aid the blind.

Barber's pattern 20-cent piece from 1875, nicknamed the "Sailor Head." The shield bearing "20" left no doubt what the denomination of this coin was. (*Courtesy Bowers and Merena*)

In any event, by mid 1876 a bill to repeal the 20-cent piece was put to a vote in Congress and the bill eventually passed. Production of circulation strike 20-cent pieces was halted in 1876, although the law did not go into effect until 1878.

CLASSIC 1876-CC 20-CENT PIECE

The Carson City Mint had manufactured 10,000 1876 20-cent pieces ($2,000 face value) by the time the bill to repeal the denomination was passed. With the exception of several assay coins sent to the Philadelphia Mint, and an obviously small quantity filtered out of the mint by employees, the entire yield for 1876 was kept in the mint's vault. This information has been public knowledge for over 120 years, which caused coin collectors to consider the 1876-CC 20-cent piece the rarest of all Carson City coins for the better part of the 20th century. In the January 1945 auction of the F.C.C. Boyd Collection, titled the *World's Greatest Collection*[1] by Abe Kosoff's Numismatic Gallery, an 1876-CC 20-cent piece was described as follows:

> This coin is seldom offered . . . we have had numerous requests for this coin but have never been able to supply it.

The "beautiful Uncirculated specimen"[2] sold for $1,500. For comparison sake, it is noted that one of the

only Uncirculated examples of an 1873-CC *Without Arrows* quarter sold for $725 in the same auction.

By 1996, the 1873-CC *Without Arrows* dime would be recognized as the rarest date in the Carson City series, and the 1873-CC *Without Arrows* quarter would rank second in rarity. The surviving populations of these two dates and denominations have remained a mystery from their issuance until the present time. Unlike the 1876-CC 20-cent piece, which has official records detailing when, where and approximately how many were melted, there have never been such records discovered for 1873-CC silver coins. Nor, for that matter, have records been located for nearly all of the date/denomination combinations from the Carson City Mint.

The scarcity of other Carson City coins has only been discovered over time, in contrast to the scarcity of the 1876-CC 20-cent piece, whose rarity has been established since the 1890s.

Augustus Heaton, writing in 1893 about the comparative rarity between the 1876-CC 20-cent piece and the 1877 Proof 20-cent piece, which had a reported mintage of a mere 350, says,

> In 1876 there were ten thousand specimens of this coin struck at Carson City, yet, while anyone can buy the proof of '77 for about three dollars, the '76 CC piece is excessively rare in any condition, and would, even if worn, command two or three times that price from a Mint-Mark collector.[3]

In this same report, Heaton reveals more of the valuable information he obtained by "investigation and experience."

> It often happens that but a portion of the registered coinage of any piece is issued for circulation, the remainder being remelted. Occasionally an entire coinage has either never left the mint or has been sent abroad and recoined there.[4]

Heaton's primary reference source was the *Annual Report of the Director of the Mint*. There was no such thing as a *Red Book* in those days and collectors did not know how many coins the mints were producing. These annual Mint Reports provided Heaton with information not available to the general public. When he realized how rare certain date/denominations were, he set his goal to obtain a com-

---

[1] Numismatic Gallery, *World's Greatest Collection*, 1945.

[2] Ibid.

[3] Augustus G. Heaton, *Mint Marks, a Treatise*, 1893.

[4] Ibid.

Coinage executed at the mints of the United States during the fiscal year ended June 30, 1875.								
Denomination.	Mint United States, Philadelphia.		Mint United States, San Francisco.		Mint United States, Carson.		Total.	
	Pieces.	Value.	Pieces.	Value.	Pieces.	Value.	Pieces.	Value.
GOLD.								
Double-eagles	238,910	$4,778,200	1,300,000	$26,000,000	98,497	$1,969,940	1,637,407	$32,748,140
Eagles	28,060	380,600	10,000	100,000	11,994	119,240	50,984	599,840
Half-eagles	348	1,740	20,000	100,000	20,393	101,915	40,731	203,655
Three dollars	20	60					20	60
Quarter-eagles	900	2,250					900	2,250
Dollars	20	20					20	20
Total gold	278,258	5,162,870	1,330,000	26,200,000	130,804	2,191,095	1,739,062	33,553,965
SILVER.								
Trade-dollars	476,800	476,800	3,379,000	3,379,000	1,841,700	1,841,700	5,697,500	5,697,500
Half-dollars	4,415,000	2,207,500	958,000	479,000	334,000	167,000	5,707,000	2,853,560
Quarter-dollars	2,003,800	500,950	492,000	123,000			2,495,800	623,950
Twenty cents	11,000	2,200	15,000	3,000	1,316	658	27,316	5,858
Dimes	4,580,600	458,060	3,430,000	343,000	885,000	88,500	8,895,600	889,560
Total silver	11,487,200	3,645,510	8,274,000	4,327,000	3,062,016	2,097,858	22,823,216	10,070,368
MINOR.								
Five-cent	1,893,000	94,650					1,893,000	94,650
Three-cent	418,000	12,540					418,000	12,540
One-cent	12,318,500	123,185					12,318,500	123,185
Total minor	14,629,500	230,375					14,629,500	230,375
Total coinage	26,394,958	9,038,755	9,604,000	30,527,000	3,192,820	4,288,953	39,191,778	43,854,708

REPORT OF THE DIRECTOR OF THE MINT.

Table from *Annual Report of the Director of the Mint* in 1875 exhibiting coinage executed at the three mints from July 1, 1874 to June 30, 1875.

plete set of all the coins issued by the mints from 1838 to 1893: 277 different date/denomination combinations according to his research. By the time his *Treatise* (as he referred to it) was published in 1893, he had acquired 270 of the possible 277. Heaton attributed his success to persistence and determination. His rankings of the rarity of many "CC" coins gave future coin collectors clues as to how rewarding it could be to obtain them. Heaton enjoyed the challenge and infected others with his passion to search for the more elusive dates.

AN EXPENSIVE PIECE OF THE PUZZLE

As it was in Heaton's day so it is today, because it is a fact that human beings like puzzles. Puzzles have been referred to as little mirrors in the search for patterns in a person's life. A coin collection is like a puzzle. For instance, a coin album for a set of Standing Liberty quarters has 38 empty spaces to fill, creating a puzzle that sets a person on a search to find the next coin to fill the gap in the album.

In 1997, the collector assembling the *Legend Collection* of Mint State trade dollars needed only a few dates to fill the gaps in his collection. Building a set of this significance and magnitude is indeed a rare opportunity that can reward a person with full satisfaction. As has been the occasion so many times, the *Eliasberg Collection* would be the source

The *Eliasberg* 1876-CC trade dollar. (*Courtesy Bowers and Merena*).

for one of the most momentous pieces of the *Legend* collector's puzzle. The Bowers and Merena auction catalog described the 1876-CC trade dollar as a "Connoisseur's 1876-CC Trade Dollar."[1] The cataloger for the sale was running out of superlatives to describe the coins in this, the most historical rare coin auction of all time. The first of the three auction sales of the *Eliasberg Collection*, held in October of 1982, comprised 1,074 lots. The next two sessions conducted in 1996 and 1997 featured 3,308 lots, bringing the total for all three sessions to 4,382. When lot 2340 appeared on the auction block, in April 1997, there were still 968 lots to go and it would take every word that a thesaurus could provide to describe them all. The description of the 1876-CC trade dollar continued, "Superb Gem Mint State, Finest known, landmark rarity in this preservation. A splendid specimen, memorable and world class. Until this piece was cataloged, no one even suspected that an 1876-CC existed in such lofty preservation. The purchaser of this coin will acquire a true numismatic rarity, which in time, may well be recognized for its significance."[2]

The winning bidder paid $63,800 for this 1876-CC trade dollar, subsequently graded MS-65 by PCGS; that grade being arguable because in comparison to other MS-65 trade dollars, it easily deserves at least an MS-66 rating and, in fact, is the finest known 1876-CC trade dollar in existence. It was eventually sold to the owner of the *Legend Collection* for $100,000 and was, by far, the most elusive piece of the puzzle needed to assemble this finest set of Mint State trade dollars. Unstoppable persistence in the search for coins needed for a collection usually brings much gratification.

---

[1] Bowers and Merena, *Louis E. Eliasberg, Sr. Collection*, April 1997.

[2] Ibid.

THE NATION'S 100TH BIRTHDAY PARTY

One of the most memorable events of 1876 was the Centennial Exposition held in Philadelphia, lasting from May to November, with 10 million visitors attending the grand affair. There were bands and marches, dances and festivals, speeches and award ceremonies, exhibits and events, food and fun. What a great opportunity for the nation to reflect on 100 years of progress, and look ahead toward limitless potential. By this time the United States had suffered through depressions, political corruption, and wars, with the Civil War dividing the North and South. But even that painful event was 11 years in the past. Expansion from sea to shining sea was something every citizen could be proud of as the nation focused on the future.

Nevada, though only 12 years old, was proud of its success and sent many delegates to the country's first multi-building World's Fair. Every state, as well as all visiting foreign countries, had their own buildings. Delegates and exhibitors from the *Battle Born* State showcased numerous examples of its heritage. The Carson City Mint was well represented and some Easterners saw coins with the "CC" mintmark for the first time. There was also a Comstock Lode display featuring examples of mining gear, pictures of the mines, and gold and silver ingots. Pioneer events were staged and displays of newspapers from the area, with special attention focused on *The Territorial Enterprise*, already known as the publication where Samuel Clemens first used the name Mark Twain.

1876 Centennial medal designed by William Barber for the Exposition in Philadelphia and sold at the Nevada Building for $1.25. Just over 2,500 medals were struck coined using silver from Nevada mines.

Mint engraver William Barber combined the obverse of a medal he had designed for the Centennial Celebration, with a specially designed reverse with a Nevada theme, to create the *Nevada – 1876 U.S. Centennial Exposition Dollar*. Using silver from the Comstock Lode, the Philadelphia Mint struck 2,526 pieces which sold for $1.25 at the Nevada Centennial building. An official certificate was issued with each medal. In the year 2003 these medals are worth between $250 and 500.

ANOTHER 1876 CARSON CITY RARITY EMERGES IN THE 20TH CENTURY

Bridging a gap of 100 or more years, it might be fitting to trace the ascent of another coin from the Carson City Mint into the 20th century. Like diamonds in the rough, several key coins minted at Carson City have

---

RENO'S TRUE NAMESAKE

Traveling back to the era in which trade dollars were produced, a bit of information related to one of Nevada's major cities might be of interest. It concerns Custer's defeat at Little Big Horn in June of 1876. What connection could this event have with the Comstock region of Nevada? A simple answer is literally none; however, to provide a little background, the city of Reno, Nevada was named after an officer in the United States Army. As it turns out there were two army officers with the last name Reno. The first was Major Marcus A. Reno who died at Little Big Horn in 1876, and until evidence surfaced in recent years, was partially blamed for the 7th Calvary's defeat.

A small number of historians and others interested in the subject have mistakenly stated that Reno, Nevada was named after Major Marcus A. Reno. But another army officer, General Jesse Lee Reno was killed by a sniper's bullet at Fox's Gap, Maryland while defending his troops in the Civil War.[1] A newspaper in Auburn, California, *The Stars and Stripes*, reported in their April 23, 1868 edition that the true namesake of the Nevada town was: "The name of the new town on the Central Pacific Railroad (C.P.R.R.), at the junction of the contemplated branch road to Virginia City in Nevada, is Reno, in honor of General (Jesse) Reno, who fell gloriously fighting in defence (*sic*) of the flag against the assault of traitors in rebellion…" So, the small railroad junction at Lakes Crossing, Nevada, officially became Reno.

It is odd how traditions become accepted as fact, sometimes without even verifying the details. After all, the city of Reno got its name in 1868 and the Battle of the Little Big Horn did not occur until 1876, unmistakably eliminating Major Marcus Reno as a candidate. The city of Reno, of course, played a pivotal role in the development of Nevada, eventually becoming the State's predominant community in the first half of the 20th century.

[1] Guy Rocha, "Wanted: The Real Reno," Nev. State Library and Archives.

emerged from relatively modest beginnings to become classics in their realms. One such example is the 1876-CC $5 half eagle from the *Eliasberg Collection*. The mint-

The 1876-CC half eagle, pedigreed to such famous collections as the Clapp family, Louis E. Eliasberg, Sr. and Henry S. Lang. (*Courtesy Bowers and Merena*)

age figure of 6,887 is low in comparison with most other $5 Liberty gold pieces minted between 1839 and 1908; however, it is certainly not the lowest and while this date is reasonably scarce, it is obtainable in grades below AU. Having said that, the *Eliasberg* 1876-CC $5 half eagle is in a class all its own. When Louis E. Eliasberg Sr. purchased the piece as part of the *Clapp Collection* in 1942, it drew little attention. However, by the time the Eliasberg family auctioned their patriarch's collection of gold coins in 1982, the Carson City 1876 $5 gold piece had achieved some notoriety. With a winning bid of $26,400 it was pronounced the highest priced Carson City gold coin in the auction. Numismatists who viewed it were awed by the stunning beauty of the coin and the competitive bidding gave evidence of how special it was. There were other scarce $5 Liberty gold coins in the sale, including an 1854-S $5, one of only three known, which realized $187,000 and the landmark 1875 Proof which brought $60,500. But very few others realized anywhere near the price of the 1876-CC.

Fast forward to 1989. David Akers is auctioning the 1876-CC gold half eagle in *Auction '89*, and it brings $60,500, destined to become a six figure coin. Another auction appearance in 1990 saw the coin bring $121,000. And the following year the 1876-CC $5 piece was sold to Henry S. Lang for $130,000+, in whose collection it remained until the summer of 2002, at which

time it sold for $138,000 in Bowers and Merena's *Rarities Sale*. This price seemed a bargain to the new owner, who had been prepared to pay in excess of $200,000 to obtain it. In 2002 there were indeed many other rare and expensive coins being auctioned at the very same time this 1876-CC $5 gold piece hit the block. Most significant was the 1933 $20 gold piece which had sold the day before the 1876-CC $5 half eagle for a record $7.59 million.

The new owner of the Eliasberg 1876-CC $5 gold piece resubmitted it to PCGS for further evaluation, and had his convictions confirmed when the grading service upgraded it from MS-65 to MS-66. This coin is securely seated aloft the highest level of coin rarity, numismatic prominence and condition rating. From its humble beginnings as one of 6,887 $5 Liberty half eagles minted at Carson City in 1876, the coin has become a jewel in the annals of coin collecting history.

GRAND

Fourth of July

CELEBRATION

AT CARSON CITY.

THE VIRGINIA & TRUCKEE RAILROAD Company will run an EXCURSION TRAIN on July 4th, to Carson and return.
Will leave Virginia City at 8:30 A. M., Gold Hill at 8:40 A. M., Mound House at 9:25 A. M., connecting with Excursion Train from Dayton.
Tickets, good on Excursion Train only, will be sold at Virginia, Gold Hill and Dayton Ticket Offices to Carson and return.

Fare...........................One Dollar
Children between 5 and 12 years....Fifty Cents

☞ Passengers are notified to purchase their tickets at the Ticket Offices before starting. Fare if paid on train will be 50 cents additional.
D. A. BENDER,   H. M. YERINGTON,
    G. F. & Pass. Agent.   General Sup't.
        je29 4t

Celebrations were always in grand style in Carson City during the late 19th century. This ad appeared in the *Carson Daily Appeal* in the late 1870s.

THE CENTENNIAL YEAR —A RECORD BREAKER AT CARSON CITY

Besides the Exposition held in Philadelphia during 1876, the Centennial year was celebrated in grand style throughout the United States. Parades, ceremonies, re-enactments of various events from the Revolutionary War, speeches, picnics, musicals, recitals, school plays and a national election were all part of the activities that proud citizens of the United States participated in. Spectacular Fourth of July pageants and ceremonies rallied the greatest nation in history to a desperately needed unity.

Eighteen-seventy-six was also a peak production year for silver coinage. All three mints ordered overtime crews to keep up with the massive volume of silver pouring into Treasury accounts. No one seemed to ask whether all the accumulating supplies of dimes, quarters, halves, and trade dollars were needed. It was similar to the Mint's

[Printer's No., 2031.

44TH CONGRESS,
1ST SESSION.

H. R. 1960.

IN THE HOUSE OF REPRESENTATIVES

FEBRUARY 7, 1876.

Read twice, referred to the Committee on Public Buildings and Grounds, and ordered to be printed.

Mr. WOODBURN, on leave, introduced the following bill:

A BILL

To provide for the improvement of the mint of the United States
at Carson City, Nevada.

1   *Be it enacted by the Senate and House of Representa-*
2   *tives of the United States of America in Congress assembled,*
3   That the sum of two hundred thousand dollars be, and is
4   hereby, appropriated, out of any money in the Treasury not
5   otherwise appropriated, for the improvement of the United
6   States mint at Carson City, Nevada, and to increase the coin-
7   ing capacity thereof; said improvement to be made, and the
8   money hereby appropriated to be expended, under the direc-
9   tion of the Secretary of the Treasury.

Bill introduced by Nevada Congressman William Woodburn in 1876 requesting $200,000 for improvement of the Carson City Mint. (*Courtesy Nevada State Museum*)

The Carson City Mint could look back to 1876 as being its pinnacle year of production. When the final tally was in, 15,839,024 coins with the "CC" mintmark had passed through the presses in 1876, a face value of $6,402,215, the highest annual total at the Carson City Mint. Dimes, quarters, and halves all reached peak numbers, and therefore are relatively easy to obtain in all conditions up through MS-64. Beyond that grade, however, they become much more difficult to locate. There are usually two or fewer 1876-CC dimes, quarters or halves in grades of MS-67 and above. The *Eliasberg* specimen of the 1876-CC half dollar is graded MS-68 by NGC. According to *The Complete Guide to Liberty Seated Half Dollars*[1] there are 24 different die marriages and three major varieties of 1876-CC half dollars. The *Small, Medium* and *Large* mintmark varieties demonstrate how mint engravers and die makers were scurrying trying to keep up with production demand.

As might be expected, the mintage of 138,441 1876-CC $20 gold pieces is the highest annual total for that denomination originating from Carson City. This date is the most readily available of all double eagles with the "CC" mintmark. In contrast, the 1876-CC gold eagles, and the $5 gold half eagle, have very low mintages.

More information concerning the silver and gold coins from the Carson City Mint in 1876 may be found in Chapter 6, *The Silver Coins*, and Chapter 7, *The Gold Coins*.

actions 100 years later, when millions of Bicentennial coins were manufactured and huge quantities remained in Treasury vaults.

---

[1] Wiley and Bugert, *The Complete Guide to Liberty Seated Half Dollars.*

❦ 1877 ❧

Mint Director H.R. Linderman arrived in Carson City from Philadelphia in 1877 on a public relations trip. Linderman inspected the mint, paying special attention to the new coin press that had been delivered the year before. After patronizing the locals and praising their mint operation, Linderman would later order Superintendent Crawford to lay off 15 female employees. Protests of gender bias caused Crawford to hire the women back and lay off 15 male workers.

IMPROVEMENTS TO THE LIBERTY GOLD $20

The wheels had been set in motion in 1876 to improve the designs of U.S. silver dollars and $20 gold pieces in honor of the country's Centennial anniversary. One hundred years seemed a long time, but at the same time, the memories and significance of the founding of the United States were near to everyone's heart.

Type II reverse of the gold double eagle displaying "TWENTY D."

Type III reverse introduced in 1877 with "TWENTY DOLLARS." (*Both photos courtesy Bowers and Merena*)

Although there had been no design changes in 1876, the patterns (or models) submitted, would introduce a change in the look of the $20 gold piece beginning in 1877. On the obverse of the coin, the head of Liberty became slightly smaller, with a sleeker appearance. The reverse of the coin featured the most significant changes. The scrolls on both sides of the shield were increased in size, and the country's motto *E. PLURIBUS UNUM* was inserted into the scroll. By widening the scroll, space was created at the bottom for both words, *TWENTY DOLLARS* (instead of *TWENTY D.*), using smaller letters. Now there were three types of the $20 Liberty double eagle, the *No Motto*, the *With Motto, TWENTY D.*, and the *With Motto, TWENTY DOLLARS.* For collectors of "CC" double eagles, there are seven dates of the Type II variety, and 12 of the Type III.

THE SEATED LIBERTY DESIGN IS CRITICIZED

Eighteen-seventy-seven was the most bountiful year for pattern coins in the history of the U.S. Mint, with over 30 different designs submitted. Public opinion about the artistic appeal of the country's coinage has often stirred many lively discussions. However, scathing criticism in the 1870s as well as monetary system weight changes prompted the Treasury to experiment with new designs. *Galaxy* magazine in 1876 wrote,

1875-CC Seated Liberty dime.

> Why is it that we have the ugliest money of all civilized nations? For such undoubtedly our silver coinage is. The design is poor, commonplace, tasteless, characterless, and the execution is like thereunto. They have rather the appearance of tokens or mean medals. One reason for this is that the design is too inartistic and so insignificant. That young woman sitting on nothing in particular, wearing nothing to speak of, looking over her shoulder at nothing imaginable, and bearing in her left hand something that looks like a broomstick with a woolen nightcap on it — what is she doing here?[1]

In the early years of the 21st century it might seem illogical that there were interest groups in the later half of the 19th century who scorned the Seated Liberty design. At the beginning of the 21st century, the historical, romantic and artifactual appeal of such relics of our country's heritage positively influence the way coin designs are viewed. The Liberty Seated Collectors Club appreciates the coin design of the series so much its newsletter is named *The Gobrecht Journal*, in honor of Christian Gobrecht one of the designers of the Seated Liberty coins. Regardless of complaints, Gobrecht's influence in U.S. coinage history is unparalleled. He died in 1844 and would be forever remembered for the silver dollars dated 1836 to 1836 and named in his honor, as well as the Seated Liberty coinage and the Liberty $2 1/2, $5 and $10 gold pieces.

THE PATTERN $50 GOLD PIECE

An array of pattern coins in 1877 was minted in gold, silver and copper. One of the most incredible coins ever minted in the United States was the pattern $50 gold piece, also called a gold Half Union. This pattern resembled the $20 double eagle, but its size was breathtaking, at least for a coin. It was 49.044 millimeters in diameter (15.044 millimeters larger than $20 gold

---

[1] Don Taxay, *The U.S. Mint and Coinage.*.

pieces), and was 3 millimeters thick, slightly thicker than a Morgan silver dollar. Weighing 2.69 ounces, and containing 2.42 ounces of fine gold it was a very impressive coin indeed.

Although the 1877 Half Union never became an authorized U.S. coin, two would later be linked to the rarest Carson City coin. William H. Woodin, who later served a short term as Secretary of the Treasury under Franklin D. Roosevelt, bought two Half Unions in 1909 for $20,000. Authorities later demanded that the Half Unions be returned to the Mint, on the grounds that the coins were never legally released. Woodin surrendered the two coins to the dealers he purchased them from and received a refund. The dealers, John Haseltine and Stephen Nagy, returned the coins to the Mint, and were fortunate to receive a large quantity of coins in exchange. This group of coins contained scores of patterns and, as tradition suggests, the unique 1873-CC *Without Arrows* dime. One can only guess the market value of these two Half Unions today. No one will ever know as both are in the Smithsonian Institution's collection, but an educated guess might be $5 million or more for each. They are certainly more interesting, more historical, and intrinsically more unique than the 1933 Saint Gaudens $20 gold, which sold for $7.59 million in 2002. The 1873-CC *Without Arrows* dime is *Unique*, and is the most expensive of all

Carson City coins, but in the year 2003 it is probably valued at $1/10$ to $1/5$ the price of a gold Half Union.

EXPERIMENTS IN GOLOID

Also in 1877, the Mint experimented with a new coin metal called *goloid*, an alloy of gold, silver and copper. The purpose of goloid was to resolve the issue of which of the two precious metals was most desirable in trade. A ratio of 16 parts silver to one part gold was established. For every two dollars in goloid coinage, there would be one dollar's worth of silver. Because the color of goloid was indistinguishable from silver, the threat of counterfeiting caused lawmakers to kill the bill in Congress.

There was no goloid, however, in Carson City, only tons of the metals used to produce it. For mine owners on the Comstock, and the brokers who traded mining stocks, life had been good. As the story goes, stockbrokers were escorting a client around the wealthy section of the San Francisco Bay in the late 1870s. The tour guides from the brokerage firm pointed out all the fancy yachts owned by successful stockbrokers. After viewing the impressive fleet, the client asked, "But where are the customer's yachts?"

DIGGING DEEPER AND DEEPER

But in 1877, it seemed that maybe even the brokers would not be able to keep their yachts. Whereas, in the

Cars coming out of a Comstock mine hauling mineral ore circa 1875. (*Courtesy National Archives*)

Hundreds of thousands of board feet of lumber stacked next to the tracks of the V&T Railroad, ready to be hauled to Virginia City to build more underground mines. (*Courtesy Nevada State Museum*)

Flumes that carried lumber from Lake Tahoe down to the Carson Valley where it could be transported to the Comstock region. This is a scene looking down from Spooner Junction toward Carson City in the late 1870s. (*Courtesy Nevada State Museum*)

Transfer yard of the Carson & Tahoe Lumber & Flume company at the bottom of Spooner Summit in the late 1870s. By this time the forests in the Lake Tahoe region were practically stripped of all trees. (*Courtesy Nevada State Museum*)

early days of the rich ore discovery along the Comstock, miners could practically pick up generous mineral deposits on the ground, gradually mining operations were forced to drill deeper below the surface. When all the valuable ore was exhausted at one level, miners developed new methods to dig deeper. By the early 1870s, the depth of the silver mines had reached 500 feet below the surface. By the mid 1870s, the 1,000-foot barrier had been broken. This was the era known as the *Big Bonanza*, as the mineral resources at deeper levels were of very high grade. Deeper levels and richer ore bodies filled the imaginations of the spirited mining company operators. One could almost hear the words pounding in their minds, "Dig, dig, dig. Drill, drill, drill. Deeper, deeper, deeper."[1]

Digging ever deeper in the mines was facilitated when Philipp Deidescheimer invented the square-set timbering system that propelled the output of bullion ore from the Comstock mines to levels never imagined. Deidescheimer's innovation solved most of the problems with dangerous cave-ins common with underground mining, and made it possible to explore significantly deeper regions below the surface. There was a downside to the success of this system, as hundreds of thousands of board feet of lumber were logged in the forests surrounding Lake Tahoe. It would be decades before the Tahoe Basin and surrounding Sierra region would be heavily reforested. Mining the Nevada silver used in the minting of the coins that would become increasingly popular with collectors would stir up controversy amongst environmentalists that would linger to present times.

The 1,650-foot level had been reached by 1877. Bankers, brokers and miners were virtually standing on the sidelines waiting to see how this game was going to end. Would it be possible to reach the 2,000-foot level? By November of 1877, one of the mines hit a vein at the 1,900-foot level. It was a low yielding strike, but it led to a richer body of ore discovered between 1,900 and 2,200 feet in the next couple of years. The table at right provides production levels over a 10-year period (1873 to 1882) at the Consolidated Virginia Mine. It is illus-

trative of the steep decline in the yield of mines on the Comstock after 1877.

CONSOLIDATED VIRGINIA PRODUCTION STATEMENT, 1873 – 1882

YEAR	TONS	GOLD	SILVER (AT $1.2929 OZ)
1873	15,750	$ 314,288.68	$ 331,293.45
1874	89,783	2,063,438.13	2,918,045.92
1875	169,094	7,035,206.54	9,682,188.22
1876	145,466	7,378,145.36	9,279,504.11
1877	143,200	6,270,518.68	7,463,500.39
1878	123,624	3,770,007.98	4,226,745.13
1879	60,227	1,198,319.68	1,283,039.15
1880	55,315	1,045,413.92	91,889.71
1881	6,816	91,889.71	52,253.72
1882	100	997.98	903.33
	809,275	$ 29,168,226.66	$ 35,948,596.03

[1]There are many excellent books on the subject, especially *The History of the Comstock Lode* By Grant H. Smith, and *The Roar and the Silence* by Ronald M. James.

ADOLPH SUTRO'S DREAM BECOMES A REALITY

In July of 1878, Adolph Sutro personally set charge to the final explosion of dynamite, which cleared the final furlong of earth leading to the other side of the massive tunnel he had been working on beneath the mining area of Virginia City. Mining operations at the time were working at the 2000 foot level which presented serious problems from steaming hot water flooding the shafts. Sutro's tunnel offered a solution to the drainage dilemma.

This project began in 1865 and took 13 long years to complete, as Sutro was at first scoffed at by mining industry leaders who did not see the need for a six mile long tunnel underground. They were not as farsighted as Sutro, however, who predicted that mineral ore would not always be as close to the surface, and as a result, operations would need to plunge to greater depths.

Sutro was finally able to secure financing and construction began in the fall of 1869. By the time the tunnel was completed in 1878 the *Big Bonanza* era had nearly come to an end. In hindsight miners saw what a valuable contribution the tunnel would have provided

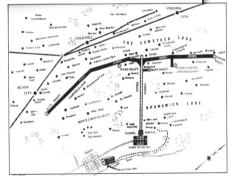

Approximate locations of mines in relation to the Sutro Tunnel in the late 1870s. Carson City is out of the picture, located in the lower left corner of the map.

during their peak years of operations. But still, the industry derived many benefits throughout the following decades from the tunnel, which had cost over $5 million; as it supplied fresh air ventilation, a mule powered railway system, and water drainage.

Sutro's success came late, but it was worth the wait, as he sold his interest in the tunnel and moved to San Francisco, where he lived the remaining years of his life as one of that city's wealthiest citizens.

There would be resurgence in silver production beginning in 1886 and continuing through 1894, as a result of mining companies breaking the 3,000-foot depth level with the help of new technology called Cornish Pumps. This would prove to be the last significant strike on the Comstock.

NEW SILVER DOLLAR PATTERNS

Coin production at the Carson City Mint after 1877 is to a degree in proportion to the declining yields of ore mined from the Comstock Lode. Silver dollars minted between 1878 and 1885 accounted for almost 80% of all coins produced during that period. There were approximately 9.37 million coins minted at Carson City between these years, of which nearly 7.5 million were silver dollars. These large *cartwheels*, as they would later be called, became the Bureau of the Mint's most heavily produced silver coin.

William Barber and George T. Morgan continued designing patterns for a new silver dollar in 1877. George T. Morgan's design that would ultimately be chosen for the silver dollar made its first appearance in 1877, although on a half dollar pattern. At least 23 different patterns in either silver or copper were submitted for the half dollar and the following year, 1878, one was selected for the new silver dollar, with only a slight variation, *HALF DOLLAR* was obviously changed to *ONE DOLLAR*.

Examining the situation at face value, it would appear that the last thing the Treasury needed to do in 1877 was to begin preparations to mint new silver dollars. The specie payments of silver coins used to retire existing fractional paper money had exceeded $36 million by 1877. As mentioned earlier, all of the U.S. mints had been very busy manufacturing coins and at the same time, it was estimated that more than $22 million in silver coins had begun to flow back into the country from neighboring lands. These mass quantities of coins had been shipped out of the U.S. during the Civil War, likely due to the profits that coinage brokers could realize because of the

premiums placed on these coins in Central and South America, Canada, and certain island territories. As Neil Carothers states in his book, *Fractional Money*:

> These coins had gone to Latin-America, served as local currency for 15 years, and then returned.

Carothers addresses the issue of why these coins returned, pointing out:

> With the value of silver going down and the value of greenbacks rising toward their parity with gold, a point had been reached where they were worth more [in the U.S.] than they were in foreign countries.[1]

MONETARY ARBITRAGE IN 1877

The trading of silver and gold coins in relationship to their comparative market value was a common practice of the era. When paper currency was added to the formula, brokers quickly took advantage of the situation. Gold had always been the popular choice as the standard on which to base monetary systems.

For example, when gold was the standard by which everything else was measured, the values of paper currency and silver were determined by how much gold either of these monetary units was worth.

For instance, if it was agreed that a one dollar paper note was worth $1/16$ of an ounce of gold when the price of one ounce of gold was equal to $15.50 in silver coin, the note was worth approximately 97 cents. Brokers exchanged these notes for $1 in silver coins, and then exchanged the $1 in silver coins for gold, ultimately exchanging the gold for paper currency. Brokers repeated these steps again, and again, as often as it was profitable, and of course it was much more profitable when larger amounts were being traded. Paper money worth $1,000 could be exchanged for $1,000 face value in silver coins, then the $1,000 in silver coins was exchanged for $1,000 in gold, which was in turn traded for $1,030 in currency. Subsequently, the $1,030 in currency was traded for $1,030 in silver coins, and then back to gold. At that point, the $1,030 in gold brought brokers $1,061 in currency, which they could use to start over again. This practice kept the coinage system of the U.S. in a disorderly state of volatility and uncertainty. The newspaper clipping below from the *Nevada State Journal*, dated November 1,

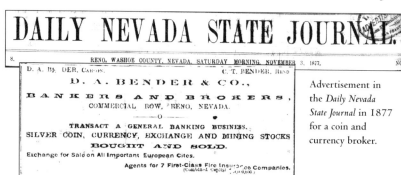

Advertisement in the *Daily Nevada State Journal* in 1877 for a coin and currency broker.

---

[1] Neil Carothers, *Fractional Money.*

1877, describes the relationship between silver trade dollars and currency.

VALUE OF THE TRADE DOLLAR – A New York Tribune Washington special says: As silver in London has fallen to [$1.20 (U.S.)] per ounce, the gold value of the trade dollar is 94 $^{1}/_{3}$ cents. The coinage charge being 1 $^{1}/_{4}$ cents at Philadelphia makes the cost of the trade dollar to the depositor 95 $^{3}/_{4}$. With gold at $1.02 $^{5}/_{8}$ (per $1 in silver) the gold value of the greenback is 97 $^{3}/_{4}$. In exchanging a trade dollar at par for greenbacks, holders of the former realize a gain of 13 $^{3}/_{4}$ per cent, and this from the use of a coin in domestic circulation intended by law for export to foreign countries only. At the present price of silver, trade dollars can be sent from San Francisco to the North-western cities and exchanged for United States notes at par and with small profit.

Coins and paper money were manufactured for the purpose of providing citizens with a standard means by which to pay and receive payment. The opportunistic enterprise of trading a nation's coinage and currency as a commodity was contrary to what a monetary system was supposed to be. Money was not intended to be used by brokers as an instrument of arbitrage for the sole purpose of making profits. If so, a nation's monetary system would be put at risk. Consider for a moment that if it became evident that the money of the United States could be sold to Mexico for more than it was worth domestically, citizens of the United States could seize the opportunity and clean out the banks. The Treasury would need to order more money be produced, placing an unnecessary burden on the Mint system. This happened between 1862 and 1876 in the U.S. – but of course at that time, the nation was at a lower rung on the learning curve concerning

DAILY NEVADA STATE JOURNAL

WASHOE COUNTY OFFICIAL PRESS

G. C. POWNING, EDITOR AND PROPRIETOR.

THURSDAY..........NOVEMBER 1, 1877.

VALUE OF THE TRADE DOLLAR — A New York *Tribune* Washington special says: As silver in London has fallen to 54¾ per ounce, the gold value of the trade dollar is 94⅓ cents. The coinage charge being 1¼ cents at Philadelphia makes the cost of the trade dollar to the depositor 95¾. With gold at 102⅝ the gold value of the greenback is 97¾. In exchanging a trade dollar at par for greenbacks holders of the former realize a gain of 13¼ per cent., and this from the use of a coin in domestic circulation intended by law for export to foreign countries only. At the present price of silver trade dollars can be sent from San Francisco to the North-western cities and exchanged for United States notes at par and with small profit.

Article informing readers how trade dollars were exchanged. For the most part, the public was confused about the value of trade dollars. (Reno *Daily Nevada State Journal*, November 1877)

monetary policy. Originally, the goal had been to establish equilibrium between gold, silver and paper money that would be fair to all, but there were just too many obstacles. Added wild cards of crooked politicians, greedy mining companies and conspiring bankers helped to thwart the original plan of the Founding Fathers. Of course, in the 20th century everything changed; there would be no plan. Money would be whatever the United States said it was and there would never be a shortage of it again. If the supply was dwindling, simply make some more. What difference would it make?

But at least back in 1877, U.S. citizens could use gold and silver in transactions if they felt insecure using paper money. Folks in the Pacific states had much more faith in gold and silver, and in Carson City and throughout northern Nevada, paper money was rarely used.

THE END OF GRANT'S PRESIDENCY

President Ulysses S. Grant successfully completed his second term in March of 1877, after leading the country through one of its most critical periods. The stress had taken its toll on Grant. He was a man with strong ethics and values, living in an era seemingly lacking these qualities. Grant was probably too often in a position where compromise was the path of least resistance. He took his record of the choices he made to the grave, and those who knew him best would attest to the strength of his integrity and resolve.

The Carson City Mint opened at the beginning of Grant's administration, and experienced some of its most momentous times through Grant's two terms; especially pursuant to the Coinage Act of 1873, which introduced the *With* and *Without Arrows* varieties, as well as the trade dollar. One wonders whatever became of that first 1870-CC silver dollar presented to President Grant. Abe Curry had seen to it that the *Battle Born* State sent the coin to the *Battle Born* President, out of respect and admiration, and many believed that Carson City's inaugural coin could not have been given to a more deserving person.

TRADE DOLLAR PRODUCTION ENDING

It was clear that the trade dollar dilemma continued to frustrate the nation throughout 1877. Mint Director Linderman staunchly supported the maligned coin, but newly appointed Treasury Secretary John Sherman declared there was no further export demand for it. In the 1877 *Annual Report of the Director of the Mint*, the fate of the trade dollar became obvious. There were more trade dollars being minted than there was need for and by the end of the year, Secretary Sherman made the decision to discontinue the Mint's practice of receiving silver deposits for the purpose of coining trade dollars. As 1877 came to an end, Mint customers still had silver on deposit entitling them to nearly 600,000 trade dollars, coins which would be minted and paid out.

Carson City minted 534,000 trade dollars in 1877, 25,000 more than the previous year's total. Although the 1877-CC trade dollar is not in a class with the ultra rarities from the "CC" Mint, it is a challenge to obtain high end Uncirculated specimens. As of 2003, PCGS and NGC had only graded 82 in Mint State, and most collectors feel fortunate if they are able to obtain one in nice AU-55 to MS-61.

OTHER CARSON CITY ISSUES FROM 1877

Dime production at the Carson City Mint in 1877 almost equaled the previous year's totals. In all, 7.7 million dimes were minted. The total of all seven denominations minted reached 13,900,577, the second highest annual total in the 21 years of coinage production at Carson City (with no coins minted in 1886, 1887, and 1888). The previous year's total of 15,839,024 coins was the highest, and the combined two-year total of coins minted in 1876 and 1877 was 29,832,392, nearly three million more than all of the other 19 years combined. In later years mintage totals would remain well below these production numbers.

As for quarter dollars from Carson City, in his study, *The Comprehensive Encyclopedia of U.S. Liberty Seated Quarters*, Larry Briggs concluded that there are 10 different reverse die varieties of the 1877-CC Seated Liberty quarter. The differences have to do with large and small mintmarks, and other slight variations. Although the values are approximately the same for all varieties, the 1877-CC quarter is a common date. A set of all 10 varieties in XF condition could be assembled for less than $1,000.

In the half dollar series, the 1877-CC is the most common date from the Carson City Mint. The finest known example of an 1877-CC half is the *Eliasberg* specimen graded MS-68 by NGC.

The low mintage (8,680) of 1877-CC $5 gold pieces is consistent with those from 1876-CC (6,887) and 1878-CC (9,054), and in the $10 gold category, there were only 3,332 1877-CCs minted, third lowest total in the Carson City eagle series. As far as the newly re-designed double eagles, a respectable number of 42,565 pieces were struck, although this represented less than $1/3$ of the quantity produced the previous year.

More information concerning the silver and gold coins from the Carson City Mint from 1877 may be found in Chapter 6, *The Silver Coins* and Chapter 7, *The Gold Coins*.

❧ 1878 ❧

The bicycle was manufactured for the first time in the United States in 1878 and cycling quickly became a popular hobby. The first electric light company opened in 1878. Joseph Pulitzer, for whom the Pulitzer Prize is named, began his publishing career in 1878.

BATTLE OVER MONETARY STANDARDS GAINS MOMENTUM

In 1878, New York City banks, with other eastern banks formed a committee to petition Congress to defeat the pending silver bill. Through 1873, slightly more than eight million silver dollars had been issued since the U.S. Mint was established, compared to more than $800 million worth of gold coins; the United States had clearly been on a gold standard. However, the amount of silver coinage increased so substantially through the mid-1870s that nearly $1 billion worth had been exported abroad. Foreign countries would either melt the coins received from U.S. exporters and re-coin them, or simply use them in circulation. Had this $1 billion in silver coins not been exported, it would have been a surplus in the United States, considered dead capital. The annual interest alone on this excess silver coinage would have been close to $50 million.

Gold standard and paper money advocates believed that the economy could survive with $50 million of silver coinage circulating. Where there once was a shortage of silver coins in circulation, now there was an overabundance. The plea coming from the anti-silver activists was "the country does not need anymore silver coins forced on it." They reasoned that producing more silver coins than were necessary for day to day transactions would be similar to producing more food than was being consumed, causing a depreciation in the value.

Silverites knew that a surplus of silver would depreciate bullion values, but they reasoned that if the excess silver was minted into coins, the monetary value would be greater than the bullion value, and all would be well. Silver miners would have a guaranteed market in which to sell their product, at a pre-determined price established by the face value of the coins. This meant that if a miner sold the amount of silver needed to produce a silver dollar to the mint, he would receive a dollar in exchange, even if the true market value of the silver was only half the face value of the coin.

Eighty years earlier, English philosopher John Locke convincingly argued that a government should not interfere with the fundamental value of the money that a country establishes as its medium of exchange. Locke illustrated that two pieces of silver of equal weight and fineness, no matter what form they were in, possessed the same value regardless if either portion of silver was minted into a coin. The only increased value of the silver coin resulted from production costs. Artificially inflating the value of coins above their intrinsic bullion value would always benefit one class of people over another, and the end result would be a depreciation of assets and either recession or depression.

THE EFFECTS OF THE SILVER ACT ON AMERICANS

At this time in the United States (1875 to 1879), the working class was at the mercy of big government (much as in the present age). If silver was artificially supported by government intervention creating a difference between silver's true value and the enforced higher value of silver coins, those who benefited would be able to pay debts with inflated money. The rest of the population would be forced to accept money that would be discounted when the time came for them to pay their debts.

Research conducted in 1878 by New York City banking firms representing banks in Boston, Baltimore and Philadelphia, led their committee to conclude that if the pending silver bill was passed, the cost to their depositors would be 10% of the money held in the depositor's names, a burdensome loss to the working class. In their report to Congress, the banking committee vividly expounded on the harsh effects that the increased mintage of silver coins would have on the population,

> The majority of the citizens of the United States, today, are laborers for wages in some form. They, with their families, constitute a majority of our population. If the purchasing power of money be reduced, their compensation would be reduced. As the nominal rate of their wages would long remain unchanged, every day would something be foregone in consequence of the depreciation of the money. In time they might get some relief, but only by demonstrating that they could no longer subsist on their reduced compensation. Whatever the disturbance and disaster to follow the demonetization of silver, they would be the first to feel the effect. They have no mode of escape. They cannot well change their places or occupations, but must toil on, as best they can, through all the calamities that befall them. The products of their labor, when gathered up into the great

reservoirs, constitute the capital of the United States. Upon them, in fact, rests the great fabric of society. To every one of them the monetization of silver would be an unmitigated evil.

The committee members inexorably placed the responsibility of protecting the nation squarely on the shoulders of Congress:

> Will Congress impose upon those whose lives are, of necessity, already condemned to severe toil, vastly heavier burdens, and subject them to new disasters which must result from the passage of the proposed measures.

According to the committee, silver mining companies, who were at the center of this controversy, would be the chief beneficiaries if the silver bill was passed. In the words of the committee:

> The favored owners of mines, [are] seek[ing] to swell into still vaster dimensions, that fabulous wealth, which is now, The Wonder of the World.[1]

This report was presented to Congress in January of 1878, at a time when the growing trend worldwide was to decrease coins in circulation, and increase paper as a form of money. The idea of introducing massive quantities of a new silver dollar coin seemed contradictory to most people.

BLAND-ALLISON ACT, MORGAN DOLLARS, AND JOHN SHERMAN

In spite of all protests, the silver bill became law on February 28, 1878 after an override of President Rutherford B. Hayes' veto. The law would be christened the Bland-Allison Act, after Senator William Boyd Allison (R-IA) and Representative Richard *Silver Dick* Bland (D-MO), who were members of the pro-silver dollar group.

Silver mining interests were reinforced. It was mandated that the Treasury purchase $24 million to $48 million worth of silver every year for the express purpose of minting it into silver dollars.

In the first year alone (1878), 22,495,550 new Morgan silver dollars were minted, 10% of that total at the Carson City Mint. Because of the enormous quantity of Morgan silver dollars issued from 1878 through 1921 (656,936,376), this series

is the most recognizable in all of coin collecting, and is the most widely collected type of coin, almost in a league of its own.

With the emphasis on minting the new Morgan silver dollars, the production of five of the seven other denominations then being minted at Carson City, was reduced by a large percentage. The chart at the bottom of the page illustrates how mintage totals decreased for the existing denominations, with the exception of the $5 half eagles (the $10 eagles only minimally).

The glut of silver coins stored in mint vaults around the country sent a clear message to the Treasury Department that there was no need to mint new coins. Barring future meltdowns, there were enough coins in circulation and stored in mint vaults to satisfy commercial needs for many years.

Secretary of the Treasury John Sherman.

John Sherman, younger brother of brilliant Union General William Tecumseh Sherman, served as the Secretary of the Treasury under Rutherford B. Hayes from 1877 through 1881. Sherman, a Republican had served as a Senator from 1861 through 1877 and was a supporter of Grant's policies during Grant's presidency from 1868 through 1876. Sherman supported the silver mining industry and had introduced the Specie Payment Act, passed in 1875, requiring the Treasury to redeem all existing fractional currency with silver coins, a major victory for silver miners. By February of 1878, Secretary Sherman suspended production of subsidiary silver coinage. Mintage totals for dimes, quarters and half dollars would be scant at all mints for the next five years. Totals for quarters and halves would remain low through the 1880s, although the need for dimes led to increased production levels beginning in 1882. John Sherman returned to Congress as a Senator in 1882 and would be forever remembered for introducing what came to be known as the Sherman Act of 1890. This act repealed the Bland-Allison Act of 1878, thereby increasing the annual quota of silver the Treasury was required to purchase for the purpose of minting silver dollars.

---

[1] *The Silver Question*, Memorial to Congress, New York, January 1878.

DIFFERENCES IN MINTAGE TOTALS BETWEEN 1877 AND 1878 AT CARSON MINT							
	DIMES	QUARTERS	HALVES	TRADE $	$5 GOLD	$10 GOLD	$20 GOLD
1877	7,700,00	4,192,000	1,420,000	534,000	8,680	3,330	42,565
1878	200,000	996,000	62,000	97,000	9,054	3,244	13,180
Increase/Decrease	(-3,850%)	(-421%)	(-2290%)	(-550%)	(+4%)	(-2 3/4%)	(-323%)

The surplus of silver coins in 1878 could be in part blamed on government interference over the years. It became a serious problem that threatened wage-earners, as well as retailers. According to Carothers:

> Wage earners were receiving subsidiary coins and trade dollars and forcing them on retailers ... Small merchants everywhere were over burdened with silver coins. Banks were refusing to accept them for deposit, and storekeepers had to dispose of them to brokers at discounts running as high as 3%. On the Pacific Coast, the discount was at one time 8%. Petitions and protests were reaching Congress from many points.[1]

COIN COLLECTORS THEN AND NOW

Coin collectors of the era paid little attention to mintage figures, coin surpluses, mintmarks, or Congressional legislation regarding Treasury affairs. There was not a reference source available equivalent to the *Red Book* of today and price lists issued by dealers usually included the dealer's buy price for certain coins, but no complete date and mintmark listings. Coins like the 1794 silver dollar, Gobrecht dollars, 1796 and 1804 quarters, Chain cents, the legendary 1804 dollar and other key dates were prized by numismatists. Collectors in the late 19th century could purchase Proof coins direct from the Philadelphia Mint. A set of Proof gold coins for example, consisting of the $20, $10, $5, $3, $2 1/2, and the $1 pieces had a face value of $41.50, and by law, the mint charged 25¢ over face value for each coin, thus a set of Proof gold coins could have been purchased for $43 in the year of issue. In today's coin market (2003-2004), an original set of Proof gold coins might bring $500,000 or more.

Pattern coins were also popular with collectors of the era. These trial or experimental pieces were used by the Treasury as part of the selection process to choose new designs for the nation's coinage. Invariably, most coin series would use the same design for many years; however, modification and improvements were continually being considered and when a new denomination or coin type was proposed, designers and engravers would submit their ideas to the Treasury. These pattern coins were struck in Proof condition, and provided impressive opportunities for collectors. Mint Director H.R. Linderman, himself an avid collector, formed a remarkable collection of pattern coins, in addition to the Proof 1804 silver dollar he acquired.

As all silver coinage, with the exception of Morgan dollars, came to an abrupt halt at the Carson City Mint in

1878, the significance of the first nine years' mintage totals to future collectors could be summed up by Heaton when he wrote, "The past will always attract the great interest of collectors"[2] Records accumulated since then provide present day collectors with compelling reasons to search for coins that have come to be known as rarities. Although it is enjoyable to collect coins with large mintages and high surviving populations, there is an indescribable feeling experienced by collectors when given the opportunity to add a key date to their collections.

Two such dates are the 1878-CC half dollar and trade dollar known as keys in the Carson City series. Mint records, which eventually became available to collectors, explain in part why the 1878-CC trade dollar is difficult to locate. In 1878 97,000 trade dollars were minted at Carson City, 56,000 in January and another 41,000 in February. In accordance with the Silver Redemption Act of February 28, 1878, 44,148 trade dollars were melted, presumably all from Carson City's stockpile of 1878's mintage. As for the 1878-CC half dollar, the mintage total was 62,000, third lowest total in the "CC" half dollar series and evidence suggests that the entire mintage was released into circulation and/or exported, accounting for a lack of high-grade pieces available today. One special example is the *Eliasberg* specimen, by far the finest known of this date, described in the catalog as an "Incredible Gem... Unsurpassable quality, possible presentation specimen."[3] Opportunities of this kind are rare, and when the author of this book purchased this coin on behalf of a client at the *Eliasberg* auction in 1997 for $77,000, was truly a memorable experience. Later on, NGC (Numismatic Guaranty Corporation) graded the piece MS-66 confirming the coin's premium quality.

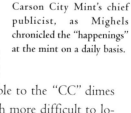

Henry R. Mighels, editor of the *Carson Daily Appeal* from 1865 until his death on May 27, 1879. The *Appeal* was the Carson City Mint's chief publicist, as Mighels chronicled the "happenings" at the mint on a daily basis.

Finishing out this grouping of coins from 1878, the 1878-CC dime, although nowhere comparable to the "CC" dimes from 1871 through 1874, is much more difficult to locate than the 1875 to 1877 dimes from this mint. The 1878-CC quarters are relatively easy to locate, being the

[1] Neil Carothers, *Fractional Money.*

[2] Augustus G. Heaton, *Mint Marks, a Treatise,* 1893.

[3] Bowers and Merena, *Louis E. Eliasberg, Sr. Collection,* April 1997.

third most common date in the "CC" quarter series. In the gold series, 1878-CC half eagles and eagles are among the rarest in their respective denomination categories, and the double eagles, though extremely difficult to locate in Uncirculated condition, do not present a challenge in circulated grades.

FAREWELL TO "CC" SEATED LIBERTY COINAGE

Eighteen-seventy-eight was the last year that more than four coin denominations were manufactured at the Carson City Mint, another turning point in the history of this institution. Familiar designs and denominations were retired into the record books, opening the door and ushering in a brand new type of coin, destined to dominate coinage operations in Carson City's final years.

When the year 1878 came to an end, there was no celebration, no fond farewell, not even a good-bye party held at the Carson City Mint to bid adieu to the four types of coins that had become like family to the employees at the mint who had seen them on a daily basis. Seated Liberty dimes, quarters and half dollars would never be struck again with the "CC" mintmark, and the same was true for the trade dollar. No pageantry, just a quiet retirement of these coins considered common and ordinary in their time.

1877-CC Seated Liberty half dollar

In the short period that Carson City produced Seated Liberty coins (1870 through 1878), many of the scarcest, most desirable coin and mintmark combinations would ultimately be counted amongst its numbers: Dimes from 1871, 1872, 1873 (*With and Without Arrows*) and 1874, quarters from 1870 to 1873, and the 1870 to 1874 and 1878 halves. Two dates from the trade dollar series, 1876-CC and 1878-CC, would eventually be nominated as key dates in their series. In the Seated Liberty silver dollar category, the 1871-CC and 1873-CC stand out; and of course the two-year 20-cent series spawned the 1876-CC rarity.

All told, the Carson City Mint accounted for nine date and variety combinations of dimes and quarters, and 10 date/variety combinations of half dollars. In the trade dollar series, six dates would proudly display the "CC" mintmark. After Heaton's *Treatise* attracted a following, coin collectors became increasingly fascinated with these *double letter* mintmark coins. By the end of 1878, all but four of the series/denomination combinations from the Carson

City Mint had passed unobtrusively from the scene. Seated Liberty coins and trade dollars minted in Carson City between 1870 and 1878 (40,900,505 in all, including 20-cent pieces) had served their commercial purpose and now they would be bequeathed to future generations of coin collectors. These captivating numismatic rarities were destined to serve a more glamorous purpose; they would become coins for the ages.

No one living at the time could have foretold how celebrated the coins from the small Nevada hamlet at the foot of the Sierra would become. For the time being, as 1878 drew to a close, the end had come for "CC" Seated Liberty coins and likewise for the trade dollars.

But there was no need to weep for their passing, for these treasured mementos from Carson City would explode in popularity in the following decades, eventually receiving all the recognition denied them during their era of mintage, truly a Horatio Alger story, if you will.

In 1879, the Carson City Mint would return to the business at hand of producing Morgan dollars and gold coins.

More information on the Carson City coins from 1878 may be found in Chapter 6, the *Silver Coins*, and Chapter 7, the *Gold Coins*.

HOTELS.

C. Y. SHARP.   H. W. SHARP.

ORMSBY HOUSE,

CARSON CITY, NEV.

SHARP BROTHERS, - - - PROPRIETORS

This Hotel is the most pleasant and conveniently located for the traveling public, being near the principal business houses and the State Capitol.

Accommodations First Class.

Rates: $2, $2 50 and $3 Per Day

Lake Tahoe Stages arrive and depart from this House.

THE ARLINGTON HOUSE.

JUDGE CAREY, Prop'r.
(Formerly of the Cary House, Placerville, California.)

The Leading Hotel of Carson

AN ELEGANT BRICK STRUCture, capable of accommodating 100 guests. Two minutes' walk from the depot. Provided with all the modern improvements. The cuisine is under the management of experienced cooks and is not surpassed in the State.

CARSON EXCHANGE

HOTEL

AND RESTAURANT

(Opposite the Railroad Depot)

E. WALKER, Prop'r.

Board, per Week $6 00
Board and Room, per Week, from .... $7 00 to 9 00

The best accommodation for the price of any house in the State.

DINNER AT TWELVE O'CLOCK.

The very best of

WINES, LIQUORS AND CIGARS Kept constantly on hand. Give me a call.

ST. CHARLES HOTEL,

Corner Carson and Third Sts.

CARSON, - - - NEV.

Four of Carson City's finest hotels in the 1870s, from an ad in the *Carson Daily Appeal.*

CHAPTER THREE

Full Steam Ahead
(1879-1888 The Morgan Dollar Period)

Carloads of silver and gold were hauled back and forth from the Comstock mines to Carson City on the V&T. (*Author's personal collection*)

The denominations of any one Branch Mint, in their irregular coinage and their relation to each other at certain periods, indicate curiously the particular needs of the given section of the land.

- Augustus G. Heaton,
A Treatise On the Coinage of the United States Branch Mints, 1893.

COINAGE RECORD UNITED STATES MINT AT CARSON CITY, NEVADA

YEAR	DOLLARS	HALF EAGLES	EAGLES	DOUBLE EAGLES	NO. OF PCS.	TOTAL $
1879	756,000	17,281	1,762	10,708	785,751	$1,074,185.00
1880	591,000	51,017	11,190		653,207	$957,958.00
1881	296,000	13,886	24,015		333,901	$605,508.00
1882	1,133,000	82,817	6,764	39,140	1,261,721	$2,397,525.00
1883	1,204,000	12,958	12,000	59,962	1,288,920	$2,588,030.00
1884	1,136,000	16,402	9,925	81,139	1,243,466	$2,940,040.00
1885	228,000			9,450	237,450	$417,000.00

Paucity is a word that has been used in numerous writings on the subject of collectibles. In the dictionary it is a noun defined as "Smallness of number: Scarcity. Dearth." It seems an old-fashioned word, especially considering that words such as rarity and scarcity are so much more familiar to the general reading audience. The meager number of 1879-CC $10 Liberty gold pieces minted, easily qualifies for whichever of these words one would choose to describe it. A quick glance at the score card comparing the mintage of 1879 gold eagles at the Philadelphia Mint with that at Carson City, clearly explains why the 1879-P $10 gold piece is priced at $400 in MS-60, while the 1879-CC eagle is listed at $55,000. Philadelphia produced 384,770 gold eagles in 1879, compared to 1,762 minted at Carson City. Of course, the price estimate for the 1879-CC $10 gold piece in Mint State condition is irrelevant, since there are no Uncirculated specimens of this date known at the present time (as of 2003).

1879-CC gold eagle, which had the lowest mintage of any date or denomination of gold coin produced at the Carson City Mint. (*Courtesy Bowers and Merena*)

THE NEW ORLEANS MINT RISES AGAIN!

The New Orleans Mint was revived in 1879 after an 18-year hiatus, and managed to eke out 1,500 $10 gold eagles that year. It had been seized by Confederate

ILLUMINATION!

In 1879 at Menlo Park, New Jersey, Thomas Edison perfected his incandescent electric light bulb, and soon, cities and hamlets throughout the United States would be all lit up. In Cleveland Ohio, that same year, the switches were flipped on the first electrical street lighting system and the public marveled.

troops in 1861 and correspondingly ceased functioning as a United States Mint office. Though the rebels in the South had plans of minting coins of their own at the New Orleans Mint, these plans never came to fruition, and for the duration of the Civil War, this southern mint was virtually out of commission as a coinage facility.

In a way, re-establishing the New Orleans Mint as a U.S. coinage institution in 1879 was a sign of reparation of broken bridges between the North and the South. After an arduous period of reconstruction, this was yet another effort by the North to officially welcome southerners back into the Union.

BUREAU OF THE MINT
FOCUSES ON MORGAN DOLLARS

By 1879, it was very clear that the new Morgan silver dollars were the Mint's chief area of focus. The Treasury Department knew the business at hand was to ensure that the operating mints under its governance were equipped to meet the annual quotas of 24 million-plus silver dollars it was, by law, committed to manufacture.

Morgan silver dollars would ultimately prove to be the collector items that put Carson City on the map. By the time the Nevada mint ceased manufacturing coins, nearly 14 million Morgan silver dollars would bear the "CC" mintmark, representing nearly 25% of all the coins produced at that mint. Only dimes would have a higher mintage total, topping 20 million.

A big silver coin like the Morgan dollar made plenty of sense for the silver rich state of Nevada. Mark Twain had called the northern part of the state "Silverland." Now here was a coin being produced in large quantities around the country, which was a natural advertisement for the region where so much of the white metal originated.

All of the mints in the U.S. tensed their rippled muscles to begin mass-producing the new silver dollars. By the time production of the Morgan dollar ended in 1921, over 650 million had been minted, nearly half being melted before the final year of their production. These big, bold silver coins were produced in numbers far exceeding any rational need, and were stored in Treasury vaults until their fateful meltdowns.

An 1878-CC Morgan silver dollar with the unpopular flatbreasted eagle referred to as a "wide pelican-bat out of the wilderness" in a Carson City newspaper.

Carson City's share of the silver dollar pie, although small in comparison, would become in many ways, the most famous. This can be attributed, in part, to the widespread publicity "CC" silver dollars would receive in the 1970s as part of the big GSA sales.

A MESSY MINTMARK

In the second year of silver dollar production at Carson City in 1879, the mintage would be trimmed to one-third of 1878's totals and today the 1879-CC Morgan is considered a key date in the series, especially in Uncirculated condition. Murky records concerning reverse die preparation cast a cloud of mystery on the question of why some 1879-CC dollars had mutilated looking mintmarks. Several of the known facts are:

1) The 1878-CC dollars displayed smaller mintmarks than those of following years.

2) The 1879-CC had a larger mintmark.

3) The Mint was under pressure to meet annual quotas of silver dollar production mandated by the act of 1878

No documents exist suggesting that the Mint first prepared reverse dies for the 1879-CC dollar using the smaller mintmark found on the 1878-CC, and then decided to use a larger "CC" instead. Nor are there any documents suggesting that after the decision was made, rather than have new reverse dies made, the engraver was told to use his tools to remove as much of the smaller "CC" as possible, punching a larger "CC" over it. However, the results speak louder than any authoritative documentation. It is certainly no stretch of the imagination to surmise that the scenario just described is close to what really happened[1] An isolated quantity of 1879-CC silver dollars was discovered to have "shattered" large "CC" mintmarks, a crude variety designated the *Capped Die*. Upon close examination, the shoddy workmanship is reminiscent of many California Fractional gold pieces.

With increased production demands, the U.S. Mint and its branches, attempted to yield upwards of 200,000 silver dollars from each pair of coin dies. In 1878, the Phila-

---

[1] Q. David Bowers, *Silver Dollars and Trade Dollars of the United States, A Complete Encyclopedia.*

delphia Mint sent enough dies to Nevada to coin 10 million silver dollars, obviously overreacting a bit. It has been reported that the Carson City Mint would strike fewer than 100,000 with each die pair (the average being 62,500). It is open to speculation at what point in 1879's production cycle dies were used for the *Capped Die* varieties.

There is a possibility that these anomalous coins originated in the first set of dies for 1879, due to the proximity of the year just past. Quite possibly, the engraver at the Philadelphia Mint was ordered to enlarge the "CC" mintmark on the 1879 dies at the last minute, and to avoid delays at Carson City, he might have sent a reverse die with a shoddily re-engraved mintmark to fill in until new dies were ready.

The coiner at the Carson Mint would most certainly have noticed the messy looking mintmarks right away, and taking pride in his mint's operations, undoubtedly would have brought it to Superintendent Crawford's attention. A letter would have promptly been dispatched to Philadelphia, and allowing for a four week turnaround, instructions (and possibly new reverse dies) would have arrived rectifying the problem. Since no correspondence exists explaining why, when and how the dies with the obliterated mintmark were created, it remains a mystery. Alhough it is not known how many *Capped Die* 1879-CCs were produced, estimates based on surviving populations range from 10% to 30% of the total mintage. Strange as the *Capped Die* variety is, it does not command a premium like other mint oddities might and, in fact, has traditionally been priced at a discount to the *normal* mintmark 1879-CC.

SILVER REDEMPTION LAW OF 1879

Picture if you will, a grandma in 1879 ordering a small amount of candies or nuts for 65 cents through the mail. She could wrap two quarters, a dime, and a nickel (or a half dime), in some tissue, stick them in an envelope and send it off to the fancy foods company. Or on the other hand, suppose an uncle wants to send his niece 50 cents for her birthday, and he encloses one of the 50¢ fractional currency notes in an envelope, and off it goes. Either method accomplishes the purpose without much difficulty. By the end of the 1870s, many of the country's citizens had grown accustomed to using the more conve-

Bags of silver dollars filled the vaults of U.S. Mint facilities across the nation during the final two decades of the 19th century. (*Author's personal collection*)

nient fractional paper money, especially for inexpensive mail order purchases. Since the passage of the Specie Payment Act, the Treasury had been redeeming the small notes in exchange for silver coins throughout the second half of the 1870s. After a 13-month pause in the redemption process, specie payments resumed in the first month of 1879, by which time, the public was not as eager to trade their paper for coins. The threat of a coin shortage had disappeared and citizens were not as survival oriented as earlier when hoarding coins from the shrinking supply seemed like insurance against hard economic times. Plus, fractional currency, as indicated worked very well for purchases less than a dollar. An almost perfect balance between silver coinage and paper money was emerging and both monetary units were increasingly more accepted.

Congress passed another act in 1879 that allowed for the redemption of silver coins for currency. As Carothers points out,

> This redemption law of 1879, intended by its framers to facilitate routine administration, was the final important step in the creation of our subsidiary system. Without being aware of its action, Congress had committed the government to a permanent policy of redeeming without limit all the subsidiary coins that it had sold to the public, whether the pieces were worn beyond the circulation point, redundant in supply, or merely unpopular in circulation. The long familiar phenomena of redundancy, depreciation, loss, and public annoyance were now impossible. The loss from wear was to fall on the government. And the mistakes of the government in choosing denominations, as in cases of the 3 cent and 20 cent pieces, would no longer have any effect on the public, since there was now a means by which the people could determine what denominations they preferred. [1]

---

[1] Neil Carothers, *Fractional Money: A History of Small Coins and Fractional Paper Currency of the United States.*

Fractional currency circulated for more than 20 years following the Civil War, until it was gradually redeemed by the Treasury.

This legislation encouraged the public to exchange silver coins for paper money. It came at a time when currency was more acceptable than it had been.

By act of this law shopkeepers and consumers would naturally be willing to trade their old worn out coins and receive the more convenient paper money in exchange. This mass redemption of silver coins during that era provides some explanation for the low surviving populations in modern times. From 1879 through the 1880s paper money became the preferred medium of exchange in most of the country, even surpassing gold coins in many states. This made it possible for the Treasury to accomplish what at one time was considered impossible. The public had become convinced that paper money was as good or even better than coins. This gave the federal government tremendous flexibility; it could issue money in any form it wanted to, and there would be no fear that the public would reject it, nor that they would hoard it – virtually power unlimited.

Even the western states gradually transitioned, from being gold and silver fundamentalists to cautiously accepting paper money. Tradition demanded, of course, that gold or silver-backed coins and currency were the preferable forms of payment.

DEATH OF H.R. LINDERMAN

Henry R. Linderman wrote his final *Annual Report of the Director of the Mint* in November 1878, and he died less than two months later in January 1879, the same month specie payments were resumed. Linderman had been at the center of all conflicts concerning monetary standards

during his service as the Director of the Mint. It is also well known that Linderman acquired many rare coins through questionable means in his appointed position.

One hundred years after his death, a magnificent 1868 16-piece pattern coin set struck in aluminum once owned by Linderman, sold in Bowers and Ruddy's 1979 *Garrett Collection* auction for $40,000. This set of coins was one of many memorable numismatic treasures from Linderman's collection. Controversy surrounding the life of this enigmatic figure in the Mint's history has persisted until modern times. For further study on Linderman's life, check out *The Crime of 1873*, by Van Ryzin, and *The U.S. Mint and Coinage*, by Taxay.

COINAGE RECORD FOR CARSON MINT IN 1879

One of the most controversial areas of Linderman's life was his relationship to the Carson City Mint; he could smile at a crowd while giving a flattering speech on Carson Street, then write contemptuous letters about the facility after returning to Philadelphia. So it was not surprising that mint workers at Carson City barely acknowledged Linderman's death as they kept to the task at hand, continuing production of Morgan silver dollars in that coin's sophomore year. By year's end, 756,000 sparkling cartwheels dated 1879-CC had been struck. Once again, Carson City's output was dwarfed by the mintages at Philadelphia (14,807,100) and San Francisco (9,110,000).

Gold half eagle production nearly doubled from the previous year's totals. But as impressive as this sounds, the mintage was still only 17,281 pieces. And being the third highest output from the 1870s, the 1879-CC is easier to locate than most other "CC" half eagle issues from this decade. However, as pointed out by Doug Winter,[1] there are probably fewer than four Uncirculated specimens known. Turning to the gold double eagle category, the Carson City Mint struck 10,708 pieces in 1879, which is the fourth lowest total for this denomination at the Carson City Mint.

Overall, coinage production for the four denominations minted in Carson City in 1879 declined sharply from 1878's output, but there were still more cutbacks to come before a brief resurgence brought new life in the 1880s.

For more information about the silver and gold coins from 1879, please see Chapter 6, *The Silver Coins*, and Chapter 7, *The Gold Coins*.

---

[1] Douglas Winter, *Gold Coins of the Carson City Mint* .

❧ 1880 ❧

More than 20 years had passed since the days when Henry Comstock, John *Old Virginny* Finney and company had first staked their claim to vast riches in *Silverland*. Grant Smith described how "Half-mad" Henry T.P. *Pancake* Comstock exclaimed to the amateur miners near Six Mile Cañon that, "You have struck it boys!"[1] Comstock reportedly "gave an old blind horse"[2] for a share in one of the first mines. None of them could have foreseen what these humble beginnings would bring forth.

EFFECTS OF HEAVY SILVER DOLLAR PRODUCTION

Morgan silver dollars manufactured at the participating mints across the nation in 1880 were beset with many surface flaws. According to the VAM (Van Allen/Mallis) book on silver dollar die varieties, there are in excess of 162 different varieties for 1880.[3] Ten "CC" dollar varieties from that year are included in this total. Collectors of VAM varieties are especially fond of the 1880-CC VAM 4, with Breen stating it is the clearest overdate of the series.[4]

Why are there so many overdates in the 1880 series? Q. David Bowers suggests that "apparently the Philadelphia Mint produced many obverse dies for 1879, and rather than waste them . . . they were overdated with 1880."[5]

This was only the third year of production for the Morgan silver dollar. By the end of the year, the three-year tally would be over 76 million, an average of more than 25 million per year. In retrospect, the government's plot to regulate the price of silver by ordering many millions of silver dollars to be minted was a major blunder. We will never know what might have happened if these silver dollars had not been produced. Coin collecting, as it is today, would certainly have drifted down another path. If it were possible to be magically swept to the highest pinnacle of history and see what the field of coin collecting would have been like without silver dollars dated 1878 to 1935, no doubt the view would be dramatically different.

There have been more *encyclopedias* written on silver dollars than on any other denomination. During the past 35 years, more articles have been written about silver dollars than all other coin series. Dare say, that from the 1960s to the present, silver dollars have been advertised as well as sold, more than any other type of coin.

And although silver dollars might be popular with coin collectors today, they were often considered a burden to the U.S. Mint during the years of manufacture. Keeping track of the dies needed to produce so many coins was one of the biggest challenges. It appears that the Mint requisitioned coin dies without knowing how many would actually be needed. There were many examples of criss-crossing obverse and reverse dies between the different mints, and as previously mentioned, the Mint took excess obverse dies from 1879, modified them, and used them to produce some 1880 dollars. Likewise, there were obviously reverse dies from 1878 in reserve when quantities of 1880 dollars were struck.

All of this helps explain the numerous varieties existing in the Morgan dollar series. One in particular is the *Flatbreast* reverse *Variety II* 1880-CC Morgan dollars, described by the *Carson Daily Appeal* as a "wide Pelican-bat of the wilderness," when it first appeared in 1878. Many explanations for inconsistencies such as this in the Morgan dollar series are lost in time, but the fact that the heavy burden of minting millions of the large silver coins was thrust upon a mint system unprepared for the task, accounts for many of the unanswered questions.

At the Carson City Mint in 1880, as reported in the 1881 *Annual Report of the Director of the Mint*, nearly 17% of the silver dollars produced were later determined to be below the standard weight based on tests performed on assay specimens and subsequently ordered to be melted. Though there never has been an explanation for the 96,000 inferior 1880-CC silver dollars, it was clearly a local problem and had nothing to do with any dies coming from the Philadelphia Mint. It proved to be another black mark against the already disparaged Carson Mint.

PRESIDENT HAYES TOURS THE COMSTOCK

Ulysses S. Grant, on a world farewell tour after leaving the White House, had stopped in Carson City in October of 1879. One of the more memorable post-Civil War photographs of Grant was taken on this tour as he and Mrs. Grant posed for a photo which also included their son, U.S. Grant, Jr., and two of the *Big Four, Bonanza Kings*, (James Fair and John Mackay).

---

[1] Grant A. Smith, *History of the Comstock Lode 1850-1997*.
[2] Ibid.
[3] Leroy C. Van Allen and A. George Mallis, *Comprehensive Catalog and Encyclopedia of Morgan and Peace Dollars*, 4th ed. .
[4] Walter Breen, *Walter Breen's Complete Encyclopedia of U.S. and Colonial Coins*.
[5] Bowers, *Silver Dollars and Trade Dollars*.

Following in Grant's footsteps, President Rutherford B. Hayes, accompanied by his wife, visited the Comstock in 1880. Hayes was escorted by prominent military leaders and cabinet members, including Ulysses S. Grant's chief Civil War officer, General William Tecumseh Sherman. A diversified committee of locals enjoyed a banquet with President Hayes and his honored escorts. This quote from the *Daily Territorial Enterprise* describes the diversification of this group, as well as Nevada's link to gambling and the spirit of the *Old West*.

> In no other place in the world would the names of leading gamblers and saloonkeepers appear on such a committee, which included Bishop Whitaker; yet there is Joseph R. "Joe" Stuart, who kept the finest faro rooms on the Comstock for years; Robert "Bob" Patterson, proprietor of the International Saloon and faro rooms; and W.D.C. Gibson [William De Witt Clinton Gibson, in full, familiarly known as "Bill"], the proprietor of a similar establishment at Gold Hill. Manhood and brains were the only tests on the Comstock.[1]

Despite presidential blessings on the Comstock and its local mint, a constituency in Washington, D.C., eager to close the Nevada facility, introduced legislation to open a new mint near the Mississippi River, perhaps in St. Louis. But once again the Carson Mint withstood a threat, as its destiny in the legacy of U.S. coinage was not yet fulfilled.

SHORTAGE OF SILVER IN THE SILVER STATE?

Despite peak levels of bullion production during the 1870s, it appeared that the *Silver State* was running out of silver. In fact, there was such a shortage in the Comstock region through 1880 and following, that coinage would be halted at the Carson City Mint on an all too regular basis. Howard Hickson informs us that:

Large bars of silver bullion were transported to and from the Carson Mint on a daily basis. (*Courtesy Nevada Historical Society*)

On March 11, 1880 . . . Crawford announced that the mint would not resume operations . . . until a two month supply of bullion was on hand . . . . Even then, on May 1, though machines, furnaces and boilers roared back to life, four months would pass before coining began again, causing production of the mint to drop below $1 million, the lowest coinage in seven years.[2]

In the 1880 *Annual Report of the Director of the Mint*, the status of the stock of bullion at the Carson City Mint was addressed,

> The Stock of bullion at this mint having become reduced at the end of October 1879, to $107,023 of gold, and $14,362 of silver; being an insufficient supply for a single month's work, coinage was temporarily suspended…[3]

Not much had improved by April of 1880, as the Director continues,

> So small an amount, however, came to the mint that, up to April 16, 1880, only $228,177 of gold and $258,427 of silver, had accumulated. This however was deemed sufficient to authorize the resumption of coinage operations, which were continued to the close of the year.[4]

Operations were intermittent through 1880, however, and the staff at the Carson Mint could only hope for a turnaround.

Several factors contributed to the shortage of silver bullion needed to mint silver dollars at the Carson Mint. The first was the ever decreasing output from the Comstock mines, which by 1880 had dropped to below 20% of its 1875 production. Another factor was a boycott, in which the controlling interests of the silver mines refused to sell their bullion to the Treasury. In late 1878, Linderman had written:

> It was found that the producers and dealers [of Comstock silver] would not sell silver to the government at the equivalent of the London rate, but demanded in addition thereto an amount equal to the cost of bringing it [silver] from London, and laying it down in San Francisco.[5]

As Robert Van Ryzin points out, the Philadelphia Mint "turned to purchasing foreign silver (in 1878) to make up for the shortfall." Mint Director Linderman also wrote in late 1878, that the mine owners had eventually reached a compromise, and began selling their silver to

---

[1] *Daily Territorial Enterprise*, September 5, 1880.
[2] Howard Hickson, *Mintmark "CC": The Story of the United States Mint at Carson City, Nevada*, ed. by Guy Shipler.
[3] *Annual Report of the Director of the Mint*, 1880.
[4] Ibid.
[5] *Annual Report of the Director of the Mint*, November 1878.

the Mint, which provided the necessary quantities "to employ the mints at San Francisco and Carson on the coinage of the dollar."[1] Complicating matters was the continuing blackball treatment aimed at the often-disparaged "incorrigible and irresponsible" mint operation in the small Nevada capital. But, as historical irony would have it, the mint that was once maligned by much of the nation has become the most treasured mint in the field of coin collecting.

Quiet afternoon street scene in downtown Carson City in the 1880s. (*Courtesy Nevada Historical Society*)

LOOKING BACK AND AHEAD FROM 1880

The National U.S. Census recorded a population of slightly more than 50 million people living in the United States in 1880, approximately 31,000 of whom lived in the Comstock region of Nevada. Carson City claimed to have a population of approximately 7,500, but people were leaving in droves, and the number was probably closer to 5,500. Regardless, these population levels would not be reached again until 1960. By the 1930s Carson City's population would decline to roughly 1,800 people, and the main highway through town would not even be paved until 1933. For decades, Carson City would boast of being *America's Smallest State Capital*.

But in 1880, there were optimists who crossed their fingers, and held their breath, wishing, dreaming and hoping that another vein of ore would be struck just around the corner. But the exodus had begun and scores of once faithful sons and daughters of the *Silver State* had begun their pilgrimage to other promised lands.

As local businesses closed, employees lost jobs, debts were outstanding and many would never be repaid. But if the memory of the prosperous times remained in people's minds, hope that those times would return, filled their hearts.

One could almost imagine the young folks of Carson City requesting of their elders:

Please tell us that story Papa. You know, the one you told us of how the large pine trees from Lake Tahoe used to come sliding down the slopes of Spooner Summit in those big flumes. And how you could hear the screeching sound of the logs scraping the insides of the flumes as they flew down those mountainsides as if they were shot out of cannons. And how those trees were milled into flat board that were used to support the underground mines and build the houses and buildings in our city.

Or

Mama, please tell that story again how the big earthquake back in 1869 shook everything so hard, and how some of the windows broke, and how all the liquor bottles fell off the saloon shelves, but how, when they checked out the new mint that had recently been built, they couldn't find any damage.

And

Remember, Grandpa, the story you told us about the time Colonel Curry gave you a tour of the new mint after it had just opened, and how he gave you one of the new silver dollars? You still have that silver dollar, don't you Grandpa? That was 10 years ago wasn't it? Do you think you could show us that silver dollar again Grandpa so we can see where those two little "C"s are?

Folks in Carson City would forever treasure their history, always striving to preserve their rich heritage for future generations.

THE UNITED STATES IN THE GILDED AGE

"What is the chief end of man?"
"To get rich."
"In what way?"
"Dishonestly if he can, honestly if he must."

Mark Twain satirically wrote these words in 1871, as the country emerged from the Reconstruction period. In the years following the Civil War, a growing trend became evident, the rich were getting richer, and the poor seemed to be getting poorer. A large percentage of households in the United States lived well below the poverty level. However, industrial and commercial giants such as Carnegie, Morgan, and Rockefeller were amassing great wealth, as they built their empires. The era in which the

---

[1] Robert Van Ryzin, *Crime of 1873: The Comstock Connection.*

Carson City Mint produced coins, 1870 through 1893, was chronologically at the center of a 50 to 60 year period known as the *Gilded Age* (c. 1855 to 1915), a phrase made popular by Mark Twain.

The word gilded is defined in the dictionary as, "to have given an often deceptively attractive or improved appearance to some thing or some one." For many people, the attractive appearance was not deceptive, because they really were wealthy. For others, there may have been an air of distinction, without much foundation. Often people would live beyond their means, giving the impression of middle to upper class status, a mindset that may be described as *Fake it 'til you make it*. The exploits of the rich were popular subject matter in the pages of newspapers and periodicals. After all, maybe some of their good fortune would rub off on the more meagerly endowed readers.

The mining regions of northwestern Nevada imported all the accoutrements of *Gilded Age* living into their communities. By 1880, the residents of Virginia City, Gold Hill, Silver City, Reno, and Carson City had partaken of just about every luxury, recreation, entertainment, cuisine, and vice that was available anywhere in the country. Images of a cultured woman, hair pulled back in a bun, with long curls flowing behind her neck, her gown gracefully draped two inches below the shoulder, a matching broach and set of earrings, and her head leaning ever so demurely into a fan of spread gold certificates, characterized the passion of the *Gilded Age*.

The residents living around the Comstock in the 1880s understood the disparity between different financial classes. Without a doubt, the bank crowd was in control and to a lesser degree, the railroad and mining industry leaders; but for many, the great riches of the 20-year mining boom were rapidly diminishing. The one thing the people of the region would always be able to salvage, no matter how desperate the situation became, was their past. More will be said about the perpetuity of the history and enchantment of this generation later, but this quote from *The Roar and the Silence*,[1] personifies the spirit that enabled Comstockers to endure even through tough times:

> . . . it will be observed that Virginians do not hang their heads like devotees of Dame Fortune in other towns less elevated. The atmosphere [in the Comstock] will not admit of it... A little growl, that hardly suggests complaint, is all that is to be heard, while good humor and pleasant sociability prevail.

In July 1880, the Virginia and Truckee railroad tore up a section of tracks connecting Virginia City to Silver City.[2] This would prove to be one of many demoralizing events that locals would have to contend with. Compare the tearing up of tracks and shutting down mines to a baseball park being torn down in a city devoted to their hometown team for many years. Unlike a major league ball park being demolished, however, these railroad tracks were not scrapped to make way for redevelopment in the area; instead, acts like these were axiomatic of the transformation of a once thriving boomtown region into a sparsely populated tourist attraction.

Ben Hur WRITTEN TO COUNTER INGERSOLL'S CLAIMS

While times grew bleak for much of the American public, the pursuit of entertainment, leisure and intellectual enlightenment during the *Gilded Age* topped the list of priorities for the middle and upper class. One of the most popular activities was listening to speeches; orators across the nation captivated audiences with lectures on a broad range of topics. Humorists, satirists, theologians, politicians, historians and philosophers were celebrities in the days before the advent of radio, television and motion pictures. Robert Ingersoll was considered to be one of the greatest public speakers of all time and his lectures were always sold out. He was paid thousands of dollars for a single speech, and he used his prestige to influence the belief systems of the crowds to whom he spoke.

In 1880, Ingersoll, a renowned atheist, was challenged in his religious convictions by a fellow Civil War officer, General Lew Wallace. Wallace yearned to be remembered for his military service. However, in 1880, he wrote *Ben-Hur; A Tale of the Christ*, forever linking his name to this memorable epic novel. Wallace had served in the Mexican War, and in 1849, at the age of 22 had entered the legal profession. Entering the Civil War in 1861, as a Colonel, Wallace rose to the rank of Major General in less than 12 months. His reputation was slightly marred during the battle of Shiloh in 1862, but by the end of the Civil War, he retired with honor. From 1865 through 1880, Wallace practiced law and served as governor of New Mexico.

Wallace was an atheist (or more accurately, agnostic), who had listened to Robert Ingersoll speak, but something about Ingersoll's beliefs on God and religion troubled

[1] Ronald M. James, *The Roar and the Silence: A History of Virginia City and the Comstock Lode.*
[2] *Virginia Chronicle*, July 13, 1880.

him. Ingersoll thought it would be in the country's best interests to convert to atheism and Wallace, not really knowing why, challenged that supposition. He was admittedly ignorant about the teachings of the Bible, but committed himself to test Ingersoll's teachings by either proving or disproving the teachings of the Church. His research culminated in the authoring of *Ben-Hur*, and Wallace himself was converted to Christianity. More than one million copies of *Ben-Hur* had been sold in the first 35 years after it was published, and it is ranked as one of the bestselling literary works of all time. Ulysses S. Grant, who was not known to read novels, finished reading *Ben-Hur* in 30 nonstop, sleepless hours. It is interesting to note that in modern times certain first edition copies of *Ben-Hur* have sold for $6,000 and more.

Hoards of 1880-CC Morgan Dollars

Not to be overshadowed by the sale of rare books, certain 1880-CC Morgan silver dollars in the finest states of preservation have sold for more than $5,000, with the record auction price being $20,700 for one at a Heritage January sale in 2001.[1]

Condition ratings notwithstanding, silver dollars struck at the Carson Mint in 1880 were at one time considered scarcer than most other Morgan silver dollars. Then, in 1938, a hoard of 50,000 Uncirculated 1880-CC silver dollars was released from the Treasury in Washington, D.C. Renowned author and coin dealer, Q. David Bowers reported that Harry X Boosel, employed in government service, obtained many 1880-CC dollars at face value, later selling them by mail-order. Years later, several more hoards of 1880-CC dollars were released, with the largest quantity surfacing during the GSA public sales, when 131,529 were sold beginning in 1973.

Carson City Gold Coins in 1880

In 1880, for the first time since the Carson City Mint opened in 1870, no $20 gold pieces were minted. As it had in most of the years since the California Gold Rush, the San Francisco Mint shouldered the majority of that burden. From 1870 through 1879 San Francisco had coined 11,689,400 $20 gold pieces while Carson City had produced

501,666, or approximately 4% of its California cousin's output. Serving vital monetary needs, the $20 double eagles were the preferred monetary units not only for large banking transactions, but also for redeeming mining company's bullion deposits, and foreign trade. It was the responsibility of the Mint Director in Philadelphia to coordinate the distribution of every coin denomination to its proper channels.

Accordingly, the Mint Director ordered the distribution of the commercial workhorses of the gold series, $5 half eagles and $10 eagles, to accommodate and supply various resource centers across the nation. The table at the bottom of the page compares distribution totals for $5 and $10 gold pieces at the four mints producing coins in 1880.

In the Carson City series, the 1880-CC $5 and $10 gold pieces are considered to be relatively common dates to locate although their mintages are very low when compared to those of San Francisco and Philadelphia. Keep in mind, the key word is relatively, for as Doug Winter estimates, there are fewer than 300 $10 eagles and 450 $5 half eagles existing in all grades.

It became clear in 1880 around the Washoe Valley, the Comstock region, and Carson City that the once bountiful mining fields were being rapidly exhausted and operations at the Carson City Mint through the 1880s would reflect that.

For the first time in its brief 11 year history, only three denominations were manufactured at the Carson Mint in 1880. Added to the mintages from the previous 10 years, over 44.5 million coins had already been struck, a figure representing over 78% of all the coins ever produced at this mint.

For more information about the silver and gold coins from 1880, please see Chapter 6, *The Silver Coins* and Chapter 7, *The Gold Coins*.

---

[1] *2002 Auction Prices Realized*, comp. and ed. by Randy Thern.

1880 $5 and $10 Gold Coin Production Totals At the Four Mints				
Denominations	Philadelphia	San Francisco	Carson City	New Orleans
$5 Half Eagles	3,166,436	1,348,900	51,017	—
$10 Eagles	1,644,876	506,250	11,190	9,200

1881

One of the nation's most humanitarian organizations, the American Red Cross, was founded on May 21, 1881.

GARFIELD'S BRIEF PRESIDENCY

James Abram Garfield was elected as the 20th president of the United States in November 1880. He was inaugurated on March 4, 1881 and shot on July 2, 1881, an event which led to his untimely death 11 weeks later on September 19, 1881, two months before his 50th birthday. Garfield had served in the Union Army during the Civil War, attaining the rank of two-star general.

In 1880, Garfield had campaigned for his friend John Sherman to win the Republican presidential nomination, but when Sherman failed to gather enough votes, Garfield himself became the dark horse candidate. As a congressman, Garfield had favored the payment of government debts in coin. He was an opponent of government interference in the valuation of silver prices, and vigorously fought for a sound monetary standard for the United States. Vice President Chester Arthur succeeded Garfield as president on September 20, 1881 and served the remainder of the term, at which time his successor, Grover Cleveland, assumed office.

SELF-SERVING POLITICIANS

In 1881, James Graham Fair, one of the *Silver Kings* on the Comstock, assumed his role as a U.S. Senator from the State of Nevada. Fair had defeated Adolph Sutro in the senatorial race in 1880 despite Sutro's attempt to buy his way into office, personally spending $250,000 on *gifts* to supporters. That sum was hardly a challenge to James Fair, listed as one of the wealthiest men in the history of the United States. With Fair's installment in the U.S. Senate, Nevada would have two native Europeans serving concurrently in that office. Senator John P. Jones had emigrated years earlier from England, and Fair was born in Ireland. Perched atop their lofty political and business standings, these two men would utilize machinations to insure a steady market

Humane and Patriotic Wall Street.

Among the dispatches received by the CHRONICLE to-day were the following :

NEW YORK, July 2.—The *Post* says: The news of the shooting of the President had no effect on the stock market.

NEW YORK, July 2—11 A. M.—Stocks opened generally firm, but a free selling movement was soon inaugurated and the entire list broke rapidly under the Washington news, declining 1 @ 1½.

These feeling telegrams from Wall street came sandwiched between others stating the chances of the President's recovery or death.

Money-making, when it becomes a passion, swallows every sentiment creditable to human nature. It renders a man a mere gold-catching sluice, and makes him lower than the brutes.

The news of the attempted assassination of the President inspired the ordinary American citizen with alarm for his country, and with grief and sympathy for the man who is lying bleeding between life and death.

Wall street rushed to look at the stock list.

Locals around Carson City cast disdainful eyes toward the Wall Street crowd at every opportunity. This blurb from the *Carson Daily Appeal* in 1881 on the occasion of the assasination of President Garfield is an example.

for the silver being extracted from the depths of their mines. Although they gave the appearance of being pro-silver, and thus supportive of local mining and minting operations, Fair and Jones were self-servers, especially Fair. This came at a time when the other Comstock businesses and the Carson City Mint, specifically, could have used a strong voice in their favor in Washington.

It was a critical year in the history of the Carson City Mint in 1881 as charges were raised of employee theft of precious metals. In his book *Mintmark: CC*, Hickson reports that when a Secret Service agent was sent to Nevada to investigate, "The loyal Carsonites gave him so much false information, and led him on so many useless chases, that the agent reported to his superiors: 'Any community where so many people seem determined to shield criminals is not a good place for a mint.'"[1] The continuing shortage of bullion needed to mint coins was also disadvantageous. Again, according to Hickson, "the Reno Weekly Gazette … charged Senator James Fair … with inactivity in getting the mint reopened in Carson City." Apparently, Fair and his partners in the Consolidated California and Virginia Mine had all of their metal refined in San Francisco at their own refinery. Hickson claims, "The bullion from Fair's mine alone would have kept the mint operating."

While the combined production totals of silver dollars at the other three mints increased by over 800,000 in 1881, Carson City's silver dollar output was cut in half. The mintage of 296,000 was the second lowest total of Morgan silver dollars ever struck in one year at Carson City, with only the 1885 total of 228,000 being lower.

TREASURY MONITORS MINING ACTIVITY

The mining industry in the United States had become inextricably linked to statistics pertinent to coin production. In 1880, the Treasury Department commissioned presiding Director of the Mint, Horatio Burchard, to include detailed statistics about mineral resources in

[1] Hickson, *Mint Mark"CC"*.

the *Annual Report of the Director of the Mint*. Burchard had served as an assistant to Mint Director H.R. Linderman and was well acquainted with the Treasury's oversight of the mining industry. Statistics about gold and silver production had been briefly incorporated into previous annual reports, but now, the subject would be exhaustively covered under the title: *Production of Gold and Silver in the United States*.

In these reports, not only would bullion production be compiled by individual states, it would also be broken down by counties. The Mint Director solicited the help of the regional mint and assay office superintendents to submit data for their states. The accuracy of the reports depended upon the representatives in each mining district passing on reliable facts and figures to the superintendents, ultimately arriving at the desk of the Mint Director. These figures would only prove to be estimates in some cases, and in others, were not without blemish. If a state, county or specific mine wished to garner more favorable reviews, a slight exaggeration in production totals was occasionally employed. When examined today, these reports are useful measuring rods for tracing the history of westward expansion, changes in the country's monetary policies, coinage production, and the history of various mints and assay offices.

Mineral resources proved to be a territory's greatest ally when seeking statehood. The Gold Rush of 1849 in California, certainly hastened that state's entry into the Union in September 1850. Gold was discovered at Grasshopper Creek, Montana, in 1862. Four years earlier, gold had been discovered at Gold Creek, Montana. Prospectors from around the nation swarmed into the *Big Sky* region and Montana gained territorial status in 1864, but waited 25 years to be granted statehood, owing greatly to increased bullion production in that state in the 1880s. *The Unsinkable Molly Brown*, otherwise known as Mrs. J. Brown, was the socialite wife of a wealthy Colo-

rado mine owner. Molly's husband made his fortune in the famous gold and silver mining boom that began along the South Platte River in what would become the 38th state. Colorado's boundaries were mapped off in 1861 when it became a territory and in 1876, President Grant signed the state's proclamation, joining it to the Union.

The Comstock, once thought to be unsinkable, left its indelible mark on many other successful mining states. Names that would be spoken almost in reverence by miners were often heard in other states where the pursuit of mineral wealth was the primary business. There is a Nevada City in Montana as well as in Colorado; and Virginia City was a name often used in mining regions around the country, with one of the well known towns of this name located between Bozeman and Butte in Montana. Workers in the mines of Nevada gained experience and passed it on like a torch to miners in other camps across the nation, and even into other nations. In his book, *A History of the Comstock Mines*, Dan DeQuille wrote:

> Men who graduated on the Comstock are now to be found in all parts of the world. They early went to Idaho, Montana, Utah, Colorado, New Mexico, Arizona, Alaska, and British Columbia. Old Comstock foremen and superintendents are today in charge of mines in Mexico, Central America, South America, Australia, Africa, China, Japan and all other regions where there is mining for the precious metals.[1]

A simple study of the statistics about gold and silver production on the Comstock Lode, as provided in the annual mint reports, uncovers part of the mystery concerning the low mintage figures for 1881 at the Carson City Mint. The table at left shows how silver production on the Comstock had risen from its underdeveloped levels of 1860, to its peak levels through the 1870s, and then declined rapidly in 1881.

TOTAL SILVER PRODUCTION OF THE COMSTOCK LODE FROM DISCOVERY AND COMMENCEMENT, BY CALENDAR YEARS, TO DATE.*	
YEARS	SILVER
1860	$ 200,000.00
1861	1,000,000.00
1862	2,350,000.00
1863	7,460,000.00
1864	9,600,000.00
1865	9,700,000.00
1866	8,944,737.00
1867	8,243,164.80
1868	5,087,861.40
1869	4,443,346.80
1870	5,222,595.24
1871	6,149,717.19
1872	7,341,839.79
1873	13,003,187.13
1874	13,486,071.09
1875	15,495,312.92
1876	18,971,196.12
1877	21,780,922.02
1878	11,796,836.47
1879	4,202,091.49
1880	3,077,409.00
1881	645,372.00

* *Annual Report of the Director of the Mint*. Compilation of different editions.

[1] *A History of the Comstock Mines*. 1889 Dan DeQuille

COINAGE VALUE OF SILVER PRODUCED IN COLORADO FROM 1859 TO 1886 *	
YEAR	SILVER
1870	$ 650,000.00
1871	1,029,046.34
1872	2,015,000.00
1873	2,185,000.00
1874	3,096,023.00
1875	3,122,912.00
1876	3,315,592.00
1877	3,726,379.33
1878	6,041,807.81
1879	12,068,930.27
1880	18,615,000.00
1881	17,160,000.00

* Annual Report of the Director of the Mint Upon the Production of Precious Metals, 1886.

Concurrent with the history of Nevada's mining production, was Colorado's ledger for its silver outputs.

At the same time the *Bonanza* period in Nevada was declining into a *Borrasca*, Colorado's silver mines were reaching peak production (shown at left). The majority of silver dollars coined at the Philadelphia Mint were made of Colorado silver.

Gold production from the Comstock mines had fallen to its lowest level in 21 years. An estimated $430,000 of gold bullion was all the mining companies in Northern Nevada could claim for their aggregate output for 1881. Just four years earlier, in 1877, the gold output had been estimated at $14.5 million. And as Grant Smith relates, the 1881 totals consisted of *unprofitable ore.*[1]

Gold coin production at the Carson City Mint in 1881 continued to decline in the wake of diminishing output from the mines. As a result, the face value totals of the two gold denominations minted that year was only $309,580, barely more than 10% of the face value of gold coins produced in 1876 at Carson City.

ROOTED IN COMSTOCK TRADITION

For numismatists, the epic stories of prosperous times on the Comstock Lode have been delightfully (and authoritatively) interwoven with the distinct characteristics of Carson City Mint coins. Life on the Comstock was indicative of life in Carson City; and the development, growth, and success of the mines along the four mile route from Virginia City to Silver City are the rea-

sons that collectors of today may possess and appreciate coins with the "CC" mintmark. To study Carson City is to study Virginia City, Gold Hill, and everything associated with the Washoe and Carson Valleys of northern Nevada. The Virginia and Truckee Railroad traveled from the mining regions near Virginia City, along the winding route down the mountain, stopping in Carson City, steaming through Washoe City to the north, eventually chugging into Reno, where it connected with the Central Pacific. Without question, the V&T Railroad, the Sutro Tunnel, the Bank of California, the Wells Fargo Company, the *Territorial Enterprise*, the Carson and Tahoe Lumber and Fluming Company, the State of Nevada itself, and the Mint in Carson City, existed because of the mineral resources that were unearthed on the Comstock.

Carson City is located less than 15 miles southwest of the Comstock region. In the days before the V&T Railroad was in operation, it was a daily event for Nevadans in this area to see a long, continuous dusty trail of wagons, oxen, mules, horses, stagecoaches, camels (sometimes), teamsters and packers hauling supplies, passengers and bullion ore back and forth between the different points on the Comstock. On many days, 2,000 animals would travel on this trail.

The history of Wells Fargo is deeply intertwined with the history of Nevada's mining and minting operations. Wells Fargo's publicity pamphlet describes how the company, "from 1866 to 1869, though operating stage lines since 1858, began using anything and everything to deliver customer's business."

Because of these strong connections, it seemed appropriate when the Wells Fargo Bank performed a well staged ceremony in 1999 as one of its signature stagecoaches pulled up in front of the Nevada State Museum (the old Carson City Mint), and bank officers officially donated the valuable *Nevada Collection* of Carson City coins which it had owned through many intermediary banks along its merger trail since 1971.

By showcasing the essential elements that make Carson City coinage such a popular topic and reflecting on the numerous ties to its exciting past it is possible to clinch a key Carson City truism:

Miners gathered around campsites like this all around the Comstock region of Nevada, as well as in other rich mineral ore centers such as Colorado and Montana.

[1] Smith, *History of the Comstock.*

Because of the themes from the Comstock Lode and the old west; history buffs, coin collectors and the general public are stimulated in their interest and enthusiasm for the heritage of this fascinating subject.

VANDERBILT'S NEW YORK MANSION

In the early 1880s the fortunes of countless numbers of locals dependent on the output from the Comstock mines were melting away as the months passed, while at the same time, notable eastern millionaires had more wealth than could be spent in a hundred lifetimes. One example was the heir to the Vanderbilt dynasty, William K. Vanderbilt, who continued his family's tradition of building monumental architectural structures, by erecting a $3 million home on 5th Avenue in New York in 1881. The cost of building this majestic house was equal to the combined wages of 25 Comstock journeymen laboring for 100 years in the mines.

ANOTHER MINE DESTROYED BY FIRE

While working men around the Comstock region could dream of striking it rich, life was anything but charitable, as hard economic times were often followed by tragedy. In Virginia City in May of 1881, a fire broke out in the mine shaft of the Consolidated Virginia and California in May 1881. The damage toll was 150 million board feet of lumber, as one writer tallied it, "enough lumber to build a half dozen small cities." By this time, the mine's ore had been exhausted. The *Nevada Historical Magazine* in 1912 reported that "when the fire burned out, the tim-

bers were removed,... the whole country[side] caved downward to fill the vacancy... [and] The whole town slid downward a little," as a result.

COINAGE RECORD OF THE CARSON MINT IN 1881

Work stoppages and low bullion supplies resulted in a lackluster year in coinage production at the Carson City Mint in 1881; resulting in the second lowest output of Morgan silver dollars in this mint's history. Surprisingly, an exorbitantly large percentage of the 1881-CC dollars have survived until modern times in Uncirculated condition, explaining why this date is not as rare as its low mintage would suggest. Hoards of Uncirculated 1881-CC dollars remained stored in Treasury vaults until the 1950s, revealing why once upon a time the date was the most expensive Carson City Morgan dollar.

At right is a review of the top five Carson City Morgan dollars according to the estimated price in Uncirculated condition in 1950:

ESTIMATED PRICES FOR UNCIRCULATED "CC" MORGAN DOLLARS FOR THE YEAR 1950	
1881	$30
1885	20
1893	17
1880	15
1889	14

In the mid 1950s, at least 50,000 Uncirculated 1881-CC Morgan dollars were released, and absorbed by collectors and investors. Then in the 1960s, over 147,000 more Uncirculated 1881-CCs were added to the government's distribution channels, and sold as part of the GSA sales in the 1970s.

Wagons full of bullion and supplies traveled between the Comstock region and Carson City for many years. (*Courtesy Nevada State Museum*)

As for gold coins from 1881, free coinage laws continued to allow the owners of raw gold ore to deposit it at regional mints, and after the bullion was assayed, receive gold coins in payment. It was the mint superintendent's responsibility to maintain adequate inventories of gold coins to pay depositors. Because of the depreciated levels of gold production near Carson City in 1881, demands for gold coins at that mint were minimal. As previously mentioned, Carson City minted $309,580 in face value of gold coins in 1881, $240,150 in the form of $10 eagles, and $69,430 in the form of $5 half eagles. The total mintage of 13,886 $5 half eagles is the sixth lowest in the series, and based on figures from the PCGS Population Report,[1] the 1881-CC $5 half eagle has the lowest population of the five dates of "CC" half eagles from the 1880s. Examples of this date in AU or above are genuine rarities.

Since for the second year in a row there were no $20 gold pieces minted at Carson City, the $10 eagle denomination filled part of the void. In fact, by Carson City's standards, it was a rather prodigious year for gold eagle production at the mint; as the mintage of 24,015 was equal to the total output of "CC" $10 gold pieces from the preceding five years combined.

Superintendent Crawford and his staff were relieved when the volatile year of 1881 ended, as coinage operations had dropped to the lowest level since 1871, with only 333,901 coins being manufactured for a combined face value of $605,508.

But fortunately, yields from the Comstock mines were on the rebound, bringing gradual relief to a hungry work crew at the Carson City Mint.

$10 GOLD EAGLE MINTAGES	
Year	Mintage
1876	4,696
1877	3,332
1878	3,244
1879	1,762
1880	11,190
Total	24,224

For more information about the silver and gold coins minted in 1881 at the Carson City Mint, please see Chapter 6, *The Silver Coins*, and Chapter 7 *The Gold Coins*.

[1] *PCGS Population Report* (Newport Beach, Calif.: PCGS, July 2003).

1882

It may have happened, it may not have happened; but it could have happened. It may be that the wise and the learned believed it in the old days; it may be that only the unlearned and the simple loved it and credited it.[1]

This quote is from the preface to *The Prince and the Pauper*, written by Mark Twain, debuting in December 1881, and already a best-seller in 1882.

These words, though written about a different time and continent, stylishly capture the spirit and soul of the story of the Comstock Lode. Collectively, the Old West, and the glory days of gold and silver mining merge together into a multifaceted union of myth and truth, legend and certainty, lore and reality, fact and fiction. For people who lived through the glory days of the Comstock Lode and the founding of Carson City, 1882 would have been like waking up from a dream. Metaphorically speaking, it would have been as if Carsonites were scratching their heads as they rubbed the sleep out of their eyes asking themselves, "What just happened during the past 10 to 20 years? Was there really a *Big Bonanza*? Or was it all a dream?" As they pieced together a timeline of events that eventually became the history of their era, it was a challenge to separate fact from fiction. But alas, it was a fact that Abe Curry set out to build a thriving city, and had left reminders of his vision behind. But in the 10 years since his death it seemed as if many of the signs of growth and success had vanished into a zephyr-like wind.

The region that Mark Twain called "The Greatest Mining Camp that America has ever known"[2] had, in fact, produced more than $300 million worth of gold and silver bullion by 1882, but the mines were depleted and the *Greatest Mining Camp* was just a shell of what it once was. And it was also a fact that the mint at Carson City had struck over $48 million in face value worth of gold and silver coins through 1882; just one of the reminders Abe Curry left behind. But even that mint's days appeared numbered. Yet still, the mines and the mint were two demonstrable vestiges of evidence that made it possible for *the wise and the learned* and the *unlearned and the simple* to believe in the *old days* and love them. There was other evidence of course: writings by journalists such as DeQuille, Twain, and Doten chronicled the events as they happened, sometimes with poetic license. Not to mention the monuments of personal wealth erected in San Francisco, financed by profits from Comstock mines.

By the early years of the 1880s much of it seemed so fleeting, and many people's dreams were shattered. The history of Nevada's mining and minting operations opens doors to questions, searches and investigations, though categorical answers are not always available. Eighteen-eighty-two served as a soul-searching year for *Comstockers*; to review where they had been, where they were, and where they were going.

REVISITING SOME OLD TIMERS

Briefly reviewing the roster in 1882 of notable names linked to Nevada's mining boom, you will discover that John *Old Virginny* Finney, the drunk traditionally given credit for naming Virginia City; had died broke. Alva Gould, the butcher who had merged his mining claim with Abe Curry's to form the Gould & Curry mine in 1859, later sold his share of what became one of the most profitable mines for a trifle (less than $1,000), and bragged how he had pulled a fast one over on his buyer. Gould had passed from the scene, a pauper at his death. Peter O'Reily, who with Patrick McLaughlin was credited with discovering the first silver mine of any significance, had gone insane and died broke. And McLaughlin spent the final years of his life cooking in Montana mining camps. And of course, "Colonel" Abraham Curry, the founder of Carson City, had died in 1873. Prominent founding member of the Bank of California, with links to Nevada, William C. Ralston succumbed to his mysterious death in 1875. Ralston's silent partner, Henry R. Linderman, Director of the Mint, and well-connected with many of the other controlling elite in Nevada, had passed away in 1879.

WHY CALL IT COMSTOCK?

By late 1882, twelve years had passed since the *half-mad, loud mouthed* con man Henry T. Comstock had taken his life. His last name had been chosen to be the epithet of a region, and an era unparalleled in the history of the United States. There was no legitimate reason to use Comstock's name as the moniker for the phenomena that was to come. But it had a certain rhythm to it, or maybe it just sounds good in hindsight because of the extended familiarity that people have had with it over the past 140 years. Try to imagine the aftereffect if one of the other names associated with Nevada's mining boom had been

---

[1] Mark Twain, *The Prince and the Pauper*.
[2] Mark Twain, *Roughing It*.

used instead: The *Grosch Lode,* the *Finney Lode,* the *Fair Lode,* the *Flood Lode,* well, you get the idea; but Comstock it became.

Consider the very name adopted for the New World, America, which has its own incredulous origins. Generally believed to be the namesake of America, Amerigo Vespucchi was the subject of controversy, and doubts have been raised about the validity of Vespucchi's records, allegedly detailing his expeditions across the ocean. Historians also found it odd that Vespucci's first name was used to honor him for his purported exploration of the North American continent. There is at least one alternative theory to the origin of the name America, however, which through the years has gained much support. Richard Amerik invested large amounts of capital in the explorations of John Cabot, who actually arrived in the New World two years earlier than the date Vespucchi claimed. As a reward for Amerik's financial support, European authorities are said to have placed his name on the new maps of the discovery. It seems like Twain's words "It may have happened. It may not have happened,"[1] are axiomatic of history in general.

CARSON MINT'S REGIONAL INFLUENCE

The Director of the Mint in Philadelphia wrote these words about the Comstock region in his annual report for 1882:

> It is a serious question whether it is available to continue operations in those mines.[2]

Although yields began to rise slightly in 1882, for the second year in a row, bullion production of the Comstock mines was a small fraction of the national total; in this case an estimated 2 1/2% of the country's output. This was of course, no match to the Comstock outputs of the 1870s that had ranged from 25% to 55% of the nation's totals. Times had definitely changed.

MORNING APPEAL.
SATURDAY .... JANUARY 21. 1882

Money is a source of comfort and a stimulant to effort.

If you want to find out a man's family secrets, buzz his neighbor's cook.

Cause and effect are not well balanced. A man with a good cause often makes little or no effect.

" Well," said an Irish attorney, "if it plaze the court, if I am wrong in this, I have another point that is equally conclusive."

It has been said that Guiteau is suffering from softening of the brain. Possibly; but no alarming symptoms of softening of his cheek have yet been noticed.

And now a Hartford man is trying to make people uneasy by saying that Mother Shipton's prophecy extends, under the old style of reckoning time, until March 24; but that is entirely too thin.

A Syracuse physician has been candid enough to file the following certificate: This is to certify that I attended Mrs. Anna Moriarity in her last illness and that she died in consequence thereof.

Editors of local newspapers around Carson City supplied daily doses of humor for their readers. Often lawyers and politicians were the subjects.

While the Comstock mines were indispensable to the Carson City Mint, the reverse was not true. Most of the gold and silver produced in the region would never get closer to Carson City than the Gold Hill, Silver City districts 12 to 15 miles away. At the same time, the Carson Mint was something the locals were proud of, just as residents of Arcadia, California are proud of Santa Anita Racetrack and people in Nashville are proud of Ryman Hall; institutions that are fascinating, prestigious and memorable, but if they did not exist, would make little difference on a national scale. Most assuredly, their influence is more localized, although in some cases, with racetracks, music halls and such, the potential is there to outgrow original surroundings. But still, when local residents pass by, they feel a sense of ownership, and although they might share their beloved institutions with the rest of the country, they know these institutions are there to serve the local population first and foremost.

No one outside Nevada gave much thought to the Carson City Mint during its years of operation. Locals knew it was there to serve the Carson and Washoe valleys, and as long as it had the authority of an official U.S. Mint it could produce coins, as well as perform assay and deposit duties. No matter how small a share of the coinage and assay business it had residents of Carson City appreciated every bit of it; although it was not always comforting to know that the majority of the gold and silver bullion produced in their backyard had been shipped off to other regions of the country.

CARSON MINT'S SHARE OF NATIONAL COIN PRODUCTION

On a consistent basis the output of coins at Carson City was substantially less than the volume of bullion produced on the Comstock. For the years, 1870 to 1882 for

---

[1] Twain, *The Prince and the Pauper.*
[2] *Annual Report of the Director of the Mint,* 1882.

example, gold production on the Comstock was approximately $81.5 million, and during the same period, Carson City minted just over $13 million in gold coins, while the nation's mints as a whole coined over $580 million face value in gold during the same period. This was also true of silver; as evidenced by the fact that from 1870 through 1882, Comstock mines produced over $122 million in silver bullion, yet the Carson City Mint struck only $16.57 million face value in silver coins during the same time.

The total face value of all gold coins ever minted at Carson City was almost $24 million. In comparison, San Francisco coined that much in one year at various times. The total face value of all the silver coins from the Carson City Mint was approximately $25.5 million, an amount also exceeded several times by the Philadelphia Mint in a single year.

Narrowing the focus to silver dollars, from 1879 to 1885, the national output of silver dollars averaged nearly $28 million per year. Carson City accounted for only $679,000 per year of that amount on average. Viewed another way, the total number of silver dollars manufactured at all mints between 1879 and 1885 was over 195 million, with Carson City producing only 2.4% of that total. From this, it is evident that Carson City's output of coins was not enough to make even a dent in the massive quantity of gold and silver bullion, which flowed from the Comstock mines.

STACK'S OF DOUBLE EAGLES AT SILVER KINGS' POKER TABLE

During this period, towers of wealth like John W. Mackay, James C. Flood, William S. O'Brien, and James G. Fair, known as the *Silver Kings,* possessed combined fortunes of more than double the cumulative value of coins produced at the Carson City Mint during its years of operation. Mackay's net worth alone was estimated to be over $25 million and his reputation for generosity and strong ethics has endured until the present. Fair, on the other hand, nicknamed *Slippery Jim,* was of dubious character. Although it may seem antiquated according to the looser, immoral standards of today, Fair was the only senator to be reportedly divorced for adultery while in office. The terms of the stormy divorce proceedings awarded Fair's wife a reported settlement of $5 million, plus the couple's primary residence.

Sensational stories (exaggerated or not) of poker games in Virginia City during the Bonanza years, told of how the *Silver Kings* played with foot-high stacks of $20 gold pieces. It has also been said that these men had so much wealth, that even winning a poker hand valued at thousands of dollars, would not so much as generate a trace of excitement in them.

These were the so-called royalty who controlled the lion's share of bullion on the Comstock and knew how to stack the deck in the high stakes games of mining and banking. Companies like the Consolidated Virginia and California, owned by the *Silver Kings,* operated their own mills in California, eliminating the need for local Nevada mills. Their counterparts amidst the bank crowd and other prominent mine owners had perfected business plans to squeeze the most out of their bullion outputs, as well as those of smaller independent miners. These powerful businessmen shipped their bullion to whomever would give them the most favorable deal, and because the cost of producing coins was highest at the Carson City Mint, San Francisco received the bulk of the Comstock baron's coinage and assay business. It was evident that the Comstock's masters of matchless material abundance knew *where and how their bread was buttered,* and apparently possessed no regional allegiance whatsoever.

Augustus Heaton had explained in his 1893 *Treatise,* that the Carson City Mint had been organized to share with San Francisco the burden of minting coins, which rich mines, rapid growth, and the Civil War had transferred in large measure to the West. Although that may have been the original plan, one certainly would have to stretch the meaning of "share the burden of minting coins" in order to validate those intentions. The San Francisco Mint had produced over $675 million face value in coins between 1870 and 1882, while during the same period, Carson City's *share* was slightly more than $28 million, approximately 4% of San Francisco's total. An oft repeated theory that presumes that the Carson City Mint handled the bulk of the mineral ore emanating from the Comstock Lode is simply not true.

GOLD COINAGE IN 1882

With reports circulating across the country in 1882 that gold bullion reserves were considerably higher than normal in Treasury vaults, the Director of the Mint used his authority to keep gold coin production levels consistent with the outputs of the preceding several years. The Philadelphia Mint shouldered the load for the $5 and $10 gold pieces, while San Francisco carried most of the burden for the $20 double eagles, also striking a considerable portion of the $5 half eagles. Carson City, while not approaching the massive output levels of the two large mints, did multiply its gold coin production fourfold from the lows of 1881.

Mint records reveal that Carson City resumed its manufacture of $20 gold pieces after a two year sabbatical, with 39,140 1882-CC double eagles being minted, nearly four times as many as had been struck back in 1879, establishing the 1882-CC as a fairly common date in the Carson City double eagle series. Of importance to coin collectors is the fact that the strike for this issue is usually among the sharpest in the "CC" $20 gold series.[1] (Carson Mint employees obviously wanted to make a good impression.)

Mintage totals for the 1882-CC $10 eagles decreased from the previous year, dropping from 24,015 to 6,764. The resumed mintage of $20 gold pieces at Carson City in 1882 apparently absorbed a considerable amount of the gold being deposited. As might be expected, the 1882-CC $10 eagle, due to its low mintage, is very scarce in Uncirculated condition. Again, Doug Winter estimates that only two Uncirculated examples exist (at this present writing, only one 1882-CC $10 gold eagle had been certified as Uncirculated, that being an NGC graded MS-62).

As for the 1882-CC $5 gold half eagles, production totals took a huge leap, with nearly six times more produced than in 1881, not to mention, this was the highest mintage total for half eagles at the Carson City Mint during its first 13 years of operation. Consequently, 1882 half eagles are readily available in all circulated grades, and relative to most of the other gold coins from the Carson City Mint, are not that difficult to locate in Uncirculated condition (again, the key word is relative, because all Carson City gold is rare in Uncirculated condition when compared to other mints). It is also interesting to note that with increased gold coin production across the country, the Philadelphia Mint manufactured only 571 business strike examples of the 1882 $20 double eagles, with 59 being Proofs, establishing the date as one of the rarest in the series.

THE *U.S. Gold Coin Collection* IN 1982

A century after 1882 gold coins were struck at the various mints in October 1982, Bowers and Ruddy auctioned one of the most famous collections of U.S. gold

Eliasberg's 1882-CC half eagle as pictured in the 1982 catalog of the United States Gold Coin Collection. The half eagle, graded Almost Uncirculated, was the only gold coin dated 1882-CC to be photographed in the catalog, as the eagle graded AU-55 and the double eagle graded only Very Fine. (*Courtesy Bowers and Merena*)

coins in history. Although his name was not used in the title of the auction as is customary, this remarkable collection was known by most numismatists to have been assembled by Louis E. Eliasberg, Sr., who had passed away six years earlier. Bowers and Ruddy labeled this grand event *The United States Gold Coin Collection*, but seasoned collectors and dealers knew whose collection it was.

This sale occurred during a cold bear market in rare coins, whereas only three years earlier, in 1979 and early 1980, the coin market had been on fire, accelerating at a crazed and frenzied pace. But in late October 1982 it was truly a buyer's market for rare coins. But still, the total prices realized for all lots in the *Eliasberg* auction soared to nearly $12.5 million, at the time a record for a single rare coin auction sale. Eight coins sold for $100,000 or more, two of them, the 1870-S $3 gold piece, and the 1822 $5 half eagle, realized $687,500, at the time the second highest price ever paid for a rare coin. There were at least five other coins in the sale that brought between $70,000 and $99,000. As an authoritative supplement to the Eliasberg gold coin auction, author and auctioneer Q. David Bowers wrote a monumental book entitled *United States Gold Coins, An Illustrated History*,[2] which is a stand-alone reference work on the subject, exhaustive in its content, featuring beautiful pictures of Eliasberg's gold coins.

Forty years before that auction, in 1942, Eliasberg had purchased the *Clapp Family Collection*, which became the foundation of his collection; Eliasberg had recognized the advantages (and joys) of coin collecting in the late 1920s and early 1930s, and although he was the owner of the Finance Corporation of America, deriving much of his income from lending out paper

---

[1] Winter, *Gold Coins of the Carson Mint*.

[2] Q. David Bowers, *United States Gold Coins, An Illustrated History* .

assets, he believed gold was a safer asset. Eliasberg was consistent and determined in his purchase of gold coins for his collection, acquiring scores of duplicates. In the 1930s, when it became unlawful for U.S. citizens to own gold, with the exception of gold with collectible value, Eliasberg truly realized the advantage of being a coin collector.

Eliasberg's name is revered in the annals of numismatics and his coin collection is considered to be the most famous of all time, while the name of John Martin Clapp is not recognized by many modern collectors. Yet it was Clapp who is credited with starting the family's coin collection, probably some time around 1882 when he would have been in his late 40s. Bowers suggests that J.M. Clapp may have been one of the very first collectors to add mintmarked coins to his collection.[1] When Clapp's heirs sold the family's collection in 1942, the following announcement was displayed in *The Numismatist:*

> Clapp Coin Collection is sold for $100,000. Comprises every U.S. Issue; Cash Price An All-Time High.[2]

In the 1982 *Eliasberg* sale, Carson City gold coins were well represented. Every date of "CC" $5, $10, and $20 gold pieces was included, and although none of them reached the record setting prices of other gold coin issues in the sale, one of each denomination of "CC" gold realized in the lower five figure range. The 1882-CC gold coins were all listed as being in circulated condition, the 1882-CC half eagle and eagle grading AU-55, and the $20 double eagle listed in VF-30.

For more information about Louis E. Eliasberg, Sr. and his fabulous coin collection, please see Chapter 9, *Three Special Collections.*

MINTAGES FOR MORGAN SILVER DOLLARS IN ASCENDING ORDER OF QUANTITIES MINTED	
Year	Mintage
1. 1895	12,880*
2. 1893 S	100,000
3. 1894	110,972
4. **1885 CC**	**228,000**
5. **1881 CC**	**296,000**
6. 1893 O	300,000
7. 1899	330,846
8. **1889 CC**	**350,000**
9. 1893	378,792
10. 1895 S	400,000
11. 1895 O	450,000
12. **1880 CC**	**591,000**
13. 1888 S	657,000
14. **1893 CC**	**677,000**
15. 1889 S	700,000
16. 1886 S	750,000
17. **1879 CC**	**756,000**
18. 1892	1,037,245
19. **1882 CC**	**1,133,000**
20. **1884 CC**	**1,136,000**
21. 1892 S	1,200,000
22. **1883 CC**	**1,204,000**
23. 1903 S	1,241,000
24. 1894 S	1,260,000
25. **1892 CC**	**1,352,000**
26. 1885 S	1,497,000
27. 1902 S	1,530,000
28. **1891 CC**	**1,618,000**
29. 1894 O	1,723,000
30. 1887 S	1,771,000
31. **1878 CC**	**2,212,000**
32. 1901 S	2,284,000
33. 1904 S	2,304,000
34. **1890 CC**	**2,309,041**

* 12,000 1895 business strikes were never released.

TAKING A GLANCE AT MORGAN DOLLAR MINTAGES

Gold coinage was not all that kept employees busy at the Carson City Mint in 1882, as silver dollars were still part of the work load. For as much as it seems as if silver dollars are synonymous with the Carson Mint, putting production totals in perspective reveals some interesting statistics: If all the Morgan silver dollars minted at Carson City are added up, the total of 13,862,041 is less than the total struck in single years at the Philadelphia Mint (1879, 1884, 1885, 1886, 1887, 1888, and 1889). In fact, out of the 96 dates in the Morgan dollar series the "CC" dates are ranked in 13 out of the 34 slots of lowest mintages (see table at left).

MORE SILVER DOLLARS MAKE HAPPY MINT WORKERS

The clanking sound of increased numbers of the shiny silver symbols of success inspired the Carsonites through 1882. Certain members of Congress, rabble-rousing in Washington once again, were attempting to push through a bill ordering a halt to the production of silver dollars. These anti-silver legislators presented ample evidence to support their bill and there were indeed, surplus supplies of silver dollars stored in Treasury vaults. But once again, the silver party, representing western mining interests had their way and silver dollars continued to roll off of the assembly lines like modern day Krispy Kreme donuts.

The quantity of silver dollars minted at Carson City in 1882 was nearly quadruple the total from 1881, with quotas rising above the one million coin mark for the first time since

---

[1] Q. David Bowers, *Louis E. Eliasberg Sr., King of Coins.*

[2] Ibid.

the Morgan dollar's inaugural year of 1878. One reason for this was that the price of silver had dropped to a level that enabled the Treasury to purchase the silver, deliver it to Carson City, mint the coins, and ship them to the eastern states for a cost less than, or equal to what the price would be if this were done at San Francisco, Philadelphia or New Orleans. This unofficial criterion had been a determining factor in the output of silver dollars from the Carson City Mint since 1879.

Another reason was the minor resurgence in silver production on the Comstock. Carson City Mint Superintendent Crawford was understandably pleased to relay the following summary in the *Annual Report of the Director of the Mint* that, "the Carson City Mint had operated the full year and coinage had increased over the previous year."[1]

Continuing his favorable acknowledgment of activities at the Carson City Mint Crawford points out that, "the difficulty in procuring silver for coinage was less than that experienced in former years."[2]

It was a fact that silver dollars were banging out of the Carson coffers to a tune of 1,133,000 pieces in 1882, and so thrilled were mint employees, that they apparently struck at least one 1882-CC silver dollar as a Proof. At least that is how the specimen in *Wayne Miller's* collection was described; in Miller's words, "it possesses deep-mirror Proof surfaces with full square rims.[3] This special piece sold at auction in 2001 for $46,000, a price that could purchase over 300 typical Uncirculated 1882-CC silver dollars which in 2003 were readily available in the marketplace.

From the ranks of the most common dates ever to be minted at Carson City, the flashy cartwheels from 1882 are always popular. Out of the original mintage total for this date, over 53% survived in Uncirculated condition

and were sold along with the other two-million plus "CC" dollars during the GSA sales in the 1970s.

JESSE JAMES AND "CC" SILVER DOLLARS

Part of the GSA's advertising when the "CC" dollars were sold in the 1970s was *The Coins Jesse James Never Got*. This was effective because Americans have a tendency to create legends out of outlaws, and Jesse James is one of the more popular examples.

It just so happened that 1882 was the year that Bob Ford shot James in the back of the head. In April of that year, Ford posing along with his brother Charlie as James' cousins for the purpose of infiltrating his gang on a bank robbery job, planned on claiming the $10,000 reward. After killing James, the Ford brothers attempted to collect the reward, but were instead charged with murder. Nebraska Governor Tom Crittenden pardoned the brothers who were later branded as cowards rather than heroes for killing Jesse James.

James' legend would be practically immortalized in the decades that followed, eventually having his name associated with Carson City silver dollars more than 90 years later when the Treasury advertised the silver dollars in the GSA sales.

Though Jesse James' life came to an end in 1882, the Carson Mint was optimistically looking forward to another successful year in 1883, with many more to follow.

For more information about the silver and gold coins from 1882, please see Chapter 6, *The Silver Coins*, and Chapter 7, *The Gold Coins*.

---

[1] *Annual Report of the Director of the Mint*, 1882.
[2] Ibid.
[3] Miller, *Morgan and Peace Dollar Textbook*.

1883

VANDERBILT, GRANT AND MACKAY

Many famous biographies were in the making during the middle stage of the Carson Mint's lifespan of coinage operations. Consider three of them in particular, all at different intervals of their own lives in 1883, beginning with William H. Vanderbilt, who arrogantly retorted, *the public be damned*, when it was suggested to him that his New York Central Railroad provide schedules that would accommodate the public. This infamous quote was reported in the *Chicago Tribune* in the year he retired as president of his railroad company in 1883. Only 62 years old at the time, his personal fortune was estimated to be over $200 million. After passing the torch of leadership to his sons, William H. Vanderbilt devoted the final two years of his life to philanthropy and horse racing.

In stark contrast to Vanderbilt's business success and accumulation of wealth, was the financial ruin of the great Civil War General, Ulysses S. Grant. In 1883, Grant invested his life savings in his son's investment firm. Fraudulent practices on the part of Grant's partners eventually forced the company into bankruptcy, with one of the partners going to jail and another fleeing the country. William H. Vanderbilt graciously loaned Grant $150,000 in 1884 to bail out the firm, but it was too late. Grant died in 1885, the same year as the elder Vanderbilt, after having just completed his memoirs through the constant urging and encouragement of his friend Mark Twain.

John Mackay's character was 24 karat. He was respected more than any of his three partners in the *Bonanza* mines known simply as *The Firm*, because he never forgot his humble beginnings as a hired hand in the Comstock mines. His acts of generosity and service toward others set him apart from the selfish and greedy businessmen of his day. In his earlier days, before striking it rich, Mackay told his friends that if he ever accumulated as much as $200,000, he would have more than he would ever need. He overshot that amount by about 125 times. But toward

John Mackay, the most respected member of the "Silver Kings" was said to have a generous heart and be of strong character.

the end of his life, after his three partners had long passed away, Mackay told a reporter that he was surprised that anyone would think that happiness depended on wealth. Mr. Mackay was probably sincere, but not everyone shared this philosophy. Sadly, for many successful people during the Comstock era, the motto was *possession and plunder*, as the passion for power and wealth had caused many to forsake ethical, moral and democratic principles. Mackay apparently was not one of them.

Mackay had been just one of the many dreamers who had swarmed into Virginia City, Gold Hill and Silver City by 1883 because of the promise of unlimited reward. The prevailing sentiment was that money was growing on trees, and that all a man seeking a fortune needed to do was go pick it up off the ground when it fell. In some instances luck conquered all; occasionally accidents did indeed become achievements, but all too often, booms became busts. The abundant silver and gold strikes had enriched a small minority, but had also cost speculators more than all the riches produced from the Comstock Lode. It is estimated that over $400 million was lost to promoters, stock manipulators and con-men, by people who were blessed with more determination than intelligence. Bewildering as it may seem, these losses total more than the combined monetary value of all the silver and gold that was extracted from the Comstock mines.

A small portion of the wealth of gold and silver excavated from the Comstock mines has been preserved in the form of coins for today's collectors, whose testimony is, "From mines to mints, to my collection."

THE TRADE DOLLAR DILEMMA

The ongoing narrative that runs through a coin collector's head is influenced by the actions taken by the federal government as it attempted to regulate monetary policies and supervise the wealth of minerals produced in the country. Certain types of coins that eventually became popular to collectors were often considered to be vexing burdens for a Treasury Department with contradictory underpinnings. At various times throughout the history of the United States, the Fed's supervisory and regulatory roles have been similar to the Dutch boy plugging the leaks in the dam with his fingers, or like a person trying to catch a feather in a tornado. Well-tailored policies sometimes ended in disaster as the governmental agencies controlling the nation's monetary system realized what a stupefying task it could be trying to keep all the plates spinning when more plates were being added all the time.

By 1883 nearly 36 million unpopular trade dollars had been minted and it was estimated that more than 27 million had been exported. Then, many of those trade dollars began to flow back into the United States, with the Treasury Department estimating that "probably five to seven million" were in circulation domestically;[1] however the correct number may have been double that amount. The silver value in a trade dollar in 1883 was 85 cents, so merchants refused to accept them at face value, and employees were cautioned to only accept fair payment for their wages. John Willem quotes the New York Mercantile Exchange's report to Congress in 1883:

> We are put to a great inconvenience…by reason of a coin known as the Trade dollar…not being able to deposit them or pay them in large amounts to our creditors, [we] are compelled to sell them to brokers at a discount for legal money. It results that there is a continual loss falling upon us, and a corresponding profit reaped by such unscrupulous persons…[2]

At the same time, the *New York Times* called trade dollars, "non-descript and bastard coins."[3] As the Treasury Department wrung its hands, it considered redeeming the trade dollars, and then recoining them into Morgan silver dollars, but the silver party vigorously opposed that idea, and the subject of trade dollars continued to be an annoying burr in the federal government's saddle; a solution would have to wait until 1887.

CHARLES BARBER'S *Cent-less* NICKEL

Meanwhile, the Philadelphia Mint was experimenting with different combinations of copper and nickel for the production of five-cent pieces. Charles Barber had become the sixth Chief Engraver at the U.S. Mint in 1879, following the death of his father, Chief Engraver William Barber. In 1882 and 1883, the younger Barber was in charge of preparing the design for the new coins, and at age 43 submitted his patterns for the new five-cent pieces. One of his interesting designs featured the head of Miss Liberty that was eventually used on the official coin; a par-

ticular design (Judd 1713) unique in that the die combination displayed *UNITED STATES OF AMERICA* on both sides.

Charles Barber's new Liberty Head nickel of 1883, the design of which did not include the word CENTS, a feature that was added later in the year.

The design ultimately chosen was controversial, for although the coin was obviously composed of a nickel alloy and bore a large Roman numeral V for the denomination, those with criminal intent gold plated many of the new coins and passed them off as $5 gold pieces. This was of course, in the days before warnings were placed on matchbooks to "close the cover before striking the match." Shortly thereafter, the Mint was alerted to the dilemma and Charles Barber had the dies modified to include the word *CENTS* below the V on the reverse. Today's collectors now find pleasure in collecting the *With* and *Without CENTS* varieties of 1883 Liberty (or V) nickels.

Charles Barber, whose career at the Mint spanned 40 years, is best known for the series of silver coins minted from 1892 through 1916: the dime, quarter, and half dollar. Barber is also given credit for his work on the 1880 $4 gold Stella, the silver coins minted for Hawaii in 1883, the first three silver commemorative issues (Columbian half dollar, Isabella quarter, and Lafayette dollar), as well as being a contributor to several other U.S. and foreign coins. In 1915, two years before his death, Charles Barber designed the Panama-Pacific 2 1/2 gold piece, and the silver half dollar in the Panama-Pacific set.

THE COSTS OF MINTING COINS

According to the Director of the Mint's *Annual Report* in 1883, silver production on the Comstock Lode rose 15% from the previous year's total.[4] Although not necessarily linked to this statistic, the silver dollar mintage at the Carson City Mint in 1883 rose 6 1/4% from 1882's output. These 1,204,000 silver dollars, bagged in canvas at the Carson Mint in 1883, still represented less than 5% of the country's total silver dollar production that year.

Each mint in the United States operated as an independent business from year to year, a system similar to

---

[1] *Annual Report of the Director of the Mint*, 1883.

[2] John M. Willem, *The United States Trade Dollar.*

[3] Ibid.

[4] *Annual Report of the Director of the Mint*, 1883.

modern day franchise stores, however, the big difference is that the profits from the individual mints were transferred into the Treasury's coffers and not the franchisee's. Conversely, if the individual mints reported losses for the year, the Treasury absorbed them. Net profits or losses were calculated upon the expenses involved in minting coins, including the purchases of metals used to mint coins, salaries of mint employees, machinery, equipment, and supplies. From this, an average cost to mint a coin was tallied; the more coins a mint produced, the lower its potential average cost per coin. Additional income could have been earned through assay charges and other services rendered. Every year when the face value of all coins minted was balanced with costs and any other income, profits (or losses) were calculated; profits generated from the government issuing money is referred to as seniorage.

The cost per coin at the Philadelphia Mint had generally been lower than that of the other mints, with the Carson City Mint ranking last in return on investment during its years of production. In the 1880s for example, the production cost per coin, less metal prices, at the Philadelphia Mint ranged between 1.33 cents to nearly two cents, while at Carson City, that rate was seven cents to nearly ten cents. During these same years the average production cost per coin at the San Francisco Mint ranged between 4.5 cents to 6 cents.

The superintendent and his staff at the Carson Mint were always grateful when given the opportunity to increase production, since every additional piece minted made it possible to lower their average cost per coin. Nevada's representatives in Congress joined with the leaders in other silver party states to get legislation passed that would once again allow producers of silver to make deposits at the mints in exchange for coins on demand, thus increasing coinage production.

Although no bills were passed to this effect, the 1878 Bland-Allison Act continued to ensure demand for at least half of the $46 million worth of silver bullion being scooped from the mines in America, and Carson City was content to settle for the bone thrown to it by the Treasury.

DIMES, DIMES, AND MORE DIMES

The only subsidiary silver coins struck in the United States in 1883 were produced at the Philadelphia Mint. Quarters and half dollars were produced in very small quantities; it seemed the Mint was only striking them to keep up the maintenance on the equipment since there was apparently no commercial or export demand for them. Dimes, on the other hand, were utilitarian coins in the United States, as evidenced by the quantity of 1883 dimes struck at the Philadelphia Mint which rose to 7,675,712, nearly double the total from the previous year.

This after all, was the era of the dime novel, dime museums, dime cigars, and dime haircuts. It cost a dime to enter Coney Island, and Frank Woolworth's new Five and Dime stores were becoming very popular, so the Treasury made sure there were plenty of dimes available. This increased production of silver dimes, however, absorbed less than 1% of the output from the mines in 1883. Consequently, dimes were not necessarily the silver miner's best friends; in fact, the silver industry had about as much incentive to have dimes minted, as the rubber industry of today has to sell pencil erasers.

GOLD COINS OF 1883

As silver dollar output remained steady, gold coin production at the Carson Mint still managed to rise by nearly 9 1/2% in terms of face value in 1883, despite the fact that the half eagle mintage was only 16.7% of that of the previous year—a mere 12,958 coins, the lowest for the series from the 1880s. Carson city gold eagle production reached a round number of 12,000 and, as Doug Winter points out, "this is a fairly easy date to find in lower grades."[1]

In the $20 double eagle category, 59,962 1883-CCs were struck, representing a nearly 21,000 coin rise from 1882, an increase in face value of more than $416,000.

Between silver and gold coinage in 1883, the Carson City Mint passed the $2 million face value mark for the second consecutive year, finishing at nearly $2.6 million. One more productive year would follow before the curtain began to drop on the first act.

GLORIFYING THE WILD WEST

The following events also occurred in 1883. The Brooklyn Bridge was hailed as the eighth wonder of the world at its opening in May 1883. Then, moving westward from New York, *Buffalo Bill* Cody staged one of his first Wild West Shows on the Fourth of July in 1883 in

---

[1] Winter, *Gold Coins of the Carson City Mint.*

North Platte Nebraska. Keep in mind that the *Wild West* era had barely begun in the United States after the Civil War, and now in 1883, it was in the infant stages of being institutionalized. Billy the Kid had been killed in 1881; Jesse James in 1882; and the gunfight at the O.K. Corral matched Wyatt Earp and his brothers against the Clanton Gang in Tombstone, Arizona in October of 1881. Gunfighter and criminal Johnny Ringo was shot and killed by a gunshot to the head sometime between July 11 and 14, 1882, historians are not sure if it was a suicide, or if Ringo had been shot in a fight.

Legendary sharpshooter Annie Oakley was 23 years old in 1883 and set to join Buffalo Bill's show. Judge Roy Bean was just getting established in Texas; for over 20 years referring to himself as the *Law West of the Pecos.* The great Apache warrior Geronimo was leading his people's defense of their homeland against the U.S. military in 1883, finally surrendering the following year in Arizona.

The lore and legacy that Buffalo Bill yearned to preserve in his day has survived for 125 years, along with the coins that people in Mr. Cody's day thought of as plain, old money. Neither Bill nor any of his spectators could have predicted the passionate enthusiasm that collectors of later generations would have for the coins Bill used to pay his employees, and that spectators used to gain admission to his shows. Legend has it that Annie Oakley could hit six silver dollars tossed high in the air before they hit the ground, and no one cared if the silver dollars were semi prooflike, prooflike, MS-63, or whatever.

For more information about the silver and gold coins from 1883, please see Chapter 6, *The Silver Coins*, and Chapter 7, *The Gold Coins.*

1884

"IRRATIONAL EXUBERANCE"

During the Bonanza era on the Comstock, as mining stock hysteria pervaded the region, prospective millionaires were as plentiful as sagebrush. A question posed by Federal Reserve Chairman Alan Greenspan more than a century later vividly illustrates the mentality of thousands of fortune hunters in the Pacific states during silver and gold rushes from 1849 through the end of the 19th century. In his speech on "The Challenge of Central Banking In a Democratic Society," Greenspan asked:

> How do we know when IRRATIONAL EXUBERANCE has unduly escalated asset values, which then become subject to unexpected and prolonged contractions?"[1]

Greenspan's phrase *irrational exuberance,* though alluding to the stock market in the 20th century, is certainly analogous to the blind optimism exhibited by many mining claimants and investors linked to the Comstock Lode. But then the busts, or borrascas came and many were left destitute and homeless. Author Ronald James called it *The Roar and the Silence.*[2] The Spanish used the terms *blue skies* (bonanza) and *barren rock* (borrasca).

Although there would be another small rally in silver and gold production in the Comstock region beginning in late 1884 and extending for another ten years, the bloom was definitely off the rose as the New Year dawned in 1884.

Virginia City had been the area's major commercial hub for 25 years: Residents from the surrounding communities of Dayton, Gold Hill, Mound House, Silver City, and of course, Carson City went shopping at the many fine stores on *A, B,* and *C* streets in Virginia City. Gallons of beer were delivered in wooden barrels to the many saloons. French, German, and Italian restaurants teamed with the traditional American eateries to provide tasty culinary delights of every kind imaginable.

In the 25 years since miners first hit mineral ore strikes, Carson City had become a respectable community in its own right, serving as the transportation center into and out of the Comstock region, providing a big boost to local businesses in town. Transportation was provided by the Virginia & Truckee Railroad, whose train it was said would wind its way through the hills, making enough turns to equal 17 circles when making a single trip from Virginia City to Carson City. A huge complex north of town housed all the engines for the railroad and gave the locals pride. The V&T's depot was located down the street from the most revered building in town, the U.S. Mint at Carson City.

Another building that inspired the town's faithful was the Nevada State Capitol, completed a year after the Mint opened, and symbolic of all that Nevada had overcome to gain a measure of respectability since the times that Mark Twain referred to when he satirized:

> Some people are malicious enough to think that if the devil were set at liberty, and told to confine himself to "Nevada Territory," he would get homesick, and go back to hell.[3]

---

[1] Speech by Alan Greenspan, "The Challenge of Central Banking in a Democratic Society." December 5, 1996.
[2] James, *The Roar and the Silence.*
[3] Mark Twain, *Mark Twain, A Biography.*

HUCKLEBERRY FINN PUBLISHED

Mark Twain's classic novel *Huckleberry Finn* was published in 1884, becoming a bestseller in 1885, when Twain was 50 years old. Although the book has nothing to do with the Comstock, northern Nevadans were always proud of Mark Twain and the fact that he first used that pen name while working as a reporter at the *Territorial Enterprise* in Virginia City. Mark Twain transcends any cultural or geographical groups he may have been associated with—folks from Missouri will always claim him as their native born son; rivermen and rascals who steamed up and down the Mississippi River considered Twain an honorary captain; and Californians from the Mother Lode and the Barbary Coast would welcome him as one of their own.

Similarly, the inhabitants of Hartford, Connecticut invite visitors to step back in time and tour the mansion Mark Twain called home for 17 of his most prolific writing years, 1874-1891. While residing in the Hartford house, Twain wrote *Huckleberry Finn, Tom Sawyer* and *A Connecticut Yankee in King Arthur's Court.* Citizens in France, Germany, Switzerland, and Italy felt privileged to share a piece of the famous American author during the Twain family's 10 year tour of Europe from 1891 through 1901. And even New York City was not big enough to contain the popularity of Mark Twain when he lived in the Big Apple during the later years of his life. Mark Twain's writings make it easy for readers to experience picturesque times, hear the vernacular of the people who lived in those times, and allow themselves to be vicariously swept back into an era which is not their own.

Somehow it did not seem fair that after coming so far by 1884, the Carson City Mint was on the verge of being closed down; the prosperity that had been taken for granted in the region might be scattering to the wind. Day after day, residents sat poised waiting to see if Carson City could rally one more time, and if the mint in this lovely city would survive.

Carson City's leading newspaper, *The Morning Appeal*, was averaging a run of 40 to 50 advertisements in each issue by 1884, as opposed to as many as 75 ads in the 1870s. Those advertisers had included hotels, restaurants, dressmakers, liquor stores, blacksmiths, drugstores, clothing stores, hardware stores, Lake Tahoe tours, and many more of the goods and services found in other thriving communities. Signs of recessionary times could be seen in the advertising section of the *Morning Appeal* which now featured occasional large blank spaces with limited ad copy inviting readers to use the paper's typesetting services. Ten years earlier, eager advertisers were placed on waiting lists to earn a spot on these pages.

Employees at the Carson City Mint stayed busy through the year, but 1884 would prove to be the facility's last full year of coin production until 1890, as only part-time conditions prevailed in two of the years between 1884 and 1890 (1885 and 1889), when limited quantities of silver dollars and gold double eagles were struck.

Although by 1884 the declining local economic conditions might not have been unexpected, the ensuing prolonged contraction would still prove to be demoralizing.

1884-CC MORGAN DOLLARS— AMBASSADORS TO FUTURE GENERATIONS

Nothing underscores the popularity "CC" coins attained in the 20th century better than the great GSA silver dollar sale. For it was in the in the 1970s, when the Treasury began selling their reserves of Carson City Morgan dollars that collectors and non-collectors alike could walk in the footsteps of the people who had lived during the times these coins were made. Of all the silver dollars in the government's hoard those dated 1884-CC were the most plentiful. An amazing 85% of the original mintage of 1,136,000 1884-CC silver dollars had been stored in the Treasury vaults in Washington D.C. for decades.

It was as if Treasury representatives in the 1880s and 1890s had planned a strategy to preserve the legacy of the Comstock era for future generations by setting these silver dollars aside, with the full intent that a century later,

people owning them would be able to look back in time as these shiny silver dollars became mirrors into the past. Those fortunate enough to behold one could see Virginia City, the V&T Railroad, saloons, stagecoaches, women in Victorian dresses, six shooters, gold miners, Mark Twain, and other visages of the *Old West* and the *Gilded Age*.

Naturally, this was not the reason these "CC" silver dollars were saved, as if stored in time capsules with instructions not to open for 90 years. However, the release of the hoard in the 1970s produced similar effects, as 1884-CC silver dollars were marketed to more people than all the other dates in the series.

Although 1884 may have been the Carson City Mint's final year of full coinage operations for five years and may have appeared to be the final curtain call for Abe Curry's masterwork, it would prove to be important to the preservation of the legend, because this "CC"-dated silver dollar would pass through more people's hands than any others. Certainly not a rarity, the 1884-CC is still special, because it is the date that was distributed as abundantly as free drinks in Nevada's casinos and it has been used to introduce multitudes of people to the joys and pleasures of collecting coins from the Carson City Mint.

Collectors in the early years of the 21st century are sure to see many 1884-CC GSA silver dollars on display at coin shows held around the country. From the original mintage, over 962,000 examples of this date have survived. Today's collector (in 2003) can purchase a nice looking Uncirculated 1884-CC silver dollar for approximately $150.

There were at least two very special examples of the 1884-CC dollar struck in Proof condition, one of which sold for $32,000 at an auction in 1991; another specimen was being offered in a Heritage September Long Beach auction as this book was being sent to the publisher (September 2003).

RESTRICTIONS LIMIT THE MINT'S USEFULNESS

Virginia City, Gold Hill and Silver City had mined the history, and Carson City had stamped the history onto the coins it produced with the two small C's on the back of each one. The fascination that generations have had with the Comstock era is a blend of the memories, the romance, the daring, the legend, the excitement, the enchantment, the charm, the magic, the lure and the lore of

The trio of dates shown above, 1882-CC, 1883-CC and 1884-CC, represented 80% of all the silver dollars sold during the GSA sales in the 1970s. The 1884-CC was the most common "CC" silver dollar sold during the GSA sales. Nearly one million of this date found their way into the hands of collectors and non-collectors alike.

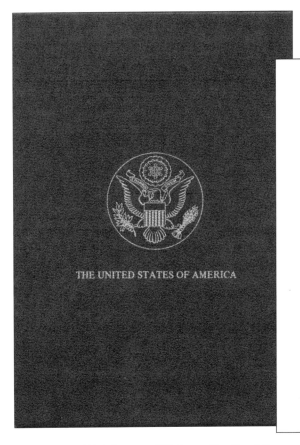

84051292

THE CARSON CITY
SILVER DOLLARS

This historic coin is a valuable memento of an era in American history when pioneers were challenging the West. The silver in this dollar was mined from the rich Comstock Lode, discovered in the mountains near Carson City, Nevada. The Carson City Mint was established there in 1870, and although it was in existence for a mere 24 years, it produced many coins which have endured as collectors' items, among them the 13 piece Morgan dollar series of 1878-1893. Their link with an historic period in our nation's history gives these dollars an added appeal.

This coin is an uncirculated specimen of the Morgan dollar, containing ninety percent silver, which somehow survived the massive coin melts of the early 1900's. They were discovered by a Treasury audit in 1964, after nearly a century of obscurity in the vaults.

This issuance by General Services Administration of the last of the uncirculated Carson City dollars will serve for millions of Americans as cherished mementos of a colorful era.

United States Government / 1972

Front of black box every GSA Carson City silver dollar was enclosed in and a copy of the certificate included with every GSA silver dollar. The first two digits in the serial number represented the date of the coin. For example, this certificate is for an 1884-CC dollar.

all that occurred in this small section of northwestern Nevada, near the California border.

Carson City is 34 miles south of Reno, 14 miles from the Virginia City region, and some 300 miles from San Francisco. But, as summarized in the 1887 *Annual Report of the Director of the Mint:*

> …The mint at Carson has at no period of its history received considerable deposits from the mines of the Comstock Lode, their product [the Comstock miners] having continued to be sent to San Francisco for coinage, the same as before the establishment of that mint [Carson City].[1]

Restrictions enforced upon the Carson City Mint by bureaucrats in Philadelphia and Washington D.C. had enabled the Treasury Department to rule over it with an iron hand. It had become conspicuously obvious by 1884 that the Carson City Mint had never been taken seriously, although the whole idea of having a mint within 14 miles of what would become the richest vein of ore in U.S. history seemed logical. After all, did it not make sense for miners to transport bullion to a location 14 miles away, rather than 300 miles, or 2,800 miles? Surely, it would have been much more expedient and cost efficient to have all their assaying, refining, and coining needs performed in their back yard, at least that was the theory. But in the beginning, northern Nevada from 1859 to 1869 was launched out of desert wilderness like a flock of quail rocketing out of the sagebrush in every direction. In rapid-fire succession, the Comstock Lode was discovered, the territory became a state, and a branch mint was established and raised. Before anyone could really absorb all that had happened, the Carson City Mint was in operation, and the Philadelphia Mint asked, *why?*

Railroad companies were vigorous in their efforts to route the major share of business out of the Reno/Carson City region. California bankers and mill operators gave lip service to the importance of the Carson City Mint, but lobbied fiercely to direct business away from it, and the federal government made it no secret that the San Francisco Mint always offered superior facilities and services. Furthermore, the Treasury Department was quick to point out that Nevada mine owners could get better transportation costs shipping their bullion deposits to San Francisco instead of Carson City. In addition, bullion depositors could be cashed out without delay at the San Francisco Mint, whereas the Carson City Mint was not authorized to pay out beyond certain limits. Another limitation that greatly influenced the perception of the Carson City

Mint's value to the country's mint system was the low annual coinage requirements assigned to it. The Director of the U.S. Mint regularly noted in his *Annual Report* that there was a "limited demand" for coinage in the region and pointing out the regularity of "excess amounts of precious metals above coinage requirements at the Carson Mint."[2]

Of course, to the coin collector of today, these limitations, restrictions, and inequitable partialities relative to the Carson City facility, make these coins that much more desirable, but during the lifetime of this volatile mint they were a source of constant bewilderment.

In 1884, however, the question looming in the mind of Superintendent James Crawford and his employees was, "Will the Mint in Carson City be allowed to either continue producing coins, or be allowed to receive bullion from depositors that would in turn be purchased by the U.S. Mint, or both?" Purchasing bullion from depositors was unlikely because of the transportation fees subtracted from the proceeds to the depositor to cover the costs of shipping the bullion to San Francisco. Other than some unusually large requests for $20 double eagles, and the token million or so silver dollars Carson City contributed to the 28 million quota for all U.S. mints that year, "the demand for local coinage," and in the Director of the Mint's words, "the coinage requirements sanctioned for this mint in general were approaching minimal levels."

HARD TIMES IN CARSON CITY

In 1884 the population in Carson City was estimated to be around 4,000 people, half what it had been when the decade began. Ads in the *Morning Appeal* informed readers of "Going Out of Business Sales," and "Best Fares To Colorado, Or Beyond." One ad in particular offered to "any interested party, CHEAP FOR CASH!… NINE HORSES & COLTS, SIXTY HOGS, 120 TONS OF HAY, AND LOTS OF WHEAT AND OATS."[3]

In the United States in 1884 the mining industry was very healthy, just not in northwestern Nevada. Business was great in mining camps in Colorado and Montana, where communities were experiencing boom times, and elsewhere there was much prosperity. But the locals in Carson City, who believed in Nevada, were forced to persevere, through true grit and crippled optimism.

---

[1] *Annual Report of the Director of the Mint,* 1887.
[2] Ibid.
[3] Advertisement in the *Morning Appeal.*

Meanwhile, on Nob Hill in San Francisco, it took the full time services of a groundskeeper to keep the block long bronze fence surrounding *Silver King* millionaire James Flood's 42-room house polished.

CARSON CITY GOLD COINS DATED 1884

Carson City minted 81,139 $20 double eagles in 1884, a last hurrah, of sorts. At the San Francisco Mint more than 10 times that amount was produced. Half eagle production rose 26 ½ % from 1883 totals, with 16,402 1884-CC pieces recorded. There were 9,925 1884-CC $10 eagles minted that year, representing a 17% drop from the previous year's mintage.

For collectors, all three gold denominations dated 1884-CC are relatively easy to locate in circulated grades. But only the 1884-CC $20 gold piece is generally available in Uncirculated condition, as the larger mintage might suggest.

PREPARING FOR AN INTERLUDE

In November 1881, a second floor had been built to the rear wing of the Carson City Mint to house a new refinery. James Crawford and his coiners, smelters, refiners, assayers, floor sweepers, and the rest of the crew, had hoped that this tenant improvement would provide longevity to their coin factory. Back in 1881 they had already been experiencing long down times, but were unaware that those had just been dress rehearsals for what would happen in the years following 1884.

Bills of Exchange on Every Part of the World!

Collections Made in Every Part of the Country!

INTEREST ALLOWED ON TIME DEPOSITS.

MINING STOCKS

Bought and Sold on Liberal Margins.

INSURANCE!

AGENTS FOR THE

Guardian Assurance Co.,

OF LONDON.

Established A. D. 1821.

Paid up Capital.......... **$5,000,000**
Cash Surplus **$7,063,135**

je20

How Many Miles Do You Drive?
THE
ODOMETER
WILL TELL

This instrument is no larger than a watch. It tells the exact number of miles driven up to 1-100th part of a mile; counts up to 1,000 miles; water and dust tight; always in order; saves horses from being over-driven; is easily attached to the wheel of a **Buggy, Carriage, Sulky, Wagon, Road Cart, Plow, Reaper, Mower**, or other vehicle. Invaluable to LIVERYMEN, SURVEYORS, PLEASURE DRIVERS, FARMERS, PHYSICIANS, DRAYMEN, EXPRESSMEN, STAGE OWNERS, &c. Price only **$5.00** each, one-third the price of any other Odometer. When ordering give diameter of the wheel. Sent by mail on receipt of price, post paid. Address **McDONALD ODOMETER CO., 2 North La Salle St. Chicago.**
☞ Send for Circular.

FOR SALE,
CHEAP FOR CASH!

NINE HORSES & COLTS,

SIXTY HOGS,

120 TONS OF HAY,

—AND A LOT OF—

WHEAT AND OATS.

Parties can arrange to purchase the above at very reasonable rates by applying to   J. W. DUFFY.
jy20

BULL STRAYED.

FROM SPOONER'S STATION,

JULY 16,

A Dark Red, White Spotted 3-year-old Durham Bull.

A suitable reward given for information or return to   M. E. SPOONER.
jy27

Ads from the *Carson Daily Appeal* on July 20, 1883. The ad at top right was posted by a resident leaving town. Times were getting tough.

Knowing what lies ahead, it is with reluctance that the author brings this section to a close. In a spirit of romanticizing, if Mark Twain were writing, he might think of a way to suspend this period in time so that the nostalgic story would be permanently halted in 1884 and relived over and over again. But, as they say, "all good things must come to an end." So now prepare for 1885, the last year of the early period in the history of the Mint at Carson City.

For more information about the silver and gold coins from 1884, please see Chapter 6, *The Silver Coins*, and Chapter 7, *The Gold Coins*.

❧ 1885 ❧

I know how vain it is to gild a grief with words, and yet, I wish to take from every grave its fear.[1]

These were the opening words spoken by Robert Ingersoll, famous orator/philosopher, at the funeral of a police detective's little boy in Washington D.C. in 1882. Ingersoll's belief system encouraged people not to fear anything, because all events are predetermined by fate and therefore unalterable by man, not always the most comforting words to hear. In 1885 the residents of Carson City through sorrow and misfortune had their fearlessness tested. Ingersoll would have probably exhorted them to "Cheer up, because it's not going to get better."

This was a year that the Carson City Mint's value to the country's coin production system would be challenged as never before. And sadly, mint employees would also have to survive the death of their superintendent James Crawford, who had held the position for 10 years, longer than any other superintendent. But, in spite of it all, the Carson City Mint was not ready for the grave yet.

SECURITY OF HARD MONEY

If a government or corporation had the freedom to issue unlimited amounts of what a society accepted as money, and was not obligated to back it up with anything but promises that the money would always be worth the amount it was issued for, the issuer would have tremendous financial power. Say for instance, if a bank needed more money for loans, or to pay off depositors, it would only need to create more money out of nothing, to obvious advantage.

Opponents of such systems, warn of the dangers inherent in them. An obvious risk is that too much money could eventually be issued, resulting in inflation. When money is created from nothing at no cost to the issuer, that money flows into circulation, with the temporary effect that people have more of it to spend, or to pay off debts. But, in time, goods and services cost more, not because the goods and services are worth more, but because there is more money changing hands.

Advocates of a gold and silver standard in the late 19th century believed that it should have been against the law to issue money without its being backed by either or both metals. It was argued by Hard Money advocates that gold and silver had been a store of value, almost since civilization began, and even if these precious metals were not used as money, they were valued in jewelry and the arts, giving them intrinsic value.

These Hard Money advocates had a plan to issue only as much paper money as there was gold or silver to back it, at least a prudent percentage of it. Their theory was that the natural resources of gold and silver mined from the earth would be a more sufficient standard by which to govern monetary policy. There would only be as much money in circulation as there was gold and silver available, and the only expansion of the money supply would come from newly discovered gold and silver deposits. Theoretically, goods and services would achieve equilibrium in their value. Since government would not be allowed to interfere with the money system, inflation would not be a threat; wages would be consistent with the value of the labor to society, and adequately provide for the cost of living.

In February of 1885, representative Thomas M. Bowen (R-CO) presented the conviction of the Hard Money advocates to Congress. Congressman Bowen said that if the Treasury would cease issuing currency not backed by bullion, and converted to a bimetallism monetary system, there would eventually be enough bullion to retire every Legal Tender note. In Rep. Bowen's words, this would:

> Leave us with a currency consisting solely of gold and silver lying in the Treasury of the United States, as a **sacred trust** with which to redeem these certificates on demand.[2] (Emphasis added)

Sacred trust or not, the Hard Money supporters lost ground in their cause when Grover Cleveland was inaugurated President of the United States in 1885. Cleveland, a well-known anti-silver adherent, bolstered his constituencies' platform, in their attempt to cease production of silver dollars and silence those demanding bimetallism. It was touch and go for a while, as both sides argued their case. Then, finally the issue was put to rest for the time being, and silver dollars continued to be produced at the Philadelphia, New Orleans, and San Francisco mints in steadily increasing numbers.

1885-CC DOLLAR RARER THAN THE 1889-CC?

Things were different at the Carson City Mint where there were only 228,000 1885-CC silver dollars minted, the lowest mintage in the Carson City Morgan dollar series. In comparison, 28,469,930 silver dollars were coined at the other three mints that year. But surprisingly, almost

---

[1] Speech by Robert Ingersoll, Washington, D.C., 1882.
[2] Speech by Rep. Thomas M. Bowen to Congress, February 1885.

a century later in the early 1960s, 148,300 1885-CC silver dollars, mostly Uncirculated, were among nearly three million silver dollars made public when the Treasury disclosed the existence of this hoard, stored for decades in Treasury vaults.

Consider for a moment that in the 1947 edition of the *Red Book* the price for an Uncirculated 1885-CC silver dollar was listed at $12.50. In comparison, the 1889-CC in the same condition, was listed at $7.50, clearly establishing the 1885-CC as the scarcer of the two. However, in the 2003 *Red Book*, which uses MS-60 and MS-63 for the Uncirculated category, prices are listed as follows:

1885-CC	1889-CC
MS-60 - $260	MS-60 - $ 6,750
MS-63 - 275	MS-63 - 16,500

Although still one of the most popular dates in the "CC" series because of its low mintage, the 1885-CC is much easier on the wallet than the 1889-CC.

AN AMAZING SILVER DOLLAR

One hundred years after the 1885-CC silver dollars were minted, some time around the mid-1980s, an example of this date wowed the eyes of all who beheld it. At the time, 1885-CC silver dollars were selling for approximately $750 to $1,000 in Gem Uncirculated condition. Gem condition was the top of the grading scale, equivalent to the MS-65's and MS-66's of today. Additional descriptive adjectives could be added to the word Gem if a coin appeared to be of even higher quality: Superb Gem, Choice Superb Gem, Premium Quality Gem or even Perfect Gem. It took all the adjectives in the book to describe this very special 1885-CC silver dollar that surfaced at a coin show in San Diego, California. It was one of approximately 148,000 1885-CC silver dollars from the GSA sales, still sealed in its plastic holder, and housed in the traditional black box as issued.

One of 148,300 silver dollars dated 1885-CC from the GSA sales of the 1970s.

First it sold for $2,800 to one dealer, then $3,000 to the next dealer, $4,000 to the next, and $5,000 to the next, who eventually submitted it to the newly organized Professional Coin Grading Service (PCGS) in Newport Beach, California.

Over the course of time, the coin graders at PCGS would go on to examine millions of Morgan silver dollars (1.5 million+ through 2002), over 12,000 of which have been 1885-CC's. But for as long as they lived, they would certainly never forget this specific 1885-CC silver dollar. Coin grading services such as PCGS do not use words to grade coins, instead utilizing the numeric 1 to 70 grade point system. All of the graders at PCGS agreed that this 1885-CC was not a perfect 70, but made sure that future generations of collectors knew how close it came, as they assigned it a grade of MS-68, which for 100-year-old silver coins is just short of divine. The next stop for this awesome coin was the finest set of Carson City silver dollars ever assembled, when coin dealer William Spears bought it for $7,500, 10 times what other Gem quality 1885-CC silver dollars were selling for. From then on, the bar for grading this date, as well as Morgan dollars in general, was raised by a mile.

CARSON CITY MINT – INDISPENSABLE OR NOT?

By 1885, the population in San Francisco had swelled to over 265,000; New Orleans' population had also topped 250,000, and Philadelphia's was over 900,000. Denver's population was over 60,000 in 1885, on its way to surpassing the 106,000 mark by 1890. But by comparison, the entire population of the State of Nevada was below 50,000 by 1885, with fewer than 4,500 people living in Carson City, a town that was not considered to be in a growth pattern at the time.

Consequently, there was no justification for an official mint in northern Nevada, especially since the other mints were in metropolitan areas, with obvious needs for higher coinage levels. Conversely, in Carson City and its surrounding communities, as it was pointed out by the Director of the Mint on various occasions, the coinage necessary to serve the needs of locals was minimal by 1885. Often miners on the Comstock received payment in goods and services, negating the need for money in the exchange process. It was also customary for miners to have cash balances in San Francisco banks, from which they could draw money to settle their debts.

Faced with a logistical problem, the Treasury Department, through its mint network, was required to ensure there were adequate amounts of metallic coin, and paper currency in circulation across the nation to accommodate trade. With a monetary system that used precious metals for all coins with a face value above five cents, this assignment presented a greater challenge than the fiat monetary system in use in the United States in the 21st century. In the Director of the Mint's 1886 report, the Secretary of the Treasury, as well as members of Congress, was briefed on the estimated stock of coins in circulation in the United States through the last half of 1885. According to the Director there was close to $970 million worth of gold and silver coins circulating in the country, split approximately 65% gold, and 35% silver. Covering all variances in his estimate the Director included the following disclaimer:

> The total…represents the potential coin circulation of the United States **diminished** by the comparatively small amount corresponding to **deperdition** [loss, or destruction] of United States coins through **vicissitudes** on land and water, **absorption** by other countries,…and by **irregular subversion** for industrial consumption…[1] (Emphasis added)

Based on the population of the United States in 1885, estimated to be between 58 and 59 million, there was approximately $16.50 in coin, per capita. Of that per capita estimate, 65% was gold, and 35% was silver. In his report the Director pointed out that gold coinage had a much higher per capita circulation percentage in the Pacific Coast states, (primarily California, Oregon, Washington and Nevada). Concerning the Director's comment about "deperdition through vicissitudes on land and water," he was certainly aware of the various shipwrecks, whose lost treasures of gold coins were to be discovered in the last part of the 20th century and early years of the next (*S.S. Central America*, et.al.).

If the coinage needs of a region were taken into consideration in the mid 1880s, based on the per capita average, the approximate 25,000 people living in the surrounding regions near Carson City would require $265,000 in gold coins, and $140,000 in silver coins for purposes of trade. The more densely populated regions east of the Sierra Nevada obviously absorbed the bulk of coins already in circulation and the new coins being minted each year. But on a more practical level, the San Francisco Mint was capable of supplying the coinage needs of the western states, Nevada included, which meant that the Carson City Mint was working on borrowed time.

THE NEVADA SILVER PURCHASE ASSOCIATION

The Nevada Silver Purchase Association was founded in the 1860s by interested parties to advocate the free and unlimited coinage of silver. Throughout most of the Association's first two decades, the Republican Party had essentially been a friend to those states with heavy silver interests, but when Democrat Grover Cleveland took over the presidency in 1885, many *mugwumps* bolted Republican Party lines and supported the new president. Moreover, the pro-silver groups lost strategic support from among their ranks, combined with the decline in Nevada's position as a silver producer, further threatening the likelihood of the *Silver State* having an active voice in related matters.

The Silver Purchase Association's lobbying efforts included sending a representative to Washington D.C. to convince bureaucrats that the mint in Carson City deserved to remain in operation. One of the Association's arguments was that the mines on the Comstock were once again producing sufficient quantities of valuable ore, although this was stretching the facts a bit. The annual gold and silver production in Storey County, Nevada was averaging $2.8 million, whereas the annual yields from mines in Colorado and Montana were over $20 million per state. But still, more ore was being produced on the Comstock than had been in the years following the *Big Bonanza* period.

Nevada lobbyists also disputed a legislative technicality, that since the mint in Carson City was still an official Treasury institution it was illegal to halt operations altogether. Keep in mind that the Association's harangues and tirades, declamatory declarations, if you will, were not just on behalf of Nevada's miners; there were other silver producing states voicing strong concerns about free-coinage rights, and the sustenance of increased levels of silver coinage production. It had indeed become a desperate situation for the mining industry as the price of silver had fallen to an average price of below 80 cents in 1885.

Since the issue of monetary standards and support for silver was of such importance to the state, the Nevada Silver Purchase Association was another in a line of silver party supporters traced back to before the Carson City Mint was established, continuing forward to include the Populist Party (1892), the National Silver Party, and

---

[1] *Report of the Director of the Mint Upon the Production of Gold and Silver in the United States, 1886.*

William Jennings Bryan's Free Silver Movement (1896). Support for silver meant support for the mining industry and reinforcement for the Mint on Carson Street.

DIRECTION OF AMERICA'S COINAGE SYSTEM

Controversy over the pros and cons of a bimetallic monetary system in the United States was the subject of much political debate from 1870 onward, well into the 20th century, when in 1965, the Federal Government ceased using silver in coinage altogether. By 1885 the government of the United States had already taken a long leap forward in establishing a monetary system independent of any backing other than promises. A comparison of three of the most powerful nations in 1885 with the United States reveals an interesting pattern developing. The table below shows the comparison at the beginning of 1886, of the supply of coins and paper money circulating in France, Great Britain, Germany and the United States on a per capita basis. You can see that the three European nations were more dependent on coins made of precious metals than they were on paper money, as the ratio in the United States, for instance, was 52% coin and 48% paper money, whereas, the ratio in Great Britain was approximately 77% coin, and 23% paper.

It was clear that the United States was moving further away from a precious metal-backed coinage system and closer to a paper currency monetary system. This, of course, posed a serious threat to the silver mining industry; yet this industry still had strong voices in Washington fighting on its behalf.

GARRARD SUCCEEDS CRAWFORD AT THE MINT

But there was more to reflect on than monetary standards in Carson City when James Crawford, the superintendent at the Carson City Mint died on March 8, 1885.

A brief eulogy appeared in the Director of the Mint's report for 1885, "Mr. James Crawford, Superintendent of the Mint at Carson, had proved an efficient and worthy officer, and was much beloved by the officers and employees of the mint."[1]

Crawford, in spite of being only 50 years old, had been ill for some time, and as an article in the *Carson Appeal* reported, "To the immediate friends of the deceased his death was not unexpected, but for a long time many had experienced a hope that his sickness would be only temporary."[2]

Just several weeks before his death, Crawford had been taken to Oakland, California to see a doctor and be nursed by his niece. His autopsy report listed the cause of death as heart disease with fatty degeneration.

On a chilly late winter afternoon, on March 10, a funeral service under the direction of the Masonic Lodge was held at the Episcopal Church in Carson City; a large crowd of mourners gathered to pay their last respects. Flags were flown at half mast throughout the entire region and expressions of sympathy poured into the mint.

Understandably, all employees at the Carson Mint regretted the passing of their beloved leader, who was known as "a man of proverbial kindness of heart, and his relations with his subordinates were of the pleasantest character."[3]

Much of the respect displayed toward Crawford by his staff came from his caring nature and impartiality, underscored by the fact that "with unlimited authority over a large force of men [and women] he never abused the power placed on him, treating them all as equals."[4]

---

[1] *Annual Report of the Director of the Mint, 1885.*
[2] *Carson Daily Appeal,* March 10, 1885.
[3] *Ibid.*
[4] *Ibid.*

COMPARATIVE TABLE OF THE SUPPLY OF PRECIOUS METAL COINAGE AND PAPER MONEY IN FRANCE, UNITED STATES, GREAT BRITAIN, AND GERMANY, PER CAPITA, JANUARY 1886 *						
	Per Capita Circulation				TOTAL	
COUNTRY	METALLIC COIN			PAPER MONEY	METALLIC AND PAPER	% IN COINS
	GOLD	SILVER	TOTAL			
France	21.05	15.53	36.58	14.17	50.75	72%
United States	10.86	5.63	16.49	15.37	31.86	52%
Great Britain	13.88	2.64	16.52	5.01	21.53	77%
Germany	7.02	4.40	11.42	5.47	16.89	68%

* *Annual Report of the Director of the Mint, 1886.*

Crawford was not only admired by his employees and friends around Carson City and the Comstock region; he was also held in high regard by his superiors at the Treasury Department. To them he was "characterized by the strictest honesty; and there has never been a loss of a single dollar which passed through his careful administration."[1]

Sadly, no photographs or sketches of Crawford were left behind at the Carson Mint; there is barely a mention of him to be found anywhere in its archives, not even a plaque on the wall. This is undeniably a major oversight, possibly compounded by the fact Crawford was a single man, leaving no children behind.

Two veritable truths about Crawford were: He would be greatly missed, and his shoes as mint superintendent would be extremely difficult to fill. Crawford had served as superintendent for 10 years and his death triggered a knee-jerk reaction in Washington; 11 days later, on March 19, 1885, the Treasury ordered that the Carson City Mint be closed for the year, resulting in an economic setback to the crestfallen townspeople of Carson City.

Crawford's successor William Garrard was appointed to the office on April 1st serving in his position as mint superintendent until 1889; he is not given much credit for anything other than laying off the entire staff of approximately 80 employees. Garrard appeared to be the fall guy for the new Democratic Administration in Washington D.C. and being in stark contrast with Crawford was never accepted by the locals in Carson City.

One of the most important duties of Garrard's term as superintendent was to supervise the transferring of close to $6 million in coins and bullion to East and West coast Treasury vaults; the largest of these shipments was a trainload of approximately three million silver dollars transferred to the Treasury's branch at Washington D.C., representing close to 80% of all the silver dollars produced at the Carson Mint from 1882 to 1885. Interestingly enough, it would be the bulk of these "CC" silver dollars remaining in the Treasury's vaults for nearly 90 years until the early 1970s, and transferred to the West Point Depository, to be processed, that would be sold during the GSA sales. Carson City dollars dated 1880 to 1885 comprised 93% of the government hoard sold at that time.

FAREWELL TO ULYSSES S. GRANT

It was also in 1885 that Mark Twain established the Charles L. Webster and Company Publishing House; and to get things off to a good start, the firm published *Per-sonal Memoirs, of Ulysses S. Grant*, as its first book. General Grant finished the book while dying of throat cancer and after laying down his pen for the last time on July 19, 1885 died four days later.

At one time a number of literary critics were of the opinion that Grant's *Memoirs* was possibly the greatest work of nonfiction ever written by an American. There was no doubt about the popularity of the book, as more than 300,000 copies were sold during the first decade and a half after publication, providing Grant's wife Julia with royalties of $450,000 during the remaining years of her life. Twain's publishing company continued to mass market Twain's own *Huckleberry Finn* in 1885, and during the next 10 years, Webster and Company would publish the memoirs of three more Civil War generals: Sheridan, McClellan and Sherman; a book on the life of Christ; as well as many other fine works of literature.

NEW ORLEANS EXPOSITION

A World's Fair was held in 1885 in another city which boasted a U.S. mint, when The New Orleans Exposition, cross-billed as *The World's Industrial and Cotton Centennial Exposition,* opened in January commemorating the 100th anniversary of the first shipment of cotton exported from the United States. At the time, the South was still suffering from the aftermath of the Civil War, which had ended 20 years earlier, and this Exposition, held in a strategic southern city, served to further heal wounds and continued to unify the country.

There were exhibits from nations all around the world, but the United States stole the show of course, taking pride in what one observer ascribed as "the unrivaled collection of American products and resources."[2] Every department of the Federal Government had its own exhibit, as did the Smithsonian Institution. Naturally, the New Orleans Mint was at its finest, offering tours to visitors as well as an exhibit on coin minting procedures at the exposition. Each state, likewise, was provided space for an exhibit and Nevadans, although not experiencing the most prosperous of times, held their heads high, and presented the splendor of the Comstock Lode, a very popular attraction with the multitude of visitors.

The themes of the *Cotton Centennial* and America's bountiful resources at the Exposition were supported by

---

[1] *Ibid.*

[2] Gorton Carruth, *A Chronology of Life and Events in America: What Happened When.*

farm and agricultural reports in 1885; it was estimated that the annual cotton crop in the mid-1880s was near $275 million, and that the number of eggs produced was in excess of half a billion dozen. But in contrast, Nevada's Comstock exhibit was only an echo from that region's past; although the mines on the Comstock had once calculated yields using impressive numbers like the cotton growers and chicken ranchers, by 1885 production was just a fraction of what it had been a decade earlier.

THE SOUTH AFRICAN GOLD RUSH

Turning to another section of the globe, a gold rush began in South Africa around 1885. Although several small gold mines had been producing limited amounts of ore prior to this, diamonds had previously been the rage in that area. But, the success of the *Forty-Niners* in California and the *Fifty-Niners* on the Comstock, raised expectations in any new mining ventures. Writing about the South Africa gold rush, author A.P. Cartwright stated, "The prospectors of 1885 were slow, agonizingly slow, in their progress towards their unknown goal."[1] Eventually, however, the diamond barons of South Africa, along with international bankers, invested heavily in gold mining in South Africa, providing the stimulus necessary to elevate the region to the highest level of production.

Veterans of the Comstock were among the multinational host who flocked to the Transvaal region in South Africa; and these veterans knew how challenging the mining business could be. Suddenly, tall tales of rags to riches experiences in California and Nevada, spurred rookie prospectors to head for the gold fields, but soon, many of these novice fortune seekers became disillusioned when they discovered that the yellow brick road did not lead them to nuggets of gold lying on the ground. Mining, like any other business, invariably required management and not carefree speculation. A.P. Cartwright offered this further description of the early arrivals to the South African Gold Rush, "They stumbled about as men do who are blindfolded, groping their way towards what they believed would be the 'Mother Lode' from which had sprung the traces of gold they had found so far. They followed false trails, they panned in all the wrong places."[2]

THE VERDICT—CLOSE DOWN THE "CC" MINT

Meanwhile, many of the citizens of Carson City probably felt they were groping their way toward a hoped-for revival of their beloved mint's operations. Director of the Mint Horatio Burchard, and his successor in Decem-

ber 1885, James Kimball, informed the Secretary of the Treasury in various reports that "the mint at Carson...has never since proved to be a bullion center like San Francisco or New York." Had they spoken these words to a local crowd in Carson City, they probably would have been booed and heckled. Furthermore, the Director pointed out the following negative factors concerning the Carson City Mint:

1. Bullion deposits made by locals resulted in costs as high as 18% of the value of the deposits. These costs were five times what they were at the San Francisco Mint.

2. Coinage operations had never been a benefit to locals (or the nation in general), other than the jobs they provided, and the residual revenues reaped by local businesses.

3. The local mining and milling industries were in a serious decline.

These facts, combined with the knowledge that the only reason the mint in Carson was built in the first place was its proximity to an important mining center, nullified grounds for its existence. Additionally, it had never been a secret that government officials scrutinized the operations at the Nevada facility with tendencies befitting nitpickers. For instance, the following findings of the Assay Commission reveal the actions of men who seemed to have more time on their hands than common sense; "...having examined and tested the reserved coins of the several mints,...it appearing that the coins are within tolerance presented by law, **with the single exception** of a silver dollar-piece from the Carson Mint, the weight of which is 1.51 grains below the standard weight." Members of the Commission favored taking action against Carson City, but fortunately at least one member listened to the voice of reason and submitted a letter originally intended to be sent with the findings, but inadvertently omitted, "To the President,...the Board of Assay Commissioners... esteem it their duty to accompany their act...to the President that the excess of tolerance as respects the silver dollar coined at Carson April 29, [1884] is so insignificant (only $1/100$ of a grain) as to be entirely immaterial in fact or in law, as to require no action;... that the excess of deviation is so small that the means of weighing necessarily used by the coiner at Carson City would not detect it."[3] Nothing so trivial would have even been considered if it had been from the Philadelphia Mint.

---

[1] A. P. Cartwright, *The Gold Miners.*
[2] Ibid.
[3] *Annual Report of the Director of the Mint,* 1885.

President Cleveland had appointed his man Daniel Manning as Secretary of the Treasury on March 8, 1885, the same day that James Crawford died in Carson City. For James Kimball and Daniel Manning to have stood in front of the Carson City Mint and make the following proclamation to the local crowd, would have required courage:

> We have recommended that this mint be finally closed [and], that its machinery and other equipment be distributed among several [other] mints and assay offices, and that the building be applied to some other public purpose.[1]

It was obviously more prudent and official (and safer), for the Directors to voice their opinions in the form of reports long distance.

By 1885, the total annual face value of all coins minted in the United States was just over $54 million. More than half of that amount was in the form of silver dollars. In 1870, when the Carson City Mint opened, the U.S. Mint service coined nearly $25 million in face value. From the opening year, through the early period of operations at the Carson City Mint, the line on the graph showed a steady increase in the nation's coinage production, peaking at almost $118 million face value in 1882. At first the Carson City Mint shared in these upswings, but now its member privileges were being revoked, and the Treasury was ready to lock it out.

THE LAST "CC" GOLD COINS—FOR A WHILE

Before the Carson City Mint closed in 1885, 9,450 $20 gold pieces were minted, representing approximately 1.3% of what San Francisco produced for this denomination. Most assuredly, the San Francisco Mint had been shouldering the lion's share of the double eagle load since the end of the Civil War. Carson City's output had crested and fallen through the years, but 1885's was the lowest total at this mint since 1870, when a mere 3,789 double

eagles had been produced. Philadelphia's mintage total for $20 gold pieces in 1885 was in a league of its own, just as the 1882 Philadelphia double eagles had been, as only 828 coins were struck (77 of them Proofs).

Silver dollars and double eagles were the only two denominations coined in Carson City in 1885. There would be just one other year, 1889, in which only two denominations were coined at the Carson City Mint.

No coins were produced at Carson City in 1886, 1887 and 1888 and the constant threat of a complete shutdown of the mint had a demoralizing effect on the locals. Only 15 years earlier, Carson City had celebrated the grand opening of Nevada's most famous landmark, and now it was on the verge of fading into the sunset.

There was no funeral dirge playing. Instead, there was a somber sobriety in the air in Carson City which had been a factory town since 1870. Now, in its 16th year of operation, the Carson City coin factory's importance to the U.S. Mint system was being seriously questioned. How could it be that there were only two employees on the payroll as the year came to an end was a question lingering on the minds of locals. But the Carson City Mint's future had turned on a dime before and surely it could again.

At this crucial juncture in 1885, a review of past operations revealed that from 1870 through 1885, nearly 88% of all the coinage ever produced in Carson City had been run through its coin presses, including some of the most legendary coins in all of numismatics.

There was still more to add, however, and this famous mint would rise again for one last hurrah a few years later.

For more information about the silver and gold coins from 1885, please see Chapter 6, *The Silver Coins*, and Chapter 7, *The Gold Coins*.

---

[1] *Annual Report of the Director of the Mint*, 1887.

❧ 1886 ❧

GREAT BRITAIN'S INTERNATIONAL INFLUENCE

In 1817, an observant newspaper reporter declared that, "The sun never sets upon the British flag." The insight behind this statement proved to be truer than ever during the final two decades of the 19th century. Countries importing goods from Great Britain were required to convert their silver-value based money into gold-value based money since Great Britain was on the gold standard, which resulted in a loss, because of the bullion value of silver compared with that of gold. This costly expense, in effect, was a hidden importation tariff, which forced many nations to trade with countries not on a gold standard. British financial elite and their counterparts in the United States feared that if free coinage of silver was put into effect by the U.S. government, pro-silver nations around the globe would form trading alliances. This could dethrone the United States as the greatest manufacturing and agricultural exporting nation in history, and since Great Britain was heavily invested in the United States, it was vital that they protect their financial interests there. British agents on both sides of the Atlantic were pulling strings to ensure this protection was in place as the 1880s pressed on.

NEVADA APPEALS TO TREASURY DEPARTMENT

The issue of free coinage of silver was of great consequence to the State of Nevada and the mint located in its capital. The Silver Purchase Association, working together with those in Nevada dependent on the mining industry (practically the total population), continued to inform officials in the Treasury Department that the Comstock mines had been producing larger amounts of bullion in the years following the severe slowdowns of the early 1880s. It was indeed true that for the five-year period from 1886 to 1890, the average annual yield of gold and silver production on the Comstock was approximately $5.3 million, whereas the average annual yield for the previous five-year period of 1881 to 1885 had been approximately $2.1 million. If the free coinage of silver were approved, Comstock mine owners would have greater incentive to deposit their silver at a local U.S. mint and since there would be no transportation costs or coinage fees to worry about, the mint at Carson City would be more than adequate as a drop-off and coin production facility for local depositors.

Millions of silver dollars were still being produced every year at the three primary mints, but not at Carson City. In Philadelphia the Treasury Department consented to have two empty vaults built in a spacious vacant area of an old post office building, for the storage of excess silver dollars that continued to accumulate. The Carson City Mint did not need an armory surrounding it, with Gatling guns on tripods, and guards with repeating rifles, as did the Philadelphia Mint. There were no silver dollars in the vaults at the Carson City Mint through most of 1886, although at some point in late 1886 or early 1887, the Director of the Mint ordered that 25,000 silver dollars be transferred back to Carson City from the San Francisco Mint. There are no records of what the dates of those 25,000 silver dollars were, but there was obviously a local need for them, probably due to the Trade Dollar Redemption Act of 1887.

GOVERNOR JEWETT W. ADAMS

As 1886 began, the Governor of Nevada was Jewett W. Adams, who had moved to Nevada in 1864, the year it became a state. He was said to have been a close friend of John C. Frémont's while living earlier near the Mother Lode in California and upon arriving in the Comstock region, Adams quickly got involved in the mining business. He served two terms as Lieutenant Governor from 1874 to 1882, at which time he became Governor. Although Adams lost his reelection bid in 1886, he remained influential in business and politics, and even served as the mint superintendent at Carson City from 1895 to 1898, by which time, the mint had closed its coining operations for good.

RENO'S RISE AND CARSON'S STATUS AS A COMPANY TOWN

In 1876, the Virginia and Truckee Railroad had hauled between 260,000 and 300,000 tons of ore from Comstock mines to Carson City mills. To accomplish this, the V&T steam engine would carry 30 to 40 carloads at a time behind it as it chugged down the mountain. By 1886 the railroad was hauling much less ore, between 50,000 to 60,000 tons a year. Most was delivered to Reno, and from there it was transferred to the Central Pacific Railroad and transported to San Francisco.

Reno was rising on the scene in 1886, as an incipient shift of power within the state's infrastructure, away from Storey (the Comstock region) and Ormsby (Carson City) counties, to Reno in Washoe County had begun. A large mineral ore reduction and milling plant was established in Reno in 1886, heralded as the most important utility service to the mining industry ever to be introduced in Nevada until that time. Access to the railroad station in Reno was a major convenience to mine operators, helping to keep costs in line. Also in 1886, the University of Nevada set up its main campus in Reno. At the time, the population of the town was approximately the same as that of Carson City; however, Reno was at the beginning of an era of growth and development, while Carson City was in a downward spiral.

Carson City was an archetype of a company town. The predominant industry in the region of course, had been the mining industry, and because of Carson City's close relationship to the Comstock, the mint became its foremost company. Carson City was synonymous with the mint and the goals of both the city and the mint were to gain as much advantage from the mining industry as they could. Whatever was good for the mint was good for the city and therefore the success of the mining industry was paramount in importance to both. As it stood, in 1886, both the city and the mint were preparing to meet destiny.

In spite of commercial stress there was one thing that Carson City was not willing to relinquish, even if their mint was taken from them, and that was their position as the state's capital. City fathers appropriated funds to build the Nevada State Printing office there, which was completed in 1886 and served the printing needs of the state government for almost 100 years. Today (2003), the old printing building is home to the Nevada State Library and Archives, where thousands of old newspapers and documents are available for anyone interested in looking back in time and reliving events related to everything about Carson City, its coins, and the era in which they were minted.

NEVADA'S VOICES ON THE POLITICAL SCENE

Since it was estimated that 80%, or more, of the silver being mined in the United States was used to mint coins, silver producers kept an ear glued to the door of the Treasury. Whenever anti-silver legislators spoke too loudly about repealing the Bland-Allison Act, or in favor of any measures that would decrease demand for silver, supporters of the mining industry would show their teeth and growl like a mother wolf protecting her cubs. For a sparsely populated state like Nevada, whose 1886 census showed less than 50,000 people, any political influence it had in the decisions made by Congress or the Executive branch seemed a long shot.

Nevada's senators had learned how to play in the big leagues; one hand would wash the other—*I'll slap your back, you slap mine.* Senator James Fair of Nevada was one of the wealthiest men in the Pacific states during the last quarter of the 19th century, and knew he could buy favoritism. Senator John P. Jones learned the game well, holding his elected position for 30 years. In 1875, only his second year in office, Jones had demonstrated his ability to pull the right strings when his successful bill authorizing the silver 20-cent piece was enacted.

Based on population, Nevada was only allowed one House of Representatives member to serve with its two senators. This minimum entitlement lasted until 1982, when Nevada finally received an entitlement of two House members.

Concurrent with the years that the Carson City Mint was shut down from 1886 through 1888, Nevada's House member was Republican William Woodburn, a lawyer, who had also served a term in the House during the *Big Bonanza* years of 1875 to 1877. Woodburn was another European immigrant in Nevada politics, having moved to the United States from Ireland at the age of 11. He was the first president of the Storey County Miner's League before being elected Virginia City District Attorney in 1870. As a lawyer who had been actively involved in mining, he knew how to communicate with the members of Congress on behalf of miners.

During the years that the Carson City Mint was on life-support and the mining industry needed assurance that the demand for silver remained steady, politics played a key role and Nevada seemed to be well represented by Senators Jones and Fair, House member Woodburn, and Governor Adams. As far as the citizenry of the state there was generally no partisanship in presidential elections, but in 1884 and 1888, Nevada voted strongly against anti-silver candidate Grover Cleveland. On one hand, Nevadans asked for help from the White House; on the other hand, they sent a message saying they would not support the president-elect. Questions would always linger regarding how much support Nevada was actually receiving from its own elected politicians; post-election actions did not always bear relationship to pre-election promises.

TREASURY SECRETARY DANIEL MANNING

At the center of political concerns was one of the pressing issues facing the federal government from 1885 to 1888: Whether the nation's currency system should be backed by gold and silver, or just gold? East Coast financial power brokers, joining with their league of international bankers, favored the gold standard (possibly looking forward to a day of *no standard*). Midwestern farmers and ranchers, and western mining operators, as well as expansionists, pressed for a silver backed currency, which would float more cash into the economy, providing the capital for new railroads and other businesses. President Cleveland's appointed Treasury Secretary, Daniel Manning, possibly bending an ear to silver lobbyists and feeling the pressure to clear out millions of silver dollars accumulating in Treasury vaults, proposed issuing paper silver certificates. These $1 and $2 notes, although not legal tender, could be exchanged for the silver dollars, which were officially accepted as tender. Now it would not matter how many silver dollars were minted, because there would be more than enough Silver Certificates in circulation which could serve as a claim on every silver dollar in Treasury vaults, and every silver dollar that the mints would produce. Congress approved Manning's bill in August of 1886, and for the next five years the average annual silver dollar output would be nearly 34 million, representing more than a 15% increase from the five previous years. Daniel Manning later resigned due to poor health in 1887, and died in December at the age of 56. His portrait appeared on a $20 Silver Certificate beginning in the 1890s with a Series 1886 and continued for over 25 years.

A New Use Found For Silver

Silver coinage production surged upward in 1886, mostly in dimes and dollars. Yet at the same time, the bullion value in silver coins had decreased. When the Coinage Act of 1873 was passed, the average value of the bullion in a silver dollar was approximately $1.00, however, by 1886; the bullion value had declined to less than 78 cents. Because of certain stipulations, the Treasury was still paying nearly 90 cents per ounce for silver to mint coins. But then, after the coins were minted, the seniorage profits were transferred to the Treasury's fund.

At the same time, another use for silver, besides coins, was introduced by the Director of the Mint in his 1886 *Annual Report*.

It will be noticed that an additional classification had been entered, covering the consumption of silver, in the form of nitrate, by photographers, and persons on the manufacture of mirrors. This has been estimated at $600,000 a year. [1]

This would open a new window of opportunity for silver producers, since anything that created more demand for the plentiful white metal was welcomed with exceeding gratitude.

Although the use of silver in photography might be grand for the mine owners, obviously it would not benefit the Carson City Mint, as there was surely not going to be any film or mirrors manufactured at that facility. Even so, locals thought there must be something their well-equipped mint could be used for.

By October of 1886, superintendent Garrard was ordered to open the Carson City Mint. It seemed at least on the surface as if the efforts of the politicians in Nevada and those united with them in the battle had delivered positive results when headlines declared, "OPERATION OF THE MINT AT CARSON OPEN AS AN ASSAY OFFICE." It was understood; the doors were open for business, but only for the receipt of bullion, and assaying. No coins would be minted. That would have to wait a few more years, but at least the mint was open, bringing good news to all concerned.

Coca Cola and American Business Enterprise

Another popular American tradition with two "C"s for its initials was introduced in 1886 when a certain Dr. John Pemberton, who for some time had been playing mixologist, and experimenting with different concoctions of leaves, extracts from nuts, wines and other fluids. At the same time he was taking heavy doses of morphine to ease the pain of his debilitating illness. In 1886, Dr. Pemberton finally mixed a drink that met his approval, a formula which included coca leaves (from which cocaine is derived) and the extract from kola nuts as its base. The new name for this drink was *Coca Cola* and it did, in fact, contain traces of cocaine, which at the time was not considered an illegal drug, and was sold over-the-counter as a pain reliever, similar to today's aspirin. Years later, the *Coca-Cola Company* would substitute caffeine for cocaine under waves of public protest and pressure from the FDA. An early 20th century investor in the *Coca-Cola Company*, Hall of Fame baseball great Ty Cobb, just happened to be born on December 16 in the year *Coca Cola* was invented and after his baseball career ended, reaped huge profits from the company.

---

[1] *Annual Report of the Director of the Mint*, 1886.

Coca Cola arrived on the scene in 1886, invented by John Styth Pemberton. Shown left to right are an early 20th century advertisement featuring baseball legend Ty Cobb, an early advertisement, as well as one of the formulas for the drink.

Another icon in U.S. business history arrived on the scene in 1886, when the Richard W. Sears Watch Company opened in Minneapolis. Originally focusing on the sale of gold-filled pocket watches, Sears eventually hired Alvah C. Roebuck, and thus began the successful mail order catalog business which became famous in the 1890s.

Technological breakthroughs were also occurring in many industries, and one innovation debuting in 1886, was the Linotype automatic typesetting machine, which could produce entire lines of type at a time. The *New York Tribune* was the first commercial company to introduce the Linotype, using it for the first time on their July 3, 1886 newspaper. Typesetting equipment would revolutionize the publishing and printing industries.

AN INSPIRING EVENT IN NEW YORK HARBOR

Casting light on one of the most monumental events of the 19th century, New York City hosted the unveiling of an inspiring symbol of everything that the United States stood for on October 28, 1886. A public holiday was pronounced, and one million people lined the streets to witness the spectacle of the French government presenting the Statue of Liberty to the United States. The following depiction issued by the American Park Network provides a glimpse of the event:

October 28, 1886 was a public holiday. It was also rainy and foggy, but the weather could not dampen the spirits of the more than 1 million people who lined New York's

bunting- and French-tricolor-draped streets to watch a parade of more than 20,000 pass by. Wall Street was the only area of the city working that day. The *New York Times* reported that as the parade passed by, the office boys "…from a hundred windows began to unreel the spools of tape that record the fateful messages of the 'ticker.' In a moment the air was white with curling streamers." And so the famous New York ticker-tape parade was born.

Dignitaries from both nations were in abundant attendance. Representing America were President Grover Cleveland and members of his cabinet, as well as the governor of New York and his staff. The French ambassador attended, accompanied by the French Committee. And, most ironically, members of some of America's wealthiest families–the same families who had not contributed a single cent to the statue's pedestal–now jockeyed for seats of prominence.

New York "was one vast cheer."

The harbor teemed with ships of all sizes. Bartholdi [the sculptor who designed it] stood alone in the head of the statue. It was to be his task to pull a cord that would drop the French tricolor veil from the face of the statue. Bartholdi was to watch for a signal from a boy on the ground below, who would wave a handkerchief. The signal would come when Senator William M. Evarts, considered one of the long-winded speakers of his time, finished his presentation speech.

[Senator] Evarts began his speech, stopped momentarily to take a breath, and the boy, thinking the speech was over, gave Bartholdi the signal.

Bartholdi pulled the cord, revealing the statue's gleaming copper face to the world. Whistles blasted, guns roared, bands played…and [Senator] Evarts sat down.

When it was President Cleveland's turn to speak, he said, "We will not forget that Liberty has made here her home, nor shall her chosen altar be neglected."[1]

MINT DIRECTOR SAYS MINERS WILL SUPPORT CARSON CITY MINT

There certainly must have been representatives from Nevada at the Statue of Liberty ceremonies that October day, however, the residents of Carson City were getting ready for winter, and perhaps having a little celebration of their own, now that the mint was open again, albeit on a part time basis. Director of the Mint James Kimball kept the Bureau of the Mint apprised of any new developments in the Carson City area. In a memo to the Secretary, Kimball informed him that mining operators on the Comstock were willing to make large bullion deposits at the mint in Carson, if they received the same treatment available at other mint branches. Kimball writes in reference to proposed appropriations that would enable the Carson Mint to resume business:

In view of the facts that representations have been made to the Bureau of the Mint of the readiness on part of the producers of bullion to deposit the same at the mint at Carson, instead of sending it to private refineries, on condition that certain benefits which it is claimed are conferred by the law, and which during the present year have been withheld from this institution, in common with some others.[2]

Kimball went on to describe the *certain benefits* that had been withheld from depositors doing business with the Carson City Mint:

It is doubtless true that the cessation of deposits at the Carson City mint was very largely due, first, to the payment of depositors by draft instead of in cash and, second, to the imposition of a "transportation charge" upon depositors for cost of transportation of refined bullion to some coinage mint or to the assay office at New York.[3]

As far as residents of Carson City in 1886 were concerned, if only a few small concessions were made, support from local Comstock miners might renew operations at their neighborhood mint.

CONGRESSMAN BOWEN CHALLENGES LONDON BANKERS

Meanwhile, political leaders from states other than Nevada were also challenging the anti-silver supporters in the nation. House member Thomas M. Bowen, from the silver producing state of Colorado threw down the gauntlet in speeches to Congress. In one of those speeches, Bowen issued a decree to all, domestic or foreign, who were trying to eradicate the use of silver as an accepted standard of monetary value:

In language too plain to be misunderstood, that this country legislates for its own people, and protects them in all their efforts, industries, and enterprises, excluding no branch, whatever it may be or wherever located within our borders. Let them also as distinctly know that **silver** is one of our **important industries**, and that this nation has planted itself firmly, unconditionally, and everlastingly upon the platform of bimetallism and will neither get off nor be knocked off.[4] (Emphasis added)

Bowen, who had served as a Union general during the Civil War was not about to surrender the nation's monetary system and the foundation of its coinage laws, to greedy international bankers. He continued:

We must have an established coinage, and our metal values must be secured against commercial vicissitudes and trading fluctuations. We hear about an "honest silver dollar,'" and we are reproached that the existing 412$\frac{1}{2}$-grain dollar is "dishonest." Who fixes the scale of metal values by which our standard dollar is rated "dishonest?" Is it the Congress of the United States? No. Who then?

Why, nobody but a coterie of bullion brokers in London, operating in Lombard street as buyers and sellers, bulls and bears; mere traffickers in a commodity, not vested with either sovereignty or responsibility, but simply bent on driving sharp bargains for themselves from day to day.

And yet the monstrous proposition is put forward here that our standard dollar ought to be made to contain whatever quantity of silver these London brokers might be willing to pay 100 cents for as bullion.[5]

All news, every report, any rumor, whether good or bad, that had anything to do with the silver issue or Bureau of the Mint decisions, was quickly disseminated among locals near Carson City. On December 31, 1886 the chilly winter kept Carsonites shivering. They were ready for a pause on New Year's Day 1887, but as they warmed themselves with hot drinks and imbibed in a toast to the coming year, they had hope in their hearts that there would be coins dated 1887-CC clanging out of their mint.

---

[1] Depiction of unveiling of Statue of Liberty in New York Harbor, October 28, 1886, *American Park Network.*
[2] Letter to U.S. Secretary of the Treasury from James Kimball, Director of the Mint, U.S. House of Representatives, 49th Congress, 1886.
[3] Ibid.
[4] Speech of Rep. Thomas M. Bowen to Congress.
[5] Ibid.

1887

How does an ounce of gold or silver get from the mines to people's pockets for the purpose of being used as money? Congress was given the power to coin money by the Constitution of the United States, and more importantly, to regulate the value of it. When the Philadelphia Mint was established in 1792, Congress set the value of silver at 15 ounces to equal one ounce of gold. Any U.S. citizen could deposit either of the precious metals at the Mint, and after an assay was performed and the fineness determined, the depositor would be paid at the 15 to one ratio, either in coins, bars, or receipt. The cost to the depositor for this service was the Mint's actual cost for preparing the bullion for coinage. In 1853, only silver dollars were available to depositors of silver, and an additional fee of one-half of 1% was charged to the depositor above the preparation cost. In 1873, depositors could no longer receive silver coins in exchange for silver deposits, as the standard silver dollar was discontinued, and the fee for gold coins was reduced to $^1/_5$ of 1%, eventually being eliminated in 1875. Valuation ratios for gold and silver were adjusted from time to time after 1834, changing to $15\,^9/_{16}$ to one, and eventually to 16 to one.

THE DEBATE OVER FREE COINAGE CONTINUES

A smoldering debate from 1886 through 1890 was whether the country should return to a free coinage system for silver bullion, just as it used for gold bullion. Silver had been under the limited coinage system since 1873, which gave the government the sole right to coin silver. As a result of the Bland-Allison Act of 1878, the Treasury produced silver dollars, which could in turn be distributed into circulation at no cost to the public. Certain silver coin production levels were required to meet the purchase limits set by Congress and after those limits were satisfied, the Treasury Secretary had the sole discretion to determine whether more coins were needed.

Pro-silver supporters were advocating that the free coinage of silver be reactivated. This would give owners of large holdings of silver bullion the right to have it coined in unrestricted amounts. Then the depositor's silver coins would have legal tender status and the exchange rates that depositors would receive would be the same fixed ratio with gold that the Treasury received. Expenses charged to depositors for turning their bullion into coins would be calculated at the same rate as that of the Treasury.

Opponents reminded Congress that when gold and silver were simultaneously under the free coinage system, one of the two metals would become overvalued. Coins made of the overvalued metal would disappear from circulation, since the value of the metal in the coins was worth more than their face value. For example, if the ratio of gold to silver on the open bullion market increased from 15 to one to 16 to one, sellers of silver could deposit 15 ounces of silver, and then exchange the coins they received for gold coins equivalent to one ounce of gold. Then the gold coins could be melted and sold on the open market for 16 ounces of silver, a simple, risk-free profit of one ounce of silver for every 15 ounces deposited at the mint. Opponents of free coinage were certain that if silver coinage were not limited, gold coins would be driven from circulation.

THE TRADE DOLLAR REDEMPTION ACT

Arguments about what to do with the abundant silver seemingly oozing out of the earth intensified each year. President Cleveland and his corps of anti-silverites probably wished silver mine production would dwindle to nothing. In early 1887, a bill was brought before President Cleveland that contained good news, and bad news. The good news was that the unpopular trade dollars were being removed from circulation through an exchange act that would pay one standard Morgan silver dollar for each trade dollar redeemed. This was a solution that would kill three birds with one stone. First, it would get rid of the disgusting trade dollars, which by now contained only 75 cents worth of silver, were not always accepted as legal tender, were a curse to merchants, and an embarrassment to the nation. Second, by exchanging them dollar for dollar with Morgan dollars, inventories of stockpiled standard silver dollars accumulating in Treasury vaults would be reduced. And third, the virtual purchase of these trade dollars would count toward the quotas of silver mandated to be purchased through the Bland-Allison Act. Oh, but wait a minute Mr. President, the third bird is the bad news, because redemptions (or purchases), of these trade dollars were not credited toward the annual silver purchases required by the Act of 1878, even though, the trade dollars would be melted and recoined into Morgan dollars.

On February 19, 1887, the Trade Dollar Redemption Act was passed and became law on March 3. President Cleveland did not sign the bill, but shortly thereafter trade dollars began pouring into the mints in Philadelphia, New Orleans and San Francisco, as they were redeemed at Treasury offices around the country. During the six-month redemption period from March 1887 to August 1887, slightly more than 7.1 million trade dollars were exchanged. At the same time, Treasury Secretary Manning also kept President Cleveland apprised on the status of the Silver Certificates project previously mentioned. Between trade dollar redemptions and Silver Certificate exchanges, the Treasury was constantly reminded of what a burden silver was.

Locally, the Carson City Mint received a shipment of 25,000 Morgan silver dollars some time before June 1887, possibly to accommodate trade dollar redemptions. The dormant Nevada mint was playing a part in a grand production number being staged across the rest of the Bureau of the Mint's network. It was a bit part, but a part nonetheless. As residents of Carson City passed by the familiar sandstone structure, lamplights glimmered through the windows, giving signs of life inside.

The Offices of the Bureau of the Mint

There were 10 offices of the U.S. Treasury's Bureau of Mint system in operation throughout the United States in 1887. Four were classified as Coinage Mints with the other six being labeled Assay Offices. The chart below lists them according to classification. The totals show how much bullion had been purchased at each facility for the year beginning January 1, 1886 and ending December 31, 1886.

In the Treasury's report, were footnotes reporting how much of each office's total included bullion returned from Europe, and there was a footnote detailing how much of the total included trade dollars that had been redeemed. Totals for Carson City are from the last half of 1886, the same time the mint on North Carson Street was preparing for increased activity in 1887 and the years following.

Why No Mints in Denver or Helena?

A question lingers. Why were coins not minted at the Denver or Helena offices in the final decades of the 19th century? Heavy loads of bullion were being deposited at those facilities, which were connected to primary railways heading in all directions. In Montana, the *Northern Pacific Railroad*, the *Helena and Red Mountain Railroad*, and the *Montana Central* were the chief systems linking to the Transcontinental. Colorado had the *Denver and Rio Grande Railway*, the *Silverton Railroad*, the *Colorado Midland*, and the *Central Pacific*. As mining boomed in each of these states, the desirability of a coinage mint in either increased. Population growth around the mining camps in these two states was definitely trending upward. Treasury officials discussed building coinage mints in strategic locations, but their experience with the Carson City Mint had very likely convinced them to take a more cautious approach before opening another mint in any location other than a thriving metropolis.

What had first qualified Carson City to mint coins? Everyone knows that the Comstock Lode was yielding temptingly large amounts of bullion ore. But the *Big Bonanza* period in the Virginia City area was still 10 years in the future when the Carson Mint was authorized, and as has already been noted, large bullion outputs did not gain the assay offices at Denver or Helena coinage mint status. So, why a coinage mint in Carson City? Was it because the Central Pacific Railroad had not yet run its tracks through the Truckee Meadows when the mint in Carson City gained approval? At the time the Carson City Mint was authorized the CPR connected San Francisco and Sacramento, and had plans to cross the Sierra Nevada, in its ultimate destiny of linking the West Coast with the East. But until the tracks reached Reno, if an assay office was not located near the Comstock region, bullion would have to be hauled by wagon train to Sacramento from the mills, in order to be transferred by train to San Francisco, where it could be minted into coins. Conjecturally speaking, if the Central Pacific Railroad had been running through Washoe Valley and the Truckee Meadows before the Carson City Mint had been authorized, it is possible that the facility would have merely been just an assay office.

BULLION PURCHASED AT COINAGE MINTS AND ASSAY OFFICES IN 1886

Coinage Mints	Philadelphia	San Francisco	Carson City	New Orleans		
Total Gold and Silver Received and operated upon	$25,634,845.87	$25,986,101.93	$58,002.73	$10,482,145.86		
Assay Offices	New York	Denver	Boise	Helena	Charlotte	Saint Louis
Total Gold and Silver Received and operated upon	$53,775,662.99	$1,458,926.11	$257,914.50	$1,570,819.63	$223,854.36	$113,520.39

In hindsight, the establishment of a coinage mint in Carson City may have been a premature act precipitated by another unknown factor, because at the time the mint was being built, Virginia City was one of the fastest growing cities between San Francisco and Denver in the Rockies, ranked in the top three with Sacramento and Salt Lake City. If that growth had continued, the coinage needs of the region would have demanded a mint to satisfy its commerce. But as history chronicles it, Virginia City was a boomtown, and like many other boomtowns, activity and growth were volatile, finally receding to a faint memory of what there once was. By 1887, the Carson City Mint was still an official coinage facility, although the Denver and Helena branches were far more deserving of the distinction. But the Treasury, having learned lessons from the past, would forevermore take a wait and see approach before authorizing any regional operations to mint coins.

Although the Denver branch had opened seven years before the Carson City Mint, it remained an assay office, and then finally, after a 32 year wait-and-see trial period, Congress provided for the establishment of a coinage mint at Denver in 1895, however, it was not until 1906 that the first coins with the Denver mintmark were struck.

Treasury Department, Ohio.

OFFICE OF THE SUPERVISING ARCHITECT.

Washington,   January 29 th.   1887

The Honorable

    The Secretary of the Treasury.

Sir :-

    I have the honor to enclose, herewith, copy of a communication from the Director of the Mint, dated January 29th. 1887, in reference to the Public Building at Carson City, Nevada, and desire to state, that if the coinage of silver is to be suspended at that place, the Mint Building can be utilized as a Court-House and Post-Office. There seems to be a question of the advisability of erecting a new building for a United States Court-House and Post-Office at an expense to the Government of one hundred thousand dollars ($100,000) if the Mint building is no longer to be used for the coinage of money.

    No work of any consequence has been performed toward the erection of the new Post-Office, and in view of the statements submitted by the Director of the Mint, I respectfully submit the matter for your consideration and instruction.

    Respectfully yours,

Supervising Architect

During the years that coinage operations were suspended at the Carson City Mint, different uses for the building were considered. This letter to the Secretary of the Treasury from the Bureau of the Mint's supervising architect proposed using the building for a court house and post office. (*Courtesy Nevada State Museum*)

NEW ORE DISCOVERY LEADS TO CORRUPTION

At the beginning of 1887, pickin's were slim in the Comstock mines, but suddenly production began to rise and whenever the sniff of riches is in the air, all too often there are con men, deceivers, and various sorts of dishonest low-lifes on the scene. Such an occasion arose when; "an excellent little ore body"[1] was discovered between the 400 to 700 foot levels in the Hale and Norcross Mine in 1887, resulting in a yield of close to $2.5 million. Locals, of course, greeted any discovery, small or large, with enthusiastic optimism.

Unfortunately fraud committed against investors spoiled the party. There had been so much corruption on the Comstock during the *Big Bonanza* years, often overshad-

owed by the magnitude of all the minerals spewing forth from the ground. But in the waning years, any crime, large or small, made the headlines.

One such story was portrayed in a fictionalized account in an episode of the popular TV series *Bonanza*, entitled *Thunderhead*; which told how a group of swindlers attempted to defraud investors by falsely claiming that a rich vein of ore had been discovered in a mine presumably swept clean of any bullion many years before. Ben Cartwright, brought in as an expert, discovered that these crooks had moved the boundary line of a connecting mine that was still profitable

America's favorite father figure from the old west, Ben "Pa" Cartwright.

---

[1] Smith, *The History of the Comstock Lode.*

over to their own exhausted mine. As all good endings go, the criminals were brought to justice; this episode being based on a compilation of actual events.

But in 1887, the true story of the Hale and Norcross scandal involved management who cheated stockholders out of their rightful share of the dividends. Charges were filed against the corrupt Hale and Norcross managers, and the investors eventually recovered judgment from the guilty parties. Newspapers throughout the region reported the details of the trial on a daily basis, and the locals were sad that one of the last successful mineral strikes had to end this way.

But they were used to egregious acts and shady characters surfacing from the mining industry. In fact one of the former owners of the Hale and Norcross was good 'Ol *Slippery Jim* Fair, the disreputable former U.S. Senator from Nevada. Living in San Francisco at the time, Fair mocked the news when informed that the long forgotten mine had hit pay dirt once again. Fair arrogantly trivialized the small ore discovery by telling reporters that he had cut his teeth on the Hale and Norcross 20 years earlier, and this was child's play in his opinion. Locals around the Comstock were just glad he was living in California instead of Nevada.

GOVERNOR STEVENSON'S TENURE

Nevada's new governor, Charles Stevenson was inaugurated in Carson City in 1887. Stevenson had moved from

BONANZA KING!

James G. Fair, *Bonanza King*, and former Nevada Senator, challenged the Southern Pacific Railroad's control of the route between San Francisco and Los Angeles in 1888. His *South Pacific Coast Railroad* tunneled through mountains from San Francisco, to Santa Cruz on the coast. It was Fair's vision to make Santa Cruz a resort destination, rivaling those in Europe and the eastern seaboard of the United States, around Newport News, Rhode Island. The Fairmont Hotel in San Francisco is named after the city's highest taxpayer from the late 1880s and early 1890s, but his scandalous divorce while he was a Senator would haunt him for the remaining years of his life. His railroad ended in failure, but he still managed to make life miserable for his competitors during the process.

New York to Nevada in 1859, at the age of 33, to work in mining, milling and agriculture, and before his election as governor in 1886, had served three terms in the State Senate, and 11 years as a Regent of the University of Nevada. Stevenson died in office in 1890 at the age of 64 from an illness he presumably contracted during his days as superintendent of the Kentuck mine. Governor Stevenson served during several critical years in the history of the Carson City Mint, and as a pro-silver Republican, it meant a lot to him to see coinage production resume at the mint near his governor's quarters before he passed away.

THE "REAL" TREASURE OF NEVADA

Reno continued to take the lead as the seat of power in the Truckee Meadows/Washoe Valley/Carson Valley region. An advertisement in the November 1, 1887 issue of *The Daily Nevada State Journal*, offered interested real estate buyers lots in "the most lovely portion of Reno." These lots were located between the tracks of the Central Pacific Railroad to the north of town, and the centrally located Truckee River to the south.

Almost from its origins, the State of Nevada faced the constant challenge of justifying its existence. Explorers like John C. Frémont soon discovered that the imposing Sierra Nevada range in northwestern Nevada seemed to guard the entrance to California and would have to be conquered by pathfinders and surveyors to open the doors to prosperity unimaginable to the human race. Nevada was the gatekeeper and must be treated with respect. But the mountain passes through Nevada were eventually overcome, prospectors replaced pathfinders, and mineral wealth secured statehood for Nevada Territory, as well as an air of respectability and importance amongst the states in the Union.

When it appeared as if the precious metals were about to be depleted, citizens of the *Silver State* began to promote its positive attributes actually closest to their hearts, advantages that were not dependent on hyperbole and the materialistic claims of the *Gilded Age*. Underscoring this, the ad in the Reno newspaper offering real estate for sale, focused on the climate, the water resources, and the ranch and farm lands, fertile and ready. Reno was also proud of its new university, and did not hesitate to mention that it was "the railroad center of Nevada."

Fifty years later, an important figure in the development of northern Nevada, Norman Biltz (whose connections to the Carson City Mint will be discussed in Chapter 9), prepared a promotional magazine entitled *Nevada, the Last Frontier*. In that magazine Biltz echoed the thoughts and emotions of the 1887 Reno newspaper ad.

Throughout much of its history the natural resources and unadulterated quality of its environment that give Nevada its individuality, have been inadequate to help it achieve deserved respectability. However, a new Bonanza period would begin in 1931 just in the nick of time. Taking the form of a worldly pastime, commonplace in many communities during the Comstock era, gambling was legalized in Nevada, ultimately producing revenues equivalent to thousands of Comstock Lodes.

Participants in the mining industry and the gambling industry have included many of the same types of rouges, greedy politicians, flimflammers, henchmen, middlemen, stalwarts and heroes. And the casino industry, like the mining industry once was, has been the dominant force of power in Nevada for over 70 years (as of 2003). Most longtime northern Nevada residents don't mind, secure in their true roots, being able to look back at

ads like the one in the 1887 Reno newspaper, and nod their heads in agreement that, "The climate is mild and genial in winter, and even healthful in summer [with] beautiful lakes and rivers, scenic mountains and wide-open spaces." Gambling in the 20th century, like mining in the 19th century, has financed the needs of the state, so residents can enjoy Nevada's true treasures.

FUTURE OF CARSON MINT STILL PENDING

As the end of the year approached, ads in 1887 editions of Carson City's main newspaper, the *Carson Appeal*, did not include real estate promotions, but throughout the year, had been keeping locals abreast of the "Happenings at the Mint." Editorial fire criticized the Director of the Mint in Philadelphia for stalling; it was true that Director Kimball waffled on his position concerning the Carson facility and when pressed, had recommended its closure. A decision would have to wait until 1888, however, and as that year began, the Carson City Mint would still be on the Treasury's roster.

Newspaper ad from 1887 promoting Reno as "a rare chance for investment and a home." These lots were in the C.C. Powning addition along "aristocratic Riverside Avenue Driveway...facing the Truckee River."

1888

Eighteen-eighty-eight was the final year of a four-year suspension served by the mint at Carson City, during which it had been allowed to put on its uniform, but had been barred from minting coins.

As daybreak dawned on the presidential election year of 1888, the winter snows and chilly temperatures had left the streets of Carson City packed as hard as frozen tundra in the shaded areas, and wet and mushy in those areas exposed to the afternoon sun. Berms of snow lined the unpaved streets in the city as locals traveled around town on horseback, by foot, horse-drawn carriages and sleighs. Strong icy winds blew the shingles off roofs, shook the rafters, and froze cheeks. Mark Twain described what kind of challenge the winds were to the residents around the Comstock in his book *Roughing It*,

> Things living and dead, that flitted hither and thither, going and coming, appearing and disappearing among the rolling billows of dust; hats, chickens, and parasols sailing in the remote heavens, blankets, tin signs, sage-brush, and shingles…doormats…shovels and coal-scuttles…glass doors, cats and little children… [it] blows flimsy houses down, lifts shingle roofs… rolls up tin ones like sheet music, now and then blows a stagecoach over and spills the passengers; and tradition says the reason there are so many bald people there, is, that the wind blows the hair off their heads while they are looking skyward after their hats…Carson Streets seldom look inactive…because there are so many citizens skipping around their escaping hats… [1]

Steam rose from the chimneys atop the Carson City Mint creating a sauna-like effect above the roof in the early months of the year. The U.S. *Stars and Stripes* would be proudly hoisted high above the smoke stacks, and every day, Carsonites could look in the direction of the mint and tell if it was shut down, or at work. So it was, in this part of the country.

Back east, around St. Patrick's Day, a severe blizzard swept through. New York City was shut off from the rest of the country. Thousands of people were without transportation and communication, at least 400 people died, hundreds became very sick, and property damage was in the millions of dollars. Residents were still digging themselves out and recuperating as spring approached, pleading with Mother Nature not to extend the *Blizzard of '88*.

As usual the price of silver was on the decline, just as the Comstock mines were staging a minor rally. Throughout 1888, the average value of the silver in a Morgan dollar was approximately 73 cents. It seemed as if the fate of the silver market hinged on the results of November's presidential election. The anti-silver Democratic Party continued to rely on getting Grover Cleveland re-elected, while Republicans rode on Benjamin Harrison's pro-silver platform. In Nevada, political party affiliation was secondary to silver allegiance, and both parties in the *Silver State* came out in favor of the free coinage of silver, with Democrats breaking party lines on this issue.

SENATOR GEORGE F. EDMUNDS AND THE SHERMAN ACT

Leaders of the anti-silver/anti-free coinage groups presented a strong case when arguing that silver was not a victim of any shortage or political schemes. Instead, in their opinion, silver had caused its own weakness in price by virtue of there being just too much of it. Republican Senator George F. Edmunds from Vermont, who served in the senate from 1865 to 1891, had a front row seat, from which to view and evaluate the most critical era in the history of silver in the United States. Senator Edmunds sat on many Judiciary Committees during his distinguished career, one of the most significant of which, also included Senator Evarts, who you may recall, spoke at the unveiling ceremonies of the Statue of Liberty in 1886. This particular committee met from 1888 to 1890, and resulted in the Sherman Anti-Trust and Silver Purchase Act of 1890. Senator Sherman was not the author of the heart of the legislation however, he merely introduced the bill. It was Senator Edmunds who drafted the most important provisions of the Act, and is credited for preparing the final draft.

Edmunds, always an ally to the silver market, was at the same time a realist and had an unobstructed view of the sweeping panorama of silver production. In an interview granted to the *Congressional Globe* after he retired, Edmunds retraced the path silver had taken from before the Civil War, through the passages of the Acts of 1873 and 1878, and past the Sherman Act of 1890. He declared an obvious fact: the output of silver bullion from the mines in the United States had increased at such a substantial rate, that it had demonetized itself. In defense of the Coinage Act of 1873, Edmunds said that it most likely had prevented more than half of the gold coins in circulation from being removed and melted for their bullion value. He concluded:

> It is very clear from these facts and figures that it was not the passage of the Act of 1873 which either demonetized silver or reduced it one half in value. In both cases, the mov-

---

[1] Twain, *Roughing It.*

ing forces have been the eternal laws of nature. If any crime has been committed against silver, nature is the culprit.[1]

Edmunds believed that the U.S. government should use every power conferred upon it, "to keep the public faith, and to preserve the parity between gold and silver, and between all financial obligations of the government."[2] And if that meant striking more silver coins to cope with the increased production levels of the metal, then so be it. The citizens of Carson City, Colorado, Montana and all the other jurisdictions directly influenced by silver usage gave a hearty, Bravo! Here Here! and Hip Hip Hooray! to that pronouncement.

DEMOCRATS TAKE CREDIT
FOR SUSTAINING SILVER

The anti-silver group agreed that silver was a victim to the laws of nature, but strongly opined that it had lost its status as a precious metal. Battle lines between the two parties were dug deeply into the strong wills of the adversaries and the issue would be hotly contended during the 1888 elections.

In the meantime, the commercial market prices of gold and silver had reached the ratio of 22 ounces of silver for every one ounce of gold and the gap appeared to be widening. Ten years earlier, in 1878 when Morgan silver dollars were introduced, the ratio had been approximately 18 to one. As Senator Edmunds and so many other observant parties had noted, Mother Nature was as much responsible for the price fluctuations of precious metals, as man-made interferences were. As they accurately stated, there was no way of predicting how much bullion would come out of the ground. And mankind's only response, according to sympathizers of the silver party, was to "prevent the depreciation of either metal as compared with the other."[3]

President Cleveland's administration felt confident that their Silver Certificate program was just what the doctor had ordered. Through 1888, just over $315 million silver dollars had been minted under the Bland-Allison Act of 1878, less than 15% of which had actually been placed into circulation. In their effort to support the country's monetary system, the Treasury Department had authorized the Bureau of Engraving and Printing to issue Silver Certificates equal to approximately 75% of the total of silver dollars stockpiled in their vaults. Democrats called it to the attention of the defenders of silver freedom, that if not for the intervention of Cleveland and his cabinet using the Silver Certificate program, the price of silver would have dropped to a much lower level. There

was no doubt that in an election year, the Democrats wanted to avoid totally alienating the silver producing states, but it was too late, they already had.

A GROWING NUMISMATIC HOBBY

While political battles were waged over the credibility of silver in 1888, numismatic auctions were attracting larger audiences than ever. Coin dealers such as the Chapman Brothers, who began in the rare coin business working for prominent numismatist John Haseltine, opening their own firm in the early 1880s, advanced the popularity of auctions. They had auctioned the *Bushnell Collection* in 1882, and raised their bar of influence every year following.

Stamp collecting was also growing in popularity in the 1880s, and many coin dealers crossed over into the philatelic field, and vice versa. Noted stamp dealer J.W. Scott sold his business to Henry Calman and Henry Collin. These partners changed the company's name to Scott Stamp and Coin Company, and in 1888, the Scott Company auctioned a portion of late Mint Director, H.R. Linderman's coin collection. The Linderman family had attempted to sell the collection the year before, but a group of pattern pieces from the collection were confiscated before Lyman H. Low & Co. could bring them to the gavel. During the 1888 auction, the Scott Company did not sell the pattern pieces either, but did sell a Class III specimen of the 1804 silver dollar which realized $407.

Still young at heart, the United States was 112 years old, and the Mint was 96 years old in 1888. Coin collecting had already established a commendable base of support. Most collectors gravitated toward the oldest coins they could find, but those with more discretionary income sought more esoteric and unique coins. Early Proof coins from pre-1840 were in demand, as were pattern coins.

Carson City coins, though beginning to draw interest, would have to wait until 1893, when Heaton's *Treatise on Mint Marks* was published, before collectors paid much attention to them. In the 20th century, numismatic authors speculated as to why so few Uncirculated coins survived from the early years at Carson City. Low mintages provided part of the explanation, but low mintage examples from the other mints of this era seemed to have higher available populations in Uncirculated grades. As Dave Bowers pointed out in his company's 1976 auction catalog, featuring the *E.A. Carson Collection* of "CC" coins:

---

[1] Sen. George F. Edmunds, interview in *Congressional Globe*, 1893.
[2] U.S. Congress, Sherman Act, 1890.
[3] Ibid.

...San Francisco was the cultural center of the West...with trappings of metropolitan success. [And] Likewise, New Orleans was the cultural and social center of its [region]. As a result, coins [from San Francisco and New Orleans] were saved in bank vaults, by persons obtaining them for gifts, and...other reasons. [1]

Of course, this only pertains to the discussion of branch mints, because the Philadelphia Mint was all of the above, and more. Bowers goes on to state:

> Not so with Carson City. That Nevada town was not glamorous. It was a functional town in a wild period in American history. Little thought was given to preserving Uncirculated coins by the miners and workers who, for the most part, lived in makeshift shacks, rude structures, and tents! [2]

A 19th century version of the Carson City Chamber of Commerce would not have appreciated that last description of their fair community very much, and obviously, there is some stereotyping in Bower's comments. Carson City, after all, was the capital of Nevada; the Virginia & Truckee Railroad depot was down the street from the mint; and Virginia City was a thriving community with many fine entrapments imported from all over the world. But, relatively speaking, Carson City and the Comstock region were nowhere near as developed as those other cultural and metropolitan cities that were homes to U.S. mints. Besides, stereotypical portraits such as this one painted of Carson City, is what adds to the glamour and intrigue of coins from that region today.

SILVER: A HOT NATIONAL TOPIC

In the days before Iraq and Iran, CNN, Saddam Hussein, al-Qaeda terrorist attacks, affirmative action, and "Sex Scandals That Rocked the White House," politicians had *Goldbugs* and *Silverites*. Provocative issues such as demonetization, remonetization, hard money and bimetallism were on par with issues such as railroad monopolies, and antitrust laws. Candidates for political office could win, or offend voters with their answer to "Should the United States be on the gold standard?" or, "What is your position on the free coinage of silver?" Arguments from both sides of these issues were reported in every newspaper, editorialized in journals, heard in every barbershop, and debated in most every session of Congress. Some politicians became career proponents, or opponents, of these contrasting economic philosophies; for some it was their reason to live. Silverites had the consummate embodiment of this type of politician in John Percival Jones, Senator from Nevada. Jones was once quoted as saying, "The money question is paramount to all others..." [3]

A large percentage of the population of the United States was not aware of the underpinnings of what was at stake. All the average poor to upper middle class wage earner wanted to know was that the plutocratic gold barons would not rob them of employment, an ample supply of money in circulation, or increase their debt. In many circles, the greedy, manipulative *money changers* on Wall Street in the U.S. and Lombard Street in Great Britain, were resented and distrusted. It was said that Lombard Street was the greatest combination of economical power and deviousness that the world has ever known.

A 19th century rumor concerning the portrait on the silver dollar designed by British native, George T. Morgan, alluded to Great Britain's powerful grip on the economy of the United States. Supposedly, Morgan in his role as Chief Engraver, strategically placed a lion's head in Miss Liberty's hair, symbolizing England's coat of arms. This lion's head can be seen when the coin is turned upside down. Was it paranoia, or perceptiveness? Only George T. Morgan knew for sure. One thing was certain: Great Britain's financial elite was opposed to a bimetallic standard, having influenced many foreign nations to demonetize silver.

COINAGE KEEPS PACE WITH POPULATION

From its inception, the United States Treasury had used the powers conferred upon it by the Constitution, to ensure that there would be a sufficient supply of coins in circulation to keep pace with the rapidly expanding population of the country. From 1794 through 1888, the mint system of the United States had coined over 216 million silver dimes, approximately 155 million silver quarters, and more than 245 million silver half dollars. Mintage figures for the quarters and halves had mostly been achieved prior to 1879 and only dimes had maintained higher production levels through the 1880s. In 1888 the Director of the Mint ordered the Superintendent at the San Francisco Mint to coin quarters for the first time since 1878 and a total of 1,216,000 were struck. Silver dollar production at the San Francisco Mint dropped below 700,000 for the first time since the Morgan dollars were introduced in 1878 possibly in response to the increased number of quarters produced there.

Three denominations of U.S. coinage were in their second to last year of production in 1888: The three cent nickel, the one dollar gold piece, and the three dollar gold

[1] *Willing Collection*, Bowers and Ruddy, June 1976
[2] *Ibid.*
[3] *Nevada State Journal*, September 5, 1894.

piece would cease production after 1889 as the U.S. Mint continued to redefine the nation's money supply.

HARRISON ELECTED PRESIDENT

During the presidential contest campaigning grew intense as the elections approached at the end of 1888. Nevada's Senators Jones and Stewart offered their full support to Benjamin Harrison in his bid to unseat President Cleveland, and when Harrison defeated Cleveland in the November election, it was considered a major victory for silverites across the country, for Nevada at large, as well as for the Carson City Mint. Senator John P. Jones, known as the *Silver Senator*, had made it clear to Harrison that the State of Nevada as well as the other silver-producing states had supported him, and now would be expecting favors and concessions. In a congratulatory letter sent to Harrison after the election, Senator Jones wrote:

Benjamin Harrison beat Grover Cleveland in the presidential race in 1888 and was expected to repay Nevada for the support he received during his campaign. (*Dictionary of American Portraits, Dover Publications*)

> I rejoiced heartily at the splendid victory achieved, and…I rendered all the assistance in my power to bring it about. To my mind the consequences involved were more momentous than those of any election since the foundation of the Government, excepting only that of Lincoln. While…I congratulate you most sincerely on your conspicuous success, after a fight in which the people thoroughly understood what they wanted, and whom they wanted, I congratulate the Republic no less that it has escaped the baleful consequences that must have followed the success of the Democratic party at this critical juncture of our economic policy."[1]

Harrison's election could only mean that the mint at Carson City stood a fighting chance of having its minting operations restored. After all, San Francisco minted over a million quarters in 1888, perhaps signaling a trend of increased silver coinage.

CASEY AT THE BAT

During a year filled with political tension, economic uncertainty, severe blizzards, and trepidations of all kinds, Americans still found time to enjoy leisurely activities. Two of the most popular forms of entertainment were reading and public recitations. One of the most cherished light-hearted literary works premiered, appearing on page four of the *Daily Examiner* of San Francisco, on June 3, 1888. It was titled "Casey At the Bat," composed by Ernest L. Thayer.

In the weeks that followed, comic actor DeWolf Hopper recited the poem on stage in different cities. This beloved poem's success is attested to by the fact that it is more popular today than ever.

Professional baseball player from the late 1880s.

Knowing the challenge that the Carson City Mint faced as 1888 drew to a close; you could have used your imagination, taking an excerpt from the poem, and inserting the name Carson City (*Carsonville*) in place of "Mudville," and the "CC" Mint in place of "Casey."

> The outlook wasn't brilliant
> for the Mudville nine that day…
> Would there be joy in Mudville?
> Or would the mighty Casey strike out?[2]

Of course the struggle to keep the mint open was not a game; it was an essential factor in the sustenance of Carson City's pride, political strengths and economy. Residents of the city were stressed over governmental decisions concerning their mint, but would have to wait until 1889 before any decisions would be handed down. So all *Carsonville* could do was wait it out, hoping the mighty "CC" Mint would not be called out on strikes and end its career.

Meanwhile, it might have expressed the sentiments of the whole town if a brief note were forwarded to the new president from the staff at the Carson City Mint.

> December 31, 1888
>
> Dear President Harrison,
> Would you be ever so kind as to sign the order
> authorizing us to mint coins again?
> Thanking you in advance.
> Signed,
> The employees at the Carson City Mint.

---

[1] U.S. Government, Library of Congress, Benjamin Harrison Papers, February 18, 1889.

[2] Ernest L. Thayer, *Casey at the Bat: A Ballad of the Republic Sung in the Year 1888*.

CHAPTER FOUR

Beginning of the End
(1889-1893)

As the new mint at Philadelphia will have a capacity equal to all existing United States
Mints, it is probable that others will be greatly restricted or even abolished in no long time,
and that mint marks will not only cease as an annual expense, but be a treasure in time to
those who have the foresight to collect them now.

- Augustus G. Heaton
A Treatise On the Coinage of the United States Branch Mints, 1893.

By the 1890s, the forests around
Lake Tahoe had been stripped
bare of their once dense growth
of evergreen trees. (*Courtesy
Nevada Historical Society*)

COINAGE RECORD UNITED STATES MINT AT CARSON CITY, NEVADA

YEAR	DOLLARS	HALF EAGLES	EAGLES	DOUBLE EAGLES	NO. OF PCS.	TOTAL $
1889	350,000			30,945	380,945	$ 968,900.00
1890	2,309,041	53,800	17,500	91,209	2,471,550	4,577,221.00
1891	1,618,000	208,000	103,732	5,000	1,934,732	3,795,320.00
1892	1,352,000	82,968	40,000	27,265	1,502,233	2,712,140.00
1893	677,000	60,000	14,000	18,402	769,402	1,485,040.00

When examining a coin, you look at the date, the mintmark, and the overall condition. There are certain features or identifying characteristics on every coin that are distinct and attributable to its type or category. For instance, on the front (or obverse) of a Morgan silver dollar, you will see a portrait, stars, the motto *E Pluribus Unum*, as well as the date. The word *LIBERTY* is inscribed in the portrait's headband, and is known to collectors as the Legend, which is derived from the Latin root *legenda*, which means, *to be read*, or *worth reading*. Usage of the word in American English has come to mean, "a collection of stories about anyone or anything that people have come to admire." And the word *LIBERTY* on a coin undeniably symbolizes the most admirable collection of stories about a courageous nation. Legends are formed when anyone, or anything, defies circumstances, and gives inspiration to those looking on. A legend, somehow, against all odds, surprises everyone by standing victorious.

In 1889, the legend of the Carson City Mint was still being compiled and the collection of stories about the famous mint would perpetually be edited, revised, and "gone over with a fine tooth comb." The year 1889 proved to be a time of the defiance of odds for the Carson City Mint; ironically, it was also the year that signaled the beginning of its end.

After the mint at Carson City was closed down at the end of 1885, it appeared there would never be another coin struck there. Nothing could have been further from the truth, for although the years from 1886 through 1888 were in all probability difficult, depressing and a true test of faith for many Carsonites, perseverance triumphed, when in 1889, the mint once again began striking coins.

No coins were produced in the first half of 1889 at the Carson City Mint as it continued functioning as an assay office, and it was still unclear when coins would once again be minted, although the prospects seemed positive. During the first three months of the year President Cleveland was busy wrapping up his affairs in the White House, in preparation for newly elected Benjamin Harrison assuming office in March; any decisions concerning the Carson City Mint's coinage operations would be on hold until then.

A TESTING GROUND

From early in the state's history, Nevada has been used as a testing ground for America. Some tests have been very innocent in nature, some have greatly benefited the United States, some have left devastating aftereffects, and for some of the tests, the results are not in yet.

In imitation of a popular method used in the indexing of subjects, here is a *Top Ten List of Topics That Nevada Has Been Used For Testing:*

 #10. Atomic bombs and nuclear weapons

 #9. U.S. Military aircraft

 #8. Irrigation and dam systems

 #7. Land speed records

 #6. Excavation of the oldest remains of mankind on the North American continent

 #5. Archaeological studies

 #4. Legalized gambling

 #3. 7/24 alcohol consumption

 #2. Legalized prostitution

And, #1. A U.S. Mint in a sparsely populated, rural area

Exhaustive studies have been made on each of the topics on this list, but the focus here, of course, is the mint at Carson City, the opening of which must surely be considered an experiment, or a test, if you will.

At the outset the Treasury Department was obliged to see if it was practicable to operate a coinage mint in a somewhat remote location, based primarily on the location's proximity to a wealthy deposit of mineral ore. If given a second chance, however, the U.S. government, in one of those "if we had it to do over again" scenarios, would probably not have established the Carson City facility as a coinage mint; it might have been an assay office, but certainly there would have been no coins with a "CC" mintmark.

A PLACE IN HISTORY

More than any individual in Nevada's history, Abe Curry was responsible for gaining approval for launching the great mint experiment in Carson City. Yet acknowledgments for his contribution were slow in coming. In fact, it was not until January 22, 1979 that one of the first significant acts of recognition came, when a statue of him was dedicated in front of the Nevada State Capitol and Legislative buildings. In a speech, the Governor of Nevada at the time, Robert List, praised Curry as "a man who accomplished more in 15 years than most men hope to accomplish in a lifetime."[1] Of course, the 15 years Governor List was referring to were from 1858, the year Curry and his partners plotted the streets in Carson City, to 1873, the year he died. Curry was the driving force behind the construction of a mint in his fair city and it was also Curry who persuaded a hesitant Washington bureaucracy to grant the new mint coinage rights. In the "two-act" story (including an intermission) of *From Mines, To Mint, To My Collection*, the U.S. Mint at Carson City from 1870 to 1888 had already accomplished enough to establish itself as a legend in numismatic history; even if it had only been a one-act story, the legacy was secured.

Statue of Abraham Curry, dedicated in 1979, stands in front of the Capitol building in Carson City.

In Latin, the word *volumen* means, *something rolled up.* Scrolls of ancient literature written on sheets of papyrus were referred to as *volumes*, as there was so much literature and history to preserve. In the same way, information relating to the Carson City Mint requires volumes to record, providing endless paths for one to travel when studying it. As a brief reminder: this book is in many ways, an enthusiast's guide to the Carson City Mint; its purpose is to inform, entice, and arouse your curiosity, hopefully bringing life to the subject. There will most certainly be information missing that readers wished to read, or information that some might challenge. The beloved nature of the Carson City Mint, and the Comstock era as a whole, only necessitates the need for further research, insuring that the coins from this glorious mint will only grow in popularity as the years pass by. Indeed, there are empty spaces on the shelves of numismatic libraries, waiting to be filled with more books on the subject. And there are many sources waiting to be explored, including old newspaper articles, diaries, journals, reference books, official documents, secondary sources, and oral histories that have been passed down.

Robert Laxalt was one of Nevada's greatest authors. His father, Dominique Laxalt, was two years old in 1889, and being raised in Basque territory in Soule, France. Dominique Laxalt would move from France to Nevada in 1906, at the age of 19. He had little education, and did not speak English, yet he built a prosperous ranching business in northern Nevada, and eventually settled in Carson City in 1926. From his family of six children, came three attorneys, a teacher, a nun, and renowned author, Robert. One of his attorney sons, Paul, went on to become a U.S. Senator, after serving as the Governor of Nevada. In a moving memoir to his father, Robert Laxalt wrote the all-time favorite, *Sweet Promised Land*. An excerpt from this book describes the spirit of so many people, who came to Nevada, and settled around the Carson City area:

> They had forsaken home and family, and gone into the unknown of a new land, with only courage and the hands that God gave them.[1]

Abe Curry brought this same passion, and more to Nevada back in 1858 and because of it, coins from the Carson City Mint are available to collectors today.

NEVADA'S DECLINING POPULATION BASE

Although the roots of a capital had been planted in Carson City and a state government was firmly established, Nevada's population continued to decline, and would continue to do so into the 20th century, as from 1889 through 1900 the state lost 10% of its population. Losing respect in the minds of many politicians across the nation, members of Congress, from time to time proposed rescinding Nevada's statehood because of its small population.

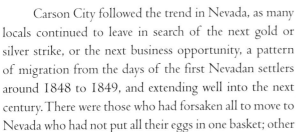

Although there is no proof, it is possible that some 1849 Mormon $5 gold coins were minted with gold from Nevada. (*Courtesy Bowers and Merena*)

Carson City followed the trend in Nevada, as many locals continued to leave in search of the next gold or silver strike, or the next business opportunity, a pattern of migration from the days of the first Nevadan settlers around 1848 to 1849, and extending well into the next century. There were those who had forsaken all to move to Nevada who had not put all their eggs in one basket; other

businesses, besides the mining industry or those related to it, were also established around Carson City, becoming the nucleus of a society that would emerge as a strong commercial and economic base 100 years into the future.

Obituaries from the Carson City area in the 1920s and 1930s give witness to many survivors who hung on when times were tough, and may have prevented Carson City from becoming one of Nevada's many ghost towns. One obituary in particular, in a 1920 issue of the *Carson Appeal*, gave due respects to a Chinese immigrant named Lee. At the time of his death, it was estimated that only 20 Chinese still lived in the area, from a once thriving Chinese population around the Comstock that warranted a small community of their own, referred to as Chinatown.

THE "EARLIEST" COINS FROM NEVADA

It has always been assumed that the first coins produced in Nevada were in 1870 at the Carson City Mint. There are however, reported to be a small group of extremely rare gold coins minted in Nevada that predate the "CC" coins by almost 20 years. The story behind these obscure gold coins is also related to the controversial debate about which is the oldest permanent settlement in Nevada. For over 150 years, the small hamlet of Genoa, Nevada has generally been credited with being the state's oldest town. Citizens of Dayton, Nevada, located just east of Carson City, however, also lay claim to this distinction. Here again, a lack of authoritative evidence shades the truth, and there are no eyewitnesses remaining, so history may just keep the secret.

Mormon pioneer John Reese was at the center of the debate concerning Nevada's oldest town and also the story about the first coins minted in the state. Reese (incorrectly named Reek in Breen's *Encyclopedia*[2]), and his brother Enoch, moved into the Carson Valley from Salt Lake City sometime between 1849 and 1851 along with other Mormon settlers who had been exploring the region seeking to extend their territorial sovereignty. The Reese brothers' settlement was known as Mormon Station, also referred to as Reese's Station.

It is now officially accepted that 1851 was the year it was established, two years later than diaries and second-

---

[1] Robert Laxalt, *Sweet Promised Land*.
[2] Walter Breen, *Walter Breen's Complete Encyclopedia of U.S. and Colonial Coins*, 655.

ary sources make reference to gold being discovered at the edge of the Carson River in what is known as Gold Canyon, near the site of present day Dayton, Nevada. Contemporary journals mentioned that John "Ol Virginny" Finney operated a trading post in that spot. Other sources tell the story of a settlement named Ragtown, which was located near present day Fallon, Nevada, being the first white-man trading post in 1849. Although the accuracy of these various accounts may never be proven to everyone's satisfaction, it is clear that an environment conducive to vigorous growth existed in the area from 1849 to the early 1850s. Whether the "First Settlement" honors are bestowed upon Ragtown, Dayton, or Genoa, the intrigue of it all, and the roles these communities and their inhabitants played in the legacy leading up to the legend of the Carson City Mint is undeniable. Readers having an interest in history (a trait shared by most coin collectors) are encouraged to visit these locales and take advantage of the tours and literature available that will most assuredly stimulate the history buff's predilection for studying the heritage of this fascinating area.

The Mormons and John Reese's Mormon Station are woven together as threads in a cross-stitch of Nevada's history with coins, beginning with Brigham Young recognizing the need for a circulating medium of exchange in the newly settled Utah Territory, and his leading elders setting up a Church Mint. New Mormon coinage was first struck in September of 1849, and continued through 1851. Another 789, give or take, $5 gold pieces would also be minted between 1859 and 1861 at Salt Lake City. These coins circulated in Utah and many of them were sent to businesses in the east in payment for commodities not available in the *Honey Bee* state. When the gold bullion (mostly gold dust) used to mint the coins was no longer available in the Salt Lake area, "The (coin) press and stamp was sold to John and Enoch Reese of Carson Valley, Nevada who minted coins from Ne-

Ragtown, Nevada, a prominent community in Carson City's early days.

vada gold dust for a brief period."[1] So although the gold coins did not bear any associative markings related to the state, they still could be considered, in a loose way, to be the first coins struck in Nevada.

By 1889, it had been 40 years since the early Mormon settlements made history in northern Nevada, and although the Territory of Utah had been created by Congress in 1850, conflicts between the residents of Utah and the federal government had prevented it from being granted statehood all those years. One of the major points of contention was Utah's allowance of polygamy. Realizing the perpetual consequences, Mormon leaders knew they were at a crossroads in 1889; it was either multiple wives for men, or statehood. The following year they made their decision and a manifesto by the Mormon Church president declared no more polygamy. It would still be a slow march to statehood, but finally in 1896, Utah became the 45th state in the Union.

CARSON MINT TAKEN OFF INACTIVE LIST

Nevada's law did not tolerate polygamy but its citizens had other quarrels with the federal government, one of which was the status of the mint in their capital city. Benjamin Harrison's election to the White House provided much needed support, a changing of the guard which occurred in the first week of March 1889. Outgoing Secretary of the Treasury, Charles Fairchild, was replaced by Harrison appointee, William Windom on March 7, 1889, beginning a chain reaction of Republican replacements throughout the Bureau of the Mint's network. Carson City's Mint Superintendent William Garrard was replaced by a popular local judge, attorney, and funeral director, Samuel C. Wright on July 1, 1889. Meanwhile, the local newspaper reported another story, with a Philadelphia dateline, that gave residents of Carson City and Nevada something to really celebrate on the Fourth of July. By order of the Director of the Mint, James P. Kimball, the coinage department of the Carson City Mint would be reopened on July 1, 1889. Mr. Kimball, known for his unfavorable attitude toward the Nevada facility, would not receive his walking papers until October of 1889, when he was replaced by the Republican Party's Edward O. Leech.

For Carson City, its mint, and the State of Nevada, having a friend in the Oval Office seemed beneficial. Nevada's Senators, Jones and Stewart, must have breathed a sigh of relief as they had probably been asked many times by locals in the state's capital, when the mint was going to start striking coins again. In a small community of approximately 4,000 people, it was obvious that politicians would have a difficult time avoiding, or evading contact with the public whom they served. Now it was time for staunch supporters of the *Silver State* to be slapped on the back and congratulated.

There was much preparation to be made, and housekeeping to be done, to ready the mint to produce its first coins in nearly four years. Out of the mouth of the frowning face of incumbent Director of the Mint Kimball came the following statement,

> The mint at Carson was reopened for coinage on July 1, 1889, **but**, owing to the dilapidated condition in which the building and machinery was found, after four years of idleness, repairs and betterment of the building and overhauling and repairing the machinery were necessary.[1] (Emphasis added)

Locals in Carson City probably would have agreed if that was all they needed to be concerned with—no problem, just get those coin presses stamping out silver and gold again.

MANIFEST DESTINY COMES TO OKLAHOMA

Nevada's sense of destiny had been revitalized. On a broader scale, the United States Congress, in its continuing mission of *Manifest Destiny*, had made the former Indian Territory in Western Oklahoma available to white settlers in April of 1889. On the count of three, on a given date, the government opened the starting gates bordering the territory on three sides, and thousands of adventurous claimstakers took off. Covered wagons, horses, mules, bicycles, pedestrians and all other types of travelers sped from the north, west, and east, and possessed all the land being offered in one day. The federal government told everyone that anyone who drove a stake in the ground in the allotted time could claim 160 acres for free. Some of the people racing to their *promised land*, cheated, and tried to get there sooner, adding a nickname to the vocabulary, *Sooners*. Oklahoma's *Cimarron* land rush of 1889 vividly illustrates the perceived notion of *Manifest Destiny*. One of the many definitions for America's sense of national destiny is, "the unstoppable right and duty to claim and develop the immense landmass allotted by Providence."[2]

A TOWERING ACHIEVEMENT

On another continent, Gustave Eiffel, a French engineer specializing in metal structural work, had built metal structures, including bridges, buildings and statues, all around the world. He had, in fact, provided the incredible metal skeletal structure inside the body of the Statue of Liberty. In Paris in 1889, Eiffel unveiled his *piece-de-la-resistance*, the Eiffel Tower, forever memorializing his name. Gustave Eiffel is quoted as saying, "It's much more famous than I am." Sad as it may seem, Eiffel was also indicted for fraud in 1889 for his company's involvement in the initial stages of the construction of the Panama Canal. He served a two-year prison sentence and paid a large fine, although the French courts later annulled his guilt and liberated him of all obligations.

The Eiffel Tower was unveiled in Paris in 1889.

Back in Nevada, Senator William Stewart had used France's monetary system to illustrate a system that was favorable to silver coins used as legal tender in harmony with gold coins, or paper currency. France's system was favorable toward the white metal, and any friend of silver's was a friend of Nevada.

Whether or not America would adopt a monetary system similar to France's, silver and gold coins would once again bear the "CC" mintmark beginning in 1889, causing this capital city to wear its reappointed responsibility like a badge of honor.

THE 1889-CC MORGAN DOLLAR

As recorded by the Director of the Mint in Philadelphia, "the coinage of gold and silver was not commenced (at the Carson Mint) until October 1, 1889,"[3] which coincided with James Kimball's exit from his position as Mint Director. October 1, 1889 was 28 years to the day, from when the first Nevada Territorial legislature had convened in Carson City, and much had taken place since 1861. None of those members, attending that first legislative meeting, could have foreseen the many roads that Carson City, and Nevada, would have traveled by 1889. And now, here again was the Carson City Mint,

[1] *Annual Report of the Director of the Mint,* 1889.
[2] *American Heritage Dictionary.*
[3] *Annual Report of the Director of the Mint ,* 1890.

revitalized and ready for another four and a half year mission to produce coins. There was nothing official in writing, declaring that the mission would only last through 1893, but when October of 1889 arrived, no one at the village mint was holding out for a longer contract. Everyone was just happy to be playing again.

Mint Superintendent Sam Wright, Chief Assayer P.B. Ellis, Vice Assayer Joseph Ryan, Melter and Refiner E.B. Zabriskie, Vice Melter and Assayer John Dennis, Coiner Charles Colburn, and approximately 67 other employers, would eventually produce 350,000 1889-CC Morgan silver dollars, beginning in October of 1889, establishing this date as the third lowest mintage in the "CC" Morgan dollar series and for some reason the scarcest date. Why this is so is unclear, but an educated guess might be that the 1889-CC was a victim of a meltdown order. One thing is certain, the 1889-CC's did not accompany other "CC" silver dollars to the Treasury's storage vaults after the Carson City Mint closed for the final time, and if there were hidden quantities of this rare silver dollar somewhere on the planet, the publicized high prices of the past 20 years most certainly would have brought them from hiding by now.

The *Eliasberg* 1889-CC dollar.
(*Courtesy Bowers and Merena*)

This date is prohibitively rare in grades above MS-64. In fact, as late as 1995, price guides made no serious attempts to estimate what MS-65 specimens might bring. In 2003, however, there is more pricing information available for 1889-CC silver dollars in MS-65 and above; it is well established that the few specimens in existence routinely sell in the $275,000 to $600,000 range.

In some ways, it seems fitting that this date is the scarcest of the "CC" Morgan series, since the reopening of the mint in 1889 was a sentimental comeback story, deserving of something special to remember it by.

ANOTHER AMAZING "CC" COIN
FROM THE ELIASBERG COLLECTION

As of 2003, no Carson City coin has ever sold for $1 million. No one would deny that when this occurs, the 1873-CC *Without Arrows* dime is the leading contender to

break through that threshold. In fact, this dime has already been advertised for sale at the $1 million mark. And so has another "CC" coin: the *Eliasberg* specimen of an 1889-CC Morgan silver dollar appeared in a 1998 dealer's catalog for that seven-figure amount. This particular 1889-CC, graded MS-68 by PCGS, realized $462,000 in Bowers and Merena's *Eliasberg* sale in 1997, and subsequently sold for $525,000 in a later auction.

At lot viewing for the 1997 *Eliasberg* auction, there was so much electricity and enthusiasm in the air; one could sense that this was not an ordinary event. Speculation about how high the prices would go for hundreds of the coins was almost a brainteaser contest. Of course, everyone was curious about the 1804 silver dollar, which would most likely set a record; if Las Vegas bookies had made a line on it; the odds would have been even money. But setting a price for the 1889-CC Morgan silver dollar was much more of a challenge; the over/under line on it may have been $275,000.

Leading up to the *Eliasberg* sale the only reported price that a Gem quality (at least MS-65) 1889-CC silver dollar had sold for, was in 1989, when a dealer to dealer transaction was reported to be in the $310,000 range. At the time this 1889-CC dollar, having been certified by PCGS, became the only MS-65 example graded by either of the two major grading services. It deservedly became a part of the *World's Finest Set of Carson City Silver Dollars.*

Graders at PCGS had originally assigned it an MS-64 grade, probably being cautious, knowing how rare an MS-65 specimen would be. But after it was upgraded, most agreed this beautiful coin deserved it.

When the *Eliasberg* 1889-CC dollar was put on display, it completely blew away all competition, similar to when the previously mentioned MS-68 graded 1885-CC Morgan silver dollar appeared in the mid-1980s. At lot viewing for the *Eliasberg* auction, the owner of the finest set of silver dollars ever assembled was certainly the prime candidate to purchase this incredible 1889-CC for his collection, but another dealer had a client ready to buy the 1889-CC if given his dealer's go-ahead. This client's dealer/agent asked the prime candidate to write down on a slip of paper the price he estimated the coin might bring, and in turn did likewise. When both papers were laid on the table, the prime candidate's number was $350,000, while the other dealer's number was $600,000. Although this dealer did not bid against the prime candidate, his client was willing to pay up to $600,000 based on the assurance his dealer/agent had given of the coin's value. There were other Carson City silver coins in the auction this dealer and his client were concentrating on, like the 1870-CC, 1871-CC, and 1872-CC Seated Liberty quarters. In the end, the prime candidate was successful in his purchase of the 1889-CC silver dollar, for an auction record price for a Morgan silver dollar of $462,000. Later on, PCGS graded the coin MS-68, affirming the stunning quality of this remarkable piece.

GOLD COINS IN 1889

Turning to the subject of gold coins; $1 and $3 gold pieces were minted for the final time in the United States in 1889 (as was the nickel three-cent piece). The $1 gold piece had debuted in 1849 and the $3 gold piece made its first appearance five years later in 1854. Neither was ever produced at the Carson City Mint, as there was greater emphasis in that location on manufacturing silver coinage and the higher denomination gold. A large percentage of the gold coins struck at Carson City were paid out in exchange for the bullion ore left by depositors, who preferred larger denomination gold coins, not to mention, there was no retail need for smaller denomination gold in that region.

Because of the late start Carson City got in coinage production, the only other denomination dated 1889-CC aside from the silver dollar, is the $20 gold piece. Bureau of the Mint records reported that there was more than $1.5 million of gold bullion in storage at the Carson Mint in 1889, yet double eagles minted that year at the Carson Mint consumed only a small percentage of it; the balance would be absorbed over the next few years.

Mintages for 1889-CC $20 double eagles totaled 30,945, and according to Doug Winter, it is a relatively easy date to locate in most states of preservation below Choice Uncirculated. Readers might find it interesting to note that Louis E. Eliasberg's 1889-CC $20 gold piece was graded XF/AU, being light-years in quality below his 1889-CC Morgan dollar.

Through the year 2003, the highest grade listed by either PCGS or NGC for an 1889-CC $20 gold piece is one lone specimen in MS-64. In May of 1993, Bowers and Merena auctioned an uncertified example of the date that was catalogued as an MS-64, "and possibly the finest known."[1] The price realized was just under $12,500, but it is worth noting that in today's market (2003), an 1889-CC $20 gold piece in true MS-64 condition would likely sell for much more. Ironically, an MS-65 specimen of an 1889-CC $20 gold piece, if one existed, probably would sell for much less than its counterpart 1889-CC Morgan dollar in MS-65; both, of course, are considered extremely rare.

Being only the second time in 21 coinage years that just two denominations were minted at Carson City, 1889 was still a milestone year for this facility. Back in action after a four year hiatus, locals welcomed the sights, sounds, and smells coming from their neighborhood landmark, and looked forward to a lively season in the mint's 20th anniversary year.

For more information about the silver and gold coins from 1889, please see Chapter 6, *Silver Coins*, and Chapter 7, *Gold Coins*.

---

[1] Bowers and Merena, *Stetson Collection,* May 1993.

❧ 1890 ❧

WHITE WINTER

Nevada is Spanish for *snowfall*. The snow fell early, and it fell hard during the winter of 1889/1890, and the residents in the area around the Comstock earned their masters degrees in the definition of their state's name. During typical winters, the snowfalls usually dust the Carson and Washoe valleys the way powdered sugar dusts a donut; but this winter the snow did not dust the valleys it smothered them. Over 100 inches fell, the heaviest total reported in northern Nevada since record keeping began. For much of the winter, travel in and out of the region was cut off, causing delays to businesses and receiving necessary supplies of all kinds.

The Carson City Mint had sufficient quantities of gold and silver bullion on hand in the early months of 1890 to keep it busy despite the challenge of inclement weather. Before that year ended the employees at the Carson Mint could hold up their heads proudly, knowing that they had produced over $4.5 million face value in coins, the third highest output in the mint's 21 years as a coinage facility.

Comstock mines were shut down most of the winter leaving many men out of work. Mine owners were reminded in local newspapers, such as *The Territorial Enterprise*, *The Carson Appeal*, *The Nevada State Journal*, and *The Lyon County Times*, that the Bullion Tax was due for the quarter ending March 31st 1890. This tax was on "the proceeds of the mines," and it was stressed in the notices that "the law in regard to their collection will be strictly enforced."[1] These taxes were welcomed into the state's coffers, just as taxes collected from gambling revenues would be 100 years later.

NEVADA WELCOMES CARSON MINT'S BONANZA YEAR

A harsh winter, and the uncertainty of the federal government's position on the free coinage of silver, would have been more distressing for residents in northern Nevada if the mint in Carson City were not producing coins again. Also reassuring was the fact that the mint was producing quantities of coins as large as it had produced during the *Big Bonanza* years of the mid-1870s. Nevada was indeed at an important crossing point. Before the Carson Mint reopened in 1889, many Nevadan's felt as if they were losing the battle. The state was in serious economic danger; it desperately needed a more diversified industrial base. No one denied that the mining industry had indeed been good to Nevada; without a doubt, the bullion ore from the mines had brought the state a long way. Nothing underscores this more than the awareness that mineral wealth had purchased statehood instead of Nevada possibly being annexed to California, or left as a section of Utah Territory. But by the end of the 1880s, and on into the 1890s, unless another *Eureka* experience occurred, Nevada's future was bleak. A newspaper reported in 1890, "just now, the state is in the dumps, and taxpayers are clamoring for a more economical government."[2]

There would be even greater opportunities for the mining industry to score a new bonanza if the price of silver increased, as this would raise the incentive for exploration and drilling of new mines. But what could possibly cause the price of silver to rise? Advocates of free coinage believed that the remonetization of silver was the answer, as it would cause demand for it to increase, resulting in higher prices. The State of Nevada, having more at stake than all others, utilized the services of a powerful brigade of politicians led by Senator John P. Jones.

NEVADA NATIONAL SILVER COMMITTEE

In spring of 1890, as the citizens of Carson City, and its surrounding areas were digging out of the winter snows, Senator Jones and his cohorts were preparing to launch an attack against the opponents of free coinage the likes of which had never been seen. Inspired by the full steam production of coins at the Carson City Mint, and fortified by the new Republican White House, members of the Nevada National Silver Committee rallied the residents of the state and charged ahead. Local newspapers kept readers abreast of anything relevant to the battle over silver, almost on a daily basis, and notices were posted in the papers declaring Nevada's stand on silver issues. The following statement is from the *Lyon County Times*:

> PAYABLE IN SILVER
>
> The Silver State says, "Citizens of Nevada now give and accept notes of hand payable in silver, as an evidence of the faith that is in them."[3]

Newspapers also ran a public service notice from the Primary Election Committee on a daily basis. The notice began by stating:

---

[1] *Lyon County Times*, May 10, 1890.
[2] *Lyon County Times*, August 16, 1890.
[3] *Lyon County Times*, June 7, 1890.

The following test will be required of every voter at the Primary Elections:

I am a citizen of this state, and I will support the nominees of the Republican Party.

Then the notice listed the resolutions that were adopted for the state's platform:

The following resolutions were unanimously adopted:

Resolved, That this committee reaffirms the State's and National Republican platform of 1888 including the declaration that "the Republican party is in favor of the use of both gold and silver as money" and that it "condemns all efforts to demonetize silver.

Resolved, That the persistent neglect of Secretary Windom to increase the coinage of silver to the maximum of four million dollars per month, coupled with his attempt to influence Congressional legislation so as to perpetuate silver demonetization, is a shameless violation of the silver plank of the National Republican platform, an attack upon the rights and interests of the miners, farmers and workers of the land, and an act of party perfidy that should call for his retirement from the councils of an administration which is pledged to help and not hinder the remonitization of silver.

Resolved, That the Republican party of this State is in favor of free and unlimited coinage of both gold and silver; that it holds to this principle as a tenet of part faith and a test of party allegiance; that it will permit of no abandonment or modification of this doctrine; that let whosoever will prove recreant to the principle of bimetallism it will remain steadfast thereto, and that it invites all voters in Nevada who favor the repeal of the iniquitous interlineated law of 1873 by which silver was demonetized, and who desire the establishment of free and unlimited coinage as the law of the United States of America, to join in electing delegates to a Republican State Convention.[1]

The language was clear. There was no middle ground on the issues.

Jones, Senator William Stewart, Congressman H. F. Bartine, and Governor C.C. Stevenson were leading Nevada's charge. There were capable commanders in the flanks as well; one was Mr. Thomas Fitch, Nevada's former Congressman, who in 1870 had bravely and eloquently defended the Carson City Mint on the floor of the House of Representatives, when it had been proposed that the mint be shut down, within two months after its opening. Twenty years later, Fitch was an active member of Nevada's National Silver Committee and was organizing a Free Coin Convention to meet in Carson City on May 18, 1890. He announced that he had "been empowered by the National Executive Silver Committee to call a convention of the friends of free coinage..."[2] Mr. Fitch had fought the battle too long to give up now.

Nevada Congressman Bartine led an advance of western state legislators in the House, threatening to block the McKinley tariff bill if the *Goldbugs* in Congress did not vote for the free coinage portion of the Sherman Bill. Conservative eastern legislators proposed a compromise if the western Congressmen would support the McKinley bill, but Congressman Bartine refused to compromise. Local Nevadan newspapers reported on the skirmish, "silver is again advancing, and it is hoped that some measure will be passed this session to make it advance rapidly..."[3] One of the papers reported that the combined legislation proposed in the McKinley and Sherman bills, "is not what is wanted by any means, and our representative, Bartine, voted against it."[4] Bartine and other allies of free coinage hoped that the certificate redemption of silver would be stricken from the bill and replaced by a free coinage measure. The newspaper concluded by attacking anyone who would threaten the security of their state: "How long would it be, if such a bill...becomes law, before Congress would be asked to issue certificates against copper, lead, iron, tin, wheat, barley, cotton, and other commodities, and make them as much of a money as silver would be under [that] bill."[5]

FOUNDING FATHERS FOUGHT FIAT MONEY

Battles over a free coinage monetary system in the United States raged from 1873, through the early years of the next century. The theory of free coinage had never really been tested; was it indeed a panacea for the economic ills of the nation? The U.S. monetary system was based on the primary unit of trade, referred to as one dollar. A dollar was evaluated in terms of how much pure silver it contained. At the time the standard was established, the accepted silver weight for a common trade unit was 371.25 grains, the same weight as the principal Spanish silver coin, which was accepted worldwide.

The origin of this specific weight is beyond the scope of this book, but there are numerous sources available on the subject. It is not without significance that it was the Founding Fathers who chose this weight when the U.S. Mint was established. These extraordinarily intelligent men set the ratio between gold and silver at 15 to one; one weight measure unit of gold would be worth 15 similar weight measures of silver. At the time, in the 1790s, that

[1] Ibid.
[2] *Nevada State Journal*, May 8, 1890.
[3] *Lyon County Times*, June 14, 1890.
[4] Ibid.
[5] Ibid.

ratio seemed expedient, for it was the Constitution that authorized the Treasury Department to govern the weights and measures of the nation's coinage system. These two important components of the coinage system were protected as if the country's life depended on them. The weight of a coin was measured in grains and the measure of the metal in a coin was determined by its fineness, and this combination specified how much pure precious metal was in each coin.

The first silver dollars, struck in 1794, weighed 416 grains, and were 892.4 fine. This meant that there were 371.25 grains of pure silver in each coin. The following year, 1795, the Mint introduced the $5 half eagle and $10 eagle gold pieces. The weight and measure of these gold coins were in harmony with the silver dollars. Based on the 15 to one ratio, the $5 gold piece weighed 135 grains, and was 916 and two thirds fine. This meant that there were 123.75 grains of pure gold in each half eagle. Correspondingly, five silver dollars contained 1856.25 (5 x 371.25) grains of pure silver, which equaled 15 times the 123.75 grain weight of the gold half eagles, and the $10 eagles contained 247.5 grains of pure gold based on their weight and fineness. Ten silver dollars contained 3712.5 grains of pure silver, equaling 15 times the 247.5 grain weight of the gold eagles. When in 1796, gold quarter eagles ($2 1/2 gold coins) were introduced, they too conformed to the system.

At the time this coinage system became law, citizens of the United States could deposit raw gold and silver bullion at the Mint and receive coins or bars in exchange. Correspondingly, the federal government relied on a steady influx of precious metal deposits at the Mint by private and business sources to provide sufficient quantities to coin money for the nation's commercial needs. If domestic sources of precious metals were exhausted, the U.S. Mint would be forced to import the required amount as there was no guarantee, one way or the other, how much mineral ore would be discovered and produced in America. Back in the 1790s, the Founding Fathers could have never foreseen the immense supply of bullion that would be dug out of the depths of the earth in the last half of the 19th century. When they were composing the nation's monetary system, they believed that Providence would provide for all of their needs; the only system that made sense to them was one that was backed by precious metals, as throughout the history of civilization's use of money, this seemed to be the most successful system. The wild card in the system was the possibility that some day, there would be a far greater supply of either of the two metals than the system could process. Other than that, the authors of the monetary system of the United States looked forward to equilibrium being achieved between goods, services, property, and mineral wealth. These men felt that it was their God-given duty to protect the system, and not allow interference with it. They seemed to be in total agreement that fiat currency (money without backing) was not acceptable. A monetary system based on paper promises, could conceivably lead to a nation's economic ruin. Even Alexander Hamilton who favored a national bank and credit money, acknowledged the need for at least a percentage of precious metal backing.

Although the country's Founding Fathers were "looking through a glass darkly" into the future, they saw that a fiat currency system would eventually cause depressions, high levels of inflation, and exorbitant unemployment. George Washington articulated his infant nation's views concerning a sound monetary system when he prophesied in 1789:

> We may one day become a great commercial, and flourishing nation. But, if in the pursuit of the means we should unfortunately **stumble** again on unfounded paper money, or any similar **species of fraud**, we shall assuredly give a fatal stab to our national credit…[1] (Emphasis added)

Was Free Coinage the Solution?

The United States has experienced many changes in its monetary policies from the time the Mint was established in 1792, to the present (2003). No one can conclude with any certainty how things would have worked out if one monetary system had been employed, rather than another. It would all be hindsight now and all conclusions would be influenced by whether the analysis was performed in an unbiased or a revisionist manner. It has been suggested that if, in the 1800s, the federal government had not attempted to fix the ratio between gold and silver, but instead had just stamped the weight and fineness on gold coins, the free market would have set the exchange rate of the price of gold in relation to the standard weight (371.25 grain) silver dollar. Free coinage rights could have remained in effect, and might have resulted in the natural absorption of all the bullion that was drawn out of the mines, without harm to anyone. Obviously, a categorical conclusion to that theory is impossible. There is one stone cold hard fact though: When performing an inflation calculation for the periods between 1800 and

---

[1] Louis Bass, *A Treatise on Monetary Reform*, 1789.

1900, and then 1901 and 2001, the cost to society of a fiat currency system is staggering. The results reveal that $100 in goods purchased in 1800, would cost $49 in 1900; making it very clear that inflation was kept in check during that century. The situation changes radically, however, when the same calculation method is used for the subsequent century. Goods worth $100 in 1901 would cost $2,045 in 2001!

NEVADA'S POLITICIANS FIGHT FOR SILVER

Political leaders in Nevada in 1890 were obviously biased in their opinions about what was the best system. Nevada's army of *defenders of silver*, in coalition with leaders from other silver producing states, applied emphatically selective reasoning in their arguments; but the fact was, in order to survive, silver producing states needed an outlet for their primary product. Silver producers were also distrustful of big business and the financial elite back east. They feared the results if eastern bankers and industrialists, supposedly in league with the financial power brokers in Great Britain, gained complete control of monetary and economic systems. It is difficult to tell if the statesmen in Nevada understood all of the machinations involved in the cause they were fighting for. It may be proper to venture, however, that they would have rallied around George Washington's cry for protection against a fiat currency system.

Senator Stewart from Nevada, at least on the surface, was a fierce warrior in the silver platform's trenches. Stewart went toe to toe with Speaker of the House Thomas Reed, who was also a Republican and considered more powerful than President Harrison concerning domestic measures. Swaying from the Republican position on the silver issue, Reed sided with the "gold men." The *Lyon County Times* reported in their July 5, 1890 edition that, "Reed...has done everything in his power to defeat any silver measure...." This article continues, "His [Reed's] last act of appointing members on the ...committee [Silver Purchase Bill] whom he knew were radical single gold standard men."[1] Senator Stewart informed the local press around Carson City and the Comstock that House Speaker Reed had insulted Senator Jones, by appointing John

A much younger William Stewart from the early days of Carson City. By 1890, whatever he had lost in youthful stamina was made up for by his experience fighting in the political trenches on behalf of silver.

Sherman to the committee that Jones had been in charge of. The silverites, believed that Senator Jones deserved to chair that committee, and Senator Stewart also felt entitled to a seat, but both were overlooked by Reed. Local papers in northern Nevada editorialized how incensed the residents were:

> The gold men... hit a heavy blow whenever they get a chance, and will rule the roost, and the poor people [working class] will continue to grow poorer by the sweat of their brow, while the usurers, thieves, and gamblers of Wall Street continue to accumulate wealth by the sweat of the same [poor people's] brow.[2]

Senator Stewart went on the offensive during the summer of 1890. The following article from August 9, 1890, reports on a new strategy employed by Stewart and his forces:

> Senator Stewart has been looking up the records on the silver question and has almost come to the conclusion that silver never was demonetized by Congress. At any rate he says he can find no record of any such proceedings, and Senator Teller, of Colorado, also says there is something mysteriously strange about the record. If it is not a fact that silver was never demonetized it is certain that some very crooked work was done somewhere in 1873. From the fact that Sherman was the one who engineered the demonetization measure, we are inclined to believe that Senator Stewart must have overlooked something, for Sherman doubtless had the matter fixed so there could be no going behind it. Whatever was done, it was the greatest swindle of the age.[3]

NEVADA CHARGES AHEAD

The winter snows were all but melted. Only the tallest mountaintops in the bordering Sierra had white on them. The Carson City Mint had been busy all year, in contrast to 1885 when the Treasury Department ordered it closed and the future had seemed grim. But 1889 had infused new life into the facility, with its reopening, and the production of nearly $1 million face value in coins.

Nevada did not just crawl back into the picture in 1890, it charged! In the midst of the action the *Silver State*

---

[1] *Lyon County Times*, July 5, 1890.

[2] Ibid.

[3] *Lyon County Times*, August 9, 1890.

even proposed that it should annex Utah in 1890, which may have caused some observers to laugh. But Nevada was serious. Their mint was banging out the coins, their politicians were fighting the good fight, and this seemed like a good time to expand borders, increase population, and add to tax revenues.

Almost daily, local papers printed the entire text of the proposed silver bill being debated in Congress. The cartel of silver supporters gained more votes when Idaho and Wyoming were admitted to the Union during the summer of 1890. It was almost high noon, and time for Senator Jones to step out into the street after being in the midst of the fight for silver all year. The *San Francisco Chronicle*, at the time the largest newspaper in California, had nothing but praise for Jones, "There is no man in either House of Congress better equipped to discuss the silver question in all its carried bearings than Senator Jones of Nevada."[1] Speeches presented by Jones, were copied, distributed, and served as manifestos for the remonetization of silver. His was a voice crying in the wilderness, admonishing the gold men, or "creditor class," as he championed the cause of those he named the "debtor class." In his words, these "were the aspiring, the hopeful, the energetic, . . .the designers, the upbuilders, the constructive force in every community."[2] Senator Jones was relentless in his attacks against the opponents of silver because he believed they were only content when in complete control. Free coinage, Jones said, threatened the *anti-silverite's* power structure. If they could not control it, they would not allow it.

Free coinage never made it to the vote, however, after the House defeated the amendment. Members of the Democratic Party who originally favored free coinage, and changed their minds, were accused of being bought off in Nevada's newspapers. After the *Sherman Silver Purchase Act* became law on July 14, 1890, the price of silver rose by approximately 10%. All of the politicians who had fought hard to get free coinage included in the legislation, were hopeful that passage of this bill might be a step in the right direction. They immediately began preparing for the next session of Congress, when they would propose the free coinage amendment once again. After all, *Grover the Great* as they referred to former President Cleveland was gone and the Republican Party was in control now, the party that pledged to restore silver to its rightful position. The road ahead, however, might only be paved with gold.

SHERMAN BILL HOLDS UP A WEARY STATE'S ARMS

Around Carson City in July and August of 1890, local papers were describing the aftereffects of the record setting snowfall from the winter just past. The *Lyon County Times* reported, "The hard winter has killed all the game in the country. There is not a quail or rabbit in the hills, and the sage hen crop is very light."[3] There had been severe flooding along the Humboldt River caused by what was now referred to as the *White Winter*. Many people lost their jobs and there was a further decrease in the population base. Reno was the only city in northern Nevada experiencing population growth and some of that growth came from the migration of residents from the Carson City and Storey County areas. So many unemployed workers had moved into the city of Reno in the summer of 1890, that the following caption appeared in a local newspaper, "Reno is overrun with tramps."[4] Gold and silver production from the Comstock Lode, after staging resurgence at the end of the 1880s, began another decline. Within five years only minimal supplies of lower grade ore would be coming out of the mines.

Because of the passage of the *Sherman Silver Purchase Act*, the U.S. Treasury practically guaranteed that they would purchase every ounce of silver produced by silver mine owners. This bill stated that at least 4.5 million ounces of silver would be purchased on a monthly basis. If that quota did not encompass the output from mines, more silver could be purchased at the discretion of the Secretary of the Treasury and the Director of the Mint. From these enormous amounts of silver, at least two million silver dollars were required to be minted on a monthly basis.

A winter scene in downtown Carson City. Snow piled up on the sides of the streets, and in the spring they would turn to mud. (*Courtesy Nevada State Museum*)

[1] *San Francisco Chronicle*, May 15, 1890.
[2] Speech by Senator John P. Jones to Congress, 1890.
[3] *Lyon County Times*, July 19, 1890.
[4] Ibid.

Trains were used as snowplows during heavy winter storms and sometimes would get derailed.

Now operating full time, the Carson City Mint was coining its share of the country's silver dollars in 1890. The total mintage figure of 2,309,041 is the highest in the history of the Carson City Morgan dollars; only the second year of 13 (1878 the other) that two million or more were produced at the mint. However, a *tale of two cities* continued to illustrate the distinction between the Philadelphia Mint, and the one in Carson City. To no one's surprise, the country's first mint struck more than seven times as many silver dollars in 1890 as did its unrefined *stepbrother* mint, out in Nevada. An 1890 population census estimated that there were over one million people living in the city of Philadelphia at the time. Whereas, the entire state of Nevada had fewer than 46,000 residents in 1890, less than 10% of them, living in Carson City.

SILVER'S BIGGEST CLIENT

The Treasury was paying an average of 92 cents an ounce for silver purchased during the years the Sherman Act was in force. The cap on what they would pay was $1 per ounce. Anywhere close to this amount was all right with the owners of the silver mines, as prices for silver may have plummeted below 50 cents per ounce without a customer like the federal government. Approximately 86% of the silver being purchased in the 1890s was used to mint silver dollars, the remainder was used to produce silver bars, and dimes, quarters and half dollars. Massive stockpiles of all denominations of silver coins accumulated in the Mint's vaults. Sellers received Treasury notes for their silver, attractive pieces of paper money often referred to as Coin Notes. They were issued in denominations of $1, $2, $5, $10, $20, $50, $100, and $1000

and stated that the United States would pay the bearer the face value amount in coin. The type of coin paid was originally left up to the request of the bearer at the time of redemption. As it became evident to the Treasury that the majority of redemptors were asking for gold coins, the policy shifted and it was left to the sole discretion of the Secretary of the Treasury which type of coins would be issued. These Coin Notes themselves were used commonly for commercial purposes. There are only two years in the Treasury Note series, 1890 and 1891; more than $155 million in face value of the notes were issued during the years of the Sherman Silver Purchase Act.

The Sherman Act was a stopgap solution to quiet dissenting voices shouting from the rooftops in western silver states. At the same time, there needed to be assurance that nothing would disrupt commerce. There was always the risk that gold coins would be hoarded and disappear from circulation, since people favored them over silver coins. If this occurred, the silver coins would be heavily discounted; a situation economists describe as *Gresham's Law*, which claims that *bad money drives out good money*, and since there was no legitimate long-term plan for silver, it would be on the *endangered species* list. However, the mintage of gargantuan quantities of silver coins as the sole salvation of silver was probably not the solution.

What has the United States learned in the more than 11 decades since the Sherman Silver Purchase Act was passed into legislation? For one, the government stopped using precious metals in its coinage: the Treasury Department under its Bureau of the Mints office has not produced silver coins for circulation since 1964. But the ghosts of silver miners and the political leaders of yesteryear are whispering into the ears of 21st century spokesmen, for example those involved in the Silver Institute, founded in 1971. This nonprofit organization includes in its goals:

1. To encourage the development and uses of silver and silver products.
2. To help develop markets for silver.
3. To foster R&D related to the present and prospective uses of silver.
4. (And so on and so forth.)

The bottom line for this organization is developing new methods to improve the welfare of the silver industry.[1]

It is not within the scope of this book to take sides on the issue of free coinage, the gold standard, fiat currency, or to support the silver mining industry; that is left to wiser and more informed sources. It is the goal of this book, however, to present information relating to or coinciding with the era in which the Carson City Mint was in operation. Issues concerning precious metals, and the changes in the coinage laws of the United States, were undoubtedly as relevant to the Carson City Mint as the quarry stones in its foundational structure.

HOW THE OTHER HALF LIVES

It is entirely possible that the publicity focused on the silver and free coinage issues back in 1890 was used by political entities to conceal intrigue of a more threatening and far-reaching nature. How much was big government's intervention in business, mining and agriculture affecting the economy of the United States? As perplexing a question as this was, there were many people who felt that the laws of the nation put *rascals into robes*, and it was said that government might possibly have been in the hands of Wall Street. And Wall Street, as many pundits asserted, was in the hands of powerful economic leaders in Great Britain.

It was estimated that by 1890, 1% of the population in the United States controlled more wealth than the other 99% combined. This disparity between

Wovoka, from the Nevada Indian tribe, had a vision of the "Ghost Dance."

the nation's economic classes was exposed in a book, *How the Other Half Lives*, written by Jacob Riis, a man known for his extensive research in the slums of big cities. In his book, Riis described the miserable living conditions of thousands of people in the inner cities of U.S.

These were not the musings of a fiction writer fabricating a story; on the contrary, Riis lived with the segment of society he was illustrating in his book, and experienced firsthand the decrepit and squalor conditions. Although glamorized at times, the *Gilded Age* was rewarding to only a small segment of the population of nearly 63 million people living in the United States.

Financial crises in Great Britain and other European countries were already causing fears on Wall Street. America felt protected by the Sherman Anti-Trust Act, which was supposed to shield the common man from big business monopolies and the control of the financial elite. But like so many laws intended to protect and regulate, the Sherman Act was being enforced about as steadfastly as the *no-skimming* laws of the Nevada Gaming Commission were enforced in Nevada casinos between 1950 and 1980. So, what were the real issues? Were the men who were shaping America holding secret meetings? If tariffs, trusts, and the Treasury's tender were brought under control, would that solve all of the country's financial woes? No one knew for sure.

GHOST DANCES AND SITTING BULL

No less perplexing was the status of Native American Indians in 1890 who had observed the westward expansion of the explorers and settlers from the beginning. To them the more the nation expanded the less land the Indians possessed and by 1890, these Native Americans were confined within certain boundaries. Small groups of Indians still believed that they could win their land and freedom back. Witness one particular Paiute Indian from Nevada, named Wovoka, who claimed to have had a vision; if the members of the various tribes would participate in what came to be known as the *Ghost Dance*, the old ways would be restored, the White Man would disappear, the buffalo would return, all the dead In-

[1] Silver Institute Website, www.silverinstitute.org September 2002.

dians would be brought back to life, and the country would be put back the way it was. In response to Wovoka's vision *Ghost Dances* were held throughout the Indian reservations.

Chief Sitting Bull, having led the attack on the 7th Calvary at Little Big Horn, was murdered by Lakota Police in December of 1890. (*Dictionary of American Portraits, Dover Publications*)

The great Indian chief Sitting Bull, who had led the attack on Custer at the Little Big Horn, had lived on and off the reservations since surrendering to the U.S. Army in 1881. During his years of captivity, he did a stint in Buffalo Bill's Wild West Show in 1885 and by 1890, Sitting Bull was living at Standing Rock near the Grand River in South Dakota.

Becoming paranoid about the outcome of the *Ghost Dances*, the U.S. Army dispatched troops to raid certain Indian villages. On December 14 or 15, 1890, Lakota Police, acting as Army agents, killed Sitting Bull after dragging him out of his cabin. Three days before 1890 came to an end, U.S. troops raided a Sioux Indian camp at Pine Ridge in South Dakota on the banks of the Wounded Knee River. After the Army had disarmed the Indians, and while having a pow wow with their chief, soldiers opened fire on the surprised Indians, massacring nearly the entire camp. This, in effect, brought to an end what had come to be known as the Indian Wars. The *Ghost Dancers* virtually "Buried Their Hearts At Wounded Knee," as one 20th century author expressed it.

BELL INTRODUCES NEW TECHNOLOGY TO CARSON CITY

Back in Carson City in 1890 a modern innovation introduced a new convenience to the locals. To provide a little background, the story begins before Nevada became a state. Inventor, Alexander Graham Bell, had developed his new telephone apparatus while living in Boston at the same time the *Big Bonanza* was lifting activities in the Comstock region of Nevada to a crescendo. Prior to that, in 1861, Samuel F. B. Morse's telegraph network had connected the American continent for the first time. Morse's first telegraphic message, a short verse from the book of Numbers in the Bible, had been sent from Washington, D.C. to Baltimore in 1844. Twenty years later, in October of 1864, at the telegraph office in Carson City, Alexander Bell's cousin Francis Jardine (Frank) Bell tapped out half of the longest telegram in history, that regarding Nevada's statehood. But, by the time the telephone was patented, Morse had already passed away.

Mr. Bell also had the privilege and honor of placing the first residential phone call in Nevada. Telephones first appeared in the state in 1878 when lines had been run from the mills and mine shafts to the mining company's offices a mile away in Virginia City. Bell's famous cousin Alexander sent the new telephone equipment with instructions in 1890, and from his house in Carson City, Frank Bell phoned the editor of the *Nevada State Journal*, C.C. Powning, in Reno, officially launching phone service in Nevada.

Frank Bell had served as state prison warden and justice of the peace, and in 1889 was appointed Lieutenant

CONNECTICUT YANKEE IN A GILDED AGE

Another observer of westward expansion was Mark Twain. The renowned American author had crisscrossed the United States many times, and had also traveled abroad on numerous occasions. Twain had been there in the early 1860s when Nevada was being born and could look back 30 years from the vantage point of 1890, summarizing events that brought America to where it was at that time. Smartly tinged with realism in his writings, Twain was not known for making observations with the help of rose-colored glasses.

His novel, *A Connecticut Yankee In King Arthur's Court* had been published in 1889, and was experiencing a broad distribution in 1890. In this story, a confident Connecticut local from the late 19th century by the name of Hank Morgan, travels to Camelot England to the court of King Arthur. Living vicariously through this character, Mark Twain had often in other places described himself as hav-

ing Missouri morals and Connecticut culture, which in his opinion made him the *perfect man.* In *Connecticut Yankee* he exposes the frivolities of both ages he is writing about: the *Age of Chivalry*, and the *Gilded Age*. Twain's protagonist, Morgan, in a moment of frustration, says, "Well there are times when one would like to hang the whole human race and finish the farce."

The year 1890 proved to be filled with trials for Mark Twain: his mother died, leaving a void in his life, and he made a fateful investment in a new business that manufactured automatic typesetting machines. Faced with the failure of this business Twain would be forced to leave his beloved Connecticut home the following year and spend the next decade on the lecture circuit in Europe recovering from financial losses. Through it all, his homespun prose and rhetoric delighted readers and audiences around the world.

Governor of Nevada when S. Chubbuck resigned. Bell became governor later in 1890, when gubernatorial incumbent C. Stephenson fell ill and eventually died. Frank Bell would only serve from September of 1890 until the next governor was inaugurated following the November elections, but his short term was not uneventful.

Frank Bell, relative of inventor Alexander Graham Bell and later Governor of Nevada.

C.C. Powning, editor of the *Reno Gazette Journal*, received the first residential phone call from Carson City in 1890.

Technology may have been ushering Carson City into the modern age, but politics seemed as old-fashioned as ever. The Republicans swept the November elections held in Nevada in 1890; all of the laws, bills, amendments, debates and elections on the political front, had serious effects on the state, both positive and negative.

After the passage of the Sherman Silver Act, the price of silver rose to its highest levels in many years, at one point, poised to break the $1.20 barrier. General Manager of the V&T Railroad, Henry M. Yerington, in a letter to Senator Stewart, gave his optimistic approval to the appearance of success.

"You have no idea," wrote Yerington, "how much the present rise in silver has helped Nevada. New mines are being opened daily, and everybody feels that there is a great, big future."[1]

There was guarded optimism, and hearts full of hope in northern Nevada at the end of 1890 as the general public trusted silver might once again be the panacea necessary to cure all its economic ills.

But by the end of the year, the price of silver had dropped below one dollar again, hitting 98 cents per ounce, and there was devastating news from London in December, when it was reported that one of England's largest financial institutions, the Baring Brothers, had gone into default. Because of the heavy investments this firm had in South America, as well as the United States, sellers on Wall Street panicked. Financial markets worldwide seemed to be on a collision course and the failure of the Baring Brothers would prove to be a trembler, a warning of monetary earthquakes to follow. Political leaders in Nevada would soon be choreographing their own *Ghost Dance* in hopes of bringing back the old ways.

Telephone service in Carson City was indeed welcomed with excitement, but who would there be to call for answers to indefinable economic problems? Of utmost priority to workers at the Carson City Mint was the perpetuation of coinage operations at their facility.

THE "CC" MINTAGE OF 1890

Approximately 25 pairs of silver dollar coin dies had been shipped to the Carson City Mint from Philadelphia in 1890; based on the average number of coins struck using each set of dies there, this would have facilitated the production of approximately 1.5 million silver dollars that year. Activity was indeed brisk at the Nevada mint in 1890 and because of the increased output ordered by the Director of the Mint, Carson City was averaging close to 100,000 silver dollars per die pair.

At some point during the year, one of the reverse dies must have accidentally been gouged on the lower left area, near where the bottom arrow feather slants downward toward the leaves in the wreath. There is no official explanation for how it happened, but the die gouge caused a raised strip of metal, visible to the naked eye, connecting the arrow feather with the leaves. It is called the *Tail Bar* variety, and is one of the more extreme die characteristics in the Morgan silver dollar series. In the pamphlet entitled *Top 100 VAM Keys*, it is suggested that the 1890-CC Tail Bar silver dollar is more common than often thought, listing the coin's price at approximately 20% higher than a common example of the same date. That might be mis-

Copyright, 1889.

"Hello! Hello!! Hello!!!"
— "Well; what is it?"
"How is your mother, this morning?"
— "Very much better; she had a real restful sleep last night; she is almost rid of her night-sweats, cough and nervousness, and is growing quite cheerful. How grateful we all are to you for that bottle of medicine."
"Don't speak of gratitude. What does the doctor say?"
— "He says he never saw so wonderful a change in such a serious lung trouble. He still thinks we are giving his medicines. I don't like to tell him."
"That's right. He's an old friend, you know. I'm sure your mother will get well now; but you won't forget the name of the medicine, will you?"
— "Never! Dr. Pierce's Golden Medical Discovery" are household words already, and it has come to stay. Do come and see what sunshine it has brought already, and let us thank you again for it."
"I will. Good bye."
    The foregoing is a fair representation of a very common occurrence. "Golden Medical Discovery" has cured severe, lingering coughs and arrested Consumption, or Lung-scrofula, in thousands of cases after doctors have failed and other medicines have been tried and abandoned as useless. The "Discovery" is guaranteed to benefit or cure in every case, if taken in time and given a fair trial, or money will be refunded.

Locals in Carson City were discovering new uses for the telephone recently introduced. In this ad from the *Carson Appeal* in 1890, a woman tells her friend about the benefits of "Golden Medical Discovery."

---

[1] Letter from Henry M. Yerington to Sen. William M. Stewart, William M. Stewart Papers, Nevada Historical Society, Reno, Nevada.

Close-up of the reverse on a 1890-CC "Tail Bar" variety silver dollar. Note the strip of raised metal extending from the arrow feathers to the wreath.

leading, since population and census reports from PCGS and NGC reveal that only 1% of 1890-CC silver dollars have received the *Tail Bar* designation through 2003. This may be due to the fact that the two grading services only recently began attributing VAM (Van Allen Mallis) varieties. Regardless, a high-grade specimen of this variety would probably command much more than a 20% premium if offered on the market, and even circulated examples rose sharply in demand during the early years of the 21st century.

Increased pressure to redeem the new Treasury Notes issued to purchase silver under the Sherman Act, combined with export demand, most likely caused higher gold coin mintages at the Carson City Mint in 1890. As a result, production of 1890-CC $20 gold double eagles tripled from the abbreviated output of 1889, as 91,209 pieces were struck, the fourth highest mintage in the series. In *Gold Coins of the Carson City Mint*, Doug Winter concurs that this date is one of the easiest of all "CC" double eagles to locate.

In denominations less than $20, there were 17,500 1890-CC $10 gold eagles minted after a five year gap for this denomination at the Carson City Mint. Though certainly not a common date, it is one of the most readily available in the "CC" gold eagle series. Production also resumed on the $5 gold half eagles after a five year break; out of the 53,800 1890-CC $5 gold pieces minted, a fair number have survived in Choice to Gem Uncirculated condition. In fact, this date is one of only five from the Carson City half eagle series that boasts specimens graded MS-65 or higher by either of the two major grading services.

All tallied, the face value of 1890-CC gold coins produced was $2,268,180, nearly equivalent to that of the 1890-CC silver dollars minted. The scales may have appeared to be balanced between the two metals, but as many silver supporters believed, it might have been time to test those scales.

The steadfast, trustworthy, and loyal employees and neighbors of the Carson City Mint had completed a successful year. In other parts of town, a new United States Post Office was under construction a couple blocks south of the mint and things looked positive for the residents of Carson City, at least for the time being. It was probably the furthest thing from former funeral director and now Mint Superintendent Sam Wright's mind as 1890 came to a close, that he might be in the early stages of preparing the city's pride and joy for its burial.

For more information on silver and gold coins from 1890, please see Chapter 6, *The Silver Coins*, and Chapter 7, *The Gold Coins*.

THE AMERICAN SPIRIT AND NELLIE BLY

The United States has always been a resilient country. Its political leaders might have been stabbing the citizenry in the back, burdening them with legislation that resulted in higher prices and lower wages, and certain segments of society might have been ignored or even abused, evidenced by everyone not possessing equal opportunities to achieve success; but in spite of adversities, improprieties, and inequities, the American spirit could not be conquered.

That indomitable spirit inspired inventors, small business owners, land rushers, ranchers, farmers, athletes, writers, entertainers, enlisted men and women and officers, doctors, scientists, ministerial staff and their faithful, and all those who pursued the American Dream. At the end of a hard day, a hard week, a hard month, the time came to step off the treadmill and take a break from labor. Americans have always loved diversionary forms of leisure-time activities, and the adventure and frolic of the last decade of the 19th century, fostered many recreational opportunities and bred daring heroes to emulate and adore.

People seeking excitement could live vicariously through these heroes who captured their imaginations. Nellie Bly (nee Elizabeth Cochrane Seaman) became the "people's hero" in 1890 when her book, *Around the World in Seventy Two Days* appeared on bookshelves. Miss Bly had first grabbed headlines in 1887, with the publication of *Ten Days in a Madhouse*, in which she described her experiences when she had voluntarily checked into a clinic for the mentally ill. The *Around the World* book turned to a merrier subject more suited to thrill seekers, and those wanting to escape the drudgeries of life. It told the true story of Nellie Bly's successful trip around the world, breaking the fictional record set by Phileas Fogg in Jules Verne's *Around the World in Eighty Days*, published in the year of *The Coinage Act of 1873*.

1891

SAN FRANCISCO FLOURISHES AT NEVADA'S EXPENSE

In 1859, when mining prospectors struck *pay dirt* on the Comstock, there were fewer than 500 people living on the land that would become Carson City. That year, the *City by the Bay*, San Francisco, had just reached the 50,000 mark, growing from a population of approximately 1,000 people in the years following the gold rush. The Comstock/Mother Lode/San Francisco connection linked many from the same cast of characters for decades, as prominent men from California made fortunes in Nevada's mining regions and then poured their wealth into the development of San Francisco. William Sharon had moved from San Francisco to Virginia City in the mid-1860s, where he amassed a fortune and was able to purchase the position of U.S. Senator. William Ralston established a branch of his San Francisco based Bank of California in Virginia City in the 1860s, commanding much power before his untimely death in 1875.

Linking the two states in another way, the most popular journalist of his day, Mark Twain, offered his talents to newspapers from northern Nevada to the Pacific Ocean, until opting to expand his horizons to other states and lands.

The *Silver Kings,* (Mackay, Fair, Flood and O'Brien, whose company was known as the *Firm*), commuted between the Comstock and San Francisco frequently. John Mackay and James Fair had been living in the northern Nevada mining region when the business was formed and the Virginia City office was referred to as *Fair and Mackay.* William O'Brien and James Flood were stockbrokers in San Francisco, and the *Firm's* branch in that city was known as *Flood and O'Brien.* Adolph Sutro, builder of the Sutro Tunnel, transferred his wealth to San Francisco, where he eventually became the mayor of the city, and at one time was estimated to own one twelfth of the available land there.

Beginning in 1849, San Francisco had been built upon the prosperity of the California Gold Rush, and in 1854, the U.S. Mint opened a branch there. During this first growth period in San Francisco, northern Nevada was considered nothing more than a passage into California's gold fields. After the Comstock Lode began to thrive, San Francisco's growth exploded; the gold rush and the Comstock Lode were the one-two punch that a city with San Francisco's bountiful natural resources and strategic location needed.

By 1891, San Francisco's population had passed the 300,000 mark, approximately six and one half times that of the entire state of Nevada. Northwestern Nevada's population at the time, was less than 23,000, and Carson City's population continued to decline, hovering around the 4,000 level. Nevada's prosperous mining industry magnates apparently had never intended to keep the bountiful wealth they were acquiring within the boundaries of the state. Other than precious metals, Nevada had undeveloped natural resources including Lake Tahoe on its western border and the territory east of the Truckee Meadows, prime for reclamation and development of thriving communities. These assets were ignored, as money from the mines went instead to California and other locales, domestic and abroad. It would be the next century before visionaries like Norman Biltz prevailed upon the state's businessmen to use their revenues to finance statewide agricultural, business, mining and irrigational development. It was not until Nevada's next cycle of mining production, which began a decade after the Comstock mines had been used up, that the men in power began filtering more profits back into the state. Towns like Tonopah and Goldfield would become the centers for new discoveries of mineral ore.

From 1900, when annual yields from Nevada's mines were approximately $2 million, another rally brought annual yields to nearly $50 million by World War I. With more of the returns remaining in the state, a 100-year growth cycle had begun in Nevada. Ironically, an interesting reversal in the relationship between Nevada and California would occur in the second half of the 20th century, when California furnished the capital and the occupants to foster Nevada's growth. However, in 1891, it did not appear that more than a faithful fragment of the mining industry cared one way or the other about the future of Nevada.

SAMUEL P. DAVIS AND THE PRO-SILVER PRESS

Samuel Post Davis was born in 1850 to a preacher's family in Connecticut. His family wanted him to go into the ministry, and while he had a quick mind and could articulate his thoughts well, he had other ideas. He gravitated toward journalism, and during his high school years, worked at local newspapers. His family brought him to California in 1872, and Sam immediately found work at newspaper offices around the Bay Area. Excited about the news he heard about the Comstock region of Nevada, he moved to Virginia City in 1873 and worked as a staff writer for the *Territorial Enterprise*. In 1879 at the age of 29, Sam Davis moved to Carson City and took the reins at the city's leading newspaper, becoming editor of the *Nevada Appeal* and marrying the widow of the *Appeal's* deceased editor, H.R. Mighels.

By 1891, Samuel P. Davis had served 12 years as head of one of the Comstock's leading newspapers and his feature articles were dispatched across the nation, due to their relevance in the battle between the *Silverites* and the *Goldbugs*. Davis inherited the genes of his sermonizing father, and was known for his oratorical and journalistic abilities when roaring from the silver platform's pulpit. Just like preachers in churches would read judgmental words from the Bible to their pew squeezing parishioners, Davis' convicting discourses aimed at the anti-silver transgressors, cut like a two-edged sword through their arguments.

Samuel P. Davis, editor of the *Carson Daily Appeal,* and Nevada State Controller. In 1913 he published his monumental tribute to his state, *The History of Nevada.*

While the *Carson (Nevada) Appeal* reported on other topics besides silver and free coinage, it was pro-silver, pro-Republican all the way; there was nothing lukewarm about it. In 1913, Sam Davis published his 1,280 page tribute to his adopted state, *The History of Nevada.* With the assistance of guest writers and scores of contributors, Davis was able to provide many eyewitness accounts of the people, the politics, the industries, the agriculture and the grandeur of Nevada. Without a doubt, the story of the Comstock Lode was given preferential treatment in the set. The pre-release of *The History of Nevada* was in observance of the state's 50th anniversary. In the preface, Davis keenly remarked that so much had happened in five decades. "It would be hard to find a state with a more eventful record of action and development compressed into the short period of fifty years..." Davis concludes in an autobiographical nature, "... the proud Sagebrusher who has learned to love the rugged mountains, the azure sky and the mysterious solitudes of his country, this history means so much."[1]

Roswell K. Colcord Takes Office

In one of newly elected Nevada Governor Roswell K. Colcord's first speeches after taking office in 1891, he predicted that the 1890 Sherman Silver Purchase Act would boost Nevada's economy.[2] Governor Colcord was inaugurated on January 15, 1891. He was another New England transplant, lured to the western mining camps in search of adventure and riches. While living in the mining town of Aurora in California, in the early 1860s, Colcord met young Mark Twain (Sam Clemens at the time), and the two formed a friendship. In 1863, Twain was a staff reporter in Virginia City, and Roswell Colcord was a mining engineer in the same area. The future governor accumulated knowledge of the essential issues facing the pro-silver forces and the mining industry and later, while serving as Nevada's leader, Colcord, together with others would be involved in one of the most critical contests in the long running battle. He was the presiding governor in 1893 when coinage ceased at the Carson City Mint and in 1898, after leaving office, Colcord was appointed superintendent of the mint, following in the footsteps of another one of Nevada's former governors Jewett W. Adams. In 1899 it would be Colcord who turned off the lights and closed the doors for the last time on the village mint's status as a coinage facility; but that's getting ahead of the story.

Free Coinage, A Panacea?

After a short holiday recess, Nevada Senators Jones and Stewart mounted their charge in January 1891 to insure that silver from Nevada's mines remained in the pocket of every American. One of their chief opponents, E.H. Conger, Congressman from Iowa, had resigned his office at the end of 1890, to accept a diplomatic position. Although a Republican, Conger had bolted from the silver platform, launching what Nevada newspapers described as "vicious attacks on western free coinage advocates..." He described the western silverites and miners as being vile, base, and exceedingly mercenary and, in 1890s parlance, accused the western mining industry of "sordidness."[3] Unabashedly supporting their side's cause, Sam Davis, in the Carson City *Morning Appeal,* expressed the urgency of a much-needed victory, when he wrote:

> The remonetization of silver concerns this state more than any and all other questions of an economic character now before the people. It means prosperous times, employ-

---

[1] Samuel P. Davis, ed., *The History of Nevada* (Nevada Publications, 1913).

[2] *Carson Appeal*, January 20, 1891.

[3] *Lyon County Times*, July 5, 1890.

ment for thousands, and a home market for the products of the farm and dairy [industries].[1]

Farmers and ranchers in the Midwest considered Nevada newspaper articles manifestos and calls to duty. A union existed between all Americans who derived their income from the country's natural resources. Farmers wanted a guarantee that next year's crop would hold its value. Ranchers worried that their grazing land would depreciate, combined with a decline in livestock prices, leaving them unable to make loan payments. Silver miners, of course, were fearful that the bottom would fall out of that market, forcing mine closures, and massive stockpiles of their product. The solution to these concerns, according to the silverites, was the re-enactment of free coinage. Veritably, the absence of a free coinage system, in the opinion of *Sagebrushers, Comstockers, Bimetallists and Silverites*, presented several oppressive dangers:

1. That corruption in government and big business would continue affording unethical men the opportunity to use their power for illegitimate goals.

2. Robber barons, corrupt political bosses, and miserly marketeers, would ally to intrude upon the property, possessions and rights of the masses.

3. The bankers, lenders, insurance companies, and the business magnates financing them, could control how much money was in circulation. These "financial magnates who, in a back room, corner the money of the world," as referred to by a staunch political advocate of free coinage,[2] would have the capability to set the value of money. They could use the flow of money like a spigot, turning it off or on, depending on their needs. If it was in their interests, money could become scarcer, resulting in higher costs for it, in the form of interest rates.

Free coinage supposedly would shift control of the country's monetary system from the clutches of the bank crowd, into the hands of the masses. Perpetual increases in the money supply would cause interest rates to fall, lowering the costs of borrowing money, making it easier to pay off loans. But if such results were beneficial, they might have also proven to be detrimental; it may have been overlooked by supporters of free coinage that expanded money supplies would have an inflationary effect on the nation's economy, as *cheaper* money being used to make loan payments would correspondingly lessen the value of goods and services. That may have been a trade off worth accepting to preserve liberty and insure the revocation of the power of the minority financial elite. Citizens represented by *silverites* and the proponents of free coinage unwillingly trusted political leaders, but at least political leaders could be controlled to some degree through the voting process. On the other hand, the working/labor/debtor class totally distrusted the banking elite, realizing that the bankers were exempt from the control of the electorate; the only hope was if the public's political leaders regulated the bankers. More than anything else, the free coinage issue seemed to be about who was in control, and often other powerful forces would merge with the bank crowd for the common goal of achieving even more control.

RUNNING ON RAILROAD TIME

Railroads had connected the United States from border to border by 1891, resulting in expansion and economic growth unparalleled in human history. There was a price to be paid, as is so often the case, as the heartland of America became dependent on railroads to transport crops and goods. The men who controlled the railways raised their freight charges to disproportional levels, and farmers and merchants, faced with no alternative, mortgaged their farms and businesses based on the credit of future crop and merchandise output. The same held true for mining operators, often forced to take out liens on future bullion production. Conversely, big corporations received discounted freight charges, making it difficult for small businessmen to compete, often resulting in bankruptcies and foreclosures.

The U.S. Post Office in Carson City was constructed in the early 1890s. This is the yard where bricks were stored for many such projects. (*Courtesy Nevada State Museum*)

---

[1] *Carson Morning Appeal*, December 1891.
[2] William Jennings Bryan, Cross of Gold speech, 1896.

Big business, railroad companies, and banks were positioned to capitalize on the misfortunes of the less powerful, while at the same time, politicians knew who held the key to their own political futures. Forthrightly, the railroads were extremely generous to the senators and congressmen in their regions and state and federal legislative offices were staffed with strong voices that boldly spoke up for the rights of the railroads. Sessions in Congress could have easily been divided into four groups: the *Banking Men;* the *Big Corporation Men;* the *Railroad Men;* and finally, the *Everyone Else Men,* representing the smallest group, including farmers, miners, and small businessmen. A persistent question being asked was, "Who was running America?"

A simple answer to that question was not available; but a possible hint was provided by how clocks were set in different parts of the country. It was clear that the U.S. was on "Railroad Time" both figuratively and literally, ever since time zones had been established in the 1880s to keep the national time in synch with railway schedules. By 1891, there were more than 200,000 miles of railway track across the nation. The combined wealth and power of the railroads, Wall Street, and the banks, monopolized America as never before, not to mention, more than 50% of the investment capital financing American railroads was estimated to be coming from Europe. Without question, the benefits of the railroad to the country were abundant, but the *Everyone Else Men* (including those from Nevada), occupying the small space afforded them in the halls of Congress were concerned about the trade offs.

Some Winds of Change

It would be a stretch to say that there was revolution in the air whiffing past the Nevada Capitol building in 1891, but the Republican Party had almost worn out its welcome in Nevada. President Harrison's loyalty to the issues of free coinage and the protectionism of silver had faded, and Senators Jones and Stewart were realigning their party affiliations by the early 1890s. The congratulatory sentiments Senator Jones had conveyed to Harrison after the election victory in 1888 had turned to resentment by 1891, and Senator Stewart became venomous in his attacks against what he considered the President's betrayal. Someone needed to be blamed for turning Nevada's number one product into junk metal, and local newspapers in the Carson City vicinity ran articles aimed at rallying voters to bolt from the Republican Party.

The towns and citizens around the Comstock were full of commotion in 1891; it was in that year, the "Edi-

torial Association of Nevada met at Reno, and passed a resolution stating that it would have nothing to do with any political party that did not include in its platform a plank demanding the free and unlimited coinage of silver."[1] Local papers refused to run the public service announcements sent by major political parties, an unprecedented act in journalism. Frederick Fairbanks, the editor of the *Lyon County Times,* believed that actions spoke louder than words, and founded the first Silver Club in Nevada. Members of the club shared concerns and proposed solutions about the silver issue.

How Can You Tell When a Politician is Lying

Rhetoric is the backbone of political maneuvering, the persuasive use of language to influence the thoughts and actions of listeners. It was axiomatic that Nevada's Senators and other legislators had a notorious track record of abusing their elected privileges for self gain, while the state's newspapers used their position to serve as watchdogs to refute the reckless rhetoric of politicians who acted irresponsibly. William Sharon, for instance, had achieved great success during his career in business and politics, but he was also an object of great derision in the Comstock area. When Sharon began his campaign for the Senate in 1872, Joe Goodman, editor of the *Territorial Enterprise* in Virginia City, showed absolutely no respect for the man, when he wrote concerning Sharon:

> You are probably aware that you have returned to a community where you are feared, hated, and despised. Your career in Nevada for the past nine years had been one of merciless rapacity. You fostered yourself upon the vitals of the state like a **hyena**, and woe to him who disputed with you a single coveted morsel of your prey. You cast your honor, honesty, and the commonest civilities aside....[2] (Emphasis added)

John P. Jones defeated Sharon in that election, despite the latter's smear campaign. But Sharon was able to buy a victory in the next senate race held in 1874, and served from 1875 to 1881, as for some reason, Senator Stewart had stepped out of that election. It appeared Stewart was simply accommodating William Sharon, because after Sharon's death in 1885, Senator Stewart had maintained a close business relationship with Will Sharon, the senior Sharon's nephew. There seemed to be something not quite right with this affiliation. For it was self-

[1] Davis, *The History of Nevada.*
[2] Irving Stone, *Men to Match My Mountains: The Opening of the Far West, 1840-1900.*

evident that the younger Sharon's allegiance was with the Central Pacific Railroad (by 1891, the Southern Pacific), and he used the political genes inherited from his uncle to manage the campaign of his second cousin, Francis G. Newlands, the husband of William Sharon's daughter.

Senator Stewart had been chief counsel for Collis P. Huntington, who was the leader of the *Big Four* owners of the Central Pacific Railroad, a quartette which also included Charles Crocker, Mark Hopkins, and Leland Stanford. Stewart's campaign was managed by Charles "Black" Wallace, known throughout northern Nevada as a master of rhetoric, and political scheming. Huntington's empire with its railroads was well represented in Nevada's political system by Stewart, Wallace, Newlands, and Will Sharon. Senator Jones from Nevada, while still aspiring to live up to press releases calling him the *Silver Senator,* winked an affirmative eye at Huntington and those under his control. Huntington's philosophy could be summed up in a compact sentence, "Everybody do as they're told, and nobody will get hurt"; politicians knew that to expect his support they would have to bow to his rules.

The railroad system connecting America was at one time referred to as the single greatest achievement (after the Declaration of Independence) in the country's history: Western states expanded, new markets were opened for farmers and ranchers, and travel became safer. But the railroad's contribution to society was not the issue; instead, the backlash came from the nefarious deeds of those who ran them. Collis P. Huntington, for instance, was congratulated to his face, but cursed behind his back; and contemporary as well as later historians chose their words carefully when describing one of the wealthiest men in history. Was Huntington a pal, a good sport, a favorite guest, a popular neighbor, and everyone's choice for being the most gracious person? Try again. A quote from *The Big Four,* by Oscar Lewis, provides a commonly shared assessment of Collis P. Huntington. "[He] was a hard and cheery old man, with no more soul than a shark."[1] It was also said that Huntington, "despised all men who sought public office as [being] exhibitionists, easily and cheaply bought."[2]

Nevada's politicians in the 1890s were faced with the challenge of convincing voters that they were not hirelings of men like Huntington.

Pause for a second and consider this familiar joke: How can you tell when a politician is lying? Answer: When his lips are moving, obviously. Now consider the vexing contradiction of how if Nevada's senators were fighting for the rights of the common man, holding the issues of silver and free coinage on banners high above their heads, could they have supported the railroad industry at the same time?

The emerging political electorate that would become the *People's Party* or the *Populist Party,* believed *silverite* senators were on their side. These *Populists* demanded that railroads be regulated as they believed that the railroads, as well as bankers and big corporations, were using their wealth to take advantage of small businessmen and consumers. An observer of the times, writing in 1941, summarized the effect the railroad had on Nevada:

> From 1870 on, the railroad **vampires**, sucked Nevada like an orange, gave nothing much in return, and kept the state needlessly a desert, in order to keep other railroads from coming west to gobble at the rich spoils of California.[3] (Emphasis added)

Questions linger concerning the veracity of the government's role in providing protection to the populace against corporate powers during the 19th century. Not wanting to open a *Pandora's Box* of conspiracy theories, perhaps it is not as audacious as one might think to suggest that the silver and free coinage issues were concocted by 19th century spin-doctors, used as seemingly valid causes, but simply camouflaging more serious plots and schemes of a diabolical oligarchy, whose goal was ultimate power and control. Was it indeed possible that a wry, eloquent and persuasive senator or congressman could be a bit delusive, a man on the take, or an outright ingratiating fraud? When ethics are cast aside, anything is possible.

The year 1891 would prove to be very decisive in the infrastructure of Nevada's political process, and the following year would bring more rhetoric and irregularities to the national conventions and elections. A vulnerable public could only hope and trust that it would not be plundered as the issues of railroads, irrigation and reclamation, and of course, whether silver would be remonetized, smoldered in the volcanic political epicenter.

As always, it was the goal of businesses to make a profit, and political leaders invariably supported business leaders in pursuit of that goal. Accordingly, business leaders returned favors, and supported the politicians, with the object being two-way maneuvering so each side got

---

[1] Ibid.
[2] Ibid.
[3] Richard G. Lillard, *Desert Challenge: An Interpretation of Nevada;* "The Desert Challenge."

what it wanted and no one got hurt. For some reason, however, protecting people from getting hurt was a big challenge.

DEATH OF WILLIAM WINDOM

While delivering a speech before the New York Board of Trade, Secretary of the Treasury William Windom dropped dead on January 29 1891, prematurely ending his appointed term. Windom had been very vociferous in his views on silver and free coinage, careful not to upset big corporations and the bank crowd with his decisions. This offended many, who felt it was his duty to protect the nation's monetary system, regardless of political, personal, or business affiliations. President Harrison himself was accused by *Populists* and *Silverites* of reneging on his platform promises from the 1888 election. In an effort to appease, Harrison spent many mind wrenching sessions with Windom, as they tried to find a solution that would satisfy all sides, but Windom was gone, and Harrison continued to waffle.

Secretary of the Treasury Charles Foster, friend of the bank crowd and Europe's financial elite, before he met financial ruin.

Windom's proposal for a new Mint building in Philadelphia to meet the needs of the increasing production of silver coins was introduced three weeks after he died. Legislation passed in March of 1891, and construction plans proceeded the following year. To honor Windom for his contributions, the president signed an order to use the ex-Secretary's portrait on a $2 silver certificate. These notes were part of the selection of denominations in the silver certificate series, being used to represent all the silver dollars minted under the Sherman Act of 1890.

Members of the blossoming Silver Party had not been comfortable with Windom's policies; so just as they had with President Harrison, they had urged Windom before he died to get off the fence and onto their side. Teeter-tottering as far as *Silverites* and *Populists* were concerned was for children, not responsible servants in government. Surely, they felt, there must be someone on the president's cabinet courageous enough to speak up for silver and free coinage.

SECRETARY FOSTER SERVES UP
U.S. GOLD RESERVES

But if *Silverites* did not approve of Windom, they certainly were not going to be pleased with his replacement, as Charles Foster, the 40th Secretary of the Treasury, made it clear from the start that he considered the free coinage of silver too inflationary. Foster, who was appointed by President Harrison and took the helm on February 25, 1891, was a wealthy businessman with strong ties to the banking and railroad industries and also part of the Rockefeller Standard Oil Corporation. At the request of an elite group of bankers and financiers Foster attended a luxurious banquet in New York City, where his remarks to this rapacious group of control seeking men, satisfied any reservations they may have had. As noted in *The Coming Battle*, "These bank presidents at once communicated the decision of Secretary Foster to their allies in Europe... The interests of the financiers of [the U.S.] and of Europe were identical." And just what were these interests? As insidious as it may have seemed, now that they had Foster's full cooperation, "the money power matured their plans to **raid the gold reserve[s]** in the United States Treasury."[1] (Emphasis added.) Suddenly, the topic of the U.S.'s monetary system rose from a grade school level to the halls of higher learning.

Smoldering with controversy, the political and economic climate of the last quarter of the 19th century serves as a backdrop to the study of Carson City, its mint, and its coins. When the first coins proudly displaying the "CC" mintmark had been introduced to the world in 1870, no one could have foretold how the events of the next three decades would reshape and transform America. When Abe Curry was granted appropriation and completed construction on the mint in the city he helped build, he had been as jubilant as a person who opens a new hometown business. In those days, the great Civil War general, Ulysses S. Grant was in the White House and somehow things seemed secure, well taken care of, unthreatening, dependable, and possibly, more innocent. Sure there had been scandals in government before, and corruption in business, payoffs, bribes, deception, and all forms of criminal behavior at every level of society. But by 1891, American financiers and European allies were raiding the gold reserve in the U.S. Treasury! How could that have happened?

Just as the Civil War had forced the country into the furnace 30 years earlier, the nation was on the verge of

---

[1] M. W. Walbert, *The Coming Battle: A Complete History of the National Banking Money Power in the United States*, 3rd ed.

being tested by fire once again; this time not with guns and bayonets, but with manipulated monetary standards and failed political promises.

CRY FOR PROTECTION AGAINST ANTI-SILVER PREDATORS

From its earliest days, the Carson City Mint seemed to have been strategically located, right in the heart of one of the richest mineral discoveries in history. Northern Nevada back in 1870 seemed as likely to evolve into a thriving, prosperous region as any other location in the western United States. In essence, it seemed like such a simple plan: Precious metals would be mined from the Comstock Lode, and be deposited in Carson City, where they would first be assayed, and then minted into coins, or poured into ingots. This would be Nevada's way of contributing to the coinage supply of an expanding nation. But by 1891, the stakes were higher. Carson City's role in the production of coinage was tantamount in 21st century terms to the contribution a small computer clone company makes in supplying the country's demand for computers. As time passed, it would become clear that minting coins in this small peaceful town was of small concern compared to other issues facing the nation.

Nevada's politicians were sounding the battle cry for a war against the enemies of silver. The state's newspapers were devoting generous space in their pages to the cause, and citizens were volunteering to serve in the fight. Residents in the *Sagebrush State* and other western silver regions viewed the *Goldbugs* and anti-silver antagonists as predators, similar to wild coyotes. Coyotes prey upon smaller, more helpless creatures; in their natural habitat, they are satisfied with wild animals such as rabbits and squirrels. However, when coyotes enter domesticated neighborhoods they take advantage of house pets such as dogs and cats, often leaving nothing more than a small leg bone or the intestines. As a sign of dominance coyotes raise their voices in blood curdling howls. Out in the desert, the wilderness, and the prairie areas, where coyotes are a threat, households take all measures and precautions to protect their defenseless house critters from savage attacks. Like those who fear coyotes, citizens of Nevada and the other silver mining states appealed to the legislators in their districts to protect them and the silver produced in their mines that was the heart of their economy. Any threat to their means of survival needed to be fought. Howling coyotes were one thing, but the blustery barking of the bigwig banking elite was another. It was fight or be conquered.

Throughout 1891, Carson City's ceaseless commitment to the Comstock Lode continued, but the question persisted: Were Nevada's legislators sticking to their guns in defense of the silver industry? Or were they looking after their own needs, at the expense of those who elected them? Their oratory and rhetoric were impressive, but what went on behind closed doors? Free coinage of silver may have appeared to many to be a cure-all for using the inexhaustible supplies of the metal. But, might free coinage merely have been like a finger plugging a dike, or a band-aid on a bullet hole?

Let the facts speak for themselves: More than 710 million ounces of silver were extracted from below the ground between 1873 and 1891; and during that same period just over 392 million ounces had been used in silver coin production, leaving a surplus of nearly 320 million ounces. Would free coinage have absorbed it all? Not in all probability, but the banking elite enunciated its fears that western silver would smother the nation with coins, just like Nevada's *White Winter* of 1890 had buried the Sierra.

Ever since Treasury Secretary Foster had promised to redeem their currency and bonds in gold, international financiers had been aggressively stockpiling the yellow metal. These power elite swore by the "golden rule"; not the one from the Bible, but rather the one that says "he who owns the gold rules." It was often said that some of the greedier members of this group, perched high upon their seats of dominance, would, "Chase a dollar into Hell."[1] In the United States, the users, manipulators, and the self-serving, in league with this international crowd, considered the nation to be in a bull market cycle, but the bubble would eventually burst during the next couple of years, and by 1893, even many of those who were on top would have hell to pay.

SEATED LIBERTY COINAGE'S GRAND FINALE

In spite of the political and economic turmoil vexing the United States in 1891, the Treasury still fulfilled its obligation to provide an adequate coinage supply. Director of the Mint Edward O. Leech once described the nation's coins as *metallic monuments*. He commented that, "The portraits and names of the great heroes of the age in which they were struck bear unequivocal witness to the truth of the historical records which have come down to us..."[2] There had been discussion at the Treasury and the

---

[1] Lillard, *Desert Challenge*.
[2] *Annual Report of the Director of the Mint,* 1891.

Bureau of the Mint for several years concerning the need for new designs on the nation's subsidiary silver coins. In the summer of 1891 Director Leech wrote, "I have told our engravers to prepare me a set of designs for the subsidiary coins to be submitted to Secretary Foster. I shall not do anything about the dollar for some time."[1]

By the end of the year, Leech reported to Congress that, "New designs for the subsidiary coins- The half dollar, quarter dollar, and dime have been prepared, ... by Mr. Charles E. Barber, the engraver, ...and with your approval have been adopted."[2]

With new designs for silver dimes, quarters, and halves on the horizon Leech seized the opportunity to, in his words, "enumerate the changes which have been made in these particular pieces."[3] First he gave a brief summation of the fundamentals which guided coinage design decisions:

> To help make the coins of the United States worthy, from the point of view of the beautiful, of our country, at the beginning of the second century of its existence, is the object of my recommendations as to new and improved designs. In modern coinage the designs in monarchial gov-

Seated Liberty dimes from the final year of the series, one from each mint that coined them: Philadelphia, New Orleans, and San Francisco. (*Photos courtesy Bowers and Merena*)

ernments consist, as a rule, of the portrait of the sovereign for its obverse and the coat of arms or seal for the reverse, thus simplifying the question of design. Republican nations have generally ignored the idea of having the portrait of their Chief Magistrate upon their coins, but have generally used some ideal head or representative; hence our coinage laws prescribe, "Upon one side there shall be an impression emblematic of liberty, with an inscription of the word 'Liberty,' and upon the reverse shall be the figure or representation of an eagle."[4]

Then Leech described the origin of the Seated Liberty coin design, which was the only subsidiary silver coin design ever used at the Carson City Mint:

> The present obverse of the subsidiary coins first appeared on the dollar of 1836, dime and half dime of 1837, half dollar and quarter dollar of 1838, and all the silver coins of 1840. It was designed by Sulley and engraved by Mr. Christian Gobrecht. The present reverse, with the exception of some minor differences, first appeared on the half dollar of 1807, dime of 1809, quarter dollar of 1815, and half dime of 1829.[5]

After several years of designing patterns and deliberating over which design was worthy to be used for the nation's silver coinage, the Seated Liberty type ended its half-century of service in glorious style to make way for the new "Barber" coinage which made its debut the following year. In spite of the fact that there were massive stockpiles of silver coins sitting in Treasury vaults, three of the nation's four active coinage mints manufactured nearly 30 million Seated Liberty dimes, quarters, and halves in 1891. No doubt the silver industry experienced some degree of consolation from the exorbitant quantities of silver coins produced that year, as this required approximately 2.8 million ounces of silver bullion in addition to the 18.2 million ounces used to manufacture silver dollars.

Dimes accounted for the highest totals, with slightly more than 23 million pieces minted; and even the New

---

ABE CURRY'S BELATED HEADSTONE

In their July 14, 1891 issue, the *Carson Appeal* lamented that "Not a stone or monument of any kind, character or description, marks the spot where the late Abe Curry is buried at Carson."* This was a sad oversight due, in part, to Curry's insolvent financial state at the time of his death in 1873. The newspaper continued by focusing on the contribution Curry is most remembered for in the city he founded: "To him [Curry], Carson was very largely indebted for the mint, through the help given him, by the late Senator James Nye, he [Curry] was able to build that monument [The mint] that adorns Carson Street."

In concluding, as the paper made its appeal on behalf of Curry, the editorial reminded everyone that he had been: "One of the very few progressive citizens that pulled the town out of the mud in 1864 to 65." And finally, "One would think the least the city could do would be to erect a stone to his memory, if it were nothing more than a plain white slab."

Apparently in 1891, city leaders had too many other concerns on their minds to address the issue of a headstone honoring their founder and, in fact, the project would be put on the back shelf for another 73 years. Then in 1964, in concert with the 100th anniversary of Nevada's statehood, a fresh new engraved stone was placed on top of Curry's gravesite in Lone Mountain Cemetery, finally replacing the old wooden marker that had rotted many years earlier.

---

* All quotations from Doris Cerveri, *With Curry's Compliments.*

---

[1] Ibid.
[2] Ibid.
[3] Ibid.
[4] Ibid.
[5] Ibid.

Orleans Mint struck 10-cent pieces, the first time the "O" mintmark had appeared on this denomination since before the Civil War in 1860. The total number of dimes minted at New Orleans was more than double that from any other year that New Orleans minted Seated Liberty dimes. Considering that there was no logical justification for "O" mintmarked dimes in 1891, it might be fair to assume they were souvenirs for citizens near that region to have something to remember the retiring coin series by. But, if this was the reason, some might ask, "Where are the 1891-CC dimes?"

In addition to dimes, the New Orleans Mint also struck quarters in 1891, also for the first time since 1860. Although the Philadelphia Mint had been issuing limited quantities of quarters and halves every year, its Seated Liberty quarter output rose substantially in 1891, as did its half dollar production. In fact, Philadelphia's half dollar mintage of 200,600 in 1891 was more than the preceding 14 years' output combined.

It was a grand display of fervent expression by the Bureau of the Mint that year honoring the Seated Liberty coin series with a fine farewell. The chart above lists the 1891 mintage figures.

COIN PRODUCTION FOR SEATED LIBERTY COINAGE IN 1891			
	Dimes	Quarters	Halves
1891	15,310,600	3,920,600	200,600
1891-S	3,196,116	68,000	----
1891-O	4,540,000	2,216,000	----
Totals	23,046,716	6,204,600	200,600

These increased production levels of subsidiary silver coins in 1891 were offset by a steep decline in silver dollar production. In 1890, a record 38 million silver dollars had jangled out of the Treasury's coinage mints, a total which dropped off by nearly 15 million in 1891. In the midst of everything the United States was experiencing, on all fronts in 1891, the price of silver had actually increased by approximately 10%; it was nothing more than a feather in the wind, as within a few years the market would surrender that gain, and then some.

THE ANA IS FOUNDED

In the same year Seated Liberty coinage took its final bow, the most recognized coin collecting organization in the world was founded. With a name similar to the American Numismatic Society, which had been established in the year Abe Curry came to Carson with his friends (1858), the American Numismatic Association followed in the senior organization's footsteps. Dr. George F. Heath from Michigan founded the ANA to foster the collegiality of coin collectors, as he believed that sharing information and experiences was the key to fulfillment. One of the earliest members of the ANA was Augustus G. Heaton, whose *Treatise On Mint Marks* demonstrated his generosity in sharing his knowledge with fellow collectors.

THE EVOLUTION OF COINAGE

The earliest specimens of coins of which we have knowledge bore the impression of a die only on the face, the reverse showing the marks of the rude punch used to force the piece of metal into the die. The idea of relief and abrasion was never considered in connection with antique coinage. The artist indulged his fancy and taste to the fullest extent, and the coins were struck as medals are now, without regard to the amount of pressure required or the number of blows from the hammer or press necessary to perfect the impression in high relief. The coins of antiquity were for the most part like those of modern times, round, the form best suited to them.

During historical times and in civilized countries, since the first invention of coinage, gold and silver have been employed whenever governments were rich enough to obtain them. The beauty of their appearance, their rarity, and the relative stability of their value during limited periods of time, are the qualities that have insured the choice of gold and silver as the monetary metals of the world during so many centuries, and in all countries in which they have been obtainable, either by mining or in exchange for other objects of value.

With the growth of technical knowledge, and in order to meet the increased demands of trade, a proportion of base metal was added to the gold or silver, and coins now are universally manufactured with an alloy of copper. The object of mixing gold and silver with a proportion of some other metal, generally copper, in coinage, is to give the pieces greater resistance to wear and tear. This proportion is called the alloy. The proportion of pure metal in the coin is called its fineness. It has been clearly demonstrated that the proportion of nine parts of gold or silver to one part of copper best accomplishes this result.[1]

[1] *Annual Report of the Director of the Mint*, 1891.

A Tour of Carson City

All of the photographs from Carson City and the Comstock region from the 19th century are in black and white, but the area, like all real life, was very colorful. In order to get a vivid picture of what the scenery was like in 19th century Carson City and the Comstock region, it is helpful to watch episodes of old TV shows, like *Gunsmoke* and *Bonanza*. Naturally, the staging in these programs was pure Hollywood; the mock-up of Virginia City in *Bonanza* was created on the back lot of NBC Studios. Regardless, when you see the hotel, the sheriff's office, the saloon, and the streets paved with dirt, it provides you with an idea of what the locals of that bygone era saw and experienced. By 1891, Carson City was actually more developed than the communities in the *Bonanza* TV series set in the 1860s and 1870s, but the streets were still unpaved, and most of the buildings from the 1870s and 1880s remained.

Even today, if you trace the route from the south end of Carson City heading north up the main street of town (Carson Street or U.S. 395), you might begin at Jack's Bar, built in 1859 and quenching the thirsts of the first settlers in the area. Several long blocks ahead is the St. Charles Hotel, built in 1862, and one of the most elegant establishments in this old west city, serving as the main passenger stagecoach arrival and pickup. (As a side note, the St. Charles was for sale in 2003) Across the street, and about five long blocks to the north, sits the Nevada State Capitol Building, the second of Abe Curry's proudest achievements, having been built in 1871. Continuing your tour, five more blocks further north, is the former U.S. Post Office building; opened in May of 1891, and considered to be the first federal office building constructed in Nevada, at that time a sign to the locals that the federal government had not given up on them. Crossing back over to the west side of Carson Street, and several blocks up, behold the structure that inspired this book, the former U.S. Mint, now home to the Nevada State Museum. To conclude this reminiscent 2.5 mile trip back into history, you cross back over to the east side of the main road and within minutes approach the old Virginia & Truckee Railroad Depot (now a Masonic Lodge). Because of the close proximity, the mint and the depot were able to keep an eye on one another.

There are many other side tours you can take through this historically rich community that will lead you to streets named after Curry and his founding partners. In addition to street names such as Musser, and Proctor, you will discover the ones named for Curry's sisters, Elizabeth and Sophia. In addition, there are houses and other buildings once belonging to William Ormsby, Duane Bliss (Fluming Co.), Governor James Nye, Secretary Orion Clemens, Senator William Stewart, and Henry M. Yerington (from the Central Pacific); all are considered state historic sites now. Not only can today's collectors view the gold and silver coins from the Carson City Mint in lifelike color, but they can also see many of the structural reminders from the era in which the coins were minted.

Clockwise from top: U.S. Post Office in Carson City, decked out for a presidential visit in 1903. Children standing in front of Abe Curry's house in Carson City, many years after the founding father had passed away. View from the Capitol building in Carson City, looking west toward the Sierra Nevada mountain range. (*Photos courtesy Nevada State Museum*)

CARSON CITY MINT PRODUCTION FOR 1891

Remembering that the 1890-CC silver dollar series featured the curiously interesting *Tail Bar* Variety, the 1891-CC series includes a novel, though less dramatic, variety, referred to as the *Spitting Eagle*; so called because a small gouge in one of the reverse dies used that year created a tiny raised drop of metal in front of the eagle's beak. It gives the appearance of the eagle spewing something out of the crop in its throat. Although there is no record of how many of this variety were produced, it is considered to be very common, with its name being its most significant trait.

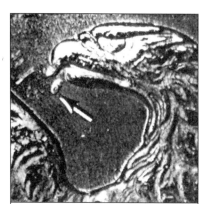

Spitting Eagle variety of the 1891-CC silver dollar.

As it had been for the previous two years since the Carson City branch had begun minting coins again, significant quantities of the 1.62 million 1891-CC silver dollars produced remained stored in that mint's vault.

Production of gold coins increased substantially at the Carson Mint from 1890 through 1891, although the face value for the two years was nearly the same. Record numbers for Carson City $5 half eagles, and $10 eagles were minted in 1891; the 208,000 $5 gold pieces produced being almost 58% of the combined total of all $5 gold pieces minted at Carson City from 1870 through 1890. The 103,732 total for 1891-CC $10 gold pieces represents the highest ever in the "CC" gold eagle series, and was equal to 42% of all those minted from 1870 through 1890. In contrast, only 5,000 "CC" $20 gold pieces were struck, representing the second lowest annual production of that denomination for the Carson City series.

FINEST KNOWN 1891-CC DOLLAR

Every silver dollar collector has his or her favorite Carson City date, and at the 1997 *Eliasberg* auction there were several "CC" dollars that were *must have* examples, for those with deep pockets. In the shadow of the 1889-CC silver dollar was an eye-popping, jaw-dropping 1891-CC. Every veteran silver dollar connoisseur present agreed that this coin deserved every bit of the cataloguer's superlatives: Written in bold above enlarged pictures of the obverse and reverse of the coin was the headline, *Marvelous Gem 1891-CC Dollar, Finest Known to Us.*[1]

And the sizzle steamed on, "Quite possibly a presentation piece.... stunning mirror like quality.... might be a branch mint proof.... This delightful coin will cause a great deal of competition, comment, and admiration."[2] Truer words could not have been spoken, as after the bidding began it was clear that a record price for this date would be established, one that would likely stand for a long time. By the time the bidding had broken the $50,000 mark, only a few brave souls hung on. At the end, there were just two fierce competitors, one outlasting the other as the final bid hit $110,000. Add another 10% for the buyer's fee, and the record price realized was $121,000, for a date available at the time in 1997 in Choice Uncirculated for $500 to $1,000.

Eliasberg 1891-CC dollar. (*Courtesy Bowers and Merena*)

This *Eliasberg* specimen was light-years above a Choice Uncirculated example, being subsequently graded by both PCGS and NGC as MS-68PL (prooflike). There is no record of a branch mint *Proof* or *Specimen Strike* of an 1891-CC silver dollar being struck; but, there is no record of 1913 Liberty nickels being struck either. In "Mint-land," anything is possible.

In the course of 10 minutes at that 1997 auction, two Morgan silver dollars struck at the Carson City Mint, had sold for $583,000, a memorable experience participants attending that *Eliasberg* auction would retain for the rest of their lives, much as spectators remember the game in which Sandy Koufax retired 27 straight; or Jerry West's half court basket as the clock ran out; or Secretariat's 31-length Belmont Stakes victory. Sales of silver dollars like 1889-CCs for $462,000 and 1891-CCs for $121,000 have a tendency to illicit emotions such as these.

[1] Bowers and Merena, *Louis E. Eliasberg, Sr. Collection*, April 1997.
[2] Ibid.

Except for $20 double eagles, Carson City's gold output had kept pace with the Philadelphia and San Francisco mints. In fact, in the $5 half eagle denomination, Carson City coined approximately 3 ⅓ times the mintage of the Philadelphia Mint, with no half eagles being minted elsewhere. In the $10 eagle series, Carson City finished the year in a virtual tie with the Philadelphia Mint, with none minted at San Francisco.

One explanation for the substantial increase in the quantities for the $5 and $10 gold pieces may have been increased exporting of U.S. gold coins in 1891 to Europe, occasioned by currency and bond redemptions from financiers on that continent. Large amounts of gold coins were sent abroad by the U.S. Treasury to supply the voracious demand of foreign depositors.

Also on a national scale, the mines in the U.S. had produced approximately 23.5 million ounces of gold between 1878 and 1891; approximately 26.6 million ounces had been used to mint gold coins during those years, slashing deeper into the nation's reserves.

Although it would be 1921 before the record output levels from 1888 to 1890 were again achieved, the Treasury and its mint network continued to produce sufficient quantities of silver dollars under the Act of 1890, with Mint records reporting that approximately $5.5 million in seniorage profit was added to the government's coffers as a result.

SILVERITES, LIKELY LONG SHOTS

Nevada is well known for gamblers betting on long shots, the house always using its edge, and eventually coming out on top. In the battle over monetary standards, there were two major opponents, the *Silverites* and the *Goldbugs*. By the end of 1891, it had become evident who the longshot bettors in the country were backing, and who was considered to be the house. During the next two years, it would be difficult to determine which side was winning at times, but when the last card was played, and the photo finish sign taken down, the longshot bettors wouldn't stand a chance.

For more information about the silver and gold coins from 1891, please see Chapter 6, *The Silver Coins*, and Chapter 7, *The Gold Coins*.

✤ 1892 ✤

I went to heaven and saw God, and all the people who had died a long time ago. God told me to come back and tell my people they must be good, and love one another, and not fight, or steal, or lie.

- From Paiute Indian Wovoka's vision, as told to James Mooney, an investigator for the Department of the Interior, in 1892.[1]

JAMES WEAVER STIRS ELECTION YEAR HOPES

Election years have a way of producing pipe dreams that will never be fulfilled and lofty promises which are never intended to be kept. For starters, how about higher prices from farm crops, lower tariff rates, eight hour work days, the common man being more powerful than corporations and bankers, and a currency system controlled by the federal government instead of the *Goldbugs* and the financial elite. Furthermore, the public owns the country's railroad system through the federal government, and the Treasury distributes millions of new silver coins into circulation, while at the same time, keeping the price of silver high.

The year was 1892, and there was actually a presidential candidate who looked voters in the eye and claimed that he could accomplish these things. That candidate was not from the Republican or Democratic parties, however. His name was James Weaver, from Iowa, and he represented the newly formed Populist Party. In the end, voters rewarded him with over one million votes and seemingly influenced the outcome of many of the political races.

WOES OF A PRESIDENT

President Harrison was afflicted with sorrows in 1892. He had lost the support of thousands of party members, an embarrassment in and of itself, considering that the Harrison family's half-century tradition in the Republican Party was well known. His grandfather, William Henry Harrison, was the ninth president of the United States, serving only one month in office before he passed away in 1841. W. H. Harrison had been a member of the Whig Party, predecessor of the Republican Party. But all of that was ancient history by 1892, and Benjamin Harrison's personal grief had surpassed his political adversities, as his wife Caroline, whom he had courted during their teenage years and had been married to nearly 40 years, was suffering from tuberculosis. Mrs. Harrison's illness grew worse as the year wore on, drawing Harrison to her bedside. With his thoughts obviously distracted, he stepped off the campaign trial. As an act of courtesy, his chief opponent Grover Cleveland limited his own public appearances during the campaign season.

Harrison had been a brave man throughout his life, serving as a brigadier general during the Civil War, and he was proud to be a member of the Republican Party that had once included Abraham Lincoln. He held deep political convictions; however, even some of his own party members were alienated from him, due to many of his policies, as well as his stiff and brusque personality, which earned him the nickname *The Human Iceberg*. Senator Stewart from Nevada (who had mildly supported Harrison in 1888) once remarked that President Harrison had, "fewer personal friends and supporters than any man who ever occupied the White House."[2] The constant criticisms, coupled with his wife's debilitating illness, wore Harrison down, leaving him fatigued and depressed by year's end. But the knockout punch would come in October when Caroline finally died, just two weeks before the election, making his loss to Cleveland anti-climatic when compared to his deeper loss.

SILVERITES AND POPULISTS SEEK SOLUTIONS

Harrison likely would not have won even if he had actively campaigned, as he was being blamed for most of the nation's setbacks. In addition, the Populist Party had undeniably had an impact on the election process. Senators Jones and Stewart from Nevada, and Henry M. Teller from Colorado, graciously extended their consolations to Harrison for his personal grief, but at the same time expressed dissension regarding their fellow Republican's "mutinous" executive decisions.

The major mining centers west of the Rocky Mountains had trusted the Republican Party to protect, defend, and support the silver market; however, the Sherman Act of 1890 had failed to produce the desired results, at least as far as the western states were concerned. Now *Silverites* were demanding that abundant quantities of silver coins and silver-backed currency be placed into circulation, while maintaining a high price for silver. In other words, they wanted an oversupply of the commodity on the one hand, resulting in an illogical increase in the value of the surplus commodity. Populist Party farmers and ranchers agreed with this strategy, as more currency in circulation would

[1] Michael S. Green and Gary S. Elliot, eds., *Nevada Readings and Perspectives*.
[2] George R. Brown, ed., *Reminiscences of Senator William M. Stewart of Nevada*.

result in higher prices for their goods and produce, meaning more money in their bank accounts, enabling them to pay debts off sooner. But then again, the only problem was that when governments print (or coin) more money to hide problems, it usually causes even more problems.

GREAT BRITAIN INFLUENCES GLOBAL DEMONETIZATION OF SILVER

Senator John P. Jones referred to silver as Nevada's "chief product."[1] The Spanish had a centuries-old tradition that professed "La plata es sangre," meaning *the silver is blood.* And the Chinese had also embraced this creed, just as many civilized nations had through the centuries. In the 400 years since the discovery of America in 1492, over 7.5 billion ounces of silver had been produced in the world, while approximately 400 million ounces of gold had been mined from the earth. In terms of the aggregate weight of the two metals, silver accounted for 95% of the total, and gold 5%. In terms of dollar value, silver represented 54 $1/2$ % of the value and gold 45 $1/2$%.[2]

Silver had indeed been the lifeblood of many countries in the world and for centuries gold and silver served side by side as stores of value, with gold always considered the more precious.

Beginning in 1867, political and economic leaders from major countries met from time to time at summits called International Monetary Conferences. Past conferences had been held in 1867, 1878, and 1881, with delegates gathering to analyze and resolve issues such as worldwide deflation, and the merits of a gold standard versus bimetallism. England had converted to a monometallic gold standard in 1816 and European nations began to follow Great Britain's leadership in the 1870s, when world silver supplies swelled. One by one foreign countries that would evolve into Euro-nations at the end of the 20th-century began converting to a gold standard: Germany in 1871; Italy, Switzerland, and Belgium in 1873; the Scandinavian Union in 1874; Norway, Sweden, Denmark and Holland in 1875; France and Spain in 1876; Austria in 1879; and Russia and India in 1893. China and Japan remained the only major powers on the silver standard by the end of the 19th century; Mexico and many Latin American nations would remain on some form of a silver standard for years.

Of course, the United States had demonetized the standard silver dollar in the Coinage Act of 1873, but the bimetallism question remained a hot topic for the remainder of the 19th century.

By 1892 the dominant financial powers in Great Britain had nearly achieved the goals of their policy making. Nations abroad kept close watch on the American silver soap opera, and English bankers like the Rothschilds, Lloyds, Barclays, and Parrs kept promoting a single gold standard. Although most of the significant monetary policies had already been decided by Great Britain and its supporting nations, the fourth and final International Monetary Conference still assembled in Brussels in November of 1892. Great Britain's representatives were the weightiest names amongst London's merchants and bankers, and their one goal was promotion of the gold standard which would guarantee their commercial and financial supremacy. The decisions brought forth at the Brussels Conference, sent a resounding message to all who favored silver coinage as a practical solution to deflationary economic times: the free coinage of silver and bimetallism would only make things worse. After all, England had been on a single gold standard for over 75 years, the attendees were reminded, and England was the most powerful nation on earth. Therefore, if a nation wanted to remain on sound footing, it should follow Great Britain's example. Following is a summary of the conclusions drawn at the end of the conference, given by Britain's Chancellor of the Exchequer:

> I may briefly recall to your recollection the history of the last International Monetary Conference which was assembled in the year 1892. The Government of the United States had taken measures to promote a conference of the European powers in order to take into consideration the condition of silver, and expressed a wish to Her Majesty's Government that a ratio might be established by the leading nations for the coinage of silver at their several mints. Mr. Goshen, while assenting to an inquiry as to the possibility of an enlarged use of silver in the currency of nations, distinctly declined to accept the invitation couched in terms which involved the adoption of a bimetallic system.

> When the conference met at Brussels the bimetallic proposals brought forward by the delegates of the United States, owing to their generally unfavorable reception, were not pressed to a division.

> At the last session of the conference an adjournment was agreed to with a view of its reassembling after an interval of six months, in order to consider some agreement (if any such could be produced) which should not infringe in any way the fundamental principles of the monetary policies of the different countries.

> It was recognized that there would be no advantage in calling the conference together again except for the purpose

---

[1] *Carson Morning Appeal*, June 10, 1892.
[2] *Annual Report of the Director of the Mint*, 1895.

of the examination of practical and explicit proposals brought forward on the responsibility of one or more of the Governments there represented, and which should conform to the condition that those proposals should not interfere with the fundamental principles governing the monetary systems of the various States.

Her Majesty's Government will not depart from the course pursued by all the Governments that have preceded them, and will give no countenance to any changes in the fundamental principles of our monetary system, nor in any discussion in which they may be called upon to take part will they admit any doubt as to their intention firmly to adhere to the single gold standard, which you justly regard as essential to our well-being as a commercial nation.[1]

Unsettling as it may have been for delegates from the *Silverite* camp, the decisions made at the conference shifted the issue of bimetallism from an international level, onto primarily American soil.

NEVADA'S STAKE IN THE FREE COINAGE DEBATE

In the United States standard silver dollars were demonetized by the Coinage Act of 1873, and for the next 27 years, the nation's position on the issue of a bimetallic monetary system would be debated, no more vigorously so than in the election years of 1892 and 1896. Many considered it an agitation, some a bothersome nuisance; to the State of Nevada and its mining industry and the mint in Carson City, it was crucial. If the free coinage of silver were reenacted, not only would it justify the Carson Mint's existence, but greater demand for silver would also revitalize mining explorations and new discoveries would sustain production levels. For as long as there was a sufficient volume of silver being supplied, portions of it would be allotted to the Nevada mint.

And future mining operations in Nevada proved that an abundance of silver was still buried below the ground even after the Comstock mines went dry, evidenced in the early years of the 20th century, when locations like Tonopah, Goldfield, Manhattan, and Berlin became Nevada's new boomtowns. However, in the 1890s, with declining silver prices and no free coinage provisions, the support and capital necessary for discovering new strikes simply did not exist. Opponents of free coinage–those who considered the matter simply agitating and annoying–did not care if Nevada ever mined another ounce of silver or of even less significance, if the Carson City Mint ever minted another coin. When finally, in 1900, the U.S. officially declared itself on the gold standard, silver producing states such as Nevada, Colorado, and Montana,

who may have considered silver to be their *chief product* or even the *blood* that flowed through the veins of their economies, were forced to begin looking in other directions for new sources of economic survival.

A REPUBLIC IS TESTED BY POWER BROKERS

Faced with political and monetary dissonance, conferences in Brussels, and debates over the free coinage of silver, most Americans living in the 1890s held firm to the belief that the United States was still a republic, meaning that the people had the right to choose their political leaders. These leaders in turn were expected to enact legislation affecting the economic, industrial, agricultural and commercial policies and serve the public interests. If political leaders were more responsive to the needs of selected groups of autocrats, the public suffered.

It should come as no surprise that the foundations upon which the republic was built were severely tested during 1892. America's big corporations, railroad companies, and banks, in harmony with power brokers in London, bought the politicians they needed in order to carry out their schemes. It goes without saying that the effects were not conducive to the fortunes of the majority of citizens in the nation. An economist writing one generation after the 1890s' calamitous string of political twists and turns described the philosophy of those who placed the public's interests below their own:

> They [*the banking elite*] viewed national interests from the windows of the bank parlour. From their point of view, industry, commerce, agriculture, wages, [*and*] employment, were but counters[2] in the skilled game of international finance. They [*the counters*] must be regulated to fit in with the monetary scheme. **The monetary scheme must not be regulated to fit the needs and necessities of the world."[3]** (Emphasis added)

A trusting public did not deserve to have their industry, commerce, agriculture, etc., used as counters in an international board game for the benefit of the powerful few. Instead they deserved the promised government: of the people, by the people, and for the people.

WHO WILL LEAD NEVADA?

From its days as a territory, Nevada had been well represented in the nation's political process, a tradition which extends to the present (2003). The seeming incon-

---

[1] *Annual Report of the Director of the Mint,* 1895.
[2] Pieces in a board game.
[3] Sir Charles Morgan-Webb, *The Money Revolution* (1935).

gruity of having a small population, but still exerting such influence earned Nevada one of its many nicknames; *The Great Rotten Borough*. Ironically, the phrase originated in Great Britain, describing any borough (political district) which contained few voters, yet retained the privilege of sending the same number of legislators to government. Senators William Stewart and John P. Jones were said to have, "equaled in ability the representatives of any state in the Union."[1] Senator Jones was acknowledged to be a gifted thinker and strategist, and received many accolades for his oratorical skills. Again Davis writes:

> He [Jones] spoke but seldom, but when he took the floor he was listened to with the most marked attention... He could cram more meaning into a fifteen-minute speech than any of his peers... Sometimes, after days of wrangling [in Congress], a short talk from the "Man From Nevada," would dispose of the question and close the debate.[2]

Senator Jones delivered one of his eloquent discourses at the 1892 International Monetary Conference in Brussels, in support of a losing cause. But when:

> The various speeches delivered on that occasion resulted in a worldwide discussion...every speech in favor of bimetallism brought forth a public response from some prominent monometalist, but no one ever attempted to answer the speech of Senator John P. Jones of Nevada, and it remains unanswered to this day [1913].[3]

At the Republican Convention in 1892, Jones told delegates that the issue of free silver coinage would necessitate the formation of a third party.[4] This was in response to the Republican Party having already coalesced with the gold standard policies of the Brussels conference, although the Republicans reluctantly included a provision for silver to continue being used as standard money in their platform.[5]

Senator Stewart, certainly not possessing the public speaking skills of Senator Jones, was a tireless lobbyist for silver and free coinage. Stewart was the author of, and sponsor to, many important mining laws enacted during his tenure. He had made many enemies, however, and was said to be rude and belligerent. Moreover, it was believed that his client, Collis P. Huntington, magnate of the Southern Pacific Railroad, had put him in office. Residing nearly full time in San Francisco prior to being elected in 1888, Stewart was scorned by many Nevadans for his apathetic attitude toward the state; critics claimed that the only reason he had won the 1888 election was because his opponent, James Fair, was more despised than he, and also because he was the Southern Pacific's link to Congress. In spite of it all, there was one surefire way to get a hearty affirmation from Nevada's *Amen Corner*. Preach the message that silver rules, and free coinage is the answer. Senator Stewart had that sermon down pat, reflected by the title to one of his more notable Congressional speeches, "Money, The Answer To All Things,"[6] to which his constituents heartily shouted *Amen!*

Stewart's silent boss, Huntington, might have agreed with the title of the speech, but not the contents of the message. Huntington's ties were to the bank crowd and big corporations, and jointly they felt that free silver coinage bordered on heresy. It is almost impossible for modern historians to fathom Stewart's motives, but like Jones, he publicly denounced the *Goldbugs* belief system, and vigorously spoke out on behalf of silver. In his memoirs Stewart recalled the 1892 election:

> After my experience with Harrison's administration, I found it would be impossible for me to further endorse The Republican Party without endorsing **the crime of John Sherman** in demonetizing silver. When it became evident that Benjamin Harrison would be nominated his own successor ..., I severed my connection with the Republican Party and joined my fellow citizens of Nevada in the organization of a Silver Party...[7] (Emphasis added)

At the local level, concerned citizens met to discuss options pertaining to the free silver coinage issue. "In Ormsby County, the Silver Club met at the Carson (City) Opera House. Organizers included Secretary of State O.H. Grey, (and) editor Sam P. Davis of the Carson City Morning Appeal..."[8] On June 24, 1892 the *Silverites* in Nevada held a convention in Reno, at which the Silver Party was officially organized. Members of the Silver Party aligned with the Populist Party, merging their major concerns into a bilateral platform: the senators from Nevada believing that aligning with the larger Populist Party would provide them with a wider audience to promote the cause of silver.

It would have been comforting for the public to know that their politicians stood independent of big corporations, railroads, and bank money; that they were fearless leaders, who like Shane in the Western movie of that

---

[1] Davis, *The History of Nevada*.

[2] Ibid.

[3] Ibid.

[4] *Carson Morning Appeal*, June 10, 1892.

[5] Harold Kirk and Donald Bruce Johnson, *National Party Platforms, 1840-1968*.

[6] Gilman M. Ostrander, *Nevada: The Great Rotten Borough, 1859-1964*.

[7] Brown, *Reminiscences of Senator William M. Stewart*.

[8] Mary Ellen Glass, "The Silver Governors," *Nevada Historical Society Quarterly* (1978).

name, remained true to their own principles, but it was simply not so.

Certainly it was true that Senator Jones had been a hero back in 1869, when the Yellow Jacket mine near Virginia City became engulfed in flames. In the midst of madness, confusion, and screams for help, Jones had climbed up and down a smoky, fiery shaft to supervise the rescue of as many men as possible, instantly becoming one of the city's most popular residents. Jones also had the good fortune to hit a big silver strike that turned him into a millionaire. If only the senator could now heroically rescue the public from deflation and falling silver prices.

FRANCIS NEWLANDS WINS THE SEAT

Just as Senators Jones and Stewart were busy bolstering their positions, another key political figure in Ne-

PATRICK McCARRAN

A distinction held in the highest esteem by residents of the *Silver State* is that of being a *Native Nevadan*. At social events, or while seated together on stools at coffee shops, people usually get around to asking where everybody is from. Since a large percentage of Nevada's population has migrated from out of state, natives are in the minority. But immediately a glow of pride is detected when a native utters, "I was born and raised here." Even the listeners are a bit impressed, and might respond by saying: "Really, you've grown up here all of your life? I'll bet you've seen lots of changes take place." Once in a while there are even quizzes in local newspaper columns, with titles like, *How To Tell If You Are A Native Nevadan*, requiring answers that presumably only state breds know. A question arising almost automatically is how to pronounce the name of the state. For locals, the acceptable answer is *Neh-vaah-dah*. Tourists and other out-of-staters on the other hand, usually pronounce it *Naah-vaaww-duh*.

One such native son was 16 years old in 1892. He grew up on a sheep ranch along the Truckee River, about 15 miles outside of Reno, and got a late start in his formal education, entering elementary school at the age of 10. At 21, he was no doubt the oldest graduating senior from Reno High School, but his maturity had given him a decided edge, both in his athletic abilities, and public speaking. His college career at the University of Nevada was cut short when he was called back to his family's ranch to take over for his ailing father. On more than one occasion the ambitious Irish lad probably walked the streets of Carson City, staring at the Capitol Building, envisioning that one day he might play a role in Nevada's political or judicial system. As it would turn out, Patrick McCarran would eventually be a key player in both; he first served as a Nevada Supreme Court Justice, and then later as a U. S. Senator.

McCarran was the first native-born Nevadan to be elected to a federal office, and depending on who is writing the biography, McCarran was either a hero, or a heel. In 1892, Senators Jones and Stewart still had 10 good years remaining in their service to the *Silver State*. But as is always necessary for the perpetuity of political leadership, new men were being raised up to enter the political arena. McCarran's senatorial career would involve many other issues besides the free coinage of silver. He would ultimately exercise more influence at a state and national level than his predecessors, but something McCarran shared with them was the question of whom he actually worked for; was he accountable to the state and federal governments and to the voters, or was he accountable to insider power brokers who pulled his strings?

Nevadans have generally been biased in regard to which issues are most important. The free coinage issue of the 1890s is one example, and although they might not have been as interested in other matters of concern across the nation, Nevadans knew what they wanted (or at least what their political leaders told them they wanted): an assurance that their chief product, their lifeblood, would be supported at the federal level, and that free coinage would be re-established.

In Pat McCarran's day, the *Nevada State Journal* made it clear what was most important to the state's residents: "The voters of Nevada don't give a hoot how he (McCarran) votes on most of the national bills that have no direct connection with Nevada, but they do want someone in Washington to whom they can turn when they need help on local problems…"[1] The article continued in its praise for McCarran, reporting that: "There has never been a senator in the history of the state who has paid as close attention to the needs of the state."[2]

As a side note; coin collectors might find it interesting to know that McCarran was linked to two individuals who were closely associated with the subject: the first was his personal secretary, Eva Adams, whose service to the Senator included superior administrative assistance as well as acting as a buffer between McCarran and the public. After McCarran passed away in 1954, Eva Adams was later honored by President John F. Kennedy in 1961 with an appointment to the position of U.S. Mint Director. The other is Norman Biltz, whose collection of Carson City coins is on permanent display at the Nevada State Museum, once the home of the Carson City Mint. Also worth mentioning is that McCarran, Biltz, Adams and President Kennedy were all closely acquainted with one another.

[1] Jerome Edwards, "Nevada's Power Broker: Pat McCarran and His Political Machine," *Nevada's Readings and Perspectives*, as cited in *Nevada State Journal.*
[2] Ibid.

vada entered the stage in 1892: Francis Newlands, the son-in-law of former power broker William Sharon. Newlands' name would become familiar because of credit given him for reclamation projects in the 20th century, when the federal government funded the irrigation of no fewer than 16 western states. On his way up the political ladder, Newlands became a welcome guest in Theodore Roosevelt's White House, and many historians consider him the most influential political figure in Nevada's history, although this appears to be unsupportable and presumptuous.

When his father-in-law, William Sharon, died in 1886, Newlands became the trustee for the Sharon estate, in spite of the fact that Newland's wife–Sharon's daughter Clara - had died in 1882 at the age of 28. In any event, by inheritance, Newlands was a very wealthy man, remarrying in 1888 and moving to Nevada in 1889. When he announced his candidacy in 1892, many of the state's citizens considered him a carpetbagger. His ties to Sharon, scorned as a *San Franciscan Nevadan*, cast suspicion on his motives; as bribery and manipulation had been at the top of Sharon's list of solutions to political problems. During those years, Nevada's politics were run by millionaires, or at least by the servants of millionaires. For good measure, Newlands' manager and political lieutenant was the deceased William Sharon's nephew, Will Sharon, who used his family's wealth to insure successful campaigns for his clients.

Efforts Begun to Reclaim Farmlands

Francis Newlands' election to the House of Representatives has been likened to a changing of the guard in Nevada's politics, witnessed by the fact that, although running on the Silver Party ticket, Newlands would eventually transition from the common concerns of the Comstock, to a program of environmental reclamation. It appeared as if mining was no longer the key to the future success of the state, and Newlands and the men he answered to proposed that the mass irrigation of land could bring Nevada's agricultural potential to fruition. Supportive of such policies, the agrarian population in the nation heartily favored such proposals, not just for Nevada, but for other western states too.

Agriculture had dominated the commercial infrastructure of the United States for the first 75 years of the 19th century. Then a dramatic shift occurred in the last quarter of that century as industrial production, abetted by new inventions and innovations, rapidly increased. Prosperity that blessed much of the nation only caused bitterness in agricultural regions where good fortune passed them

by. The price of wheat had dropped more than 55% in the 20-year period since 1873, and the value of the dollar had risen substantially at the same time.

Undergirding its monetary standards, the federal government's policy of removing currency from circulation in its attempt to align with British and international gold-backed monetary systems, caused the per capita money supply to drop dramatically. This combination of falling crop and land prices, with a shrinking currency supply, caused farmers facing insolvency to "sit up with kerosene lamps studying pamphlets about money, trying to understand what had gone wrong."[1] They also struggled with "the railroads...[who] were hated for plucking the farm districts through localized high freight rates, rebates, and other transgressions."[2] If it is true that misery loves company, most certainly, the country's farmers and Nevada's mining industry of the 1890s proved to be a match made in heaven; as Ostrander put it, "These ills required radical remedies."[3]

Two New Parties Merge

In search of solutions, the Populist Party, representing farmers and the working class, united with the Silver Party, representing the mining industry. Populists had items in their platform that were of vague consequence to the Silver Party, but the bridge, of course, was the free coinage of silver; the *Silverites* were virtually one-dimensional in their political agenda. Populists knew they were fortunate to have the wealthy mining industry on their side; otherwise the party's war chest would have been light on funds. However, they were not entirely supportive of a monetary system backed by any precious metal, whether it was gold or silver, their primary objective being that the government increase the money supply.

Both groups had an apparent enemy in the railroads, although a few of the leaders from the silver camp simultaneously were on the railroad's payroll. Farmers had won minor regulatory victories against the railroads through legislation, but still desired to loosen the perceived stranglehold railroads had on them. Nevada's relationship with railroads was deeply rooted; from the days of William Sharon's V&T, to the border-to-border connection of the Southern Pacific, the state was totally dependent upon the railway system. At times it appeared as if the railroads were taking

---

[1] Kevin Phillips, *Wealth and Democracy: A Political History of the American Rich.*
[2] Ostrander, *The Great Rotten Borough.*
[3] Ibid.

advantage of their power and might not have been that concerned with the interests of their *Silver State* customer. Again, historian Richard Lillard, writing in the early half of the 20th century, assessed the influence the railroads had on Nevada in the last decades of the 19th century:

> Nevada was retarded for four decades by the Southern Pacific. From the first, it made passenger and freight rates low enough to kill competition from stages and wagons. Once [the] competition was good and dead, it raised its rates. It enforced the vicious long and short haul system to make huge profits at the state's expense. For example, [during one period] the railroad's charge was $300 to take a carload of coal oil from New York to San Francisco. [But] from New York to Reno, a trip three hundred and six miles shorter, the charge was $536. Goods destined for Nevada towns were shipped to San Francisco, and reshipped back.[1]

Lillard continued by presenting his opinion of the effect this had on the state, "This system of rates prevented any Nevada towns from rising to occupy the place of Salt Lake City…or…Denver."[2] Accusations that the Southern Pacific had attempted to buy the members of Nevada's legislature incited the indignation of the public—strong statements, to be sure. The election years of 1892 and 1896 would prove to be forums for all the discontented members of society to vent their bitterness, complaints and wrath.

THE POPULIST'S PLATFORM IN 1892

The Preamble to the Populist Party's 1892 platform provides insight into the convictions of many Americans at the time:

> The conditions which surround us best justify our cooperation: We meet in the midst of a nation brought to the verge of moral, political, and material ruin. Corruption dominates the ballot box…The people are demoralized… The newspapers are largely subsidized or muzzled…our homes [are] covered with mortgages, labor impoverished, and the land [is] concentrating in the hands of capitalists…we seek to restore the government of the Republic to the hands of the "plain people," with whose class it originated…[3]

A majority of Nevada's population approved the principles declared by the Populist Party, although several of the demands made by the populists were extraneous to the *Silverites*. In particular was the crop-warehousing proposal, referred to as the Sub Treasury System, which would permit farmers to store up to 80% of their annual harvest and draw funds against it. Populists would compensate the *Silverites* for supporting their party on such issues, by sponsoring strong free silver coinage demands in their platform. Mutual items of agreement in the drafted proposal were:

The Money

1-We demand free and unlimited coinage of silver and gold at the present legal ratio of sixteen to one.

2-We demand that the amount of circulating medium be speedily increased to not less than fifty dollars per capita.

Next came:

Transportation

Declaration

We believe that the time has come when the railroad corporations will either **own the people**, or the **people must own the railroads**.

1-Transportation being a means of exchange, and a public necessity, the **government should own and operate the railroads** in the interest of the people.[4] (Emphasis added)

---

[1] Lillard, *Desert Challenge.*
[2] Ibid.
[3] *The Omaha Platform, Populists,* 1892.
[4] Ibid.

Parades, like this 4th of July celebration, were popular events in Carson City. The streets were wide, but could easily fill up when crowds gathered. (*Courtesy Nevada State Museum*)

At the time of these proposals, the true market ratio between gold and silver was much higher than the Treasury's antiquated legal rate. Circulating media (money in circulation) wavered between $10 and $16 per capita. Obviously, the *financial reformers* (Populists, Silverites, etc.) had their sights aimed high. On the other side, the *financial conservatives* (Bank Crowd, Goldbugs, etc.) blamed silver's depreciation on overproduction and believed that the gold standard was superior to all others. This side, represented by big corporations, bankers, and the *Goldbugs* believed that the National Banking System was the best model. Private banks, as well as state banks, were growing in size and influence and the banking community, especially the large eastern banks, let Congress know that the less government regulation, the greater opportunity for growth and prosperity. In answer to the agriculture industry's plea for help in credit matters, bankers scourged farmers for using inefficient business practices. These *financial conservatives* predicted that the remonetization of silver would plunge the nation into an economic panic and attacked the *financial reformers'* demand for the ratio between gold and silver to be set at 16 to one, reminding them that this ratio was only half of the true market relationship between the two metals. They warned that "since 50 cents worth of silver bullion would buy a legal dollar's worth of goods, silver would be preferred, and remain in circulation, and gold would be hoarded or exported. Bimetallism at sixteen to one would have resulted in a monometallic silver standard."[1] There was also the possibility that foreign countries would dump mass quantities of silver onto the U.S. Treasury.

A Double Minded Press?

Both sides of the debate regarded money as the key to the future success of society, the disagreement was over who controlled it, and who determined the value of it. Who were the heroes, and who were the villains? The *Populists* and *Silverites* had no doubts, and neither did scores of the nation's journalists and editors. A raging political battle over monetary standards produced as much propaganda, investigative reporting, and character slandering as any other issue since the Civil War. In his book *Striking For Life*, former *New York Times* editorial page editor, John Swinton, cast his spin on the events that rocked the nation during this turbulent time.

> We know the powers that are defying the people ...Our Government is in the hands of pirates. All the power of politics, and of Congress, and of the administration is under the control of the moneyed interests...The adversary has the force of capital, thousand of millions of which are in his hand...He will grasp the knife of law, which he has so often wielded in his interest. He will lay hold of his force in the legislature. He will make use of his forces in the press, which are always waiting for the wink, which is as good as a nod to a blind horse...Political rings are managed by skillful and unscrupulous political gamblers, who possess the "machine" by which the populace are at once controlled and crushed.[2]

Earlier in his career, Swinton had addressed a group of fellow journalists at a banquet. His brutally honest attempt to dissipate smokescreens and expose deceptions offended his peers.

> There is no such thing, at this date of the world's history, in America, as an independent press. You know it and I know it.

> There is not one of you who dare to write your honest opinions, and if you did, you know beforehand that it would never appear in print. I am paid weekly for keeping my honest opinion out of the paper I am connected with. Others of you are paid similar things, and any of you who would be so foolish as to write honest opinions would be out on the streets looking for another job. If I allowed my honest opinions to appear in one issue of my paper, before twenty-four hours my occupation would be gone.

> The business of the journalist is to destroy the truth, to lie outright, to pervert, to vilify, to fawn at the feet of mammon, and to sell his country and his race for his daily bread. You know it and I know it, and what folly is this toasting an independent press?

> We are the tools and vassals of rich men behind the scenes. We are the jumping jacks, they pull the strings and we dance. Our talents, our possibilities and our lives are all the property of other men.

> We are intellectual prostitutes.[3]

Senators Jones and Teller Address Republican Convention

The public political arena in the 1890s was a "world of sound bites and shouting matches."[4] Senator Teller of Colorado mocked President Harrison's apparent double-minded appeal to the financial reformers that the proper course of action to restore the world to the bimetallism standard, was to accumulate as much gold

---

[1] Gretchen Ritter, *Goldbugs and Greenbacks: The Antimonopoly Tradition and the Politics of Finance in America, 1865-1896.*

[2] John Swinton, *Striking for Life: Labor's Side of the Labor Question: The Right of the Workingman to a Fair Living.*

[3] W. J. Ghent, *Our Benevolent Feudalism.*

[4] J. Budziszewski, *Revenge of the Conscience* (Spence Pub., 1999).

as possible. There was a major problem with this strategy, as Teller pointed out:

> We cannot keep our gold if Europe wants it…as long as she [Great Britain] holds our securities, and the balance of trade is not in our favor.[1]

At the Republican Convention in the summer of 1892, Senator Jones from Nevada, working closely with Senator Teller, sounded the call that:

> The American people, from tradition and interest, favor bimetallism, and the Republican Party demands the use of

---

THE TEN VARIETIES OF MONEY BEING USED IN THE UNITED STATES IN 1892

First: Gold coin, with unlimited legal tender for all debts of every kind, public and private.

Second: Gold certificates, limited to the amount of gold deposited in the Treasury, not legal tender, but could be counted as part of national bank reserves. They were redeemable in gold coin alone. They were the paper representatives of the gold as a more convenient form of the coin. Their denominations ranged from $20 to $10,000

Third: Silver dollars, the coinage of which since 1878 had been limited; Of full legal tender for all debts.

Fourth: Silver certificates, limited to the amount of silver dollars deposited in the Treasury by their holders, not legal tender. Redeemable in silver dollars alone, their denominations ranged from $1 to $1,000.

Fifth: United States notes, unlimited legal tender for all debts, public and private, except duties on imports and interest on the public debt.

Sixth: Currency certificates, limited by amount of United States notes deposited. Therefore, not legal tender. Their denominations ranged from $5,000 to $10,000.

Seventh: Treasury notes of 1890, issued for the purchase of silver under the Sherman law.

Eighth: National bank notes, printed by the Government, and given to national banks, limited to 90% of the United States bonds deposited therefore in the Treasury. Legal tender for payment of debts to national banks. Also redeemable in gold. The circulating notes of national banks could be presented to the Treasury Department for redemption in greenbacks. Then could be immediately presented for redemption in gold.

Ninth: Subsidiary silver coins. Legal tender not to exceed five dollars. Denominations of ten cents, twenty-five cents, and fifty cents.

Tenth: Minor coins. Denomination of copper cents and nickel five cents.*

*Acknowledgement to Walbert, M.W., *The Coming Battle*.

---

both gold and silver as standard money…as will secure the maintenance of the parity of values of the two metals, so that **the purchasing and debt paying power of the dollar whether silver, gold, or paper** shall be at all times equal. The interests of the producers of this country, its farmers, and its working men, demand that **every dollar, paper or coin… shall be as good as any other.**[2] (Emphasis added)

Support of this section of the *Silverite's* plank still was not enough for the Republican Party to carry the states of Colorado, Idaho, Kansas, and Nevada, all of which cast their votes for the Populist Party. It did not matter, for as Senator Teller questioned in one of his speeches:

> Does anyone suppose that the men who hold the credits of the world [The banking elite]… and who take by reason of the present condition of affairs… nearly 40% more from the people who owe the debts than they would under a **proper system of currency** [free silver coinage], will tamely and quietly surrender…?[3]

A CRADLE OF DECEPTION

Colorado's Senator Henry Moore Teller earned the title role "Defender of the West" for championing the cause of the public's interests in his Rocky Mountain area. In his biography of Senator Teller, Elmer Ellis quotes him as saying, "I must answer to my conscience, and not to my neighbors."[4] Teller was another Republican who would bolt to the new Silver Party, and later, when the era of free silver coinage came to an end, he switched to the Democratic Party. His biography describes his devotion to the silver cause, and another senator is quoted as saying, "Teller helped to rock the cradle of these infant states and has ever been a watchful guardian of their interests."[5]

But the hands rocking the cradle of the western mining states were not always watchful guardians. Citizens felt they were being held in the safe, defending arms of state and local government, giving them the secure feeling of a baby being held by a loved one. But at the other end of the hand rocking the cradle was not the state's benevolent political leader; the hand was attached to the banking elite and railroad owners. The citizenry had been rocking to a false sense of security all this time, without even knowing it. In 1892, public groups around the country met to decide who their leaders should be, and many were realizing that the traditional political parties, trusted

---

[1] Elmer Ellis, *Henry Moore Teller, Defender of the West*.
[2] Ibid.
[3] Ibid.
[4] Ibid.
[5] Ibid.

to preserve, protect and fulfill their rights in a democratic republic, might be wolves in Little Red Riding Hood outfits. As a result, parties like the Populist, People's, and Silver were organized, at a time when the economy was based on steel, oil, railroads and machines. Although dominant businessmen like Rockefeller, Carnegie, and Morgan were controlling huge capital resources, these new emerging political parties were attempting to establish where farmers, ranchers, and miners fit into it all.

THE LAND OF OZ

Several years after the elections of 1892, on the heels of the final deathblow to free silver coinage, an allegorical story related the *financial reformers'* version of the controversy. Dorothy is the main character, a typical Midwestern farm girl, who believes in good old American values. She represents the agrarian community of the United States, believers in truth, justice, and the American way. Suddenly Dorothy is swept up in a tornado, symbolizing the chaos, confusion, and conflict of the battle for monetary standards. After crash landing in a make-believe land, Dorothy is told by the strange inhabitants to follow the yellow brick road to the city of Oz (the abbreviation for ounce), where she can meet the Wizard, who will help her return home: this *yellow brick road* is the gold standard, and returning home speaks of restoring the prosperity of the farmlands.

Along the way, Dorothy meets the Scarecrow, stuffed with hay, and apparently not too smart. He represents the average farmer who later proves to be brave, and much smarter than he thought. Next she meets the Tin Man, who claims he does not have a heart, representing the industrial worker whose long overtime hours in the factory have taken the spirit right out of him. As the threesome skips along the yellow brick road, a ferocious lion jumps out and scares them. This lion's ferocity is quickly exposed, however, as it turns out he is really a coward; he eagerly joins the group on their journey, and at times even attempts to protect them. Some interpretations suggest this Cowardly Lion must be compared to William Jennings Bryan, whose roar proved to be bigger than his bite after the 1896 elections.

Dorothy and her comrades arrive at the Emerald City and are instructed to wear green tinted glasses, and are subsequently allowed to enter the Emerald Palace. Again, by way of interpretation, the symbolism suggests that the Emerald City is Washington D.C., the Emerald Palace is the White House, and the green tinted glasses

symbolic of the color of money. The Wicked Witches in the story depict the motherhood of the *Goldbugs* whose banking elite were sometimes described as *sons of witches*. Lastly, a Great Wizard speaks with an intimidating voice of authority, and promises to have the answers to all of Dorothy and her escorts' problems; his character portraying a ménage of politicians and the presidential candidate who promises the world, but eventually delivers nothing. Later, the Wizard is exposed as a fraud, and ultimately cannot save anyone but himself.

Finally, the Good Witch instructs Dorothy to click the heels of her silver slippers whereupon, Dorothy is supernaturally transported back to the safety of her farmland, where she reunites with her family and friends, who are ready to rebuild after the devastating effects of the tornado. According to some interpretations, the meaning suggested in the finale reveals that the *Goldbugs* were imposters, and when they were finally removed, it was proven that the *Silverites* had the solution all along.

Of course, the name of this story is the *Wizard of Oz*, written by free silver supporter, L. Frank Baum after William Jennings Bryan was defeated in the 1896 election.[1] Was it childish amusement, or a parable of real-life events? There were strong opinions coming from both sides of the issue.

THE CAPITAL OF THE UNDERDOG STATE

The American experience is replete with stories about the underdog challenging the *Goliath* and bringing the giant to its knees (maybe even cutting off its head). Nevada seemingly has always played the role of the underdog.

For instance, as the state's economy weakened, and the population dwindled through the final decade of the 19th century, there was some talk of revoking its statehood. At the time, there was serious conviction, especially in the east, that "the state was going to die or they'd just hang out here a little longer hoping it would somehow bloom."[2]

In 1892, life moved along as usual in Carson City. The people who stayed, even as multitudes fled to more promising parts of the country, were convinced that even without silver flowing from the nearby mines, other business opportunities existed, as the area and surrounding

---

[1] Acknowledgment to: H. Rockoff, "The Wizard of Oz as a Monetary Allegory," *Journal of Political Economy* 98 (August 1990).
[2] Michael Green, Nevada historian, interview.

land offered other desirable natural resources. Family names like Dangberg, Settlemeyer, and Springmeyer were among the successful farmers and ranchers in the area during the 1890s. There were doctors, lawyers, druggists, brewers, blacksmiths, and merchants of all sorts. A prominent furniture store in town was operated by the Kitzmeyer family. Wells Fargo & Co. ran a bank, and the Olcovich brothers owned a mercantile store. Congressman H.H. Bartine, who lost his House seat in the 1892 election, remained in the capital the rest of his life, and became well known for his journal, *The National Bimetallist*. Though only a child in 1892, Clark J. Guild, born in Dayton in 1887, would later became a well-known district judge, and as a longtime Carson City resident, Guild would play a major role in the preservation of the old mint during the 20th century. George W.G. Ferris, Jr., had grown up in the house once occupied by Orion Clemens at the corner of Spear and Division streets. His family's landscaping business helped beautify many of the city's Main street buildings. In 1892, George W. G. Ferris, Jr., unveiled his amusement ride invention, in Chicago, forever to be named the Ferris Wheel. This attraction would be premiered at the following year's Columbian Exposition. Young Ferris received inspiration for his invention while watching the big water wheel at Cradlebaugh's bridge turn round and round as he sat on the banks of the Carson River.

Carson City itself was considered a *runt* among state capitals. Almost incessantly, the political bullies in Washington D.C. and big business put many obstacles in the city's path. But to most, the peaceful town had never been considered dangerous; even in the 20th century, when southern Nevada was home to mob killings and union strikes, Carson City's small casino industry was shielded from that sort of melodrama. Strong-arming its way to the top was not in the town's profile. Although shaped in the American West, it had a reputation of being a polite city in most ways, more casual in its approach to life, an environment that was more New England than Dodge City. Commercial buildings and residential areas were a mixture of the Midwest and small villages back east, although the culture may not have been as refined, and the people sounded more like the way Mark Twain wrote. There might have been rowdy occasions from time to time, for example if a person got mud slopped on them by another person and broke into the 19th century version of *road rage*. In short, disputes were not settled with gunfights and hangings, as in old west towns like Tombstone; instead, life proceeded at a calmer pace. Excitement might come when

the train pulled into the depot, or the stage arrived with passengers. Instead of a sheriff's jail, there was a men's prison and even the red light district was on the outskirts of town to keep things more respectable. Residents possessed great pride in their capital city; many trees and shrubs were planted, and houses were kept in shape. And there was the mint, that lovely, prestigious, wonderful mint; it had been there since 1870, in its prominent location in town, the prize of prizes, having brought much credibility, dignity, and respect to the fair city for 22 years.

By 1892, Carson City had become accustomed to being grateful for any crumbs that fell off the federal government's table. Now there was more talk that the Treasury was once again thinking about closing the city's mint. Would *Carsonites* protest? Of course they would, at least to a degree; but would they stage rallies and demand that Congress keep their mint open? Not hardly. There was one thing mint employees could be counted on to do: faithfully keep to their task, and as long as the doors were open and the work orders coming in, steam would continue to rise from the stacks on the roof.

CHARGES AGAINST CARSON MINT BREAKING BULLION DEPOSIT RULE

There was a law in 1892 limiting the amount of silver bullion a person could deposit at a U.S. mint, to 10,000 ounces, one of many such laws passed by the federal government through the years placing restrictions on money or precious metals. At the present time (2003), for example, a person who makes a purchase with $10,000 or more in cash must fill out an IRS form; and another law requires a bullion dealer to fill out an IRS form for any client who sells 25 or more ounces of certain gold bullion coins, or 1,000 or more ounces of fine silver. Of course, on occasion, people employ different methods to circumvent these laws, such as staggering cash payments in amounts less than $10,000 over a period of time, or selling only 24 ounces of gold at a time.

In 1892, a complaint was filed by a San Francisco organization against the Carson City Mint, charging that employees there had circumvented the 10,000 ounce silver deposit rule by splitting up larger deposits between multiple depositors, even though the silver was coming from only one source. Congress authorized an investigation, and when questioned, Carson Superintendent Sam Wright readily admitted that his mint had indeed split large deposits between multiple depositors when the deposits belonging to only one person had exceeded the limit. But, as Mr. Wright told the investigator, all of the country's mints followed the same practice, and if the Carson Mint was guilty, so were the other mints. Investigations ceased and charges were dropped.

NEW COIN DESIGNS INTRODUCED

Few decades in the nation's history have been as economically challenging as the 1890s. As the battle over monetary standards drew the discernible lines of separation between *financial conservatives* and *financial reformers*, the Treasury Department, through its Bureau of the Mint, hastened to deliver increasing quantities of coins. Defying all logic, 1892 turned out to be a stellar year in the Mint's history, at a time when coinage might have been expected to take a back seat due to pending policy decisions. For the first time, a commemorative coin was issued by the Mint for mass distribution, as the 1892 Columbian half dollars were struck in standard silver composition for the Columbian Exposition, to be held in Chicago. This Exposition

Commemorative half dollar issued to celebrate the 400th anniversary of Columbus' discovery of the new world.

and the coins minted for the occasion commemorated the 400th anniversary of Columbus' voyage to the New World.

Columbus' portrait on the obverse was designed by Charles E. Barber using a likeness from a popular sculpture based on a painting in Madrid; the reverse was designed by George T. Morgan, featuring a conceived replica of the *Santa Maria* atop two globes, representing the old and new worlds. These half dollars were sold for one dollar each, the proceeds going to the fund-raising for the Exposition, originally scheduled to open in October of 1892, but delayed until May of 1893. Coin production be-

gan in November of 1892, with 949,896 commemoratives eventually issued bearing that date; another 1,548,300 were issued the following year, dated 1893. Congress had authorized up to five million of each date, but obviously amidst hard economic times the coins were not as popular as had been anticipated. To publicize the event, the Bureau of the Mint staged a ribbon-cutting introduction of the new half dollar, selling the first Proof specimen off the press to the Remington Typewriter Company for $10,000, equivalent to $1 million today (2003).

Any sensible pollster would have probably advised the Mint not to overdo it with coin production in the election year of 1892. Columbian half dollars were one thing as they were linked to a worthy celebration, but on the matter of new dimes, quarters, and half dollars, would a wait-and-see approach have been more advisable? There were those who believed that perhaps Congress and the Treasury should just get through the election, and see what happened with the free silver coinage issue. On the other hand, 1892 was the Centennial year of the opening of the Philadelphia Mint and new silver coin designs would seem appropriate to acknowledge the anniversary. Furthermore, the issuance of increased quantities of new subsidiary coins, combined with the release of the Columbian halves, would be ample proof that the government supported silver as much in 1892 as it had in 1792. Whatever rationale was used, new Liberty Head dimes, quarters, and halves began appearing in January of 1892, and production con-

The new Barber designs, which made their debut in 1892. (*Courtesy Bowers and Merena*)

tinued nonstop at the mints in Philadelphia, San Francisco, and New Orleans through the year. As Dave Bowers notes, in reference to half dollars, "The restricted mintages of the [1880s] were left behind, and again half dollars were produced in large quantities for circulation."[1] All told, the three participating mints struck two million half dollars in 1892, compared with the previous year's total of 200,000. In addition, there were 11,840,079 quarters minted, nearly double 1891's total, and nearly 17 mil-

---

[1] Q. David Bowers, *United States Dimes, Quarters, and Half Dollars.*

lion dimes, approximately six million fewer than 1891's Seated Liberty grand finale. These new Barber coins would be issued for nearly the full 25 year term required for U.S. coin designs, before they were replaced by the stylish designs of 1916.

This increased subsidiary coin production in 1892, combined with the Columbian halves, tapped into nearly 4.4 million ounces of the Treasury's silver reserve. A counterside was that there were only 6,333,245 silver dollars minted, generating little net benefit to silver producers in the country. Worth pointing out, is that this steep decline in the production of silver dollars had continued since its peak in 1890. From that year's mintage figure of 38 million, mintages had fallen to 23.5 million in 1891, 6.3 million in 1892, continuing to fall to approximately 1.45 million in 1893. This was, of course, during the years of the Sherman Silver Purchase Act, and despite the dramatic drop-off in silver dollar mintages, the Treasury continued to buy the mandatory amount of silver bullion directed by the Act. Through the end of June of 1892, the Treasury reported holdings of approximately 79 million ounces in storage. Unfortunately, the market value of this silver would decrease by nearly 40% over the next few years, causing the coinage value to be much greater than the bullion value, and the challenge would be to get anyone to accept it.

At the same time the production of silver coins continued to decline during the 1890s, gold coin production rose substantially. The table below exhibits this trend which occurred during the first five years of the 1890s, beginning with the year of the Sherman Silver Act.[1]

While silver coin mintages were falling to their lowest levels since the Coinage Act of 1873, silver bullion production in the United States was reaching record highs. Treasury documents reported that approximately, 63.5 million ounces of silver had flowed from the nation's mines

in 1892. Colorado was the chief producer, with a reported output of 24 million ounces in 1892; Montana was in second place, with 17 million ounces reported, and followed by Utah's 8 million ounces. Nevada was no longer a major player in silver mining, but still reported 2.2 million ounces for 1892.[2] Secretary of the Treasury Sherman was ordered to temporarily suspend the Sherman Act silver purchases after the November election, and although the purchases would resume, there would be serious debate as to the economic soundness behind the act, leading to its repeal in 1893.

COINAGE AT CARSON CITY IN 1892

By order of the Mint Director, the Carson City Mint was not allowed to produce the new Liberty Head coins; its staff stuck to the task of manufacturing silver dollars and gold coins. Amidst rumors that the Treasury might shut the mint down again, folks in Carson City were satisfied with whatever work they were given.

Theodore R. Hofer, Carson City Mint Superintendent and prominent citizen in town.

Although 1892 was a year in which there were fewer Morgan silver dollars minted in the country than in any previous year, the Carson City facility had the distinction of surpassing the totals at both the San Francisco and Philadelphia mints, the first time that this occurred during the Morgan dollar era. It was of little consequence, however, especially in light of the extenuating circumstances behind it (like Columbian halves and Barber coins at the other mints). Still, it must have been rewarding to Carson Mint workers to experience the distinction at least one time. It would happen again the following year that the Carson Mint topped all other mints in silver dollar production.[3]

Mintage figures for 1892-CC silver dollars totaled 1,352,000, as workers delivered a monthly average

---

[1] *Annual Report of the Director of the Mint,* 1895.
[2] Ibid.
[3] For more information, see the next section on 1893.

COINAGE OF GOLD AND SILVER COINS AT THE U.S. MINTS FROM 1890 TO 1894				
	Gold		Silver	
	Fine Ounces	Face Value	Fine Ounces	Face Value
1890	990,100	$20,467,182	30,320,999	$39,202,908
1891	1,413,614	29,222,005	21,284,115	27,528,857
1892	1,682,832	34,787,223	9,777,084	12,641,078
1893	2,757,231	56,997,020	6,808,413	8,802,797
1894	3,848,045	79,546,160	7,115,896	9,200,351

of 110,000 pieces during the first seven months of the year. Operations at the mint were temporarily suspended on August 1, 1892, (four days before the Columbian commemorative was authorized) when Mint Superintendent, Sam Wright, suddenly died at the age of 61. Mr. Wright's replacement was the chief clerk at the mint, Theodore R. Hofer, who had also been employed as a cashier at the Carson branch of the Bullion and Exchange Bank. Hofer had first moved to Carson City in 1869 to become a messenger boy for the opening of the mint and by 1892, had become a respected citizen of the capital city. After serving as mint superintendent he became very wealthy in the mining industry around Goldfield and Tonopah. His oldest son, Theodore Robert Hofer, Jr., was appointed Postmaster in Carson City in the late 1890s.

Nearly two and a half weeks of production time was lost, as Mr. Wright's funeral was arranged, and Mr. Hofer made the transition into his new position; but by the end of August the mint had produced another 40,000 silver dollars, maintaining a steady pace through the end of the year. By this time it had become standard policy to release only limited quantities of new outputs and nearly the entire mintage of 1892-CC silver dollars was added to the previous three year's output and stored on premises.

ESTIMATING "CC" DOLLAR POPULATIONS

In the Treasury's *Annual Report* an account was given that approximately 3.4% of Carson City's silver dollar production from October of 1889 through July 1, 1892 had been distributed. For coin collectors, this might provide a clue in the never-ending search for accurate population statistics.

Understandably, collectors want to know how many examples of certain dates of coins survive, as this will aid in determining values. The original mintages, of course, have already been provided, but unfortunately, except on rare occasions, the Treasury does not report meltages, and it is this meltage data that is most critical when researching surviving populations.

Say, for example, the mintage figure on a certain coin was 10,000, and the Treasury disclosed that 9,980 were melted, leaving 20 survivors. If all 20 pieces can be accounted for, the mystery is solved and collectors then know the entire population of that coin. But in the real world, with few exceptions, information like this is not provided, and requires the use of detective work.

Returning to the "CC" silver dollars from 1889 to 1892, if the Treasury disclosed that approximately 3.4%

Bullion and Exchange Bank at the corner of Carson and Proctor. Theodore R. Hofer, one of the mint superintendents at Carson City was also employed at this bank. (*Courtesy Nevada State Museum*)

of the silver dollars minted between 1889 and 1892 were distributed, after doing the math, a number of 145,274 pieces is arrived at. From this starting point it becomes necessary to track the remaining silver dollars held in storage; how many were distributed in each successive year. And if at some point in the future, the Treasury reported that the stored coins were transferred to another facility, further tracking would be required, possibly leading to any announcements of meltdowns or further distributions. At this point, collectors are at the mercy of the Treasury and its records; all that is left now is making educated guesses and sound judgments.

Questions lingering are: has the Treasury distributed any silver dollars once held in storage? And what about the mass melting's? In the early years of the 21st century there is more population information, Mint reports, and auction records available than at any time in history, providing numismatists with ample resources when conducting research. Many have gone before who have taken the giant leap of faith when estimating populations extant; some have been fairly accurate, whereas some have missed the mark by a mile. It goes without saying that some questions will never be answered; but the important thing to remember is that this is what makes numismatic research and study so intriguing.

As for the "CC" dollars in question, since the Treasury did not disclose in its 1892 *Annual Report* from which date, or dates the 3.4% distribution came, one can only surmise as to whether or not the coins were distributed evenly between the four dates (1889 to 1892), or if only one date was used as a source.

Assuming the distribution was spread evenly, the table below exhibits the Mint's distribution through July 1, 1892 (previous years distributions are also provided).

During the years that followed, an additional 493,636 silver dollars were distributed from the Carson City Mint through 1901, bringing the total number distributed to 1,308,805. In 1900, the remaining five million silver dollars minted at Carson City from 1889 to 1893 were transferred to the Treasury.

TRYING TO MAKE SENSE OF THE DATA

In truth, there are too many variables to draw solid conclusions from calculations such as these; of course, the Treasury did not provide any such percentages for the distribution breakdown by date and distributions could have just as easily been weighted in favor of one date, at the exclusion of others. As R.W. Julian pointed out, "There was a policy of [The Treasury] notifying a Mint superintendent that a particular year of coins could be released, however, **not** - so far as can be determined at present – **a legal requirement** found in a law passed by Congress."[1] (Emphasis added) Apparently this policy was not strictly enforced, because if a superintendent violated the policy and changed the distribution order, "he might have gotten a slight reprimand had the action been discovered, but otherwise it was simply a matter of convenience…"[2] The main purpose of the Treasury dictating the order in which coins were to be released, according to Julian, "was merely to see that the oldest coins were paid out first."[3]

In 1892, at the Carson City Mint, this would have meant that all 350,000 1889-CC silver dollars would have been distributed by July 1, 1891, a fact not validated by the surviving population of 1889-CC dollars. If 100% of

CARSON CITY MINT'S DISTRIBUTION OF 1889-1892 SILVER DOLLARS THROUGH JULY 1892

Date	Mintage	Year	Distributions	Percentage	Balance
1889-CC	352,764*	1890	41,626	11.8%	311,138
		1891	45,924	14.76%	265,214
		1892	9017	3.4%	256,197
1890-CC	2,309,401	1890	128,384	11.8%	2,180,657
		1891	321,865	14.76%	1,858,792
		1892	63,199	3.4%	1,795,593
1891-CC	1,618,000	1891	131,069	14.76%	1,486,931
		1892	50,556	3.4%	1,436,375
1892-CC	1,352,000**	1892	22,508	3.4%	1,329,492
		Total	814, 148		

*2764 Silver dollars carried from 1888
**662,000 minted through July 1,1892

(Variable 1,020 coins)
(815,169 actual)

[1] R.W. Julian, Article, *Numismatic News* (October 1, 2002).
[2] Ibid.
[3] Ibid.

that date were distributed, why do less than 5% survive today? Unfortunately, the Bureau of the Mint simply did not supply an answer to this question. But, the Mint did supply useful information in the form of distribution totals, and the record of the transfer of those five million "CC" silver dollars in 1900 sheds light on the question of how many silver dollars could have been in circulation at one time; 1,308,805 is the number to use as a starting point. As far as the five million figure is concerned, it will remain a mystery unless evidence surfaces that this group was included in the mass silver dollar meltdown begun in 1918. Likewise, any portion of the 1,308,805 distributed coins could have been sent to the melting pot as well. Another point to consider is that "distributed" does not always mean "placed into circulation." Rolls or even bags of any of the later date "CC" dollars could have been stored in their original Uncirculated condition by those who claimed them. In fact, there have been reports of an Uncirculated bag or two of some of these dates from the Carson City Mint entering the marketplace during the

1940s and 1950s: witness the Redfield Hoard, discovered in Reno during the early 1970s, said to have included two or more bag quantities (1000 coins) of several of the dates in question in Uncirculated condition.

And without a doubt, the most publicized hoard of Carson City silver dollars of all time was the GSA holdings in the 1960s and 1970s. At right is a table exhibiting the sparse quantities of later date "CC" dollars included in that group.

In the century or so since these dollars from the Carson City Mint were listed on the Treasury's balance sheet, relative rarities of the dates compared to other silver dollars in the Morgan series have become well known. David Bowers, in his encyclopedia on silver dollars, estimates that anywhere from 31.5% to 60% of the distribution total of 1,308,805 has survived.

1889-CC TO 1893-CC SILVER DOLLARS IN GSA HOLDINGS
1889-CC I
1890-CC 3949
1891-CC 5687
1892-CC I
1893-CC I

BUREAU OF THE MINT'S RECORD FOR THE YEARS 1890-1901 DISTRIBUTIONS AND MINTAGES OF CARSON CITY SILVER DOLLARS*						
Date of Distribution Record	Date of Coin	Date of Record of Mintage	Mintage	Distributed from Mixed Dates	Percentage of Surviving Population	Balance
July I, 1890	1889-CC	Jan I, 1890	352,764**			
	1890-CC	July I, 1890	1,088,000	170,531	11.84%	1,270,233
July I,1891	1890-CC	July I,1891	1,221,041			
	1891-CC	July I,1891	888,000			3,379,274
				498,914	14.764%	2,880,360
July I, 1892	1891-CC	July I, 1892	730,000			3,610,360
	1892-CC	July I, 1892	662,000			4,272,360
				145,724	3.41%	4,126,636
July, I,1893	1892-CC	July I,1893	690,000			4,816,636
	1893-CC	July I, 1893	677,000			5,493,636
				95,181	1.73%	5,398,455
July I, 1894				53,228	1%	5,345,227
July I, 1895				176,833	3.3%	5,168,394
July I, 1896				31,276	.6%	5,137,118
July I, 1897				40,993	.8%	5,096,125
July I, 1898				56,688	1.1%	5,039,437
July I, 1889				30,885	.6%	5,008,552
July I, 1900				1,505	.03%	5,007,047
July I, 1900			Transfer to Treasury	5,000,000		7,047
July I, 1901				7,047	100%	0

*Annual Reports of the Director of the Mint, 1890 to 1901.
** 2764 Carried from 1888

On the low side for the 1892-CC dollar for example, Bowers suggests that there might be 107,000 surviving pieces in both Uncirculated and circulated condition; his highest estimate being 196,000. Obviously, there is no way to know what the exact count is; final answers will always remain veiled in uncertainty, but investigative research, as described above, may lead to more accurate estimates in the future.

Using Population Reports in Numismatic Research

Using the 1892-CC silver dollar as an example, the *PCGS Population Report* (December 2002) listed a total of 4,312 certified in all grades, with Uncirculated grades accounting for 4,095 of that total. In rank order the highest grade is MS-67 (out of 70), with a population listed of three pieces. Next in highest grade is MS-66, with 15 listed, followed by MS-65, with 171 examples reported. Comparatively, the *NGC Census Report* (December 2002) listed approximately 2,100 1892-CC's in all grades, with approximately the same ratio between Uncirculated and circulated grades as recorded in the PCGS report. Allowing for resubmissions of a certain number of coins, the combined total of 1892-CC Uncirculated silver dollars graded by PCGS and NGC through 2002 was approximately 6,000.

Using the same deductive process mentioned earlier, an estimate can be made of how many surviving 1892-CC's which have not been sent to the grading services remain in Uncirculated condition. Once again, using David Bowers' figures as an example; an estimate of between 32,000 and 56,800 Uncirculated 1892-CC's is arrived at, leaving the possibility open that populations of this date could swell at any point in the future as more examples are submitted for grading.

So what percentage of the original 1.35 million 1892-CC silver dollars survived into the 20th century? Perhaps a reasonable estimate, based on the approximate distribution rate for "CC" dollars dated 1889 to 1893 as reported by the Treasury is 20%. And through normal attrition, this percentage has probably been cut in half (through 2003). Out of this extant population in all grades, probably 20% or less of the 1892-CC dollars are in Uncirculated condition.

Gem quality 1892-CC Morgan dollar from the *Eliasberg Collection.* (*Courtesy Bowers and Merena*)

Once upon a time, coin dealers and collectors spoke of bag (1,000) quantities of Uncirculated 1892-CC silver dollars being available; but in today's rare coin marketplace, a roll of 20 Uncirculated 1892-CCs is considered a major event.

Collecting "CC" Coins in the 19th Century

Back in 1892, famous collector John Martin Clapp was actively assembling his family's coin collection which would later become the foundation of Louis Eliasberg's fabulous set of coins. Mr. Clapp ordered Proof sets directly from the Philadelphia Mint at the time, living near enough so he could pick them up in person. Besides Proof sets, Clapp also ordered examples of various coin denominations from the branch mints through agents around the country. Mr. Clapp had apparently become extremely interested in the Carson City Mint by 1892, and enthusiastically began playing catch-up as it neared the end of its operation as a coinage facility.

A year after Carson City ceased coinage operations, Clapp purchased an 1892-CC silver dollar in gem quality with prooflike surfaces for approximately $2.50 at the J. Colvin Randall auction held in March of 1894. At the 1997 *Eliasberg Collection* sale, 103 years later, the same coin sold for $8,525. Two other dates in the Carson City Morgan dollar series Clapp was fortunate to purchase at the 1894 Randall sale were an 1890-CC and 1893-CC; both became prized additions to collector's sets more than a century later.

A Decline in Gold Mintages

Due to sharp declines in total gold coin production at the Carson City Mint, half eagle and eagle mintages dropped off in 1892; in terms of face value, 1892's total was 37 ½% less than the previous year's figure and the number of coins minted decreased by more than 52%. In spite of these reductions, the 1892-CC half eagle is the second or third most common date in the "CC" $5 gold series, probably tied with the 1890-CC; only the 1891-CC is more common. According to Doug Winter, the surviving population of 1892-CC half eagles is estimated to be fewer than 500 pieces.[1]

---

[1] Douglas Winter, *Gold Coins of the Carson City Mint.*

Although output of gold eagles at Carson City fell from over 100,000 in 1891 to 40,000 in 1892, it is still the second highest mintage in the series, and like the half eagles, 1892-CC eagles are fairly common.

In the gold double eagle category, demand from the redemption of Treasury Notes remained constant and large quantities of the big gold pieces were being shipped to Europe to satisfy the longings of the financial elite. As usual, the San Francisco Mint was the chief producer of the Treasury's heavy duty utility gold coins. At Carson City, though double eagle production was just a speck in a prospector's pan compared to San Francisco's output of 930,150, the 27,265 pieces minted represented a significant increase from the previous year's output of 5000. From a collector's viewpoint, the 1892-CC is not considered one of the rare dates in the series, but like any double eagle with a "CC" mintmark all specimens are quickly absorbed when brought on to the market.

CLEVELAND'S VICTORY SIGNALS DEFEAT FOR FREE COINAGE

In November 1892, many close elections were *aided* if necessary as the financial elite, railroads, and big business rigged the game whenever it was necessary. In effect, powerbrokers left nothing to chance in their attempts to keep men in office who suited their agendas. Harrison was out and Cleveland was in, after an already distraught Harrison had been stifled with even more anguish when his management of the labor strikes at the Homestead Steel factory and the Couer d'Alene mines were harshly criticized before the elections. For him, it was now over, and for the first time in nearly 40 years, Harrison had to cope with life's problems without his dear wife by his side.

Republican, Populist, and Silver Party losses in the 1892 elections were to the free silver coinage movement what the losses at Vicksburg and Gettysburg had been to the Confederacy; there would be more battles to come, but this movement's fate was sealed.

Although it would be campaigned more mightily than all others before it, the 1896 election would be the final wrap-up to the lost cause of free silver coinage.

CARSON MINT'S TIME RUNNING OUT

November's elections in 1892 also resulted in a new Congressman for Nevada, as the state welcomed Francis Newlands, who over the next 25 years would play a key role, not only in Nevada's political scheme, but also in the

---

A PATRIOTIC TRADITION BEGINS

A Boston magazine aimed at young people, *The Youth's Companion* published a 22- word statement, intended to be recited at public gatherings; school children across the nation would stand in their classrooms in ceremonies honoring Columbus' 400th anniversary, reciting the pledge. The first version of this pledge was introduced as follows in October of 1892:

> I pledge allegiance to my flag,
> and to the Republic for which it stands,
> One Nation, Indivisible,
> with Liberty and Justice for all

This recitation would, of course, eventually be known as *The Pledge of Allegiance.* Changes would be made through the years, until President Eisenhower authorized this final version in 1954:

> I pledge allegiance to the flag
> of the United States of America,
> And to the Republic for which it stands,
> one nation, under God, indivisible,
> with Liberty and Justice for all.

In 1892, as in so many years, the country needed a unifying pledge to help mend the brokenness; it had only been 27 years since the Civil War ended; and the nation was once again in danger of dividing, but this time, the slavery being debated, was of a different nature.

---

nation's. As for the outcome in the presidential race, employees at the Carson City Mint knew that Cleveland's victory was not viewed as a positive sign for Nevada, and especially for the future of their facility. Workers at the mint were ready to take one more ride around on the merry-go-round in 1893, but sensed that their admission tickets were running out.

But the future of the *Silver State,* and especially the Carson City Mint always seemed to be up in the air, locked into a perennial wait-until-next-year mentality. The author of *Nevada, the Great Rotten Borough,* described what he felt was indicative of the uncertainty that residents of Nevada experienced through the years when he declared that Nevada was, "a state whose history has been marked by some odd aspect not anticipated by the Founding Fathers."[1]

Finally; a song debuted in 1892, perhaps fitting to be used as a theme for events that would occur in 1893; the title of the song was *After the Ball Is Over.*

For more information about the silver and gold coins from 1892, please see Chapter 6, *The Silver Coins,* and Chapter 7, *The Gold Coins.*

---

[1] Ostrander, *The Great Rotten Borough.*

1893

Grab your coat, and get your hat,
Leave your worries on the doorstep.
Just direct your feet, to the sunny side of the street.
If I never have a cent I'll be as rich as Rockefeller,
Gold dust at my feet, On the sunny side of the street.[1]

IN THE THROES OF ECONOMIC CRISIS

In terms of significance in the history of the United States during the last half of the 19th century, three years from the final 40 tower above all others, 1861, 1865, and 1893. The last plunged a nation still recovering from the crippling effects of the first two into cataclysmic distress. Untold losses to the United States during the Civil War included human lives with estimated casualties over 600,000. Primary losses during the Panic of 1893 were, on the other hand, financial; a severe depression lasted until 1897, and by then masses of people wondered if their feet would ever be back on the sunny side of the street again. The republic was in a dire state of affairs when Grover Cleveland was inaugurated for his second term as president in 1893, and thousands of citizens west of the Appalachian Mountains already blamed him.

Eastern newspapers, fueled by the *Goldbugs*, insisted that the Sherman Silver Purchase Act was the root of this dawning economic crisis. An attack on silver purchases came immediately after the New Year's recess, when sena-

tors began introducing bills to repeal the Sherman Act. Banking interests in the United States, buoyed by European strongholds, began lining up an army of businessmen and legislators to overwhelm the enemy forces. You might recall that in a speech by Treasury Secretary Foster, it was revealed that Europe's goal was to raid America's gold reserves; by 1893, this was in deployment as the export of U.S. gold coins was rapidly increasing. The stability of the U.S. Treasury was becoming frighteningly dependent on international financiers. By the middle of summer, Great Britain manipulated its domination of India (one of the last major silver countries in the world) and announced that Calcutta was ready to abandon silver as their standard coinage.

The price of silver was already plummeting. Banks in the New York financial district began to recall loans in the western states, and farmers in the Midwest grew increasingly anxious. Rumors spread that the mining states were considering seceding from the Union. In meetings being held in cities from Peoria, Illinois to San Francisco, California, citizens proposed that debtors default on their bank loans, and that the mining states should begin minting their own silver coins. Populist Governor from Colorado, Davis H. White, shouted from the podium that, "if the money power shall attempt to sustain its usurpations by the strong hand, we shall meet that issue when it is forced upon us. For it is better, infinitely better, that blood should flow to the horses' bridles, than that our national liberties should be destroyed."[2] A conservatively biased press flashed headlines of revolution and anarchy. Influenced by this anti-silver smear, some people went as far as to claim, "that all the ills of life— scarcity of money, baldness, the comma bacillus, [etc.] are due to the Sherman bill… If it is repealed, sin and death will vanish from the world…"[3] The eastern media called the *Silverites* unpatriotic, and the journalistic rag, *Harper's Weekly*, labeled the silver senators, "Enemies of the Public Welfare."[4] President Cleveland laid

Residents posing for a picture at a formal ball in Carson City, sometime in the 1890s. The mood is not as festive as it was at social gatherings in more prosperous years, but heads are still held high, and there are even a few smiles in the crowd. (*Courtesy Nevada Historical Society*)

[1] Dorothy Fields, song, "On the Sunny Side of the Street."
[2] Elmer Ellis, *Henry Moore Teller, Defender of the West.*
[3] Ibid.; *John Hay, Letters and Diaries, 1838-1905.* Brown University.
[4] Ibid.

his cards on the table at the opening bell and systematically used his power of appointment to fill the ranks of government with yes men, "taking no heed of the destruction of his own party."[1]

THE SILVER WAR INTENSIFIES

The commanders of the *Grand Army of the Silver States* positioned their regiments against the eastern flank of the *Goldbug* forces. Senators Jones and Stewart from Nevada, Senator Teller from Colorado, Senator Dubois from Idaho, Senator Cannon from Utah, and Representative Bryan from Nebraska, campaigned relentlessly across the nation, and in the halls of Congress. Their subordinates stood by, ready to hold up the arms of their leaders, often substituting when the leaders grew weary. Filibustering was tirelessly used as a strategic weapon in the silver arsenal; during one session, Senator Stewart, had been on the floor for 37 hours, "boasting that he could talk forever."[2] Senator John P. Jones as usual, was the hero of all those on the side of silver, and later in 1893, Jones spoke for nearly eight days with almost no rest during a two-week session— a speech more than 100 pages in the *Congressional Record.* As Leonard Schlup remarks, "Silverites hailed the published work as a compendium on the subject."[3] Although heroic feats like these impressed the underdogs and even a few fence sitters, the side backed by New York and international bankers barely raised an eyebrow.

The press that rode in the money-power's hip pocket, countered every minor *Silverite* victory with venomous diatribes of the inferiority of the "mining camp and Sagebrush Senators."[4] Libelous names slung by eastern reporters, included, "fanatics, disloyalists, traitors, and lunatics."[5] It was a common stratagem for the press to belittle the mining states by pointing out that populations were higher in many eastern state counties, than the entire populations of those rural western states. A constant barrage of journalistic and political ammunition being fired at the *Army of the Silver States* wearied it, but did not entirely crush it. This vignette from Senator Teller's experiences during 1893 describes both desperation and courage, "Nervous and worn out after several sharp exchanges with opposition senators, he [Teller] began to describe the probable effect of repeal on the mining states." Apparently, Teller did not withhold his emotions in front of his fellow Congressmen, as his "voice tremulous with emotion, and his eyes wet with tears, he pictured the misery he saw in the future for the people whom he loved. The spectacle was so striking and unusual that it riveted the attention of every

senator." As if a spirit more powerful than himself anointed him, Teller passionately proclaimed his convictions, as every listener caught up in the drama of the moment, beheld the event. Then, "when with [a] clenched fist, he denounced the 'damnable bill,' the galleries burst forth with applause." The final scene cast a somber spell on the meeting, "when [Teller] concluded he sank to his seat, buried his face in his hands, and presented a living picture of the misery he had so touchingly described."[6]

H.A.W. TABOR

In 1883, when Senator Teller was appointed Secretary of the Interior by President Chester Arthur, H.A.W. Tabor, one of the wealthiest men in Colorado, bought for himself the remaining month of Teller's 1882 senatorial seat. Colorado legislators then elected Thomas Bowen, another wealthy miner, to succeed Tabor for the next four-year term. When Tabor asked Teller for support in his senate bid, Teller expressed his indifference to Tabor's generous financial contributions and flatly denied the request. Exhibiting no respect for Tabor, Senator Teller replied: "You are mistaken in supposing that I could elect you if I wished…I would not if I could…I know you are not fitted by education, temperament, or general personal equipment for that office."[7] When you're worth $20 to 50 million, perhaps education, temperament, or "general personal equipment" are unnecessary.

H.A.W. Tabor was another example of being in the right place at the right time, striking it rich in the silver mines of Colorado when two German shoemakers cut him in on a claim that had not yet revealed its potential. Tabor dedicated himself to the venture, and it paid off beyond anyone's wildest imagination, as he reached the pinnacle of financial success. He could say, as did Sandy Bowers from Comstock fame, "I have enough money to throw to the birds."[8] Tabor not only threw money, he spent it in heaps. He had a vision of Leadville becoming a cosmopolitan city like San Francisco and by 1879 he had his own fire and police departments, town hall, and opera house. He learned early the power of money after he was

---

[1] Ibid.

[2] Ibid.

[3] Leonard Schlup, "Nevada's Doctrinaire Senator: John P. Jones and the Politics of Silver in the Gilded Age," *Nevada Historical Society Quarterly* (Winter 1993).

[4] Elmer Ellis, *Henry Moore Teller, Defender of the West.*

[5] Ibid.

[6] Ibid.

[7] Ibid.

[8] Stone, *Men to Match My Mountains.*

elected Lieutenant Governor; Tabor thought nothing of writing checks for $1 million or more to invest in anything anyone pitched to him. Among other guests Tabor invited General Ulysses S. Grant to Leadville and gave him the royal treatment, wining and dining the entire city.

While serving as lieutenant governor, Tabor, in his 50s, fell in love with a girl 33 years younger than he and the romance became his obsession. Her name was Baby Doe, and from all accounts she was beautiful, with natural blonde hair, a soft complexion, and eyes that could melt a man's heart. Baby Doe's first husband had moved her to Colorado with promises of riches and a lifestyle worthy of her beauty. He had more longing than luck, however, and became a $4 an hour mining camp laborer, wages that could never satisfy Baby Doe's lust for life. She set her sights on Tabor and his millions and eventually had her own suite in the elegant Windsor Hotel in Denver; Tabor commuted often from Leadville to carry on the secret liaison. His first wife begged him not to divorce her, but his passion for Baby Doe was greater than his common sense, so he sent his wife away, with a sizable settlement of cash and real estate. His marriage to Baby Doe tarnished his reputation in Colorado, and was one of the reasons Senator Teller openly disrespected him. Tabor's fantasy lifestyle continued for over 11 years, producing two children, the second, born in 1890, was a daughter named Silver Dollar by Tabor's friend William Jennings Bryan, in honor of Colorado's chief product.

Bryan warned Tabor about the coming crisis stimulated by eastern bankers and *Goldbugs* attempting to destroy the silver market and put the nation on the gold standard. Tabor thought it an interesting argument, but at the time he had more money than he could count, and did not see any threat. That would soon change.

As the so-called *Panic of 1893* began sweeping the nation, Tabor recklessly spent money on himself, his family, and his friends. His daughter Silver Dollar turned three years old in 1893, and Tabor celebrated the occasion with gifts of diamonds and expensive hand tailored clothing. By the end of the year, a crash in the silver market combined with his own irresponsibility, left Tabor and his family suddenly destitute. He was almost 66 and Baby Doe was 33, and it shocked everyone when Baby Doe stuck by her man through the remaining six years of his life. Stories of peoples' descent from affluence to poverty became more common beginning in 1893.[1]

TREASURY SECRETARY FOSTER DECLARES BANKRUPTCY

It seemed no one was sheltered from the ravaging effects of the *money power's* raid on America's economic system. Even those who held high positions in federal government were not immune as former Secretary of the Treasury Charles Foster, from President Harrison's cabinet, declared bankruptcy in 1893 when his liabilities exceeded $1 million. Foster, as you recall, was somewhat of an insider to the schemes of the *money power* and had assured New York bankers who had hosted him at Delmonico's, that as long as he was head of the Treasury, all of their Treasury Note redemptions would be paid in gold. Foster had virtually transferred control of the government's monetary system to the financiers and now he was broke. Members of Congress had no sympathy for Foster's sudden reversal of fortune. Many of them had never forgiven him for his cowardly surrender to the bank crowd back in 1891 and labeled him, along with President Harrison, as a traitor to the cause of bimetallism. When Foster "called upon his New York banker friends for aid, they laughed in his face."[2] These were indeed, merciless times.

John G. Carlisle had replaced Foster in the Treasury Department in March, when Grover Cleveland took office, becoming as bewildered as anyone over the nation's economic crisis.

CARSON CITY MINT'S 9TH INNING

Carson City, as well as the rest of northern Nevada, was shifting into deceleration. When the year began, the Carson City Mint was similar to a weary Major League baseball pitcher walking to the mound in the ninth inning of a losing game, still hanging in there, hoping his team might rally in the bottom half, and turn the game around; it would have been difficult to wager on the outcome though. Granted, the future of silver dollars seemed bleak, but there was at least an ever-increasing demand for gold coins, and Carson City was situated near enough to the gold mining regions in the Pacific states to be an auxiliary gold coin producer if the San Francisco Mint's workload became too heavy. But instead it was the Philadelphia Mint that picked up most of the slack for supplemental gold coins needed to redeem Treasury Notes and supply export demand, knocking Carson City out of contention.

---

[1] For a complete story of H.A.W. Tabor, see David Karsner, *Silver Dollar: The Story of the Tabors*.
[2] Walbert, *The Coming Battle*.

In fact, in response to increased demand, Philadelphia's $20 double eagle output in 1893 rose to its highest level since 1888, jumping from 4,523 pieces in 1892, to 344,339. The nation's chief mint also increased its gold half eagle and eagle production, more than doubling from the previous year. A large percentage of the country's gold coin output occurred in the second half of the year, keeping pace with the constant demand brought on by bank closures and Europe's unrelenting drain of the nation's gold reserves. During the early months of the year, the Treasury allowed the Carson City Mint to continue manufacturing silver dollars at its typical monthly average rate of 120,000 to 150,000 pieces; and Carson City's gold coin production was also on its normal course.

As the ninth inning began, there was no word whether this would be the final game of the Carson City Mint's career, but it was clearly apparent that the team with the "CC's" on their cap was beginning to turn gray with age.

HERITAGE OF THE COMSTOCK FROZEN IN TIME

Whatever the outcome, there was no doubt that events in the Comstock region of northern Nevada had made a significant impact on the growth of the United States in the last half of the 19th century. Historians past and present have been impressed by how Comstock miners were able to reach the depths beneath the ground that they achieved. Also impressive was the ability of enormous milling operations to process such massive amounts of bullion, and the lumber and fluming industry's ability to generate so much wood for the mines. One of the most magnificent engineering feats, in many people's opinion, was the building of the V&T Railroad.

One auspicious distinction that set these accomplishments above similar ones in other locations, was the isolation of the Comstock area. Virginia City was located on the side of Mt. Davidson, and the railroad, the mills, and the lumber industries merged with the mines in ways that defied comprehension; the *crookedest railroad in the world* still baffles architectural engineers. It is undeniable that it would be difficult to replicate some of these efforts even today, let alone in the 1860s, 1870s and 1880s. When President Rutherford B. Hayes had visited the region in 1880, he "expressed his wonderment and praise" for the achievements to a proud audience of Comstockers. Hayes was, "impressed with the prosperity of the Comstock despite the area's relative isolation," and told the folks, "Yours is a barren region, but you have surrounded yourselves with all the comforts to be found in the most favored lands."[1]

Countless other observers have been equally impressed with this area of northern Nevada. In many ways, these accolades and complementary observations are interesting as Virginia City and its surrounding communities were not cities of the future, but more cities of the past. Their enduring legacy comes not from what they are doing now, but from what they did then.

When Nevada's *valley of vision* began to fade into the distance during the 1890s, and depression set in, it had the effect, "of freezing Nevada in time…, into sort of a mold of the wild mining west," says historian William Rowley. This aura would turn the region into a tourist attraction, "as 20th century America urbanizes, modernizes, and [then] romanticizes this past." Anything, and every place, associated with the conceived, "rollicking kind of society," became desirable to own, or attractive to visit.[2] Collectors, historians, and simply tourists, are thrilled to own some relic, artifact, or souvenir, from Virginia City, Gold Hill or Carson City, or have their picture taken in front of one of the vestigial landmarks, so blessedly preserved by time and human effort. Once the Carson City Mint struck its last coin in 1893, the potential inventory from this time-honored site was sealed forever, and meltdowns and natural attrition would further diminish supplies. Considering that the Carson City Mint produced slightly more than 56.6 million coins during its term as a coinage facility, there would only be enough for one out of every five U.S. citizens to own one, not to mention collectors outside the country. That is, of course, if all the coins had survived, but it is well known, that only a fraction of the original mintage of "CC" coins survives today and the limited supply naturally causes increasing desirability. Advanced collectors know this all too well, as prices for the scarcer "CC" dates have risen exorbitantly in the past several decades. If you have not done so already, purchase a piece for yourself and you too will savor the charm of the *Silver State's* heritage that was *frozen in time.*

NEVADA'S IMAGE MARKETED IN THE 20TH CENTURY

In reaction to the calamitous collapse of the silver mining industry and related business failures, Nevada sought new sources of revenue in the 1890s. Capitalizing on its *rollicking kind of society* image, legislators decided to

---

[1] Guy Rocha, "Wanted: The Real Reno," *Reno Gazette-Journal.* February 17, 2003.

[2] William Rowley, Interview, "The Nevada Experience," KNPB (Reno, Nevada).

loosen divorce laws, which sent a message to the rest of the country that "this is where you can get a divorce."[1] While the national trend was to reduce divorce by legislating stiffer laws; the publicity Nevada received because of the divorce issue ultimately brought in more business, but the enterprise of looser moral standards was certainly not a sufficient base for the state's economic survival. When the *sky was falling* during the 1890s, Nevada, like many states, looked for solutions. Historian Rowley suggests that "the liberal divorce law probably would not have existed if Nevada had been more prosperous in the [last decade of the 19th century]."[2] Nevada's merit to the rest of the Union was as usual in question, and one Midwest newspaper editorialized the beliefs of many in the land, when it discredited the *Battle Born State* by making the following derisive comments:

> The silver mines which made her all she was have been exhausted. She has no agriculture resources. She has **nothing to attract people;** and as a consequence, she is flickering out.[3] (Emphasis added)

And this slam continued, when papers from across the nation were demanding that this shameful *den of iniquities* was not entitled to senatorial representation, just as Confederate senators had been denied during the Civil War. In a twist of irony, many heirs to these judgmental journalistic syndicates from bygone eras would hold their conventions years later, in the *Entertainment Capital of the World*, Las Vegas, Nevada.

The bridge between looser divorce laws and the "Entertainment Capital" was reclamation and irrigation, opening the door to the Boulder Dam, which harmoniously dovetailed into the gambling industry. Although mining eventually revived in the state during the 20th century, gambling would forever dominate.

Nevada, like many of the other mining states, had a one-crop economy during the final four decades of the 19th century; precious metals had been to Nevada what cotton had been to the southern states before the Civil War. When the *bullion crop* could no longer be harvested, Nevada fought courageously to thwart efforts calling for the rescission of its statehood, until finally the seeds of gambling were sown, a crop which the state continues to bountifully reap in the 21st century.

Nevada also took advantage of its *hell-bent-to-leather* reputation in its attitudes toward prostitution, an issue that raises eyebrows even in the most liberal open-minded parts of the country. As Nevada was pulling itself out of its valley of uncertainty from the 1890s to the 1930s, prostitution seemed like a friendly bedfellow (if you will) to gambling and divorce. There had been *red light districts* on the Comstock, even one in Carson City, just a couple miles south of the mint. Thus, as the reasoning concluded, there should be brothels to complement the gambling, saloons, divorce, and the *helldorado* Wild West mining camp environment. Just make sure the brothels were on the outskirts of town, and not near schools, churches, respectable businesses, and government buildings, especially government buildings. Moral vices in Nevada have not been prohibited through the decades, just regulated. For example in a classic case of old-habits-die-hard, a headline on the front page of the *Reno Gazette Journal* reported, "Lawmakers Consider State Brothel Tax." And what year do you think this headline appeared— 1893? Or perhaps 1903? Guess again. In fact it was not in the 19th century, or even the 20th century, but this headline was at the top of the page in the February 9, 2003 edition. Picture if you will what locals would think if an article about prostitution in their state appeared in a newspaper in Davenport, Iowa, or Sudbury, Massachusetts, or any state other than Nevada for that matter?

Longtime residents of Nevada know there is a whole lot more to their state than, "gambling, and drinking, and wild-wild women,"but it is the view from the outside looking in, that evokes a great deal of this imagery. Nevada has survived on the strength of this imagery for the past 110 years since the severe financial trials set off by the Panic of 1893 nearly killed the state's silver mining industry and indirectly closed down its mint.

POLITICAL PATRONAGE WHILE A NATION CRUMBLES

The Carson City Mint operated during a period in the nation's history that was marked by corruption, political patronage, scandal, fraud, and forms of depravity that had plagued the United States since it was founded, and would reach advanced levels as the 20th century progressed. But the period between 1869 and 1895 represents a turning point, almost a point of no return, in the audacious manner in which the banking elite, big corporations and politicians would foist their self indulgent schemes upon the American people. An English historian, named Edward Gibbon, wrote a colossal six volume panoramic history in the 1780s entitled, *The History of the Decline*

---

[1] Ibid.

[2] Ibid.

[3] Quote from Chicago Tribune, in Lillard, *The Desert Challenge.*

and Fall of the Roman Empire. In it he describes history as being "indeed little more than the register of the crimes, follies, and misfortunes of mankind."[1]

Whether by folly or by crime, the United States was on the brink of economic meltdown in 1893. Both the Goldbugs and the bank crowd had entered the year with confidence that a contraction in the nation's money supply was the best way to curb inflation and maintain a steady economy. Events leading up to a crisis signaled that their plan might not be foolproof; one of the major railroads in the country, the Reading, went into receivership at the end of 1892 and banks and businesses dependent upon the railroads began to fail. Gold reserves in the U.S. Treasury dropped below the crucial threshold of $100 million, as foreigners continued to redeem Treasury Notes and securities for the only precious metal considered to be a safe store of value. The Cleveland administration was slow to act; outside collaborators, speaking through the voices of politicians, assured the president that short-term financial crises were just part of the business cycle, and everything would quickly recover.

An undercurrent of political and financial skullduggery was related in some ways to the battle over monetary standards, but was unmistakably an independent issue that influenced decision-making in 1893. For the first 90 years of the 19th century, agriculture, textiles, mining, and railroads attracted the lion's share of investor capital; bankers played the role of the house, taking their rake-off on every wager. The securities market in the 1890s, seeking a new angle, turned from its old favorites, to the rising star of big corporations. There were more ways to shelter profits, offer kickbacks, control prices, rub out competition, and tempt politicians, than even William Sharon from the old Comstock days had imagined. And the bank crowd loved this new game, as long as they got their cut.

But many concerned citizens felt big business was a threat to small independent companies and the employees working in them. Small regionalized factories, mills, retail stores, and wholesale firms felt the threat of being bought out, surrendering profits, or being shut down. Tariff bills legislated by members of Congress, who also sat on the boards of corporations, destroyed small companies' hopes of free trade abroad.

An anti-monopolistic attitude prevailed in the land, as the public grew alarmed that large corporations would take control of wholesale and retail profit margins, as well as wages. The theory was that if big business was left unregulated, it would rule America and eventually the public

would be told what kind of goods they could buy, and when they should update, or replace those goods.

Railroads were too vital to the industrial growth of the nation to be totally left out of the picture and corporate giants worked in tandem with railroads, although not always on friendly terms. Efforts of senators and congressmen were split between large corporations, railroads, and banking in a trilateral power structure which was seemingly self-governing. A brief peek behind the curtains, offers a glimpse into the meaning of political patronage, and power brokering; it was common to hear one political agent say to another, things like "At one time all the papers have been **fixed,** [as well as] many of the principle **wire-pullers** in different sections" or "Stewart forces had successfully **purchased control of the senate**...."[2] (Emphasis added)

There had been a time when the mining states had been able to use profits from their bullion to finance political maneuvering, but by the 1890s, their money was like *flea-pee* in the ocean compared to the finances of big business and bankers. Men representing the Silver Party and the Populist Party could inspire the crowd, but their hidden allegiances prevented them from accomplishing the goals the crowd was shouting about. The state of Nevada was a perfect illustration, as "the Southern Pacific [Railroad] Political Bureau in the nineties, was ...acknowledged as the only real political machine in the state, and one which commanded the loyalties of all the smaller politicians and county statesmen."[3]

Beneath the surface of Senator Stewart's political maneuverings, for instance, was the fact that his political manager was "Southern Pacific's C. 'Black' Wallace, [who] dominated the politics of the state during the decade."[4] Stewart and Wallace were instrumental in founding the Silver Party, yet paradoxically at the same time their boss, Collis Huntington "opposed the Silver Party, which his political agent[s] [were] helping to create." Huntington was also opposed to the Populist Party and their "platform, including certainly, its plank on the nationalization of the railroads."[5]

Political patronage is all about a favor received for a favor given. Huntington realized that superficial support of the Silver Party would ease the prejudice of the public

[1] Edward Gibbon, The History of the Decline and Fall of the Roman Empire.
[2] Ostrander, The Great Rotten Borough.
[3] Ibid.
[4] Ibid.
[5] Ibid.

toward the railroads, and as it is in many bilateral relationships, the win-win outcome meant that, "Nevada got its Silver Party," but more significant, "Huntington got its Silver Senators."[1]

One man fighting for silver in 1893 might have come from the breed of men who stay true to their principles in the face of temptation. Biographers claim that Senator Henry Teller from Colorado was a *Defender of the West.*[2] Looking at a portrait of Teller in his later years, you see the stern face of a man with a call to duty. His trimmed white beard, (minus a mustache), and his dark penetrating eyes, dividing his chin from his neatly brushed hairline of distinguished gray hair, gave him the appearance of a Quaker, or a prominent doctor of medicine. Teller might just have been that unimpeachable stone wall of a man who had never put himself up for sale in the political market. But if Senator Teller knew anything about the corruption, political payoffs and patronage occurring while he was in office, and did not step forward and expose the crimes, he categorically must be considered guilty by association. Senator Teller worked side by side with *hired men* in Congress who took their cues from outside sources. A man of his intellectual stature and discernment, would have had to possess a tremendous amount of trust in the integrity of his peers, to overlook their weaknesses. Only Teller knew for sure.

In a perfect world, which the 1890s in America was not, political guardians would have had purer hearts than those they were entrusted to guard, but temptation then, as always, had a way of revealing hidden faults in people. Though political leaders might have begun their careers with virtue and integrity, when the enticing aroma of personal gain was held beneath their noses, it required consciences forged in steel to stand firm. But if their consciences had become seared, a descent into a morally unprincipled state of mind was inevitable; and the more reprobate politicians became, the more difficult it became to control them.[3]

Looking back on the political scene in the 1890s, it appears as if chaos and corruption permeated the corridors of democracy; and nothing short of a shaking of the

President Grover Cleveland held office during one of the worst economic nightmares in U.S. history. (*From Dictionary of American Portraits, Dover Publishing*)

foundations on which the country was built would bring about repentance.

James Madison, the framer of the Constitution, believed that the way to inhibit the buying of votes was to increase, as much as possible, the size of the districts voters lived in; he believed that larger districts, greater sums of money and more acts of patronage would be required than candidates might be willing (or able) to dispense. But the one glitch was that when it became too costly, or too time consuming for candidates to influence voters in their districts, they could turn to power brokers and political machines for support. Ultimately, there would be no district, region, or country too large that a *money powered elite* would not be equal to the task.

For better or worse, government in the 1890s was controlled by international financiers, large corporations, and the railroads. Congressmen were the buffers protecting the true leaders from the public, simply because it would have outraged the citizens of the United States, to see the president of J.P. Morgan, or the head of Standard Oil, or the managing owner of the Southern Pacific Railroad, or the director of the leading bank in England, standing on Capitol Hill giving President Cleveland orders. None of these men had been elected to any office; but whose words were actually being spoken when a senator or congressman opened his mouth? The only clues came from legislation being passed; if laws were enacted enriching one group at the expense of another, patterns of favoritism could be detected—low taxes for large corporations, generous loans to railroads, and less government intervention in banking policies seemed overtly accommodating. But what about the issues of the free coinage of silver, farm subsidies, and lower tariffs? These issues were highly politicized, receiving lots of press, and even having two parties formed on their behalf, but in retrospect they did not appear to have received much support where it really counted. What were these special interest groups to do; what recourse did they have other to submit to those in power?

---

[1] Ibid.

[2] Elmer Ellis, *Henry Moore Teller, Defender of the West.*

[3] Acknowledgement to Budziszewski, *Revenge of the Conscience.*

When the government turns a deaf ear to the needs of certain segments of society it sends a strong message that the concerns of these citizens are being ignored, like Humphrey Bogart's line in the movie *Casablanca* about the affairs of a couple of people, "not amounting to a hill of beans."

This was the message coming from the Cleveland Administration concerning the free silver movement and other issues affecting many Americans during the early 1890s. When President Cleveland brushed off the panic of 1893 as just another natural stage in the business cycle, he was listening to the voice of denial, not reason, hoping that life would somehow go back to normal. But it was no comfort to *Mr. Scarecrow* farmer and *Mr. Tin Man* factory worker to be told not worry, that if they would just press on it would all be over in a few years and they could return to their ordinary lives.

Cleveland might have been able to say that to the head of a corporation who was worth $200 million before the Panic and saw his pile dwindle to $150 million. In actuality, thousands of businesses had failed, hundreds of small banks were shut down, repossessions and foreclosures were at all time highs, and record unemployment forced millions out into the highways and byways, desperate for jobs. It seemed cruel indeed for the government to have treated its populace as if their affairs, "didn't amount to a hill of beans," but in 1893, the *American Dream* came to a temporary halt and in the midst of the panic, bankruptcies, unemployment, and depression, the public wondered what had happened. The government in which they trusted, had led them down a slippery slope, and they had begun to feel the disastrous effects. Yet millions of people responded faithfully and patriotically, choosing to remain loyal to the government, for that was all they had to cling on to.

SILVERITES' VIEW ON THE ECONOMIC PANIC

At the same time, millions of other people continued to listen to *Silverite* orators heralding the soundness of free silver coinage and bimetallism, and demand from banking and creditor groups to have the Sherman Silver Purchase Act repealed gave rise to more vociferous appeals from the Silver Party. Senator Jones from Nevada assured his supporters, that a free silver/bimetallic monetary system would provide every man, woman, and child with the comforts of life. The cause of the Panic of 1893, as far as Jones was concerned was a contraction of the money supply. In short, the Treasury had been redeeming all currency with gold, and not issuing new currency to replace it, so Jones told his followers that the country needed more currency in circulation which would occur when the Treasury began accepting silver from citizens and mining companies. He also professed that gold was the money of the affluent, and silver was the money of the working class and poor, an interesting belief coming from a multimillionaire, who represented super wealthy individuals like Alvinza Hayward and D.O. Mills, men who had little interest in free silver. In fact, Jones had married Hayward's sister and Mills of course, was from the old Bank of California crowd. At best, Senator Jones teetered atop a delicate fence of compromise.

In his political appeals for silver Jones made it clear that he wanted to exclude British financiers from America's monetary system, but he was too late for that, as Great Britain's bankers were firmly entrenched in America's monetary system. Too often overlooked was the fact that British banking interests had rushed to San Francisco in the 1860s and opened five banks to purchase bullion from the Comstock and California's Mother Lode. Although these British bankers were competitors of Mills, Sharon, and Ralston's Bank of California, deals were made, and bonds were formed. Only time will reveal the hidden truth of Great Britain's influence in America's economic policies.

Jones' rally cry called for a standard of justice, from which it can only be assumed that Jones was saying that the gold standard was unjust, with the silver standard being the just one. In an equitable sense, it might have been fitting if "standards of justice," as Senator Jones earnestly demanded, had been applied to the senator's own motives, either exonerating or incriminating him.

A NEVADA MELODRAMA

Senator Stewart, stepping outside of his glass house, threw stones at President Cleveland all year. Stewart would later describe Cleveland's second term in office as "probably the worst administration that ever occurred in this or any other civilized country."[1] Axiomatic of the adage about people in glass houses throwing stones was the constant backbiting and political infighting that unfolded in Stewart's relationships with his anti-silver benefactor Huntington, his blossoming rival, Congressman Newlands, and the Silver Party at large. This melodrama begins with Mr. Huntington, who as head of the Southern Pacific Railroad became wealthy by persuading Congress to invest

---

[1] Brown, *Reminiscences of Senator William M. Stewart.*

millions in his company through grants and low interest loans. Huntington had tried his hand as a mining prospector when he first arrived in California in 1850, but after half a day, he decided he was better suited to supplying goods to the miners and used his paltry bank roll to begin a trading company. In the 50 years following until his death in 1900, Huntington's only interests in silver were the quantity of supplies the miners bought from him and how much ore they shipped on his trains.

In the early years of building his railroad, Huntington formed strong bonds with the bankers in San Francisco; at one point he and his partners offered 80% of their Central Pacific to D.O. Mills from the Bank of California. Keenly ambitious, Huntington's interests were corporate power, banking connections, and favors from Congress for his railroad. Always seeking new opportunities to expand his empire, he looked beyond Nevada's crumbling mining industry and saw the potential in cultivating the state's agricultural growth. In the last years of his life, Huntington told one of his wealthy friends from Nevada, "If I were a young man, I would devote my life to developing irrigation in Nevada,"[1] a comment suited to the next character in this melodrama, Congressman Francis Newlands. Having no background in Nevada, no interest in silver, and seemingly no ties to Huntington, but having a lot of money, Newlands was not the one being purchased, he was the one purchasing. There was an obvious link between Newlands and the bank crowd in California, since he was William Sharon's son-in-law and trustee. An instant rivalry formed between Newlands and Senator Stewart, because Stewart considered the newcomer a threat to his senate seat.

From the beginning of his political career in 1893, Newlands spoke of reclamation and irrigation as the key to Nevada's future, an apparent coincidence because Senator Stewart's boss, Huntington, had also voiced an interest in that subject.

Out of the four main characters in this melodrama, Senator Stewart is the only one that was an outwardly loyal supporter of the Silver Party, being one of its founders. In fact those who knew him related how the senator prided himself in being a champion of the rights of the downtrodden silver miners; Stewart capitalized on this persona in later years as his weekly newspaper, *The Silver Knight* (the watchtower publication for the silver cause) premiered in the mid-1890s and reached a circulation of over 100,000 subscribers.[2]

Comrade in arms to Stewart was the other *silver senator* from Nevada, John P. Jones, whose backers included D.O. Mills and the Southern Pacific. Although Jones' affiliation with Huntington was not as pronounced as Stewart's, Huntington had *owned* Jones' loyalty since 1877.

Whereas Stewart had bolted from the Republican Party at the earliest opportunity, Jones hedged in the beginning, waiting a year to officially

Senator John Percival Jones, "Silver Senator" from Nevada.

join the Silver Party, although he would stubbornly adhere to a strict agenda of silver for the masses, until he declared the movement dead in 1901. Neither *silver senator* seemed that interested in reclamation or irrigation, but in an effort to fuse all subordinate issues in order to combat the so-called "money-power," both men offered their perfunctory support. Long after the fight had been lost, *silverites* would read Stewart's speeches in meetings. But, by then, when any message about silver was presented in Congress, yawning throughout the room was the norm, as the words would go in one ear and out the other of those that bothered to stick around. By the end of its days in 1900, the silver message had become *a beaten horse.*

All of the men in this live drama seem to have been related in some way. Senator Stewart, although a broken record with his silver speeches, worked for Huntington, who did not seem to give a *toad's rump* about silver; Senator Jones was just as involved, sharing similar connections with Stewart, though more covert. Senator Newlands represented the bank crowd (and mostly himself), and voiced his passionate beliefs on reclamation. Cracking through the underpinnings, Senator Stewart and Congressman Newlands were political rivals, with seemingly separate agendas, yet beneath the surface, Newlands shared similar notions with Stewart's boss Huntington, who really was only concerned with how big an empire he could build for himself. Collectively, there was so much money available to the four of them, enabling them to buy anything (or anybody) they wanted. In hindsight, it is almost impossible to fathom who, or what these men represented, and

[1] Lillard, *Desert Challenge.*

[2] Davis, *History of Nevada.*

any public political disagreements between them would have seemed pointless and farfetched at best, comparable to the modern day *sport* of professional wrestling—mostly just for show.

CARSON CITY DESTINED TO SURVIVE WITHOUT MINES OR A MINT

In 1893, Reno was the fastest growing, and most highly populated city in Nevada, climbing to nearly 9,000 people by the end of the decade. Winnemucca and its surrounding county were nearing 4,000 in population, and in central Nevada, situated on what is known as *The Loneliest Forty Miles In America*, Austin claimed fewer than 2,200 inhabitants. Over in eastern Nevada, White Pine County's largest city, Ely, had grown to slightly under 2,000, and closer to the state's capital, Storey County, home to the Comstock Lode and its famous Virginia City, accelerated its population decline, as it dropped to near the 5,000 mark. At the southern tip of the state, Las Vegas' approximate population of 600 gave no indication of what was to come; while at the same time, Nevada's capital, Carson City, continued losing residents, eventually dropping below 3,500 in the immediate years following 1893.

Carson City, being Nevada's capital, required that measures be employed to insure its survival. Although it was not a mining camp town whose primary industry was producing precious metals, the mining district in Carson City's backyard certainly stimulated its growth and prosperity. The mint itself was an obvious by-product of the mining boom, as were the mills, the lumber businesses, and the railroads. From the earliest days, vehement arguments about the life-giving role that the Comstock Lode played in the development of the northwestern section of Nevada were expressed, as characterized by this statement made just five years after mining fever broke out in the region: "But for the mines, all your stores would be removed, your farms would dry up, and be abandoned, and your wagons would stop in the streets…everyman you see…looks directly to the miner…"[1]

It is undeniable that Nevada owes its existence to mineral wealth, but Abraham Curry and his friends founded Carson City the year before the rush to the Comstock began, and whether or not Curry and his friends anticipated a mining boom in the region, Curry must be given credit for the vision he had of "a city with a central square upon which the capitol building of an independent state would be erected."[2] From that vision arose the first territorial post office, established in November of 1858, giving the new city status as an official town site. In the months and years following, Curry and his friends erected commercial buildings and residential houses as fast as they could. In those days, Carson City was a little over one mile square, and the "wide streets were laid out, and Curry reserved a plaza of four acres in the center of town for a public square."[3] William Ormsby built a retail store, and operated a hotel in the bottom floor of his two-story house. One of the founders Benjamin Green owned a jewelry store and gunsmithing business. John Musser and Frank Proctor, Curry's other two partners, had a law partnership and, "although times were hard, food scarce, and the weather severe, the [first] settlers were a cheerful lot who liked good company and merriment."[4] One of Curry's great pleasures in life was throwing parties and staging balls; locals would dance and eat, drink and tell stories, and engage in all sorts of amusements. With the Comstock Lode and its wealth, everything happening in town was amplified to the highest pitch, but the vision the founders had for Carson City was independent of this windfall. Years later, in 1893, the venerable city would find out if it could survive without the

---

[1] Speech by Charles Delong at Nevada Constitutional Convention in 1864, from Lillard, *Desert Challenge.*
[2] Cerveri, *With Curry's Compliments.*
[3] Ibid.
[4] Ibid.

Landscape view of the Capitol building in Carson City, site of much political activity in the 19th century, carrying forward to the new millenium.

support of the mines. If in fact, like the man had said back in 1864, its "stores would be removed, farms be abandoned, and wagons would stop in the streets."[1] After midyear in 1893 Carson City would also have to survive without its mint.

Besides mining and minting if Carson City had another predominant industry in the 19th century it would have been politics. Vividly illustrated whenever the state legislature was in session, the atmosphere in town pulsed with hustle and bustle as more than 100 politicians would fill the seats of the Capitol chambers. At the conclusion of each day's session, those same men accompanied by their wives hit the streets, causing greater than normal pedestrian traffic. Abe Curry had made sure the streets were wide, but they weren't that wide, and this assemblage of politicians could block the path of passing carriages, as local restaurants and saloons hastened to stock up with ample foodstuff and libations to serve the overflow business. One of the more popular hangouts was the Arlington Hotel, on the same side of the street, heading one block south from the mint, said to offer the most appetizing meals. And always the central focus of the peaceful community was the grand Capitol building, which came to life when it was time for politics.

No one would argue that the Comstock connection had played the most influential role in the Carson City's past, and an especially meaningful role in the establishment of the mint, but this city outlasted the mining towns surrounding it. Though the mint is more revered than any reminder from the state's past, it is because Carson City is the state's capital that the community has maintained its sense of political and historical permanence through the years.

AUGUSTUS G. HEATON

Memorable events in the history of coin collecting illuminated the scene in 1893, the same year that the author and numismatist often credited with introducing collectors to the thrill of collecting mintmarked coins turned 49. Having been an active collector for years, Augustus Goodyear Heaton would be indelibly linked to the gratifying experience of collecting coins from every U.S. mint. In the years leading up to 1893, Heaton had been writing articles on various topics for the *Numismatist*, a publication introduced in 1888, and later the voice of the American Numismatic Association (ANA) after its establishment in 1891. In Heaton's opinion, the coinage of the United States had boring designs, and being an artist himself, he appealed to the Treasury to enlist creative designers to refashion the nation's coinage. Heaton declared that collectors in the 1890s drew pleasure from

---

[1] Speech by Charles Delong, in Lillard, *Desert Challenge.*

Across the street from the beer company is the popular Arlington Hotel, famous for its culinary delights. In the background is the Carson Mint with its flag raised high. (*Courtesy Nevada State Museum*)

searching for the earliest U.S. coinage, but even that could become tiresome, despite there being at least 50 varieties of the 1794 cent and just as many for the 1795 half dollar. Certainly variety collecting offered some fascination, suggested Heaton, but in many cases the differences in varieties were so trifling, there wasn't much to get excited about. Proof issues from the several decades before his writings appeared, also offered slight interest to collectors, due mostly to the stunning mirrorlike qualities of the coins. In Heaton's *Treatise on Mint Marks* from 1893, he acknowledged that, "some well meant attempts have, to be sure, been made in the new dies of 1892 [Barber Coinage], and in the Columbian half dollar, to awaken numismatic and artistic interest." Unfortunately, Heaton was still bored, and he assumed the new coin designs of 1892 would, in his words, "greatly dispose the collector to slumber again,"[1] until such a time that coins worthy of the collector's interest appeared.

Since 1893 was the 100th anniversary of the Mint's first coins, Heaton patriotically appealed to the romanticized senses of the collectors. He challenged the creative minds of the Bureau of the Mint in his declaration, that "we should, on the centennial year of the first United States coinage, advocate a return to the superb designs of our earliest dates...Let us hope [that] some imaginative brain and skillful hand, may yet be authorized to produce new coins with the dignity, beauty, and simplicity of the old."[2]

From Heaton's day until the modern age, everyone has had his or her own opinion about which denomination, series type, or variety category is the most interesting, a component that gives coin collecting its broad diversity. For collectors in the 21st century, nostalgia often makes the past look better than the present and just about every U.S. coin type from 75 to 200 years ago offers some curiosity and interest. Time and again, it has been the author's experience, that whenever a collector is shown a complete *type set* (one example of every U.S. coin design), there are levels of fascination with every coin. In such a comprehensive display of America's coinage as in a type set featuring coins from the year the Mint was established to the present, there is a greater appreciation for the sum of the parts, especially for beginners and novices. There is no denying that viewing the artifacts, relics, antiquities, coins and collectibles from a nation's past is intriguing, piquing most people's curiosity.

As for Heaton, the coins in circulation during his day were not satisfying enough to awaken the collector spirit in him, and being ever resourceful, Heaton discov-

TYPE AND VARIETY CATEGORIES AVAILABLE TO COIN COLLECTORS	
• VAMS (Van Allen/Mallis)	Silver dollar varieties
• Full Head (FH)	Standing Liberty quarters
• Full Band (FB)	Mercury dimes
• Full Bell (FBL)	Franklin half dollars
• Full Step (FS)	Jefferson nickels
• Sheldon/Noyes	Large cent varieties
• Crosby	Half cent varieties
• Browning	Bust quarters
• Overton	Bust half dollars
• Bolender	Bust silver dollars
• Blythe	Half dimes
• Snow	Flying Eagle and Indian cents
• Various References	Error coins

ered a way to enliven collecting even the most commonplace coins in circulation, "In the meantime, [that is, until more creative coins are designed] there is a generally overlooked or neglected means of dispelling all apathy in connection with our modern coinage."[3] Heaton's revelation of the overlooked or neglected means was of course, the subject of his treatise, collecting by mintmarks; it was like a light bulb had been turned on in the minds of numismatists, a concept so obvious, but needing someone to announce, *gentlemen, start your engines.*

Concerning the categories of various coins available to collectors, the options in the present age (2003) are more numerous than at any point in history. Collecting by dates and mintmarks does not generally fall under the category of *Varieties*, although there are, of course, varieties within the mintmark listings. Heaton proposed that the pursuit of mintmarks would serve as a suitable alternative to variety collecting. He stated that: "The various sizes of the mintmarks... ranging from capital letters of average book type, to infinitesimal spots...as well as the varied location...defy any accusation of monotony... [these mint marks] are far more distinguishable than the characteristics of many classified varieties..."[4] For a par-

---

[1] A.G. Heaton, *A Treatise on Mint Marks.*
[2] Ibid.
[3] Ibid.
[4] Ibid.

tial list of the options available to coin collectors today, see the side insert on the previous page.

By 1893, coins from the Carson City Mint were already a gleam in many a collector's eye and Heaton's *Treatise*, which made its debut that year, increased interest. Auction companies were already using adjectives like rare, scarce, and uncommon, in their catalog descriptions of "CC" coins, and in an age without population studies and computer databases, numismatists often used the *simple-formula-first* approach to determine rarity. Heaton's postulation suggested that if certain dates and mintmarks, "in the possession of collectors and dealers are **proportioned relatively** to the original coinage, the date[s] [with the lowest mintage] should be the most difficult to find."[1] (Emphasis added) Using that criteria as a reference for "CC" Morgan dollars, Heaton declared that the "1885 is quite scarce and the 1889 moderately so."[2] At the time it seemed logical, since the 1885-CC had the lowest mintage, and the 1889-CC had the third lowest. For a time, auction prices realized supported this rationale, as 1885-CC silver dollars were already bringing substantial premiums.

To illustrate, in the 1894 Frossard sale of the *W.M. Friesner* collection, an Uncirculated 1885-CC silver dollar sold for $2.30, while an Uncirculated 1881-CC silver dollar brought $2.60, and an 1878-CC dollar sold for $2.00. In comparison, an 1893-S silver dollar in Uncirculated realized $1.10. Decades would pass before anyone knew about the significant quantities of Uncirculated examples of 1881-CC and 1885-CC silver dollars in storage in Treasury vaults; as if the coins had been strategically preserved for future generations of coin collectors. Of equal importance to collectors as mintages and extant populations is the quality rating of coins, and concerning this Heaton stressed how rare many mintmarked dates had become in Uncirculated condition, stating that, "Any prominent dealer could soon fill an order for one hundred strictly Uncirculated Philadelphia coins of any silver denomination and date (with few exceptions) between 1840 and 189[3], but would find an equal number of any Branch Mint pieces very difficult to gather in [Uncirculated]."[3]

With his knowledge of the subject, it was no surprise when Heaton compiled his *Leading Coins* list that "CC" dates ranked at the top in every denomination, except in the half dollar category, where they ranked sixth. Years later, even the scarce date "CC" half dollars would be eclipsed only by one of the top dates on Heaton's list, the

1838-O. Future generations of collectors—following in the footsteps of notable numismatists like Heaton, George Heath of the ANA, and auctioneers like the Chapman brothers, and Ed Frossard—would certainly possess more knowledge, thanks in part to the chronicles left behind by these men of their experiences, which stimulated the learning process, and instilled a greater sense of appreciation for the subject.

UNITED STATES BRANCH MINTS

By the time Heaton published his *Treatise* in 1893, the Carson City Mint had been in operation for 23 years, the San Francisco Mint had been in operation 39 years, and the New Orleans Mint, 55 years. Charlotte and Dahlonega, the other two branch mints, had opened 55 years earlier but had been closed for over 30; neither of these two southern mints produced silver coins, but the gold coins struck at these facilities, ranging from $1 to $5 denominations have become rare to exceedingly scarce in the early years of the 21st century. Of great interest to collectors are the $3 gold coins struck at Dahlonega in 1854, the only year either southern mint issued this denomination.

A loyal following for all "C" and "D" (Dahlonega) gold coins has grown through the years, but nothing compared to the "CC" series collector base, in spite of the fact that all three of these mints only manufactured coins for less than 25 years, and played major roles in the expansion of the country, exuding their own unique charm and alluring appeal. But why aren't coins from Charlotte and Dahlonega as popular as those from Carson City? Some enthusiasts will probably claim that they are, but truth is in numbers. Many collectors have never heard of these two mints and even some of those familiar with them have a difficult time pronouncing Dahlonega correctly (Dah-law-neh-guh). Certainly the limited denominations available from the two southern mints, lessens widespread saturation in the collector market; it is entirely conceivable that if these two mints had issued subsidiary silver coins, silver dollars, and $10 and $20 gold pieces, the collector base for them might be substantially larger. Another point to consider, unrelated to coin collecting in general, is the universal popularity of the "Old West" theme as compared to that of the "Old South." Both have their merits, but the choice would probably be obvious to most.

---

[1] Ibid.
[2] Ibid.
[3] Ibid.

Keep in mind, there are no losers in such comparisons, for all U.S. mints are evocative, having made tremendous contributions to the country they serve.

Of the five branch mint coinage facilities from the 19th century, only Dahlonega, situated in Lumpkin County, Georgia, having a population of less than 25,000, shares small town status with Carson City. Dahlonega itself is reported to have a population less than 4,000; nestled at the base of the Chattahoochee National Forest; it is approximately 100 miles from Chattanooga, Tennessee to the north, and 60 miles south to Atlanta. Closed for over 17 years by 1878, the old Dahlonega Mint was destroyed in a fire that year.

In contrast to size, the home of the Charlotte Mint in North Carolina, is one of the south's major cities, with a population of approximately 600,000 (in 2003). But in modern times it has shared similar status with the facility in Carson City, as the old mint in Charlotte has been a museum since the 1930s, preserving the history of southern heritage.

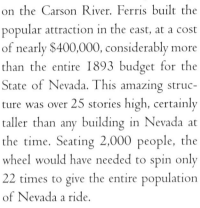

2003 POPULATIONS OF CITIES HOME TO BRANCH MINT COINAGE FACILITIES FROM THE 19TH CENTURY	
(As of 2003 • All approximate)	
City	Population
Charlotte, North Carolina	600,000
Dahlonega, Georgia	3,800
New Orleans, Louisiana	500,000
San Francisco, California	775,000
Carson City, Nevada	54,000

Traveling south from Charlotte, New Orleans has also grown into a large metropolis with a population of approximately 500,000 people; at one time it was considered to be the banking and financial center for the Gulfport states. New Orleans is known for its hospitality and recreation industries a similarity it shares with Carson City's home state of Nevada; the French Quarter once boasted of gambling houses, saloons, opera houses, restaurants, and even a red-light district. The New Orleans Mint is still a popular tourist attraction today, as it has been preserved and is open to daily tours.

Out west, San Francisco's population of over 775,000 people (2003) establishes it as the largest city that is home to one of the original branch mint coinage facilities. Through the years the San Francisco Mint has been renovated; and is currently awaiting a decision about its status as a museum.

WORLD'S COLUMBIAN EXPOSITION OPENS

On May 1, 1893, the Chicago World's Fair, officially the World's Columbian Exposition, opened to cheering crowds. Authorized by Congress in 1890 and originally scheduled for the fall of 1892, the Exposition attracted more than 27 million visitors during its six month run; all 44 states, as well as over 70 foreign countries, displayed exhibits.

Amusement rides mystified the crowds, one of the most popular being the *Ferris Wheel*, created by George W.G. Ferris, Jr., son of a family from Carson City. Ferris told everyone that the inspiration for his invention came from the big water wheel as it turned near Cradlebaugh's bridge on the Carson River. Ferris built the popular attraction in the east, at a cost of nearly $400,000, considerably more than the entire 1893 budget for the State of Nevada. This amazing structure was over 25 stories high, certainly taller than any building in Nevada at the time. Seating 2,000 people, the wheel would have needed to spin only 22 times to give the entire population of Nevada a ride.

The new Columbian commemorative half dollars, as well as silver quarters honoring Queen Isabella were sold at the fair, but proved not to be as successful as the Philadelphia Mint had hoped. *Treatise on Mint Marks* author A.G. Heaton designed a cover with a Columbus theme for a 50-cent stamp that proved popular with attendees.

All in all, the Exposition was a rousing triumph for a country in the throes of economic disaster, and might have been the last semblance of gaiety many Americans would experience for several years.

As a boy, George W.G. Ferris, Jr., sat by the river at Cradlebaugh's water wheel, dreaming of the amusement ride he would one day invent.

SALE OF $300 MILLION IN TREASURY BONDS

Though not anticipated by planners, the World's Fair ran simultaneously with a financial panic that began in 1893. Just four days after the event opened, the stock market took the first of many plunges, as transfers of millions of dollars were made between banks in New York and others in the east, in an attempt to avert closings. During the summer, President Cleveland ordered the sale of nearly $300 million in Treasury bonds to New York City banks in exchange for gold, to be redeemed on four different occasions beginning later in the year. As investment and credit capital flowed into New York, it severely contracted the nation's money supply. New York banks were able to loan the money to borrowers of their choice and banks in the west, as well as the south, were passed by in favor of eastern banks. These loans became assets on the lender bank's balance sheets, enabling those banks to make loans, using the loans as security.

Simply stated, a bank's assets consist of the money on hand, plus the credit it has issued. For illustrative purposes, imagine that a bank has $1 billion in cash and that the bank has loaned out $1 billion. The bank can lend the $1 billion in cash (less required reserves), plus, it can lend on the $1 billion in loans that it has already issued (less required reserves); at that point it would have loans of $2 billion (less reserves) listed as assets on its balance sheet entitling it to offer loans on that $2 billion in assets, plus any new cash deposits received. This creation of money by issuing credit could continue until laws prevented it or an economic panic shipwrecked it; since it is all done on paper, it is difficult for outsiders to track. Therefore, the flow of money between banks, corporations and creditors takes place on a higher plane than 99% of the public is familiar with, and by the time a nation's economic system goes in the dumper, the public can only rub its eyes, and wonder "What went wrong?"

Although cloaked in mystery, one can only surmise that banks at the very top of this inverted pyramid (wherever that top may be) are continuously accumulating frightening amounts of wealth and power, reinforcing the link between the concentration of wealth into a financial banking elite, and the rise of industrial and corporate capitalism.

GOLDBUGS SCORN FREE COINAGE OF SILVER

During the summer debates over monetary standards in 1893, the *Silverites* and the *Populists* fought to free the country from the lock-grip of the banks, corporations, and *Goldbugs*; leaders in these two parties were the so-called defenders of the middle class and common citizens, arguing that if the Treasury remonetized silver, the nation would have a purer monetary system. *Silverites* declared that precious metals were *natural money*, not like the credit-based money created by the banks. They pled for the use of it, basing their pleas on the constitutional and biblical legitimacy of silver, using the economic crisis enveloping the country as prime evidence of the dangers of a gold standard controlled by an elite few.

Opponents of the free silver coinage movement were referred to by many names: *Goldbugs, Financial Elite, The Money Power, The Bank Crowd, Conservatives, Monopolists,* and *The Anti-Silver Group*—and those were the polite names. Leaders on this side of the battle insisted that the *Silverites* were to blame for the messy state of financial affairs the nation found itself in, saying the glut of silver burying the country caused the panic. These *Conservatives* supported a bill to repeal the Sherman Act, and assured the public that after the burdensome flow of *debased money* was brought to a halt, the panic would end, and the nation would be strengthened by the gold standard, and be back on its feet in no time.

In the midst of the debates, one of the gold advocate's spokesmen, Representative Samuel McCall argued before Congress:

> Now, Mr. Speaker, not withstanding the reduced demand for silver, caused by the demonetization of 1873, you will find that, in the face of that decreasing demand, the **product of silver has constantly increased**, and today [1893] the annual output of that metal is nearly 250% greater than it was in 1873. [Silver production] has gone up so much, that today silver can hardly be ranked among the precious metals....[1] (Emphasis added)

One can only imagine the catcalls, and boos coming from the *silvermen* after that statement, as one by one the *Goldbugs* portrayed silver as being despicable, gross, sickening, and the dross of the earth.

There were men of compromise in the debate, however, who did not see free silver coinage as the issue, but rather the enactment of it as legal tender, believing that any form of *good money* does not need legal tender status to make it acceptable. Michael Daniel Harter, a Congressman from Ohio who probably did not hold silver in high regard, still challenged the government to let citizens decide what kind of money they wanted to use. Harter asked Congress why it did not just, "open the mints to the free

---

[1] Ritter, *Goldbugs and Greenbacks.*

coinage of **both gold and silver** with no legal tender quality imposed upon either?" (Emphasis added) Stating that international traders of the world used that method, Harter asked them, "Is not this the best and fairest way out of our financial complications?" Why not just, "leave both metals to stand upon their own merits as money, without the aid of any legal tender enactment?" Probably knowing what the result would be Harter concluded, "it would soon be demonstrated **which metal the people preferred to use as money.**" (Emphasis added)

It was then, and forever will be debatable whether free silver coinage and bimetallism would have been the wisest choice, and more specifically if a monetary standard of that nature would have prevented the depression. But the battle over monetary standards was more a battle for control, as those in control were not willing to relinquish it, and the ones being controlled were trying to lift the restraints of tyranny. Leaders at the highest level in the country, who had sworn oaths to preserve and protect the Constitution, had allowed tremulous conditions to shake the lives of the citizens who had elected them. St. Thomas Aquinas, writing on political theory stated that: "If the ruler has been elected by the people, he may justly be checked, or even deposed for abuse of power…If no remedy can be found in human procedures, [the people] must turn to God…He, if He wishes, may change the heart of the tyrant."[1] By the end of 1893 the nation's citizens would be on their knees, seeking help from anyone who might have mercy on them.

PRECURSOR TO FIAT MONETARY SYSTEM AND DEBATE OVER SHERMAN ACT

Following the timeline through America's monetary history it became clear that neither *Goldbugs* or *Silverites* would achieve their goals; by 1933 it became illegal for U.S. citizens to own gold and the nation's money was backed by nothing but *faith and promises.* In 1964, the Treasury would cease using silver in coins altogether; "silver and gold have I none, but such as I have, give I thee."[2]

A paradigm shift from a monetary system backed by precious metals to a *fiat* money system was in progress in the United States in 1893, and in the future, it would not matter where gold and silver mines were located, because mints could operate from anywhere that was convenient, as coins would not require precious metals or possess intrinsic value. From that time on, the hands of the financiers, bankers, and governments around the world, would never again

be tied since the ability to control the amount of money in circulation would be solely in their power, and never again would they need to be concerned whether the money was worth anything. Furthermore, the Bureau of the Mint could strategically place coinage facilities where they were capable of accommodating mass distribution of their product.

At the beginning of the 21st century, governments would be toying with the idea of cashless societies, an interesting concept, as bureaucrats would probably support cashless monetary systems, especially bureaucrats running governments that consider hard cash outdated, old fashioned, and hopefully obsolete.

Senator William M. Stewart in the later years of his political service.

Coin collectors are waiting on the sidelines to see if coins and paper currency will eventually become dinosaurs from the past, only increasing demand for them.

In Ancient Rome leaders convinced the citizens that imperialism was the key to their future success. Eventually, trade with foreign countries increased and the empire's exporters and high level government-backed businesses grew wealthier, but the agrarian culture in Rome became unprofitable, and eventually, the economy of a large middle class was destroyed. Something similar loomed in the United States, and in her review of America's economic shake-up of the 1890s, Gretchen Ritter writes, "History suggests that the antimonopolists [Populists, et. al.] were right. Financial concentration skewed economic opportunities in favor of some regions and groups, and contributed to the rise of a concentrated corporate economy."[3]

Throughout the ensuing death march to financial insolvency, President Cleveland remained committed to what he believed was the solution, "On August 8, 1893, [he] urged Congress to repeal the purchase clause of the Sherman Act…A bill for repeal was introduced on…August, 11."[4] Immediately, *Silverities*, Teller, Bland, Jones, Stewart, Bryan, and their silver compatriots stomped to the front. First, Congressman Bland called for a fixed

[1] St. Thomas Aquinas, *St. Thomas Aquinas Summa Theologica* .

[2] Acts 3:6, *The Bible.*

[3] Ritter, *Goldbugs and Greenbacks.*

[4] Don Taxay, *The United States Mint and Coinage.*

ratio between gold and silver at 16:1 to be added to the bill; his enemies scoffed, reminding everyone that the true market ratio between the two metals was currently closer to 32:1. Then Senator Stewart pulled one of his canned speeches out of the cupboard, and harangued about "The Rule of The Gold Kings," attacking those who did not consider silver to be *honest money*. Pulsing with emotion, the blood vessels in Stewart's forehead were probably bulging when he hurled his attacks at Cleveland, Harrison, Treasury Secretary Carlisle, Mint Director Preston, Great Britain, Germany, the Republican Party, the Democrat Party, that senator over there from Maryland, and anyone else who criticized silver! But, by now his arguments had lost much of their impact; everyone had heard it all before. He continued to speak because legislative protocol allowed him to for as long as he wanted.

Senator Teller counterattacked the repeal bill by asserting that, "It was legislative action being forced upon the country by powerful special interests, without any chance for ascertaining the popular will." And he challenged his colleagues in Congress to, "Go to the people with this question. Take the public sentiment on it, and if they elect [to support the pro-repeal leaders]...Then we will surrender."[1] Teller was not willing to give up without a fight, however, and used every legislative weapon available to him to attack his opposition. Finally it was Senator Jones' turn, who by then was in all essence a member of the Silver Party, although his official bolt from the Republican Party would take place the following year. He later said, "I can no longer, as an honest man, true to my convictions, remain with a party whose principles on the main issue are so repugnant to my own views."[2] Jones' filibuster, just days before the vote on the bill, is the classic manifesto from the *Silverite* camp. During this critical period, another setback for the silver camp came from the other side of the globe on June 27, 1893, when India ceased free silver coinage. As fall approached, the situation worsened.

SILVER DOLLAR PRODUCTION DECLINES AS THE CARSON MINT CLOSES

After the first quarter of 1893, there had been little doubt that this would not be a big year for silver dollar production in the United States. In January and February, the Philadelphia Mint began striking silver dollars as usual, but did not produce any in March. Other than a mere 28,000 in April, the nation's chief mint would not coin another silver dollar the rest of the year. At the New Orleans Mint, the entire output for the year (300,000) was struck in January, with not a single silver dollar coined from February through December. San Francisco issued the rarest business strike Morgan silver dollar in the entire series that year, striking only 100,000 1893-S dollars in January and none thereafter.

Meanwhile, at the Carson City Mint, production of silver dollars progressed at the normal steady pace: 130,000 in January, 150,000 in February, and 140,000 in March, probably engendering a sense of reserved optimism among employees there. Of graver concern than the number of coins being minted was the gloomy forecast that the country was heading toward depression. Adding to the Carson Mint's insecurity was President Cleveland's comment about repealing the Sherman Act. Rumors floated around that the Treasury was considering shutting down operations at the Carson facility, and although locals had grown accustomed to rumors like that they knew their mint was a vulnerable target of the Bureau of the Mint's downsizing proposals. This was sure to be the most challenging year ever, and all the faithful employees at the Carson City Mint could do was remain steadfast and hope for the best.

Through the years the Treasury Department had become an old pro at deciding whether to bolster one of their facilities with tenant improvements and new machinery, or close one down. Back in the 1830s, even the main Mint in Philadelphia was itself considered a heavy burden on the government; there had been debate in Congress whether the Philadelphia Mint should be closed down, or fortified and supported until it became profitable. Congress auspiciously voted to keep the national mint open, and provide whatever means was necessary to ensure its success. Then, after the Civil War, the Treasury and Congress were faced with decisions about their southern branch mints, one in particular, the Charlotte Mint, which had closed in 1861 when war broke out. After the war ended citizens in North Carolina appealed to the Treasury to reopen that mint, but their wishes were never fulfilled.

In 1893, the time was nearing to make a decision about the Carson City Mint. Faced with realization of an impending bleak outlook, residents in Carson City knew very well how dismal mining production had become on the old Comstock and surrounding regions, and they could only hope for a turnaround of some kind to validate their mint's existence.

---

[1] Elmer Ellis, *Henry Moore Teller, Defender of the West.*

[2] Speech by Sen. John P. Jones of Nevada, Senate of the United States, Government Printing Office, 1894.

Superintendent Hofer ordered the coin presses to be fired up in April and another 120,000 silver dollars were produced; in May another 137,000 silver dollars were delivered, bringing the five month total to 677,000, a far greater quantity than any of the other three mints. In fact, Carson City's total equaled 87% of the combined output from those mints, in a year that represented a steep decline in silver dollar production in general. The table below shows the rapid reduction of silver dollar mintages from 1890 through 1893 for all mints combined.

ANNUAL COMBINED SILVER DOLLAR PRODUCTION FROM ALL U.S. MINTS FOR THE YEARS 1890-1893	
Year	Total
1890	38,043,004
1891	23,562,735
1892	6,333,245
1893	1,455,792

Then it came—the news Nevadans and especially Carsonites had known was inevitable: on June 1, Director of the Mint Robert E. Preston, by order of Secretary of the Treasury Carlisle directed Carson City Mint Superintendent Theodore R. Hofer to suspend coinage operations at his facility. For the more optimistic in Carson City the word suspend did not sound like *close up for good*, or something permanent; however more than half of the employees were immediately given their walking papers. Some of the employees had already experienced this before as the Carson City Mint had been closed or suspended several times in its 23 year history, the latest being 1885. Maybe it would open again; sometimes it had taken six months, and once it took four years. But was there reason to hope? Somehow, this time, the suspension seemed more final. But no one could say for sure, and until that magnificent building that Abe Curry had put there was demolished, there would always be hope.

PROOF (AND NON-PROOF) 1893-CC DOLLARS

At some point in 1893, mint employees struck 12 1893-CC silver dollars as Proof specimens for presentation to officials in honor of the mint's closing. Examples of these Proof 1893-CC silver dollars have appeared in auctions from time to time; one of the more recent being at the 1997 Heritage ANA sale in New York City; where the price realized was $41,400.

Between the two major grading services, PCGS and NGC, a total of 15 specimens have been graded, an inflated number due to resubmissions of several of the same coins, with the highest being an NGC Proof-67.

Existence of 1893-CC Proof silver dollars was revealed to coin collectors 50 years after their production by coin dealer Wayne Raymond. It would be another 30 years after that before the first specimen was actually seen by the larger coin collecting community, appearing at the 1973 RARCOA auction where it realized a record price for a Morgan silver dollar at the time of $18,000, the first of that series to sell for over $10,000.

One of the 12 specimens of the 1893-CC Morgan silver dollar in Proof condition.

At the 1997 Heritage ANA auction, the cataloguer estimated that only five of the original 12 were traceable. At the time, the specimen being offered was encased in an ANACS (American Numismatic Association Certification Service) holder, but has reportedly been *crossed over* to a PCGS holder. Certain 1893-CC Proof dollars, if shown to a person without introduction, might be mistaken as business strikes which have been cleaned or polished; but several of the pieces in the finest grades are stunning.

How glorious it would be if all 12 of the original examples were recovered and displayed together, similar to how all five 1913 Liberty nickels were displayed at the 2003 ANA convention in Baltimore.

Aside from the Proof issues, the 1893-CC silver dollars in business strike (non-Proof) are considered to be the second rarest of the 13 dates in a set of "CC" Morgan dollars, surpassed only by the 1889-CC; and this date's rarity is further evidenced by there having been only one example available during the GSA sales in the 1970s; a distinction it shares with the 1889-CC and 1892-CC.

Prices have risen dramatically for 1893-CC dollars since the 1970s, especially for examples in MS-65 condition, which routinely sell in the $50,000 range, as much or more than some of the Proof specimens bring (In 2003).

A RECORD OF THE CARSON MINT'S GOLD OUTPUT FOR 1893

The demand for gold coinage increased at a deliberately frenzied pace in 1893, as the Treasury rushed to fulfill its currency redemption obligations both home and

CARSON CITY GOLD AND SILVER COIN PRODUCTION BETWEEN 1889-1893

Years	Coins	Total Mintage	Total Face Value
1889-1893	Silver dollars	5,696,741	$5,696,741
1889-1893	Gold Coins	752,821	$7,232,580

LIFETIME COINAGE RECORD AT THE CARSON CITY MINT IN TERMS OF FACE VALUE AND QUANTITIES

Years	Coins	Total Mintages	Total Face Value
1870-1893	Silver	54,762,546	$25,445,009.30
1870-1893	Gold	1,873,573	$23,829,425.00
		Ratio – (Gold)1:1.0678(Silver)	

abroad. Consequently, the ratio between the face value of gold and silver coins produced at all mints, approached a level not seen since before the Coinage Act of 1873. For 20 years the ratio fluctuated in a steady range from 2.5:1 to 1:2. But in 1893, the ratio widened to 6.5:1, followed in 1894 with an 8.7:1 ratio, and the face value of gold coins minted in 1893 was higher than it had been since the first three years of the 1880s.

At the Carson City Mint a consistent ratio of approximately 1.27:1 had been maintained between gold and silver coins during its final five years of production. The first table above exhibits the quantities and face values of the gold and silver coins produced at that mint from 1889 to 1893.

This characteristic marginal ratio between the face value of the gold and silver coins minted at Carson City, resulted in a near dead heat when the mint's lifetime totals were tallied as exhibited in the second table above.

In Carson City's final year, the ratio was approximately 1.79:1; as $808,040 in gold coins were minted, compared to $677,000 in silver dollars. Dominating gold coin output at the Carson City Mint were half eagles, just as they had in the preceding four years, but only in terms of pieces minted, because $20 double eagles, once again, led in terms of face value, though the quantity was much smaller than the previous year's.

In the $10 eagle category, far fewer 1893-CCs were produced than either of the other two gold denominations, a consistent pattern extending through much of the Carson Mint's coinage years.

For collectors in the early years of the 21st century, all three denominations are relatively easy to acquire in the Almost Uncirculated grades, becoming much more of a challenge in Uncirculated conditions.

It is not certain when the gold coins manufactured at the Carson Mint in 1892 and 1893 were released, as Treasury records indicate that there were at least two years of gold coin production still in the mint's vaults after it closed on June 1, 1893. This was reported when Treasury inspectors visited Carson City to settle accounts, and listed the total face dollar amount of coins in holding at $8 million. From this amount, nearly $5.5 million were unreleased silver dollars still in the Carson Mint's vault, leaving approximately $2.5 million in face value of gold coins. For the two year period ending in June of 1893, $2,168,180 in face value of gold coins had been produced at Carson City, which when added to the silver dollars in storage, would still have been several hundred thousand dollars short of the $8 million settlement amount.

There had been large quantities of gold half eagles and eagles minted at Carson City in 1891 and possibly some of these were still in storage on closing day. Although the actual release date of the stockpile of gold coins stored

GOLD COINAGE RECORD AT THE CARSON CITY MINT FOR 1893, 1889-1893, AND 1870-1893

Denomination	1893 Mintage	1893 Face Value
$5 Half Eagle	60,000	$300,000
$10 Eagle	14,000	140,000
$20 Double Eagle	18,402	368,040
Denomination	**1889-1893 Mintage**	**1889-1893 Face Value**
$5 Half Eagle	404,768	$2,023,840
$10 Eagle	175,232	1,752,320
$20 Double Eagle	172,821	3,456,420
Denomination	**1870-1893 Mintage**	**1870-1893 Face Value**
$5 Half Eagle	709,617	$3,548,085
$10 Eagle	299,778	2,997,780
$20 Double Eagle	864,178	17,283,560

at the Carson Mint after July of 1893 is unknown, millions of dollars in gold coins were being exported at the time, and invariably Carson's inventory was included in shipments abroad. To be sure, small hoards of Carson City gold coins from the 1890s which might otherwise have been extremely rare returned from overseas and Latin America in the last half of the 20th century.

But aside from exports such as these, there have not been any reports of large quantities of Carson City gold coins lost in transit, similar to the well-known shipwreck losses of San Francisco coins in the 1850s and 1860s. Only occasionally have small hoards of "CC" gold coins surfaced, one of the largest reported being approximately 1,500 pieces, mostly double eagles, that hit the coin market in the late 1990s. There have been rumors of similar hoards, one in particular being a family's approximate 1,000 piece accumulation of "CC" gold coins, reportedly including several of the extremely rare 1870-CC $20 double eagles. Trustees of this hoard are said to be saving the coins for their kids' education; if they hold onto the coins long enough, they might be able to buy a college.

SUBSIDIARY COINS, SENIORAGE PROFITS AND TONS OF SILVER

Though gold coins dominated the nation's money supply, silver grabbed the headlines with unceasing recurrence, as followers observed that silver prices took dips, short bursts, and dives throughout 1893. When the Carson City Mint was ordered to halt coinage operations on the first of June, it sent an incipient message to western silver states that the party might be over. It was not just the Carson Mint, for all the mints in the country had been ordered to cease silver dollar production. The bullion value represented in every silver dollar hovered around 60 cents through the year and now the White House called upon the Treasury to do something to restore confidence in the weak U.S. silver dollar that had become the scourge of bankers around the world, adding further incentive for a repeal of the Sherman Silver Purchase Act.

Neither the Sherman Act of 1890, or the Bland/ Allison Act of 1878, were considered free coinage measures, or bimetallic endorsements, or changes in the official monetary standards, but were basically subsidiary coin laws; subsidiary coinage is silver coins that are worth more as money than the market value of their metal content, and in 19th century America, this included at various times

dimes, quarters, half dollars, and silver dollars. Smaller denominations were referred to as *minor coinage*, consisting of cents and nickel five-cent pieces. Silver bullion was purchased on the government's account, coined into money that was worth less as bullion than face value, and then distributed to the public at a seniorage profit to the government, profits derived from the positive balance of the coins' face value above the cost of the metal in them. Costs of production were also expensed against gross profits, and if, by chance, the cost of the bullion and production costs exceeded the monetary value, a loss would be recorded in the Mint's accounting ledger.

Alexander Hamilton, the designer of America's monetary system, had not been in favor of a seniorage profit system, but instead argued that the metallic value and the monetary value in coins should be at par. Under a seniorage system temptations would inevitably become too great for those controlling the country's purse strings.[1] Free coinage, as being promoted by the *Silverites* and *Populists* in 1893 would have been impracticable to the government, if only on the grounds of seniorage, mainly because seniorage had been an exclusive right of the government, which was unlikely to give up its profits to the public.

As 1893 solemnly trudged on, *Gilded Age* ideologies like *eat, drink, and be merry* began reaping the latent vicissitudes of, *for tomorrow we shall die.*[2]

Cleveland's administration apparently lacked a competent risk management team; the country was short on wise economists and long on corporate and political blindness, driven by the obsession for increased revenues and power. Spokesmen defending the rights of the common masses against an abusive and manipulative government promised that free silver coinage would realign the balance of economic power.

Half a century later, economist Elgin Groseclose, an authority on the subject of monetary standards, crystallized the essence of what the free coinage movement in 1893 advocated, "The function of government is to maintain the integrity of the [monetary] standard...It is as corrupt to vary the standard of value... as [it is] to change the length [in a] yard... or the [measure] of a bushel."[3] Proponents of free coinage stood for freedom from gov-

---

[1] Acknowledgements to Neil Carothers, *Fractional Money: A History of Small Coins and Fractional Paper Currency of the United States.*

[2] Isaiah 22:13, *The Bible.*

[3] Elgin Groseclose, *Money and Man: A Survey of Monetary Experience.*

ernment monopoly of money, influenced by the banking elite. Free coinage philosophy argued that there should never be a contraction, or an over-saturation of the money supply, but rather a balance. Groseclose stated that: "The mechanism by which the circulation [of money] is always adequate to the needs of trade is that of free coinage…under this system, the free market, rather than a bureaucracy, determines the amount of circulating [money]."[1] The problem of an inflexible currency standard was that it led to a contraction of the money supply, allowing a concentration of financial power controlled by select groups representing the heads of banking and corporate monopolies. Free coinage theorists believed that their plan was the only way the nation could maintain a currency supply that would conform to population and industrial growth; and according to their plan, this system would eventually act as a democratic lever in directing the course of economic change.[2]

Nevada, Colorado, and the rest of the western mining states, were just as concerned about support for their chief product as they were for a sound monetary standard. Free coinage and silver were inseparable parts of the pecuniary puzzle. *Silverites* needed a stronger support base for their silver, and would have been just as content if Congress had proposed a solution even at the exclusion of free coinage; the undeniable fact was that millions of ounces of silver were still being mined from the ground. Pro-silver groups rallied through 1893, desperate to protect their primary source of revenue from becoming worthless. In Butte, Montana an advertisement sounded an alarm for any slumbering silver supporters to wake up and heed the call, "This is a serious crisis, and a failure at this time to respond to the call of duty and self interest…will betoken [represent] an indifference which can only result in serious criticism of our motives, and the justice of our cause."[3] Another article appeared in *Harper's Weekly* editori-

alizing the dilemma facing the country already headed into depression and burdened with a glut of silver: "But we are now [concerned] with the load of silver bullion which the government is storing. It is difficult to foresee what will be done with this amount of material. Even if the Sherman law is repealed, there it is [the silver], and if the government undertakes to sell it, the silver market will go even lower…the silver miners insist that the government shall buy and maintain the price of their product, although the Treasury vaults now hold **4900 tons** of it which it cannot sell…" In a portent of things to come, the article, in the spirit of fairness, argued that, "If the silver miners have the right to demand this [Treasury silver purchases], why is it absurd for the farmers to demand that the government store their crops, and loan them money on them?"[4] (Emphasis added)

CONGRESSMAN RAYNER COUNTERS SILVERITE ADVANCES

Silverites in Congress fired their final salvos as they led the charge against their enemy's center flank. Congressman Richard Bland continued to use conspiracy allegations as a primary weapon, accusing the Treasury of conspiring with eastern bankers and Great Britain in an attempt to bulldoze Congress to repeal the Sherman Act and place the United States on the gold standard. Senator Sherman frequently expressed his opinions in the debate over repealing the Act bearing his name. Many of his speeches and writings were compiled in his book *Silver and Gold*, from which comes the following:

> If we adopt the single standard of gold without aid from silver, we will greatly increase the burden of national and individual debts…[and] still further reduce the value of silver, of which we now have over $593 million…On the other hand, if we continue the purchase of silver, we will eventually bring the United States to the single standard of silver…[5]

Sherman further insisted that the United States had always been a bimetallic country, and that the strength of the nation's monetary system depended on remaining on that standard. He outlined his plan for maintaining parity between both metals, essentially by the free coinage of only the more valuable metal (gold), and setting a legal ratio

---

FORMULA TO DETERMINE THE MARKET VALUE OF METAL IN U.S. SILVER DOLLARS

Standard Unit of Measure – 480 grains in one troy ounce of bullion
Silver content in silver dollars – 371.25 grains (.999)
Mathematic Formula: 480÷371.25=1.29.

Use of 1.29 As Factor

Silver Price	Equation	Value of Silver in Coin
$1	$1÷1.29	.77519
$0.90	.90÷1.29	.69767
$0.75	.75÷1.29	.58

---

[1] Ibid.
[2] Acknowledgment to Ritter, *Goldbugs and Greenbacks*.
[3] Q. David Bowers, *Silver Dollars and Trade Dollars of the United States, A Complete Encyclopedia*.
[4] *Harper's Weekly* (July 1893).
[5] *Silver and Gold*, Collections of Sen. John Sherman, 1895.

between it and the cheaper metal. Sherman realized that this would only be a regression and he further proposed the use of the *fiat* system as the means by which the government would support the value of the cheaper metal. His rationale was:

> This necessarily imposes upon the government [at all times] the duty of buying the cheaper metal and coining it into money…If the bullion falls in price, the government must make it good; if it rises in value the government gains…The Government is thus always interested in advancing the value of the cheaper metal…This is the kind of bimetallism I believe in.[1]

One way or the other, the government was being called upon to subsidize silver.

From their lookout posts, the opposition calmly viewed the troop movements of the *Silverites* throughout the year. One of their secondary commanders, Congressman Rayner from Maryland, called for unconditional surrender of the army that supported the Sherman Silver Purchase Act. In his speech before Congress, Rayner boldly stated: "I am not in favor of purchasing another ounce of silver, or coining another dollar of it…Now, in saying this, I desire to add that I have no hostility whatever to the use of silver upon a proper basis…" Regardless, the Congressman from Maryland enumerated all the disasters, financial ruins, and fallen civilizations, brought about by the improper use of silver in monetary systems. Rayner then stated that if the U.S. government continued to support silver the country might as well, "lock hands with every bankrupt government on earth that believes in the cheap manufacture of wealth, in cheap money, in broken contracts, and in repudiated debts…" Rayner judged that all those who ever believed that silver could be used as sound money "have been excommunicated as heretics from the roll of civilized communities, and banished from the field of honor." He proceeded to assure his colleagues in Congress, that the rumors about an eastern banks/Great Britain conspiracy were completely bogus. One of the roles of the Treasury, during the past 15 years, in Mr. Rayner's assumption had been, "to act as a pawn broker's shop for the benefit of the Colorado and Nevada mines." In total condemnation of free silver coinage, Rayner tells Congress the solution is so simple: "If more money is needed, can we not increase our currency upon a legitimate basis? Is there no method known to the ingenuity of man…to enlarge the circulating medium of the country?"[2] (Twenty years later, Mr. Rayner's inquiry would be answered in spades— Federal Reserve, 1913). Congressman Rayner

Publications such as this reminded readers of the glut of silver coins being held in Treasury storage vaults.

concluded his remarks by demanding the dissolution of the partnership between the government and the silver mining industry, "I ask what earthly right have the silver mine owners to haunt these halls demanding protection for their investment? Is the Government bound to guarantee to them a profit upon their enterprise? Is the Government in partnership with the mine owners? I deny it."[3]

THE SHERMAN ACT IS REPEALED

After a smashing filibuster by Senator John P. Jones in mid-October momentarily halted the frontal attack of his opposition, Senator Teller from Colorado was called upon to fire the final offensive. The outcome hung in the balance, and the repeal of the Sherman Act, if passed, would be a crushing blow to the cause of silver. Both sides had fought hard all year as the battle between the Repeal and the Anti-Repeal forces had weakened an already stag-

---

[1] Ibid.
[2] Taxay, *The U.S. Mint and Coinage.*
[3] Ibid.

gering economy. Casualties of the Panic of 1893 were enormous, growing worse, as time passed. *Silverites* were not just fighting for their beliefs on legislative issues, they were fighting for survival. If the Sherman Act was repealed, their losses could swallow them back up into the earth from which their silver had come from. On the other side, the *Goldbugs* and their Pro-Repeal allies had less to lose, as their economic bases, also being shaken by the panic, were more diversified than the *Silverites*. Without a doubt, the Sherman Act was certainly an obstacle in their paths and a constant source of agitation, but even if it remained, they could hurdle past it.

It appears as if by late October of 1893, the outcome had been unofficially decided long before, and was simply awaiting proper approval. Senator Teller spoke in Congress on October 27, 1893, "in a chamber as 'silent as death', and in words which will 'long be remembered for their solemnity, [for] the thrill of sympathy which they aroused... and for the sincerity and earnestness which emphasized each word." Teller's passionate appeal, "addressed not the Senate so much as the country at large." He identified with Colorado and the nation's silver miners, when he edified them saying, "we are neither cast down nor dejected...we know what it [will mean] to turn out our 200,000 silver miners ...we are ready and willing to meet the occasion... But, Mr. President the iron will enter into our souls." Teller went on record to say that the repeal of the Sherman Act, and the defeat of the free silver coinage bill "is the most terrible moment of my legislative life...I fear that we are entering upon a financial system from which there is absolutely no escape."[1] There was no doubt in the senator's mind who masterminded this insidious plot:

> I know that it is the combined capital of the world...I know they have the power to control the great agencies of thought.... The men who own the money of the world, the bonds, the interest-bearing securities, know that if they can put

this country upon a gold standard [they will control prices and men's freedom]...It strikes me to my very soul...I warn the American people, that if they do not now resist, they will speedily enter upon a system of industrial slavery which will be the worst known to the human race.[2]

Three days later, on October 30, 1893, Congress and President Cleveland finally broke through the gridlock of political debate, and repealed the Sherman Silver Purchase Act of 1890, one day before Nevada's 29th birthday. The vote was in, the repeal was passed, the President signed it, and that was that. There was a loud boom, and then silence. In hindsight, Gretchen Ritter, writing over 100 years after the repeal, remarks:

> Their [the repealer's] victory does not prove the superiority of their monetary system...Having gained control over the government, and eventually over the regulatory structures, the financial conservatives implemented their world view. The telling of history belonged to the victors.[3]

Ms. Ritter also surprisingly draws the conclusion that "there is no evidence of collusive activities by individuals to seek control of the national economy." It seems that more research might be necessary to concur with that presumption, as it is indeed unfathomable, to infer that the Panic of 1893, the subsequent depression, and the upheaval in monetary standards occurred through a series of unrelated and disunified decisions. Nevertheless, as Ms. Ritter accurately declares, "The telling of history belongs to the victors."[4]

History may never reveal the truth of what actually happened during the turbulent 1890s. Lacking wiretaps, surveillance cameras, computers, and other forms of modern day security technology, investigators were dependent upon informants, and document searches. Misdeeds done behind closed doors, and in hidden political and corporate

Cartoon depicting the *Silverites* defeat after the Sherman Act was repealed in 1893. Senator William Stewart is sitting on the ground, Senator John P. Jones is upside-down, falling halfway down the side of the building, and Senator Henry Teller is just being thrown out of the Senate's window at the upper left.

[1] Elmer Ellis, *Henry Moore Teller, Defender of the West.*
[2] Ibid.
[3] Ritter, *Goldbugs and Greenbacks.*
[4] Ibid.

CHAPTER FOUR • BEGINNING OF THE END (1889-1893)   189

chambers, are not included in the archives available through the Freedom of Information Act. Only *Father Time* and the omniscient *Keeper of the History Books*, decides what and when the truth is told.

But the Coins Remain

Coins of the realm, on the other hand, provide a more definitive history. These *impressions in metal*, often speak louder than words, as they preserve a nation's heritage. The Carson City Mint, for example, really did manufacture 56,636,119 coins, a fact that cannot be denied. What happened to all those coins after they left the mint is a topic ripe for researchers. But today a collector holds a "CC" coin in his or her hand, and suddenly can almost hear a recitation about who designed the coin, when and where it was struck, how many were minted, what the metal content is, what the different symbols, legends, and mottos mean, which other types of coins were struck, who the assayer was, who milled its planchet, who pressed it into the dies, what it sounded like when other coins clanged together in canvas bags, who the mint superintendent was, and what the two "C"s stood for. A coin may also be a window back into the events from the year in which it was manufactured, reminiscent of the fashions, politics, inventions, wars, economics, literature, and other essential information needed to understand the country's past; it is left up to the beholder to take it as far as curiosity leads.

An 1893-CC silver dollar for instance, reminds collectors of many facets of the history of Carson City and the mint that operated there for 23 intermittent years. Looking back 30 years before the colorful Comstock coin-processing plant shut down, Abe Curry's son Charles had died at the tender age of 27, in 1863, when the town of Carson City was only five years old. In 1873, the year of the Coinage Act, Abe Curry died at the age of 58, and a decade before the mint closed, in 1883, prominent Carson architect and businessman, Peter Cavanaugh died after suffering for 11 years from the effects of a stroke, which left him crippled in the prime of his life. Before his paralysis, Cavanaugh had built Carson City's central Catholic Church, St. Theresa's, and his structural masterpiece, the state Capitol building. And finally, returning to the year the 1893-CC silver dollar was made, collectors are reminded that this was when the beloved mint ceased its coinage operations.

It is axiomatic of nostalgia buffs in America that the chosen people, places, and things, whose times have been cut short are treasured forever, focusing on the specific memories admirers wish to keep of the objects of their adoration and curiosity. Just like J.F.K., the Pony Express, James Dean, Marilyn Monroe, Sandy Koufax, the World Trade towers, and all whose time was cut short, the Carson City Mint will be remembered the way it was in its prime.

Every coin, every object, every document, and every piece of the historic building on Carson Street, or chips of wood from the trees surrounding it will become increasingly more revered as time passes by. If the GSA (General Services Administration) were to hold sales of three million "CC" silver dollars today (2003), a one-day sell-out would most likely be guaranteed. If the time ever came, (God forbid) that a decision was made to demolish the Carson City Mint building, it probably would not be presumptuous to suggest that chunks of the sandstone exterior, and boards from the wood floor, would be easy to market as souvenir items.

There are several hundred pieces of correspondence between Abe Curry and the Philadelphia Mint that would sell like hotcakes in bibliographic auctions. There is a gold watch on display at the Nevada State Museum (the old mint building) that was presented to Abe Curry in 1871 by the employees at the mint inscribed, "To A. Curry from the officers and employees of the U.S. Branch Mint, Carson City, Nevada, January 1, 1871." If this piece were ever auctioned, the bidding would most assuredly be lively. (Hopefully, if this occasion ever arose, the State of Nevada would be the winning bidder.) Curry, himself loved to give friends and visitors tours of the mint. In his short term as superintendent from 1869 through the middle of September 1870, Curry was fond of passing out newly coined 1870-CC silver dollars, now eagerly sought, as are all coins with the "CC" mintmark.

Many distinctions have been credited to the Carson City Mint's record books, including issuing the rarest Seated Liberty silver dollar, and striking the first trade dollar west of Philadelphia. Back in 1869 the Director of the Mint James Pollock, had expressed his assessment of the purpose of the Carson City Mint: "...it will be much more of an assay office than a mint....The power to make coins may be an **occasional benefit**...this branch may fully meet the expectations of **its friends** [locals, Comstockers, etc.], and greatly promote the general prosperity of that **interesting portion of our country**."[1] (Emphasis added)

It was no secret that the Carson Mint had never been taken as seriously as other mint facilities around the

---

[1] *Annual Report of the Director of the Mint*, 1870.

country; after all, what credibility could a mint have whose superintendent passed out its newly minted silver dollars to his friends like they were cigars, was delinquent on his personal loans, and often had liens against him appear in the local papers? But in the mint's early years there was so much silver in the region the Treasury simply could not ignore it.

By 1893, with the nation facing an economic debacle, and the silver mines around the Comstock stopped in their tracks, the Carson City Mint was in the wrong place, at the wrong time. The glorious Comstock Lode had contributed so mightily to the westward expansion of the United States, and now the mines and the mint that had once served them had come to the end of the line.

Remarkable as it may seem in retrospect, prior to the discovery of vast mineral wealth in Nevada, and subsequent silver bonanzas in states like Colorado, the U.S. government faced a shortage of the metal and the Treasury had actually been concerned about where to get bullion for the country's silver coinage. Sources in Mexico, South America, and Europe had been considered and the Mint Director placed advertisements around the globe to purchase silver; little did anyone at the time know that silver would become so plentiful, it would be coming out of the nation's ears.

THE SILVER DOLLAR PRESSES SHUT DOWN

But in 1893, the brakes came screeching to a halt on Government purchases of silver; the Sherman Act had been repealed, and the Treasury said, "Enough already." At the time, over 550 million ounces of silver coins and bullion were stuffed into the Treasury's vaults. No more silver would be purchased and no more silver dollars would be minted, at least for the time being. Finally, after 15 years of voluminous silver dollar production, the presses shut down at Philadelphia, New Orleans, and San Francisco. Not only was an out-of-service sign placed across Carson City's coin press, a gone-out-of-business sign was posted on the front of the building.

The overwhelming supply of silver dollars in storage across the country remained on hold, as the only areas of the nation that experienced general circulation of these large coins was the South and West. In the South, still recovering from the adversities caused by the Civil War, there was a scarcity of gold coins, especially among former slaves. Readers might find it interesting to note that according to Carothers, "the colored population refused to use greenbacks with their **printed symbols** [but] they gladly

accepted the new silver coins."[1] (Emphasis added) Western states, of course, had been the primary source of the silver used in the coins, and generally favored *hard money* over soft currency. The rest of the country virtually shunned the bulky silver dollars contributing to the huge stockpiles remaining in Treasury vaults. Carothers described the situation (from a 1930 perspective) as, "The millions in the vaults are merely an undigested mass of stamped metal, of discreditable history, and no present use…they should be eliminated."[2]

America's grand experiment with the production of large coins, designed to utilize the nation's vast silver supply, had been temporarily discontinued, an operation that would remain stalled, until a logical excuse for the silver dollar's existence could be discovered. From 1894 through 1904, and then from 1921 through 1935, silver dollars were produced resulting in millions more being added to Treasury supplies. From 1918 through 1920, approximately 260 million silver dollars minted prior to 1905 were melted at Treasury facilities. At the time, the public held enormous quantities of silver certificates, redeemable in silver dollars and as these certificates were recalled, the Treasury again began producing silver dollars in 1921, continuing intermittently through 1935. Seniorage profits, to the government this time, were substantial, due to record low silver prices. Then finally in the mid 1960s, the price of silver rose above the monetary value of the coins, and the Government reneged on its promise to redeem paper money for hard money.

In modern times (2003), silver dollars are in the hands of collectors, investors and accumulators, and the antiquated practice of the Treasury redeeming currency for silver coins will seem as odd to many children growing up in the 21st century, as the belief in Santa Claus.

However, one state discovered a legitimate use for silver dollars in the 20th century. Millions of tourists visiting Nevada's casinos were thrilled at hearing the jangle of the old coins dropping out of slot machines. Since the theme and ambience of most of the state's casinos was Old West, tourists spent their vacations living vicariously as *cowboys* and *cowgirls*, placing stacks of silver dollars on the gaming tables. From the 1930s through the mid 1960s, hundreds of thousands of silver dollars were shipped back to Nevada at the request of casino owners in a splendid marketing tactic. Tourists loved holding those nostalgic

[1] Carothers, *Fractional Currency.*
[2] Ibid.

tokens in their hands; and there was a sense of poetic justice in the return of those silver dollars to the source from whence they came.

THE END OF AN "ENTERPRISE"

Another casualty of the hard times in 1893 was the *Territorial Enterprise.* This famous newspaper originally went to press in Genoa, Nevada, in 1858, the year Carson City was founded. Soon the owner moved the *Enterprise* to Virginia City in one of the most newsworthy beats on the planet. How many times will you hear that Mark Twain (Samuel Clemens) got his start as a cub writer at this paper? Another renowned journalist at the *Enterprise* was Dan DeQuille (William Wright). His chronicle of the rise and glory of the Comstock Lode was published in 1876 as *The Big Bonanza.*

Not only popular in Nevada, the *Enterprise* was popular in all parts of the country, and even abroad. Readers would wait with curious anticipation for news about the Comstock region; there is no question that Virginia City's own *Territorial Enterprise* was the public relations voice of the area. Sam Davis, editor of the *Carson Appeal,* spoke respectfully about the closing of his paper's competitor, when he wrote, "Its loss was felt everywhere." Davis' epithet fondly declared: "The history of journalism in Nevada begins with the 'Territorial Enterprise' ... The leading journals of the United States published sympathetic and stirring obituaries...[when the Territorial Enterprise] 'died with its boots on' in Virginia City, January, 1893."[1]

THE WELLS FARGO COMPANY

One of the most emblematic images depicting the American West is the stagecoach. With six horses in full gallop across the wilderness, two large wooden wheels in the rear, two smaller ones forward, luggage stacked on the roof, the driver seated at the helm holding the reins, his comrade at his side, the cash and bullion safely secured, and the passengers bouncing in the cab, a passing stagecoach was a sight to behold. The Concord Stagecoach Company, a.k.a. the Abbott and Downing Company, originally designed the stagecoach in New Hampshire in 1826, and from the 1850s, into the 1890s travel by stage was as common as rapid transit is today. Travelers were advised on how to survive their trips:

- The best seat ...is the one next to the driver...
- Never [travel] in tight boots or shoes...
- Don't...lop [fall] over on your neighbor when sleeping.
- Don't ask how far it is to the next station until you get there.
- Don't discuss politics or religion.
- Expect annoyance, discomfort, and some hardships.
- If you are disappointed, thank heaven.[2]

Wells Fargo Express and Banking Company was the most powerful institution in the western states during the expansion that coincided with the Comstock era, once said to be more trusted than the federal government. Towns emerged along Wells Fargo express routes, and a Wells Fargo bank could be found in every major city. By the time Wells Fargo started using the stagecoaches, the original design had been improved, achieving travel speeds of approximately ten miles per hour with four horses, and up to 50% faster with six horses. These "cradles on wheels,"[3] as Mark Twain described them, played a significant role in the development of the American West, but by 1893, the era of the stagecoach had practically come to an end. Wells Fargo still had *express* wagons that were used for short trips and small hauls, but railroads had dominated transportation in the country for more than 20 years. Wells Fargo had acquired access to 7,750 miles of Southern Pacific's rails by 1893, but *SP* owned one third of Well's Fargo's

---

[1] Davis, *History of Nevada.*

[2] *Hints for Plains Travelers, Omaha Herald,* 1870.

[3] Mark Twain, *Roughing It.*

This familiar sight from the old west era had all but passed from the scene by 1893. Wells Fargo's stagecoaches had virtually been replaced by railroad trains. (*Courtesy Wells Fargo Bank*)

stock. Eventually, in 1900, when Collis Huntington died, his nephew Henry, sold the Southern Pacific Railroad to Wells Fargo, and the merger was complete.[1] The company identified by its stagecoach service was changing with the times and rarely dispatched those fabled overland chariots across sagebrush-laden paths after the early 1890s. Wells Fargo and Company's Bank in Virginia City, Nevada ceased its banking operations in 1893. It was a year for demises.

GOULD AND CURRY REVISITED

One life that came to an end in 1893 was only a faint memory from the Comstock's past. Alva Gould, Abe Curry's partner in the famed Gould and Curry mine, had lost everything and was seen around the Reno railroad depot peddling fruit in the last years of his life. He died on September 28, 1893, in poverty and a broken man; if Abe had still been alive he would not have heard of it. Only the obituary in the *Reno Gazette- Journal* acknowledged Mr. Gould's death, illustrating how 34 years can separate a man from his dignity.[2]

Abraham Curry had not left much behind for his family after he died. Here was a man who could have been the *owner and operator* of northern Nevada. He could have been like Ben Cartwright on the *Ponderosa*, with more land and money than big corporate executives. However Abe Curry

Charles C. "Black" Wallace, the most powerful political manager in Nevada in the last two decades of the 19th century.

was a man possessed with vision but not with ambition for worldly gain. Curry loved what he could hold in his hand today, but gave no thought for tomorrow. He wasn't irresponsible; he just lived life like it would last forever. One of his contemporaries said that if Abe Curry wanted to he could live for 1,000 years; but of course, he only made it to 58. His wife Mary was still living in Carson City when the mint closed in 1893, taken care of by her daughter Mettie (Mary Elizabeth). They did all right, nothing fancy, but surely not representative of the way the first family of Carson City would be expected to live. Mettie died in 1895, and Abe and Mary's other daughter Elvira took care of her mother, along with her own son, William, who was 32 years old. Mary Curry, Abe's beloved wife, lived until 1912, dying at the age of 95; she had outlived Abe by 39 years, one year longer than they had been married.

NEVADA NEVER SAYS DIE

It was not the merriest Christmas for much of the population of the United States in 1893 as the financial hits taken by the public were devastating. They say that hope springs eternal, but in this case the hope was really gone; in the face of coming sadness and personal failure, the nation prayed and hung on. People were finding it difficult to "leave their worries on the doorstep"[3] because times were tough, and they seemed to be getting tougher.

In Carson City, the Treasury had closed down their mint. Nevada's survival had depended on mining for so long, but now it was time to look elsewhere. Many had lost their fortunes and their hope, but not their spirit.

Men like H.H. Springmeyer, and Fred Dangberg continued to forge Nevada's heritage on their ranches in the valley at the base of the mountains separating them from Lake Tahoe. There was also dark-haired and darkly sinister Charles Wallace, whose appearance earned him the nickname, "Black" Wallace. He would later tell H.H. Springmeyer that he would get him elected as a U.S. Senator with the stipulation that, "we want a man favorable to the Southern Pacific…and we want only laws which the Southern Pacific says are all right." But Mr. Springmeyer, of German descent, was a man of principles who had fought for everything he had, without compromise. Springmeyer's granddaughter, writing nearly 90 years later, stated: "No man in Nevada had ever fought the Southern Pacific and won, but he [Springmeyer] did not care… [My grandfather] had not journeyed halfway around the world to bend a servile knee before the Southern Pacific." Almost before "Black" Wallace finished uttering the words of his offer, H.H. Springmeyer roared back, "There's no railroad collar around my neck, I'll vote as I damn well please." "All right Herman," said "Black" Wallace quietly as he stood up, "then you will lose. Hank Martin will be the [next] senator. We'll buy the votes for him."[4]

[1] Philip L. Fradkin, *Stagecoach: Wells Fargo and the American West* (New York: Simon & Schuster Source, 2002).

[2] Cerveri, *With Curry's Compliments.*

[3] Dorothy Fields, song, "On the Sunny Side of the Street."

[4] Zanjani, Sally Springmeyer, *The Unspiked Rail* (Reno: University of Nevada Press, 1981).

Nevada would need individuals with the grit of Springmeyer, and others who saw hardships as opportunities. Carson City and its outlying regions would experience increasing social problems, unemployment, poverty and loss of population, at a faster pace in the years following 1893, than in the prior 13 years. Residents around the Comstock had seen the handwriting on the wall since the early 1880s, and now their worst fears had been realized. Carson City had experienced a gradual decline, pushing them to the edge of the abyss, while for the rest of the country, the crash was sudden. If you have ever driven through an intersection, and been broadsided by a vehicle running a red light, you will have a sense of what the panic of 1893 was like for much of the nation.

Carson City was a casualty, just like the rest of the country; its survival was due to a strange combination of *Rotten Borough* politics, represented by men like "Black" Wallace, and the "Don't Fence Me In"[1] men, like H.H. Springmeyer. The Newlands Reclamation bill would be a hot political item for the next decade, and when the bill was passed, 87,000 acres were irrigated in the Fallon, Nevada area northeast of Carson City. It was Springmeyer in his forward thinking visionary style, who had pushed through legislation in 1889 for the creation of the Nevada Reclamation Commission, as he and his ranching neighbors were already looking for new sources of revenue to supplement the state's sagging mining industry. Indeed, it was Springmeyer who took Francis Newlands on a tour of acreage in need of reclamation and irrigation. So, Newlands got credit for the passage of the bill, but resourceful Nevadans were way ahead of him. Approximately 27 miles north of Carson City, Reno was beginning to blossom into its own distinct municipality. In Reno, Newlands, by now anticipating the growth in northern Nevada after the reclamation bill would be passed, told H.H. Springmeyer that it would be wise for him to invest in property near the Truckee River in the rapidly expanding city of Reno. Springmeyer replied in his typical independent manner by replying to Newlands, "Hell no. I've got too much sagebrush of my own."[2]

CARSON MINT'S CAREER COMES TO A CLOSE

The V&T railroad was still chugging into the Carson City depot in 1893, and its familiar sounds enlivened the locals. This hallowed railroad would continue running in and out of the state's Capital for many more years. Just as it had hauled the silver in from the mines so the Carson

This closed door at one of the Carson City Mint's main storage vaults is symbolic of closed operations at that facility. (*Photo by S. Klette, 2003*)

Mint could strike coins, now it would transfer the coins from the mint during the next eight years—it must have been a sight when the very last of the silver dollars were removed from the Carson City Mint, and loaded onto the V&T. (Does anyone have a picture of the event?)

It was the ninth inning and the last pitch had been thrown; the game, the season, and the career were over. The stats for 'Ol "CC" were in the record books, and all that awaited, was the decision to retire the beloved mint's number. It certainly was not among the biggest, and indubitably was not a contender for the best in the Bureau of the Mint's system, but like the emotional highs that visi-

---

[1] Cole Porter, song, "Don't Fence Me In."
[2] Zanjani, *The Unspiked Rail.*

tors experience in the small township of Cooperstown, New York, home to baseball's hallowed shrine, the Carson City Mint evokes pleasant sensations in the minds of coin collectors. Both Cooperstown and Carson City are demographically small, but so historically significant.

When Mark Twain penned his classic *The Prince and the Pauper* in 1881, he had observed 20 years of boom and bust economic cycles and would himself experience personal financial failure in the years to come that would rip the heart out of him. But even in his satiric, snickering style, Twain probably could not have foreseen in 1881, the Grim Reaper's destruction that would test America's endurance in 1893. Twain's words from *The Prince And The Pauper* serve as a fitting exhortation for future generations to never forget their misfortunes:

> As long as the King lived, he was fond of telling the story of his [past] adventures…and thus keep [those] sorrowful spectacles fresh in his memory, and the **springs of pity** replenished in his heart.[1] (Emphasis added)

At least a few parents might have been inclined to name new born male children *Ichabod* in 1893, as a fitting reminder of the financially distressed times, that, "God has left this place."[2]

The country eventually pulled itself out of the miry trenches of misfortune brought on by the Panic of 1893. Mark Twain would most likely concur with the time-tested adage that, "those who fail to learn from the mistakes of the past are doomed to repeat them in the future."

If you were reading about Carson City and its coins for the first time, and had never seen a *Red Book*, nor heard anything about this Nevada capital, you might be inclined to believe that the year 1893 brought it to ruins. But Carson City did not wind up in ruins, and the legacy of the town has been powerfully publicized and glamorized by the coins its old mint left behind. Carson City is like the *phoenix* of ancient mythology that first had to perish, before it rose renewed from its ashes. The United States institution in Nevada closed the books on its first career in 1893 and then spent 80 years (1893 to 1973) preparing for its second career as the distinguished progenitor of the most famous and glamorous offspring of coins in all of numismatics.

For more information about the silver and gold coins from 1893, please see Chapter 6, *The Silver Coins*, and Chapter 7, *The Gold Coins*.

---

[1] Mark Twain, *The Prince and the Pauper*.
[2] I Samuel 4:21, *The Bible*.

CHAPTER FIVE

Searching for a New Identity (1894-1941)

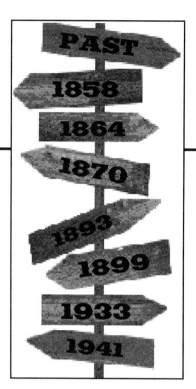

1894-1896

Afterthe Carson City Mint's coinage activities came to a halt in June of 1893, the town lost a piece of its identity. In the course of 35 years, this unpretentious hamlet at the base of the Sierra Nevada Mountains had grown out of nothing more than the vision of Abe Curry and a few friends into a respectable seat of state government and home to a U.S. Mint. No one knew for sure what the future held, but collectively the town's folk hoped to preserve their heritage and avoid the course of neighboring cities like Empire, Gold Hill and Silver City. Even the once thriving Virginia City was on the brink of insolvency by the mid 1890s.

But life could go on without a mint; it was a matter of redirecting priorities. Of course there were people in town who were confident that the Treasury would again order coining operations to resume, with their optimism predicated upon potential victories of the Silver Party and *free coinage* advocates. In fact, the political battle for monetary standards practically dominated all other topics of discussion in the years immediately following the Carson Mint's shutdown.

Splinter groups formed in and around Carson City to rally support for the remonetization of silver and free coinage. A leader of one such group was Hirsh Harris, melter and refiner at the Carson Mint, who organized his fellow mint workers to bolt from the Democratic Party and support the silver ticket. A convention was held in Carson City in September of 1894, at which Harris and his fellow delegates nominated their own men for the upcoming election. At the same time, another convention of traditional Democrats was held in Carson City, with delegates also calling for the free coinage of silver. A counterside to this party's platform however, was their endorsement of the ar-

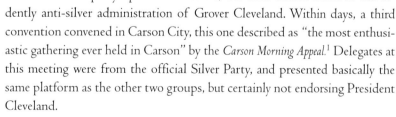

dently anti-silver administration of Grover Cleveland. Within days, a third convention convened in Carson City, this one described as "the most enthusiastic gathering ever held in Carson" by the *Carson Morning Appeal.*[1] Delegates at this meeting were from the official Silver Party, and presented basically the same platform as the other two groups, but certainly not endorsing President Cleveland.

A Scandal or Two Won't Do

Hirsh Harris had been appointed to his position as melter and refiner at the Carson City Mint on June 1, 1894 and was joined in his new job by the President's selection for new mint superintendent, Jewett W. Adams. Both men came highly recommended, viewed as being honest and of strong character. Whenever changes in personnel occurred at any mint facility, a formal settlement of accounts was conducted to ensure that the departing officer's books were accurate. Once approved, all responsibility for balanced accounts in the future rested on the replacement's shoulders.

Jewett William Adams, former Governor of Nevada from 1883 to 1886, appointed to the position of Superintendent of the Carson City Mint in June 1894.

[1] *Carson Morning Appeal,* September 5, 1894.

Harris' predecessor, E.B. Zabriskie's books were reckoned to be exact, though Zabriskie himself had died. In December of 1894, operating on bullion leftover from Zabriskie's time in office, Harris began using a new process for parting gold from silver. An alarming discovery was made when bars of bullion stamped with certain weights and finenesses of gold were found to contain large percentages of silver and copper instead.

When all of the leftover bullion was reassayed, there was a shortage of over 4,000 ounces of gold. Harris and Superintendent Adams reported this inaccuracy to the Director of the Mint who immediately dispatched the Superintendent of the New York Assay Office, Andrew Mason, to investigate. Careful measures were implemented to uncover the truth in this awkward matter and it was soon determined that the missing gold had disappeared between 1891 and the close of business in June of 1893. Narrowing the theft down into this time frame automatically absolved Harris and Superintendent Adams, and instantly implicated John T. Jones.

With detective-like precision Andrew Mason with the assistance of other government agents, uncovered evidence proving that John T. Jones had altered his accounting books, removed pages from ledgers, substituted silver and copper for gold in bars of bullion, and falsely stamped the bars with incorrect weights and values. Mason also concluded that Jones could not have acted alone, and the investigation continued to locate accomplices.

Local newspapers reported the day-to-day events surrounding this case. As a result of the publicity, a tip was provided by H.H. Beck, owner of the Reno Reduction Works Company, who told authorities that James H. Heney deposited over $20,000 in fine gold to be assayed. Heney was employed as a silver dissolver in the refinery department at the Carson Mint during the time that the gold was stolen, and with Jones was the chief accomplice in the crime (although there were others involved).

A small-time participant in the case was William J. Pickler, who failed to satisfy investigators when he could not account for the approximately $150 in bullion found on his premises. Pickler had been a deposit melter at the mint when Jones and Heney committed their crime, and though he was also guilty of stealing, the government was

Hirsh Harris, appointed melter and refiner at the Carson City Mint in June of 1894.

not convinced it was connected with their main case. Pickler's part in the pilfering at the mint was surrounded by mystery, only enhanced when he suddenly died in his sleep on July 31, 1895, just as the investigation came to a crux.

Two other bit players in this crime drama were Joseph Langevin and Barney Brule, both connected with James Heney. Langevin's son had been hired by Heney to drive him to Reno in the elder Langevin's wagon in August of 1893. Langevin's son later told investigators that Heney ordered him to stop the wagon on the outskirts of Carson City, at which time Heney picked up two heavy canvas bags and then the two men proceeded to the Reno Reduction Works. Then in 1895, after investigations began on the stolen gold case, Barney Brule, acting as the payoff man, gave Joseph Langevin $400 to make his son disappear, and another $400 to keep his own mouth shut. This was not revealed during Heney's first trial, which ended in a hung jury. But at the second trial, the whole Langevin family sang like birds.

Defense lawyers tried numerous tactics to win Heney's freedom, even calling a metallurgist to the stand to testify that it was possible for more than 4,000 ozs. of gold to have dissolved during improper acid works in the mint's refinery. In another instance of shameless jurisprudence, Heney's defense team told the jury that the two main sewers in town were connected to the mint and tons of gold and silver bullion were flushed out to nearby streams, fields and meadows, even supplying samples of smelly mud laced with gold dust to prove their point. One group of samples came from a potato farm, and when assayers visited the site, they did indeed find gold dust mixed with the spuds. Local newspapers later alleged that this potato patch had been salted with gold by Heney's lawyers' aids.

In the end, James Heney was convicted by a jury on December 21, 1895. Three days later, Judge Hawley, upon sentencing the felon to eight years in prison and a $5,000 fine, spoke to him in a somber tone, "You with your family have resided near me, and I have always known and regarded you as a sober, industrious young man... I sincerely regret the disgrace you have brought upon your family."[1] Heney was then taken to the prison to spend his first Christmas behind bars.

[1] *Nevada State Appeal*, December 25, 1895.

This whole affair caused a solemn pallor to settle over the typically genial city. And now the question was, "will he make a full confession and tell who his accomplices were? … Men who have been employed in the mint say it is impossible for any one person to have stolen any considerable amount of gold…without the knowledge of others…will Heney tell who those persons were?"[1] In a plea for full cooperation of every citizen in town to preserve the integrity of their mint, an article titled **"LET NO GUILTY MAN ESCAPE"** warned of the consequences if they did not unite:

> There is no denying the fact that rumors of crookedness at the Carson Mint have been in circulation for some time…. As it has been ascertained that there is a shortage in the mint, it is due the honest men who have been employed in that institution that the guilty ones should be hunted down and punished. The fair name of the state is involved, and unless the mass of the people admit that it is a crime for those employed in the mint to rob it, and that authorities should be assisted rather than obstructed…they will have no just cause for complaint if **the mint is dismantled.**[2] (Emphasis added)

John T. Jones awaited his trial as 1896 began and after a couple of postponements, he appeared in court on March 2, 1896. Despite overwhelming evidence, the jury failed to convict Jones after a two week trial. No time was wasted, and Jones was back before a new jury on April 20, 1896. This time the prosecution did everything except show videotape of the crime actually being committed,

and Jones was pronounced guilty on May 2, 1896 after a few minutes of deliberations by the jury. Judge Hawley issued the same sentence to Jones as he had to Heney, and a dreadful page in the history of Carson City was finally turned to the next chapter.

Commenting on this spurious and embarrassing affair, chief investigator Andrew Mason wrote: "The real cause of the shortage of gold in the Carson Mint had been made evident. These men (Jones and Heney) had not only stolen from the Government the gold entrusted to their care, but had endeavored to fix the guilt on others. The present officers of the mint have been completely relieved of the imputation cast on them."[3] At least for a while.

Indications of illegal deeds at the Carson Mint were observed long before charges were brought against Jones and Heney. In the Director of the Mint's 1894 report, suspicion was cast upon the procedure employed by melter and refiner E.B. Zabriskie on large silver deposits during the 11

Judge Thomas Hawley presided over the hearing of Heney and Jones during the stolen gold scandal in Carson City in the mid-1890s.

---

[1] *Nevada State Journal,* December 22, 1895.
[2] *Nevada State Journal,* December 27, 1895.
[3] *Annual Report of the Director of the Mint,* 1896.

Street scene in front of the Carson City Mint looking south in the 1890s. The scenery here changed very little until the 1930s.

months prior to his death. When the superintendent at Carson, Theodore R. Hofer submitted his report explaining why 600,000 ounces of silver with a fineness of .991 to .992 had been melted and refined to .9975 and above, the Mint Director declared this act to be "clearly injudicious."[1] Furthermore, "Measures have been adopted that will prevent this course of treatment of bullion in the refinery hereafter."[2]

According to the Mint Director, these 600,000 ounces were well within government regulations, rendering it unnecessary (not to mention irresponsible) to refine them again. At the time, no further allegations were made, and only after the gold shortage scandal surfaced were inferences drawn connecting the two events. Carson City had grown accustomed to being under the scrutinous eye of the government, and would become even more so as the 1890s pressed on.

Rumors of clandestine coining activities followed the Carson Mint throughout its history. One objection often raised casting doubt on these rumors was that any criminal actions would require the cooperation of many employees to accomplish the acts. Other allegations included, but were not limited to, silver dollars being minted at night using bullion purchased by employees for their own accounts, and 80,000 illegal 1893-CC silver dollars discovered in the vault at the State Treasury office. In regard to the former, supposedly employees at the Carson Mint in partnership with representatives from a local mill were buying silver from the mill at 60 cents an ounce and secretly coining it into silver dollars at night. If true, the conspirators reaped a profit of nearly 70 cents on every dollar produced based on the ratio between face value and intrinsic value.

In the case of silver dollars in the State Treasury office, a Reno paper reported that, "The Director of the Mint has heard that the State Treasurer of Nevada had a large quantity of the coinage of 1893 on hand.... the presses were ordered to be dismantled [After June 1, 1893] and he did not think there could have been any secret coinage. An investigation is being made."[3] This controversy came at the most inopportune time for Carsonites who had just suffered through the second James Heney trial. All at once, they were relieved that Heney was behind bars, but dismayed about the new scandal.

A question on everyone's mind was voiced in the news article, "How did 80,000 dollars of the mintage of 1893 find their way into the State Treasury?" There were no records of the Bureau of the Mint transferring the dollars there, neither for the State or County Treasurer. Tax payments did not account for this windfall of dollars in the State's Treasury, as only $15,000 had been collected for the year, and as the article reminded everyone, even if State revenues were that high, taxes were not paid "in sacks containing 1,000 silver dollars each."[4] Then with a bit of sarcasm alluding to the trial just concluded, the paper asked again, "...how did the dollars get there? The Mint sewer does not discharge into the State Treasurer's vault, consequently they must have reached through some other channel."[5]

In conclusion, the article expressed confidence that an investigation would clear up the matter, but then shifted responsibility onto the preceding Treasurer, who the paper remarked, "could do so without investigation, and why he does not is a subject of such comment."[6] But once again, crucial testimony in a scandalous case concerning the Carson City Mint was lost, this time due to the death of the State Treasurer, John F. Egan. Egan had held this office from 1891 through the time of his death on April 14, 1894, and if unauthorized 1893-CC silver dollars had been minted, it would have been some time during the last year of Egan's life. An interim Treasurer, George W. Richard, filled in until the new one took office in January 1895. It was probably Richard to whom the newspaper article referred when questioning why the preceding Treasurer did not come forth and set the record straight. In fact, Richard claimed that the surplus of dollars came from tax revenues, but the books contradicted him.

It was newly elected Treasurer William Westerfield who revealed the existence of the dollars when he assumed office in 1895 and it remains a mystery why it took nearly 12 months before an investigation was ordered. When the coins were examined, "some...have been found to be defective, as if rushed through the mint in a hurry," as one news article described them.[7] Confusion set in when it was reported: "The records were examined to see what the coinage of 1893 should have been. The amount on hand was counted, as was the amount paid out by the mint, and then the $80,000 that was in the State Treasury was added..., and it made just the correct total."[8] Sud-

---

[1] *Annual Report of the Director of the Mint*, 1894.
[2] Ibid.
[3] *Nevada State Appeal*, December 24, 1895.
[4] Ibid.
[5] Ibid.
[6] Ibid.
[7] *Carson City News*, December 24, 1895.
[8] *Carson City News*, December 31, 1895.

denly the issue was not whether the dollars had been manufactured illegally, because the official mintage figure balanced, even with the 80,000 coins added. Instead, investigators were concerned with how the dollars were moved from the mint, since there was no record of them being paid out. And of course the big question: with no record of the Treasury office receiving the dollars, who had put them there, and why?

Years later, Samuel P. Davis, former editor of the *Carson Daily Appeal*, linked two scandals together when he wrote: "It was also charged that silver bullion worth but 60 cents an ounce was taken from the Mexican Mill at Empire and brought to the Mint at night where it was coined into dollars…It was further charged that this [the dollars] went through the Bullion and Exchange Bank and from there **into the state Treasury** to be exchanged for gold."[1] (Emphasis added) This account was written nearly 20 years after the events had allegedly occurred, and facts may have been muddled with time. On the other hand, if Davis' version is correct, it entails the involvement of a rather large ring of clever people over the course of at least a 12 month period.

At the top of the list of men who might have been the ringleaders are Carson Mint superintendent Theodore Hofer (who coincidentally was an officer at the Bullion and Exchange Bank), and State Treasurer John F. Egan. Hofer, one of the most respected men in the community, was never accused of wrong doing. Other members of this team of criminals might have included employees at the Mexican Mill, and an experienced crew from the Carson Mint including the melter, refiner, coiner, pressman, someone in the assaying department, engineer, night watchman, cashier or bookkeeper, and possibly a few general assistants. In addition, a few teamsters would have been needed to haul over two tons of silver, and at least several

clerks in the State Treasurer's office and the bank would have been necessary to assist with minor details, all in all a very challenging caper to pull off. Apparently, the case had not been solved by 1913, for when Davis summed up the event he wrote, "The charges relative to the presence of Carson Mint dollars in the State safe, which had never been officially coined, **was never investigated** by the Government."[2] (Emphasis added)

As the record stands, the mintage figure for 1893-CC silver dollars is 677,000, and the whereabouts of 80,000 of them allegedly sitting in the State Treasurer's vault in January of 1895 are unknown. Unfortunately, the negative publicity from these scandals further destroyed what little credibility the Carson Mint still had with the federal government and became something Carson City could never shake.

Similar events occurred in other parts of the country, but when they happened in Carson City it seemed to be blown out of proportion. For instance: "In September of 1893, it was discovered that gold bullion of the value of $113,423.85 had, with criminal ingenuity, been abstracted from one of the vaults in the Philadelphia Mint. Suspicious circumstances pointed to the weigh clerk of that institution as the culprit. He was arrested, confessed his guilt, and gave information leading to the recovery of about $90,000 of the stolen property. He was promptly tried, and convicted. The Government is not likely to lose anything from his crime."[3] Many such examples at all mint facilities around the country can be told, but usually in a more matter of fact manner than when the Carson City Mint is involved.

There was something about that Nevada institution that provoked bureaucrats in Washington D.C. and Philadelphia, similar to the way the press treats controversial celebrities in the early years of the 21st century. When celebrities experience the same things that happen in the lives of everyday people it suddenly becomes a media event. Headlines around the world scandalize the events—some deserving, many exaggerated. Though it was never part of the original plan for the Carson City Mint to achieve celebrity status, it just happened, and publicity, often

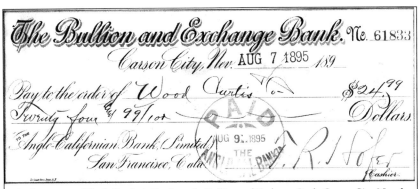

Check written to Wood, Curtis & Co. from the Bullion and Exchange Bank, Carson City, Nevada, in 1895. Signed by cashier T.R. Hofer, former superintendent at the Carson City Mint.

[1] *History of Nevada*, Samuel P. Davis, 1913.
[2] Ibid.
[3] *Annual Report of the Director of the Mint*, 1893.

negative, comes with the territory. Make no mistake about it though; the Carson City Mint was not a victim. It had served its purpose and achieved more than in anyone's wildest imaginings. For a mint that was on the verge of being shut down from the day it opened, it lasted far longer than expected.

1897-1899

Somewhere along the way Carson City got lost on the road to self-discovery. By the late 1890s the wealth of the Comstock was a faint memory, and the gradual exodus of people from the region continually shrank the population. Businesses in Carson City that once served the thriving mining industry were forced to close and both the owners and employees moved on. Although the V&T Railroad still chugged into town, passengers and freight were minimal compared to the glory years. And of course the local mint was not in the coining business any more.

Apart from government, ranching, farming, and sporadic tourism, there really was no strong business base to support more than a small population. Many of the town's folk preferred it that way and as long as there were nice homes to live in, good restaurants and saloons to patronize, doctors, barbers, drug stores, hardware stores, livery stables, schools, newspapers, a bank, an opera house, dry goods stores, a post office, clothing stores and all the other goods and services necessary for a modest life-style, the majority of residents were content.

Carson City became known as a *living cemetery* because outsiders considered the town so dull that "men fell asleep in the middle of the street going from one groggery to another." An oft-repeated jibe poked at the calm city said, "If someone died on the courthouse steps in Carson on a Saturday, he would not be found until Monday morning."[1] It probably was not that dull, but by the late 1890s the train pulling into town might be a major event, and for real excitement, a group of people would stand in the street to pose for a picture.

HEAVYWEIGHT CHAMPIONSHIP
DECIDED IN CARSON CITY

In 1897, organizers in Carson City decided to try something new. While much of the nation was committed to banning the sport of boxing, Nevada decided to give it a shot, with the capital, Carson City, chosen as the site for the first match. All of a sudden the town came alive, and for a month prior to the March fight between

Gentleman Jim Corbett and challenger Bob Fitzsimmons, crowds were transported into town via the V&T Railroad, and hotels were booked solid. Flags and banners were draped over every public building, parties were held, reporters from out of state sent dispatches back to their hometown papers, and within a short time Carson City was again on the minds of thousands of people around the country. Many visitors saw Lake Tahoe for the first time, and nearby Reno, known for its looser life-style, drew curious crowds.

This heavyweight championship fight set the stage for Nevada's reputation as the prize fighting capital of the world in the 20th century. Fitzsimmons beat Corbett for the crown and within 24 hours Carson City had put away the decorations and resumed life where it had left off.

LOCAL PAPERS FOLLOW SILVER MARKET

Nevadan senators and legislators continued to give lip service to the fight for silver as the 19th century came to a close. At the National Silver Party convention in 1896, Congressman Francis G. Newlands had acted as Chairman, but after the Silver Party's defeat in the elections, morale throughout the State of Nevada weakened. Nearly 25 years had passed since the Coinage Act of 1873 became law, and the battle over monetary standards had raged for the duration. Silver supporters stood their ground the whole time, but their strength had abated and their plan of attack had become monotonous. It did not help Nevada's cause that its mining industry was experiencing lean times.

Yet through it all, local newspapers in Carson City kept the public abreast of daily happenings in the silver market. For instance, in the *Carson Morning Appeal* on October 8, 1897, an article titled "THE PRICE OF SILVER" made the following petition: "We beg our readers to note the sensitiveness of silver in the market. It has recently risen nearly 7 $^1/_2$ cents above the low price of September 1, and the only reason that experts can give for it is a *rumor* that purchases have been made for India."[2] Reasons given for India's sudden interest in silver seem to have implicated the Bank of England, who the writer of the article refers to as "the money manipulators of the world."[3] According to the editor, Great Britain was taking advantage of the low price of the metal, "loading up with cheap silver,"[4] supposedly

[1] Sally Springmeyer Zanjani, *The Unspiked Rail.*
[2] *Carson Morning Appeal*, October 8, 1897.
[3] Ibid.
[4] Ibid.

in anticipation of a free coinage law being passed in the United States during the 1900 elections. This sudden reversal in Great Britain's attitude toward the free coinage of silver was strictly mercenary, because as the article stated, "When free coinage wins, the world will have to turn to these men for the supply."[1]

Though it angered many people that Great Britain would in part support a silver standard after being diametrically opposed to it for years, others welcomed reinforcement for the metal from any direction. News about England's involvement in the silver market was published every day in local papers throughout the remainder of 1897 and into 1898. With the price of silver hovering between 55 and 60 cents per ounce through 1897, the mining industry longed for it to rise to higher levels. Unfortunately, prices would fall again, and it would be another 20 years before silver rebounded to the 85 cent to $1.00 level of the early 1890s.

TREASURY INDECISIVE ABOUT CARSON MINT'S FUTURE

In 1898 the Carson City Mint's coinage operations had been shut down for five years, although during that time the facility's doors had been open to the receipt of gold and silver deposits. However, due to declining yields from the Comstock mines, and bullion owners choosing San Francisco over Carson, business had dwindled to a pittance.

Congress had authorized minimal appropriations to keep the Carson Mint open on a part time basis through the final years of the 1890s, and for reasons unknown, over five million silver dollars remained stored on location. Paltry quantities of those silver dollars were released annually during the last few years of the decade. The table below exhibits the distributions for the fiscal years 1897 through 1899.

Carson City was not the only mint facility with a surplus of silver dollars stored on its premises, as millions

of cartwheels filled the vaults of the nation's Treasury offices. Yet in spite of the overstock, Congress authorized millions more to be minted at the outbreak of the Spanish American War. Starting in June of 1898 and continuing through 1904, over 108 million silver dollars were produced in compliance with this so called War Revenue Act. What purpose these additional coins served is a matter of speculation, though the official explanation was to support the U.S. economy during the war; most would be melted under the Pittman Act in 1918 and 1919.

Regardless of why the dollars were produced, Carson City benefited by supplying silver from the local mint's refinery. Locals were perplexed why silver dollars could not be struck at their mint since it had not been officially shut down, but the Treasury was not interested in having Carson City's coining equipment taken out of mothballs. Besides, the Director of the Mint was pressuring Congress to close the Nevada branch down for good. He wrote in his report for 1898 that precious metal output in Nevada had dropped below $3 million in 1897, and that 80% of it was deposited out of state. Furthermore, it was more cost effective for bullion producers to send their product to the San Francisco Mint, therefore, "it is… recommended that the mint at Carson be discontinued. If it is considered desirable to continue an assay office there, and the institution can be relieved of the care of the silver dollars now on storage in it, the annual outlay can be reduced to about $12,000."[2] As far as Director George E. Roberts was concerned, Carson City was old business, and it was time for the Treasury Department to concentrate on its new facilities. He also wanted to close the St. Louis Assay Office, reasoning that, "The saving which might be made by abolishing this office (St. Louis) and the mint at Carson would meet the new outlay incurred by establishing an assay office at Seattle."[3] Carsonites had been hearing appeals like this for 28 years from government officials, but somehow their local mint had survived, often by a thread. At this point in 1898, the Carson Mint was all but closed anyway.

A NEW SUPERINTENDENT TO USHER IN THE NEW CENTURY

In September of 1898, Superintendent Jewett W. Adams ended his stress-filled four year stint at the helm of the controversial mint. He was replaced by another former Governor of Nevada, Roswell K. Colcord, who

ANNUAL DISTRIBUTION OF SILVER DOLLARS AT THE CARSON MINT FOR FISCAL YEARS 1897-1899*

YEAR	TOTAL
1897	40,993
1898	56,688
1899	30,885

*Annual Reports of the Director of the Mint, 1897, 1898, 1899.

[1] Ibid.
[2] *Annual Report of the Director of the Mint*, 1898.
[3] Ibid.

would remain at the mint until 1911, first as Superintendent, then as Assayer in charge. Colcord, originally from Maine, moved to Nevada in 1863 at the age of 24. Before he became governor in 1891, Colcord had a distinguished career as a mechanical engineer and mining superintendent. After his retirement from the Carson Mint at the age of 72, Colcord lived another 28 years in his adopted city, where he died one day short of Nevada Day in 1939 at the age of 100. Mr. Colcord served as a reminder of Nevada's heritage to a new generation, as he strolled the streets of Carson City in his old age.

Colcord was well aware of the conflict associated with the local mint when he assumed office, and was dedicated to preserving whatever integrity could be salvaged. As old memories die hard, the gold shortage scandal from 1895 was briefly brought to the forefront in 1898, when the Treasury Department filed suit "against the estate and sureties of E.B. Zabriskie, deceased, who held the position of melter and refiner of the Carson Mint during the period the [gold] was embezzled. The recovery of any part of the amount is very doubtful."[1] Zabriskie's assistant John T. Jones, who replaced his boss after Zabriskie died, was the culprit. Charges had never been filed against the deceased, but in 1898 there had been pressure on Congress to relieve the deficiency of the stolen gold off the books. Bringing suit against Zabriskie's heirs was a last ditch effort to appease those who complained that the $75,000 shortfall should not just be excused.

Putting all that aside, R.K. Colcord led the struggling mint facility into 1899, promising to do all he could to secure appropriations from Congress. In his report to the Director for 1899, Colcord acknowledged that, "it is safe to say that coining will not be resumed at the Carson Mint."[2] Then he proposed that, "if this mint, operating as an assay office, was authorized to receive ore samples for assay, it would add very materially to its operations and earnings and I would earnestly recommend that such authority be given."[3]

It was a good move on Colcord's part. As the Carson facility had been operating as an assay office anyway, ever since coining ceased in 1893, why not make it official? His strategy paid off, as noted in this statement by the Director of the Mint, "without explanation it might ap-

Roswell Colcord, former Governor of Nevada, became Superintendent at the Carson City Mint in 1898.

pear strange that with mint facilities at present inadequate, the mint at Carson, Nev., should be reduced to an assay office. The explanation lies in its location. It could not be used for the coinage of silver except by the shipment of bullion from Philadelphia, and the subsequent shipment of coin eastward. The mint at San Francisco is able to execute the coinage of all the gold produced…on the Pacific coast and of all the silver coin required there…at much less expense… For this reason the Carson mint was at the close of the fiscal year [June 30, 1899] reduced to an assay office."[4]

Some blamed Congressman Francis Newlands for the mint's loss of official coinage privileges, but the likelihood of it retaining that status was doubtful. Newlands had become unpopular with many in northern Nevada, and the local press constantly derided him for playing both sides of the fence. Articles appeared frequently about Newlands with such headlines as "NEWLANDS ON TWO OPPOSING PLATFORMS," and "ANYTHING TO GET INTO OFFICE." He was accused of joining the Silver Party not because he was a silver supporter, but only because he knew it would win. A letter from Newlands to Treasury Secretary Lyman J. Gage showing how the free silver coinage bill could be defeated was published in the *Carson Morning Appeal* in late 1898. After Newlands included his clause in the mint appropriations bill giving the Secretary of the Treasury the option to choose between mint or assay office status, the knee-jerk reaction was to blame Newlands for the outcome. But the Secretary did not need Newland's two cents worth to make a decision; he could do whatever he wanted, even close the Carson Mint permanently. Nevertheless, on July 1, 1899 the Carson Mint was ushered into its final role as a branch of the United States Government, and Colcord's official title switched from Mint Superintendent to Assayer in charge. It was not the preferred outcome for those in Carson City, but it was better than being closed down all together. Besides, it was inevitable that U.S. coinage would never be minted at the facility again. There was

[1] *Annual Report of the Director of the Mint*, 1898.
[2] *Annual Report of the Director of the Mint*, 1899.
[3] Ibid.
[4] Ibid.

THE MORNING APPEAL.

VOL LXIV.   CARSON CITY, NEVADA, FRIDAY MORNING, JANUARY 13, 1899.   NO. 81.

Francis G. Newlands was a perennial target for the local press in Carson City. He was wealthy enough to buy his way into Congress, but it was difficult to buy friends.

NEWLANDS ON TWO OPPOSING PLATFORMS.

Pledged to Senator Stewart.

Pledged Against Senator Stewart.

ANYTHING TO GET OFFICE.

Silver Measures In Congress.

Dodged by Mr. Newlands.

MR. NEWLANDS' TREACHERY.

His Letter to Gage Showing How Silver Coinage Can Be Defeated.

He Advocates Seigniorage on Coinage and Royalty on Mining, Then Withdrawing Mines From Sale.

RENO, NEV., *Nov. 1, 1898.*
HON. F. G. NEWLANDS,
Reno, Nevada.

SIR: You were elected as a silver man to Congress for three terms, and you are now a candidate for re-election on two platforms—one Silver, and the other Democratic—which make free coinage at the ratio of 16 to 1 by the independent action of the United States the paramount issue. Were you while in Washington faithful to the cause of silver?

In the second session of the Fifty-third Congress, during President Cleveland's administration, Mr. Bland, of Missouri, introduced a bill to issue silver certificates on the idle bullion in the treasury, then amounting to over $50,000,000, and requiring that the silver should be thereafter coined. The bill passed both Houses of Congress by an overwhelming majority. President Cleveland vetoed it. An attempt was

NEWLANDS—"I assume the utmost good faith on both sides; that you will support me for Congress and I will support you for the Senate."

Mr. Newlands presents Secretary Gage with three clubs.

NEWLANDS—"You know I was always a Democrat.—"

NEWLANDS ENTERING THE RACE

THE HO USE THAT SELLS THE BEST GOODS

We are sole agents for Thomson's genuine Glove Fitting corsets At the prices quoted, the best corsets on the market---4 hook, short hip corsets, the latest creation in these goods, kept ONLY by Us---are remarkably cheap at $1.25

Then we have the extra long, 6 hook ones and in fact all styles and shapes of this well-known brand You'd better give them a trial

ISAAC OLCOVICH

Ad appearing in an 1899 Carson City newspaper offering women the latest in fashion, a $1.25 corset.

no justification for it as the population in the region was so sparse, and the mines were virtually exhausted.

Later in 1899, Colcord supervised the transfer of Carson City's coin presses and other related coinage material to Treasury offices as ordered by the Director of the Mint, along with the leftover silver dollar dies mentioned earlier. Then Colcord and crew marched forward with the backbreaking task of removing five million silver dollars from the mint's vaults. Local newspapers covered the events of this conveyance of equipment, accessories and coins on a daily basis and spectators lined the street between the mint and V&T depot watching with sadness and wonder as the 12 and 18 ton coin presses were transported to waiting railroad cars, and hearing the clanging noise of bags of silver dollars being hauled away. If there had been any doubt whether coinage would resume, the matter was firmly settled. A new sign with the words U.S. Assay Office replaced the old sign, but nothing could remove the memories.

1900-1910

On March 28, 1900 Congress authorized the Assay Office at Carson City to receive ore samples for assay, in response to Assayer in charge Colcord's appeal for government assistance to help increase deposits at the floundering Nevada branch. Colcord reported to the Director of the Mint after the authorization for the receipt of ore samples went into effect that, "I caused the fact to be published throughout the State...but in order to avoid competition with private assayers, the charge for each as-

Carloads of Silver

The Journal is informed that orders have been received from Washington for the removal of all of the silver at the Carson mint. There are eight or ten carloads of dollars and bullion in storage there. As the white metal appears to be a drug on the Washington market, why not leave it in Nevada where it was extracted from the womb of mother earth? Nevadans could find a use for it, if Uncle Sam would give them the chance.

Announcement appearing in the *Nevada State Journal* during the summer of 1899 when the Carson City Mint's vaults were emptied.

say was fixed at $3, as against their charge of $1, consequently our work in this line is necessarily limited."[1] Unless another significant mineral discovery was made in Nevada, prospects for the Carson Assay Office seemed dim.

TONOPAH AND GOLDFIELD REVIVE NEVADA'S SAGGING ECONOMY

In the early years of the 20th century, two obscure roadside stops in west central Nevada became the state's next thriving mining districts. Tonopah's mining boom began in 1900 when local resident Jim Butler picked up a stone to throw at his mule, and realized he had rich mineral quartz in his hand. There is some question as to what is history and what is myth, but the key point is that within no time prospectors were swarming this isolated area seeking fortunes. Within two years, gold was also discovered about 40 miles south of Tonopah in a region the Shoshones called *Gran Pah*, and soon after, gold was being extracted from these bountiful fields, leading miners to rechristen the area Goldfield. Yields from this region were second only to those on the famous Comstock Lode.

What was noticeably different about these new strikes was that controlling interests were held by Nevadans instead of men from California and the powerful San Francisco bank crowd. These Nevadans invested their windfalls into developing business in the state, planting many banks in key centers like Reno, Winnemucca and Carson City. Three dominant leaders emerged from this new bonanza period, Key Pittman, George Nixon and George Wingfield. Pittman, achieving much success in Tonopah, would go on to become Nixon's successor in the U.S. Senate, and gain notoriety in 1918 by sponsoring the silver meltdown act named after him.

Bullion deposits from these new mining centers were shipped in varying degrees to the Carson City Assay Office, some 250 to 280 miles to the north. Receipts of these deposits would gradually increase through the first decade of the 20th century, boosting the Carson branch's production. Still, the work staff at Carson was kept to fewer than 10 people most of the time. In the Mint Director's *Annual Report* for 1907, R.K. Colcord stated that seven employees were on staff that year, and had operated

---

[1] *Annual Report of the Director of the Mint*, 1900.

on approximately $811,000 in gold. By the end of 1907, Colcord sent an appropriations request to the Treasury to increase annual salaries by $1,250 for the purpose of hiring an additional clerk and another melter. He advised the Director of the Mint that deposits had increased so rapidly that employees were forced to work overtime, and even then were unable to keep up.[1]

These new mining booms breathed life into Nevada's economy at a crucial period when railroads had practically abandoned the state, and Comstock mines were barren. Nevada's population had dropped to just over 42,000 people, the lowest level since 1870 when the state was only six years old. Moreover, the United States had officially gone on the gold standard, consequently crippling whatever silver mining still existed in Nevada.

FAREWELL TO SENATORS JONES AND STEWART

Beginning in 1901 and continuing through 1902, Congressman Francis Newlands campaigned for new legislation which would open up Nevada's vast desert lands to reclamation through government subsidized irrigation projects. On June 15, 1902 the Newlands Reclamation Act was passed, becoming the Congressman's single most celebrated achievement as a Nevada politician. Discord between Newlands and longtime political patriarch Senator William Stewart temporarily cast a shadow on Newlands' triumph, but in the end the Congressman's name would be indelibly etched in Nevada's political hall of fame for this act.

Further success came to Newlands in the November election when he won the U.S. Senatorial seat vacated by the retirement of Senator John P. Jones. Nevada's proclaimed *Silver Senator*, realizing the fight for silver had been lost and that he had grown very old, ended his 30 years of public service when Newlands was sworn in on March 4, 1903.

Another familiar name was cast into the senatorial race when Judge Thomas P. Hawley, of the gold shortage trials fame, announced his candidacy. Senators Jones and Stewart stumped on behalf of Hawley in an attempt to defeat Newlands, but the *Reclamation* man simply had too much money along with the momentum of his recent legislative victory, and won hands down.

In May of 1903, President Teddy Roosevelt visited Carson City and addressed a large gathering in front of the Capitol building. His speech was supportive of Nevada's planned irrigation projects and served to cheer the rebounding state on to optimistic growth in the future. Senator Stewart, still bitter over Newlands' victory in the senatorial election, seized the opportunity of Roosevelt's visit and told the press that it was the President who was responsible for the passage of the Reclamation Act. In truth, President Roosevelt, a pro-environmentalist, probably did influence the decision, but in the end, Newlands' name would be identified with the act.

In the early years of the 20th century, the political scene was rapidly changing in Nevada and Newlands' success only served to focus attention on the demise of the old guard in the state. Whereas at one time the Silver Party and the railroads had dominated, by 1901 their influence was superseded by supporters of reclamation, labor movements, women's suffrage and bipartisan politics. New power brokers were emerging who would control Nevada's direction throughout the first half of the new century. These men had been passed a torch by Nevada's most powerful political manipulator of the 19th century, Charles "Black" Wallace.

Referred to in unflattering terms as "the finest political coyote that ever got into Nevada,"[2] Wallace, in his role as spokesman for the railroad companies, was a WASP-ish version of an Italian mafia godfather for 20 years. Practically no election was decided without his supervision and issues crucial to the welfare of the state required his approval. If a man spoke out against Wallace, he did so at his own risk, knowing that Wallace could destroy his career.

But eventually Wallace's influence had waned, evidenced by the losses of his endorsed candidates in the 1900 elections. Under the growing pressure of government regulation, railroad companies had become faint glimmers of the powerful forces they had once been. Realizing he had been de-clawed, Wallace shut down his Nevada office, escaped to safer ground in California, and on January 31, 1901, the once feared "Black" Wallace died, bringing to an end one of Nevada's most turbulent eras.

Today

and for three weeks we will sell for

$8.⁴⁵

(SEE THEM IN OUR WINDOWS)

One Hundred Men's and Young Men's
SUITS

These Suits are all this season styles made first-class from worsteds, cheviots and all the latest fabrics. These Suits represent the odd and broken lines left after the largest clothing business done in Reno. Compare these values with others advertised, that's all.

M. Frank & Co., Modern Clothiers and Haberdashers
WE GIVE SAVING STAMPS

Ad for men's suits at a downtown Reno store in 1906.

[1] *House of Representatives, Doc. 356*, December 12, 1907.
[2] Sally Springmeyer Zanjani, *Nevada State Journal*, September 1, 1910, from *The Unspiked Rail.*

With Wallace gone, Senator Stewart found himself without the political manipulation necessary for him to win another election. Like Senator Jones two years earlier, Stewart knew the free silver issue was a lost cause and so the last vestige of Nevada's 19th century *rotten borough*, railroad influenced, silver-supporting politics, retired from his Senate seat in March of 1905.

Not many months later, Stewart traveled to the new boomtowns of Tonopah and Goldfield. Four years later, while living in Washington D.C., this man who had seen Nevada grow up from nothing more than a sagebrush plant, died on April 23, 1909, leaving a legacy, although what that legacy was is not entirely clear.

DULL ENOUGH FOR A TEMPERANCE RALLY

In 1909, the same year that Senator William Stewart died, Nevada adopted the direct primary system for its elections. This was a step away from controlling political machines deciding which candidates would be on the ballot, and beginning with the elections of 1910, voters would select party candidates in this supposedly more democratic system. This method would work as long as the voters could not be bought off, and theoretically political power brokers would have more favors to pass out than under the old system whereby delegates selected the candidates. Yet in Nevada, the voting population was only about 15,000 men, a very manageable size for those enterprising souls ready to seize opportunities.

At the Carson City Mint, now ending its first decade as an assay office, bullion deposits continued to arrive in from various locations in Nevada, including the Comstock. Though no comparison to the glory years of the past, yields from Comstock mines averaged $600,000 annually through the 10 year period ending in 1909 and a percentage of this mineral ore was assayed at the old Carson City Mint. Chief custodian Colcord performed his duties with aplomb, regularly submitting appropriation requests to the Director of the Mint. In 1905 Colcord ordered new telephone service, and in 1907 requested, "a new and up to date safe for this mint."[1]

A wall of 10 tall and mature poplar trees in front of the old mint partially obscured its view in the summer, and looked like malnourished, multibranched stick figures during the winter. Neighborhoods surrounding the mint changed little from their 19th century design. Visitors to Carson City were generally of the opinion that it was more sophisticated than most towns out west. People commented how the architectural design of the houses and most of the public buildings was like that found in New England. And life moved at a slow pace, at times very slow.

When nothing in particular was going on, locals might rouse attention by stirring up a fuss; like the time Reverend Yorkum, a visiting temperance preacher rallied a crowd on Carson Street and smashed and burned all of businessman Joe Kelly's liquor and tobacco. This event occurred five days before Christmas in 1909, and undoubtedly caused a few people in Carson City to have a dry and smoke-free New Year celebration. It is a good thing Abe

[1] *Mint Documents dated October 18, 1905 and November 7, 1907.*

Visiting on a cold December day in 1909, Reverend Yorkum turns Carson City dry during a temperance rally in front of a local liquor store.

Curry was not around; he probably would have ridden the good rev' out of town on a rail.

Temperance leagues aside, Carson City was always ready to throw a good party or have a parade. Fourth of July was one of the more festive occasions, as everyone would get dressed up and flags would be hung everywhere. Bicyclists, marching bands, Masons, wagons, buggies, fire department vehicles, ladies with parasols, and other participants would parade down Carson Street hooting, hollering and cheering.

Because of the new wealth being accumulated in Goldfield and Tonopah, Nevada's population grew steadily. By the end of the first decade of the 20th century there were nearly twice as many people living in the state as there had been in 1900. Carson City's share of this population boom was steady, but barely noticeable, especially since there were still only one third as many people in town as in 1880. For Carson City and beyond, there were imminent changes on the horizon that would eventually reshape the state in unimaginable ways.

1911-1930

A political power base formed in Nevada between 1911 and 1930 that became unshakable until the mid-1950s, as men like George S. Nixon, Key Pittman and George Wingfield were indomitable. Nixon and Wingfield were business and political partners while Pittman was their foe, and all three told everyone else what to do.

WINGFIELD, NIXON, AND PITTMAN

George Wingfield arrived in Tonopah in 1902 looking for work. His first job was as a dealer in a gambling club where a stroke of luck gave him the stake he needed to amass a fortune. Eventually Wingfield bought majority shares in many lucrative mining companies with his partner George Nixon. Together, the two men owned most of the banks in Nevada, hotels, acres of cattle ranches, and controlling interests in the rich gold and silver mines in Goldfield and Tonopah. By the time Wingfield lost everything as a result of the stock market crash of 1929 and subsequent depression, he had become the most powerful man that had ever lived in Nevada.

George S. Nixon had the political moxie that Wingfield lacked. He honed his skills in the desert stopover town of Winnemucca in the 1890s and joined Francis Newlands' political team. After Newlands won the seat vacated by Senator Jones in 1903, it seemed inevitable that Nixon would follow suit and win the next seat up for grabs in 1905. In his 1910 re-election bid, Nixon was opposed by Key Pittman in one of the most contentious political fights in Nevada history. In the end Nixon's money and power secured the victory, further strengthening his invincible partnership with Wingfield. Then in 1912, Nixon died establishing Wingfield as a one man show.

Key Pittman, like so many others also strolled into Tonopah in the early years of the 20th century. With a degree in law, he quickly offered his services to flourishing mine operators often receiving his retainers in the form of mining stocks, and within a few years he had become wealthy. Pittman first considered challenging George Nixon for the 1905 senate seat, but thought better of it, being well aware of Nixon's power. As the 1910 election approached, Pittman felt more confident, especially after substantially increasing the size of his bankroll thanks to the continued success of mining stocks. After losing bitterly to Nixon, Pittman spent the next two years preparing and in 1912, following Nixon's untimely death, Pittman won the special election and became his former opponent's successor. Pittman never lost an election again, serving until he too died in office in 1940. During his time in the Senate he emerged as an influential leader in Congress, serving on many high level committees, but his claim to fame is the Silver Purchase Act of 1918 which bears his name. In support of the silver industry, he sponsored and pushed through legislation calling for the meltdown of up to 350 million silver dollars. Then in a reciprocal move, the Treasury was to purchase the same amount of replacement silver at $1.00 per ounce, despite the market price being much lower, another in a long line of acts legislating government subsidization of the silver industry. No one was necessarily calling for the free coinage of silver anymore, just that the government always support the price of the metal.

COLCORD RETIRES

After 13 years of faithful service as Mint Superintendent, Assayer in charge, and Custodian, Roswell K. Colcord retired from the U.S. Assay Office at Carson City. He had been there when the Treasury changed the status of the old mint to an assay office in 1899 and then supervised the shipment of the five million silver dollars remaining on the premises in 1900. Dedicated to his job, to his employees and to the city of Carson, Colcord did everything within his power to keep the mint facility/assay office open, and secure as much in appropriations as possible.

Andrew Maute, Assayer in Charge at the U.S. Assay Office in Carson City shown above (seated) while on a family outing at Lake Tahoe. Maute replaced Colcord as Assayer in 1911. (*Above photo courtesy Nevada State Museum*)

ANNIE MARTIN BECOMES HEAD OF CARSON ASSAY OFFICE

Women have always played an active role in Nevada's history and have generally received support to achieve their goals. At the Carson City Mint it had been a tradition to fill as many staff positions as possible with females. Abe Curry's original team of employees counted no fewer than 12 ladies on it, and even after the mint's status was changed to that of an assay office years later, women were included as part of the small crew.

Assayer in charge Colcord hired one of Carson City's trendsetting women, Annie Hudnall Martin, as a clerk in 1908. Prior to that, Ms. Martin had been one of Curry's original staff members, having moved on to become one of the most popular teachers in Carson City's school system for 13 years, later achieving success in the mid-1890s as the owner/editor of the *Carson City News*.

After Colcord was replaced by Andrew Maute, Annie Martin was promoted to Chief Clerk in 1913 and served in that position until 1921, at which time she was appointed Assayer in charge when Maute retired. Although Ms. Martin supervised a staff of only three employees, she is still distinguished as being the first woman to be in charge of a Bureau of the Mint facility.

For seven years, Annie Martin sent her annual report to the Director of the Mint and capably administered her duties, earning high marks in Philadelphia and Washington D.C. She held this position until her death in 1928 at the age of 71 years old. Her funeral was well attended, as flags throughout the city flew at half-mast.[1]

An inscription on her gravestone expresses the local community's sentiments,

Youthful portrait of Annie Martin, taken around the time she was the editor of the Carson City News. She has the distinction of being the first woman to serve in the senior position at a U.S. Mint facility. (Courtesy Nevada State Museum)

Certainly it must have been somewhat rewarding when bullion deposits increased during the decade from 1901 through 1910. In his role, Colcord received nothing but accolades from the different Mint Directors he served under. Though his requests were relatively small, Treasury officials took them seriously, knowing that Colcord only asked what was absolutely necessary. He was the kind of supervisor businesses appreciate: detail oriented, frugal, and accountable. Other than James Crawford, the Carson facility never had a more capable leader.

Colcord's successor was Andrew Maute, a native of France, who was 67 years old when appointed on July 11, 1911. Prior to his job at the old mint, Maute worked in the newspaper business as both a foreman and editor at the Nevada State printing office and also served as a State Senator for Nevada.

Details concerning Maute's term in office are sketchy. Bullion deposits were still being brought in during the second decade of the 20th century. In fact, yields from the Comstock mines increased sharply from 1911 through 1913, averaging $1.2 million annually, nearly double what it had been in the preceding decade, the first time production had passed the $1 million mark since 1894. But just as quickly as output had risen, there was a steep decline in 1914, with annual yields for the four year period ending in 1917, averaging $380,000.

Andrew Maute retired in 1921 and lived in Carson City with his wife Louise until he died in 1926 at age 82.

---

[1] Elbert T. Clyde became Assayer in charge upon Ms. Martin's death and held the position until the assay office ceased operations on July 1, 1933. Clyde also served as an editor of the *Carson City News*.

"Annie H. Martin 1857 to 1928: Dedicated to the memory of Annie H. Martin, by her bereaved students and classmates, in loving remembrance of her great devotion, unfailing kindness, unselfish service and sterling womanhood."[2]

On occasion, Annie Martin's portrait is displayed at the Nevada State Museum; not for her service as a mint employee, but rather in a "Historical Women of Nevada" exhibit.

WOMEN'S SUFFRAGE IN NEVADA

Another side to feminism in Nevada was women's right to vote, which had been a key topic of conversation in Carson City and surrounding regions for at least 20 years. It was not until Anne Henrietta Martin (no relation to Annie Martin) spearheaded the movement beginning in 1911 that real progress was made. Martin was president of the National Woman's party and organized rallies and protest marches. She was respected as the head of the history department at the University of Nevada, Reno, and gained the support of many influential women nationwide and in her home state. One of her key allies in Carson City was the former first lady of Nevada Janna Adams, wife of Governor and Mint Superintendent Jewett W. Adams.

Motivated by women winning the right to vote in western states such as Colorado (1893), Utah (1896), Idaho (1896), Washington (1910), California (1911), and Arizona and Oregon (1912), Nevada's voters joined those in Montana in November of 1914 and approved the legislation. Nevada and these other progressive states were six years ahead of the national act which was adopted in 1920 when the 19th Amendment was ratified.

NEWLANDS' FINAL YEARS

Some historians have lauded Francis Newlands as "one of Nevada's most valuable contributions to the nation…,"[3] while others have viewed him as a lucky opportunist who married a wealthy woman to attain his goals. Regardless of perceptions, Newlands did win eight successive elections, five in the House, and three in the Senate, and will forever be acknowledged for the Reclamation Act of 1902. He was also known for his defense of minorities, though he was not in favor of the unlimited immigration of Asiatic peoples, which he saw as a threat to domestic labor forces.

When Newlands won the election in November of 1914 by a mere 40 votes, he was 66 years old and perhaps planning to make it his final term in office. Unfortunately he

never had a chance to make that decision, because on December 24, 1917, Francis Griffith Newlands died at the age of 69.

Now all three of Nevada's U.S. Senators from what Mary Ellen Glass refers to as the age of "Silver and Politics in Nevada," were gone.

PITTMAN ACT BOOSTS PRICE OF SILVER

At the time America entered World War I in 1917, the price of silver took a sharp rise to nearly one dollar an ounce, up from an average of approximately 57 cents during the preceding 15 years leading up to the war. Nevada Senator Key Pittman drafted a bill during his first term in office (1913 to 1917) designed to support the price of silver through the process of melting down millions of silver dollars. His plan was adopted in 1918, and during the next four years at least 270 million Morgan silver dollars were melted.

This action had an immediate effect on the silver market, as prices reached nearly $1.40 per ounce in 1919 and 1920. Mining exploration around the Comstock region staged a renewal of interest, leading to a mild resurgence in productivity. Between 1918 and 1922 yields averaged $640,000 annually, and then from 1923 through 1926, rose to $2.1 million a year.

This spike in bullion production brought renewed activity at the Carson City Assay Office, but did little to revive a sagging local economy. In the years leading up to these new mineral ore discoveries, Nevada's population base had decreased by nearly 7% from the highs reached in 1910. Carson City lost 1,000 residents between 1911 and 1920 as the population dropped to its lowest level since before the mint opened in 1870.

In spite of the healthy support the silver industry received from the Pittman Act and the introduction of new Peace silver dollars in 1921, prices fell into a downward spiral through the rest of the decade, which resulted in annual averages of approximately 58 cents per ounce.

PROHIBITION YEARS

With the ratification of the 18th amendment at the end of 1919, prohibiting the manufacture, sale, or transportation of intoxicating liquor, America was poised for a dry 1920s, at least in theory. In Carson City, locals were still searching for an identity, as it became increasingly more evident that the Comstock mines were in for

---

[2] *Gravestone at Lone Mountain Cemetery, Carson City, Nevada.*
[3] Gilman M. Ostrander, *Nevada, the Great Rotten Borough, 1859-1964.*

a long dry spell, and the old mint turned assay office was all but extinct.

Many Nevadans had already taken advantage of the Reclamation programs offered by the government and were using irrigation to develop the state's natural resources. Reno took advantage of its proximity to the Southern Pacific's railroad depot as well as the Truckee River to develop a city independent of mining, and by the end of the 1920s, was the fastest growing city in Nevada. Prospects of catering to the tourist crowd visiting nearby Lake Tahoe also engendered optimism.

George Wingfield's banking empire was firmly entrenched in Reno and Carson City. In all, Wingfield was the principal controlling partner in 12 banks in northern Nevada and also owned the two largest hotels in Reno, plus thousands of acres of real estate throughout the state. One thing Wingfield apparently lacked was a vision to make Nevada a better place, at a time when the state desperately needed a man with vision.

About that time, a 25 year old budding entrepreneur made his first visit to the North Shore of Lake Tahoe. It was spring of 1927 when Norman Biltz, formerly of Connecticut and New York, stopped at the Cal Neva Lodge in Crystal Bay, Nevada to see his new acquaintance Robert Sherman. Biltz was just the man of vision needed and eventually he created a political power machine the likes of which the *Silver State* had never seen. (More about Norman Biltz can be found in Chapter 9.)

But first, the severe stock market crash of 1929, and subsequent depression of the 1930s would test residents of Nevada, as well as the nation at large. By the end of the 1920s, Carson City was accurately described as the smallest capital in the United States; and though it was 3,000 miles from New York, no doubt the crash on Wall Street reverberated all the way to the modest white houses in this city.

But Carson City's livelihood was not dependent upon stocks traded back east, as it had instead relied for sustenance on the surrounding natural resources and the business of politics conducted in the highly esteemed Capitol building in the center of town.

1931-1941

A severe drought in 1930 and 1931 forced dozens of Nevada's ranchers into bankruptcy at a time that even banks were finding it difficult to survive. Men like Norman Biltz rushed to the aid of the ranchers, seeking financial support from out of state sources to prevent thousands of acres in Nevada—cultivated for nearly three decades through reclamation and irrigation projects—from again becoming barren.

THE GREAT DEPRESSION

Not since 1893 had America suffered as severe a financial depression as that of the 1930s. In his inaugural speech of March 4, 1933, newly elected president Franklin

View of downtown Carson City in the 1930s. The Arlington Hotel can be seen on the right. (*Courtesy Nevada State Museum*)

D. Roosevelt assured the nation that his administration would pull it out of the economic emergency. His classic pronouncement that "The only thing we have to fear is fear itself,"[1] strengthened and comforted many weary souls.

Bank failures caused panics across the country in the early 1930s as the public frantically attempted to draw out what little savings they had, and when unsuccessful, were left helpless and despondent. In Nevada, the most powerful banker in the state, George Wingfield, held onto the mast as the storm blew violently past him. Finally, he ran out of resources and all of his banks were closed. Almost at once he was wiped out, reduced to the lowly financial condition he had been in 30 years earlier when he strolled into Tonopah.

A faltering stock market dragged silver down with it and between 1931 and 1933, prices for the white metal fell to all time lows, slipping below 26 cents per ounce several times. This served an almost fatal blow to the mining industry around the Comstock region. Annual yields from mines in that area dropped to the $60,000 level in 1930 and 1932, its lowest point since mineral discoveries were first made in the 1850s.

Nevada's venerable Senator Key Pittman went to work again on the floor of Congress and sponsored a new silver purchase bill. Legislation was passed in 1933 and the Presidential Silver Purchase Act was one of many programs under the umbrella of FDR's *New Deal* campaign. Initially the price of silver rebounded, rising above 60 cents per ounce on several occasions. But Roosevelt shifted his emphasis to the gold market and authorized that the official price be set at $35 per ounce. At the same time, the Gold Reserve Act was passed, officially taking the United States off the gold standard and making it illegal for the public to own any form of gold bullion or gold coins, with the exception of those possessing numismatic (or collector) value.

Apparently, by the end of 1933, the government believed that Americans needed a strong drink and the 21st Amendment was ratified, repealing the 18th Amendment prohibiting liquor consumption. Nevada had a jump on the rest of the nation since alcohol had never been totally forbidden, especially since the defining year of 1931 when gambling was legalized in the state. After all, who would go to a casino where alcohol was not served?

Nevada's decision to introduce gambling coincided with the Boulder Dam project begun in 1931. With so many workers moving into the area, it seemed a sure bet to lure them into legitimate houses of games. Otherwise, the workers would be stuck in the middle of the desert looking for other ways to amuse themselves.

Reno was the leader in taking advantage of legalized gambling, seeing the potential to consolidate all elements of the loose life-style, old west reputation that already characterized it. Carson City on the other hand was still searching for an identity. While it could certainly use the revenue from gambling, its population of only 1,800 people by 1931, and its reputation for being a lazy, dull town seemed to limit its allure.

Of course Carson City, because it was the state's capital would always be linked with gambling regardless of where casinos were set up, as lawmakers there regulated the industry and decided how much tax it would pay. Later on, casinos would make sure that their representatives held the offices that were responsible for creating the regulations and deciding the tax rates, but that is getting ahead of the story.

By 1933, with slumping silver prices and Comstock mines in hibernation, the Assay Office in Carson City had come to the end of the line. Requests for appropria-

---

[1] *Inaugural address, Franklin Delano Roosevelt,* March 4, 1933.

Treasure hunters paid $600 for the privilege of placer mining the yard around the Carson City Mint in the 1930s. The U.S. Government allowed them to dig for six months, resulting in a gross return of approximately $1,800. (*Courtesy Nevada State Museum*)

The U.S. Post Office was over 50 years old by the 1940s when this photo was taken.

tions to keep up maintenance on the facility had been denied in recent years. With the nation in a depression and banks failing, the Treasury Department had little concern whether or not bullion deposits were brought into the Carson office. Finally in June of 1933, Director of the Mint Nellie Taylor Ross sent notice to Carson City that the old mint and assay office should officially cease operations as of June 30, 1933.

Director Ross included instructions as to how the shut down should proceed and over the course of the next few months all stored inventory was shipped out, all machinery and equipment was dismantled and sent to various locations, all documents were carefully packed, sealed and delivered, and employees were given their final wages. When it was all over, it looked very empty inside, with very few reminders of the times when three coin presses were running full steam banging out thousands of gold and silver coins.

Every vault was a hollow cave with only dirt and other debris on the floor. Instead of the smell of sulfuric and nitrate acids billowing through the building, there was now only a musty scent, mere traces of the familiar aromas from the past.

A custodian kept a key so he could check on it occasionally, as well as let Treasury officials in from time to time. There was no need for watchmen as there was nothing to guard. Quietly the old building just stood there. Old timers told stories about it to the children in town as realtors pondered different uses for the building. But what was worthy enough to occupy this monument to the heritage of Abe Curry's city?

In time there was talk about demolishing it and erecting a commercial building, usually resulting in loud protests from locals. Yet no one was quite sure what it could be used for and still maintain its dignity. Beginning in 1930, a relief agency office shared the building with the remnant of an assay operation, a temporary situation during the bleakest years of the great depression. Later on, the old mint was put under the jurisdiction of the New Deal Works Project Administration and used as a regional office for that agency. There really was no hurry to make a decision about its future, for after all, Carson City was not in a growth and developmental stage at the time. So it just stood there and waited; it was not costing the city anything, as volunteers even took on groundskeeping duties so the yard would not be overrun with weeds and tall grass.

What the mint needed more than anything was a person with vision.

THE HONORABLE CLARK J. GUILD

Three months before the old mint and assay office in Carson City was permanently closed, Patrick A. McCarran became the first native born Nevadan to be elected to the U.S. Senate. McCarran had lost earlier bids to win this seat, having been involved in Nevada government since 1903, and serving as the Justice of the Nevada Supreme Court from 1913 to 1918.

McCarran's rise to national stature in 1933 coincided with the emerging business endeavors of Norman Biltz. Both of these men would play key roles in the even-

Patrick A. McCarran, U.S. Senator, 1933-1954.

tual outcome of the Carson City Mint and by the end of the decade they had become inextricably linked, gaining a reputation for pulling practically every political string in the state.

Throughout the mid 1930s the old mint lay dormant. While no longer under the jurisdiction of the Bureau of the Mint, the building was still the property of the United States government. It was categorized as surplus real estate, being placed under the supervision of the WPA. By reason of a clause in the original statute from 1865 authorizing the mint, the property was not eligible to be sold publicly.

When Judge Guild walked by the old mint building in 1938 he saw this "For Sale" sign to the left of the front door. (*Courtesy Hal V. Dunn*)

Inquiries from individuals interested in acquiring the property came in on a regular basis. In 1938, Senators McCarran and Pittman introduced a bill requesting that the old mint property be conveyed to the State of Nevada free of charge. Though the bill was dismissed, Congress did pass an act authorizing the public sale of the Carson Mint. Almost at once offers from private parties were presented, ranging from $3,000 to $11,000.

Then in the summer of 1938, on a lazy Sunday morning in Carson City, popular local judge Clark J. Guild walked by the old mint, and discovered "a sign on the building [reading] 'For Sale.'" In the judge's own words, "it rather upset me…." He then walked over to a group of men standing in front of the Arlington Hotel and told one of them, "Bill they're going to sell the old mint building." To this Bill replied, "Well Judge, do you want to buy it?" Pausing for a second, the Judge then uttered the visionary words that would seal the old mint's fate, "No I can't buy it, but it ought to never be sold. It would make a wonderful museum."[1]

From that point on, Judge Guild devoted his undivided attention to seeing that statement fulfilled. Immediately, he pledged to put up $1,000 toward the purchase price, and began soliciting more donors. Senator Pat McCarran was called upon for support and hurriedly submitted a bill authorizing Nevada to buy the mint for its appraised value. Guild later said that if McCarran had not acted so promptly, "we never would have gotten the building, because when it became known that the building was only appraised at $6,000, several private parties commenced to put bids in for it."[2]

---

[1] *Clark J. Guild, Memoirs*, Oral History Program, UNR, 1971.

[2] Ibid.

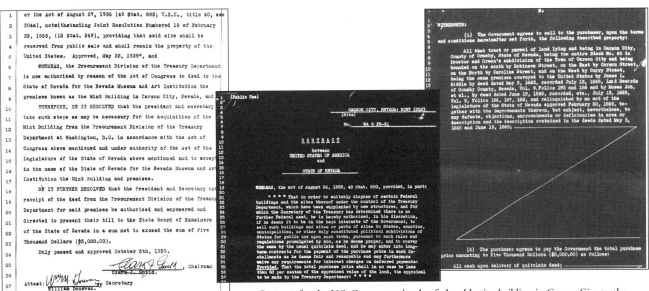

Purchase order signed by Judge Clark J. Guild on behalf of the State of Nevada for the purchase of the old mint building in 1939.

Contract for the U.S. Government's sale of the old mint building in Carson City to the State of Nevada for $5,000.

In short time, the Judge organized the Nevada Museum and Art Institute, and received sanction from the state to proceed with the purchase plan. All Guild needed now was a generous benefactor, so he "wrote to Major [Max C.] Fleischmann and asked him if he wouldn't assist us and be our advisor."[1] At first the good Major declined the request, but Judge Guild was tenacious, appealing to Fleischmann from every angle, and finally Fleischmann agreed to have a meeting to discuss the matter. When the two men met, Fleischmann asked Guild, "What do you know about a museum?" And Guild answered, "Major, I don't know anything, but by gum, we're going to have one here in Nevada. I've been around. I've been to large cities. I've been to many museums. This may be a dream of mine, but I hope to see it consummated..." Fleischmann was impressed with Guild's spirit and said, "Well I like your guts. I'm going to give you $5,000 to get started."[2]

What a relief to Judge Guild, for he knew how crucial Fleischmann's support would be to the project, and not only financially. Museums were Fleischmann's hobby, one of his proudest achievements being the gifts he had made to the magnificent museum in Santa Barbara, California. Fleischmann also loved his adopted state of Nevada and had originally established his residence there when Norman Biltz sold him on the state's favorable tax advantages. For many years Fleischmann's passion for the *Silver State* was beneficial to its development.

Major Fleischmann's involvement attracted many more supporters to the project, and by late 1939 everything was in place to close the deal. A contract was drafted between the United States of America and the State of

A parade passes in front of the Carson City Mint on Nevada Statehood Day on October 31, 1939.

Nevada on December 8, 1939, stating in part, "Whereas, the Carson City, Nevada, old mint site and building..., for which there is no further Federal need, and the sale of which will be in the best interests of the Government... Now therefore, the Government agrees to sell the purchaser...the following described property."[3] A description of the property, providing the names of the four bordering streets, as well as the details of the original purchase in 1865 followed next, and then the purchase price of $5,000. Signatures completed the sale and Nevada now officially owned the beloved old mint that had been standing on Carson Street for 70 years.

For the next two years the building was cleaned up and refurbished, as preparations were made for the transition from mint to museum. Judge Guild garnered many volunteers to assist with the improvements, and Major Fleischmann's personal contractor completed the work at a cost of $19,000.

Then on October 31, 1941–appropriately commemorated as Nevada Statehood Day–the new State Museum opened. More than 5,000 toured the premises on opening day and learned that it was the goal of this new institution to procure, house, and display exhibits reflective of Nevada's heritage. For the past 62 years (through 2003) dedicated staff workers have remained faithful to this goal.

Carson City locals, as well as people from the entire State of Nevada, know how indebted they are to Judge Clark J. Guild for the devotion he displayed while spearheading the purchase of the old mint and its transformation into a museum. It was also Judge Guild who organized the first Nevada Admission Day in 1938, which eventually became a state holiday celebrated on October 31.

As a district judge, Clark Guild served on the bench from 1925 to 1953, first in Churchill County and then in the Carson City district. He was a familiar figure around the town he held dear to his heart, his reputation for stepping forward and assisting in any way possible was above reproach, and he was unquestionably one of the greatest living advertisements for Carson City and Nevada. One of his last major contributions to the preservation of local history occurred in 1958, when he saved the Carson City Mint's old number one coin press from the scrap yard in San Francisco. Visitors today (2003) are still privi-

[1] Ibid.
[2] Ibid.
[3] *Real Estate Contract, United States of America,* December 8, 1939.

Judge Clark J. Guild holding on to old coin press #1 when it was delivered to the Nevada State Museum in 1958.

leged to see this historic press on display and operating at the museum.

Old mints should have their glory preserved after they are closed down and retired. Out of their offices, rooms, and departments have come America's coins, stamped with the dates of bygone eras, and these buildings and coins are icons of the nation's past, filled with the memories of those olden times.

Being converted into a museum after retirement is the perfect way to preserve an old mint. In the case of the Carson Mint, this was no small challenge because small towns with populations of only 3,500 people generally do not have museums. But that is where a man with vision like Clark J. Guild comes in; he was there at just the right time to help the Mint on Carson Street end its search for a new identity.

The old coin press #1 being hoisted through the front door of the Nevada State Museum in 1958.

A crew returns the old coin press #1, after Judge Clark J. Guild rescued it from the scrap heap for a paltry $225. (*All photos on this page courtesy Nevada State Museum*)

CHAPTER SIX

The Silver Coins of the Carson City Mint

As an introduction to this date-by-date, denomination-by-denomination chapter about the silver coins minted at Carson City, readers are encouraged to consider the scope of this category. There are 54 different date, denomination, and major variety combinations in a complete set of silver coins: Eight dimes, two 20-cent pieces, nine quarters, ten halves, four Seated Liberty dollars, six trade dollars and thirteen Morgan silver dollars. Dimes and quarters from the early years (1870 to 1874) had very low mintages, while half dollars had relatively higher mintages through the consecutive date run from 1870 to 1878. Twenty cent pieces had low mintages for the only two years they were minted, with the 1876-CC being one of the scarcest coins in all of numismatics. Production reached its highest levels for the dimes, quarters, and halves from 1875 to 1878 as a result of the Treasury's *Specie Payment* program, part of the plan to redeem all the fractional paper currency in circulation.

There were three different designs of silver dollars, the Seated Liberty, Trade, and Morgan; Seated Liberty's being coined in only four years, from 1870 to 1873, resulting in some of the lowest mintages in the entire Carson City coinage series. Trade dollars were issued as *Legal Tender* coins in the beginning, eventually losing their *Legal Tender* status; and subsequently being discontinued after a short six-year run.

Morgan silver dollars have the second highest combined mintage of all "CC" coins (dimes are first), with a total of 13,862,041 being produced from 1878 to 1893 (none minted in 1886, 1887, and 1888). Morgan "CC" dollars are the most widely collected series out of all coins issued from this mint, featuring some of the highest graded, most eye-appealing specimens of silver dollars surviving today (2003).

In the following sections, each series of silver coins produced at the Carson City Mint, are presented as complete sets, with each date given special attention. Aside from elementary data such as mintages, other pertinent information will include: "Finest Knowns," "Notable Pedigrees," "Survival Estimates in All Grades," "Survival Estimates in Uncirculated, and XF/AU," as well as "Total Certified Examples in All Grades."

FORMAT

In the "Finest Knowns" category, statistics are taken from PCGS and NGC population data. Though other specimens not graded by either of these two services may exist, the certified populations encompass a vast majority of the Condition Census specimens extant. Under "Notable Pedigrees," an effort has been made to acknowledge the most recognizable names associated with each date. No attempt has been made to provide a comprehensive pedigree list, which will invariably result in qualified names being left out; often in the case of Carson City coins, auction companies omit pedigree information, making it difficult for researchers to track. As far as the more common dates are concerned, pedigree information will be classified as "*Various.*"

For survival estimates, five primary sources have been employed: auctions, population reports, secondary references such as encyclopedias, general market observations, and without a doubt, intuition or educated guesses. Fortunately in this regard there is so much more *grass beneath the collector's feet* concerning surviving populations than at any time in history. As an example, when Augustus Heaton wrote his *Treatise on Mint Marks* in 1893, the only information available for him to make his rarity estimates were original mintages and a small number of auction appearances. Even access to mintages was a relatively new advancement in numismatic research in Heaton's time. But in the early years of the 21st century, it seems doubtful that estimates in most cases will be off by long margins, especially on the extremely low population dates. Percentage variables will obviously be more error-sensitive for low population dates. If, for instance, a second 1873-CC *Without Arrows* dime is discovered, survival estimates will be off by 100%. On the other hand, if it is revealed that there are 1,100 1877-CC quarters in Uncirculated the estimate of 800 will be off by 37.5%. In relation to dates with the highest population estimates like 1884-CC silver dollars, a 15% error to the lower end would mean there were more surviving dollars than were minted! And yet for other high population dates like 1890-CC dollars, if estimates are off by 100%, the question lingers: where are they all? One important reminder about estimates is, that is all they are—estimates. For the purposes of this book, a thorough effort has been made to arrive at these estimates, yet undiscovered hoards, estate holdings, and other factors, leave room for error.

Without a doubt, 20 or 30 years from now (2003), future numismatic authors will have access to a far greater information base, facilitating more precise survival estimates.

Throughout this book, two grading services, PCGS and NGC, are used as representatives for the certified coin market. Though not every Carson City coin submitted for grading is sent to these two companies, time has proven that most are, especially the key dates.

Acknowledging that the category "Total Certified Examples" does not include every certified Carson City coin in existence, it is nevertheless the author's opinion that population data from PCGS and NGC is sufficient for this study.

As with any time-sensitive information, the most current data available was used (July 2003), prior to this book being sent to the publisher.

Under the "Reflections" category, comments are included relative to each date, concerning, but not limited to: the history of the Carson City Mint, early collector interest (1875 to 1950), noted auction appearances, pedigrees, varieties, general price histories, and the availability of examples in various grades. In the Morgan silver dollar section, the "Reflections" have been organized in a slightly different format, as well as abbreviated. This is in recognition of the extensive library of literature already available on the subject. Correspondingly, throughout each set of silver coins, readers are encouraged to select from other works that are provided, for further exploration and research.

It cannot be emphasized enough that the Carson City Mint and its coins comprise a nearly inexhaustible subject; there are so many paths to travel and side-routes to take, and it is the author's desire that readers will discover something of interest while examining each series that will lead to further study. Resources in the National Archives in Philadelphia and Washington D.C. are available to all researchers, as are the archives at the Nevada State Museum and Historical Society. Undiscovered references are hidden in old newspapers from the Carson City Mint era as well as unpublished oral histories from the times. Auction catalogs, *Coin World Almanacs,* old price guides, newsletters from the *Gobrecht Journal* and other specialized coin clubs, offer further sources for investigation.

Variety collectors as well, may have a field day with Carson City coinage; in the Morgan dollar series alone, VAM collectors can search for fascinating "CC" varieties and assemble interesting and rewarding sets or subsets.

There truly is something for everyone within the complete set of silver coins from the Carson City Mint, so please take your time and find exactly what suits you—if you have not done so already.

(Photo courtesy Bowers and Merena)

Dimes were first struck at the Carson City Mint in 1871 and continued to be coined there through 1878. There are nine dates in the set, with the year 1873 featuring two well-known varieties, and the 1875 offering two more minor variants—bringing the total of the Carson City dime set to 11 pieces.

The first five dimes in the set are extremely rare, and since there is only one known specimen of the 1873-CC *Without Arrows* dime, the completion of an 11 piece set is limited to one collector at any given time.

The bulk of the "CC" dime population was minted in the three years starting in 1875 and continuing through 1877; the combined total for those three years was 20,615,000, which represents 99% of all "CC" dimes produced.

Of the later dates, the 1878-CC dime is much scarcer than those from the mid-1870s. Collectors building 10-piece "CC" *Type Sets* (one example of every denomination) generally settle for one of the three high mintage dates from the mid-1870s.

BUREAU OF THE MINT DATA FOR CARSON CITY DIME PRODUCTION

Total Combined Mintage:	20,901,108
Total Face Value:	$2,090,110.80
Total Ounces of Silver Used:	1,511,133 ozs.+
Design Type:	Seated Liberty (Legend Obverse)
Designers:	Obverse: Christian Gobrecht
	Reverse: James B. Longacre
Metal Composition:	.900 silver .100 copper
Actual Gross Weight:	2.49 grams
Actual Fine Silver Content:	.0720 oz. (1871-1873)
Actual Gross Weight:	2.5 grams
Actual Fine Silver Content:	.0723 oz. (1873*-1878)
Value of Silver in One Dime Between 1871-1878:	$.083-.096

(* After April, 1873)

1871-CC

(Photo courtesy Bowers and Merena)

Mintage: 20,100

Finest Knowns°:

    NGC MS-65 (1)

    PCGS MS-64 (1)

    PCGS MS-62 (1)

    NGC MS-62 (1)

    NGC MS-61 (1)

Notable Pedigrees:

    Neil Collection (1947)

    Holmes Collection (1960)

    Norweb Collection (1987)

    James A. Stack (1990)

Survival Estimates in All Grades: 50-100
Estimated in Uncirculated: 3-5
Estimated in XF to AU: 10-12
Total Certified Examples in All Grades (PCGS and NGC)*: 30

(° As of July 2003)

REFLECTIONS:

The 1871-CC dime was greatly undervalued in high grades until the *James Stack* specimen reached the $50,000 mark in 1990. Even in the early 21st century, when scarcity and popularity factors are taken into consideration, the present prices for 1871-CC dimes remain undervalued. Uncirculated examples currently (2003) hover around the $100,000 level and will most likely advance beyond that mark in the future. In 1987, when the *Norweb* specimen sold for $12,100, collectors were shocked that it had reached such a high level; but in the present market (early 21st century), the *Norweb* specimen would easily bring many multiples of that price.

The *James Stack* specimen is currently encased in an NGC MS-65 holder, and someday it will probably be designated a Branch Mint Proof, or at minimum, a Specimen strike. Empirical evidence insists upon this, because of the coin's attributes.[1] The old adage, *if it walks like a duck, and quacks like a duck, then it must be a duck,* is applicable here. Though there may be no connection between the *Stack* specimen and the one in the 1947 *Neil* sale, coin dealer B.

Max Mehl described the *Neil* specimen as, "A beautiful Proof specimen."

Prices for most Carson City coins have lagged behind in their relation to the coin market in general through the years. Surviving population information for "CC" coins remained shrouded in uncertainty for decades; and as more data became available during the past several decades, prices for "CC" coins began playing catch-up; the 1871-CC dimes are vivid examples.

Even lower grade circulated examples of this date will bring at least double the listed wholesale prices (in 2003).

Many of the lowest grade 1871-CC dimes are corroded, have surface etchings, are brushed or cleaned, or have been repaired; the lucky collector who finds a problem free circulated piece has found a true treasure.[2]

---

[1] A Proof coin is being described in this context as a coin struck on a polished planchet and receiving multiple die strikes. The result is a coin with deeply mirrored surfaces, fully squared rims and sharper than normal definition on the portrait and devices.

[2] One of the *Top 25*.

(Photo courtesy Bowers and Merena)

Mintage: 24,000[1]

Finest Knowns*:

    PCGS MS-61 (1)

    PCGS AU-58 (1)

    NGC AU-55 (1)

Notable Pedigrees:

    Anderson-Dupont Collection (1954)

    Empire Collection (1957)

    Eugene Gardner (1965)

    R.L. Miles, Jr. (1969)

    E.A. Carson (1976)

    James A. Stack (1990)

Survival Estimates in All Grades: 75-150
Estimated in Uncirculated: 3-4
Estimated in XF to AU: 15-18
Total Certified Examples in All Grades (PCGS and NGC)*: 45

(* As of July 2003)

REFLECTIONS:

U.S. Bureau of the Mint records list a mintage figure of 24,000 for 1872-CC dimes, the total used by numismatic reference works for over 100 years. For the past 25 years, however, some reference books have added 11,480 pieces to the original Mint's total. Not surprisingly, this increase on paper has not resulted in an increase in surviving specimens.

The survival factor of approximately .5% of the original mintage corresponds with the other "CC" dimes from 1871 to 1874. The 1872 is ranked fifth in rarity order in the Carson City dime set, and is securely positioned in the top 10 within the complete 116-piece Seated Liberty dime set. As of the date of this writing (2003), only one Uncirculated 1872-CC dime has been certified by either of the two major grading services. Stack's auctioned an Uncirculated specimen in 1965, which they had also sold in 1957 in their *Empire Collection* sale. Another Uncirculated 1872-CC dime was sold in 1954 as part of the *Anderson-Dupont Collection*. The *Empire* specimen was sold for the third time in a 20-year span, when Bowers and Ruddy auctioned the coin as part of the *E.A. Carson Collection* in 1976. Also worth noting, the *James A. Stack* sale in 1990 also featured a multicolored Uncirculated example, possibly one of the coins mentioned above.

Each of the 1872-CC dimes in the *Eliasberg, Norweb*, and *F.C.C. Boyd* collections were in circulated condition. This date, like all pre-1875 silver coins, is rapidly increasing in popularity; and gaining respect in the collector community. Problem-free circulated 1872-CC dimes easily bring double, triple, or whatever the prices that are listed in wholesale or retail guides; a resistance point will eventually be reached, but that appears to be a long way off.

If offered at public sale, the Uncirculated specimen will most likely sell for a price comparable to the 1871-CC, 1873-CC *With Arrows*, or 1874-CC dimes.

Many of the lowest grade examples are victims of corrosion, surface etchings, buffings, cleanings, or repairs. Planchets used for many of the dimes were not of the highest quality, resulting in abnormal surface porosity. Although random coins from the Carson City Mint were sent to Philadelphia for assaying every year, the Assay Commission found nothing significantly subpar with them. Still, rumors abounded that the Carson City Mint's employees were careless, often bypassing certain procedures,

[1] From *Annual Report of the Director of the Mint*, 1901.

although there was no proof of this. The verdict will be left to metallurgists and assayers of the modern age to perform tests on these early silver coins from the Carson City Mint to determine if the metal content conformed to U.S. Mint standards. Anything is possible, of course, but almost without fail, Carson City Mint employees were very proud of their operation, and exerted great effort to ensure quality control.

Today's high values of early "CC" silver coins like 1872-CC dimes would probably deter most modern *detec-* *tives* from cutting one in half to prove whether they were of substandard metal quality. (Modern metallurgist tests are performed with sophisticated technology of course, not requiring the physical destruction of coins.)

There are two minor reverse varieties; the earliest one displaying a clear mintmark, and the second variety features a die crack through the mintmark just like that found on 1873-CC and 1874-CC dimes.[1]

---

[1] One of the *Top 25*.

1873-CC
Without Arrows

(Photo courtesy Bowers and Merena)

Mintage: 12,400

Finest Knowns*:

    NGC MS-65 (I)

Notable Pedigrees:

    William H. Woodin (1915)

    Charles Williams (Menjou) (1950)

    Louis E. Eliasberg, Sr. (1996)

Survival Estimates in All Grades: I

Estimated in Uncirculated: I

Total Certified Examples
   in All Grades (PCGS and NGC)*: I

(* As of July 2003)

REFLECTIONS:

This date is the *Crown Jewel* of the Carson City coin series; rising to prominence on a national scale in 1950 when Louis E. Eliasberg, Sr. purchased the only known surviving specimen for the reported sum of $4,000. Since then, the 1873-CC *Without Arrows* dime has received much press coverage and with its *Unique* status, only one collector at a time can own a complete set of coins from the Carson City Mint. It is generally listed as *Uncollectable* or *Unique* in price guides and reference works,[1] and has the distinction of being the first dime to sell for $500,000 or more. Correspondingly, it is the most valuable of any of the coins with a "CC" mintmark.

Counterfeiters are faced with a considerable challenge if attempting to reproduce this rarity, for if a cast copy were manufactured, familiar diagnostic comparisons would quickly expose it as a fake. Adding a mintmark to an 1873 *Without Arrows* dime from the Philadelphia Mint would require first, that a *Closed Three* variety be used, and second, that the "CC" mintmark display the diagnostic die crack crossing through the center, extending to the ribbon on the bow. A third option for an unscrupulous coin alterer would be to remove the arrows from a genuine 1873-CC *With Arrows* dime; a bold tactic indeed, reserved only for the gutsiest gambler, because if the attempt were not successful (which it would not be), the crook would lose the costly value of the coin used for alteration. As with any highly publicized rarity, when a new discovery is introduced, cautious examination is employed to authenticate it, preventing anyone save the most brainless from attempting to reproduce an 1873-CC *Without Arrows* dime.

The only known example of this date was catalogued in the Bowers and Merena sale of the *Eliasberg* collection as, "MS-65 or finer."[2] It has since been graded first by PCGS, as an MS-64, and then by NGC as an MS-65; trivial details, of course, when referring to a date with only a single piece extant. Most likely, the query will never be made, "What is the bid price on an 1873-CC Without Arrows dime in MS-64 and MS-65?"

This date will always be esteemed as the rarest dime in the history of U.S. coinage, and its association with the Carson City Mint adds to its eminence in numismatic circles.[3]

---

[1] For example *Complete Guide to Liberty Seated Dimes*, Brian Greer, Chapter 5.
[2] Bowers and Merena, *Louis E. Eliasberg, Sr. Collection*, May 1996.
[3] One of the *Top 25*.

1873-CC

With Arrows

(Photo courtesy Bowers and Merena)

Mintage: 18,791

Finest Knowns*:

    NGC MS-65 (Norweb) (I)

    NGC MS-65 (Stack) (I)

Notable Pedigrees:

    F.C.C. Boyd (1945)

    Norweb Collection (1987)

    James A. Stack (1990)

    Waldo E. Bolen, Jr. (1995, 1999)

Survival Estimates in All Grades: 50-75
Estimated in Uncirculated: 3
Estimated in XF to AU: 3-6
Total Certified Examples in All Grades (PCGS and NGC)*: 42

(* As of July 2003)

REFLECTIONS:

Minted in response to the *Coinage Act of 1873*, the *With Arrows* variety increased the silver content by a whisker. This date is the only collectable "CC" dime from 1873, and is slightly more available than the other *With Arrows* dime from Carson City. The term *more available* is used frugally, however, since the only other "CC" dime in the *With Arrows* variety series (1874-CC) is prohibitively scarce. The *Red Book*[1] does not even list a value above the Extra Fine grade for the 1873-CC *With Arrows* dime.

The survival rate for this date seems to parallel the percentages for the 1871-CC, 1872-CC, and 1874-CC dimes; certain numismatic researchers (Breen, as an example) have placed their survival estimates at 1% of the original mintage.[2] In relation to current (2003) populations, it seems reasonable to lower that estimate to perhaps one-third to one-half of 1%.

With the continuous operations of the professional grading services approaching their 20th anniversaries, owners of recognized coin rarities, whether dealers, collectors, or non-collectors, have witnessed that certified coins sell for more than uncertified coins. There are exceptions of course, but, using universally accepted statistics, sellers wishing to reap the highest return, will get their coins certified. And with the dissemination of information in these early years of the 21st century at the most technologically advanced stage in history, the public is exposed to more facts, news, and trivia than it is almost able to assimilate. Relative to the coin market, publicity about $7.6 million $20 gold pieces, and $215,000 1943 copper cents reaches every town and hamlet, nook and cranny in the United States; the point is that owners of rare Carson City coins (like all rare coins) have a greater awareness of what they have, and as a result, have more incentive to get their coins certified. This overwhelmingly suggests that a very large percentage of surviving "CC" dimes from 1871 through 1874 have already surfaced, and as more time passes, the likelihood of undiscovered specimens of these rare dates will further diminish.

Armed with knowledge of the total population (or as near as possible), collectors and dealers will feel more confident when establishing valuations: Using the unique 1873-CC *Without Arrows* dime as an example, if the buyer is certain that only one specimen exists, the high price will not cause as much anxiety as it would if there were rumors of additional specimens. Turning back the hands of time to 1950, one can recall that the rarity and value of the 1873-CC *Without Arrows* dime was unknown to 99% of the public. News of the sale caused widespread searches of attics, drawers, safes, coin albums, bank shelves, and

---

[1] *Guide Book of United States Coins*, R.S. Yeoman, edited by Kenneth Bressett.

[2] *Walter Breen's Complete Encyclopedia of U.S. and Colonial Coins*, Page 318.

pocket change, in the days before the Internet and other broad means of disseminating information.

Witness, for example, the revelation that 99.8% of the 1876-CC 20-cent pieces had been melted, which promptly established the date as the rarest in the "CC" series (an honor later bestowed upon the 1873-CC *Without Arrows* dime). To further illustrate, it is worth noting that less than 70 years after the coin was minted, a specimen of the 1876-CC 20-cent piece sold for $1,500 in 1945 as part of the *World's Greatest Collection*; the total prices realized for the entire sale was $169,806, with the 1876-CC 20-cent piece firmly seated on the top ten list of highest prices from that auction.

Of the two known Uncirculated examples of the 1873-CC *With Arrows* dime, the *Norweb* specimen is superior in eye appeal to the *Stack* specimen although both coins have been graded MS-65. At best the *Stack* coin grades MS-64 on the obverse, with an MS-65 reverse; a severe ice-pick-like scratch is well hidden on Ms. Liberty's right arm from below the elbow to her hand, and there are other scattered scratches and hits located on the obverse, all of which are concealed by toning. The *Norweb* 1873-CC *With Arrows* dime, on the other hand, scores high points for overall visual appeal, luster, and minimal surface marks. Both coins are free of the porosity associated with many lower grade circulated specimens of this date.

At the *World's Greatest Collection* sale, held in 1945, a lovely Uncirculated specimen of the date was offered, but unfortunately its path was not traced beyond that sale. There is a possible connection with the specimen the Norwebs purchased from the *Numismatic Gallery* in 1954.

As for higher grade circulated examples of the 1873-CC *With Arrows* dime, the *R.L. Miles* sale in 1969 offered one listed as being in XF, with slightly porous surfaces, and NGC has certified one 1873-CC *With Arrows* dime as an AU-50 (as of July 2003). Other than that, there are no other high grade circulated pieces known.

An interesting side note about the 1873-CC *With Arrows* dime relates to the Eliasberg collection. In an example of stark contrasts, Mr. Eliasberg's famous 1873-CC *Without Arrows* dime was listed as being in Gem Uncirculated condition while his 1873-CC *With Arrows* dime was listed as a VG (Very Good). Two other significant collections of Carson City coins settled for circulated examples of this date as well; the *Empire Collection* sold in 1957, included a near problem-free specimen listed as being in Fine condition and the *E.A. Carson Collection* that sold in 1976, featured an 1873-CC *With Arrows* dime in Very Fine.

All specimens of this date are the *Open Three* variety, and display the diagnostic die crack through the mintmark with the second "C" higher than the first.[1]

---

[1] One of the *Top 25*.

1874-CC

(Photo courtesy Bowers and Merena)

Mintage: 10,817

Finest Knowns*:

    PCGS MS-63

    PCGS MS-62

    NGC MS-62 (2)[1]

    NGC AU-53 (1)

Notable Pedigrees:

    Anderson-Dupont (1954)

    Empire Collection (1957)

    R.L. Miles (1969)

    Buddy Ebsen (1987)

    Norweb (1987)

      ex: Anderson-Dupont

    Waldo E. Bolen (1995)

    Nevada State Museum (Current)

Survival Estimates in All Grades: 25-35
Estimated in Uncirculated: 5-6
Estimated in XF to AU: 6-8
Total Certified Examples in All Grades (PCGS and NGC)*: 26

(* As of July 2003)

REFLECTIONS:

The 1874-CC dime completes the *Fearsome Foursome* (or *Five-some*) of the Carson City dime series. It has the lowest mintage in the "CC" dime set and is the key to the collectable dates in the Seated Liberty dime series, towering above all other dates except the early "CC"s.

Uncirculated examples of this date are typically well struck, but coarse-grained with brilliant frosty luster, or semi-prooflike obverses. A large percentage of lower grade circulated pieces have rougher surfaces, with various levels of porosity. Like so many silver coins from the Carson City Mint's early years, circulated 1874-CC dimes are often found damaged, as surface graffiti, rim dings, and buffing plague many specimens.

A characteristic die crack extending through the mintmark is found on all 1874-CC dimes, and there are a few examples that have been observed with what Kam Ahwash referred to as a *Broken S* on the top serif stem of the first letter in STATES.[2] If the date itself was not so rare, the *Broken S*, would be an interesting and possibly valuable variety; but whether you find a *Broken S*, a *Full S*, or one with porous surfaces, the thrill of owning an 1874-CC dime is all that matters.

The Norweb family purchased their specimen for $950 in the *Anderson-Dupont* Sale auctioned by Stack's in

1954. This sharply struck and semi-prooflike piece is one of the handful of known Uncirculated 1874-CC dimes. A detracting dark oxidation spot covers the tops of the T and A in STATES and there is a rim nick to the lower left of the U in UNITED. If this were a more common date dime, this defect would be an obstacle for the discriminating collector to overcome. But the Norwebs were pleased to add the coin to their collection, as was the buyer who paid $15,700 for it at the *Norweb* sale in October of 1987.

Earlier in that year, an absolutely stunning 1874-CC dime was sold for $26,400 as part of the *Buddy Ebsen Collection.* The cataloger at Superior Galleries claimed that it was the "Finest Known 1874-CC Dime."[3] That same piece was again offered in 2003 as part of Superior's February auction, but the appearance of the coin had changed drastically. Covering its obverse surface were over 30 unsightly dark spots splattered across it, and unflattering discoloration blanketed both sides. Beneath the unpleasant top layer was a well-struck prooflike coin, with characteristic coarse-grained obverse centers. It was bought back by the consignor and was subsequently graded by PCGS

---

[1] Two MS-62s listed, possibly the same coin, or possibly the PCGS coin.

[2] Kamal M. Ahwash, *Encyclopedia of United States Liberty Seated Dimes 1837-1891.* (1977).

[3] Superior Galleries, *Buddy Ebsen Collection*, June 1987.

as an MS-63, after which it was consigned to another Superior auction in September of 2003, where it realized $162,000, setting a record for the date.

1874-CC dime. PCGS MS-63.

The *World's Greatest Collection* specimen was cataloged in 1945 as being a beautiful Uncirculated coin, and sold for $200. Its path after the sale was not tracked, but it was possibly the same coin sold in the *Empire Collection* in 1957 for $775. Another 1874-CC dime listed as Uncirculated sold in 1969 for $2,400 as part of Stack's *R.L. Miles* auction.

There is a possibility that the coin sold as part of the *Waldo E. Bolen Collection* by RARCOA/Akers in 1995 may have been one of the previously mentioned Uncirculated pieces. It was described as "Choice to Gem Brilliant Uncirculated,"[1] and realized $31,900. A key identifier found on this coin is a noticeable scratch between Liberty's ankle and the *A* in AMERICA. One other notable 1874-CC dime is in the *Nevada State Museum Collection*, and is a candidate for a top spot in the Condition Census for this date. It is entirely possible that this piece is one of the listed Uncirculated specimens sold pre-1970 (the year the *Museum* collection was completed).

There was one other Uncirculated 1874-CC dime that sold at Stack's *Lovejoy Sale* in October 1990 for $20,900. This specimen had been purchased for $7,000 at a Superior auction in June of 1982. The most recent appearance of this piece was in the Stack's October sale

of 1997, where it realized $37,400. This coin has not as yet been certified (2003). An identifiable rim bump on the reverse will aid in attributing this coin in the future. In November 1989, still another Uncirculated 1874-CC dime appeared in a Bowers and Merena auction and realized $17,050; as far as is known, the location of this specimen is not public knowledge (2003).

The *Eliasberg* collection could only boast of a VG-8 specimen; *James A. Stack's* collection featured a pleasing XF; and the *E.A. Carson* "CC" set included an attractive VF specimen. Throughout the decades the annual rare coin auction circuit has historically offered one 1874-CC dime per year, and some years not even one.

Buyers are lined up ready to compete at every given opportunity.[2]

---

[1] *Numisma "95"*, RARCOA/Akers, 1995.
[2] One of the *Top 25*.

Register of the Uncirculated 1874-CC Dime Appearances Mentioned in this Section

1 *World's Greatest Collection* (F.C.C. Boyd), 1945 .... $200

2. *Anderson-Dupont*, 1954 .... $950

3. *Empire Collection*, 1957 .... $775

4. *R.L. Miles*, 1969 .... $2,400

5. *Nevada State Museum*, circa 1965-1970 .... Price Unknown

6. *Norweb*, 1987 (*Anderson-Dupont* coin) $15,700

7. *Buddy Ebsen*, 1987 .... $26,400

8. *Bolen*, 1995 .... $31,900

9. Superior Sale February 2003 (*Ebsen* coin)
.... No Sale (Reserve not met)

10. Superior September Sale 2003 (*Ebsen* coin) ... $162,150

1875-CC
Mintmark in Wreath

(Photo courtesy Bowers and Merena)

Mintage: 4,645,000

Finest Knowns*:

NGC MS-67 (3)

PCGS MS-66 (13)

NGC MS-66 (4)

Notable Pedigrees:

Numerous

Survival Estimates in All Grades: ... 9,000-16,000
Estimated in Uncirculated: 300-500
Estimated in XF to AU: 500-1000
Total Certified Examples in All Grades (PCGS and NGC)*: 325

(* As of July 2003)

REFLECTIONS:

When the arrows were removed from silver dimes in 1875, Chief Engraver William Barber fancied himself in a creative light, and just for good measure placed the mintmarks below the word DIME inside the wreath on the reverse of the coins. This uncharacteristic position proved to be impractical, however, precipitating a change midway through the year. In the second half of 1875 the mintmarks were returned to their customary location below the wreath. This circuitous handiwork did not accomplish anything other than to substantiate Barber's authority, but it did result in another variety for the collector. Barber's staff also experimented with the width of the distance between the letters in the "CC" mintmark, resulting in a *wide-spaced* mintmark and a *compact* "CC" mintmark for the *In Wreath* variety.

Reverse of 1875-CC
"mintmark above wreath."

Without a doubt the *In Wreath* 1875-CC dime is the more common of the two 1875-CC dime varieties, with even Choice Uncirculated examples being relatively easy to locate. Several of the highest grade specimens display beautiful multicolored toning, and there are small quantities of bright lustrous, untoned examples available as well.

Lower grade Uncirculated specimens are generally covered with more small contact marks than dimes of equal quality from the other mints. The luster on these MS-61s, 62s, and 63s is usually adequate, except on washed out pieces which have been dulled due to improper cleaning. Even on these, the "CC" mintmark often helps collectors overcompensate for any such detractions.

1875-CC
Mintmark Below Wreath

(Photo courtesy Bowers and Merena)

Mintage: Included in the 4,645,000 for this
year***

Finest Knowns*:

NGC MS-66 (1)

PCGS MS-65 (2)

NGC MS-65 (7)**

Notable Pedigrees:

Numerous

Survival Estimates in All Grades: 3,500-7,000
Estimated in Uncirculated: 75-175
Estimated in XF to AU: 150-400
Total Certified Examples in All Grades (PCGS and NGC)*: 36

(*As of July 2003)

(**Possible resubmissions of one or more of the same coins.)

(***Rough estimate is 30% of the total)

REFLECTIONS:

The Mint reverted to traditional mintmark placement in the second half of 1875; this *Below Wreath* variety
displays larger more tightly bunched letters in the mintmark. Other diagnostics for this date include: a die crack
line running through the mintmark, characteristic of the
1872 to 1874 "CC" dimes, no longer appears, and the
second "C" nearly touches the ribbon on the bow. On the
obverse, the *Broken S* in the first letter of STATES is seen
on many examples.

This variety, although scarcer than its *In Wreath*
cousin, generally does not command a premium commensurate with the population differential. Both varieties are among the most affordable "CC" dimes. In the
late 1940s, Choice Uncirculated pieces could be purchased for $2; famous collector John J. Pittman purchased
his 1875-CC *In Wreath* dime for $2.25 during that de-
cade. Today the *Pittman* 1875 *In Wreath* dime is encased in
an NGC MS-66 holder and retails for approximately
$4,500 (2003).

1876-CC

(Photo courtesy Bowers and Merena)

Mintage: 8,270,000

Finest Knowns*:

    PCGS MS-67 (2)

    NGC MS-67 (3)

    NGC Specimen-66 (1)

    NGC Specimen-65 (3)

Notable Pedigrees:

    Numerous

Survival Estimates in All Grades: . 35,000-80,000
Estimated in Uncirculated: 700-1,500
Estimated in XF to AU: 1,750-4,000
Total Certified Examples **in All Grades (PCGS and NGC)*:** 385

(* As of July 2003)

REFLECTIONS:

This is the highest mintage date in the "CC" dime series. A memorable centennial anniversary in the United States, combined with a contrived need for more silver coins, resulted in 1876 being a big production year for all three of the nation's coinage mints.

One of the reasons coin collecting is such an interesting hobby is because of its diversification. Collectors have the option of selecting any series of coins and branching off into many divergent offshoots of that series. A set of coins begins with the basic *one-two-threes* of obtaining one example of each date in the series, and from that launching pad, a collector has the option of searching only for full strikes of the selected series, or maybe just problem-free examples, or maybe toned or untoned specimens. There are always the error coins within a series, and of course, varieties provide seemingly endless opportunities, as the thrill of finding *discovery coins* displaying previously unknown varieties sustains countless numismatic detectives in their searches. Classic reference works from the past illustrate the intensity exerted by many collectors. In any fully stocked numismatic library you will certainly find copies of books on Bust quarter, half, and silver dollar varieties, large cents, half cents, half dimes, Flying Eagle, Indian and Lincoln cents, Morgan and Peace dollar varieties, and of course, the Seated Liberty denominations, just to name a few.

With the cascade of coinage flowing from the nation's mints in 1876, opportunities abounded for a multitude of various die strikes to be produced: re-punching of digits, re-engraving of mintmarks, an incessant demand for more coin dies, and the overtime work of employees at breakneck speeds, resulted in an abundance of varieties.

Carson City coinage offers its own share of this vast pool of varieties. For example, there are two reverse types of the 1876-CC dime; the differences are not dramatic, with the key identifier being the distance of the *E* in ONE from the wheat stalk; another slight difference on the reverse is found in the left tip of the ribbon extending from the bow. On the *Type 1 Reverse* dimes, the left tip of the ribbon is split, and the *E* in ONE nearly touches the wheat stalk, and on the *Type 2 Reverse*, the end of the ribbon is singly pointed as it flows into the fields, with the *E* in ONE situated approximately 0.3 mm. from the wheat stalk.

The variety options do not stop here on the 1876-CC dimes; collectors are now faced with variant combinations of different mintmark locations, double die lettering, *Large Knob* and *Small Knob 6s*, cudding, die breaks, re-punching, and many other justifiable excuses for the ownership of a high-powered coin loupe (magnifying glass).

This date is plentiful in circulated grades, and moderately so in lower Uncirculated condition, and the rarity factor fluctuates between the numerous varieties, with price premiums usually of minor significance from one variety to another. In the case of the *Type 2 Reverse*, researchers agree that it is by far the rarest variety. There are probably instances of variety collectors paying ten times the listed book value for a *Type 2 Reverse* 1876-CC in circulated grades, but it would be highly unlikely for Choice to Gem Uncirculated specimens of this variety to command a premium at all.

One version of the 1876-CC dimes that commands a substantial price tag is the Proof or Specimen strikes.[1] As of the date of this writing (2003), NGC lists four of the 1876-CC Proof dimes as having been certified. Although the Carson City Mint was not ordered to strike Proof coins, and there is no record of how many 1876-CC *Proof* dimes were indeed minted, it is certainly conceivable that Superintendent Crawford authorized a few of the special coins to be struck, if for nothing

Prooflike 1876-CC dime.

more than to serve as mementos of the Centennial year. The legitimacy of the 1876-CC Proof dimes has been validated through the years, as collectors have been willing to pay strong prices to own them; as recently as March of 2003, one example graded Proof-65 by NGC sold at a Heritage auction for $48,875.

For further study on the varieties for the 1876-CC dime, refer to the works by Kam Ahwash, or Brian Greer. [2]

---

[1] A Proof coin is being described in this context as a coin struck on a polished planchet and receiving multiple die strikes. The result is a coin with deeply mirrored surfaces, fully squared rims and sharper than normal definition on the portrait and devices.

[2] *The Complete Encyclopedia to Liberty Seated Dimes*, Brian Greer, *Encyclopedia of U.S. Liberty Seated Dimes*, Kamal Ahwash.

COMPARISON OF DIME PRODUCTION AT THE
CARSON CITY MINT WITH THE
PHILADELPHIA MINT'S FROM 1871 TO 1878

DIME MINTAGE TOTALS		
Year	Carson City	Philadelphia
1871	20,100	907,710
1872	24,000	2,396,450
1873 *Without Arrows*	12,400	1,568,000
1873 *With Arrows*	18,791	2,378,500
1874	10,817	2,940,000
1875 All Kinds	4,645,000	10,350,700
1876	8,270,000	11,461,150
1877	7,700,000	7,310,510
1878	200,000	1,678,000
TOTAL	20,901,108	40,991,020

1877-CC

(Photo courtesy Bowers and Merena)

Mintage: 7,700,000

Finest Knowns*:

    NGC MS-68 (3)

    PCGS MS-67 (3)

    NGC MS-67 (5)

Notable Pedigrees:

    Numerous

Survival Estimates in All Grades: .	40,000-80,000
Estimated in Uncirculated:	1,000-1,750
Estimated in XF to AU:	3,000-6,000
Total Certified Examples in All Grades (PCGS and NGC)*:	451

(* As of July 2003)

Reflections:

In 1877, the Carson City Mint was in the third year of its big dime-a-thon. Nearly 99% of all the dimes minted at Carson City were credited to the years 1875, 1876, and 1877, a total of more than 20 million dimes having been struck during that run. Only the combined mintage totals for "CC" Morgan dollars and trade dollars would approach that production level at the Carson City Mint. That being said, the dimes produced at Carson City afforded more probability of diverse varieties than any of the other denominations, and in 1877, just as they had in 1876, the coiners at the Carson City Mint used the two distinct reverse types.

The chief engraver at Philadelphia was busy trying to keep up with demand from the branch mints for reverse dies with mintmarks. In that regard, the "CC" was always a challenge, as two letters were needed rather than one, requiring two separate blows of the same letter punch, allowing more room for human error in positioning.

In 1877, there are at least five different mintmark positions, and when viewing them side-by-side one can almost sense the die puncher's frustration as he attempted to align the letters. On one variety you will see the second "C" placed higher than the first; on another variety, the second "C" drifts lower. One variety displays the mintmark nearer to the left side of the ribbon; on another, the second "C" is touching the right side of the ribbon; and on another variety, the mintmark appears to be placed dead center between both sides of the ribbon. All of these mintmark variations provide collectors with added pleasure when attempting to acquire one example of each.

In addition; the die cracks, clashed dies, repunched digits, rusted dies, granular surfaces, and many other irregularities have established the 1877-CC dime as a target for variety specialists and diagnostic experts, although the date itself is the most common in the Carson City dime series. A few of the varieties are extremely scarce, but so far in the early years of the 21st century, they have not commanded premiums commensurate with their rarity. For further study, you are encouraged to read the works of Greer and/or Ahwash.[1]

---

[1] Ibid.

1878-CC

(Photo courtesy Bowers and Merena)

Mintage: 200,000

Finest Knowns*:

> PCGS MS-68 (I)
>
> NGC MS-68 (I)
>
> NGC MS-67 (2)
>
> PCGS MS-66 (I)
>
> NGC MS-66 (7)

Notable Pedigrees:

> Auction '81 (Unknown consignor)
> (1981)

Eliasberg (1996)

Knoxville Collection (2003)

Survival Estimates in All Grades:	300-500
Estimated in Uncirculated:	65-80
Estimated in XF to AU:	100-125
Total Certified Examples in All Grades (PCGS and NGC)*:	88

(* As of July 2003)

REFLECTIONS:

The production of dimes slid into a deceleration phase beginning in 1878 that lasted for several years as the primary focus of the nation's coinage operations was on the newly introduced Morgan silver dollar. Millions of silver dimes, quarters and half dollars remained stockpiled in Treasury vaults because there simply was no urgent need for any more silver coins. The Carson City Mint would bid farewell to dimes after 1878, as well as quarters, halves, and trade dollars.

A nice round number of 200,000 1878-CC dimes were manufactured and the scarcity of this date suggests that only a small percentage of the mintage made it into circulation. There appears to be a disproportionate amount of Uncirculated specimens relative to the surviving population for 1878-CC dimes, probably due to the traditional practice of locals saving specimens of a final year as keepsakes. There is also the possibility that the grading services' population figures for Uncirculated pieces might be a little skewed due to multiple submissions of the same coins in attempts to get them upgraded. For instance, the total of 17 listed in the NGC Census Report for MS-64 1878-CC dimes seems inordinate, but if accurate, collectors would certainly be delighted, since there is always a demand for more Uncirculated specimens of the date, especially in MS-64 quality; however, the empirical evidence suggests otherwise.

The two finest known 1878-CC dimes are the *Elias-*

berg coin, and the *Knoxville Collection* specimen. The latter piece, graded MS-68 by NGC, sold for a record $22,000 at Superior's January sale in 1993; and the Eliasberg specimen though not graded as high, brought $5,500 in Bowers and Merena's May 1996 sale, and was last seen in an NGC MS-67 holder. A third Gem quality 1878-CC dime worth noting sold in Paramount's session of Auction '81. Finally, in the early years of the 21st century, a second 1878-CC dime was awarded the grade of MS-68, this time by PCGS, but it is uncertain whether this piece is an upgrade, crossover, or a newly discovered specimen.

The coin market has become accustomed to infrequent auction appearances of the 1878-CC dimes; in fact, in certain years not even a single specimen crosses the block, and for the majority of years only a single example or at best two, appear in public auctions.

There are two reverse types for 1878-CC dimes just as there were for the 1876-CC and 1877-CC; some of the reverse dies from those two years were left over and most likely used on the 1878-CC dimes. One of the varieties is more dramatic than any of the other later date "CC" dimes, as the left ribbon is nearly missing, and the tops of the mintmarks are extremely weak, caused by a shattered die during the minting process.

For further information on the Seated Liberty dimes from the Carson City Mint, please see the books by Greer and/or Ahwash. [1]

---

[1] Ibid.

(Photo courtesy American Numismatic Rarities)

The 20-cent piece is the most celebrated denomination that the Carson City Mint ever turned out. Origins of this odd subsidiary coin can be found in the political history of Nevada, and the specie recommendations of Thomas Jefferson. Challenges faced by the early founders of America's monetary system arose from the merger of coinage distributed by the U.S. Mint with coinage from foreign countries that widely circulated across the nation. Attempts were made to replicate the monetary systems of foreign countries, while at the same time maintaining a distinctly American signature. The dollar was the standard unit of monetary value from which all other measures were based. For monetary values exceeding one dollar, gold coins in increments of $2 \frac{1}{2}$, $5, and $10 seemed to be a viable solution. Ordinary commerce in the public marketplace was usually transacted with denominations less than one dollar. This required coinage with values of a half cent, one cent, five cents, 10 cents, $12 \frac{1}{2}$ cents, 20 cents, 25 cents, and 50 cents. Such a complex array of denominations resulted from the unnatural amalgam of circulating currency required for assimilation with coins from foreign nations. If Thomas Jefferson's coinage recommendations had been adopted, America's fractional coinage would have consisted of the half dollar, fifth dollar, tenth dollar, 20th dollar, and hundredth dollar, with no quarter dollar in this monetary system. But Jefferson's plan was not adopted in its entirety; the Treasury instead chose the quarter dollar over the fifth dollar, using the rationale that a quarter dollar was in greater conformity with the Spanish two reales coin.

Superintendent of Finance, Robert Morris, had proposed the quarter dollar in the 1780s. In the years immediately following America's independence from Great Britain, the new nation's leaders took the issue of a monetary system very seriously. They shouldered the complex burden of establishing a sound system that would be unique, but would also survive. A collapse in their system would be ridiculed by the rest of the world, who watched in anticipation of whether the *Union* would succeed. Superintendent Morris, aided by his assistant Gouverneur

Morris (no relation), believed if the United States could create *good* money, it would drive out the *bad* money of foreign nations. After all, how independent could a new republic be if its citizens used the currency of other lands instead of their native country's money? Thomas Jefferson was in total agreement with the fundamentals of these principles; however he felt that a fifth dollar would be in truer alignment with the rest of the nation's monetary system. But he was overruled.

For over 80 years, quarter dollars were one of the nation's primary subsidiary coins. They served their purpose well—until a shortage of $^1/_{20th}$ dollars (or half dimes) in the West and parts of the South caused chronic problems in the nation's retail markets. Customers using quarters to pay for items priced at ten cents often received only a dime in return. Merchants claimed to be out of smaller denominations. In saloons all throughout the western states, a glass of beer cost five cents, and well drinks were commonly priced at $12 \frac{1}{2}$ cents. Beer drinkers had no problem, but customers imbibing in shots of liquor faced the annoyance of being shortchanged when paying for the drink with a quarter, as bartenders often tendered only one dime in change. Obviously many tavern patrons would order two drinks at a time, either being accompanied by a friend or simply accelerating their own inebriation.

Who else came to the rescue, but newly elected Nevada Senator, John Percival Jones? In a short five year run, Jones had gone from a fast talking, out of luck, story-telling, poker player extraordinaire, to a multimillionaire, story-telling local hero—and feared poker player. He had been the superintendent of the Crown Point and Yellow Jacket mines in 1869, living on meager wages, when a disastrous fire broke out in the core of the Yellow Jacket. Jones was heralded in the local papers in April of 1869 as one of the heroes during the fire, risking personal danger attempting to save his men. Within two years, Jones used his poker skills to bluff and outmaneuver the powerful William Sharon and obtain a large stake in Sharon's Crown

Point. Jones eventually ousted his former employer, and reaped rewards far beyond even a storyteller's wildest imagination. He parlayed his lucky streak, reportedly spending $500,000 to buy a U.S. Senate seat—it was but a small wager considering Jones's windfall wealth.

As a U.S. Senator, Jones soon learned that money could buy more money (lots more money). He was a successful silver mine owner, and like any shrewd businessman he was always looking for new markets for his product. So what was one of the primary uses for silver in the 1870s? It does not take three guesses to resoundingly answer, silver coins. Between 1873 and 1875 Jones busied himself securing the passage of a bill that would create a new silver coin denomination, the 20-cent piece. Trade dollars were in their second year of production in 1874, and would eventually require the Treasury to purchase over 30 million ounces of the white metal. The new 20-cent coin was of minor consequence in terms of silver usage and would become the shortest-lived series of any U.S. coin. Senator Jones discovered something very important during his work on the 20-cent piece legislation: Congress was like a big poker game. If a player's bankroll was large enough and he could keep his opponents off guard, there were many pots that could be bought off. Considering that Jones was only in his sophomore year as a U.S. Senator in 1875 when the 20-cent bill was passed, he had already accomplished more than some senators do in their entire political careers—and Jones had 28 years to go!

After only two years of production the 20-cent series was discontinued in 1876. There are only two dates in the "CC" 20-cent series, and fortunately for collectors one of them is relatively easy to locate. Proof specimens were issued by the Philadelphia Mint in 1877 and then again for a final time in 1878, after which the Bureau of the Mint could begin preparing for the new Morgan silver dollars.

BUREAU OF THE MINT DATA FOR CARSON CITY 20-CENT PRODUCTION

Total Combined Mintage: 143,290

Total Face Value: $28,658

Total Ounces of Silver Used: .... 20,727.16 ozs.

Design Type: Obverse: .... Seated Liberty
            Reverse: Eagle similar to Trade Dollar (No Legend or Motto)

Designers: .... Obverse: Gobrecht, William Barber,
                                            Reverse: William Barber

Metal Composition: .... .900 Silver .100 copper

Actual Gross Weight: .... 5 grams

Actual Fine Silver Content: .... .14468 oz.

Value of Silver in One 20-Cent Piece: .... $.167-.18 (1875-1878)

1875-CC

(Photo courtesy American Numismatic Rarities)

Mintage: 133,290

Finest Knowns*:

    PCGS MS-66 (4)

    NGC MS-66 (4)

    PCGS MS-65 (14)

    NGC MS-65 (27)

Notable Pedigrees:

    Auction '80 (Consignor Unknown)

    Eliasberg (1997)

Survival Estimates in All Grades: ... 7,000-10,000
Estimated in Uncirculated: 750-1250
Estimated in XF to AU: 1,250-1,500
Total Certified Examples   in All Grades (PCGS and NGC)*: 708

(* As of July 2003)

REFLECTIONS:

Production on 20-cent pieces at the Carson City Mint began on the first of June in 1875. Employees at this mint facility had made a concerted effort to beat San Francisco to the finish line in the race to be the first mint west of Philadelphia to strike the new coin. The race resulted in a virtual dead heat, but Carson City claimed the victory. Senator Jones was presented with the first 1875-CC 20-cent piece minted. Locals were proud to celebrate the issuance of a coin that one of their own political leaders was credited with introducing. The specimen given to Jones was probably struck with extra pressure using polished dies with a specially prepared planchet; several other *first strike* 1875-CC 20-cent pieces were presented to distinguished residents as well. The whereabouts of the *Jones* specimen is not known today (2003), but if it surfaces, there will certainly be much interest in the coin.

Authorities at the Bureau of the Mint had decided to manufacture 20-cent pieces with unconventional plain edges, one of several solutions Mint officials decided might help avoid confusion in the marketplace between quarters and the new coins. There were two additional distinctive features, both on the reverse: the motto *In God We Trust* was removed, and the U.S. Mint also chose to use *TWENTY CENTS* as the denomination on the reverse. Other possibilities had been *Fifth Dollar* or *Double Dime*, since using the word *CENTS* was traditionally reserved for minor coinage such as *FIVE CENTS* and *ONE CENT*. One solution that

might have proven to be more successful was a William Barber design that featured a more youthful portrait of Ms. Liberty on the obverse, and a large heraldic shield with the numerals *20* boldly centered in the middle and the word *CENTS* beneath the shield near the rim. This beautiful pattern coin is listed in Judd's book as #1392.

In terms of grading, a typical no-problem 1875-CC 20-cent piece in grades above MS-60 will have subdued to nearly brilliant luster, generally not on par with Philadelphia or San Francisco specimens. Also worth noting is that 1875-CC's with full strikes are rare. As on many examples the top of the eagle's shoulders are weak, with corresponding weakness at the central areas on the obverse. There is also typical weakness on Liberty's head on most examples. In circulated grades the weakness is of lesser importance, since natural surface wear blends with the weak strike to produce similar results. The word *LIBERTY* on 20-cent pieces is struck in raised relief, giving the letters an embossed effect. On circulated specimens with weaker strikes, the central letters *BER* are either almost or totally missing.

One of the finest known 1875-CC 20-cent pieces was sold in Auction '80 for $9,000; the cataloguer having described the piece as being "Evenly toned and sharply struck…this is the finest example we have ever seen…"[1] This coin is currently encased in a PCGS MS-66 holder,

---

[1] Superior, *Auction '80 Catalog.*

and reportedly sold for $17,500 in 2002. From time to time, semi-prooflike 1875-CC 20-cent pieces have appeared, but these are certainly the exception, not the rule. Coin collectors are fortunate that sufficient quantities of this date were minted, otherwise there would not be collectable examples of this denomination with the "CC" mintmark. Even at that, there is a limit to how many type sets from the Carson City Mint can be assembled, as the quantity of 1875-CC 20-cent pieces extant is estimated to be fewer than 10,000. If you have not done so already, do yourself a favor and obtain an example of the 1875-CC 20-cent piece and avoid the rush.

COMPARISON OF 20-CENT PRODUCTION AT THE
CARSON CITY MINT WITH THE
PHILADELPHIA MINT'S FROM 1875 TO 1876

20-CENT MINTAGE TOTALS		
Year	Carson City	Philadelphia
1875	133,290	39,700
1876	10,000	15,900
TOTAL	143,290	55,600

1876-CC

(Photo courtesy Bowers and Merena)

Mintage: 10,000

Finest Knowns*:

    PCGS MS-66 (2)

    PCGS MS-65 (2)

    NGC MS-65 (3)

Notable Pedigrees:

    Clapp (1942)

    F.C.C. Boyd (1945)

    Knapp (1945)

    Atwater (1946)

    Q. David Bowers (1956-1959)

    Empire Collection (1957)

John J. Ford, Jr. (1957-1959)

R.L. Miles (1969)

S. Benton Emery (1984)

Norweb (1987)

Eliasberg (1997)

Nevada State Museum (Current)

Survival Estimates in All Grades:	17-20
Estimated in Uncirculated:	15-16
Estimated in XF to AU:	1-3
Total Certified Examples in All Grades (PCGS and NGC)*:	17

(* As of July 2003)

REFLECTIONS:

For nearly 60 years after coinage operations ceased, this date was the solitary representative from the entire production of the Carson City Mint to be included in *Classic Rarities* lists. The rarity of the 1876-CC 20-cent piece had been established within 17 years of the date of its production, as one preeminent author, most famous for bringing mintmark collecting to the limelight, certainly must have had access to the now legendary document sent from Mint Director Linderman to Carson City Superintendent Crawford in 1877, ordering Crawford to melt the entire (or nearly entire) mintage of 1876-CC 20-cent pieces, and thus create a numismatic classic. This author of course was Augustus G. Heaton, who in 1893 wrote in his *Treatise* that the 1876-CC 20-cent piece was "excessively rare."[1]

For the 57 year period from 1893 to 1950, the 1876-CC 20-cent piece served as the Carson City Mint's claim to fame. Rare coin auction companies in the first half of the 20th century always devoted extra word space in their catalogs whenever an example of this special date was offered. Premier coin collections of the day were graced by counting this elusive coin among their holdings, and coin dealers and researchers were in agreement with their estimates of 10 to 12 pieces known during that time.

After Louis E. Eliasberg, Sr. purchased his 1873-CC *Without Arrows* dime in 1950, the rarity of the 1876-CC 20-cent piece was bumped to second place in the standings of scarce Carson City coins. Eventually, the 1873-CC *Without Arrows* quarter would be recognized as the second scarcest in the Carson City series, relegating the 1876-CC 20-cent piece to third place. In the final two decades of the 20th century, other selected coins from Carson City's progeny of rarities proved to be scarcer than the 1876-CC 20-cent pieces in terms of condition rarity, but the 1876-CC will always be spoken of reverently by numismatists.

Estimates of the number of surviving specimens have risen over time; general consensus opinion is an extant population of between 16 and 18 survivors. No one has ever seen that many 1876-CC 20-cent pieces in one place at one time, but auction appearances and private treaty sales over the years suggest that the current estimates are fairly accurate.

The Carson City Mint sent a customary small sampling of the 1876-CC 20-cent pieces to Philadelphia for assay purposes. Based on the percentage of other coin denominations sent to the Assay Commission, it is probable that six to twelve 1876-CC 20-cent pieces were reserved for this purpose. In addition to the Assay specimens there

---

[1] Augustus G. Heaton, *Mint Marks, A Treatise*, 1893.

238

are several other reasonable sources to consider when estimating how many pieces escaped the melting furnace. First, of course would be local interest in the coins; Superintendent Crawford or any members of his crew at the Carson City Mint could have simply exchanged two dimes for a 20-cent piece just to have one as a memento. Motivation to do this would have increased greatly beginning in July of 1876, when a bill was introduced to repeal the production of 20-cent pieces, and then especially in March of 1877 when the order was dispatched to melt all 20-cent pieces in storage. Even the most casual observer would have realized that a rarity was being created. Secondly, Director of the Mint Linderman and other officials in the Treasury Department would have had first hand information that the 20-cent piece denomination was doomed, and might have been tempted to secure a few specimens of the 1876-CC for themselves. It is well known that Director Linderman was never shy about increasing his numismatic holdings with coins not available to the public at large.

The year in which these rare 20-cent pieces were minted, 1876, was of

Reverse of 1876-CC 20-cent piece.

course the Centennial anniversary of the nation's independence. Millions of coins were produced; employees at the three coinage mints took certain liberties, for either personal or patriotic reasons, and it would be impossible to fathom all of the exchanges that might have occurred in that year. Keep in mind that there were over 85 million gold and silver coins made, not to mention the minor coins, minted in 1876. It would have been easy for a handful of 1876-CC 20-cent pieces to have been *lost* in the melee. All of this is pure speculation, however, and the true facts will probably never be discovered. There is one thing that 125 years accomplishes though: certain established numismatic theorems line up like ducks in a pond as more time passes.

The 1876-CC 20-cent piece from the Eliasberg Collection traces its pedigree back to the *J.H. Clapp Collection* purchased in 1942; the Clapp family acquired the piece from the *Dr. S.L. Lee Collection*, auctioned by the Scott Stamp & Coin Company in 1899. Clapp family patriarch J.M. Clapp was pleased to add this prized "CC" classic rarity to his cabinet. One of his acquaintances, Augustus G. Heaton had championed the notoriety of the 1876-CC 20-cent piece in 1893, and as Bowers pointed out, "Perhaps, the first specimen to attract notice in a catalogue

was sold in the *Davis Collection* by New York Coin & Stamp Company, January 20-24, 1890."[1]

As the 20th century began, 1876-CC 20-cent pieces were selling for $25 to $40. Noted collector S. Benton Emery purchased a high quality specimen for $28 in 1900 at Frossard's *J.G. Hubbard* sale. In those days, auction cataloguers would describe just about any coin with a "CC" mintmark as rare or very scarce; every time an 1876-CC 20-cent piece was offered, extra effort was exercised to distinguish the date as being *extremely* rare, always making sure to give the coin its due respect and often referring to it as the *key* to the Carson City series. As a result, 1876-CC 20-cent pieces were always thought of as prized numismatic treasures; adding a sense of prestigious achievement to a collection. As late as the 1920s, estimates placed the surviving population of 1876-CC 20-cent pieces at six; but by the 1940s, the generally accepted estimate was 10 pieces or fewer. Prices had risen dramatically by then, and 1876-CC 20-cent pieces were routinely bringing $1,500 to $1,600 at auction, nearly 70 years after Linderman had ordered Superintendent Crawford to melt all the 1876-CC 20-cent pieces.

This date has secured its ranking on *Top 25* lists of the scarcest coins in the nation's history and just like other rarities from the Carson City Mint, makes only infrequent market appearances. The task of estimating surviving populations or making price evaluations for any of the truly rare coins is not always easy. Consider Eliasberg's 1873-CC *Without Arrows* dime, for example, a coin that was off the market for 46 years after he purchased it in 1950, and no one was sure whether it was the only specimen, or if others existed during that period. Since no other examples surfaced during this nearly five decade hibernation, the *Unique* status (only one in existence) of the coin endured, and the $550,000 price realized in 1996 seemed justified.

But on the other hand, 1876-CC 20-cent pieces have appeared more frequently in auctions than 1873-CC *Without Arrows* dimes, thus making price analysis slightly more calculable. To illustrate, readers can track the *William Knapp* specimen beginning in 1945 using the chart at the bottom of the following page.

---

[1] Q. David Bowers, *Louis E. Eliasberg, Sr., King of Coins.*

The *Knapp* specimen grades AU 55, and occasionally has been described as Uncirculated. It has traded hands on several occasions since the Auction '80 sale, but its whereabouts are unknown as of the writing of this book (2003).

In 1995, the *Atwater* specimen that James A. Stack had purchased in 1946 for $1,625 nearly broke the $100,000 barrier, just missing the prestigious six figure mark by $1,000. Finally, in 1997, Eliasberg's 1876-CC 20-cent piece smashed the six figure barrier, selling for the then record price of $148,500. Everyone in attendance knew the historic significance of this event: it was as if a signal had been given and the door was literally blown off the hinges for the prices of the rest of the Carson City coins in that sale. Almost without warning new records were established for many of the "CC" Condition Census rarities.

Since the 1997 *Eliasberg Sale*, the *S. Benton Emery* 1876-CC 20-cent piece set a new record for the date when it sold for just the third time in 101 years for the staggering price of $161,000 at Superior's 2001 Mid-Winter ANA Sale. In 2003, this specimen appeared again in Superior's May Pre-Long Beach Sale, shattering all records for this date, when it realized $253,000. There is no doubt that future Condition Census specimens of this date appearing on the market will test new price territories.

A group of eight very special 1876-CC 20-cent pieces was discovered in the Baltimore area sometime around 1956 to 1957. Q. David Bowers related how "Baltimore dealer Tom Warfield found a group of seven, eight, or possibly nine splendid Mint State coins in his home town. Each piece was a lustrous gem, delicately toned and virtual perfection." Prominent dealer John J. Ford purchased four of the examples, selling two to Stack's Rare Coins, and two to private collectors. And likewise, Bowers purchased four pieces for his own account, subsequently selling one to collector Charles A. Cass, which later sold as part of Cass' auction consignment in November of 1957 for a price realized of $3,800 (the *Empire Collection*).

Details of the *Maryland Hoard* of 1876-CC 20-cent pieces are sketchy. The only thing anyone knows for sure is that these coins were struck at the Carson City Mint in 1876. Where they were for 80 years and who owned them remain mysteries. It is also not known what dealer Tom Warfield paid for the rarities, the price at which he sold them to Ford or Bowers, and there has never been conclusive evidence that there were only eight coins in this hoard, for some reason the estimate has always been seven to nine pieces. If Ford and Bowers each bought four specimens, the minimum total is eight, and one cataloger (Breen) suggested as many as 10. It is conceivable that there were more than eight, since the dealer who served as the instrument to pass them on to future generations of coin collectors could have kept one or even sold one to someone else. Questions linger, but one thing is certain: the *Maryland Hoard* of the 1950s doubled the surviving population of 1876-CC 20-cent pieces known to numismatists.

In the succeeding 45+ years since the discovery of the *Maryland Hoard*, the coin community has largely absorbed them into the fold, as witnessed by the appreciating prices. An approximate aggregate value of the hoard in the late 1950s was $30,000 (based on eight coins). In the current market (2003) the aggregate value of the eight coins would be near $1.5 million. Augustus Heaton predicted the appreciation potential of 1876-CC 20-cent pieces back in 1893, although the prices 110 years later would have no doubt bowled him over.

The most significant die characteristic of the 1876-CC 20-cent piece is the doubled *LIBERTY* on the shield. Correlating to this is doubling on some of the stars at the left rim, as well as the first letters in *TWENTY* on the reverse. The letters in the mint-mark are spaced wider apart than on any "CC" issue, with the first "C" being above the *Y* in *TWENTY*, and the second "C" being located on the other side of the arrow feathers almost directly above the *C* in CENTS. This effect is visually stimulating; and if you concentrate hard enough, you can practically see the words "Carson City."[1]

[1] One of the *Top 25*.

KNAPP SPECIMEN 1876-CC 20-CENT PIECE			
Price Appreciation From 1945 to 1980			
Year	Pedigree	Auction Company	Price Realized
1945	Knapp	Mehl	$1525
1947	Neil	Mehl	$1700
1963	Wolfson	Stacks	$7,750
1969	Miles	Stacks	$16,000
1978	Henderson	Ivy	$39,500
1980	Unlisted	Auction '80	$85,000

(Photo courtesy Bowers and Merena)

Much can be said about the quarter dollar series from the Carson City Mint. For the past 125 years, the image of certain dates in the set has been cultivated, refined, and grown immensely in stature. The inclusion of an 1873-CC *Without Arrows* quarter in a person's collection has earned elevated esteem for that collector, as the absence of one of the scarce "CC" quarters in a collection is likewise noted. For example, a typical line in auction catalogs reads, "Not even the famous Neil, Atwater or Garrett collections possessed a specimen of the scarce 1873-CC 'No Arrows' quarter."

The Carson City Mint began producing quarters during its rookie season, one of six denominations coined in that exciting year of 1870. There are eight dates in the "CC" quarter series, the most famous of which is the 1873–divided between the two well-known varieties–resulting in a nine piece set. There are also many sub-varieties in the set, offering die specialists hours of stimulation. Unlike the dime and half dollar series, there were no quarters minted at Carson City in 1874, the final year of the *With Arrows* era. When quarter production resumed in 1875 at the Carson Mint, a mere 140,000 pieces were coined. During the last three years quarters were minted in Carson City, approximately 98% of the output for the entire series was struck, and if 1875's totals are added, the percentage increases to 99.6%.

Mintage figures for 1872-CC quarters have been disputed during the past several decades. For 105 years, beginning in 1872, the Bureau of the Mint listed a total of 9,100 for the 1872-CC quarter in their official records, but sometime around 1977, numismatic publications began listing the mintage for 1872-CC quarters as 22,850. If this total is accurate, it would mean that quarter production at the Carson City Mint more than doubled from the previous year. This increase would have been feasible in light of San Francisco's 168.6% increase in quarter production from 1871, and Philadelphia's 53.5% increase during that same two-year period.

On the other hand, it seems illogical that an accounting error such as the one in question would not have been audited sooner. If there was an additional $3437.50 face value in quarters minted in 1872 at Carson City, it does not seem possible that it would have gone unnoticed by the Treasury's accounting department. A similar oversight reportedly occurred on the ledger sheet for dimes minted there in 1872; supposedly, the Treasury's records understated 1872-CC dime production by 11,480 pieces. Adding the two denominations together, this would have caused the Treasury's books to be off by $4,585.50 during Carson City's fiscal year of 1872, and considering that the total face value for both denominations as originally reported in 1872 was only $4,675, this would have been hard to overlook. Even if the revised mintage figures are used, the total face value is still only $9,260.50, still a significantly small sum, leaving little room for bookkeeping oversights. It appears that someone, somewhere, either in 1872 or 1977, made a royal boo-boo.

There is no doubt that the Treasury's mintage reporting procedures left something to be desired at certain intervals during the later half of the 19th century, causing a great deal of confusion for numismatic researchers in later years. Prior to 1857, the Director of the Mint's fiscal year ran concurrent with the calendar year; but on February 21, 1857, the fiscal year was changed by Congress to extend from July 1 to June 30th of each year, precipitating a change in the way mintage figures were reported. Totals for annual mintages, as listed in the *Director's Report* would now be for coins minted in the last half of one year and the first half of the next year. In 1873, as part of the *Coinage Act*, Congress revised the Director of the Mint's reporting duties, requiring a report to be sent to the Secretary of the Treasury at the close of each fiscal year. Starting in 1880, mintage figures were once again reported in calendar years.

By 1887, the *Annual Reports of the Director of the Mint* listed complete mintage records from the founding of the

Mint in 1792 through 1886. These mintage totals had been audited, consolidated, and edited, to conform to generally accepted accounting procedures. All mintages were listed in face value dollar amounts. All one needed to do to determine the actual number of pieces minted was simply divide the face value by the denomination for gold coins, and multiply the face value by the denomination for silver and minor coins. For example, the face value listed for 1870-CC quarters is $2,085; by multiplying that by four, a mintage total of 8,340 pieces is arrived at.

The *Guide Book of United States Coins* (*Red Book*) has been the authoritative source for mintage figures since its first edition was issued in 1947. Almost without exception, the *Red Book* has used the totals provided by the Mint Director's *Annual Reports*; however, the aforementioned Carson City dates are instances in which the *Red Book* no longer correlates. Some records from the Carson City era are lost in time, and discrepancies involving certain dates may never be resolved. Regardless of the outcome, the quarters, as well as the other coins struck during the first five years at the Carson City Mint will remain scarce and highly prized.

BUREAU OF THE MINT DATA FOR CARSON CITY QUARTER PRODUCTION

Total Combined Mintage: 10,316,792

Total Face Value: $2,579,198

Total Ounces of Silver Used: .... 1,868,367 ozs. +

Design Type: .... Seated Liberty *With Motto*

Designers: Christian Gobrecht is generally given credit for being the designer; nonetheless, all of the following men contributed in some way: John Reich, William Kneass, Thomas Sully, Robert Ball Hughes, James B. Longacre, Anthony Paquet, and William Barber

Metal Composition: .... .900 Silver .100 copper

Actual Gross Weight: .... 6.221 grams

Actual Fine Silver Content: .... .1800 oz. (1870 to 1873)

Actual Gross Weight: .... 6.25 grams

Actual Fine Silver Content: .... .18082 oz. (1873* to 1878)

(* After April 1873)

Value of Silver in One quarter: .... $.208-.239 (1870 to 1878)

1870-CC

(Photo courtesy Bowers and Merena)

Mintage: 8,340

Finest Knowns*:

    NGC MS-64 (I)

    PCGS AU-55 (I)

    NGC AU-53 (I)

Notable Pedigrees:

    J.H. Clapp (1942)

    R.L. Miles (1969)

    Eliasberg (1997)

Survival Estimates in All Grades: 39-49
Estimated in Uncirculated: 2
Estimated in XF to AU: 8-11
Total Certified Examples in All Grades (PCGS and NGC)*: 36

(* As of July 2003)

REFLECTIONS:

Prior to 1997, the only quarter with the "CC" mintmark that had sold for $100,000 or more was the 1873-CC *Without Arrows*. Then in April of 1997 the most spectacular 1870-CC quarter crossed the auction block for $187,000! This event was another in the slowly progressing chain reaction of rising "CC" price evaluations that began at the *Menjou Sale* in 1950. That sale, of course, hosted the smashing performance of the 1873-CC *Without Arrows* dime that sold for $3,650, at the time the highest price ever paid for a coin from the Carson City Mint. This triggered a series of sales of 1876-CC 20-cent pieces that pushed prices for this classic rarity over the $3,000 threshold. As the 1950s passed, the 1876-CC 20-cent pieces were poised to break the $10,000 barrier.

These price increases gave the signal to coin collectors that "CC" coins were just as worthy of their bankrolls as other well-known rarities. The major obstacle did not manifest itself in the form of price resistance, but rather in the lack of scarce "CC" coins in the marketplace. By the time of the 1996 *Eliasberg Sale*, an 1873-CC *Without Arrows* quarter had already broken the $300,000 mark (1990). Classic rarities from other mints had reached the $500,000 level and beyond. When the 1873-CC *Without Arrows* dime, previously from the *Menjou Sale*, sold for $550,000 at the May 1996 *Eliasberg Sale*, Carson City coins were *kicked up a notch*. The three major rarities from the Carson City Mint had been validated by the collecting community and were keeping pace with the steady price appreciation in the rare coin market at large. But still, there were only a few other "CC" date/denominations that were on the list of *also eligibles*, and prices for these were for the most part contingent upon the coins being Condition Census rarities. Several dates from the "CC" gold coin series were on the list as well, including the 1870-CC $20 double eagle in just about any grade, and the Gem quality 1876-CC $5 half eagle from the 1982 *Eliasberg Sale*. Similarly the "CC" dime series was well represented on this list by the 1871-CC, 1873-CC *With Arrows*, and the 1874-CC, all dependent on them being Condition Census coins of course. In the silver dollar category, an 1889-CC in MS-65 had sold for $310,000 in 1989, but circulated 1889-CC dollars were available for less than $1,000.

The buyer who paid $187,000 for the 1870-CC quarter at the *Eliasberg Sale* had no precedent to stretch that high for an example of this date, but the rarity of the piece and its superb condition provided the incentive. The under bidder obviously felt the same way, just not quite as strongly. A stage had been nicely set for this *Eliasberg* 1870-CC quarter to soar to its sky-scraping price, when earlier that evening, Eliasberg's 1876-CC 20-cent piece sold for $148,500 setting a new record. The 1870-CC in the *Eliasberg Sale* was the only Uncirculated specimen known, and surely if Uncirculated examples of 1901-S Barber quarters were selling for six figures, it qualified as well. Eliasberg had purchased this 1870-CC quarter as part of the

Clapp Collection back in 1942, but there is no record of what it would have sold for separately at that time.

The only other 1870-CC quarter described as Uncirculated had last been sold in 1974 as part of the *H. Philip Speir Sale*, realizing $5,250. Prior to that sale, this coin had sold in Stack's *R.L. Miles* auction in 1969 for $1,250. As of the writing of this book (2003) the collecting community does not know the whereabouts of this specimen. Described by the cataloguer as being "Brilliant Uncirculated, some proof-like surface… One of the Finest Known." The description also notes that the coin is "softly struck on the upper portion of the obverse and correspondingly on the reverse."[1] A picture of the coin in the catalog does in fact show a rather weak head; on the reverse, the second "C" is nearly missing and the *R* in QUAR is also very faint. It is very possible that this coin has been submitted to the grading services, but because of the weak strike, has not received an Uncirculated rating. Notwithstanding, the fact remains that this coin sold for $5,250 in 1974, at the time the highest price ever paid for an example of this date. The *Eliasberg* specimen (subsequently graded by NGC as an MS-64) sold for $187,000 in 1997 and the roof, as they say, had been raised on the pricing for 1870-CC quarters.

Numismatic researchers have long debated the quantities of 1870-CC quarters that the Carson City Mint actually released. Bureau of the Mint records reveal that 1870-CC quarters were first struck on April 20, 1870 when 3,540 pieces were credited to the local mint's inventory. No one knows for sure how many of these first 1870-CC quarters were released into circulation, but there is no doubt that 40 pieces were promptly reserved either for assay purposes or to be given as mementos of the event to mint officials and other locals in Carson City. Considering that 40 quarters is only $10 face value, one quickly realizes that it was not a large sum of money in question, and the face value of the remaining quarters was still only $875–simply not very much money.

Whether $875 in quarters would have been needed for commercial purposes in the Comstock/Carson region is purely speculative. The population in the Carson City area was estimated to be 21,000, six inhabitants for each 1870-CC quarter. But as some numismatic scholars (Breen for one) have declared, Superintendent Abraham Curry was ordered by the Director of the Mint to withhold all small silver coinage from circulation.[2]

Whatever the findings might be regarding distribution, the Carson Mint struck another $350 face value (1,400 pieces) of quarters the following month. On August 15, one month before Abe Curry resigned, the final $850 (3,400 pieces) face value of 1870-CC quarters were minted, bringing the total face value to $2,085 worth of quarters produced in Carson's first year. The added mystery of whether only those selected 40 pieces ever left the Carson Mint's vaults or if all 8,340 were released, will beguile collectors forever. Today's (2003) estimates of surviving population figures for 1870-CC quarters favor the former theory.

More than 60% of known 1870-CC quarters are in the Very Fine grade or lower. Many of the lowest grade specimens are seen with corrosion, porosity, severe scrapes, scratches, graffiti, and cleaned surfaces. Treasure hunters in the Comstock region, using metal detectors, have unearthed some of these specimens, lending credence to the idea that at least small quantities were released into local circulation.

The famous *Eliasberg* specimen is obviously one of the first 1870-CC quarters issued, as it has all the attributes of an early die state piece. This coin's surfaces are prooflike, the strike is awesome, and numerous raised die polishing lines cover certain areas in the fields. On typical 1870-CC quarters, raised die scratch lines on and around the portraits, lettering and devices are visible. For comparison it would be interesting to examine the *Miles/Speir* specimen.

The probability of the Eliasberg 1870-CC quarter having been one of the pieces sent to Philadelphia for Assay purposes is increased by the awareness of the coin's first public appearance. It was purchased by John Clapp from New York dealer Harlan P. Smith sometime around the early 1900s. Smith's coin business, known as the New York Stamp and Coin Company, was located in Union Square. He was more of a collector than a dealer and his coin store afforded him the opportunity to satisfy all of his numismatic desires. Like many East Coast collectors, Smith was fortunate enough to be offered many splendid coins that had passed through the Assay Commission's hands.

The 1870-CC is unquestionably the second rarest date (behind the 1873-CC *Without Arrows*) in the Seated Liberty quarter series, the rarest in Uncirculated condition, and is considered one of the most desirable classic rarities in all of U.S. coinage.[3]

---

[1] Stack's *H. Philip Speir Sale*, March 1974.
[2] *Walter Breen's Complete Encyclopedia of U.S. and Colonial Coins.*
[3] One of the *Top 25*.

1871-CC

(Photo courtesy Bowers and Merena)

Mintage: 10,890

Finest Knowns*:

    PCGS MS-65 (1)

    NGC MS-65 (1)

    PCGS MS-64 (1)

Notable Pedigrees:

    Pezzo (1941)

    F.C.C. Boyd (1945)

    James A. Stack (1975)

    Norweb (1988)

    Eliasberg (1997)

Survival Estimates in All Grades:	35-45
Estimated in Uncirculated:	3-4
Estimated in XF to AU:	6-7
Total Certified Examples in All Grades (PCGS and NGC)*:	24

(* As of July 2003)

REFLECTIONS:

Six months had passed between the last delivery of Carson City quarters in 1870 (August 18, 1870), to when the first delivery of 1871-CC quarters was recorded (February 1871). Superintendent Curry had resigned in September of 1870 to seek political office. His successor at the mint, H.F. Rice (officially appointed by President Grant in February 1871), received the new obverse dies for 1871 quarters in December of 1870. There had been no need for additional reverse dies for 1871 since production totals were so scanty in 1870; in fact, there was no justification for new quarters to be minted in 1871 at Carson City in the first place, especially if small silver coins were not even being released from this mint during its first few years of operation.[1]

The mintage figure for the first delivery of 3,490 quarters in 1871 was curiously nigh unto Carson City's initial quarter delivery of 3,540 back in April of 1870. Similarly, the first delivery of quarters in 1871 also approximated 1870's final delivery of 3,400 pieces. It quickly became clear that the Treasury's need for small silver coins from the Carson City Mint was negligible. As the year ended, only $2,722.50 face value in 1871-CC quarters had been produced, representing a slight $637.50 increase from 1870.

The odd amount of $22.50 face value, or 90 individual quarters was included in the first delivery total for 1871, probably representing the amount divided between assay coins, and those distributed to key residents in the area. Readers will also remember that in 1870 a somewhat extraneous total of 40 quarters was minted at Carson City for similar purposes. Today's depleted populations of 1871-CC quarters imply that no more than 90 pieces ever escaped from storage vaults at the Carson Mint.

What if the $2,700 face value of 1871-CC quarters was never released and then subsequently melted in 1873 (or later) along with nearly the entire mintages of other small silver coins from the first few years at the Carson City Mint? An interesting question, and in response, it has long been the author's goal to discover official mint correspondence between Directors Pollock and Linderman and Carson Superintendents Rice and Hetrich relating to meltdowns of silver coins produced at Carson City from 1870 through April of 1873. One of the only examples of such a document is a letter dated May 19, 1877 in which Linderman directed Carson Superintendent Crawford to melt all stored 1876-CC 20-cent pieces, a letter known to coin collectors for over a century. Indeed it would be a masterstroke of numismatic research if

[1] *Walter Breen's Complete Encyclopedia of U.S. and Colonial Coins*, page 354.

letters similar to this were discovered pertaining to the small silver coins minted from 1870 to 1873 with "CC" mintmarks.

As for die characteristics, the numerals in the date on 1871-CC quarters are not as evenly spaced as on 1870-CC quarters, as the top right backside of the *7* nearly touches the extending top serif of the second *1*, with the gap between the *8* and *7* being disproportionately wider, and the first *1* tilting to the left. On the reverse, the same die used for 1870-CC quarters was again used for the 1871-CC's. The distance between the two letters in the mintmark is approximately adequate to fit a third "C" of equal size, with the first "C" being centered above the *A* in *QUAR*, and the second "C" centered above the *R*.

The three known Uncirculated 1871-CC quarters exhibit commonalities, but at the same time possess distinctive signature qualities. Without question the *Eliasberg* specimen is breathtaking with its prooflike obverse, pinpoint sharp strike and nearly perfect reverse. Evidence of special die preparation is provided by die polishing lines which weave side-to-side, up and down, and cross-angled. Both sides of the coin are layered with a delicate blend of light toning and have smooth blemish-free surfaces. It is a leading contender for *finest known* honors substantiated by its amazing price of $165,000 at the 1997 auction.

Not to be overshadowed is the *James A. Stack* specimen. The obverse on this magnificent piece has mirrorlike surfaces leaving little doubt that the dies received special care while being prepared to strike this jewel. Shades of violet, green, blue, red, yellow, russet, and orange blend together, forming an artistic masterpiece that gracefully blankets the prooflike obverse. It takes high magnification to spot any well hidden diminutive ticks on the obverse surfaces. The reverse is frosty and non-prooflike, and the original mint luster peaks through light patches of multi-colored toning. You can truly examine this piece from every angle for hours on end and find new qualities that will excite you. The *Stack* coin and the *Eliasberg* coin are very special in their own unique ways and it would take the "Wisdom of Solomon" to choose the better of the two.

With all of this being said, the *Norweb* specimen of the 1871-CC quarter also deserves much respect, for if not for the preceding two coins, it would stand head and shoulders above all others of the same date and rank high on all-time greatest lists of U.S. coins in general. With brilliant satiny surfaces, the absence of prooflike quality on this piece does not diminish its eye appeal. Both the obverse and reverse are evenly silhouetted with rich antique gold patina. There are a couple of very minor surface marks visible under magnification and a few light hairlines in the fields. Collectors know how challenging it is to find silver coins from the 1870s that match this level of eye appeal. Because of the *Eliasberg* and *Stack* specimens, the *Norweb* coin must be ranked third in the Condition Census. There are no boo-hoos necessary, for one must keep in mind that the *Norweb* specimen is an 1871-CC quarter in Uncirculated condition, and coins such as these do not come around often.

Circulated 1871-CC quarters with no problems are also extremely difficult to locate. The *R.L. Miles* specimen in AU is arguably the fourth finest known. Examples of this date in Fine to Very Fine are on many collectors' want lists. Dealer wholesale price guides list the 1871-CC quarter on equal terms with the 1870-CC in grades below MS-60.

In Mint State grades, the 1870-CC is of course the second rarest behind the 1873-CC *Without Arrows*, with the 1871-CC being the third rarest date in all grades in the "CC" quarter series, just slightly beating out the 1873-CC *With Arrows*.[1]

---

[1] One of the *Top 25*.

1872-CC

(Photo courtesy Bowers and Merena)

Mintage: 9,100**

Finest Knowns*:

  NGC MS-66 (1)

  PCGS MS-62 (1)

  PCGS AU 55 (1)

  NGC AU-50 (1)

Notable Pedigrees:

  J.H. Clapp (1942)

  Norweb (1988)

  Eliasberg (1997)

  ex: Clapp

Survival Estimates in All Grades:	55-70
Estimated in Uncirculated:	3
Estimated in XF to AU:	6-7
Total Certified Examples in All Grades (PCGS and NGC)*:	44

(* As of July 2003)
(** Some sources say 22,850)

REFLECTIONS:

Until the 1990s the 1872-CC quarter was listed as "unknown" in Uncirculated condition. Then the Norweb specimen (originally catalogued as an AU-55) was graded MS-62 by PCGS. In 1997 an 1872-CC quarter appeared in the *Eliasberg Sale* that was mountain tops above any other known specimen. Auctioneer Dave Bowers described the piece in his catalog as "Far and Away the Finest Known to Exist." He graded it "MS-66 or finer," and it was in every way a "Landmark 1872-CC quarter." [1]

Since the 1872-CC quarter is considered a major rarity in grades above Extra Fine, the *Eliasberg* specimen is spellbinding. The author described the piece as "Unbelievable with only the faintest hairlines, which are the only things keeping it from the MS-68 grade...A no question MS-66+!" At the *Eliasberg Sale* the coin realized $99,000, making it one of the grandest bargains in this or any auction. The obverse of the coin has semi-prooflike surfaces and the reverse has a frosty look, equating it in some measure to certain other early date "CC" silver coins. There is a darker patch of carbon toning on the reverse to the left of *Q* in *QUAR* that in no way detracts from the glorious eye appeal of this coin. It was subsequently graded MS-66 by NGC, establishing it as the no-question finest known example of the date. Eliasberg obtained this 1872-CC quarter in 1942 as a part of the bountiful collection he purchased from the Clapp family. The extent of Condition Census rarities from the Carson City Mint in the Clapp family's collection is mind-boggling.

Some of the landmark "CC" rarities had gained respect among numismatists by the 1940s, but were largely overshadowed by early gold and silver type coins, as well as pre-1858 Proof coins. The 1876-CC 20-cent piece had already risen to the ranks of *classic rarities*, and the 1873-CC *Without Arrows* quarter was steadily moving up the ladder. Uncirculated quarters dated 1870-CC, 1871-CC and 1872-CC, however, were not viewed in the same light as specimens of 1796, 1823/2, and 1827/3 (original) quarters.

When Eliasberg purchased the *Clapp Collection* in 1942, the 1872-CC quarter may have been figured in the deal at approximately $70, whereas the *Original* 1827/3 Proof quarter in the collection may have been valued at approximately $700. And if the Clapp's 1827/3 quarter had not been circulated, it might have brought $1,200 or more in the context of the deal. The disparity in the value between a Choice Uncirculated 1872-CC quarter and an 1827/3 quarter is no longer 10 or 20:1, however, for in today's market (2003) the two coins might be at par with one another. This is also true regarding price comparisons between Uncirculated 1872-CC and 1823/2 quarters.

[1] Bowers and Merena, *Louis E. Eliasberg, Sr. Collection*, April 1997.

During the first few years of coinage at the Carson City Mint there was little need for more than one or two sets of dies to produce the smaller silver denominations. The typical die life was approximately 200,000+ coins, but a mere 44,792 (58,542 in some sources) quarters were struck at the Carson City Mint between 1870 and 1873, so only minimal stress was put on the dies used there. Naturally, the only requirement for each new year was for an obverse die with the date on it. Lightly used reverse dies could be held over and used in subsequent years until they were worn out. Minimal quarter mintages at Carson City in those early years posed no threat to the dies wearing out prematurely, and consequently, in 1872, the same reverse die that was used for "CC" quarters in 1870 and 1871 was put to work again. Mint superintendents at Carson City would routinely put in orders for additional dies every year during the early 1870s, but it was more out of formality than necessity. After all, if the production output was only 10,000 to 20,000 dimes or quarters a year, what need was there for requisitioning multiple dies capable of producing 500,000 or more coins? In the late fall of 1871, Mint Superintendent H.F. Rice customarily ordered more dies for the following year's production. The usual optimism prevailed, leading Rice to order enough dies to strike more than a million coins, but of course, that was not going to happen. A somewhat bizarre situation did develop which created a feigned urgency in coinage production during the first few months of 1872 at the Carson City Mint. Instead of a needless quantity of extra dies being delivered, a heavy snowstorm lingered in the Sierra passes temporarily shutting off railroad transportation into the area.

In Philadelphia, Director of the Mint Pollock assured Superintendent Rice that new 1872 dies would be delivered by one means or another. A cargo ship transported one order of Carson City dies into the port at San Francisco, that did not arrive until March, while the Union Pacific Railroad had already delivered another order of "CC" dies after the rails were cleared of snow in late February. It remains a mystery as to what precipitated the urgency for the Carson City Mint to coin new dimes and quarters in early 1872. Accentuating this already unexplainable pressure to mint more coins at Carson City in 1872 are the added details that Superintendent Rice was in such a hurry to mint coins that he "borrowed a set of obverse dies from the San Francisco Mint"[1] to begin production. There is something very peculiar about the events

that transpired within that time frame, and apparently records that could have set the story straight have been lost or destroyed. Statistics about how many dimes and quarters were minted at Carson City do not help either.

If there had indeed been such an urgency to produce coins, it quickly dissipated and mintages remained extremely low. Although enough dies had been delivered to manufacture over one million quarters in 1872, only 9,100 (22,850 by some accounts) were actually struck.

Storing extra dies at the regional mints was not all that unusual. Mint superintendents had no way of predicting if a die might break or in another manner become unusable. At the Carson City Mint, precipitation during the fall and winter months would seep into structures, causing certain levels of dampness. All precautions were taken of course, but in an era not equipped with the sealants used in today's (2003) building construction, problems did arise. Carson City Mint employees took extra precautions to keep the interior spaces as free of moisture as possible, always on guard against machinery and tool rust. Coin dies of course were always susceptible to contaminants and signs of the use of rusted dies are seen on many issues in the "CC" silver coin series. Toxic vapors were released into the air during refining, and excessive moisture filtering through the interior spread these vapors from room to room. Although the machinery and die equipment were kept well greased there was still heavy exposure to oxidation on anything made out of metal and prolonged exposure to corrosive toxins could have contaminated coin dies that were not properly protected. The resultant small specks of rust on the dies would leave granular impressions on corresponding areas of the coins. Attempts by the coiners to polish off rust accounts for minor variations on numerous issues. Silver planchets were also occasionally victims of exposure to the damp interiors of the storage vaults. It has also been suggested that from time to time the Carson City Mint used below average silver that was not alloyed to government specifications. Many coins surviving today that were struck at the Carson City Mint provide valid testimony of counterproductive conditions and practices. Even the finest known 1872-CC silver quarter, which sold in the *Eliasberg* sale in 1997, has minuscule patches of porosity caused by the rusted reverse die.

The obverse on the 1872-CC quarters is distinguished by an interesting millimeter long die obtrusion that begins at the eighth vertical line in the shield and

---

[1] Howard Hickson, *Mintmark "CC"*.

ends at the base of the rock pointing approximately toward seven o'clock. Why did Superintendent Rice and his crew choose this obverse die, when they must have had at least five dies to choose from? Possibly because this die with such a noticeable scratch was the best of the lot. An upside to the apparent poor choice in obverse die selection is that today's collectors are left with another memorable trademark that adds diversity to their collecting experiences.

If an additional 13,750 1872-CC quarters were minted, as some sources have suggested since the late 1970s, it has not affected the population of survivors. If universally accepted survival percentages for the early "CC" silver coins are used (.3%-.5% of original mintage) for the revised mintage figure, there should be approximately 41 to 69 more 1872-CC quarters surviving than had previously been estimated—but, if so, where are they? [1]

---

[1] One of the *Top 25*.

1873-CC

Without Arrows

(Photo courtesy Bowers and Merena)

Mintage: 4,000

Finest Knowns*:

NGC MS-66 (Stack)

PCGS MS-64 (Eliasberg)

NGC MS-64 (Norweb)

Notable Pedigrees:

William H. Woodin (c. 1905-1915)

H.O. Granberg (1919)

F.C.C. Boyd (1945)

Harold M. Budd (c. 1954)

James A. Stack (1975)

Norweb (1988)

Eliasberg (1997)

Survival Estimates in All Grades:	5
Estimated in Uncirculated:	3
Estimated in XF to AU:	I
Total Certified Examples in All Grades (PCGS and NGC)*:	4[1]

(* As of July 2003)

REFLECTIONS:

Why are there so few surviving specimens of the 1873-CC *Without Arrows* quarter? Part of the answer of course, is the reported low mintage of 4,000 pieces, but even a modest original quantity such as this might suggest that the surviving number extant would be perhaps 10 to 20.

Probably the most logical reason that 1873-CC *Without Arrows* quarters became the rarest business strike date of the denomination is that the entire mintage, except for a few examples, was melted down in compliance with the *Coinage Act of 1873*.

New dies for the 1873-CC coins had arrived promptly at the end of 1872 and Superintendent Rice was apparently anxious to begin using them as soon as the new year arrived. He ordered that 4,000 new quarters be minted in mid-January of 1873, followed by 12,400 new dimes during the first few days of February. There is no clear rationale for Rice's actions, certainly not a shortage of small silver coins. Unless further evidence is uncovered, one might surmise that the staff at the Carson Mint was simply looking for something to occupy their time during the slow winter season. Or, possibly, Rice and company believed that steadiness in their operations would help justify their existence in the eyes of the Bureau of the Mint. Of course, there is always the outside possibility that the Carson City Mint had been releasing its entire annual outputs of quarters into circulation from the first year it opened and the local economy was demanding more. But if so, why weren't mintages increased on a regular basis every year? Considering the paltry mintage of 10,890 in 1871, for instance, if the need for more quarters had been foreseen by Rice, it would not have taken much effort to mint more coins.

Until 1977, the mintage figure listed in all coin price guides and reference works, was 9,100 for 1872-CC quarters. In 1977, after 105 years, numismatic researchers proposed that the traditionally accepted mintage figure for the 1872-CC quarter was understated by 13,750. If true, it could mean local commercial needs had indeed existed

---

[1] PCGS and NGC each list one MS-64, but in fact, it is the same *Norweb* coin.

in 1872. As has been stated, new information in 1977 revealed that 4,000 quarters were struck on December 31, 1872 at the Carson City Mint. Could this total represent the reported 4,000 1873-CC *Without Arrows* quarters produced just 18 days later, or was there really a need for 8,000 quarters in a 19 day span? The revised mintage figures surfacing in 1977 also reported that 5,100 quarters had been minted at the end of September in 1872 at Carson City, implying that 13,100 quarters were coined from the end of September 1872 to January 18, 1873, less than 115 days, at a time when silver coins were not being issued by the western mints except in exchange for gold.[1]

Depositors of gold wishing to exchange it for silver coins were faced with a 2% discount in the process. Since half dollars were normally used in gold-to-silver-coin exchanges anyway and there were no coin shortages in the Pacific states, all incentives for the Carson City Mint to produce more than minimal amounts of dimes and quarters were nonexistent.

The *Coinage Act* that passed on February 12, 1873, served as a reset mechanism that later sent substantial percentages of previously minted silver coins to the melting pot. When the time came, the books would be wiped clean of all the silver coins struck at the Carson City Mint in its first three and one half years of operation. None of those 4,000 1873-CC *Without Arrows* quarters (except for a few reserved for the Assay Commission and perhaps a few snatched by employees), ever left the building, at least not in their original form. After the quarters were melted, they were re-coined, using the new *With Arrows* design.[2]

For most of the first 100 years after the 1873-CC *Without Arrows* quarters were minted, numismatists were unsure of how many surviving pieces existed. The specimen that later became identified with the *James A. Stack Collection* made its first public appearance at E.D. Cogan's sale of the *John Swan Randall Collection* in May of 1878. In the catalog, the quarter was described as, "1873-CC. Old Style. Nearly Uncirculated."[3] The coin's humble beginning in this auction in no way foretold the prestigious position to which it would later rise within the numismatic community. The winning bidder who at the time paid 35 cents to obtain the coin had no way of knowing the significance of the treasure he now possessed. By the 1940s one of the three known Uncirculated 1873-CC *Without Arrows* quarters was purchased by Eliasberg for $725 in the *World's Greatest Collection* auction (*F.C.C. Boyd* specimen). Every time

a famous collection came onto the market, it was asked whether there was an 1873-CC *Without Arrows* quarter in it. One by one, headliner collections came up for auction, minus the 1873-CC *Without Arrows* quarter. Significant names like Neil, Atwater, Dunham, Hall, Colonel Green, Charles M. Williams (*Menjou Sale*, 1950), Anderson-Dupont, and King Farouk were all missing this scarce date. Even famous collections like *Brand's* and *Garrett's* were denied. Eventually the *Stack* specimen would sell for $80,000 in 1975, and then $341,000 in the *Apostrophe* event, *Auction '90* in 1990. In 112 years the coin had appreciated over 97 million%! In a previous section of this book, a comment was made about how prices for Carson City coins had lagged behind prices of the coin market in general for many decades. But when the cork was finally popped, "CC" coins unleashed a fury of accelerating appreciation that by the early 21st century resulted in more accurate price levels being established.

A.G. Heaton announced in 1893 that interest in U.S. coins with mintmarks was beginning to catch on and he predicted that collecting coins by mintmarks would become a "permanently established department of numismatic science," adding that "This activity is none too soon."[4] These words were written just 20 years after the 1873-CC quarters were minted. Heaton proposed that the 1870, 1871, and 1872-CC quarters were scarcer than the 1873-CCs; he did not seem to regard one 1873-CC quarter variety over the other, concluding, "Both are exceedingly rare"[5]

One of the earliest enthusiasts of "CC" coins was New York dealer/collector Harlan P. Smith; and one of his prominent clients, John H. Clapp, who carried the torch passed to him by his father, purchased some blockbuster Carson City dates from him. Transcendent to all other "CC" coins pedigreed to H.P. Smith was the 1870-CC quarter. Mr. Smith obviously had connections to have been able to obtain a prized piece of this significance, probably passed down to him through someone with authority, such as a Mint official. The *Smith* pedigree is also associated with certain spectacular half dollars from the Carson City Mint, including the gem 1873-CC *With*

---

[1] Neil Carothers, *Fractional Money*, 1930.

[2] It is the author's opinion that at least 98% of all the silver dimes and quarters dated 1870-1873 (*Without Arrows*) from the Carson City Mint were melted as a result of the *Coinage Act of 1873*.

[3] E.D. Cogan Auction, *John Swan Randall Collection*, May 6-9, 1878.

[4] Augustus G. Heaton, *Mint Marks, A Treatise*, 1893.

[5] Ibid.

Arrows and 1874-CC that wound up in the *Eliasberg Collection* via the Clapp family.

Harlan P. Smith also reportedly owned an 1873-CC *Without Arrows* quarter at one time and sold it to A.G. Heaton. The patriarch of the Clapp family, J.M. Clapp, wrote about Heaton's purchase in the 1890s, but went to his grave in 1906 never owning one. His son John H. Clapp was likewise unsuccessful in his pursuit of an 1873-CC *Without Arrows* quarter.

This date became a target for Louis E. Eliasberg from the time he purchased the *Clapp Family Collection*, and several years after he obtained the famous collection, he notched another victory when he acquired the *F.C.C. Boyd* specimen. Numismatic researchers have never been able to track the transference of ownership of the *H.P. Smith/A.G. Heaton* coin, although some have speculated that it might be the *Stack* specimen, which sold for 35 cents at the *Randall Sale* in 1878.

H.P. Smith was 38 years old in 1878, and probably just getting his feet wet as a dealer/collector. A couple years later, he threw all of his chips in the pot when he formed a partnership to conduct coin auctions, a career that lasted another 22 years until his death in 1902. Whether he was the winning bidder at 35 cents for the 1873-CC *Without Arrows* quarter in the 1878 *Randall Sale*, or whether he obtained an example years later, there is no doubt that he acquired an interest in "CC" coins at some point.

Mintmarked coins were more curious than costly in Harlan P. Smith's day. A collector could enjoy the novelty of owning them with little strain on the wallet. In retrospect those times seem like a coin collectors' paradise.

On the obverse of the 1873-CC *Without Arrows* quarters the date is the *Closed 3* variety. It is evenly spaced and well centered between the base of the rock and the rim, in contrast to the 1872-CC quarters, and both the *1* and the *3* tilt slightly to the right. Surprisingly, a different reverse die than the one seen on the 1870, 71, and 72-CCs was used. The right "C" in the mintmark is positioned slightly different than the left "C" when compared to the other three years, and the right "C" also has a signature diagonal raised line caused from a die crack running from the right serifs to approximately the 7:00 position.[1]

---

[1] One of the *Top 25*.

1873-CC

With Arrows

(Photo courtesy Bowers and Merena)

Mintage: 12,462

Finest Knowns*:

    NGC MS-65 (Norweb)

    PCGS MS-64 (Eliasberg)

    PCGS AU-55 (I)

Notable Pedigrees:

    F.C.C. Boyd (1945)

    R.L. Miles (1969)

    E.A. Carson (1976)

    Norweb (1988)

    Eliasberg (1997)

    Nevada Collection (1999)

Survival Estimates in All Grades:	30-35
Estimated in Uncirculated:	2-3
Estimated in XF to AU:	5-6
Total Certified Examples in All Grades (PCGS and NGC)*:	27

(* As of July 2003)

REFLECTIONS:

Orders originating from various coinage acts in the first few years of the 1870s informed the regional mints that silver coins would only be paid out in exchange for gold. Furthermore, the minimum amount in an exchange was set at $100. Therefore, the only other reason a mint would release small silver coins was if small amounts were necessary "for change less than one dollar in settlement for gold deposits."[1] The Philadelphia Mint was the only Treasury institution authorized to release silver coins into circulation for commercial purposes, meaning that all of the small silver coins minted at Carson City continued to stockpile in their vaults, most likely reserved only for the melting pot.

By the time the *Coinage Act of 1873* was passed on February 12, 1873, the Carson City Mint had produced the three silver coin denominations that were destined for greatness in numismatic circles; the 1873-CC *Without Arrows* dimes, quarters and halves sat in the vault awaiting orders from the Philadelphia Mint as February 12 came and went. A few weeks later, in March, the final 1,300 of a total mintage of 2,300 1873-CC Seated Liberty silver dollars were struck. Now there were four coin denominations dated 1873-CC that would eventually be among the

most coveted dates in all of coin collecting. Impetus for the extraordinary rarity of these 1873-CC silver coins is provided by mass meltings that reportedly occurred in the second half of 1873, at which time, two of the denominations (dime and quarter) faced near extinction, while the other two (half and dollar) were placed on the endangered species list.

There was a four month suspension of silver coin production as workers at the Carson City Mint waited for new dies with the arrowhead devices placed on either side of the date. Concurrent with the design makeover on the small silver coins was the discontinuance of the Seated Liberty dollars; the gap in production of silver dollar-sized coins was almost immediately filled by the new *Coinage Act*-inspired trade dollars.

Finally at the end of June in 1873 the new dies were arriving and coin production resumed, and at the Carson City Mint, the first 3,500 new 1873 quarters with arrowheads next to the date were struck. A month later, the final delivery of 1873-CC *With Arrows* quarters went through the coin press, bringing the total to 12,462.

---

[1] *Coinage Act of 1873, Amendments 1874*, U.S. Mint.

The question of why those two extra quarters were minted has never been answered. Perhaps Superintendent Rice felt it necessary to round off the extra 50 cents carried forward from the quarter production of 1871.[1] Or perhaps two extra quarters were struck especially for presentation purposes. Whatever the reason, it must have been a purely subjective act, as there certainly was no rational basis for minting two extra quarters. A lack of existing correspondence associated with the Carson City Mint leaves many such unanswered questions.

Curiously, the mintage figure of 12,462 for 1873-CC *With Arrows* quarters is identical to the first year total of silver dollar production at the Carson City Mint. Perhaps Superintendent Rice viewed the new coin designs as a rebirth of the Carson City Mint and wanted to commemorate the event by returning to a special number synonymous with the mint's origins, all fanciful conjecture of course, since no one knows for sure.

The finest known of the two Uncirculated specimens of the 1873-CC *With Arrows* quarter first gained national attention in 1988 when it sold in Bowers and Merena's *Norweb Collection* sale. Surprisingly, the catalog description did not include pedigree information; considering that the price realized was $44,000, ranking it in the top 14 out of 1,269 lots, the lack of a record of ownership seemed a bit odd. Likewise, the *Eliasberg* specimen, which sold for $88,000 in 1997, was not pedigreed. Since all of the coins in Eliasberg's collection had been purchased prior to 1951, his 1873-CC *With Arrows* quarter is not traceable to any listed auction from 1873 to 1950, or surely the cataloguer would have referred to it. In July 1919, B. Max Mehl in his sale of the *Granberg Collection* described the 1873-CC *With Arrows* quarter as being, "Uncirculated." Although there has never been a connection made between this coin and either the *Norweb* or *Eliasberg* specimens, there appears to be a high probability that it is one of the two. In the absence of solid data, speculation is the only course one can take.

In the spirit of pure romanticism, it would be thrilling for numismatic researchers to one day discover that the *Norweb* and *Eliasberg* specimens were, in fact, those two extra quarters minted at Carson City in July of 1873, which brought the total to 12,462.

The obverse die used to strike the 1873 *With Arrows* quarters at all three mints was the *Open 3* variety. There had been discussions in Philadelphia about the *3* in the *Closed 3* design used earlier in the year; some officials believed it was too similar to an *8*, so the decision was made to change it. At the left of the date, the arrow on "CC" quarters is higher, the end of the shaft pointing just below the top serif on the *1*. Conversely, the right arrow is placed lower, the shaft pointing toward the lower curve of the *3*. The lower left curve of the *8* is close to the base of the *1* and the *873* tilts slightly to the right. Although there were many reverse dies on hand, employees at the Carson City Mint decided to employ the same one used to coin the 1870, 1871, and 1872 quarters–begging the question: why did the employees choose not to use the same reverse die that produced the 4,000 1873-CC *Without Arrows* quarters, especially since it is well known that this reverse die was put to use again in 1876?

After being utilized in three previous seasons, the reverse dies used on the 1873-CC *With Arrows* quarters began to show signs of wear and rust. Conspicuous weakness and porosity can be seen on the letters of the denomination, especially on the bottom half of *QUAR*. Lower grade circulated pieces usually have the porosity worn away. On some specimens numerous raised die lines can be seen diagonally crossing the bottom lower reverse surfaces below the mintmark, most prominently through the letters *QUAR*.

A low mintage, combined with even lower commercial demand, contributed to the rarity of the 1873-CC *With Arrows* quarters, for apparently no more than a handful was released by the Carson City Mint. Combined with the fact that no quarters were minted at Carson City in 1874, this provides further evidence that commercial requirements for the denomination in the Comstock region were practically nil.

It does not, however, explain why the stockpiled coins were melted, and if the 1873-CC *With Arrows* quarters were still part of Carson City's coinage inventory in 1875 it means none were released in spite of the U.S. Mint's stepped-up silver coin production. The explanation given for why the pre-*Coinage Act of 1873* inventories were melted has always been the lower silver content in the coins, but what about the *With Arrows* coins? The silver content in them was at par with the revised standards of the 1873 coinage laws. If these coins were kept in storage from 1873 through 1874 and were still surviving in 1875 and 1876, surely some of them would have been included in the mass

---

[1] If the revised figures reported in 1977 are accurate, the extra 50 cents was already rounded up to the nearest dollar by the additional quarter output from 1872.

distributions during the specie payment years of the latter 1870s. But as has already been mentioned, the Treasury's vaults were gushing with excessive amounts of stored silver coins and there was no serious need for new supplies until after 1885. Even then, the Bureau of the Mint had no problem staying ahead of demand.

Regardless of what really happened concerning the nation's mintages and meltages during the final three decades of the 19th century, the overwhelming evidence suggests that only a small fraction of 1870 to 1873 silver dimes and quarters from the Carson City Mint ever left

that building. It would be very surprising to discover that more than 62 1873-CC *With Arrows* quarters found their way into the hands of the public, and even if 462 of them had been distributed, it would not explain the scarcity of this date today (early part of the 21st century).

In lieu of the absence of concrete evidence, it might be safe to assume that the quantity of 1873-CC *With Arrows* quarters melted was 12,400, and if anyone has evidence to prove otherwise, let him or her come forth.[1]

---

[1] One of the *Top 25*.

1875-CC

(Photo courtesy Bowers and Merena)

Mintage: 140,000

Finest Knowns*:

    PCGS MS-65 (1)

    NGC MS-65 (4)**

    PCGS MS-64 (5)

    NGC MS-64 (5)

Notable Pedigrees:

    Eliasberg (1997)

    John J. Pittman (1998)

Survival Estimates in All Grades:	300-500
Estimated in Uncirculated:	45-70
Estimated in XF to AU:	50-75
Total Certified Examples in All Grades (PCGS and NGC)*:	68

(* As of July 2003)

(**Possible multiple submissions with the same coin being counted twice)

REFLECTIONS:

After a one year hiatus, quarter production resumed at the Carson City Mint. The arrowheads were no longer a part of the design and there was a significant right shifting of the mintmark.

As usual, Treasury and Mint records are foggy and do not provide an explanation as to why there were no 1874-CC quarters produced. This one year curtailment was more than compensated for in 1875, however, as 140,000 quarters passed through the coin presses, a rather slim figure in comparison to the 4,293,500 struck at Philadelphia, but for Carson City it was a sizable increase. In fact, the 140,000 1875-CC quarters produced at Carson City was 3 ½ times the combined quarter production from that mint during its first four years of operation.

At one time the Treasury Department had reported that quarters were in fact minted at Carson City in 1874. The *Annual Report of the Director of the Mint* in 1886, for instance, lists 8,962 pieces for 1874. Paradoxically, the same report states that there were **no quarters** minted in 1875 at Carson City, a statement that simply is not true. As has been mentioned, discrepancies in mintage figures were due in part to *fiscal* versus *calendar year* accounting practices used by the Treasury. A major effort was made to update Mint records in 1886 to 1887, and annual mintage figures were compiled based on *calendar year* standards. This

"Valuable"[1] information, had "been compiled with no little care and research."[2] Authorities used "original sources of information, such as the workbooks and delivery books of the coinage mints."[3]

Every coin ever produced at a U.S. mint from 1792 through 1886 was accounted for and listed in its appropriate calendar year. Nearly $2 billion in face value—representing millions of coins—was documented and all denominations from half cents to $20 gold pieces were included in this massive study. Some of the records were obscure—in several instances missing—and Mint officials admitted that "early records...are neither complete nor in conformity with modern detail(s) of statement."

One of the most confusing obstacles to researchers in 1887 still confounds numismatists in the early years of the 21st century: Why do mintage figures for specific dates differ depending on which reference charts are used? This "difficulty" arose, explained Mint Director Kimball, "from the change from calendar to fiscal years."[4] Calendar years were used from 1792 to 1857 at which time fiscal years were employed, but only "until 1880, when statements were also made for calendar years."[5]

---

[1] *Annual Report of the Director of the Mint*, 1887.

[2] Ibid.

[3] Ibid.

[4] Ibid.

[5] Ibid.

From 1887 on, if discrepancies arose, "in any respect from the figures heretofore presented...original accounts on file in the office of the Register of the Treasury"[1] would be consulted. In every *Annual Report* henceforth an updated table showing the coinage of all previous and current mints would be included. Director Kimball and his staff were proud of this achievement and the fact that information like this "has never before appeared."[2] Collectors of "CC" coins in the early years of the 21st century have solid assurance that the Bureau of the Mint's time-honored mintage records are accurate.

Quarters dated 1875-CC are much more elusive than the mintage figure would suggest. Less than 1% of the original 140,000 survive, maybe even less than .33%. Curiously, the 1875-CC 20-cent pieces with a comparable mintage total are considerably easier to obtain. Even back in 1947, B. Max Mehl commented in the *Neil Collection* sale that the 1875-CC quarters were "in very few collections and very few dealers' stocks."[3] This date was even missing from the *World's Greatest Collection* in 1945, although most likely due to an oversight, considering that the consignor (F.C.C. Boyd) owned almost every major rarity.

Throughout the 1950s it became routine for auction catalogers to describe 1875-CC quarters as underrated. In the shadows of giants such as the 1873-CC *With* and *Without Arrows* quarters, as well as the 1870 to 1872-CC issues, 1875-CCs were not given much consideration. But ever since the *Holmes* specimen sold for $33 in 1960, this date has been on an upward trajectory. In 1965, the coin in the *Stadiem–Gardner* sale sold for $240, and four years later the *R.L. Miles* specimen realized $425. Consummate coin collector John J. Pittman purchased a Choice Uncirculated 1875-CC quarter for $6.50 in the late 1940s to early 1950s, and in 1998 when the second of three parts of his famous collection was sold by Pittman's heirs, the price realized for the coin was $10,450.[4] It is currently encased in an NGC MS-65 holder and is one of the finest known specimens.

Another great example of an 1875-CC quarter is the *Eliasberg* specimen, which when it appeared in the 1997 Bowers and Merena *Eliasberg Sale* impressed numismatists with its prooflike qualities. Like so many pieces in the *Eliasberg* collection, this quarter had been part of the *Clapp* estate, and when Eliasberg purchased the Clapp family's collection in 1942, this 1875-CC was probably valued at no more than one dollar. According to the cataloger of the *Eliasberg* sale, this coin had been purchased by J.M. Clapp

in a two-piece lot with an 1876-CC quarter from the *Richard B. Winsor Sale* in December of 1895. The price realized was 35 cents for both quarters (you can do the math). At the *Eliasberg Sale* the price realized was $5,720 to the fortunate bidder.

In 1875 the Carson City Mint possessed more coin dies than it had in nearly all the previous five years combined. An increase of nearly 500% in total coins produced kept mint employees working at maximum capacity. This proved to be the make-it-or-break-it year that showed what the Carson coiners were made of. If they passed this test there would be support for further advancements. Every worker in the melting and refining department, the assay room, and the coining section came to work early and left late. Deposits of gold and silver bullion had reached peak levels between 1872 and 1877 as the mines on the Comstock blazed through their *Big Bonanza* phase.

Odorous fumes rose through the chimneys on the roof, filling the air outside with smells worse than rotten eggs. Improvements were made so residents neighboring the mint would not have to hold their noses all the time. An innumerable amount of dimes, 4,645,000, were minted in 1875 compared to 10,817 in 1874. Half dollar production increased from 59,000 in 1874 to over one million in 1875. A new 20-cent piece was added to the fray. Trade dollar production continued to rise, as gold coin production was dominated by $20 double eagles.

James Crawford replaced Superintendent Hetrich in 1874 and one of Crawford's improvements was the addition of a small coin press to absorb some of the load. Crawford actively participated in this incredible climb to the summit in production levels at the Carson City Mint, and would be there 10 years later when the avalanche began. He lobbied the government for tenant improvement funds, pleas that were ignored at first, but appropriations would be granted in the future.

In the meantime, 1875-CC quarters were minted using only two identifiable pairs of dies. One of the obverses displayed a similar alignment of the numerals in the date as seen on 1873-CC *Without Arrows* quarters. One obvious difference was that the date on the 1875-CCs was shifted approximately 0.3 mm to the left. Chief Engraver William Barber continued experimenting with

[1] Ibid.
[2] Ibid.
[3] *Will W. Neil Collection*, B. Max Mehl, 1947.
[4] *John Jay Pittman Collection*, David Akers, May 1998.

Longacre's original reverse design, eventually altering the spacing of *TATE* in *STATES.* These dies were shipped to all mints. At Carson City, Chief Coiner W.S. Doane had at least five reverse dies and eight obverse dies to choose from. He chose two reverse dies with only slight variation in mintmark placement. Doane must have reworked obverse dies and/or planchets on occasion, as some examples are seen with prooflike surfaces. However, the majority of Uncirculated 1875-CC quarters display frosty satiny-sheen surfaces. Many examples of the date display minimal signs of the die rust usually associated with small silver coinage from the Carson City Mint.

Properly graded specimens in Fine to MS-63 are most desirable. In higher grades this date is very elusive, and although the 1875-CC quarter does not qualify for the *Top 25* list, it deserves respect.

1876-CC

(Photo courtesy Bowers and Merena)

Mintage: 4,944,000

Finest Knowns*:

    PCGS MS-67 (1)

    NGC MS-67 (2)

    NGC MS-66 (11)**

    PCGS MS-66 (4)**

Notable Pedigrees:

    Various

Survival Estimates in All Grades: ... 5,000-10,000
Estimated in Uncirculated: 500-600
Estimated in XF to AU: 1,000-1,500
Total Certified Examples in All Grades (PCGS and NGC)*: 302

(* As of July 2003)
(** Possible Resubmissions)

REFLECTIONS:

Prior to 1876 the quarter was a very low mintage denomination at the Carson City Mint. Just like dimes in 1875, however, quarters were given a coming-out party in 1876 at Carson City and made up for six years of lost time as employees produced an average of 412,000 pieces a month through 1876. It is difficult for those living in the early years of the 21st century to fathom what it must have been like to experience such increased output. What did the dedicated crew at Carson City think about it, as just three years earlier they were lucky to mint 5,000 quarters or dimes in a three month period? Now they were averaging 220 times that amount every month! Plus they were producing approximately 162,000 half dollars per month, plus trade dollars, and gold coins were still on the agenda.

Although the number of coins produced doubled in one year, and had increased 2,800% since 1873, personnel increased by only 14%. Superintendent Crawford managed to get his budget appropriations raised, and managed to secure a badly needed third coin press to facilitate striking an average of approximately 45,000 coins a day. Keep in mind that two days' output in 1876 equaled the entire **annual** output from 1870. This would be like a small mom and pop hamburger stand suddenly serving the starving needs of the lunch crowd in Times Square, with maybe an extra fry cook, an additional counter helper, and one more griddle. But obviously, the workers at the

Carson City Mint must have appreciated the opportunity bestowed upon them, as most of them were denied raises, and some even took slight pay cuts to defray the costs of equipment and tenant improvements.

In the midst of it all there must have been times when it resembled a frat party on initiation day. There is no way that Superintendent Crawford and his staff could have supervised all the activities taking place, especially considering that operations were nearly on a 24/7 schedule. But given the circumstances, it appears that everyone at the Carson City Mint performed admirably through 1876, although taking certain liberties was no doubt too tempting to resist.

The most memorable event concerning the Carson City Mint in 1876 will always be the 10,000 20-cent pieces that were struck and subsequently melted, except 18-20 pieces. But there were many other aftereffects which became significant to future numismatists that occurred in 1876 at the Carson City Mint. One example is the reported four Proof 1876-CC dimes coined that year.

Regarding the 1876-CC quarter varieties, Briggs' *Comprehensive Encyclopedia of U.S. Seated Liberty Quarters* lists 14 obverse and 12 reverse dies that have been identified as being used to produce nearly five million coins,[1] a variety collector's dream come true: a common date "CC" quar-

---

[1] Larry Briggs, *Comprehensive Encyclopedia of U.S. Liberty Seated Quarters.*

ter with multiple die variations, and all affordable. What more could a coin diagnostician ask for?

While operations at the small village mint in Carson City pressed on, Philadelphia's mass coinage distribution center hurled out more than 17.5 million 1876 quarters. Over 100 obverse and 100 reverse quarter dies were used at Philadelphia that year.[1] Modern day die variety researchers in the early years of the 21st century might be tempted to "cry uncle" when attempting to attribute Philadelphia quarters from 1876. But Carson City's entry in the contest of coin die diagnostics is neat, tidy and compact. At right is a chart exhibiting some of the more interesting variety characteristics seen on 1876-CC quarters.

None of the varieties of the 1876-CC quarter command high premiums in Uncirculated grades. Collectors will, however, pay multiple percentages for circulated specimens in order to fill out their sets. In the *Guide Book of United States Coins* a footnote states that "Variety with fine edge reeding (153 reeds) is scarcer…"[2]

---

[1] Walter Breen, *Complete Encyclopedia of U.S. and Colonial Coins.*
[2] Whitman Coin Products, *A Guide Book of United States Coins.*

Diagnostic Die Attributes on 1876-CC Quarters

General Reverse Types

Type I Reverse – (TATE closely spaced)
Type II Reverse – (TATE spaced wide)

Reeds On Edges

113
122
153

Mintmarks

Small CC spaced wide
Small CC closely spaced
Small CC medium spaced
Small CC same as 1873-CC *Without Arrows*
Large CC

Numerals in Date

Upright numerals, evenly spaced
Slightly tilted to the right
Date centered between portrait and rim
Date lower, nearer rim
Repunched numerals

Miscellaneous Die Impartations

Die crack through mintmark
Die cracks through upper denticles
Raised die polishing lines
Recut letters
Repunched stars
Doubling on devices and lettering
Prooflike surfaces
Die rust causing corrosive look
Tooling marks
Clashed die impressions

1877-CC

(Photo courtesy Bowers and Merena)

Mintage: 4,192,000

Finest Knowns*:

    PCGS MS-67 (6)

    NGC MS-67 (4)

    PCGS MS-66 (8)

    NGC MS-66 (5)

Notable Pedigrees:

    Numerous

Survival Estimates in All Grades: **5,000-7,500**
Estimated in Uncirculated: **600-800**
Estimated in XF to AU: **700-900**
Total Certified Examples   in All Grades (PCGS and NGC)*: **590**

(* As of July 2003)

Reflections:

Over $18 million in face value in silver dimes, quarters, and halves were produced by the three working mints in 1876, nearly $10 million more than the previous year's record setting total. As the year 1877 began, it seemed highly probable that the momentum would harvest another record breaker. Enactment of the *Specie Payment Act* in 1876 set the federal government's plan in motion to issue millions of dollars in silver coins which would in turn be used to retire the outstanding fractional currency, estimated to be between $35 and $45 million. When public response to fractional currency redemptions lagged far behind the Fed's expectations, a glut of silver coins stockpiled in Treasury vaults. Concurrent with this stockpiling was the unexpected deluge of U.S. silver coins flowing back into the country from foreign nations.[1]

Mass quantities of silver coins continued to be manufactured during calendar year 1877. It did not seem to matter to the Treasury Department that silver coins were virtually coming out of the country's ears. Not only were silver coins being exchanged for fractional paper money, but now the Treasury also began issuing silver coins in exchange for greenbacks. Banks and merchants in Nevada and the Pacific states opposed the coins-for-paper standard, choosing instead their traditional silver-coins-for-gold system.

Institutions, businesses and residents in this region were dissuaded from exchanging gold for silver coins, however, because of the discounts incurred, at times 8% or higher.

By the end of the year the Treasury slammed the brakes on its silver coinage production, eventually leading to a radical cutback in 1878, followed by more than a decade of contraction. New standard silver dollars introduced in 1878 filled the gap, and consumed all (and more) of the silver previously used for dimes, quarters and halves. The table below exhibits the rise and subsequent decline in silver dime, quarter, and half dollar production from 1875 to 1878.

At the Carson City Mint subsidiary silver coin production took an orderly descent in 1877. The mintage

---

[1] See Chapter Three.

SUBSIDIARY SILVER COIN PRODUCTION (IN FACE VALUE) AT U.S. MINT'S BETWEEN 1875 AND 1878:				
Year	Dimes	Quarters	Halves	Totals
1875	$2,406,570	$1,278,375	$5,117,750	$8,802,695
1876	3,015,115	7,839,288	7,451,575	18,305,978
1877	1,735,051	6,024,928	7,540,255	15,300,233
1878	187,880	849,200	726,200	1,763,280

(Twenty cent pieces and trade dollars were also minted during these years. Morgan silver dollars were minted in 1878.)

COMPARISON IN SUBSIDIARY SILVER COIN PRODUCTION AT THE CARSON CITY MINT FROM 1876 TO 1877 (IN QUANTITY)				
Year	Dimes	Quarters	Halves	Totals
1876	8,270,000	4,944,000	1,956,000	15,170,000
1877	7,770,000	4,192,000	1,420,000	13,382,000
	about 7%	about 15%	about 27.5%	about 12%

comparisons shown above indicate how gradual the decline was.

These were still sizable quantities being produced according to Carson City Mint standards. The coiner there had had so much fun (or aggravation) in 1876 experimenting with the dies available to him, he diligently kept to the task at hand again in 1877. At least 10 different obverse and 10 different reverse dies were employed, averaging a commendable 419,200 coins per die pairing. Some of the obverse dies were contaminated with rust, resulting in minimal to excessive granularity on the coins. Reverse dies –based on consensus opinion– are all of the *Type II Variety.*[1] All but one of the mintmark combinations are *Large* or *Tall* "CC" varieties. At center is a table exhibiting the different categories 1877-CC quarter varieties are classified in.

None of the *Large* "CC" varieties command a significant premium over another, although some collectors desiring to complete a die variety set of 1877-CC quarters might pay extra for a specific example.

A single *Small* "CC" variety is known (Briggs Rev. D.) It is similar to one of the 1876 varieties (Briggs Rev. I), although shifted slightly to the left.

Spacing Between *C*'s

Wide

Medium

Close

Opening At Mouth of *C*'s

Open

Medium

Closed

Position of Right *C* in Relation to Left *C*

Higher

Lower

Virtually Equal

Distance of Left *C* From Arrow Feather or Right *C* From Stem

Closer

Medium

Farther

In 1988, Breen said this variety was "very rare,"[2] but like the *Large* "CC" varieties it does not command a premium.

There are at least 11 different varieties of the 1877-CC quarter that have been identified (as of the early years of the 21st century). One of the recognized grading services that attribute die varieties on Carson City coins is ANACS (American Numismatic Association Certification Services). A complete certified set of 1877-CC die varieties, although not valued at much of a premium, makes for an interesting display. Repunched dates, providing a doubled-die effect, clash marks, raised die crack lines, small dots of raised metal, and coarse granulated devices, add to the fascination when studying these coins. For a date that is considered very common, more space has been allotted in some research volumes than for coins that are much rarer.

Uncirculated examples of 1877-CC quarters often exhibit the highest quality of eye appeal characteristics of any of the dates minted at Carson City. Many of the 1877-CCs possess needle-point sharpness and the most satiny smooth, pearl-like luster. One of the finest specimens appeared in RARCOA's *Auction '90.* It was graded MS-67 by NGC and sold for $20,300,[3] at a time when MS-65's were priced at $1,200. In terms of availability, the 1877-CC is the easiest "CC" quarter to locate in Uncirculated grades (with the exception of MS-67 specimens selling for $20k).

---

[1] *TATE* in *STATES* widely spaced.
[2] Walter Breen, *Complete Encyclopedia of United States and Colonial Coins.*
[3] RARCOA, *Auction '90.*

1878-CC

(Photo courtesy Bowers and Merena)

Mintage: 996,000

Finest Knowns*:

    NGC MS-67 (1)

    PCGS MS-66 (4)

    NGC MS-66 (4)

Notable Pedigrees:

    Various

Survival Estimates in All Grades:	600-900
Estimated in Uncirculated:	300-400
Estimated in XF to AU:	150-200
Total Certified Examples in All Grades (PCGS and NGC)*:	322

(* As of July 2003)

REFLECTIONS:

With the advent of new standard silver dollars–fulfilling the Bland/Allison Act of 1878–Carson City's spirit was revived. Superintendent Crawford continued his aggressive campaign to procure much needed improvements for the pride of Carson City. A new addition to the building was constructed, to house the new boilers that would provide the power necessary to run all three presses at full capacity. One of these coin presses, the first ever used at Carson City, received a much needed overhaul at the V&T's machine shop.

Crawford continued petitioning Mint Director Linderman for additional tenant improvement funds, and his perseverance became a burr in the Treasury's saddle. In late February, Linderman ordered Crawford to cease production of trade dollars, the first casualty of an ever-changing (at times befuddled) Treasury Department. All three denominations of Seated Liberty coinage were also retired at the Carson City Mint, vanishing into the sunset by year's end.

More than 1.85 million ounces of silver had been used in 1877 to mint dimes, quarters and halves at Carson City. In 1878 only 218,650 ounces were needed. Counting trade dollars, silver usage in 1878 totaled 295,028 ounces as opposed to nearly 2.3 million ounces in 1877. There had clearly been a steep decline in the manufacturing of subsidiary silver coins at the Carson City Mint, but because of the new Morgan silver dollars introduced in 1878, another 1.7 million+ ounces were consumed.

Sufficient supplies of silver were still being used in 1878, albeit for different purposes. This would be the last time, however, that the Carson City Mint would use two million or more ounces of silver in a single year. Twelve years later, in 1890, would be the closest it ever came, when 2,309,041 silver dollars were minted, requiring 1,785,873 ounces.

One of the most interesting die characteristics on any U.S. coin is seen on approximately 33% of the surviving 1878-CC quarters. Running diagonally from Ms. Liberty's right elbow to her left knee is a severe die gouge. Branching off from this long raised die obtrusion are several smaller die gouge lines. In the absence of a clear explanation for this peculiarity, one might venture a guess that cancellation of this die was given a second thought. Perhaps this obverse die was given a partial whack with a sharp-edged chisel, but was spared the final blows. If the die was then set aside, maybe it was later put to use to manufacture the final month's coin output. If this is true, it indicates that there were only three obverse dies available to the Carson coiner in 1878. This is certainly feasible, since the Bureau of the Mint was more focused on the new Morgan silver dollars, and subsidiary silver coinage was being brought to a halt. Whatever the reasons are for the existence of these semi-cancelled or die-gouged 1878-CC quarters, it is the most extreme die variety on any U.S. coin. Added to the diagnostic characteristics on this variety are heavy signs of die rust, mostly at the center of Liberty's body. All three known reverse dies are *Type*

Two varieties with *Large* "CC"s, very similar to the 1877-CC quarters, one reverse die being in fact from 1877.

As with most of the other varieties of "CC" Seated Liberty coinage, there are no premiums for many of the 1878-CC varieties. In fact, on occasion, the *semi-cancelled* 1878-CC variety is viewed as a problem coin and sells at a discount; on one instance, the author submitted a specimen to a grading service and it was returned ungraded, with the explanation being "long scratch" (the misunderstanding was later corrected).

Numismatic markets can be incongruous at times. If certain die varieties in the Carson City series belonged to other U.S. coin categories they might be prized rarities. Picture if you will, an equivalent of the 1878-CC *semi-cancelled* variety being in the Overton[1] half dollar book. Even if only Rarity-3 (201-500) or Rarity-4 (81-200) interest would be intense. Currently, in the early years of the 21st century, there is no such demand for most "CC" Seated Liberty varieties. If by chance, sectors of the collector community became enamored with "CC" varieties, as for example, E.A.C.[2] members are with theirs, or *Overton* specialists and VAM[3] zealots, prices could soar. Availability of many varieties in the "CC" series would certainly be inadequate to satisfy demand.

Aside from variety collectors, Choice Uncirculated specimens of 1878-CC quarters are relatively easy to locate, but even slight growth of demand would quickly diminish supplies. This date is much scarcer than the two preceding years of Carson City quarters. As far back as the 1940s, auction catalogers suggested that 1878-CC quarters were rarer than generally realized. During the post-World War II era, and continuing into the 1950s, Uncirculated 1878-CC quarters routinely sold for $5 to $12. In 1963 the *Wolfson* specimen sold for $38 in a Stack's auction, and then in 1976 that same coin realized $525 in Bowers and Ruddy's sale of the *E.A. Carson Collection*. A lovely specimen of the *semi-cancelled* variety sold at Superior's *Boys Town* sale in May of 1990 for $5,775, at a time when Choice Uncirculated examples were selling for $1,000 or less. Price appreciation eased for high grade 1878-CC quarters through the 1990s, and as of the writing of this book (2003) they are at bargain levels.

---

[1] A. C. Overton, *Early Half Dollar, Die Varieties.*

[2] *Early American Copper Club.*

[3] Leroy Van Allen and George Mallis, *Van Allen and Mallis Silver Dollar Varieties.*

Comparison of Quarter Production at the
Carson City Mint with the
Philadelphia Mint's From 1870 to 1878

QUARTER MINTAGE TOTALS		
Year	Carson City	Philadelphia
1870	8,340	87,400
1871	10,890	119,160
1872	9,100	182,950
1873 *Without Arrows*	4,000	212,600
1873 *With Arrows*	12,462	1,271,700
1875	140,000	4,293,500
1876	4,944,000	17,817,150
1877	4,192,000	10,911,710
1878	996,000	2,260,800
TOTAL	10,316,792	37,156,970

(Photo courtesy Bowers and Merena)

A coinage law enacted by Congress in February of 1853 amended the existing laws relative to the nation's small silver coins. Henceforth, the bullion required to mint half dimes, dimes, quarters, and half dollars would only be supplied through government procurement. Private citizens were no longer allowed to deposit silver and receive small silver coins in exchange—only silver dollars were available unless the depositor chose gold coins or either silver or gold bars. All silver coinage would be credited to the Mint's account, later to be paid out in exchange for gold coins. The minimum for such exchanges was set at $100. From time to time the Director of the Mint was authorized to have silver coins transferred to regional distribution centers. A further stipulation applied to silver denominations less than the half dollar: authority was given to the Secretary of the Treasury to regulate the amount of small silver coins produced, resulting in half dollars being in a separate classification. The reasons why Congress did this are not clear; perhaps they were anticipating increased demand for the half dollar, since it was the largest subdivided denomination of a dollar.

With the price of silver bullion drifting between $1.32 to 1.35 per ounce in the early 1850s, depositors would most likely not be asking for silver dollars in exchange. At these rates, the market value of a silver dollar exceeded its face value, almost assuring lower mintages for these larger silver coins, and in turn half dollars would fill the gap in commercial channels. Even though half dollars did not qualify for free coinage as silver dollars did, they could be useful for gold exchanges that met the $100 minimum. Exportation needs were also considered, as lower supplies of silver dollars would put pressure on foreign demand for the largest silver denomination available, as millions of silver coins were transferred abroad in the decade leading up to the Civil War.

Proof of the utilitarian use of half dollars in America's monetary system can be seen in the Mint's records. From the beginning of coinage operations at the United States Mint in 1793, through the year before the opening of the Carson City Mint, half dollars reigned. The table below shows comparable mintage figures of dimes, quarters, and half dollars between 1794 and 1869.

Half dollars continued to fulfill this role until midway through 1878, at which time the Morgan silver dollar was crowned king of the heap.

In spite of the disparity in mintage totals between the half dollar and the dime and quarter, survival ratios between the three denominations are surprisingly proportional, even in the Carson City series. Before anything else is said, however, let it be understood that dimes and quarters minted at Carson City between 1870 and 1874 are without equal in terms of rarity. Nonetheless, when original mintages are considered, half dollars minted at Carson City during that same five year period are unbelievably rare. From the time the first 2,000 1870-CC halves were delivered in April of 1870 until the last delivery in 1874, a total of 862,627 had passed through the coin press. In contrast, the **combined** mintage total for dimes and quarters in the same time frame was 130,900. But as you will see, several "CC" half dollars are extremely rare, especially in Uncirculated grades.

Approximately 82.5% of all the half dollars minted at Carson City were coined during the peak production years of 1875 to 1877. Although this represents a lower percentage than the corresponding dime and quarter ratios, it provides further confirmation about the exuberant business climate. Billows of steam persistently rose from the Carson City Mint's smoke stacks during that industrious period.

Coinage of Dimes, Quarters, and Half Dollars At All U.S. Mints 1794 to 1869 (Face Value)*			
Years Covered	Dimes	Quarters	Half Dollars
1794 to 1869	$8,376,184.10	$21,727,878.00	$95,509,284.50

Annual Report of the Director of the Mint, 1900

Half dollars accounted for the lion's share of production in terms of pieces coined at Carson City during the early years. Even when trade dollars were introduced in 1873, half dollar production generated 62% of the total combined coinage output from all eight denominations. The table at right demonstrates the predominance of half dollars from 1870 to 1873.

Higher mintages meant more coins released. Half dollars could be arbitrarily delivered in exchange for gold in $100 minimum increments, whereas dimes and quarters were subject to the discretionary dictums of the Director of the Mint. Without a doubt, vastly greater numbers of Carson City half dollars circulated than did "CC" dimes and quarters, leading one to believe that "CC" half dollars are relatively common. This notion tends to be true for the 1876-CC and 1877-CC half dollars, but certainly not for the other dates in the series.

Small surviving populations of the Carson City half dollar series suggest that nearly 99% of the original mintages have been lost, as multitudes of "CC" half dollars went to the melting pots. San Francisco's half dollar production during the Carson City years far surpassed its western state neighbor's mint. It is likely that huge percentages of "CC" half dollars were transferred to San Francisco and subsequently shipped abroad. From that point on the course of these coins is unknown.

Other than several small hoards (including a 90-piece holding described later) of various dates in the "CC" half dollar series there have not been any notable findings. The possibility always exists for discoveries of previously unknown quantities, but in all likelihood, there will not be any significant increase in the population of "CC" half dollars.

ANNUAL TOTAL OF ALL COINS MINTED AT CARSON CITY COMPARED TO HALF DOLLAR PRODUCTION 1870 TO 1873			
Year	Half Dollars	All Denominations	Percentage of Half Dollars
1870	54,617	92,791	58.86%
1871	139,950	214,958	65.106%
1872	272,000	360,380	75.47588%
1873	337,060	545,882	61.746%
Totals	803,627	1,214,011	66.196%

There are nine dates in the Carson City half dollar series; one year (1873) includes two major varieties. Within this 10-coin set many die variations exist, none of which are listed in *A Guide Book of United States Coins.* Several of the die varieties are much scarcer, but normally do not bring premiums in excess of what the date would sell for sans attribution. In the case of 1870-CC through 1874-CC half dollars, the rarity of individual dates would far overshadow any subordinate attribution factors.

Regarding rank in terms of rarity in the "CC" half dollar series, the 1870-CC stands alone. Second place honors are shared by the 1874-CC and 1878-CC, followed by the 1871-CC and 1872-CC; close behind is the 1873-CC *Without Arrows.* Although the 1873-CC *With Arrows* half dollar surpasses a large percentage of other dates in the Seated Liberty series, it must settle for seventh position in its family of origin. Three so-called common dates complete the "CC" half dollar series, with the 1875-CC clearly the rarest of that trio. A complete 10-piece set of "CC" half dollars consisting of problem-free circulated coins is a rewarding achievement, and an Uncirculated set would be a very impressive feat. Several dates are nearly impossible to locate in Uncirculated, with only one 1870-CC having been certified in Mint State as of the writing of this book (2003).

BUREAU OF THE MINT DATA FOR CARSON CITY HALF DOLLAR PRODUCTION

Total Combined Mintage: 5,308,627

Total Face Value: $2,654,313.50

Total Ounces of Silver Used .... 1,919,246 ozs.

Design Type: .... Seated Liberty *With Motto*

Designers: .... Christian Gobrecht is generally given credit for being the designer;
nonetheless, all of the following men contributed in some way:
John Reich, William Kneass, Thomas Sully, Robert Ball Hughes,
James B. Longacre, Anthony Paquet, and William Barber

Metal Composition: .... .900 Silver .100 Copper

Actual Gross Weight: .... 12.442 grams

Actual Fine Silver Content: .... .361 oz. (1870 to 1873)

Actual Gross Weight: .... 12.50 grams

Actual Fine Silver Content: .... .36164 oz. (1873° to 1878)
(*After April of 1873)

Value of Silver in One Half Dollar: .... $.418-.478 (1870 to 1878)

(Photo courtesy Bowers and Merena)

Mintage: 54,617

Finest Knowns*:

    PCGS MS-62

    PCGS AU-55

Notable Pedigrees:

    Anderson-Dupont (1954)

    Empire (Cass) (1957)

    Eugene H. Gardner (1965)

      ex: Empire

    Reed Hawn (1973)

    Donald Groves (1974)

      ex: Eugene H. Gardner

    E.A. Carson (1976)

Robison (1982)

    ex: Donald Groves

James B. Pryor (1996)

    ex: Reed Hawn (1973)

David Queller (2002)

    ex: Robison, et. al.

Eugene H. Gardner (Current)

    ex: Queller, et. al.

Survival Estimates in All Grades:	125-150
Estimated in Uncirculated:	2-3
Estimated in XF to AU:	12-15
Total Certified Examples in All Grades (PCGS and NGC)*:	69

(* As of July 2003)

REFLECTIONS:

On February 10, 1870 the stars seemed to be properly aligned and Carson City was ready for the first coins ever bearing the "CC" mintmark to be delivered. These 2,303 silver dollars set in motion the timeless love affair rooted in the operations at the Carson City Mint. Two months later, the half dollar became the second silver denomination struck at that legendary institution. Ten days later, on April 20, 1870, quarters were produced, thus rounding out Carson City's inaugural year offering of silver coins. Three denominations of gold coins had also been introduced in February and March. By the end of the year, the combined mintages of the five denominations excluding half dollars totaled 38,174. On the other hand, 54,617 halves were minted at Carson City in 1870, establishing this denomination as the primary product in terms of quantity issued, a status it would maintain for the first four years.

Beginning in April 1870 the half dollar would be the only denomination produced every month, and almost without exception they were minted in round number quantities. In July, however, an odd number of 7127 pieces was coined. There is no explanation for this onetime break from conformity, but it is interesting that 27 is the number of assay coins that would have been required relative to the total mintage, this requirement being based on a minimum of one assay specimen reserved for every 2,000 coins minted.[1] There is no proven connection here, but it is an interesting coincidence.

While it might be true that dimes and quarters minted at Carson City from 1870 through 1873 were withheld from the public, half dollars were released into circulation, accounting in part for the steady flow of production and higher mintage totals for this denomination. As long as exchanges met the $100 minimum and were made in gold, depositors could request half dollars. As with all other related matters, the Director of the Mint in Philadelphia had the final say on coinage distribution. In the absence of detailed documents from the Carson City

---

[1] *Annual Report of the Director of the Mint,* Various laws.

era, it is impossible to estimate with authoritative accuracy how many 1870-CC half dollars were actually placed into circulation. Once again, the scanty original mintage—especially compared to those at the Philadelphia and San Francisco mints—begs the question of whether there was any real need for the coins in the first place. Other than for the sake of convenience to the occasional gold depositors requesting silver coins, the benefits of local coin production as opposed to having coins transferred from San Francisco are negligible. After all, the distance between the two regions was only 300 miles. There were over one million half dollars minted at San Francisco in 1870, with Carson City's output being only 5.5% of that number, limiting the substantive evidence numismatists might possess attesting to distribution scenarios. One such hint is the diminutive survival ratio, for if estimates are relatively accurate, less than 0.3% of the 1870-CC half dollars survive from the original mintage. As with many of the other Carson City dates, this suggests that very few ever saw the light of day, or that nearly all of the total mintages were exported, never to return.

Approximately 100 years after the 1870-CC half dollars were minted, numismatists estimated that no more than 40 pieces existed. In the late 1970s and early 1980s, information about a hoard double that size came to light. When the time came, numismatic researcher Randall E. Wiley confirmed the existence of a 90 coin hoard. Wiley examined this significant hoard in 1986, attributing varieties and assigning grades. No fewer than 55 pieces graded AG to VG, 23 were F to VF, and nine received the XF rating. Only three coins qualified for the highest grade in the lot, that being Almost Uncirculated (AU). During the early 1970s to early 1980s when the "CC" half dollar enthusiast assembled this momentous collection, prices gradually increased. Although it is not known what the man from Louisiana (later identified as Roy Pohler) paid for his triumphant cache, estimates place the total cost at less than $65,000. This figure is derived from the helpful breakdown of grade ratings by Wiley, and price guides from

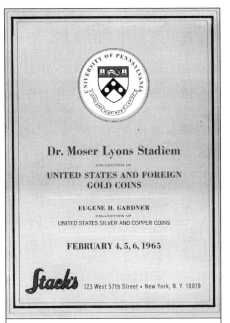

Auction catalogue from 1965 featuring Eugene Gardner's 1870-CC half dollar.

the era the collection was assembled. In the present market of the early years of the 21st century, the value of this hoard if replicated would be estimated to approach the $250,000 mark. Also worth noting is the fact that the *Louisiana Hoard* did not include an Uncirculated example.

And there is good reason for this, as Uncirculated 1870-CC half dollars are practically nonexistent. The consensus is that there are no more than three to four Uncirculated pieces extant, ranking this date in the top three based on rarity in Mint State condition. A quick scan of the most famous U.S. rare coin collections substantiates just how scarce 1870-CC half dollars are in this grade classification. During the years the *Louisiana Hoard* was being put together, only three Uncirculated specimens appeared in auctions, two of which were offered on two separate occasions, one eventually winding up in the James B. Pryor collection, commonly referred to as the *Pryor* coin. The other of these two specimens is the subject of a thrilling saga complete with a novice collector's delight of acquisition, and subsequent sacrifice on behalf of his family.

The year was 1957 and Eugene H. Gardner was a college sophomore being groomed to work in his own investment company. Young Eugene had caught the coin collecting bug while studying at Harvard and was fascinated by key dates in many U.S. coin series. In November of 1957 when Stack's auctioned the *Empire Collection* consigned by Charles Cass, Eugene Gardner traveled from Boston to New York City to participate in this sale and drool over the extensive smorgasbord of tasty numismatic morsels. He was attracted to dozens of coins in the catalog, but focused on two in particular: An 1872-CC dime in Uncirculated condition, and an 1870-CC half dollar described by Stack's as "Brilliant Uncirculated Gem. . . Just beginning to tone about the edges." There was also a note by the cataloguer that the coin had previously sold in "the Dupont sale 3 years ago."[1] Price guides at the time listed the 1870-CC half dollar in Uncirculated at $100, but collectors knew it was worth at

---

[1] Stack's, November 1957 *Empire Collection*

least twice that amount. After all, said Stack's, "it realized $200 in the Dupont sale."[1]

Gardner followed his strategy, first winning the 1872-CC dime for $260, and then 610 lots later, picking up the 1870-CC half dollar for $210. He managed to obtain several other coins in the auction and was well on his way to forming a quality collection. Eight years later, while still a young businessman in his late 20s, the vicissitudes so often encountered in life forced Gardner to sacrifice his coin collection for the sake of his growing family. His prized coins were consigned to a Stack's sale in February of 1965, which came to be referred to as the *Stadiem-Gardner* sale. Gardner scored well—his 1872-CC dime brought $540, and the 1870-CC half dollar realized $1,500, reflecting that coins from the Carson City Mint had begun to receive well-deserved recognition in the marketplace by then.

Out of all the wonderful pieces Gardner sold in that 1965 auction, perhaps the most difficult to say goodbye to was the 1870-CC half dollar. One thing was certain: his conviction that rare date "CC" coins were grossly undervalued was being proven in full measure. From a price realized of $200 in 1954 to his purchase for $210 in 1957, and now in 1965 the 1870-CC reached uncharted territory at the $1,500 level. The *Flagship* of the "CC" series at that time was the 1876-CC 20-cent piece which had already broken the $10,000 barrier. Yet this period in the last half of the 20th century would be remembered by Eugene Gardner and countless other collectors as the *Good Old Days*. Prices for "CC" mintmarked coins did not climb steadily, they skyrocketed. *Bang zoom, right to the moon Alice!* Those who missed this chance to get in the game would have to pay up later.

Well, Eugene H. Gardner did not have the opportunity to jump back in immediately following the liquidation of his collection in 1965, as he put the needs of his family first. After his children were put through school and his business began to thrive, he got out his loupe again and began seriously studying auction catalogs in the 1990s. One by one he began to pick off those key dates that he still believed so firmly in, and even though prices were much higher he resolved to buy the finest quality available. By the time the final *Eliasberg* sale rolled around in 1997, Gardner had assembled an impressive collection. He went to the *Eliasberg* auction loaded for bear, but it would take a brave trapper to snag some of the magnificent game in that sale. This auction was filled with the classic American rarities—an 1804 dollar, an 1822 quarter (in Gem Proof!), an 1885 Proof trade dollar—but for the Carson City enthusiast it was ecstasy.

Anyone so inclined could have bought every "CC" coin in the sale, but it would have cost a mansion in Beverly Hills. Bidders would need to be selective, choosing the "CC" coins they absolutely had to have, and even at that many eager participants went home empty. Eugene Gardner made sure right from the start that his trip had not been made in vain; he was the winning bidder on the fifth lot of the evening, the 1876-CC 20-cent piece in Gem condition. Gardner had to pinch himself after that one, to make sure he had really just paid $148,500! Forty years earlier in that same *Empire Collection* sale where he really got his feet wet, another 1876-CC 20-cent piece had sold for $3,800—Ah, the *Good Old Days!*

Throughout the rest of the auction record prices were being set left and right. One coin in Eliasberg's collection was somewhat of a disappointment though. In the midst of all the colossal coins was an 1870-CC half dollar in VF, not the one Gardner wanted, but it still brought $3,960 even in such a low grade—2 ½ times more than Gardner's glorious Uncirculated specimen had sold for 32 years earlier.

As the 20th century came to an end, there had been no sign of Gardner's 1870-CC half dollar since 1982, when it sold for $21,000 in Stack's *Robinson* sale. At that time Eugene had not quite finished raising his family and growing his business, but a small fire still burned in his heart for that coin. In the aftermath of the *Eliasberg* auctions and the subsequent *John J. Pittman* and *Harry Bass* sales, it was clear that truly rare coins were never going to be cheap again, a comment someone could have made in each of the past generations.

Who could have predicted what classic U.S. rarities would sell for at the dawning of the 21st century? An 1804 silver dollar had broken the $4 million barrier. Then in July of 2002 the record-shattering price of $7.6 million was paid for a 1933 $20 gold piece. Carson City coins had established themselves in their own right. Eliasberg's 1873-CC *Without Arrows* dime had sold for $550,000 in 1996, and then $632,500 in 1999. Other famous "CC" rarities like the 1873-CC *Without Arrows* quarters and 1876-CC 20-cent pieces had routinely been selling for six figures, but many dates were still finding their marks.

---

[1] Ibid.

In early autumn of 2002, Stack's sent out a catalog featuring the *Queller Family Collection*. As Eugene Gardner turned to page 178 he could hardly believe his eyes. It was as if he had just seen a long lost friend, missed, but never forgotten. There it was accompanied by a beautiful color photo–his 1870-CC half dollar–aged a little, just like Eugene, but unmistakably the ultimate coin. Gardner, as he had done so many times before, planned his strategy for the auction. There were other "CC" half dollars in the sale that he was interested in, but he would not be satisfied unless he got his 1870-CC back. Price speculating became like a competitive game of bridge–what would the finest known 1870-CC half dollar sell for in 2002? One of the other three reported Uncirculated 1870-CC half dollars, the *James B. Pryor* coin, had sold for $39,600 in January of 1996, before the *Eliasberg Collection* established new price records for dozens of coins. At the time, the *Pryor* coin was touted as the finest known of the date, but curiously, it had not been certified by one of the major grading services. Population reports for both PCGS and NGC told the tale of the date— no 1870-CC half dollars were certified in the Mint State category.

1870-CC half dollar, the *Gardner* specimen.

On the evening of October 16, 2002 Eugene Gardner was poised and waiting to get his long lost pal back. It might take double what the *Pryor* coin sold for only six years earlier; even at $80,000 it would set a new record for a "CC" half dollar. Bidding finally began and five or six other determined auction participants jumped in with Gardner. As the price reached the $80,000 mark, everyone but Gardner, another bidder, and the current author had dropped out. Soon it was just Gardner and your author, neither of whom had anticipated the other's presence. At $125,000 bidding was at a stalemate–the auctioneer called for $130,000 and Gardner nodded. Then it was $135,000 to your author who wondered, "Could this finally knock Gardner out?" The hand went up– "$135,000 on my right," said the auctioneer, "$140,000 is next, do I hear $140,000?" A pause that seemed like an hour, but was only a second and Gardner nodded again– "I have $140,000 do I hear $145,000, called the auctioneer." Several seconds passed, sweaty palms and a pounding heart, trying to contemplate the opponent's next move. Again the auctioneer called out the conditions for this match, "I have $140,000, do I hear $145,000?" It was time to accept defeat, your author shook his head no.

At the beginning of the sale, Eugene's estimate of $80,000 had seemed reasonable, and $100,000 seemed like a no-brainer victory, but nothing was going to stop Eugene H. Gardner that night. He was not just competing for another coin in his collection; he was on a mission to recover something that he had never really relinquished since he first bought it in 1957 for $210. This was an act of poetic justice, and after Gardner realized that with the buyer's fee of 15%, he had just paid $161,000, he brushed price aside and was just jubilant over his ultimate conquest. What a night!

Since that auction, PCGS has graded Gardner's 1870-CC half dollar MS-62, the only Uncirculated example graded by the major grading services. It is much nicer than that, and it will remain on the throne, crowned king of the "CC" halves until another comes along to challenge it.

One challenger of course, is the *Pryor* specimen. Although it has yet to be certified by one of the grading services, (2003) the coin is captivating. James Pryor purchased this piece out of Stack's *Halsell* sale in 1984 for $18,700. It had previously sold in Stack's *Reed Hawn* sale in 1973 for $13,500. There has been some disagreement whether the *Pryor* coin or the *Gardner* coin came out of the *Anderson-Dupont* sale in 1954. In the *Empire Collection* Stack's described the *Gardner* coin as being the *Dupont* coin, but in their *Queller Family* sale in 2002 the same company declared that, "in many ways it resembles the Dupont specimen, but we cannot be absolutely certain."[1] On the other hand, Breen stated that the *Pryor* coin was in fact the *Dupont* coin,[2] a claim refuted by Stack's.[3]

When the *Pryor* specimen sold in January of 1996, Bowers described it as, "Prooflike...perhaps possible that this was intended as a Proof or Specimen striking to mark the opening of the Carson City Mint."[4] Perhaps this coin has not been assigned a certified grade by one of the major grading services (as of 2003) because graders are uncomfortable with the hairlines on the coin, but unless some-

[1] Stack's October 2002, *The Queller Family Collection*.
[2] *Walter Breen's Complete Encyclopedia of U.S. and Colonial Coins*, 405.
[3] Stack's *Queller Family Collection*.
[4] Bowers and Merena, 1996, *James Bennett Pryor Collection*.

one has harshly altered the surfaces on this coin since the 1996 auction it deserves an Uncirculated rating. James B. Pryor was a very picky coin connoisseur who specialized in the Liberty Seated half dollar series, and when he obtained his 1870-CC half dollar in 1984 he considered it to be the cornerstone of his entire collection. Any coin purchased by Pryor, first had to pass his strict grading criteria and other collectors and dealers respected his high standards.

Besides the *Gardner* and *Pryor* specimens, a third Uncirculated 1870-CC half dollar was offered in a Bowers and Ruddy auction in 1976. This coin, which realized $3,100, was part of the *E.A. Carson Collection* of Carson City Mint coinage,[1] described as being, "Brilliant Uncirculated."[2] The cataloguer suggested that the coin might be the *Anderson-Dupont* specimen, apparently because he was not aware of the *Gardner* or *Reed Hawn* specimens. Although the *E.A. Carson* specimen possesses Uncirculated characteristics, it has been heavily cleaned, and would possibly rate MS-60 at best. Nevertheless, it is still the third finest known example of the date and deserves much respect.

Concerning die varieties for the Liberty Seated half dollar series there is no greater authority than *The Complete*

Scene on the floor of a rare coin auction.

Guide To Liberty Seated Half Dollars.[3] Three obverse and three reverse dies are listed in this *Guide* as being used for 1870-CC half dollars. Although at one time the so-called *No Drapery* variety was considered scarcer than its counterpart

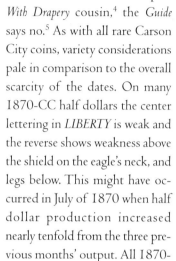

With Drapery cousin,[4] the *Guide* says no.[5] As with all rare Carson City coins, variety considerations pale in comparison to the overall scarcity of the dates. On many 1870-CC half dollars the center lettering in *LIBERTY* is weak and the reverse shows weakness above the shield on the eagle's neck, and legs below. This might have occurred in July of 1870 when half dollar production increased nearly tenfold from the three previous months' output. All 1870-CC half dollars display the *Large* "CC" mintmark, centered below where the stem and the arrow feather dissect.

This is one of the most rewarding dates in the wide spectrum of U.S. coinage to own. Well preserved, problem-free circulated examples will always command a premium.[6]

[1] Bowers and Ruddy, 1976, *Dr. Edward B. Willing Auction.*
[2] Ibid.
[3] Randy Wiley, Bill Bugert, *The Complete Guide to Liberty Seated Half Dollars.*
[4] Walter Breen , *The Complete Encyclopedia of U.S. and Colonial Coins.*
[5] Randy Wiley, Bill Bugert, *The Complete Guide to Liberty Seated Half Dollars.*
[6] One of the *Top 25.*

(Photo courtesy Bowers and Merena)

Mintage: 139,950**

Finest Knowns*:

    PCGS MS-64 (I)

    PCGS MS-62 (I)

    NGC MS-62 (I)

    NGC MS-6I (I)

    PCGS MS 60 (I)

Notable Pedigrees:

    Anderson-Dupont (1954)

    R.L. Miles (1969)

Reed Hawn (1973)

James Stack (1975)

James Pryor (1996)

    ex. Reed Hawn (1973)

Survival Estimates in All Grades:	200-300
Estimated in Uncirculated:	5-7
Estimated in XF to AU:	30-40
Total Certified Example sin All Grades (PCGS and NGC)*:	68

(* As of July 2003)

(** Some sources say 153,950)

REFLECTIONS:

One of the three rarest dates in the "CC" series, surpassed only by the 1870-CC and 1874-CC. Though not as scarce as the three other silver denominations issued in 1871 at the Carson City Mint, the 1871-CC half dollars are respected by numismatists.

In the first half of the 20th century it became evident that Uncirculated examples of this date were missing from most trophy collections. The *World's Greatest Collection* (F.C.C. Boyd) could only boast of a Fine example. Not incidentally, this same notable collection included a dime and quarter dated 1871-CC, both in breathtaking Uncirculated condition. Even the 1871-CC silver dollar in the *World's Greatest Collection* was, "a splendid example… much proof-like lustre [*sic*]."[1]

Eliasberg's 1871-CC half dollar, although described as, "MS-61/63 prooflike,"[2] had numerous hairlines from a harsh cleaning. Using the strict market grading of the early years of the 21st century it would only be assigned an AU-58 rating, still much higher quality than usually found for this date. The *Norweb Collection* featured a pleasing example of this date, but only in XF condition. Even the *Empire Collection* from whence came the finest known 1870-CC half dollar, only had a VG example. Although

the mintage for the 1871-CC half dollar had nearly tripled from the preceding year, the number of Uncirculated specimens surviving is less than that for many other recognized numismatic rarities.

Prices for 1871-CC half dollars did not rise in proportion to the rarity of the date, especially in Uncirculated grades. In the *Anderson-Dupont* sale in 1954 a beautiful Mint State example sold for $170, just minutes after one of the few known 1870-CC half dollars sold for $200. In comparison, a Choice Uncirculated 1893-S silver dollar sold for $285 and a gorgeous Proof 1895 silver dollar hit the block at $300.

In 1975, the *James Stack* 1871-CC half dollar grading Brilliant Uncirculated Gem sold for $3,800, the second highest price for the date up to that time. Two years earlier, the *Reed Hawn* specimen brought $4,000 in a 1973 Stack's sale. It was becoming accepted practice to pay several thousand dollars for some of the scarcer "CC" coins by the end of the 1970s. And of course, the 1873-CC *Without Arrows* quarter and the 1876-CC 20-cent piece were pushing the upper limits of the five figure range. In 1985 a Gem Uncirculated 1871-CC half dollar realized $8,250

---

[1] Numismatic Galleries, 1945, *The World's Greatest Collection.*

[2] Bowers and Merena, 1997, *Louis E. Eliasberg, Sr. Collection.*

at Stack's session of *Auction '85*. It would only be a matter of time until the $10,000 barrier was broken for this date, and then prices would set sail.

At the *James B. Pryor* sale in 1996, the bar was raised to new heights for 1871-CC half dollars, as the *Pryor* specimen realized $35,200. But then things stalled, more due to a lack of new high grade examples being offered than anything else. A reported private sale in the $40,000 to $45,000 range was as high as the 1871-CC half dollar would climb by the end of the 20th century.

In October of 2002, at the *Queller Family Collection* sale, an MS-63 quality 1871-CC half dollar sold for $29,900, and it would be safe to assume that if an example in Gem MS-65 condition hits the market in the first decade of the 21st century it will test the $100,000 mark. And of course, that is a big if, since there is still only one MS-64 specimen at the top of the Condition Census, with no challengers on the horizon (as of 2003).

Other than being placed into circulation, what is one of the worst things that could happen to an Uncirculated coin? Aside from receiving the usual bagmarks, PVC damage, ugly toning, etc., harsh cleaning is the kiss of death. Dozens of unsightly hairlines across the surface of an Uncirculated coin is tantamount to the hood of a brand new car being scraped with a heavy duty garden rake, but unlike a coin, the hood of a car can head for the body shop.

There seems to be a disproportionate number of 1871-CC half dollars that are technically Uncirculated coins, but display the aftereffects of improper cleanings. A portion of these altered 1871-CC half dollars have retained much of their original prooflike qualities, including razor sharp strikes and mirrored surfaces. Auction companies routinely describe these coins as Uncirculated and prooflike in their catalogs, yet the grading services typically rate them as AU-58 or AU-55, occasionally returning them ungraded due to *improper cleaning*. Some of these altered 1871-CC half dollars exist because of the one-sided Proof characteristics found on them, often tempting collectors owning heavily toned examples to remove the tarnish, hoping to uncover hidden beauty, as the mirrorlike surfaces tend to glow beneath heavy layers of toning more than frosty surfaces do. But mirrorlike surfaces are also more susceptible to hairlines when carelessly wiped, scrubbed or cleaned in any way.

DIVISION OF 28 OUNCES* OF PROOF SILVER BETWEEN FOUR DENOMINATIONS			
Denomination	Fine Silver Content	Share of Total	Possible Number of Coins Minted
Dime	.07199	7 ozs.	97.23
Quarter	.181	7 ozs.	38.67
Half Dollar	.361	7 ozs.	19.39
Silver Dollar	.773	7 ozs.	9.05
			(* Price of fine silver at $1.325 per oz.)

One of the curious things about the year 1871 at the Carson City Mint was the coiner's use of polished planchets and or dies for a small number of silver coins, including dimes, quarters, half dollars, and even a special 1871-CC silver dollar which will be discussed later. A letter sent by Carson Superintendent Abraham Curry, in August 1870, to Director of the Mint Pollock acknowledged receipt of proof silver (as well as gold). What does *proof silver* mean? One person's guess is as good as another's. Curry received this proof silver at his request in exchange for a 5 3/4 ounce gold bar he sent to the Philadelphia Mint. This was not a normal request and as far as anyone knows, was never made again by a Carson Mint superintendent.

Of course, Curry was long gone by the time the 1871 silver coins were struck and any Proof or Specimen strike coins dated 1870 are thought to have been minted as grand opening keepsakes before receiving these specially prepared planchets. But if Curry's order was fulfilled as requested, the Carson City Mint would have received approximately 28 ounces of proof silver. If this was indeed in the form of proof silver planchets, there would have been enough to produce approximately $36 to $39 face value in silver coins. Put another way, the Carson Mint could have struck approximately 390 dimes, 156 quarters, 78 half dollars, 36 silver dollars, or any combination of the four. The table above exhibits the mintage possibilities if the 28 ounces of proof silver was divided equally between the four denominations.

Since it is not clear what Curry was referring to when he wrote "proof silver," this whole exercise may be for naught, but it leaves the door open for further investigation.[1]

---

[1] For more information see Randy Wiley, Bill Bugert, *The Complete Guide to Liberty Seated Half Dollars*.

One thing is certain: prooflike coins, one-sided prooflike coins, Proof quality coins and Specimen strike coins, somehow wound up outside of the Carson City Mint bearing those very familiar "CC"s on the reverse. Whether the planchets used for these coins were part of Curry's mysterious order in 1870 or were specially prepared on location will probably never be revealed, and there is always the possibility that the coiner at Carson City polished dies on occasion—certainly when attempting to remove corrosion or other defects. There is also the evidence of exceptionally sharp strikes on certain surviving specimens, which of course only occurs when multiple blows of the coin press are made.

If being prooflike adds to the eye appeal of 1871-CC half dollars, then it is indeed important to make such distinctions. On the other hand, if such labeling is for identification purposes only, premium prices will most likely not be necessary to acquire cleaned or in any other way problem-coins even if possessing prooflike qualities.

In an entirely different manner this is also true for various die varieties of 1871-CC half dollars, for although diagnostic studies serve as useful means of identifying diverse surface characteristics, the rarity of the 1871-CC far exceeds any separate variety designation.

One of the known reverse dies used on the 1871-CC half dollar was also used on 1870-CC half dollars. At least four other reverse dies were put in service in 1871, all of which bore the *Large* "CC" mintmark. Philadelphia's engraver produced one obverse die with each number in the date spaced evenly from the others. A second obverse had wider spacing between the 8 and the 7, which moved the 7 and 1 much closer to one another. Breen referred to this as "71 about touching."[1] This obverse is seen on many 1871-CC half dollars, while the bulk of the mintage from that year has the normal spaced date similar to the one on 1870-CC half dollars.[2]

[1] *Walter Breen's Complete Encyclopedia of U.S. and Colonial Coins.*
[2] One of the *Top 25.*

(Photo courtesy Bowers and Merena)

Mintage: 272,000 ***

Finest Knowns*:

    PCGS MS-63 (5)**

    NGC MS-63 (3)**

    PCGS MS-60 (1)

Notable Pedigrees:

    Anderson-Dupont (1954)

    Terrell Collection (1973)

    James A. Stack (1975)

    James B. Pryor (1996)

    Eliasberg (1997)

    Douglas Noblet (1999)

      ex: Eliasberg

    Queller Family (2002)

Survival Estimates in All Grades:	400-500
Estimated in Uncirculated:	8-10
Estimated in XF to AU:	50-75
Total Certified Examples in All Grades (PCGS and NGC)*:	87

(* As of July 2003)

(** Some multiple resubmissions of the same coins)

(*** Some references list 257,000)

REFLECTIONS:

As early as 1893 the 1872-CC half dollar was described as scarce in numismatic writings. Augustus Heaton conceded that none of the dates in the "CC" half dollar series had mintages low enough to qualify for rare coin status but the 1870-CC, 1874-CC, and 1878-CC half dollars had already defied the numbers and dates like the 1872-CC, and both varieties of the 1873-CC were gaining respect.[1]

No one is certain when mass meltings of pre-1874 silver coins took place, but it is entirely possible that there was no rush—as is commonly believed—to send them to the furnaces after the *Coinage Act of 1873* became law. The Treasury Department stockpiled millions of dollars in silver coins during the decade of the 1870s and was much more dedicated to producing coins than to destroying them.

But still, mass meltings did occur and account in part for the smidgen of surviving dates in many categories of coins. Half dollars of course, were to the silver series what one cent pieces were to minor coinage, as there was a legitimate need for half dollars beyond any semblance of patronage between politicians and silver miners. And of course, Nevada's senators and legislators certainly welcomed the mintage of any coin capable of consuming the seemingly unending supply of bullion flowing from their supporter's mines.

Yet beneath the surface of the denomination's relationship to silver, half dollars would have been minted even if there had been no such things as *Big Bonanzas*. Commercial transactions, money changers, and foreign trade needed a coin of substance, worth less than gold coins, but of sufficient size to minimize the tedious task of counting out change in larger transactions and exchanges. Bags of 10,000 dimes, or even 4,000 quarters would have obviously been more cumbersome than bags of 2,000 half dollars when silver coins were required for deals involving higher dollar amounts. Silver dollars would have been handy too, but the bullion value of a silver dollar was almost seven cents more than the silver value in two half dollars. Besides, half dollars provided more flexibility than silver dollars, especially in transactions under $10.

So in 1872 the mints in the United States produced $866,775 in half dollars, compared to a combined total of $519,113.50 in all other small silver coinage. A surprising 36.5% of the small silver coinage came in the form of half dimes, as there was a shortage of five cent coins in the East and the Treasury had also been issuing 5¢ frac-

[1]For more background see Augustus G. Heaton *Mint Marks, A Treatise* 1893.

tional paper money to solve the problem. Remembering the comparison mentioned above concerning the quantity of silver coins required in a $1,000 transaction–imagine someone presenting 20,000 half dimes.

Of course this is exactly why the coinage law favored half dollars. None of the other small silver denominations could be used in large exchanges such as this, and small silver coinage was considered lawful legal tender only up to five dollars.

The Carson City Mint never produced half dimes, but in 1872 plenty of half dollars rattled out of that facility. Only 3,150 silver dollars were minted at Carson City in 1872, compared to 272,000 half dollars. This was way out of proportion with the silver dollar/half dollar ratio at the Philadelphia Mint, which tallied 1,106,450 silver dollars, as well as 881,550 half dollars. At San Francisco the ratio was nearer to Carson City's: 580,000 1872-S half dollars compared to 9,000 silver dollars.

There is no questioning the demand for half dollars. Look at the even distribution of this denomination between the eastern and the western United States–Philadelphia's total is just a shade more than the combined mintages of the two western mints.

Carson City's half dollars must have been transferred to San Francisco in 1872 (as they were every year they were minted), probably for foreign export. This better explains why "CC" half dollars are scarce than does the theory of mass meltings. If hundreds of thousands of half dollars were exported, it is likely they never returned. Foreign countries appreciated the versatility of half dollars and this denomination could have easily been adapted to diverse international monetary systems.

For the collector of "CC" half dollars, this virtually guarantees smaller surviving populations. It is worth noting, that a date like the 1872-CC, with a relatively high original mintage, can claim only MS-63 as the highest grade known. Yet dates from the Philadelphia Mint like 1879 through 1890, are plentiful in grades of MS-65 and above in spite of low mintages ranging from 4,400 to 12,000.

Just as with so many other rarities from the Carson City Mint, the 1872-CC half dollar is elusive in higher condition ratings, even to the most advanced collectors. For example, the *Atwater* (1946), *Neil* (1947), and *Empire* (1957) collections contained VF examples and Mr. and Mrs. Norweb owned a high end XF specimen. It should also be pointed out that not all notable coin collectors strive to obtain Condition Census quality coins in every series. Although a common trait shared by celebrated numismatists

might be assembling the most comprehensive collections possible, some target specialized series and reserve their capital for high grade purchases in those series. Ideally a collector would desire to have a Condition Census quality coin for every date in a collection, but there are limitations. Though a person would long to have Uncirculated examples of every "CC" date ever minted, time, capital, and availability will determine who the fortunate ones will be.

Two such privileged collectors were Louis E. Eliasberg, Sr. and James A. Stack; Carson City coins from these men's collections are the stuff dreams are made of. Proof of this has been seen over and over again in earlier pages of this book and it is not surprising that the 1872-CC half dollars in both of these collections are the two finest known–each is inspiring in its own way. If a person were forced into an arm wrestling contest to decide the finest of the pair, the *Stack* coin would probably win. In the catalog for the *James Stack Sale* in 1975, the auctioneer estimated that the piece was, "Well worth a bid of $1000." At the sale, it sold for three times that amount.[1]

A close look at the *Eliasberg* specimen shows why the cataloger commented, "possibly the finest known," and "A prize for the advanced specialist and connoisseur."[2] After being graded MS-63 by PCGS the *Eliasberg* specimen traded hands several times in the final years of the 20th century, and so far into the early years of the 21st century the coin has remained off the market. As it said in the *Eliasberg Collection* catalog, "Where can you find another?"[3]

Four obverse and four reverse dies have been identified as being used to coin 1872-CC half dollars. Snow-packed mountain passes in late 1871 had delayed delivery of these dies until early 1872, but once the dies arrived, production proceeded on schedule, averaging nearly 27,000 coins per month. All 1872-CC half dollars bear the *Large* "CC" mintmark, with minor shifts in position. On the *Eliasberg* specimen for instance, the right "C" is considerably lower than the left. But on the *Stack* specimen the two letters are nearly even. Some specimens exhibit sharply struck, prooflike surfaces, whereas others are seen with weakly struck lettering in *LIBERTY* and frosty surfaces. The majority of pieces are, of course, circulated, many having been harshly cleaned and/or brushed. Typical low grade examples have cuts, scratches and heavy wear. As the "CC" series increases in popularity, problem-free circulated 1872-CC's will command substantial price premiums.[4]

[1] Stack's, 1975, *James A. Stack Collection.*
[2] Bowers and Merena, *Louis E. Eliasberg Sr. Collection,* April 1997.
[3] Ibid.
[4] One of the *Top 25.*

1873-CC
Without Arrows

(Photo courtesy Bowers and Merena)

Mintage: 122,500

Finest Knowns*:

    PCGS MS-67** (1)

    PCGS MS-66** (1)

    NGC MS-67 (1)

    NGC MS-66 (1)

Notable Pedigrees:

    R.L. Miles (1969)

    Harry X. Boosell (1972)

    James A. Stack (1975)

    Garrett Collection (1979)

    James Pryor (1996)

    Douglas L. Noblet (1999)

    Waldo E. Bolen (1999)

      ex: Garrett

    Queller Family (2002)

      ex: Miles

Survival Estimates in All Grades: 300-400
Estimated in Uncirculated: 10-15
Estimated in XF to AU: 30-50
Total Certified Examples in All Grades (PCGS and NGC)*: 67

(* As of July 2003)

(** Possible resubmission of the same coin)

REFLECTIONS:

This is the only collectable date from the *Without Arrows* "CC" silver coin series. But even with that distinction there is a short supply and like so many dates from the Carson City Mint, any examples entering the market are snapped up as quickly as prime lakefront properties.

Official U.S. Mint records show that production of the 1873-CC *Without Arrows* half dollars picked up where it had left off at the end of 1872. A reported total of 22,000 pieces were minted in January of 1873, following on the heels of the 54,000 recorded for the previous month. After January, however, mintage figures become foggier.

On February 12, 1873 the Coinage Act was signed into legislation by President Grant and silver coin production ceased until the new *With Arrows* dies arrived, an interim period of two months. Why then do Mint records report that 100,500 1873-CC *Without Arrows* half dollars were coined in March? Generally the Carson City operation had minted between 10,000 and 20,000 halves per month during the two preceding years—the highest total

being 54,000 in December of 1872. This suspicious quantity of 100,500 seems out of place, especially for March, when coinage was supposed to be temporarily halted. Price guides and reference works have used this number since the 1960s to arrive at a mintage figure of 122,500 for the 1873-CC *Without Arrows* halves. However, in the 90 or so years after the date was first minted, references would simply state that it was included in the combined total of 337,060 for both varieties.

To add to the mystery, only 18,000 new *With Arrows* halves are listed as having been minted in April of 1873 after the new law went into effect. Is it possible that a portion of the 100,500 credited to March should have been listed for April's delivery, meaning there are fewer *Without Arrows* halves than previously recognized? These are unsettled questions, but what is undeniably clear is that the mintage for "CC" *Without Arrows* halves was much higher than for the corresponding dimes and quarters; as a result there are more surviving *Without Arrows* half dollars extant and a relatively handsome number of Uncirculated specimens.

Out of the approximately 10 to 15 examples in Uncirculated grades the *Garrett Collection* specimen is clearly the finest. When it was described by the cataloger in the 1979 *Garret Collection* sale—before PCGS and NGC—not only was it "just a whisper from …a full MS-70," it was "unsurpassed in condition by **any** business strike Liberty Seated half dollar." This accolade was not just relative to 1873-CC *Without Arrows* halves (or any "CC" halves for that matter), it was in reference to any date or mint the auction company had ever seen.[1] Bidders obviously agreed, as the price realized was $30,000, in an era when Choice Uncirculated examples of this date were listed at $2,000 to $2,500.

More than a decade later, after professional grading services set the standards for the industry, the *Garrett* specimen 1873-CC *Without Arrows* half was given the MS-66 grade—not an MS-70, but heading in that direction. In fact, in the early years of the 21st century this piece was resubmitted and was upgraded to MS-67. This is just one of those coins that stirs the senses. In 1999 the *Garrett* specimen sold at a public auction for $69,000 when it was still in an MS-66 holder.[2] After being upgraded to MS-67 in 2002, the coin was offered for sale in the $120,000 plus range.

Another special example of the date is the *R.L. Miles* coin, auctioned by Stack's in 1969 and described as probably "the finest known of this great rarity" as the *Garrett* specimen would not enter the scene for another decade. Still, the *Miles* specimen realized $1,200 and eventually became part of the *Queller Family Collection*, also sold by Stack's 33 years later in October of 2002. This time, the coin brought $55,000 and was subsequently graded MS-65 by PCGS.

Population reports for PCGS and NGC are a little skewed in their data for Uncirculated 1873-CC *Without Arrows* half dollars, due to the multiple resubmissions and upgrading of various examples. For example there are 16 Mint State specimens listed between the two services, but in reality there are probably 10 or fewer extant. This is not the kind of statistical error that will generally affect prices however, as known pedigrees and infrequent auction appearances provide numismatists with more accurate population data for coins like this.

Every 1873-CC *Without Arrows* half dollar was struck using a redesigned reverse die with a *Small* "CC" mintmark, as described by Breen in his *Encyclopedia* as the "smallest roundish 'CC'."[3] Both letters are level with the other, and form a neat compact hallmark of the coin's origin. The numerals in the date are uniform and tightly spaced with a *Closed* 3 at the end. Many higher grade specimens exhibit random raised die lines which appear to be a trademark of Seated Liberty coinage from the Carson City Mint.

Fortunately for collectors there are occasional opportunities to obtain circulated examples of this date, however problem-free circulated pieces will always command premiums. Since the other two *Without Arrows* 1873-CC denominations are prohibitively scarce, the half dollar is a popular option to own a memento from this historic time in the nation's coinage.[4]

---

[1] Bowers and Ruddy, *The Garrett Collection Sale I*, November 1979
[2] Heritage Numismatic Auctions, *CSNS Sale — Waldo E. Bolen, Jr. Collection.*
[3] *Walter Breen's Complete Encyclopedia of U.S. and Colonial Coins.*
[4] One of the *Top 25.*

One of the finest known specimens of an 1873-CC *Without Arrows* half dollar.

1873-CC

With Arrows

(Photo courtesy Bowers and Merena)

Mintage: 214,560

Finest Knowns*:

    NGC MS-66 (1)

    NGC MS-65 (2)

    PCGS MS-65 (1)

Notable Pedigrees:

    Anderson-Dupont (1954)

    Baldenhofer (1955)

      ex: Dupont

    Empire Collection (1957)

    E.A. Carson (1976)

James B. Pryor (1996)

Eliasberg (1997)

John Jay Pittman (1998)

Waldo E. Bolen, Jr. (1999)

Survival Estimates in All Grades:	500-700
Estimated in Uncirculated:	20-25
Estimated in XF to AU:	70-100
Total Certified Examples in All Grades (PCGS and NGC)*:	144

(* As of July 2003)

REFLECTIONS:

From a collector's standpoint, 1873-CC *With Arrows* half dollars offer a relatively affordable opportunity to own a "CC" variety from a pivotal year. Since the only other date of the *With Arrows* "CC" half dollars (1874) is much scarcer, the 1873-CC fits thriftily into a Carson City type set (thriftily being a relative term of course).

Issued as a result of the Coinage Act from the same year, 1873-CC *With Arrows* halves were first introduced in April of 1873. No coins were minted in May, and then 98,000 pieces were delivered by the Carson coiner in June, nearly equal to the 100,500 supposed *Without Arrows* halves minted in March. In truth, it seems a little odd that approximately 71% of the total output for 1873 was produced half way through the year. Yet the reason for this is found in the introduction of trade dollars, as beginning in July of 1873, these "beautiful and massive coins" —as described by the *Carson Daily Appeal*[1]— absorbed much of the silver being deposited at the Carson City Mint, as well as a proportionate amount of the labor force.

Across the country, the nation's mints doubled half dollar production from the previous year while simulta-

neously sharply increasing in the quantities of dimes and quarters being struck. For silver dollar sized coins, trade dollars virtually swapped places with the outgoing standard silver dollars, all of these activities were directly related to the passing of the Coinage Act.

Arrowheads placed at either side of the date on the half dollars alerted the public that the amount of silver in each coin had been increased. To illustrate the significance (or insignificance) of this increase, two half dollars now had .0045 of one cent more silver. In other words a $1,000 face value bag of half dollars contained $4.47 more silver than before. An additional 3 1/3 ounces of silver were now required to produce 2,000 half dollars. Someone probably benefited from all of this, but it was not readily apparent who.

At the Carson City Mint in 1873, half dollar production increased by only 23% from 1872's total and surprisingly, the output at the San Francisco Mint was cut in half during this same period. Philadelphia as usual was responsible for the lion's share of half dollar mintages. When San Francisco was informed of the new coinage

---

[1] *Carson Daily Appeal*, April 3, 1873

laws, only 5,000 1873-S *Without Arrows* half dollars had been struck. This date is unknown in any collection.

Carson City employees used four different obverse dies and two reverse dies to coin *With Arrows* halves in 1873. One reverse die had the *Small* "CC" mintmark punched into it, and the other reverse die used a *Large* "CC" mintmark similar to the one seen on the 1870 to 1872-CC halves.

In Wiley and Bugert's book, mention is made of the *Orlando* hoard containing 230 1873-CC *With Arrows* halves, split evenly between *Large* and *Small* mintmarks.[1] Four coins in the hoard are said to have rotated reverses of 20% or more. The existence of hoards such as these, and the *Louisiana* 1870-CC halves account for substantial percentages of surviving populations.

One of the foremost numismatists of the 20th century was John J. Pittman. When his collection was auctioned on three separate occasions, the total prices realized was over $28 million. Mr. Pittman concentrated on rare Proof coins from the 19th century, patterns, early type, and all facets of American and world numismatic treasures. His want list was the *Guide Book of United States Coins (Red Book)*, and if it was listed in its pages, Pittman wanted it. Although not a specialist in Carson City coinage, he obtained as many fine "CC" pieces as he could. Among the many highlights in his collection from the Nevada mint was a splendid example of an 1873-CC *With Arrows* half dollar. In the description, the cataloguer noted that Pittman had purchased this coin in a 1940s auction for $22.50. Like most of the delights in Pittman's collection this "CC" half had appreciated over the years; the winning bidder paid $38,500 to own it. Later on, the coin was graded MS-65 by NGC.[2] When great collections are sold, Carson City coins are usually well represented.

---

[1] Wiley and Bugert, *The Complete Guide to Liberty Seated Half Dollars.*
[2] David Akers Numismatics, *John Jay Pittman Collection Part II,* May 20-21, 1998.

1874-CC

(Photo courtesy Bowers and Merena)

Mintage: 59,000

Finest Knowns*:

    PCGS MS-66 (I) **

    PCGS MS-65 (I) **

    NGC MS-64 (2)

    PCGS MS-64 (I)

    PCGS MS-63 (I)

    NGC MS-63 (5)

Notable Pedigrees:

    World's Greatest Collection (1945)

    Atwater (1946)

    Anderson-Dupont (1954)

    R.L. Miles (1969)

    Reed Hawn (1973)

    Norweb (1988)

    RARCOA Auction '90 (1990)

    James B. Pryor (1996)

      ex: Norweb

    Eliasberg (1997)

    Noblet (1999)

    Queller Collection (2002)

Survival Estimates in All Grades:	100-125
Estimated in Uncirculated:	9-15
Estimated in XF to AU:	21-30
Total Certified Examples in All Grades (PCGS and NGC)*:	66

(* As of July 2003)

(** The PCGS MS-65 AND PCGS MS-66 listings are possibly for the same coin.)

REFLECTIONS:

One of the most popular spots at the Carson City Mint in the 1870s was located just inside the front entrance on the right, where depositors received payment for bullion they had dropped off. A sign on the wall identified it as the *Paying Teller's Office.*

Directly behind the teller's office was another room where the coining press produced the mint's primary product. Hour after hour, day after day, the constant banging and clanging of coins being struck was heard, further jingling came from the sound of the virgin metal discs rattling into bins at which time employees inspected, inventoried, and then stored them in vaults located in the basement. A sufficient quantity of coins, cash, and certificates of deposit were at hand in a smaller vault in the paying teller's office.

All aspects of the Carson Mint's operations were lifted to a new level in 1874 when production, as measured by face value, increased over 400%, with gold coins and trade dollars accounting for most of this rise. For some reason, dime and half dollar production actually decreased during this upturn and there were no quarters minted in 1874 at Carson City, with 20-cent pieces still a year off.

Only two obverse dies and one reverse die were in service to manufacture 1874-CC half dollars, indicating that low mintages had been projected. In light of a tenfold increase in trade dollar production, all other silver coinage was kept at a minimum.

At the time, only one press occupied the coining room; the following year a second coin press would be added at the behest of new superintendent James Crawford. Frank D. Hetrich, Crawford's predecessor, had supervised the installation of new refinery equipment before leaving office, which combined with added personnel facilitated the boost in production beginning in 1874.

During the minting process the coiner and his staff could have looked out the window facing north in the direction of the V&T depot where the bullion necessary to mint coins arrived on a continual basis. A loud screech and a jet of steam announced that the train was back in town. Approximately 90 tons of silver and five tons of gold were transported to the Carson City Mint in 1874, a portion of this mass of metal was returned to depositors in the form of unparted bars, but a larger share was turned into parted bars and, to a lesser extent, coins.

Comstock miners were in the early stage of a six-year bull run later immortalized as the *Big Bonanza.* Annual production had already risen from $8 million in 1870 to over $22 million in 1874. In spite of this, bullion deposits at the Carson City Mint, though sufficient to maintain full workloads, were not keeping pace.

For instance, in 1874, although the mines grossed over $22 million in bullion product, only 22% went to the local mint, half of which was reserved for trade dollars.

By 1878, one of the peak years on the Comstock, this percentage had dropped to 8.75%, as only $3.185 million in bullion was deposited locally out of the $36.5 million brought forth from the ground. Director of the Mint Linderman and his successors attributed Carson City's mediocre record of securing depositors to the fact that it was more expedient and cost effective to ship bullion to San Francisco. As usual, employees at the Carson City facility were grateful just to be working and as far as they were concerned a 400% increase in production was a positive sign.

None of this would have been possible without the tenacious spirit of Abe Curry, displayed a decade earlier. But Curry was gone now, having died in October of 1873. Since he did not have a male heir to extend his lineage, Curry's tradition would be passed on by his wife and daughters, one of whom, Lucy Ann, married the Carson Mint's Assayer Frank Hetrich in April of 1872. One month later, Hetrich was appointed mint superintendent and held that position for two years. His tenure, though short, ran concurrent with decisive events in the Carson Mint's history.

These were the *With Arrows* coinage years and more significantly, the inaugural years of the trade dollars. Hetrich had been part of Curry's team during the first year of operations in 1870, and was at the helm just when the *Big Bonanza* period sounded its wake-up call. From those humble beginnings in 1870 when annual production had been a meager $215,090, Hetrich was there in 1874 to witness output rise to $4 million. Like everyone directly involved with the Carson City Mint from those early years, Hetrich certainly had many stories to share: the mint was only five years old in 1874 and Nevada itself had been a state for only 10 years. So much history had been packed into this short period: long telegrams, trips back and forth between Nevada and Washington D.C., congressional debates over statehood and the merits of a branch mint, jealousies, animosities and backbiting amongst fellow Nevadans, coinage acts, *Crimes of '73*, railroads, Capitol buildings, and two-letter mintmarks.

In the early years of the 21st century many of these stories are revived and relived almost daily, at the Nevada State Museum located in the old Carson City Mint building. Visitors are welcomed at the former paying teller's office, where a friendly receptionist gives directions for the tour. Now instead of paying depositors, the staff member sells admission tickets and passes out souvenir programs. In the room once occupied by coining presses, visitors are seated in a mini-theater to watch a 20 minute documentary. Sitting in the same room where some of the rarest and most historical coins were minted is an exhilarating experience. After watching a short film, visitors can turn around facing north, and look out the window in the direction of the old V&T depot; the trains and station are gone and a lodge building rests on the site, so now individuals must rely on their imaginations.

An active imagination is an essential trait common to many coin collectors which allows them to picture what times were like when a coin was minted, how many collectors have previously owned a certain coin, what a coin looked like before it became tarnished, or before someone carelessly cleaned it. They can imagine discovering a new variety, what it would be like to own a one of a kind, the joy of completing a set and maybe ranking number one in a Registry category (PCGS Registry Sets). They can also imagine buying coins 60 years ago when prices seemed so cheap and then look ahead 20 years when coins might be worth much more than they are now. And Carson City collectors can dream about finding a Gem Uncirculated 1874-CC half dollar.

1874 was the last year of the short run *With Arrows* coinage, as the Treasury assumed everyone had gotten the idea. You could say that the silver content in half dollars had increased, just like you could say that one of the whiskers in Senator William Stewart's beard was too long. Anyone who considered this additional .00169 of an ounce to be an increase might just have been a candidate for an accountant position at *Ebenezer Scrooge & Company*. Examining it from another angle, the additional silver in the *With Arrows* halves added up to 3 ⅓ ounces for every 2,000 coins, equal to $4.47 more than 2,000 of the previous *Without Arrows* halves would have been worth in bullion value, based on current silver market prices at the time. Actually, this is not entirely true as there was a five cent drop in the price of silver from the time the Coinage Act was passed to the last half of 1874, striking a chord about *the best laid plans of mice and men*. Ironically, if the Bureau of the Mint had so chosen, the older lighter weight planchets could have been used for the *With Arrows* coinage, as they were technically within the weight variances allowed by the law.

At the Carson City Mint in 1874 the only two small silver coins manufactured were dimes

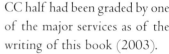
Stunning 1874-CC half dollar.

and halves, both being extremely rare. Estimates at the beginning of this section suggest that between 100 and 125 1874-CC halves exist in all grades. Heaton acknowledged in 1893 that this was the second scarcest date in the "CC" series, trailing only the 1870.[1]

Choice to Gem Uncirculated specimens are prohibitively scarce, with the *Eliasberg* specimen possibly being the only example that deserves a Gem rating. Conservatively graded in the auction catalog as MS-63/64, the cataloger still suggested that it might be the finest known. Purchased by Louis E. Eliasberg, Sr. in 1942 as part of the *Clapp Collection*, this stunning beauty realized $60,500 at the 1997 Bowers and Merena Sale. It was subsequently graded MS-65 by PCGS, and is the no-question leading candidate for *finest known* honors. In 2003, an 1874-CC half was listed in the *PCGS Population Report* as being graded MS-66 which might very well be the *Eliasberg* specimen.

Several other examples of this date deserve worthy mention, including the *Anderson-Dupont* coin, previously purchased in 1908 from dealer Henry Chapman and sold at the *Dupont Sale* in 1954 for $150. By the turn of the 21st century this coin would probably sell for $30,000 or more. Another notable specimen was offered as part of the great *Norweb Collection* of coins in 1988, where the cataloguer called it "MS-60 to MS-63 prooflike ...perhaps made as a presentation piece."[2] The winning bidder paid $5,060 and eight years later, in January 1996, it realized $15,400 as part of the *James B. Pryor Collection*, described

as a solid "MS-63...Prooflike." A comment by the cataloguer confirmed the ever-increasing demand for rare "CC" coins, "Once sold, an offer of twice the price realized probably could not secure a duplicate the morning after the sale."[3] Statements such as these are difficult to prove, simply because once coins like this are purchased they tend to stay off the market for extended periods of time; collectors for high grade "CC" rarities sometimes wait a decade or more for the right coin to come around. It is not known whether the *Norweb* 1874-CC half had been graded by one of the major services as of the writing of this book (2003).

One deterrent to some scarce "CC" coins being certified by major grading services is previous cleanings. On many occasions, when these "CC" coins retain moderate amounts of toning PCGS and NGC have generously overlooked hidden hair lines and scattered bagmarks, especially on prooflike specimens where raised die polishing lines and hairlines from previous dippings blend together. Under layers of multicolored patina (toning), these mint-made and man-made lines generally do not detract as much from the eye appeal. But often when the patina is wiped away, the hairlines can jump out at you. Grading services tend to be more conservative when alterations to the original surfaces of a coin are visible to the naked eye. Prior to the advent of professional grading services in the 1980s, collectors and dealers alike, tended to be more aggressive—and frivolous—in their attempts to enhance the appearance of coins, frequently stripping the color off until the bright shiny surface appeared. In the modern era (early years of the 21st century), these *makeovers* from the past often result in coins being returned from the grading services in *body bags* (vinyl flips) instead of plastic slabs, accompanied by a tag saying *cleaned* or *altered surfaces*. Many previously captivating coins have been victims of carelessness (or ignorance) such as this.

Although the combined population of Uncirculated 1874-CC halves listed by PCGS and NGC is 14, the actual figure may be 50% of that amount. As usual, the reason for this is multiple submissions of the same coin,

---

[1] Augustus G. Heaton, *Mint Marks, A Treatise, 1893*.
[2] Bowers and Merena, *Norweb Collection*, November 1988.
[3] Bowers and Merena, *James Bennett Pryor Collection*, January 1996.

as the practice of seeking upgrades has at times turned into sport. If a coin is submitted in its original holder and is subsequently raised a point, the grading service will delete the former grade from their population database and update it with the new one. But when individuals break coins out of holders and resubmit them without sending the grade certificate, the services will keep adding to their databases without the corresponding deletions.

Two grade levels that seem suspect for the 1874-CC halves are found in NGC's MS-63 column, and PCGS's MS-62 listing, where there is a combined total of eight coins between the two. In truth, it is more probable that the total might be closer to three to four.

Another submission stratagem tending to skew population data is sending the same coin to both grading services; one of the most obvious examples of this is the 1873-CC *Without Arrows* dime. Everyone (or almost everyone) knows there is only one specimen of this famous U.S. classic, yet NGC lists an MS-65 in their report, and PCGS, until July of 2003, claimed it in their report as an MS-64. Fortunately, PCGS relinquished control of the listing for this coin as it cannot be cut in half!

Returning to the 1874-CC half, although it is possible there are 14 certified examples in the Uncirculated range as the population reports suggest, logic, auction appearances and gut feeling say no. Even if this total was accurate it does not come close to meeting demand. For it is safe to say, that small crowds are waiting on the sidelines for every high grade specimen that enters the market.

Circulated examples are in just as high demand, if not higher. Problem-free circulated pieces will probably command significant premiums for years ahead, as auction appearances for this date in any grade are infrequent; there have been years when not a single specimen was offered. Although the 1874-CC half dollar has been considered a rare date since the 1890s, it is still very underrated, and as the popularity of the "CC" series increases as a whole, so will prices for this date.

Variety collectors derive much enjoyment from examining examples of this date; for although there were only two obverse dies and one reverse die used, 1874-CC halves offer a mini-lesson in diagnostic study. One of the most striking characteristics is the position of the arrowheads beside the date. Instead of projecting on a horizontal line, each arrow slants upward at slightly more than a 5° angle. Another dramatic effect found on some specimens is numerous raised die lines and mounds of metal no bigger than pinheads. One string of vertical lines cuts directly across the second *T* in *STATES*.

If readers are interested in the study of varieties, a good reference to use for further exploration is *The Complete Guide to Liberty Seated Half Dollars*.[1/2]

---

[1] Wiley and Bugert, *The Complete Guide to Liberty Seated Half Dollars*.
[2] One of the *Top 25*.

1875-CC

(Photo courtesy Bowers and Merena)

Mintage: 1,008,000

Finest Knowns*:

    PCGS MS-66 (1)

    NGC MS-66 (1)

    PCGS MS-65 (2)

    NGC MS-65 (1)

Notable Pedigrees:

    Reed Hawn (1973)

    James A. Stack (1975)

    E.A. Carson (1976)

| Survival Estimates in All Grades: ...... 1,500-3,000 |
| Estimated in Uncirculated: .... 80-100 |
| Estimated in XF to AU: .... 200-300 |
| Total Certified Examples in All Grades (PCGS and NGC)*: .... 153 |

(* As of July 2003)

REFLECTIONS:

Silver dimes, quarters and half dollars were minted without arrows for the first time since 1873 as coin production in 1875 reached the highest level in the history of the United States. Nothing even approaching this output had been seen since before the Civil War, but Treasury officials were convinced that an abundance of new coins was the solution to many of the nation's financial woes.

Half dollars had always been the stalwart coins in the country's monetary system, and in 1875 they again led the way. In 1874, 2.8 million halves were produced at the country's three mints and in 1875, more than 10 million were delivered, with the Carson City Mint supplying 10% of that number.

Compared to the Carson City Mint's output in 1874, 1875-CC half dollar production skyrocketed over 1700%. In fact, there were more halves manufactured in Carson City in 1875 than that mint had produced in the five preceding years combined. Superintendent Crawford managed to gain approval for an appropriation of funds to purchase an auxiliary coin press and with two coin presses, an expanded staff, and around the clock work-shifts, Carson Mint employees nearly kept pace with demand.

Comstock mines continued their growth with production rising 18% from 1874's output. Yet, the Carson City Mint only received 12.5% of this increase as the largest portion was shipped to San Francisco. It was still a great year in the history of the Carson City Mint, with the new 20-cent pieces, millions of coins, and a take-charge superintendent.

One of Superintendent Crawford's tasks during the final months of 1874 and the early months of 1875 was conferring with his coiner to decide how many coin dies would be needed to ensure there would be a sufficient supply on hand. Of course trade dollars would require plenty of backups, and dimes as well, as between these two denominations more than 6.2 million pieces were coined—over 81% of the combined total for all eight denominations.

At least nine obverse dies and six reverse dies have been identified as being utilized to manufacture 1875-CC half dollars. A new mintmark was introduced that was midsized between the *Small* and *Large* "CC"s, today known as the *Medium* "CC". In 1893, Augustus Heaton wrote the following about the mintmarks on 1875-CC halves: "The first variety has small upright CCs, but widely separated... The second shows the very small rounded close mintmark placed as before."[1] Breen also described the mintmark on 1875-CC halves as a "small roundish CC."[2] He also refers to a *Large* "CC" mintmark for the date that is the precise measurement (.042 inches) of the ones seen on the 1871-CC, 1873-CC *With Arrows*, and 1876-CC halves. In Wiley and Bugert's book, the *Medium* "CC" is the only mintmark listed, with two variations.[3] From personal inspections and auction photographs, it appears that the *Medium* "CC"'s are the general rule for 1875-CC halves.

Surfaces on Uncirculated specimens are generally frosted and satiny and there is a noticeable absence of prooflike specimens as seen on several other dates in the "CC" series. Portraits and devices are, as a rule, sharply struck, with virtually no signs of weakness. Occasional traces of die rust are seen on random examples, as well as raised lines and die cracks. An interesting story about an 1875-CC half with multiple clash marks is told by Weimar White in the *Gobrecht Journal Collective Volume #4.*

Though not classified as one of the rarities in the Carson City series, the 1875-CC half is much scarcer than the date's mintage would suggest. If survival estimates are in the ballpark, less than 0.2% of the original mintage still exists. Once again, minuscule survival ratios like this in the Liberty Seated half dollar series are probably due to exportations and, to a lesser degree, mass meltings. Choice to Gem Uncirculated examples of this date are very elusive. In fact, the only Liberty Seated half minted between 1875 and 1891 that is rarer in MS-65 is the classic 1878-S. Only two MS-65s and one MS-66 1875-CC

1875-CC half dollar in near Gem condition. (*Courtesy of Weimar White*)

halves have been graded by PCGS (through 2003), and one in each of these grades at NGC, less than even the 1878-CC.

Premiums above the more common date "CC" halves were not paid for Uncirculated 1875-CCs until the late 1950s. In a Stack's sale in April of 1957 a reported "record" price of $16 was paid for a Brilliant Uncirculated example. At the *Empire Collection* sale in November of 1957, a Gem Uncirculated specimen shattered the $20 barrier, realizing $22. By 1969 this date had ascended the $100 barrier as the *Miles* specimen sold for $120, this compared to a Brilliant Uncirculated 1876-CC half in the same sale, which brought $37.50. When the *E.A. Carson* specimen sold in 1976 it realized $650, but it would not be until 1994 that an 1875-CC half would reach the mid-four figure mark at a Heritage auction where the price realized was $6,215.

Without a doubt, the 1875-CC half is one of the most underrated of all dates from the treasury of coins from the Carson City Mint. Choice to Gem Uncirculated examples will eventually reach a price resistance level, but this appears to be quite far in the future (As of 2003). And, as prices begin to rise for the relatively small surviving population of Uncirculated specimens, attractive XF and AU pieces will be in greater demand. As with many Carson City coins, the slightest increase in collector activity reveals how empty the barns holding existing inventory are. It is no wonder that the record auction price for Uncirculated 1875-CC halves rose from $16 in 1957, to $120 in 1969, to $650 in 1976, to $6,215 in 1994; and then beyond?

---

[1] Augustus G. Heaton, *Mint Marks, A Treatise*, 1893.
[2] *Walter Breen's Complete Encyclopedia of U.S. and Colonial Coins.*
[3] Wiley and Bugert, *The Complete Guide to Liberty Seated Half Dollars.*

1876-CC

(Photo courtesy Bowers and Merena)

Mintage: 1,956,000

Finest Knowns*:

NGC MS-68 (1)

NGC MS-67 (1)

PCGS MS-66 (4)

NGC MS-66 (2)

Notable Pedigrees:

Various

Survival Estimates in All Grades: 3,000-5,000
Estimated in Uncirculated: 200-300
Estimated in XF to AU: 250-500
Total Certified Examples in All Grades (PCGS and NGC)*: 197

(* As of July 2003)

REFLECTIONS:

No one had been quite sure how much silver coinage the U.S. Mint system was capable of producing in a single year. Then in 1876 the gates opened wide and a mass of silver coins, the likes of which had never been seen, filled the Treasury's vaults. Superintendents from the three coinage mints hastened to manufacture as many coins as their employees and equipment were capable of producing. Having achieved record levels in 1875 when silver coinage crossed the $15 million mark, the Bureau of the Mint shattered the $24 million barrier in 1876.

Carson City and the nearby Comstock mines were major players in the hell-bent-to-leather dash to deliver wagonloads of new coins. It was another record-setting year on the Comstock, with gross deposits of over $34 million and this time, the Carson City Mint received 24% of the mine-owner's mineral ore, the highest percentage since 1873. A large share of the bullion deposits were turned into coins, resulting in the highest annual output in the Carson Mint's history.

More than $3.5 million in face value of the $6.4 million produced at Carson City were silver coins, nearly 15% of the total from all three U.S. mints. Once again, half dollars were plentiful as almost two million were minted, the highest total ever at the Carson City Mint. None of this would have been possible if Superintendent Crawford had not been able to secure a third coin press in mid-1876.

This would be the last coin press that the Carson Mint would receive, which was just as well, since space was getting a little cramped inside the building by then.

While America celebrated the centennial year in many ways, employees at the Carson City Mint commemorated the grand anniversary by striking a small quantity of Proof-quality specimen coins. As far as is known, none of these special coins were considered official Proof strikings, as only the Philadelphia Mint was authorized to issue such pieces. But there is no doubt about the prooflike characteristics of certain 1876-CC coins, including several 1876-CC half dollars. In fact, one such example is accompanied by a letter of authentication (or blessing) from Walter Breen attesting its Proof status. When this coin appeared in Stack's *Floyd T. Starr* sale in January of 1993 it was catalogued as "Brilliant Proof."[1]

To date, neither major professional grading service (PCGS or NGC) has agreed with this designation, perhaps reluctant because official mint records do not confirm the existence of branch mint Proofs for this date. Of course, this does not mean that coins appearing to be Proofs are not Proofs; it only means that prices will not be commensurate with the rarity of the coins in this unconventional category. Apparently the letter from Breen did not convince bidders at the *Starr Sale* that the 1876-CC half was a Proof, as the price realized was only $6,500,

[1] Stack's, *Floyd T. Starr Estate,* January, 1993.

at the time a fraction of what a Proof specimen would have brought. If PCGS or NGC certified an example in Proof or Specimen strike condition, bidding competition would probably drive the price to the same level as 1876-CC dimes with similar grade designations (in 2003, approximately $50,000).

One of the most captivating 1876-CC half dollars is the *Eliasberg* specimen, which sold for $25,300 at the memorable Bowers and Merena auction in April of 1997. It was catalogued as an MS-66, but NGC subsequently graded it MS-68 after the sale. The obverse is fully prooflike and the reverse is frosted and satiny. Probably an early die state specimen, the coin is sharply struck with numerous raised lines crisscrossing the fields. A series of die cracks connecting several digits and also extending around the periphery through the stars adds to the allure. This breathtaking beauty traded hands privately in the upper five figures in 1997, and then appeared in a *Coin World* advertisement at the end of that decade for $49,500.

To provide for the huge increase in production in 1876, the superintendent at the Carson Mint ordered a greater number of dies than for any other year in this mint's coinage operations. As many as 30 obverse dies and 18 reverse dies for half dollars were shipped, in addition to an unknown quantity of reverse dies which remained in house from previous years. A close estimate of the number of dies actually

Examples of Small, Medium, and Large "CC" mintmarks on half dollars.

used appears in Wiley and Bugert's book,[1] recommended reading for collectors seeking to explore die varieties, rarity rankings, and other useful information concerning Liberty Seated half dollars. These authors suggest that approximately 20 different obverse and 20 different reverse dies were employed to strike 1876-CC half dollars. From this combination, approximately 25 die marriages have been confirmed. Given the mintage figure for 1876, the number of coins struck from each die pairing averaged between 80,000 and 85,000, far exceeding the typical average for the Carson Mint up to that time.

All 1876-CC half dollar reverse dies are referred to as Type I's on which the berry on the branch above the *H* has a groove down the center. Breen reported that there were also Type II reverses known for this date, on which the berry was not split.

There is debate concerning this, but regardless of the debate, none of the varieties of the 1876-CC half commands a premium.

Also fascinating are the three sizes of mintmarks that are available which, just like soft drinks at a restaurant come in *Small, Medium,* and *Large.* Reverse dies with the *Large* "CC"s were left over from 1871, thus providing one of the commonalities so often shared between staggered dates from the Carson City Mint.

---

[1] Wiley and Bugert, *The Complete Guide to Liberty Seated Half Dollars.*

(Photo courtesy Bowers and Merena)

Mintage: 1,420,000

Finest Knowns*:

    NGC MS-68 (1)

    PCGS MS-67 (1)**

    NGC MS-67 (2)**

    PCGS MS-66 (2)**

    NGC MS-66 (4)

Notable Pedigrees:

    Various

Survival Estimates in All Grades: ...	7,000-10,000
Estimated in Uncirculated:	450-750
Estimated in XF to AU:	1,000-1,500
Total Certified Examples in All Grades (PCGS and NGC)*:	263

(* As of July 2003)
(** Possibly one of the coins listed has been resubmitted
or crossed over and is counted twice)

REFLECTIONS:

Pausing briefly to take a deep breath after the record year of 1876, Carson City Mint employees fired up the engines and rushed into another banner year in 1877.

Demands were heavy and workloads were strenuous, but as usual the faithful at the Carson Mint were grateful for the success of their operation. Elsewhere coin production was just as brisk and the San Francisco Mint achieved record levels for quarters, half dollars and trade dollars. Reliable as ever, the Philadelphia Mint maintained peak production levels and combined, the three coinage mints reached another milestone in silver coin output in 1877, passing the $28 million mark for the first time.

Though not matching 1876's output, the Carson City Mint still delivered over $3 million in silver coins, although gold coin production dropped sharply. Yet it was another record year on the Comstock, as miners brought forth nearly $35 million in bullion. A significant decline in the percentage of bullion being deposited at the local mint seemed like a precursor of things to come, as only 15.5% was sent to the Carson Mint, compared to 24% in 1876.

When production began on 1877-CC half dollars it appeared as if 1876's record number would be toppled. For the first 10 months of the year the Carson Mint was on a pace to surpass the previous year's total, but then

Secretary of the Treasury Sherman prepared the nation's mint system for a slowdown.

At Carson City, Superintendent Crawford and his coiner William S. Doane utilized at least 15 die pairings for half dollars. There were probably another 10 obverse dies available to them, but with the slowdown at the end of the year these were not needed. Experience gained from the previous two years of peak production taught the Carson coiner how to maximize output with each set of dies, averaging nearly 95,000 coins per each pairing.

Both Type I and Type II reverses were used on 1877-CC halves, with *Small* and *Medium* mintmarks. Breen lists six specific varieties of this date, although Wiley and Bugert disagree with his "smallest cc" with a Type II die. One of the most dramatic varieties displays recut *7s* in the date. Numerous prooflike specimens are known to exist, a characteristic shared with many dates from the Carson Mint.

At least two examples possess attributes of branch mint Proofs or Specimen strikes, one of which was featured in a Stack's auction in May of 1993 as part of a consecutive three-lot set that Stack's described as an "Incredible Trio of 1877 Carson City Silver Coins."[1] Each coin was fully prooflike with a razor sharp strike. After

---

[1] Stack's, *Public Auction Sale*, May 1993.

the dime and quarter were bought back by the consignor it was the half dollar's turn. Everyone in attendance agreed that it was head and shoulders above the two smaller denomination coins, yet just like the dime and quarter, the date was the most common in the "CC" series. In Stack's opinion, "This remarkable coin presents the most reflective glass-mirror fields imaginable." It was obvious that the auction company would not have had a problem calling the coin a Proof, but the only problem was that, "Breen's listing of Branch Mint Proofs included no 1877-CC [halves]." Still not willing to concede, the cataloguer appealed for at least *presentation piece* status, arguing that, "obvious care [had been] taken in preparing a special polished planchet and [also] striking this coin." [1] None of this polished prose helped convince bidders however, and the coin was also bought back by the consignor.

One of the finest known 1877-CC half dollars. (*Weimar White pedigree*)

Though NGC was not willing to designate this 1877-CC half as a Proof, they did grade it MS-67 with a *STAR* for excellence. If at some point in the future, one of the major grading services awards this coin Proof or Specimen strike honors, expect a substantial leap in price.

In order for a coin to be minted with prooflike qualities, the coiner is faced with the further task of preparing a treated planchet and then applying increased pressure when striking it. During peak production periods this would be counterproductive, as operations needed to proceed at a rapid pace with no dalliance. Everyone at the Carson City Mint in 1877 knew there was no time to putter with Proof coins, but apparently this did not prevent them from doing so on at least a few occasions.

Today (2003-2004) at the old mint in Carson City—home to the Nevada State Museum—tourists are treated to a coin striking exhibition. Volunteer staff

member Ken Hopple operates the famous *Number One* coin press in a much calmer environment than Carson Mint workers experienced in 1877. Hopple has the opportunity to devote full attention to the preparation of the planchets and then takes his time and lets the power of the press imprint fully struck impressions of commemorative tokens. This is one of the highlights of a tour through the historic museum.

In the *Gobrecht Collective Volume #4*, Weimar White describes a high grade 1877-CC half dollar he was fortunate enough to acquire, attributing it as a Type I variety with the *Small* mintmark. White's specimen is Choice Uncirculated, prooflike, and a very beautiful coin. In Wiley and Bugert's study on Liberty Seated half dollars, this variety is listed as *Unknown* in Mint State (Uncirculated). For further information about this special piece see page 491 of the *Collective Volume #4.*[2]

By far the most awesome specimen of an 1877-CC half dollar was part of the *Eliasberg Collection.* Like hundreds of coins in this famous set, the 1877-CC was described with a dozen superlatives and when the hammer fell at the 1997 auction, the price realized was $16,500, for a date considered common. This coin is currently encased in an NGC MS-68 holder, like the 1876-CC half from the same auction.

For collectors not wishing to put pressure on their bank accounts, hundreds of examples of this date are available in circulated grades. Many problem-free VF's, XF's, and even AU's exist for under $500 (2003 price levels). Fortunately, the "CC" series of coins includes a generous assortment of dates like this, affording everyone, regardless of budget, the opportunity of ownership.

---

[1] Ibid.

[2] *Gobrecht Journal Collective Volume #4*, LSCC, 1996.

1878-CC

(Photo courtesy Bowers and Merena)

Mintage: 62,000

Finest Knowns*:

    NGC MS-66 (1)

    PCGS MS-65 (4) **

    NGC MS-65 (1) ***

Notable Pedigrees:

    William M. Friesner (1894)

    W.F. Dunham (1941)

    World's Greatest Collection (1945)

    William C. Atwater (1946)

    Will W. Neil (1947)

    Samuel W. Wolfson (1963)

    Reed Hawn (1973)

    James A. Stack (1975)

    Norweb (1988)

    James B. Pryor (1996)

    Eliasberg (1997)

      ex: Friesner

    Heritage Long Beach Sale (1998)

    Douglas L. Noblet (1999)

    Queller Family (2002)

      ex: Reed Hawn

Survival Estimates in All Grades:	80-120
Estimated in Uncirculated:	8-10
Estimated in XF to AU:	20-30
Total Certified Examples in All Grades (PCGS and NGC)*:	45

(* As of July 2003)

(** Possibly only two or three)

(*** Possibly one of the PCGS MS-65s)

REFLECTIONS:

Seized with the realization that the monetary system of the United States needed an overhaul, Treasury Secretary John Sherman put a halt to subsidiary silver coinage in 1878 and a three-year resurgence in dime, quarter, and half dollar production abruptly ended. Cutbacks were greatest at the western mints and out of the 6,728,000 small silver coins produced in 1878, the Philadelphia Mint delivered nearly 80% of them.

At Carson City the retrogression was dramatic as mintages for dimes, quarters and halves fell 99% from 1877 to the end of 1878. Mint employees must have thought, "Just when business started to boom, the bottom fell out," a bitter lesson that became all too common for Carsonites.

Morgan dollars made up for some of the slack, but still there were 10 million fewer coins of all denominations struck at the Carson City Mint in 1878 than in the previous year. In addition, there was also an order that came in late February of 1878 to discontinue trade dollars. Up to that point, the Carson City Mint had been on pace to equal 1877's production of 534,000, but when the order was issued, a mere 97,000 1878-CC trade dollars had been minted.

Ironically this subsidence in silver coin production coincided with an all-time record year of bullion yield from the Comstock mines. According to U.S. Treasury records, over $36 million worth of gold and silver ore was unearthed by *Big Bonanza* barons, less than 9% of which was deposited at the Carson City Mint. Of the estimated 20 million ounces of silver from the Comstock Lode in 1878, only 2.3 million was turned into coins bearing the "CC" mintmark. Most of the silver went to the San Francisco Mint where nearly 14 million 1878 trade and Morgan dollars were struck.

Even gold coin production at Carson City took a precipitous drop this year. A steep slide, which had begun in 1877, sent the face value-total of coins minted to

$341,310, the lowest since the year the mint first opened. Unless the Bureau of the Mint sent the Nevada institution a life preserver, employees would have to find busy-work to occupy their time in 1878.

Whereas in both 1876 and 1877, monthly coin production averages were well over one million pieces, 1878's average was approximately 300,000. If Morgan dollars are subtracted the number drops to 115,040. The scanty number of 1878-CC half dollars could have easily been manufactured in one month.

Only one set of obverse and reverse dies were used and all 1878-CC halves are the Type II variety with the *Closed Bud* on the berry. A noticeable downward slope of the second "C" in relation to the first is an attribute of the *Medium*-sized mintmark, giving it a rather distinctive appearance, fitting for a final year of issue coin. A second reverse die variety with parallel mintmark letters is said to exist, but has not been substantiated.

Because the mintage was so low for this date, there are no signs of severe die deterioration on known specimens, although several die cracks can be seen in the form of raised lines in various locations, and several protruding dots of metal appear on Liberty's body from her mid-torso downward. As with most issues from the Carson City Mint, the date alone is too scarce for any variety factors to warrant premiums—just finding an example is reward in itself.

Certain 1878-CC half dollars exhibit unquestionable prooflike qualities. One such piece is the *Louis E. Eliasberg, Sr.* specimen. Featured in April of 1997 in a public auction for the first time since 1894, the coin caused the hair on viewer's arms to stand up and was capable of giving ladies a chill. Once again, the cataloguer honed his skills of adulation in his description: "INCREDIBLE GEM 1878-CC HALF DOLLAR…Unsurpassable Quality… magnificent…memorable. One of the finest known…of this highly prized date…from an aesthetic viewpoint—completely unsurpassable."[1] And this was just the introduction! From there the description complimented the piece for its prooflike qualities and the gorgeous spectrum of colors adorning its surfaces. In conclusion, this special 1878-CC half was heralded as a, "Possible Presentation Piece."[2] As they say, words were not enough to describe this beauty; you had to be there.

When the bidding ended, the new owner had paid $77,000, more than any "CC" half dollar had ever sold for up to that time, and worth every nail-biting penny of

it (and more). Later the half was submitted to NGC where it was given a grade of MS-66 and is still the finest known, and probably will be forever.

Another splendid prooflike example is the *Douglas L. Noblet* specimen. Though not in the same league as the *Eliasberg* coin, the *Noblet* specimen probably has deeper mirrors. Many raised diagonal lines crisscross the surfaces giving evidence of polished dies and a specially prepared planchet. Detracting hairlines caused by a past cleaning caused PCGS to lower the technical grade to MS-62; for a date with limited Mint State examples to choose from, it will satisfy most discriminating collectors. When this coin sold in Bowers and Merena's *Rarities* sale in January of 1999 the winning bidder paid $17,250–at the time a very fair price.

In 1946, dealer B. Max Mehl wrote in his auction catalog that the *Atwater* 1878-CC half dollar was almost equal to a Proof, and likewise in 1947, he described the *Will W. Neil* 1878-CC half as being prooflike. Both pieces sold for $105. Mehl had commented that Mr. Neil paid $75 for his specimen a number of years earlier.

Uncirculated examples did not only come in prooflike condition, however. Two noteworthy auctions from earlier in the 1940s offered Brilliant Uncirculated examples. One was the *W.F. Dunham Collection* in 1941, where the 1878-CC half realized $26, and the other was the *World's Greatest Collection* specimen, which sold for $85 in 1945. Both of these prices cause collectors in the early years of the 21st century to burn with envy.

In 1996, another frosty Uncirculated specimen was sold at auction by Bowers and Merena as part of the *James B. Pryor Collection*. It was graded by PCGS as MS-64 and possessed every attribute of a Gem Uncirculated coin except for a few extra bagmarks. Collectors and dealers in the era before professional grading services would not have had any problem referring to it as a Gem. The price realized for the coin in the *Pryor* sale was $20,900, at the time the highest price ever paid for an 1878-CC half. But this was 15 months before the *Eliasberg* specimen knocked all the doors down. Later on, the *Pryor* coin was upgraded to MS-65 and was reportedly being offered for sale in the $45,000 range (2003).

Like so many other key dates from a collection encompassing a complete set of coins issued by the Carson City Mint, the 1878-CC half dollar smashed one price

[1] Bowers and Merena, *Louis E. Eliasberg, Sr. Collection*, April 1997.
[2] Ibid.

barrier after another through the 20th century. After a choice multicolored Uncirculated specimen sold for $7,700 in Paramount's session of *Auction '79* there was little doubt that the $10,000 level was not too far off for this date. Just four years earlier the *James A. Stack* specimen, described as "Brilliant Uncirculated...prooflike condition,"[1] had sold for $950. In 1973, the stunning Gem Uncirculated *Reed Hawn* specimen provided a glimpse into future price performance of this date when it sold for $2,300.

Near Gem quality 1878-CC half dollar.

After the *Pryor* coin in 1996, and the benchmark *Eliasberg* specimen in 1997, collectors would be expected to pay strong five figure prices to obtain Condition Census quality examples. An impressive piece graded MS-65 by PCGS, exhibiting a sharp strike and glowing cartwheel luster, sold at a Heritage sale in September of 1998 for $31,050.

When the calendar page turned to the 21st century, prices for 1878-CC halves lost no momentum, as the *Reed Hawn* specimen surfaced again in 2002 and sold for $32,500, this time as part of the *Queller Family Collection*. In 29 years, it had appreciated over 1400%, representing an average annual rate of appreciation of approximately 10%. If the value of this coin continues to appreciate at this pace for 29 more years it will be worth over $500,000 in 2032! Inconceivable? Certainly. Impossible? Not really. Keep in mind, that if a coin collector during the World War II era were told that the price of Uncirculated 1878-CC halves would rise

from $105 to $2,300 in 29 years, skepticism would most likely have mocked the absurdity of it. In 1973 there is the same scenario, only the numbers are larger: $2,300 to $32,500 in 29 years. Did the skeptic's voice howl again in laughter?

Some readers in the early years of the 21st century will not be around in 2032 to witness if it happens again, but it appears that the word impossible should never be used in reference to price appreciation for rare Carson City coins.

Though not as scarce as the 1878-S half, the 1878-CC has been considered one of the key dates in the Liberty Seated half series since Heaton's *Treatise* was published in 1893. It is the third date out of three that Heaton described as being very scarce. Indeed, any collector fortunate enough to obtain choice specimens of all three of Heaton's rare threesome of "CC" half dollars will have prizes to treasure. Picture if you will, owning the Eliasberg specimens of the 1874-CC and 1878-CC, and the Gardner 1870-CC (everyone can dream a little).

Whenever 1878-CC halves in any condition are sold, buyers are waiting and eager. Problem-free circulated examples will generally bring a premium and are well worth it. As of 2003, this is truly a date seldom seen in dealer inventories or auction catalogs. [2]

---

[1] Stack's, *James A. Stack Collection*, March 1975.
[2] One of the *Top 25*.

COMPARISON OF HALF DOLLAR PRODUCTION AT THE
CARSON CITY MINT WITH THE
PHILADELPHIA MINT'S FROM 1870 TO 1878

HALF DOLLAR MINTAGE TOTALS		
Year	Carson City	Philadelphia
1870	54,617	634,900
1871	139,950	1,204,560
1872	272,000	881,550
1873 *Without Arrows*	122,500	801,800
1873 *With Arrows*	214,560	1,815,700
1874	59,000	2,360,300
1875	1,008,000	6,027,500
1876	1,956,000	8,419,150
1877	1,420,000	8,304,510
1878	62,000	1,378,400
TOTAL	5,308,627	31,828,370

Set of Seated Liberty Silver Dollars from the Carson City Mint

(Photo courtesy Bowers and Merena)

In the beginning, the U.S. Treasury created the silver dollar. From this genesis arose a new monetary system using the silver dollar as its vanguard monetary unit. When Treasury officials and Bureau of the Mint authorities spoke about silver dollars, they referred to them as *standard silver dollars*, and every other denomination was based upon its proportion to the *standard silver dollar*: ten dollars, quarter dollars, $1/100\text{th}$ of a dollar, etc.

From 1794 to 1804, 1,439,517 silver dollars were minted in the United States and then silver dollar production was suspended for 32 years. When the time came, a new Seated Liberty design was introduced to the American public. First issued between 1836 and 1839 in limited quantities, these artistic coins were called Gobrecht dollars, after the name of the chief designer. Modifications were made in 1840, with the reverse being totally redesigned. Without interruption, Seated Liberty dollars were minted until 1873, when Congress voted to eliminate silver dollars from the nation's monetary system. Over the course of time 6,591,721 Seated Liberty dollars were manufactured, bringing the total of all silver dollars produced between 1794 and 1873 to slightly over eight million.

Nearly 85% of the total mintage of Seated Liberty silver dollars was produced at the Philadelphia Mint. Out of the 34 years these dollars were struck, branch mints coined them in only eight. Twelve dates with mintmarks were struck and one, the 1873-S, is unknown in any collection.

By 1870, the first year of the Carson City Mint, silver dollars were worth more as bullion than as money and Congress was already deliberating their demise. Few were found in circulation by then as it was more profitable to melt them than to spend them. But still, depositors could request them in exchange for bullion, and hundreds of thousands of silver dollars were used in foreign trade.

When Carson City struck its first Seated Liberty dollars on February 10, 1870, only four years remained until the series would be retired. All design changes had already been made for this coin, the last significant one being the addition of *IN GOD WE TRUST* on the reverse in 1866. Mintages for all four "CC" issues were negligible. One numismatic author (R.W. Julian) suggests that, "The Carson City dollar coinage was mainly designed to impress Californians with the importance of the Nevada Branch Mint."[1] This may or may not have been the reason, but in any event, very few were made.

Local Carsonites, though maybe not trying to impress their neighbors to the west, were very proud of their new facility and the new coins being minted there. Stories about Abe Curry handing out new silver dollars, and other accounts of Uncirculated specimens being found in local cornerstones, add to the lore.

Three of the four "CC" issues pose a formidable challenge to the collector, especially in grades above XF or AU. Though the 1870-CC Seated dollar is more readily available than the other three dates, it is still considered scarce, and demand for the first year of issue puts pressure on existing supplies. For the first 20 years after "CC" Seated dollars were produced, examples could be purchased for small premiums above face value, usually between $1.25 and $1.75, occasionally as much as $2. Then in the 1893 to 1895 era, prices jumped to 15 times face value, in part due to Heaton's *Treatise on Mint Marks* encouraging collectors to get in while the getting was good. He obviously knew what he was talking about, as by the early years of

---

[1] Q. David Bowers, *Silver Dollars and Trade Dollars of the United States: A Complete Encyclopedia*, Section on Liberty Seated Dollars.

the 21st century, certain "CC" Seated dollars were selling for the price of a nice house.

When the final Seated Liberty silver dollar was struck at the Carson City Mint in 1873, the 80 year reign of the standard silver dollar came to an end. Five years later, in 1878, a new silver dollar would be introduced, though it would never achieve the status of America's standard monetary unit once afforded to Seated Liberty dollars.

BUREAU OF THE MINT DATA FOR CARSON CITY SEATED LIBERTY SILVER DOLLAR PRODUCTION

Total Combined Mintage:.. 19,288

Total Face Value:... $19,288

Total Ounces of Silver Used: .... 14,910 ozs.

Design Type:..Seated Liberty

Designers: Obverse:....... Christian Gobrecht and Robert Ball Hughes; after drawings by Kneass, Sully, and Peale.

Reverse: .... Longacre; after Reich and Hughes

Metal Composition: ....900 Silver .100 Copper

Actual Gross Weight:.. 26.73 grams

Actual Fine Silver Content: ....77344 oz.

Value of Silver in One Dollar: .... $1.004-1.027 (1870 to 1873)

1870-CC

(Photo courtesy Bowers and Merena)

Mintage: 12,462**

Finest Knowns*:

    PCGS MS-63 (8) ***

    NGC MS-63 (3)

    PCGS MS-62 (3)

    NGC MS-62 (1)

Notable Pedigrees:

    World's Greatest Collection (1945)

    R.L. Miles (1969)

    Fairfield Collection (1977)

    Auction '84 Stack's (1984)

    French Family (1989)

       ex: Auction '84

James A. Stack (1995)

Eliasberg (1997)

Sonnheim Collection (1998)

Dr. John C. Wong (2001)

L.K Rudolph (2003)

Survival Estimates in All Grades:	450-650
Estimated in Uncirculated:	20-25
Estimated in XF to AU:	200-300
Total Certified Examples in All Grades (PCGS and NGC)*:	335

(* As of July 2003)

(** Some Sources Say 11,758)

(*** Possible resubmissions of several of the same coins)

REFLECTIONS:

Carson City is on the line of the old Virginia and Truckee Railroad, 14 miles from Virginia City and 34 miles from Reno. When the mint in this quiet settlement opened for business on January 8, 1870, a whoosh of chilly winter air blew through the front door and filled the entryway. Superintendent Abraham Curry stood at the open door and waved to passers by. No matter what degree of progress or growth Carson City would achieve in the future, it would always be remembered for this coinage facility.

Abraham Curry was raised in New York and was a business owner in Cleveland before moving west at the age of 40. He spent a short time in San Francisco before backtracking and heading east, eventually lowering his anchor on the property that became Carson City. Curry knew that his new home did not compare to the metropolises he had left behind. Populations in cities like Cleveland, Ohio and Syracuse, New York (near Curry's birthplace)

were larger than the entire population of the state where Carson City was located. He could have remained in any of those thriving communities and used his entrepreneurial spirit to become part of the infrastructure. But something in Curry drove him to establish his own thriving community—an infrastructure of his design.

When he stood at the front door of the Carson City Mint on that January morning in 1870 he must have been one of the most gratified men in the country. His town now had a government facility reserved for only a few select locations: Philadelphia, San Francisco and now, Carson City. What would his friends back east think?

A month later, on February 10, 1870, it was time for the sound of the coin press to finally roar and from morning until night that big 12-ton Morgan and Orr clanged out 2,303 new 1870-CC Seated Liberty silver dollars. Curry had already planned who the first coin was going to be reserved for: the number one citizen in the United States, President Ulysses S. Grant. There is no record of who struck that first silver dollar; it could have been Coiner E.W. Staley, or perhaps Curry himself performed the honor.

Whomever the honor was bestowed upon, it is certain there was a wide-eyed crowd surrounding the press observing the historic event. Each new blank planchet would be loaded into the lower die and then 150 tons of pressure would impress the image of the coin into the blank silver disc, creating miniature works of art. Uncirculated examples offered a century later would send chills down the spines of coin collectors who viewed them.

Surviving 1870-CC silver dollars with Proof or prooflike attributes give evidence that special preparation and care were exercised in the minting process. A planchet could have been polished before it was loaded into the lower dies and then two blows of the 150-ton press would sharpen the details on the coin and impress a mirrorlike finish on its surfaces.

As mentioned, Curry gave silver dollars away to his friends and distinguished locals, as well as persons of high standing in other parts of the country. His friend Alf Doten, one time reporter for the *Territorial Enterprise* and later editor of the *Gold Hill Press,* recounted many of his experiences with the Carson Mint's first superintendent. Doten wrote that, "Superintendent Curry had given me a tour of the Mint on February 12, 1870, and then handed me one of the new shiny silver dollars."[1] Doten, often in financial straits, probably spent the piece, but what a numismatic prize it would be to modern collectors if this or any of the 1870-CC silver dollars presented as gifts suddenly appeared.

Journalist Alf Doten was given a tour of the Carson City Mint by Abe Curry in 1870.

Some very fortunate souls were privy to one such appearance in the 1970s at Carson City. According to Robert Nylen, curator of the Nevada State Museum in 2003, when the cornerstone at the Capitol building was opened in 1977, one example of each of the three 1870-CC silver denominations was discovered and all three coins, wrapped in soft material were in Mint State condition! After all the artifacts were examined, the entire bounty was carefully placed back in the cornerstone to be preserved for yet future generations to admire. Though the three coins–quarter, half dollar, and dollar–equaled $1.75 in face value, their numismatic value in 2003-2004 is well over $500,000. For a state whose government always claims to be broke, one wonders if Nevada's political leaders are tempted to reopen the cornerstone. If they do, collectors are lined up waiting to cash them out.

One 1870-CC silver dollar displaying prooflike or *Presentation piece* qualities is pedigreed to Weimar White. Mr. White's coin has been featured in numismatic publications and mentioned in reference books. It has mirrored surfaces that White says he can read "a newspaper in when spaced a foot apart."[2] Although this piece has not been certified by PCGS or NGC as a branch mint Proof or Presentation piece, it is as much a Proof as any Philadelphia issue designated as such. In time, it is almost certain that more "CC" coins will be awarded either Proof, Presentation piece, or Specimen strike status. Curry and his successors seemed to have had strong inclinations to flaunt their coins from time to time, all the better for generations of collectors.

Possible Proof 1870-CC silver dollar. (*Courtesy of Weimar White*)

In terms of varieties, the 1870-CC silver dollar is known to have two basic obverses and two basic reverses. Obverses are seen with the date slightly shifted either to the left or the right, and reverses come with either a *Closer Spaced* or *Wider Spaced* "CC". Apparently prooflike specimens were struck in different months of the minting cycle, since known specimens are seen with several different variety combinations. An array of die cracks, die chips, lumps of metal, rotated reverses and raised lines can be seen on various examples of this date and occasionally, examples exhibit weakness at the center of the obverse.

For an issue with a mintage of approximately 12,000, there seems to have been a disproportionate amount of dies used, resulting in more varieties than would be expected. If coin delivery ledgers for the Carson City Mint are accurate, the entire output of silver dollars from 1870 was completed

---

[1] Alf Doten, *The Journals of Alf Doten.*
[2] *Letter from Weimar White,* dated September 19, 2002.

by June. Readers interested in learning more about the different varieties for "CC" Seated Liberty silver dollars are encouraged to seek out Bowers' *Silver Dollar Encyclopedia*, and numerous articles from the *Gobrecht Journal*.[1]

One of the most interesting statistics uncovered from official Bureau of the Mint records reveals that two sets of dies were made for 1869-CC silver dollars. Although the obverse dies were never used, could one or more of the reverse dies have been put to use in 1870? Empirical evidence suggests that they were, since only two reverse dies were reported to have been made for 1870-CC dollars. Even the reverse dies for 1869 and 1870 do not account for a fifth mintmark variety discovered in the 1980s, posing the question: are Mint records always accurate and did everything that happened at all of the regional mints get reported? No one knows for sure.

To illustrate occasional discrepancies in Mint records, consider the reported mintages for 1870-CC silver dollars:

COMPARISON OF REPORTED MINTAGES FOR 1870-CC SEATED LIBERTY SILVER DOLLARS			
Coin	Monthly Reports as Per Carson City Mint[2]	Assay Report Deliveries as Per Director of the Mint[3]	Corrected Totals After 1887 as Per Director of the Mint Report[4]
1870-CC Silver Dollar	12,158	11,758	12,462

Yet another report, the Director's fiscal year statement from 1871, lists 304 "CC" silver dollars minted between July 1, 1870 and June 30, 1871. These dollars are suspended somewhere in time and space because they were supposedly struck during a 12 month period when no silver dollars were delivered. Both the *Monthly Returns* report and the *Assay* report show that June 1870 was the last month silver dollars were minted that year, with production on this denomination halted until August of 1871. But if no "CC" silver dollars were struck at Carson City from June 30, 1870 to August of 1871, where did the 304 come from?

The Treasury admitted in 1887 that errors had been made in its annual financial reports. But rather than concede failure the Treasury, "compiled with no little care and research, from original sources of information, such as the workbooks and delivery books of the coinage mints..." a record of all annual mintage figures from the foundation of the U.S. Mint through 1887. Director

Kimball claimed with confidence that "it (the mintages) is as nearly perfect as can be made..."[5] Treasury financial reports regarding its Bureau of the Mint system had gone through a major audit and all records were set in balance. In the scheme of things, Carson City's puny silver dollar mintage for 1870 was equivalent to one spike along the tracks of the Transcontinental Railroad. When the dust settled, the Treasury officially declared that 12,462 1870-CC silver dollars had been delivered at the Carson City Mint in calendar year 1870 and this figure has been used in *Annual Reports* ever since.

Additionally, in Bowers' *Silver Dollar Encyclopedia* Dr. Harry Salyards comments, "...is the recorded mintage accurate?...the market doesn't value it (1870-CC dollar) like a coin with a mintage of only 12,462. So, could that reported mintage be in error?" Dr. Salyards votes to increase the figure, not lower it.[6] If readers still aren't satisfied, perhaps spending a week at the National Archives, in the Mid Atlantic Region in Philadelphia, and then heading to the branch in the D.C. area for round two will reveal some hidden facts. If the *Holy Grail* of mintage records from the Carson City Mint is discovered, the findings should be sent to *Coin World*, for the rest of the world to see.

Why were so few silver dollars minted at Carson City in 1870 anyway (whether 11,758, 12,158, or 12,462) and why are there no listed mintages for 1870-S silver dollars? One would think that the two western mints would have been natural choices to produce much greater quantities of the big silver coins.

In truth, there were several reasons, chief among which was the high price of silver at the time. For every thousand coins a silver depositor requested he would lose $27, plus mint charges, which was not much incentive. Also, though California's Mother Lode and Nevada's Comstock Lode are known for the enormous amounts of bullion that spewed forth from their mines, yields were much lower in 1870 than in other years. On the Comstock alone, production was a tad over $8 million for the year,

[1] *Gobrecht Journal Collective Volumes 1, 2, 3, and 4.* In Volume 2 for example, see page 355 for four reverse varieties, and page 360 for the two obverse dies.
[2] R.W. Julian , Article *Coins Magazine*, May 1977.
[3] *National Archives.*
[4] *Annual Report of the Director of the Mint, 1887.*
[5] Ibid.
[6] Q. David Bowers, *Silver Dollars and Trade Dollars of the United States: A Complete Encyclopedia*, page 826.

and from the outset, limited percentages of Comstock bullion yields were deposited at the local coinage facility. The table below illustrates the ratio of bullion output and deposits.

This clearly shows that silver bullion was in short supply at the Carson City Mint in 1870, and even when silver was deposited ($28,262) it was returned in the form of unparted bars (bullion ore mixed with gold and silver). Nearly all silver bullion yielded from the Comstock mines was sent to San Francisco to be shaped into bars, which resulted in a greater return to depositors than silver dollars would provide.

In 1893, Augustus Heaton mentioned the two reverses of the 1870-CC silver dollars. Although he did not elaborate on eight different varieties or whether there were any Proof specimens known, he did acknowledge that the date was rare. As mentioned, all dates in every "CC" denomination category (save for the Morgan dollar) are intrinsically rare without concern for variety factors; this is certainly true for 1870-CC silver dollars.

When any pressure is placed on supplies at hand, demand always exceeds inventories and auction appearances. If every *Coin World* subscriber, for instance, wanted an example of a "CC" Seated Liberty silver dollar, it would be first come-first serve, and available supplies would sell out as fast as box seats at a World Series game. As the most common of the four dates in the Carson City series, the 1870-CCs would be swooped up first.

Back in 1945, a brilliant prooflike 1870-CC sold for $55 in the *World's Greatest Collection*—not much more than an Uncirculated 1903-S Morgan dollar realized in the same sale. A quarter of a century later, in 1969, the *R.L. Miles* 1870-CC silver dollar brought $475, and in 1977, the *Fairfield* specimen sold for $3,400. Continuing the progression of price increases for Uncirculated 1870-CC dollars, a near Gem Uncirculated piece, catalogued as "the

finest known,"[1] sold for $16,500 in 1984. In the early years of the 21st century two examples sold for $36,800 (2001) and $35,650 (2003) respectively. What will the next record level be? No one knows for sure of course, but based on the ever-increasing popularity of Carson City coins, hefty gains seem attainable.

For many collectors, Uncirculated examples of this date do not fit into budgetary restraints and perhaps a pleasing AU or even XF coin would bring satisfaction. At the high end of the AU grade is AU-58, often viewed as Borderline Uncirculated. If population data for PCGS and NGC were accurate, a total of 19 1870-CC silver dollars have been certified as AU-58 (through 2003). Unfortunately, this total is doubtful due to multiple submissions of several of the same coins; the incentive exists to resubmit borderline coins since there is a wide price margin between AU-58 and MS-60 to MS-61 examples.

In the pre-1980 period it was common for auction companies to describe brilliant prooflike specimens of this date as Uncirculated in spite of obvious signs of minimal wear. As grading standards tightened in the late 1980s however, small quantities of 1870-CC dollars once considered to be Uncirculated were downgraded to AU.

Many 1870-CC dollars that have been certified as AU-50 are unattractive, often displaying signs of cleaning. In the mid-AU grading range—AU-53 to AU-55—patient collectors can find worthwhile bargains, and original examples in AU, if they exist, are worth ample premiums.

Problem-free examples in grades below AU also represent excellent values in today's market (2003-2004). Supplies are anemic, and as interest in 10 piece Carson City type sets broadens, tremendous demand for 1870-CC dollars will put pressure on existing populations.

---

[1] Stacks, *Auction "84"*, July 1984.

	Comstock Production Gold and Silver	Deposits at Mint			Coinage By Calendar Year		
Year		Gold	Silver	Total	Gold	Silver	Total
1870	$8,319,700	$124,155	$28,262**	$152,417	$173,235	$41,855.50	$215,090.50

DEPOSITS AND COINAGE AT THE CARSON CITY MINT IN 1870 *

* *Annual Report of the Director of the Mint,* 1887.
**For Unparted Bars Only, (No coins).

(Photo courtesy Bowers and Merena)

Mintage: 1,376

Finest Knowns*:

    PCGS MS-64 (1) (Stack)

    PCGS MS-63 (1) **

    NGC MS-63 (1) **

    NGC MS-61 (1)

Notable Pedigrees:

    E.A. Carson (1976)

    Norweb (1988)

    James A. Stack (1995)

Sonnheim Family (1998)

    ex: Norweb

L.K. Rudolph (2003)

    ex: James A. Stack

Survival Estimates in All Grades:	100-125
Estimated in Uncirculated:	3-4
Estimated in XF to AU:	35-50
Total Certified Examples in All Grades (PCGS and NGC)*:	104

(* As of July 2003)
(** The same coin)

Reflections:

More than 13 months had passed since the last silver dollars for 1870 were minted at Carson City and it was not until August of 1871 that the first and only "CC" silver dollars dated 1871 were produced. There were no silver dollars struck at the San Francisco Mint during those two years, at least officially, since a handful of 1870-S pieces do exist. With the price of silver hovering around $1.326 per ounce, depositors gained more from bars than coins. Each silver dollar contained approximately $1.026 worth of precious metal resulting in a net loss to anyone willing to exchange bullion for coin, and as a result, the western mints did not attract any customers for silver dollars.

At the Philadelphia Mint, although there was not much demand from domestic silver depositors, silver dollar production increased dramatically in 1871 and 1872. There was still a demand for the large coins among bullion and money traders for export purposes as Latin American countries, as well as merchants in the West Indies, preferred U.S. silver dollars for commercial exchanges. To meet this need, Philadelphia minted nearly 2.2 million

Seated Liberty dollars between 1871 and 1872, compared to 4,526 at the Carson Mint.

Legislation had been introduced in 1869 that would reform America's coinage system. Though the draft of the bill would not gain full momentum until 1871 to 1873, the House Committee on Coinage and the Senate Committee on Finance vigorously deliberated the issue from 1870 on. One of the controversial elements in the proposed Mint act was the elimination of silver dollars from the nation's coinage profile, and a supposed conspiracy railroaded this article of the bill past a slumbering Congress. But for three years before the bill became law in 1873, the intents of the Congressional Committees were boldly displayed in capital letters across the legislative documents, "THE SILVER DOLLAR—ITS DISCONTINUATION AS A STANDARD."

Nevada's mining industry was at risk. If the silver dollar was retired, the price of silver would surely decline. But in 1871, only a pittance of Comstock silver was being used to produce silver dollars, or any silver coins for that matter. This came at a most inopportune time, because the production of precious metals in Lyon and Storey Counties (The Comstock) had just begun to thrive, with nearly a 35% increase in yield, from 1870 to 1871 alone.

Yet demand for silver dollars was nil, with none minted during that 13 month gap from 1870 to 1871. It does seem surprising that during a period highlighted by flourishing silver mines the Carson City Mint would produce fewer silver dollars than had been produced at the Philadelphia Mint in 1794, especially knowing how sparse silver supplies were in George Washington's day.

But the story of 1871-CC silver dollars is the story of the lowest mintage date–save for the mysterious 1873-S–in the Seated Liberty *With Motto* silver dollar series. Although overshadowed by the 1873-CC silver dollar in terms of rarity, the low mintage of the 1871-CC merits notoriety within the ranks of elite numismatic classics, and the estimate that no more than 10% of the original mintage survives, adds to the allurement of the issue.

In 1976, a cataloguer for Bowers and Ruddy reckoned that there were, "several dozen extant specimens,"[1] and in the 1980s, author Weimar White arrived at a number of 55 pieces or fewer.[2] As late as the early 1990s it was estimated by some numismatists that fewer than 100 1871-CC silver dollars survived in all grades. Though the precise total may never be known, population and census reports compiled by PCGS and NGC shed some light on the mystery: through July of 2003, the combined total of certified examples of 1871-CC dollars was 104. It must also be noted that a variance of at least 10% must be applied to this number due to multiple resubmissions of certain coins.

As time passes, population and census data will result in greater accuracy when estimating the number of coins extant. Is it possible that figures for the 1871-CC dollar will double from where they are in the early years of the 21st century? Certainly, but not likely. Attrition rates for silver coins from the pre-1876 era are generally high, especially for Carson City coinage. From dimes through dollars, survival rates for these early "CC" dates range from $1/3$ of 1% to 10%; with the upper end seldom surpassed.

Melting and exporting accounted for substantial losses of Seated Liberty silver dollars. Some researchers have speculated that 1871-CC dollars circulated in the Carson City area, and Q. David Bowers for one, believes that domestic use explains a higher survival rate than the low mintage suggests.[3] But even if these theories are true,

the higher bullion value through 1872 would have motivated owners of silver dollars to export them or have them melted. In the early years of the 21st century, many retail stores have jars at the cash register that hold pennies tossed in by customers for use by all, two cents here, and three cents there. But in the early 1870s those two or three cents would have been a matter of consequence.

It seems doubtful that 1871-CC silver dollars would have been saved by collectors during the short time in which they circulated, especially if Heaton's assertions about a general disinterest in mintmarked coins prior to the 1890s are true. He wrote in 1893 that coins from the "Carson City Mint…received little present attention…" and that the small mintages of early Carson City coinage "will always attract the greatest interest of collectors."[4] So although Carson City issues would eventually begin to attract interest, prior to Heaton's *Treatise* it was widely believed that coin collectors ignored them.

As mentioned, annual mintage figures were unknown to the public at large. Heaton made it clear that when he began his research the hobby "lacked any guide-book"[5] to aid collectors in determining low mintages. His discovery of the annual Mint reports "was valuable as indicating what dates a collector should look for, and what should be accounted scarce or rare from limited coinage."[6] With the exception of staff workers at the Carson City Mint in 1871, no other locals were privy to mintage totals, and this was true across that nation.

Silver dollars obviously circulated around Carson City in the early 1870s, as evidenced by the number of worn specimens extant, but how many remains a mystery. Heaton reminded his readers that data like this was only uncovered, "by investigation and experience,"[7] and speaking of the conflict between Mint reports of annual mintages versus quantities actually released, he observed that: "It often happens that but a portion of the registered coinage…is issued for circulation, the remainder being remelted. Occasionally an entire coinage has either never left the mint, or has been sent abroad…"[8] Any of these three scenarios could have applied to the Carson City Mint, especially the limited or zero releases of certain year's mintages.

[1] Bowers and Ruddy, *Dr. Edward B. Willing Collection*, June 1976.
[2] Weimar White. *The Seated Liberty Dollar 1840-1873*.
[3] Q. David Bowers, *Silver Dollars and Trade Dollars of the United States*.
[4] Augustus G. Heaton, *Mint Marks, A Treatise*, 1893.
[5] Ibid.
[6] Ibid.
[7] Ibid.
[8] Ibid.

Heaton's investigation and experience must have revealed statistics that enabled him to draw conclusions on the scarcity of silver dollars dated 1871-CC to 1873-CC, and his rarity ratings have held true since 1893. When Heaton observed that there were only "about 2000 dollars coined annually at Carson City,"[1] during those three years he was only using the average (2,275) of the combined totals, for it is well known that he had access to the annual Mint reports. It does seem odd considering his preoccupation with low mintages that Heaton chose not to isolate the 1871-CC dollar's small quantity.

There are no confirmed documents revealing why silver dollar production was recommenced in August of 1871 at the Carson City Mint after a 13 month hiatus. It would indeed be a major breakthrough in the study of the Carson City series to discover who ordered the 1,376 1871-CC dollars to be struck, and consequently what happened to them after they were minted. Apparently there was little demand for the dollars, since six months passed before another small quantity (2,150) was manufactured in March of 1872. These long intervals between scanty production runs were typical at Carson City all the way through the final month that Seated Liberty dollars were minted in 1873.

Certain numismatic authors have suggested that a percentage of Carson City's Seated Liberty silver dollars were melted after the passage of the Coinage Act in 1873. This is questionable, however, because there would have been no reason to melt them, as the price of silver had fallen, resulting in the bullion value being almost at par with the face value. One possible motivation may have been to exchange standard dollars for the heavier weight trade dollars, but this would have occurred after July of 1873.

Another explanation for the disappearance of a majority of the dollars is found in Heaton's third scenario: exportation to foreign countries. While the numbers might be trivial, it is possible that 90% or more of the 19,288 silver dollars minted at Carson City between 1870 and 1873 were sold to moneychangers and subsequently sent abroad.

Still another avenue of pure speculation involves the Chinese population in the western states. It is well known that Chinatowns existed all over Nevada and northern California, and those living in these areas certainly had connections in the Orient, making it very possible that silver dollars were sent by Chinese emigrants to their native homeland. Considering that during this period fewer than 29,000

silver dollars were manufactured at the Carson City and San Francisco mints, it is probable that export demand exceeded supply, as new steamship lines like the *Pacific Mail Steamship Company* advanced trade between San Francisco and China. Still, the exportation of silver dollars was predicated upon buyers willing to pay premiums over the bullion value in the coins, and there was always the competition of Mexican silver dollars to contend with. Yet there seemed to be a trace of popularity for U.S. silver dollars in China, making the above scenario very feasible.

Theories aside, the three items of most importance to modern coin collectors are: how many 1871-CC silver dollars survive, where can one be found, and how much will it cost? Part one of this question has already been addressed. Part two is a tough one, because this date is very elusive, but generally auctions are where they most often surface. And lastly, how much do 1871-CC dollars cost? In the early years of the 21st century, the answer to this question changes rapidly, as it does for most coins with a "CC" mintmark.

From the year it was issued until the 1940s the price history of 1871-CCs paralleled that of the other three dates in the Carson City Seated Liberty dollar series. By the 1950s, the 1871-CC, along with the 1872-CC and 1873-CC, had pulled ahead of the 1870-CC. For example, at the *Anderson-Dupont* sale auctioned by Stack's in 1954, XF specimens of the 1871-CC and 1873-CC sold for $300 and $500 respectively, while an 1870-CC in the same grade went for $30. Then in 1969 at the *R.L. Miles, Jr.* sale, 1871-CC and 1873-CC dollars in AU were purchased for $1,300 and $2,100 respectively. At the *Norweb* sale in 1988, one of the two finest known 1871-CC dollars in Choice Uncirculated realized $19,800. Ten years later, the same coin brought $101,500 as part of the *Sonnheim Family Collection* at a Bowers and Merena auction in 1998.

This impressive price jump had not occurred without precedent, however. In 1995 at another installment of the *James A. Stack* sales, an absolutely mind blowing specimen surprised everyone in attendance when it sold for $137,500. It had become clear that Uncirculated 1871-CC silver dollars were now six-figure pieces of merchandise; by the turn of the century, lovers of Carson City rarities anxiously awaited the next appearance of an Uncirculated 1871-CC dollar.

On Wednesday May 14, 2003, the *James A. Stack* specimen made an encore performance in New York City,

---

[1] Ibid.

this time as part of Stack's *L.K. Rudolph* sale. There was a standing room only crowd waiting to participate in this sale which featured a complete set of Seated Liberty silver dollars. Records were shattered as the auction progressed, then came the 1870-S silver dollar (also a *James A. Stack* specimen). At the 1995 *Stack* sale, this coin had sold for $462,000, so everyone expected a fireworks show; those in attendance witnessed the 1870-S become the first Seated Liberty dollar to crash the $1 million barrier ($1,092,500).

Next came the 1871-CC dollar, a stunning example of this date–"possibly the finest known" in the words of the cataloguer.[1] Bidders who had come hoping to catch this piece at close to, or slightly more than it had brought in 1995 knew that was a joke, especially after the record-setting performance of the 1870-S dollar minutes before. Though at the time this 1871-CC dollar had not been certified by PCGS or NGC, it was unquestionably considered to be a Choice Uncirculated coin. Raised lines are scattered in every direction across the fields, interacting with hairlines from an old cleaning. Like several of the other "CC" coins from the *James A. Stack* collection, this 1871-CC has a deep-mirror-prooflike appearance. When held vertically, there are at least six inch mirrors on the coin and around the rims is gorgeous blue, green, purple, and yellow toning, which accents the resplendent central areas. A number of detracting hits and one significant scrape in the right obverse field keep it from the Gem category, but on a coin with the eye appeal and rarity of this one, criticism should be used cautiously.

When the bidding ended, another record was established, this time for $218,500. After the sale, several bidders regretted that they had not been more aggressive, but the buyer certainly had no regrets; he knew he had a winner. And on that May evening in 2003, another chapter was written in the price history of coins from the Carson City Mint.

For the collector not interested in mortgaging his house to buy a coin, what are some other price alternatives for 1871-CC dollars? A problem free example in grades below VF can be purchased for anywhere from $1,500 to $6,000 (2003 prices), but interested parties had better hurry, because when the recoil of the $218,500 price realized hits, it will drive all prices upward.

One interesting variety feature on 1871-CC dollars is a small die chip that connects two denticles at the lower obverse rim, located below the 7 slightly left of the large round curve on the left side of the numeral's base. All examples have the *Widely Spaced* "CC", and the date is evenly set. A small number of examples are seen with prooflike surfaces, although none compare with the *James A. Stack* specimen in this regard.

All things considered, this is one of the most fascinating dates in the entire Carson City set of coins—well worth acquiring. For further study, check out the *Gobrecht Journal Collective Volumes.*[2]

---

[1] Stacks, *L.K. Rudolph Collection*, May 2003.
[2] One of the *Top 25.*

(Photo courtesy Bowers and Merena)

Mintage: 3,150

Finest Knowns*:

NGC MS-65 (1)

NGC MS-64 (2) **

PCGS MS-63 (2) **

PCGS MS-62 (3)

Notable Pedigrees:

Jack Roe-Waltman Sale (1945)

Atwater (1946)

Anderson-Dupont (1954)

Wolfson (1963)

E.A. Carson (1976)

Garrett Collection (1980)

Harold S. Bareford (1981)

Auction '84 Stack's (1984)

Norweb (1988)

Auction '90 Akers (1990)

Auction '90 RARCOA (1990)

Superior May Sale (1992)

Superior May Sale (1993)

Eliasberg (1997)

Sonnheim Family (1998)

Dr. Wallace Lee (1999)

Dr. John C. Wong (2001)

L.K. Rudolph (2003)

Survival Estimates in All Grades:	250-300
Estimated in Uncirculated:	16-19
Estimated in XF to AU:	65-85
Total Certified Examples in All Grades (PCGS and NGC)*:	167

(* As of July 2003)

(** Possible resubmissions of the same coin)

REFLECTIONS:

This was the year that the delivery of new coin dies to the Carson City Mint was delayed when snowfall blocked the mountain passes. Superintendent H.F. Rice might have stressed over some of the other denominations, but silver dollars had not been produced at his mint for five months anyway, and apparently there was little pressure to manufacture more of them. When silver dollar production finally resumed in late February or early March of 1872, a mere 2,150 pieces were minted. This would suffice until the final 1,000 silver dollars for the year were struck in July, bringing the annual total to 3,150, the highest mintage for the three year run from 1871 to 1873.

Numismatic researchers have long speculated as to what happened to those 3,150 1872-CC silver dollars.

Were they distributed to local depositors in exchange for silver bullion, or perhaps exported? One theory, which seems contrary to reason, is that the mint withheld delivery and subsequently melted the dollars in 1873 or thereabouts. This would not have benefited any of the parties concerned. Coinage laws granted banks, merchants, and private citizens the privilege to deposit bullion in exchange for silver dollars for a fee of $1/2$%. Additionally, the Mint treasurer was authorized to order silver dollars at his discretion. Essential to this system was the charge to provide sufficient supplies to meet both the domestic and international commercial needs of the nation. If the 3,150 1872-CC silver dollars were ordered, it is almost certain that there was a target destination for them. It was not until 1878 that silver dollars would be minted, stockpiled and withheld from circulation.

Mint reports reveal another interesting twist to the perplexing question concerning the origin and eventual destination of 1872-CC silver dollars. According to official deposit records from 1872, there was no silver exchanged for coins that year, only for unparted bars. In fact, from 1870 through 1873 all silver deposits at the Carson City Mint were for unparted bars.[1] This suggests that no silver dollars were ordered by private citizens, and might suggest that the Mint treasurer authorized all silver dollars produced during those years. If this is true, the Director of the Mint could have ordered the dollars to be withheld and subsequently ordered the Carson City Mint to melt them. Actually it leaves the door open to many scenarios, one being the sale of silver dollars to local banks or merchants, which still allows for the inference from the section on 1871-CC dollars about exportation to the Orient. All postulations concerning the issue should be considered suggestive rather than definitive, as unfortunately, too many documents have been lost or destroyed. An open-minded approach seems to be the most sensible; a dogmatic position seems ill-fit on this subject.

It is not known whether the 3,150 1872-CC silver dollars were released into circulation, claimed by bullion traders, banks, or merchants, held in the mint's vaults, exported to China, buried in the ground, hoarded or melted—or, a combination of any or all of the above. Regardless what happened to them long ago, it appears that no more than 10% of the original mintage survived to the early years of the 21st century.

Augustus G. Heaton told his readers that he had not seen an 1872-CC silver dollar as of the writing of his *Treatise* in 1893. Readers are well aware of his affinity for "CC" coins by now; he was enamored with them and as far as he was concerned all four of the Carson City Seated Liberty dollars were extremely rare. Years after Heaton had passed away, the ranking order of rarity was more clearly defined for these issues. Today's collector (2003-2004) knows that the 1873-CC is the rarest, with the 1871-CC a close second, and 1872-CC edging out 1870-CC for third place.

Reviewing auction records from 1972 to 2002 provides insight into the relative rarity of 1872-CC dollars compared to the other three "CC" dates. In all, the 1872-CC made 191 appearances, averaging slightly more than six per year. As expected, this is below the average for 1870-CC and considerably higher than both the 1871-CC and 1873-CC. Of course these 191 appearances do

not represent 191 different coins as there are multiple appearances of many of the same pieces. A large percentage is seen in grades below AU, although there are very few listings for coins in grades below Fine. There are a fair amount of Uncirculated specimens for such a rare date, although it is evident that Gem quality examples are prohibitively scarce. In fact, as of the writing of this book (2003) only one 1872-CC silver dollar has been graded MS-65 by either PCGS or NGC.

Turning time back to 1906, Uncirculated examples of the 1872-CC were practically unknown. In the famous *Harlan P. Smith Collection*, sold by the Chapman Brothers in 1906, a specimen described as being in Fine condition sold for $5.25. Uncirculated pieces began appearing with more regularity by the 1940s. In 1945 at the *Waltman* sale held by B. Max Mehl, a specimen Mehl described as being "almost equal to a proof" sold for $132.50.[2] This piece was pedigreed to the *Jack Roe Collection* sold as a part of the *Waltman* sale. Then in 1946 at Mehl's *Atwater* sale, another prooflike specimen sold for $127.50.

Moving forward into the 1950s, the *Anderson-Dupont* sale conducted by Stack's featured a breathtaking 1872-CC that the cataloger boldly described as being "Prooflike" and "Unsurpassed in condition, the Finest Known"[3] which realized $330. At Bowers and Ruddy's *Dr. Edward B. Willing* sale in 1976, a specimen the auctioneer described as, "An absolutely unbelievable coin: probably … a presentation piece"[4] sold for $3,100. It was a part of the noteworthy *E.A. Carson* set of Carson City coins. By 1998 specimens of the 1872-CC dollar in Uncirculated condition were bringing nearly $30,000; the *Sonnheim Family* coin auctioned by Bowers and Merena sold for $28,750 that year.

Thanks to the relatively high survival rate for a coin with such a low original mintage, there are many acceptable circulated examples available. Of course the $5.25 price tag for *Harlan P. Smith's* example in Fine condition is ancient history, but collectors in the early 21st century might be able to locate a piece in that grade for approximately $2,000. Problem-free specimens in any grade will be good deals at up to double the listed bid prices in dealer wholesale guides.

[1] *Annual Report of the Director of the Mint*, 1887.
[2] B. Max Mehl, *Waltman Sale*, 1945.
[3] Stack's, *Anderson-Dupont Collection*, 1954.
[4] Bowers and Ruddy, *Dr. Edward B. Willing Collection*.

When considering "CC" coins, two thoughts prevail: dwindling supplies and rising popularity. It would not take more than one major advertising campaign to sell every Carson City coin on the planet. Once upon a time in 1973, the GSA (General Services Administration) sales of "CC" Morgan dollars were not instant sell outs, as the collector market for "CC" coins was only getting its feet wet; but today it would be all over, quick. It is not without significance that there were nearly three million of those dollars, a totally different story than the Seated Liberty series.

Variety specialists do not get too excited about 1872-CC dollars. Only two obverse dies were shipped, and only one was necessary for such a small mintage.

The Philadelphia Mint did not even bother to send a reverse die, and a leftover from 1870 served the need. The reverse features the *Widely Spaced* "CC" and displays a small raised line stemming upward from a bottom denticle between the *O* and *L* in *DOL.* Two attributes on the obverse are a repunched *2* at the top of the date and occasional weakness in *BER* in *LIBERTY.* Fully struck specimens of this date are relatively easy to locate.

(Photo courtesy Bowers and Merena)

Mintage: 2,300

Finest Knowns*:

    NGC MS-65 (1)

    NGC MS-64 (1)

    NGC MS-61 (2)

    PCGS MS-60 (1)

Notable Pedigrees:

    World's Greatest Collection (1945)

    Fairfield Collection (1977)

    Harold S. Bareford (1981)

    Auction '81 Stack's (1981)

    Norweb (1988)

    Sonnheim Family (1998)

      ex: Bareford

    Waldo E. Bolen, Jr. (1999)

Survival Estimates in All Grades:	80-100
Estimated in Uncirculated:	4-6
Estimated in XF to AU:	45-50
Total Certified Examples in All Grades (PCGS and NGC)*:	89

(* As of July 2003)

REFLECTIONS:

Silver dollars were still being produced in the first two months of 1873, in spite of pending legislation designed to eliminate these big coins from the nation's assortment of denominations. Philadelphia minted more than 293,000 Seated Liberty dollars before the Coinage Act was passed in February, and the Carson City Mint toddled along barely eking out 2,300 pieces before the cutoff date. Delivery ledgers found in the National Archives record the final 1,300 coins being minted in March at Carson City. Technically this could have happened since the law did not become effective until April 1, 1873, but it would not have been practical. Silver dollars as a denomination were doomed as their 80 year reign as America's primary unit of account ended on February 12, 1873. At the time, the silver value in dollars was at par with their face value, but this was steadily decreasing, and within a year the intrinsic value would drop below the face value.

Silver depositors, wary of this trend, may have made last-ditch attempts to exchange their silver at the buck-a-coin rate, knowing that the face value would soon be worth more than the metal content. Or, those last 1,300 1873-CC silver dollars may have been minted in February and not recorded until March; no one knows for sure what happened. Most important is the awareness that only 2,300 pieces were coined, ranking the date as the fourth lowest mintage in the Seated Liberty dollar series (with the exclusion of the 1873-S).

Certain numismatic authors (Breen for one) have suggested that most if not all of the final 1,300 1873-CC dollars were melted after the Coinage Act was passed, possibly along with a portion of the 1,000 pieces struck in January. Reasons for this presumption were not provided and it would not have made sense for the Treasury to order that the coins be melted. If that had been the case, a nationwide recall for Seated Liberty dollars would have been necessary, but hundreds of thousands of the old standards were still in circulation, not to mention the masses being held by foreign countries. The silver dollar as a denomination might have been abandoned, but it was not forsaken.

What other reasons might precipitate the act of melting silver dollars? Bullion value, as mentioned, offered no advantage, for this would have resulted in a push no matter how it was computed. There is the possibility that silver dollars were exchanged for trade dollars, for if a depositor received a one-on-one exchange he would have gained the extra 6.75 grains of silver in the heavier weight trade dollar, netting a return of $.01825. Multiplying that by the 1,300 aforementioned pieces equals a $23.75 gross profit. In addition, trade dollars had legal tender status, whereas Seated Liberty dollars had lost theirs. In time, the federal government would toy with the legal tender issue so much that the public would not know which end was up.

Theories about melting certain dates seem unsupportable, unless official Treasury documents detail such occurrences. This is why open-mindedness is preferable to rigidity when researching these "riddles wrapped in mystery."[1] Indeed there are many mysteries in the field of numismatics, and especially on the subject of coins from the Carson City Mint.

But since there are so many unanswered questions about various coins from the Carson City Mint, numismatists often find it necessary to solve mysteries through the deductive process. Certainly the relative scarcity of 1873-CC dollars presents a challenge. It is no surprise that a date with such a low mintage would be scarce, but if low mintage was the criteria, then the 1871-CC with a figure of 1,376 would rank ahead of the 1873-CC. Such is not the case, however, and in the Uncirculated category, the two dates are nearly equal, with a slight edge to the 1871-CC. However in terms of surviving populations in all grades, the 1873-CC appears to be 25% to 30% scarcer, and as for auction appearances, there are some years when not a single example of an 1873-CC is offered.

Pricing comparisons between the two dates presents more of a challenge. In AU condition, with all things equal, the 1873-CC is generally priced at least double what the 1871-CC sells for. This ratio holds true from XF down to VG; but in Good condition, the 1873-CC often brings at least three times the price of the 1871-CC.

In the Uncirculated category comparisons become difficult as it readily becomes apparent how scarce the two dates are in this grade range. Paralleling is imperfect, but auction records between 1983 and 2003 indicate that there were slightly fewer appearances of the 1873-CC in Mint State condition. Both dates were featured in the Norweb sale held in 1988 and realized prices of $19,800 for the

1871-CC, and $15,400 for the 1873-CC. In 1995, the *James A. Stack* 1871-CC dollar went to the winning bidder for $137,500, the second of only two Uncirculated 1871-CCs that were auctioned during that 20 year span. Then in 1998, the second of only two Uncirculated 1873-CCs auctioned during these years sold as part of the *Sonnheim Family* collection and realized $64,100. This specimen had sold in October of 1981 in the *Harold S. Bareford* sale for $12,000. There would be two more appearances of the two Mint State 1871-CC dollars, but neither of the two 1873-CCs in Uncirculated would be seen again in a public auction during this period.

Complicating price comparisons is the difference in grades between the Uncirculated specimens of these two dates which have recently appeared in auctions. Whereas both examples of the 1873-CC dollars are in the MS-60 range, the two Mint State 1871-CCs grade MS-63 or better, explaining in part why the 1871-CCs broke through the $100,000 barrier twice, and recently in 2003, one of them even passed the $200,000 mark. It is reasonable to believe, however, that if one of the higher grade 1873-CC specimens listed in NGC's *Census Report*[2] were offered at a public auction in the early years of the 21st century, it would shatter the 1871-CC dollar's price record, which must put a smile on the face of the collector who owns the Gem quality 1873-CC. In fact, as this book went to press, it was reported that a private treaty sale was in negotiations for this coin in the neighborhood of $300,000.

As prices continue to appreciate for many scarce Carson City coins, collectors will marvel when looking back, and seeing what the coins sold for "once upon a time." For example, at the *World's Greatest Collection* sale in 1945, an Uncirculated 1873-CC dollar described as "lustrous, with light cabinet frictions"[3] was hammered down for $110. In October of 1977 at the *Fairfield Collection* sale hosted by Bowers and Ruddy, a "Choice Borderline Uncirculated" specimen brought $3,700.[4] These trails back to the past provide collectors with the paths to follow when evaluating the growth in popularity of their hobby.

Commentaries appearing after the *Norweb* sale in 1988 expressed awe at the prices being paid for coins then, including amazement gushed over the set of Seated Lib-

---

[1] Phrase coined by Winston Churchill.
[2] *NGC Census Report*, July 2003.
[3] Numismatic Gallery, *The World's Greatest Collection*.
[4] Bowers and Ruddy, *The Fairfield Collection*, 1977.

erty silver dollars that sold for over $500,000. In today's market (2003-2004), a single Gem Uncirculated 1873-CC dollar and a Choice Uncirculated 1871-CC would probably bring more than that.

One of the stories from the library of Carson City coin lore concerns the discovery of three Uncirculated 1873-CC silver dollars. As the story goes, a local company in Carson City was contracted to demolish a building in 1973. Apparently the structure had been erected in 1873, and following a Carson City tradition in the 19th century, objects and artifacts were placed in the cornerstone as construction began.[1] Coins were popular items back then, and when the crew opened the cornerstone of this particular edifice in 1973, they ruffled through the assortment of memories stored a century before, and quickly opened three small folded handkerchiefs containing three brand new 1873-CC silver dollars. From this point in the story, the details become fuzzy. Who actually witnessed this event is unknown, and what happened to the coins is lost over 30 years as second and third-hand renditions were passed down. Coin dealers got involved and allegedly one of the dollars traded hands for $5,000 in the second half of 1973. Another of the three reportedly traded hands around 1977, and the whereabouts of the third piece, if it exists, has never been revealed. In the absence of pedigree information, tracking these rarities will be impossible. Maybe some day the truth will surface.[2]

A story like this and the one about the 1870-CC coins found in the Capitol building cornerstone stirs the imagination. One can only wonder what would be discovered if the whole downtown of Carson City were torn down; there might be more numismatic wealth in the cornerstones and rubble piles than anyone thought possible. (Don't worry Governor, this is not a threat, just a dream).

1873 was the year the nation came to grips with its

commitment to the gold standard or bimetallism. Germany had demonetized silver two years earlier, and converted to the gold standard. They professed to not be switching to gold because gold was good, but rather because Great Britain was good. There was not anything special about gold per se, but there was something special about England, and if gold was good for England, then gold was good for Germany, and many other countries around the world.

Nevada was understandably concerned about the silver issue. In the *Territorial Enterprise* at the end of 1872, looking ahead toward the passage of the *Coinage Act*, an editorial described the impending fate of silver dollars,

"The dollar is therefore worth intrinsically $4\frac{1}{2}\%$ more than the half dollar, which virtually excludes the former from circulation..."[3]

This came to pass on February 12, 1873, just when silver production in Nevada and especially the Comstock region was beginning a steep climb upward. Increased silver supplies, combined with declining demand for silver coinage, posed a serious threat to the economy of Nevada and the other mining states. But Congressional committees planned to circumvent plunging silver prices by introducing trade dollars, which began production in July of 1873, just several months after production of Seated Liberty silver dollars had been put to rest.[4]

---

[1] See the story about the 1870-CC coins in the section on the 1870-CC silver dollar in this book.

[2] Another version reports that a local construction worker in Carson City found a tobacco can full of "CC" coins while working on the reconstruction of the Nevada State Museum. Included in the group of coins were three 1873-CC seated dollars that were sold to a local coin dealer in Carson City who subsequently sold two uncirculated examples to a California dealer for $10,000 a piece.

[3] *Territorial Enterprise*, December 18, 1872.

[4] One of the *Top 25*.

COMPARISON OF SEATED LIBERTY DOLLAR PRODUCTION
AT THE CARSON CITY MINT WITH THE
PHILADELPHIA MINT'S FROM 1870 TO 1873

SEATED LIBERTY $1 MINTAGE TOTALS		
Year	Carson City	Philadelphia
1870	12,462	416,000
1871	1,376	1,074,760
1872	3,150	1,106,450
1873	2,300	293,600
TOTAL	19,288	2,890,810

(Photo courtesy American Numismatic Rarities)

What an interesting topic trade dollars are. It is no surprise that so much has been written about this controversial denomination, not just in numismatic literature, but also in books on political history, economics, and finance. Many adults living in the United States in the early years of the 21st century have never heard of trade dollars, let alone seen one. These enigmatic coins were conceived around 1870, introduced in 1873, aborted in 1878, and issued as Proofs through 1885, at which time they were given their last rites. Short-lived denominations were nothing new in America's monetary system; from 1864 to 1873 two-cent pieces debuted and departed. In the trade dollar era, the incongruous 20-cent piece flashed and crashed. When trade dollars first appeared the smart money bet against their success and later numismatic authors like Walter Breen blasted the coinage as an "expensive mistake."[1]

Indeed, trade dollars were and are easy targets, for even at the time of issue, few knew the new coin's purpose. Charges that the legislation authorizing them was corrupt soon made the headlines. Did political patronage between wealthy silver miners and congressmen push the bill through? If so, how was that different from the way things worked anyway? After all, the railroads were receiving political favors right and left, as were big banks and corporations. But for some reason, the issuance of the trade dollar was for many the unpardonable sin.

More than anything else, the *Coinage Act of 1873*, which authorized trade dollars, surreptitiously sentenced standard silver dollars to expulsion. But weren't the new coins called *dollars* too? If the nation was simply exchanging one silver dollar for another, what difference did it make? A design change for the old dollars was overdue, and the new dollars even contained more silver than the old and many thought that was good. More silver meant more security and more profits for the mining industry, and would guard against falling prices in the wake of higher bullion yields.

Anyone could purchase trade dollars from the Mint by exchanging 378 grains of silver, which in 1873 was worth approximately $1.022 in gold, plus a coining fee that covered "the actual average cost to each mint...of the material, labor, wastage, and use of machinery employed."[2] From the depositor's point of view, trade dollars were no bargain during that first year, but as silver prices declined, they provided an obvious advantage.

Yet bullion depositors were not the primary source of trade dollar production, this distinction belonged to the Treasury which purchased silver with money in a bullion fund. As the cost of manufacturing trade dollars decreased due to lower silver prices, coinage profits were credited to the Treasury Department. This became a lucrative business for the Treasury, but soon the public protested against overvalued trade dollars, and only bullion depositors favored the continuation of the series at that time. But once again the Treasury stepped in and this time, revoked the legal tender status of the trade dollars in 1876. This stripped bullion depositors of their domestic profit—making opportunities, although there were still advantages from exportation.

In general, the public was baffled by trade dollars, and exploitation permeated the country. Unwary merchants and consumers were assured by licentious brokers that trade dollars were worth one dollar in gold, or close to it. Then, upon attempting to use them for payment, merchants and retail customers alike were subject to losses due to discounting. Finally, in October of 1877 a proposal was made to discontinue further issuance of trade dollars; but since

[1] *Walter Breen's Complete Encyclopedia of U.S. and Colonial Coins.*
[2] *Coinage Act of 1873,* section: 3524.

orders were pending for more trade dollars to be exported to China, the authorization to cease production did not come until February of 1878.

By then the Carson City Mint had manufactured 97,000 1878-CC trade dollars. Combined with the previous five year's production, mintages totaled 4,211,400, representing approximately 11.7% of the nation's entire output. On the other hand, the San Francisco Mint, strategically located for commerce in the Orient, manufactured approximately 74% of the country's trade dollars.

Popular or not, trade dollars minted at Carson City accounted for approximately 39% of all of the silver used to produce coins between 1873 and 1878. In the small company environment at the Carson Mint this was a welcome addition. Any businessman can appreciate what a godsend a supplemental increase of 39% would be, especially to the Carson City Mint and its 80 to 90 employees, seemingly always facing the prospect of closure.

There are six dates in the "CC" trade dollar series, not including the multiple varieties. Although the 1875-S/CC is listed separately in all numismatic publications, it is claimed as a date in a set from both mints. For the purposes of this book, the 1875-S/CC will be included in the section on the 1875-CC, and categorized as optional to the set.

Assembling a six (or seven) piece set of "CC" trade dollars is challenging in any grade and becomes an exacting task in Uncirculated. Key dates in all grades include the 1873-CC, 1876-CC, and 1878-CC, and the 1875-CC is by far the most common, as its higher mintage suggests. Two dates, the 1874-CC and 1877-CC, are considered mid-range on the rarity scale. In strict Uncirculated condition, the 1873-CC, 1876-CC, and 1878-CC are in a virtual deadlock for scarcest date honors. All dates are practically nonexistent in MS-65 or higher, generally classified as having a population of 1, if available at all.

Because of the preponderance of scholarly reference works on the subject of trade dollars, only the briefest of overviews will be provided in this book. Readers are encouraged to explore such helpful literature as Q. David Bowers' *Silver Dollars and Trade Dollars of the United States* and John M. Willem's, *The United States Trade Dollar.*

BUREAU OF THE MINT DATA FOR
CARSON CITY TRADE DOLLAR PRODUCTION

Total Combined Mintage: 4,211,400

Total Face Value: $4,211,400

Total Ounces of Silver Used: .... 3,316,057 ozs.

Design Type: .... Trade Dollar

Designer: .... William Barber

Metal Composition: .... .900 Silver .100 Copper

Actual Gross Weight: .... 27.22 gr.

Value of Silver in One Trade
    Dollar Between 1873 and 1878: .... $.90-1.03

(Photo courtesy American Numismatic Rarities)

Mintage: 124,500

Finest Knowns*:

NGC MS-65 (1)

PCGS MS-64 (2)

NGC MS-64 (4)**

Notable Pedigrees:

James Swan Randall (1878)

Anderson-Dupont (1954)

Empire Collection (1957)

R.L. Miles (1969)

Fairfield Collection (1977)

Bowers and Merena (1988)

Waldo E. Bolen (1999)

Legend Collection (Current)

Survival Estimates in All Grades: 750-1,000	
Estimated in Uncirculated: 50-75	
Estimated in XF to AU: 125-250	
Total Certified Examples in All Grades (PCGS and NGC)*: 186	

(* As of July 2003)

(** Possible resubmissions of one or more of the same coin)

REFLECTIONS:

When the trade dollars debuted in Carson City in July of 1873 they were the talk of the town. Every newspaper in the surrounding area *puffed* the new attractive examples of what silver was meant to be used for. These big glistening coins had "commercial" written all over them. A poised and confident *Liberty* is seated on bales of packaged goods, surrounded by agricultural produce facing toward the Far East. Her right hand is outstretched with an olive branch symbolizing peace. At the base is the inscription *IN GOD WE TRUST*, not necessarily expressing the sentiments of every citizen now that the Civil War was over. This motto had been added to America's coinage in 1864 amidst turmoil and trepidation, affirming an old adage proclaiming that "there are no atheists in foxholes"; and explaining in part the general acceptance of the pledge at that time. However, when wars end, people tend to abandon spiritual inclinations and retreat to more secular beliefs. But anyway, there it was, boldly displayed on the obverse of the trade dollar in 1873, sending a message to the rest of the world that America was not a pagan nation.

On the reverse was found an obvious expression of commercialism: *TRADE DOLLAR*, leaving no doubt about the purpose of the coin. Metal weight and fineness were stamped below the eagle similar to the hallmarks seen on bars of bullion. A dual philosophical message is clutched in a more lifelike eagle's claws; a sprig of olive calling for peace, and arrows just in case.

Mintage of these new congressionally inspired dollars coincided with the limited production of the *With Arrows* coins, emanating from the same *Coinage Act of 1873*. By the end of July, 16,500 1873-CC trade dollars had been manufactured, most being shipped to San Francisco for export to Asia. Local depositors, excited to participate in the event, secured a small percentage of the fresh output. Production dropped off through summer, then accelerated in October, when 37,000 "CC" trade dollars were minted. San Francisco was outpacing Carson City by a wide margin, and in the final month of the year, 200,000 1873-S trade dollars were minted, compared to a respectable 43,500 at Carson City. End of the calendar-year tallies were 397,500 at Philadelphia, 703,000 at San Francisco and 124,500 at Carson City.

From the start, a small mintmark, seemingly disproportionate to the size of the coin, was used on Carson City trade dollars, and surprisingly it would get smaller in 1874 before reversing course and being enlarged. All three known mintmark varieties feature parallel letters. On two of the varieties, the letters are uniformly close together, and on the third variety, the two "C"s are spaced wide apart. Some Uncirculated examples are seen with die cracks shooting every which way downward from *ADE* and *DOL* to the denticles. On the obverse, certain specimens show a recut 7. Many examples of this date exhibit granularity in spots.

Throughout the production years of the trade dollars, two different obverse and two reverse designs were utilized within the mint system and three known design marriages resulted: the Type I/I, I/II, and II/II. All 1873-CC's fall into the Type I/I category, and although varieties within the "CC" trade dollar series offer hours of satisfying research to the specialist, virtually no significant market exists other than for the recognizable 1875-S/CC. *Cherrypickers* and diehard diagnostic devotees might disagree, but the coin market is all about pricing, and excluding exceptions, prices for "CC" trade dollars are based on date and condition, not variety. One of the most complete sets of trade dollars by variety was assembled by the foremost authority in his day, John M. Willem. His collection was auctioned in 1980 by Henry Christian, Inc. and provides a virtual textbook on trade dollar varieties, including chopmarks.

A survey of price appreciation for 1873-CC trade dollars in Uncirculated condition reveals two points of interest. First, this date, like most from the trade dollar series, was not in demand until the 1940s and even at that time, the trade dollar series was being ignored by most coin collectors. For example, in the *William C. Atwater* sale in June of 1946 an Uncirculated 1873-CC trade dollar

"with frosty mint surface" sold for $27. In comparison, a 1903-S Barber half in Uncirculated realized $57.50, and a sharply struck 1921 Standing Liberty quarter in Uncirculated brought $50. Of course there is no way to determine what point rating these coins would have received using modern (2003) grading standards, but all things being equal, the 1873-CC trade dollar was a bargain. Then in the 1954 *Anderson-Dupont Collection*, an Uncirculated specimen described as "very scarce" was purchased for $45. In this same sale, a "Brilliant Uncirculated" 1893-CC Morgan dollar realized $62.50, and a 1919 Walking Liberty half sold for $47. There is no question which of these three coins would be the scarcest today (2003), notwithstanding Consensus Condition rankings. For instance, in the early years of the 21st century, an MS-66 or 67 specimen of an 1893-CC dollar would outprice an 1873-CC trade dollar in MS-63 or MS-64. Using the same reasoning, a 1919 Walking Liberty half graded MS-69 would probably surpass both the 1873-CC and 1893-CC in price if these two were in grades below MS-65. It is all relative of course. A snapshot of modern (2003) prices for these three dates in the table below serves to illustrate further how undervalued Uncirculated 1873-CC trade dollars were in the 1950s.

Moving forward from the 1950s to 1977, Uncirculated 1873-CC trade dollars had reached the $1,000 level. At Bowers and Ruddy's *Fairfield Collection* sale, memorable for a dazzling assortment of Carson City trade dollars, a "Choice Brilliant Uncirculated" 1873-CC trade dollar brought $1,000; less than 20 years later, it was routine for legitimate Uncirculated specimens of the 1873-CC to bring strong five figure prices when sold at auction. In the early years of the 21st century, this date is highly respected among numismatists, especially in grades of MS-64 or higher.

Circulated examples offer good value when found in problem free condition. And of course, there is no way to determine how many specimens exist in all grades, but it seems safe to predict that there are no large hoards waiting to be discovered. That being said, the number of collectors who could own one example for themselves is probably limited to 1,000, including chopmarked pieces.[1]

2003 UNCIRCULATED PRICES FOR 1919 HALF DOLLARS, 1873-CC TRADE DOLLARS, AND 1893-CC SILVER DOLLARS

Grade	1919 Half	1893-CC Dollar	1873-CC Trade Dollar
MS-60	$ 900	$ 2,000	$ 4,000
MS-63	2,500	3,500	20,000
MS-64	3,200	6,000	40,000
MS-65	4,500	40,000	100,000

---

[1] One of the *Top 25*.

(Photo courtesy Bowers and Merena)

Mintage: 1,373,200

Finest Knowns*:

    PCGS MS-66 (1)

    NGC MS-65 (4)

    PCGS MS-64 (10) **

    NGC MS-64 (13)**

Notable Pedigrees:

    James Swan Randall (1878)

    Empire Collection (1957)

    Wolfson (1963)

    Amon Carter (1984)

Notre Dame Sale – Stack's (2001)

    ex: Amon Carter

Legend Collection (Current)

    ex: Amon Carter

Survival Estimates in All Grades:	2,000-3,000
Estimated in Uncirculated:	185-225
Estimated in XF to AU:	300-500
Total Certified Examples in All Grades (PCGS and NGC)*:	307

(* As of July 2003)

(** Possible resubmissions of one or more of the same coin)

REFLECTIONS:

After a productive December in 1873, the Carson City Mint reduced its trade dollar output by 78% in January of 1874. This proved to be a brief pause, however, because the rest of the year trade dollars were hauled out in larger quantities than any previous "CC" silver coins. In fact, the 1,373,200 trade dollars produced at Carson City in 1874 surpassed the combined quantities of all other silver coins minted there from 1870 through 1874, including the 1873 trade dollars. Added together, the dimes, quarters, halves, and standard dollars minted during those years, plus the 1873 trade dollars, totaled 1,137,315 pieces.

Of course trade dollars took precedence over all other silver coinage in 1874; half dollar production fell off 82.5%, no quarters were struck, and dime mintage was a meager 10,817 pieces. It was clear that the Treasury was committed to its new trade dollar program; all three mints were at full steam ahead.

At first trade dollars were welcomed by silver coin-starved Americans who were sick of paper money, but gradually the attraction began to wear off. By the end of 1874, the silver value in a trade dollar was worth less than its face value. For silver depositors this was good news, but for merchants and consumers it was a pain in the neck. Ever resourceful bullion traders however, made the most of it, and export demand for trade dollars was steady. Merchants in the Far East found the U.S. coins as tradable as any other country's offerings, and the reputation of the United States as an international power was growing rapidly.

It has been estimated that as many as 98% of the 3.9 million plus trade dollars minted between the Carson City and San Francisco mints in 1874 were exported, which would have left nearly 80,000 pieces stateside, 27,000 or more in Carson City alone. These figures could be off by a small percentage, but chances are they are very close, and if 27,000 is near the correct total for the 1874-CC trade dollars, one piece per person would have been available for residents living in the surrounding region at the time.

From the supply of 1874-CC trade dollars reserved for local business perhaps as many as 90% were melted in the years to follow. If these estimates are close to accurate it means that less than .3% of the original mintage may have survived. Of course, small quantities of 1874-CC trade dollars were imported back into the United States years later, but stripped of legal tender status they were doomed to the melting pot.

In the second half of the 20th century, any specimen discovered abroad would have drawn the interest of coin collectors in the U.S. It is also worth noting that many 1874-CC trade dollars with the trademarks (chopmarks) of Chinese merchants have been returned to U.S. markets via different channels, causing this date to be considered the most common chopmarked "CC" trade dollar.

With a price history similar to "CC" trade dollars in general, the 1874-CCs were ignored by the majority of collectors. Again, Heaton provided insight as to why this was true when he wrote, "the amount in circulation before the recall was not limited enough in any date to cause...scarcity."[1] Heaton does give special recognition to the 1878-CC though; presuming that since this date had the lowest mintage it must therefore be scarcer than the other dates. As a general rule, Heaton based his rarity rankings strictly on original mintages, which is surprising, knowing that he used the Directors' *Annual Reports* for most of his references. Certainly he would have had a copy of the 1887 report with the recapitulation of trade dollar exports for every year they were issued. The table below clearly exhibits that more than 80% of all trade dollars minted had been exported, resulting in a much smaller playing field. If, for the sake of ascertaining rarity factors, 80% of the original mintages for "CC" trade dollars were subtracted, certain dates would rank much higher in scarcity. Additionally, the export percentages for the earlier "CC" dates were much higher than 80%.

Of course Heaton had his reasons and it is a tribute to him that his work has stood as a standard in the study of branch mint coins for more than 110 years.

Regardless of the accuracy of Heaton's analysis of the scarcity of "CC" trade dollars, his view was shared by numismatists for decades. Evidence of the general disregard for trade dollars as a series, including the "CC" issues is found in auction catalogs from 1873 through the 1930s. It was routine for trade dollars to sell for below their face value in the 1880s and 1890s. Gradually auction prices rose, and by the turn of the century, certain pieces were realizing prices slightly above face value. Two coins from the *Norweb* collection, the 1873-CC and 1874-CC trade dollars, are illustrative of this as both coins graded AU and were purchased in 1908 at a Henry Chapman auction for $1.25 each. By the 1930s "CC" trade dollars were pushing the $2 and $3 envelope; for example an AU 1878-CC crossed the block for $2.50 at B. Max Mehl's 1930 *Lusk and Leopard* sale.

Price gains for "CC" trade dollars were lackluster through the 1950s, though they had blasted past the $15 mark. At the *Anderson-Dupont* sale in 1954 the winning bid for a Choice AU 1874-CC was $16 and at the 1957 *Empire* sale an attractive Uncirculated specimen realized $45. Into the 1960s, prices continued to increase at a snail's pace; for example, a Brilliant Uncirculated 1874-CC, "just about Gem," sold for $65 at Stack's *Wolfson* auction in 1963.

A sweeping tide of rare coin activity beginning in the late 1970s, turbocharged just about any round object made out of metal with a date on it and trade dollars were finally invited to join the party. It had been a long 100 year wait, but they had finally arrived.

EXPORTS AND IMPORTS OF TRADE-DOLLARS TO SEPTEMBER 4, 1887.

Fiscal years.	Exports.	Imports.
1874	*3,000,000	
1875	*4,500,000	
1876	*4,500,000	
1877	8,672,596	
1878	5,166,006	
1879	1,238,749	
1880	43,383	783,062
1881	20	92,397
1882	3,600	
1883	1,000	
1884	225,500	
1885	1,073,150	
1886	354,848	
1887	10	766,483
1888 (to September 4, 1887)		64,078
	28,778,862	1,706,020
	1,706,020	
Net Export	27,072,842	

* "Partly estimated." (Annual Report of the Director of the Mint, fiscal year 1879, p. 130.) Total exports prior to November 1, 1878—exact period not stated— 25,703,950. (Annual Report of the Director of the Mint, fiscal year 1878, p. 12.)

Of the total imports of trade dollars, 830,561 have been imported into the United States since the passage of the act of March 3, 1887, authorizing their redemption. (*Annual Report of the Director of the Mint,* 1887)

[1] Augustus G. Heaton, *Mint Marks, A Treatise,* 1893.

No "CC" trade dollar could have better represented the series than the *Amon G. Carter, Jr.* 1874-CC, when it sold in 1984 at the Stack's auction. Described as a Gem Uncirculated, pristine specimen, it set a record for the date at $10,450. Seventeen years later this coin appeared in a 2001 Stack's auction featuring properties belonging to *Notre Dame*. After a knock-down-drag-out bidding session the winner paid $54,625. To no one's surprise PCGS graded the coin MS-66 and it fits like a glove into the *Legend Collection*, the finest set of trade dollars as of 2003. Collectors' reservations about the popularity of trade dollars, especially Carson City issues, have vanished, and future offerings of show-stopping specimens, like the *Amon Carter* 1874-CC, should bring more price records.

Just like choices for clothes sizes, the 1874-CC trade dollar offers four sizes of mintmarks; *Micro, Small, Medium,* and *Large*; die specialists have been busy investigating this date much to their delight. When 1874 began, a smaller mintmark than that used in 1873 was employed. By the end of the year, the direction had been reversed and the *Large* "CC", also known as *Tall,* seemed more appropriate considering the coin's size.

In the ongoing saga of Proof coins from the Carson City Mint, auction catalogs in the past have listed certain 1874-CC trade dollars as being "Proofs." Yet to date, (2003-2004) there have been no "Proofs" authenticated.

In circulated grades up to XF, 1874-CC trade dollars are priced just like common dates, establishing them as exceptional bargains. Problem free examples in circulated condition are worth at least double, if not triple, current wholesale prices. In AU condition, this date begins commanding a premium over common dates in the trade dollar series. Examples in the two lower AU grades (AU-50, AU-53) typically have been cleaned and tend to have a washed-out look; these coins should only be considered at discounted prices. In contrast, Choice AU to Borderline Uncirculated (AU-55 to AU-58) specimens that are problem free, are worth almost double the wholesale prices listed for MS-60 coins.

(Photo courtesy Bowers and Merena)

Mintage: 1,573,700

Finest Knowns*:

   1875-CC   PCGS MS-66 (I)

                  NGC MS-65 (3)

   1875 S/CC PCGS MS-65 (I)

                  NGC MS-65 (2)

Notable Pedigrees**:

       Atwater (1946)

       Amon G. Carter (1984)

       E.A. Carson (1976)

       Eliasberg (1997)

Survival Estimates in All Grades**:	3,500-5,000
Estimated in Uncirculated**:	350-400
Estimated in XF to AU**:	600-1,200
Total Certified Examples in All Grades (PCGS and NGC)*: 1875-CC:	359
1875-S/CC:	88

(* As of July 2003)
(** For 1875-CC Only)

REFLECTIONS:

Congress passed the *Specie Payment Act* on January 15, 1875 which, "authorized and required, as rapidly as practicable, to cause to be coined at the mints of the United States, silver coins of the denomination of ten, twenty-five, and fifty cents…, and to issue them in redemption of an equal number and amount of fractional currency of similar denominations." This was to continue until, "such fractional currency outstanding shall be redeemed."[1] This would have the effect of thrusting silver coin production into overdrive, and it could not have come at a better time for the mining industry in Nevada. Annual yields on the Comstock were approaching $30 million in 1875, and this was just a warm-up. Members of the silver party were in a festive mood during the *Bonanza* times. For all of a sudden it was time to test the Bureau of the Mint's multi-tasking capabilities: not only were millions of the smaller denomination silver coins going to be manufactured, the trade dollar program was in full swing. Of greatest consequence to the mining industry, with all the minting ahead, more silver would be used than at any other point in the nation's history.

Operations got off to a resounding start at Carson City in 1875 when 225,000 trade dollars were delivered in January, culminating a prolific six month run extending back to August of 1874 that resulted in 1,236,500 trade dollars being struck. Of course, the mint did not sustain this pace that would have resulted in an annual output of nearly 2.5 million pieces. But still, workers were placed on overtime schedules, and none of the increased production would have been possible had Superintendent Crawford not purchased a second auxiliary coin press.

It seemed as if everyone in the nation had been bitten by the silver bug. Even foreigners, hearing of the outpour of wealth being discovered on the Comstock, journeyed long distances to seek fortunes. The following, from the *Carson Daily Appeal*, relates how 30 immigrants arrived in town, "with large canvas sacks in which to begin 'salting down' (salting away) the trade dollars that they are to commence earning on the day they land…." With a hint of sarcasm, the article goes on to describe how these inexperienced treasure seekers planned to grab silver off the side of a mountain that locals had overlooked, convincing themselves that they had worked out the plan hundreds of times before arriving. To this the article adds, "in their dreams."[2]

At San Francisco, mint workers were on a torrid schedule that nearly doubled the trade dollar output from the previous year. During one of the peak production

---

[1] *Annual Report of the Director of the Mint*, 1875.

[2] *Carson Daily Appeal*, February 27, 1875.

months in 1875 orders must have been issued to send at least one altered reverse die originally prepared for Carson City to San Francisco, possibly because there was a surplus of "CC" reverse dies on hand at Philadelphia. Upon arrival, the coining department at San Francisco was instructed to use the crude reverse showing the "CC" mintmark, until new dies with their normal "S" mintmark were sent. Of course this might have been slightly offensive to rival mint San Francisco's pride. One thing was certain, there was much more demand for dies at San Francisco than at Carson City.

What had been a common act of resourcefulness during a stressful production schedule provided later generations of coin collectors with a popular variety. Remnants of the two *Large* C's are visible to the sides of where San Francisco's "S" mintmark is located. Though officially struck at the California mint, 1875-S/CC trade dollars are claimed by collectors of sets from both mints. Although it is difficult to say for sure what collector response would be if the situation were reversed, as far as collectors of Carson City coins are concerned, if it has "CC"s on it, they want it!

Of course, there are numerous examples of overmintmarked coins with other combinations of mints, but the popularity of those coupled with a "CC" mintmark is undeniable. Of the three other mints active during the Carson City era, only Philadelphia does not share a mintmark combination with the Carson Mint; just imagine if there had been a Philadelphia silver dollar with just the slightest trace of the two "C"s, allowing Carson City to have teamed up for twosomes with all three mints. Added to the 1875-S/CC and 1900-O/CC, this Philadelphia edition would have formed a pleasing three piece set; but alas, "only in our dreams."

The 1875-S/CC variety was unknown to the broad numismatic community until the early 1960s when it was considered an extremely scarce variety. Premiums were paid to obtain this peculiar variety, though trade dollars as a series still lagged far behind mainline denominations. As more examples of the 1875-S/CC were discovered, the date's rarity status was re-evaluated and lowered to semi-rare. Yet in Uncirculated condition it is considered one of the scarcer dates in the series, and through the years premiums have risen dramatically. As of the writing of this book, the 1875-S/CC is valued at three to four times more than the 1875-CC. A brief survey of auction prices realized for selected Uncirculated specimens from 1977 to 2001 is displayed at right.

Concerning regular issue Carson City trade dollars from 1875, prices have risen consistently since the 1960s. Though hardly a blip on the coin pricing screen in 1946, when a Choice Uncirculated example sold for $13.50 at the *Atwater* sale, by the 1970s high grade specimens were attracting more attention. At the *E.A. Carson* sale in 1976, a Choice Uncirculated specimen was hammered down for $750, but it was not until the *Amon Carter* sale in 1984 that the roof was raised on the price for this date. Of course the *Carter* specimen is the one by which all other examples of this date will be measured, yet the audience at that 1984 auction was still surprised when it passed the ten grand mark at $10,175. Years later this coin became the only example of the date to grade MS-66, and is one of only four "CC" trade dollars graded this high, three by PCGS, and one by NGC.

Many examples of this date were struck on porous planchets and display various degrees of granularity on the surfaces. Both Type I and Type II reverses were used on 1875-CC trade dollars and all known examples feature either *Large* (Tall) or *Medium* "CC"s. One reverse variety shows doubling across various sections of the lettering, but is not considered a premium priced issue.

Though the 1875-CC is certainly the most common date in the Carson City trade dollar series, it is doubtful that more than .5% of the original mintage survives in all grades. When compared to modern issues such as American Silver Eagles and the proliferation of U.S. commemoratives, the supply of 1875-CC trade dollars is rather small. Once again, a massive national sales promotion would most likely result in a sellout of every available 1875-CC trade dollar on the planet.

AUCTION PRICES REALIZED FOR 1875-S/CC TRADE DOLLARS IN UNCIRCULATED – 1977 TO 2001			
Year	Auction Company	Grade	Price Realized
1977	Bowers & Ruddy – Fairfield	Uncertified Uncirculated	$1,250
1992	Stack's – September	Uncertified Gem	6,875
1994	Stack's – January	Uncertified Gem	11,500
1998	Heritage – March	MS-62	5,175
1998	Heritage – January	MS-64	13,500
2000	Superior – February	MS-63	10,120
2001	Heritage – August	MS-64	14,375
2001	Bowers & Merena – November	MS-64	17,250

(Photo courtesy Bowers and Merena)

Mintage: 509,000

Finest Knowns*:

PCGS MS-65 (1)

NGC MS-64 (4)

Notable Pedigrees:

John Swan Randall (1878)

Atwater (1946)

R.L. Miles (1969)

Fairfield (1977)

Stack's – September (1992)

Eliasberg (1997)

Legend Collection (Current)

ex: Eliasberg

Survival Estimates in All Grades**: .. 1,000-1,500
Estimated in Uncirculated**: 50-75
Estimated in XF to AU**: 275-600
Total Certified Examples in All Grades (PCGS and NGC)*: 183

(* As of July 2003)

(**Includes Double Die Variety)

REFLECTIONS:

It was business as usual at the Carson City Mint as 1876 began, and by the end of January 216,000 trade dollars had been delivered. Then an emphasis on dimes, quarters and halves, combined with a major shift in trade dollar production to San Francisco, curbed Carson City's output. Supplies of silver were compounding by the minute and the silver industry did not care where trade dollars were minted, as long as large scale production continued.

This was a peak year for silver coinage during the *coin-drive* that spanned from 1875 through 1877. Of course, 1876 was also known for the classic 20-piece minted at Carson City that year. The abundance of coins being produced was so great it was almost as if when each new silver piece fell from the coin press, the silver miner's cash registers went *ka-ching*.

At Carson City, Superintendent Crawford supervised the installation of the third and most powerful coin press in May. This had no impact on trade dollar production however, which had finished for the year at the end of April. Corresponding with the Carson Mint's proclivity to experiment with Proof strikes in 1876, a number of

trade dollars were struck with one or two sided prooflike surfaces, several of which have relatively deep mirrors.

Though once thought to be much scarcer in Uncirculated condition, professional grading services have certified a relatively large number in Mint State. Yet close to 90% of these certified 1876-CC trade dollars are in MS-63 and lower, with most lacking in eye appeal. Even the majority of MS-63s and MS-64s are quite ugly, and some display hideous artificial toning.

Just as the rarity of this date in the higher Uncirculated grades might suggest, there is only one known specimen graded MS-65 by PCGS or NGC.[1] Aside from this Gem specimen, population data for all other grades of this date is slightly skewed due to multiple resubmissions, as significant price increases from one grade to the next provide obvious incentive for resubmitters hoping to squeeze the last ounce of value out of their coins. Attractive, problem-free examples of this date are very scarce, and are worthy of substantial premiums. Even Choice AU specimens are a challenge, and if encountered are greatly undervalued in today's market (2003-2004). Circulated pieces are easy

---

[1] You can read about this coin in Chapter 2, section 1876 of this book.

to locate, but as the popularity of Carson City coins increases, existing populations of this date will rapidly be absorbed. Additionally, the 1876-CC provides variety collectors with multiple opportunities for exploration.

Primary of course, is the *Double Die Reverse* variety, which displays dramatic doubling in *E. PLURIBUS UNUM*, and in the area above the word *FINE*. If this type of error were attributed to coins such as Lincoln cents, Buffalo nickels, or any 20th century series for that matter, higher price premiums would naturally prevail. But in the early

years of the 21st century, examples of this variety are often sold at non-error prices.

Yet another area of interest on 1876-CC trade dollars for variety and die specialists, are the three mintmark sizes: *Micro* (same as in 1874), *Medium*, and *Large* (*Tall*). All known examples of this date come with Type I obverses, which are married to both types of reverse design (*Berry* and *No Berry* below claw). At the present time, (early years of 21st century) prices for varieties of the 1876-CC trade dollar do not exceed prices for the date in general.

COMPARISON OF TRADE DOLLAR PRODUCTION AT THE
CARSON CITY MINT WITH THE
PHILADELPHIA MINT'S FROM 1873 TO 1878

TRADE DOLLAR MINTAGE TOTALS		
Year	Carson City	Philadelphia
1873	124,500	397,500
1874	1,373,200	987,800
1875	1,573,700	218,900
1876	509,000	456,150
1877	534,000	3,039,710
1878	97,000*	900
TOTAL	4,211,400	5,100,960

* 44,148 Trade Dollars were melted on July 19, 1878.

(Photo courtesy American Numismatic Rarities)

Mintage: 534,000

Finest Knowns*:

    PCGS MS-66 (1)

    NGC MS-65 (1)

    PCGS MS-65 (1)

    PCGS MS-64 (7)**

    NGC MS-64 (8)**

Notable Pedigrees:

    John Swan Randall (1878)

    Atwater (1946)

    Anderson-Dupont (1954)

    R.L. Miles (1969)

    Lamborn (1974)

    Stack's – September (1992)

    Legend Collection (Current)
        ex: Stack's September 1992

Survival Estimates in All Grades:	500-1000
Estimated in Uncirculated:	75-100
Estimated in XF to AU:	250-400
Total Certified Examples in All Grades (PCGS and NGC)*:	159

(* As of July 2003)

(**Possible resubmissions of one or more of the same coins)

REFLECTIONS:

Negating all optimistic plans that the Treasury Department originally had, the trade dollar became a problem child by 1877. Intended to serve as the primary unit of account for trade in the Orient, while simultaneously providing sustenance for a runaway silver market, the denomination now gave brokers an edge, diminishing merchants' and consumers' buying power. Yet another source of consternation to the Treasury was the growing advantage to depositors who exchanged depreciating silver for trade dollars, reaping profits generally reserved for the federal government. Congress had abrogated the legal tender status of trade dollars in July of 1876 in an attempt to curb domestic demand, and reinforce the original intent of exporting the coins. But as the price of silver continued to plunge, the enticement of scoring easy profits led depositors to ignore the change in status. Legal tender or not, they could still deposit 90 cents in silver and receive a big coin with the letters *ONE DOLLAR* on it. Maybe it could not be used to pay government obligations, but someone could be found who would accept it at face value.

Realizing the crisis at hand, Secretary of the Treasury John Sherman directed that the deposits of silver for trade dollars be discontinued in October of 1877, but not before the San Francisco Mint had delivered nearly nine million of the offensive coins. Despite the order of discontinuance, the western mints were given an extension to receive deposits for trade dollars, supposedly to fulfill exportation obligations. Later on, it was discovered that the majority of trade dollars produced during this probationary period were not exported at all, but instead remained in California.

At the Carson Mint, almost 13 months had passed between the last trade dollar deliveries in April of 1876 and the first production in 1877. Beginning in June, business proceeded briskly as over 530,000 trade dollars were struck from June through August, but slowed again as a mere 3,000 were minted from September through December.

There had been a decision to concentrate trade dollar production in the western states at San Francisco, and from January through May of 1877, monthly trade dollar deliveries at the California mint averaged 957,400. If not for a temporary cutback at San Francisco in June (312,000 pieces), perhaps Carson City's output would have been much smaller. But by the last half of July, San Francisco was fired up again and by August, managed to bang out over 1.3 million trade dollars. Accordingly, Carson City's trade dollar activity was brought to a halt, resuming for only a short spurt in December.

By then, general silver coin production had been suspended across the nation. Merchants on the Comstock and surrounding regions let their opinions of the vexatious trade dollars be known in advertisements in local papers and signs posted in public places. It was common to open the *Carson Daily Appeal* or the *Territorial Enterprise* in 1877 and see "Trade Dollars Will Be Discounted," or on storefront signs, "Trade Dollars Not Accepted!" These big coins containing a generous measure of silver had been heralded in 1873 as the saviors of the silver market, but now they were the scourge of the nation.

It is not known whether the glut of trade dollars in and around the Comstock region were native breds from the Carson Mint or if some had come from California. Apparently, nearly all of the 531,000 1877-CC dollars minted during the summer were earmarked for shipment to San Francisco presumably for exportation. Combined with the 9.5 million produced at San Francisco in 1877, nearly 10 million trade dollars were available for export. It has been suggested that a substantially large percentage of these coins were exported to the Far East. If so, why was Secretary Sherman alarmed at the end of 1877 about large quantities flooding domestic markets? If exportation was the goal, and if the bulk of the mint's output was being exported, what was the problem? It seems there are inconsistencies in theories surrounding the domestic/exportation uses for trade dollars minted in 1877 and 1878 and it is reasonable to assume if the exportation market for trade dollars remained brisk, the program would have been deemed successful and would have continued. Since domestic circulation seemed to be more of a problem, it implies that export demand was declining. If so, not all of the 531,000 1877-CC trade dollars allegedly reserved for exportation actually left the state of Nevada. Author John Willem for one, speculated that the

only 1877-CC trade dollars available locally came from the final 3,000 coins minted in December.[1] Of course there are no documents to support this, just as there are no documents to support most speculation concerning Carson City coins, but if it is true, the 1877-CC is conceivably much rarer than previously estimated.

Today's coin collector, living in the early years of the 21st century, has references such as population reports, auction prices realized, and sophisticated price guides, as well as the accumulated numismatic wisdom of more than a century since the Carson City Mint ceased coinage operations. From these resources it is observable that the 1877-CC date ranks fifth in rarity among "CC" trade dollars. An argument could be made that it outranks the 1876-CC when all grades are considered, but the verdict is still out. In grades of AU and above, rarity ranking between "CC" trade dollars becomes more clearly defined. For instance, see the list below that shows approximate wholesale prices for all six dates in the Carson City trade dollar series in grades of AU and MS-60.

As grades move higher up the scale, prices jump in leaps and bounds. In MS-65 or above, new price levels are tested at every auction appearance.

Fueled by the meteoric rise in market value that Uncirculated Carson City trade dollars experienced in the late 20th century, the 1877-CC date flashed its brightness. Beginning at the *Atwater* sale in 1946 when a "Brilliant Uncirculated" example described by B. Max Mehl as "just as perfect as the day it was minted"[2] sold for $27.50, prices went up as a similar specimen realized $47 at the 1954 *Anderson-Dupont* sale and at the 1969 *R.L. Miles* sale another crossed the block at $300. The stage was set for propulsive price appreciation during the final quarter of the 20th century.

A heavenly example of an 1877-CC trade dollar appeared out of nowhere in March of 1980 at a Stack's auction. Somehow bidders forgot that this was supposed to be a relatively common date, driving the price realized to $9,000. In hindsight, the coin market was experiencing a phenomenal bull market at that time, causing wild price gains in all categories;

TRADE DOLLAR WHOLESALE PRICES FOR 1873-CC TO 1878-CC IN AU AND MS-60*		
Year	AU	MS-60
1873-CC	$ 925	$2,100
1874-CC	265	900
1875-CC	215	500
1876-CC	400	1,800
1877-CC	425	600
1878-CC	2,350	7,500
* As of August 2003		

---

[1] John M. Willem *The United States Trade Dollar*.
[2] B. Max Mehl, *William C. Atwater Collection*, 1946.

one month later, on April 18, 1980 the bubble burst, and there was *blood in the streets*, so bad, that at one point it seemed like coin dealers could not give their inventories away. But the fortunate individual who purchased the 1877-CC trade dollar knew he had a winner.

At the time, trade dollars were bid at $500 in MS-60 and $2,600 in MS-65 (1980s grading standards). Gem quality "CC" specimens were selling for $3,700 to $4,750 at auctions, and a high end key date 1878-CC brought $22,000 in July of 1980. So at $9,000, it was obvious that the 1877-CC from the March Stack's sale was special, notwithstanding 1980's hyper-inflated market.

Although the background of this particular 1877-CC trade dollar is unknown, and pedigree information beyond the 1980 sale has not been revealed, it can possibly be linked to another Stack's sale in September of 1992. This time it was part of what the cataloguer described as "unquestionably the finest or nearly finest set of Business Strikes ever offered at a public auction sale."[1] Stack's had a right to puff this group of trade dollars as it included several exquisite pieces, none of which compared to the 1877-CC as attested by the $23,100 price realized. Stack's noted that the collector had spent 20 years assembling the set and in his opinion the 1877-CC was "Unique" in the condition it was in.

At the time of this 1992 auction, none of these trade dollars had been graded by PCGS or NGC. Subsequently, the 1877-CC was awarded the lofty rating of MS-66 by PCGS, an honor it shares with only three other "CC" trade dollars (1874, 1875, and 1878). In due season, this *wonder coin* found its way into a set of trade dollars fit for a king.

When a collector competes for top honors for his or her set, he/she will invariably be forced to pay for the privilege. But suppose you were competing for *finest known set* laurels and were so far ahead that your competition had no chance? Your position would be secure and the only challenge would arise when competitors "kept you honest" as they bid against you while pursuing individual coins they were desirous of, whether they were building a set or not.

An example of a set with no equals is the *Legend Collection* of trade dollars, which consists of many specimens listed as "Pop-Ones," precluding any competition. When there is only one example of a date or dates in the highest grade, there can only be one *finest known set*; and it is in the *Legend Collection* that the 1877-CC graded MS-66 by PCGS resides. It is in good company, and for the Carson

City specialist the splendor of this remarkable assemblage is exhilarating. Picture if you will, an 1874-CC, 1875-CC and 1877-CC each in PCGS MS-66, and all the other dates in MS-65! Once upon a time these six trade dollars could have been purchased for $25 to $50 apiece (1940s). But of course, the specific coins mentioned made fewer appearances than reclusive movie stars, remaining in prestigious collections such as those of *Louis E. Eliasberg, Sr.* and *Amon G. Carter, Jr.* for decades. If and when dates like the 1877-CC from the *Legend Collection* are offered to 21st century collectors, competition will start afresh.

For collectors at all levels, 1877-CC trade dollars represent great value. Problem-free circulated examples are easily worth double current listed wholesale prices (2003 to 2004). For instance, certain coin guides estimate that AU examples are in the $700 to $1,000 range, but for problem free specimens these would be bargain prices. When more collectors start building Carson City type sets (a virtual certainty), increased demand will quickly absorb existing supplies of "CC" trade dollars. Other factors include the potential for advanced interest in building sets of trade dollars, and the outside possibility of more brave collectors starting complete 111 piece sets of Carson City coinage.[2]

There are two mintmark sizes for the 1877-CC, *Medium* and *Large (Tall)*, and all known examples were struck using the Type II obverse and reverse. Variety specialists have focused on the many characteristics found on the date for this issue. On some specimens the *1* and *8* touch, and on others there is space between them. One variety of the *Spaced 18* displays the date higher than usual above the center position, and on one variety of the *Close Date 18*, repunching is seen at the numerals in the date. An attribute of the *Close Date 18* varieties is a bolder strike on the date, in contrast with one of the *Spaced 18* varieties that exhibits a lighter strike.

A commonality that the 1877-CC shares with many other Carson City issues is rusted dies and porous planchets. Some specimens display extreme roughness and porosity, often outlining *Liberty's* silhouette with what looks like a cancerous growth. At times these rough surfaces extend from *Liberty's* middle torso to her ankle. There are also many examples with various degrees of die erosion, usually only seen on Uncirculated specimens.

[1] Stack's, New York, *Stack's September Sale*, 1992.
[2] For more information about the diversity of sets available in the Carson City coin series, see Chapter 10 *Collecting Opportunities*.

1878-CC

(Photo courtesy American Numismatic Rarities)

Mintage: 97,000

Finest Knowns*:

    NGC MS-66 (1) ***

    PCGS MS-65 (1)

    NGC MS-65 (1)***

    PCGS MS-64 (9)**

    NGC MS-64 (7)**

Notable Pedigrees:

    Jack Roe – Waltman Sale (1945)

    Anderson-Dupont (1954)

    Fairfield Collection (1977)

    New England RCA – July (1980)

    New England RCA – January (1982)

Superior Auctions (1988)

RARCOA Auction '90 (1990)

Superior – Boys Town (1990)

Legend Collection (Current)

Survival Estimates in All Grades:	300-500
Estimated in Uncirculated:	60-75
Estimated in XF to AU:	150-250
Total Certified Examples in All Grades (PCGS and NGC)*:	152

(* As of July 2003)

(**Possible resubmissions of one or more of the same coins)

(*** Possibly the same coin)

REFLECTIONS:

By 1878, a paradigm shift occurred in America's silver coinage operations, transferring the spotlight away from minor silver coins and trade dollars onto Morgan silver dollars. Treasury and mint vaults were packed with millions of silver coins that had been produced during the previous five years, and additionally, millions of silver coins began flowing back into the U.S. from foreign nations, drawn like magnets to higher face value over bullion value ratios.

Treasury Secretary Sherman had authorized the discontinuation of trade dollars in October of 1877, but loopholes in his order allowed San Francisco and Carson City to proceed with trade dollar production after that date. It proved to be a triviality at the Carson Mint, with only 3,000 1877-CC trade dollars delivered through the final two months of 1877, and then continuing at low speed as 1878 began. In contrast, the San Francisco Mint struck more trade dollars in December of 1877 than the Carson Mint had produced in either 1876 or 1877. Then in the first four months of 1878, the sound of more than 4.1 million trade dollars kept noise at high decibels inside the chief mint in

the western states. According to Sherman's directive, mintage of these supplementary trade dollars was allowed to meet a supposed demand for export, but it was discovered that most of the coins were placed in circulation locally. Sherman later denied having knowledge of this duplicitous plan, but there were inferences that he might have been a willing participant in political patronage.

One important conclusion to be drawn from these maneuverings is that there was no export demand for the paltry 97,000 trade dollars minted at Carson City in 1878. Although 44,148 trade dollars dated 1878-CC were eventually melted in July, it is plausible that the remaining 52,852 pieces circulated domestically, most likely not all in the Carson City area, but nevertheless in the western states. This would explain the incongruity of a low mintage and at the same time a higher survival ratio. If the average percentage of those trade dollars had been exported, coupled with the meltdown of a portion of the remaining coins, the 1878-CC would be super rare. Based on typical attrition rates for pre-1879-CC silver coins there might have been fewer than 50 specimens extant.

But, of course the surviving population is nearly 10 times that amount, still scarce, but not prohibitively. Like most Carson City issues it was customary for dealers and auction companies in the early 20th century to spice their descriptions with words like rare or scarce, certainly warranted, but decades might pass before anyone would know for sure just how rare certain dates like the 1878-CC trade dollar was. Even Augustus Heaton could not claim with complete accuracy that the 1878-CC trade dollar was scarcer than any of the other dates. Yet he could make an educated observation, surmising that because of the date's low mintage it "should be the most difficult to find."[1]

Dealers and auction cataloguers in the first half of the 20th century agreed with Heaton's presumption, therefore it almost became tradition to describe the six "CC" dated trade dollars as extremely scarce, very scarce, very rare, rare, scarce, and for the 1878-CC, "the rarest date in the series." But exactly how rare was a matter of speculation. The most valuable references from bygone years relate to Uncirculated specimens, because circulated trade dollars were not given much respect, still selling for only $2 to $5 each.

By the 1940s, the 1878-CC trade dollar in Uncirculated condition began to break away from the pack and auction prices for this date were generally higher than similarly graded specimens of other "CC" dates. It was becoming apparent that many of the finest collections did not have an Uncirculated example of the 1878-CC, and some pre-eminent collections did not even include an example of the date in any grade. For example, B. Max Mehl alluded to the absence of an 1878-CC in a notable collection to illustrate the superiority of his consignor's piece, "Uncirculated with frosty mint surface...The rarest trade dollar of this mint... Not in the great collection of dollars recently sold at auction."[2] Mehl was of course referring to the *World's Greatest Collection* sale held five months earlier in January 1945. It is ponderable whether this famous collection did not include an 1878-CC trade dollar because Mr. F.C.C. Boyd (the owner) could not locate one, or because it was inconsequential to him. Regardless, Mr. Mehl's consignor (Jack Roe) received $52.50 for his Uncirculated specimen.

At the *Anderson-Dupont* sale, a Choice Uncirculated specimen sold for $170, not quite reaching the record mark of $190 for the date. Then at the *Wolfson* sale in 1963, an Uncirculated 1878-CC trade dollar hit the block at $310. By the early 1970s, prices for Uncirculated specimens approached the $1,500 mark, more than two to four times what other "CC" dates were bringing in similar grades. From 1975 through the end of the decade, collectors could

expect to pay a minimum of $3,000 for Choice Uncirculated pieces, rising to the $5,000 level and beyond. But this was only the beginning.

After the rare coin market tumbled from its lofty heights in April of 1980, many collectors and dealers were wary of stretching to obtain most coins. Right at that time, a sensational specimen of an 1878-CC appeared. It was time to see how the torpid market would affect rare "CC" issues; would dates like the 1878-CC retreat back to their mid-1970s levels? The answer came loud and clear; no retreats for this date, as a record price of $22,000 was paid at the July auction, establishing the 1878-CC as the leader of an already enthusiastic price rally in the "CC" trade dollar series. This sustained rate of appreciation continued through the 1980s, and lost no momentum as the next decade began. At the Superior *Boys Town* sale in May of 1990, a Choice Uncirculated specimen, graded MS-64 by PCGS, sold for $28,600; and later that year, in the midst of another icy cold bear market, an NGC MS-65 1878-CC trade dollar was purchased for $55,000 at Auction '90.

True to form, the 1878-CC, like most Carson City issues, had gotten off to a slow start, not impressing many along the way. But when the time came, advances were made in leaping strides. Other dates in the "CC" trade dollar series, like the 1873-CC and 1876-CC, have caught up with the 1878-CC in grades above MS-63, but in MS-60 and below, prices for this date confirm its status as the key to the set; not just for "CC" coins, but for the entire trade dollar series. At today's levels, (2003 to 2004), the 1878-CC is not as undervalued as some other "CC" dates. However, for problem-free examples in circulated grades through AU, expect to pay hefty premiums. Since MS-65 specimens are few in number, a decade or more may pass before one appears on the market. Expect to see perpetual price records whenever Gems are offered.

Two obverse varieties exist for this date, one with a *Normal 8*, and the other with a *Repunched 8*. Three reverse dies are known, all with *Large* "CC"s, one with a parallel mintmark, a second, same as an 1877 die with the left "C" slanting lower than the right, and a third with the mintmark shifted to the right, located above *DO* in *DOLLAR*. Since few if any 1878-CCs were exported to the Far East, chopmarked specimens are extremely rare, if not *Unique*.[3][4]

---

[1] Augustus G. Heaton, *Mint Marks, A Treatise*, 1893.

[2] B. Max Mehl, 1945 *Waltman Sale*.

[3] If you have not done so already, consider doing some research on chopmarked trade dollars and "Opium" dollars.

[4] One of the *Top 25*.

(Photo courtesy Bowers and Merena)

During the *age of silver politics* in America a bill entitled, "AN ACT TO AUTHORIZE THE COINAGE OF THE STANDARD SILVER DOLLAR, AND RESTORE ITS LEGAL TENDER TO CHARACTER" became law on February 28, 1878.[1] In effect this legislation was a *re-authorization* with modifications. As stated, it was enacted, "that there shall be coined at the several mints of the United States, silver dollars of the weight of 412 ½ grains troy of standard silver, as provided in the Act of January 18, 1837."[2] In essence the standard *unit of account*, discontinued in 1873, was restored to the nation's monetary system. Two major provisions from the past were altered under the new law: free coinage was nixed, and the Treasury was directed to purchase $2 to $4 million worth of silver per month.

As usual, this made some people happy and angered others. Congressman Richard Parks Bland coauthored the legislation, presumably to appease silver miners, with whom Bland had ties from his short residence in Nevada. Representative Bland had held public office in Carson County, Nevada in the 1860s, being mentored by Senator William Stewart. By 1878, political maneuverings placed Bland in a well-timed position as a Missouri House member, fully committed to the silver industry. Almost everything about his silver dollar bill pleased the silverites, except the lack of a free coinage statute. Senator John P. Jones from Nevada filibustered on the free coinage issue for several days, and his speech became a manifesto for the cause. Jones' 20-cent bill, successfully sponsored in 1875, would also be repealed in 1878.

In some ways the silver industry reaped tremendous benefits from the various coin acts, however, there always seemed to be a hole in the bottom of their sack. But it was hard to complain about the required government purchase of at least $2 million worth of silver each month, even if individuals were not allowed to deposit silver in exchange for silver dollars. It really came as no surprise that the federal government refused to give up its special *seniorage* privileges to public silver depositors. In 1878, for instance, the Treasury could purchase bullion to produce a silver dollar for approximately 90 cents, resulting in an 11% gross profit per piece. By 1889 the profit margin was 38% and would increase with each passing decade. Advocates of free coinage would fight for an individual's right to a share of those profits on into the 20th century, but to no avail.

Morgan silver dollars brought work to the Carson City Mint at just the time production ceased on minor silver coins and trade dollars. Had it not been for the *Silver Dollar Act of 1878*, Carson City would have been limited to a trifling amount of gold coins by 1879. If the 756,000 1879-CC silver dollars minted had been subtracted from that year's coinage, only 29,751 gold coins would have been produced, hardly enough to keep a full crew busy. News of the new silver dollars was on lips and pens all around Carson City and the Comstock. Mint workers were grateful for the revitalization at their facility while officials at Philadelphia, Washington D.C. and San Francisco continued to see little value in the Nevada minting operation.

There was no rationale for the Carson Mint to manufacture silver dollars; after all, the Treasury was obligated to purchase silver on behalf of this regional coin plant to supplement deposits from Comstock miners. Paradoxically, this same silver was being mined just 14 miles from Carson City, but transportation costs and preferential treatment, lured producers to sell their bullion in San Francisco. As if this was not enough to erode the validity of maintaining a coinage facility in Nevada, operating expenses were higher at the Carson Mint then anywhere else.

In the wake of a slew of negative factors, one angle in favor of sustained operations at the Carson City Mint would have been if there had been sufficient local demand for coinage, but a diminishing population in the region eliminated that need.

---

[1] U.S. Treasury, *Coinage Laws of the United States*.
[2] Ibid.

But in spite of the odds against it, Carson City proudly performed the duties of a U.S. Mint producing a respectable total of nearly 13.9 million Morgan silver dollars between 1878 and 1893. Out of this yield originated 13 dates, with optional varieties for the collector, such as the 1879-CC *Capped Die*, 1880-CC *Flatbreast* and 1890-CC *Tailbar*. Even the 1900-O/CC, though not minted at Carson City, attracts enthusiasts who cannot get enough "CC"s to satisfy their craving. From the vaults at this legendary mint emerged key dates such as the 1889-CC and 1893-CC, with honorable mention to all the dates in the GSA sales.

Because of the disproportionate amount of "CC" Morgan dollars that have survived, these historic numismatic mementos afford collectors at all levels the opportunity to own a cherished "CC" coin. For decades, these silver dollars that Augustus Heaton described as having an "Ornate Head"[1] have symbolized the Old West. Nevada with its rodeos, *rough and tumble* image, *Helldorado Days*, and *howdy pardners* has provided a picture perfect backdrop for the *cartwheels* to be promoted.

For this very reason, it came as no surprise in 1964, when two large vans from Washington, D.C., escorted by an armored car, delivered 1.5 million assorted silver dollars to Reno casino owners. Western politicians had been lobbying Congress in 1964 to authorize production of 150 million new silver dollars, but instead the value of the precious metal rose, and there was talk of melting existing surpluses of the old dollars. Fretting extinction of the species, casino owners pooled together to ensure that the sound of the big silver coins would continue to be heard in slot machines and on gaming tables. As luck would have it, within two years, the casino owner's plans were foiled when the value of silver increased, causing a run on the gambling house's coin supply by the public. Realizing replacement was impractical, casinos switched to copper-nickel tokens for use in slots and table games.

Because of the popularity of Morgan silver dollars, library shelves and bookstores are stocked with reference works on the subject, and it is not within the scope of this book to elaborate on the topic. Each date in the "CC" series will be covered briefly, with peripheral information provided

about major varieties, but the author sees no purpose in reinventing the *cartwheel*.

Estimates of surviving populations in grades below MS-60, except for key dates, are based on unsupportable hunches. Through a process of elimination, totals can be narrowed to realistic ranges; however in many instances the ranges are very wide. These estimates should be used as a starting point for further research and postulation. For grades above MS-63, estimates, although not scientific, should be more exact, attributable in part to the extensive population and census data from PCGS and NGC, as well as Treasury records.

For more advanced study on Morgan silver dollars in general, and Carson City dates in particular, readers are encouraged to explore such valuable reference works as *Silver and Trade Dollars of the United States*, by Q. David Bowers, and the *Comprehensive Catalog and Encyclopedia of Morgan and Peace Dollars* by Leroy C. Van Allen and A. George Mallis.

---

[1] Augustus G. Heaton, *Mint Mark, A Treatise*, 1893.

Price of silver per fine ounce.	Value of pure silver in a silver dollar.	Price of silver per fine ounce.	Value of pure silver in a silver dollar.	Price of silver per fine ounce.	Value of pure silver in a silver dollar.
$0.50	$0.387	$0.77	$0.596	$1.04	$0.804
.51	.394	.78	.603	1.05	.812
.52	.402	.79	.611	1.06	.820
.53	.410	.80	.619	1.07	.828
.54	.418	.81	.626	1.08	.835
.55	.425	.82	.634	1.09	.843
.56	.433	.83	.642	1.10	.851
.57	.441	.84	.650	1.11	.859
.58	.449	.85	.657	1.12	.866
.59	.456	.86	.665	1.13	.874
.60	.464	.87	.673	1.14	.882
.61	.472	.88	.681	1.15	.889
.62	.480	.89	.688	1.16	.897
.63	.487	.90	.696	1.17	.905
.64	.495	.91	.704	1.18	.913
.65	.503	.92	.712	1.19	.920
.66	.510	.93	.719	1.20	.928
.67	.518	.94	.727	1.21	.936
.68	.526	.95	.735	1.22	.944
.69	.534	.96	.742	1.23	.951
.70	.541	.97	.750	1.24	.959
.71	.549	.98	.758	1.25	.967
.72	.557	.99	.766	1.26	.975
.73	.565	1.00	.773	1.27	.982
.74	.572	1.01	.781	1.28	.990
.75	.580	1.02	.789	1.29	.998
.76	.588	1.03	.797	*a* 1.2929	1.00

***a* Parity.**

The value of pure silver in a silver dollar at prices of silver per ounce fine from $0.50 to $1.2929. (*Annual Report of the Director of the Mint*, 1887)

FORMAT FOR CARSON CITY MORGAN DOLLAR SECTION:

1. In addition to original mintage listings, GSA populations will be provided. These figures are from the official Treasury reports documenting the hoard of "CC" dollars revealed in the 1960s.

2. Pedigrees will generally be listed as *Various* because for decades "CC" dollars were too common for auction companies to devote much space to.

3. Because the grading for silver dollars presents more variables than other denominations, the following statistics for each date will often combine varieties, as well as non-prooflike, prooflike, and Deep-Mirror-Prooflike, especially in the "Total Certified Examples" column.

BUREAU OF THE MINT DATA FOR CARSON CITY MORGAN SILVER DOLLAR PRODUCTION

Total Combined Mintage: 13,862,041

Total Face Value: $13,862,041

Total Ounces of Silver Used: .... 10,719,520 ozs.

Design Type: .... Liberty Head

Designer: .... George T. Morgan

Metal Composition: .... .900 Silver .100 Copper

Actual Gross Weight: .... 26.73 grams

Actual Fine Silver Content: .... .7733 oz.

Value of Silver in One Silver Dollar Between 1878 and 1893: .... $.60-.90

1878-CC

(Photo courtesy Bowers and Merena)

Mintage: 2,212,000

GSA Population: 60,993

Finest Knowns*:

PCGS MS-67 (4)

NGC MS-67 (1)

PCGS MS-66 (181)

PCGS MS-66PL (10)

PCGS MS-66DMPL (3)

NGC MS-66PL (9)

Notable Pedigrees:

Jack Lee

Mike Gilley

ex: Jack Lee

Survival Estimates in All Grades:	.180,000-275,000
Estimated in Uncirculated:	100,000-125,000
Estimated in XF to AU:	15,000-20,000
Total Certified Examples in All Grades (PCGS and NGC)*:	18,470

(* As of July 2003)

REFLECTIONS:

EARLY HAPPENINGS

Employees at the Carson City Mint were given two months after the last trade dollars of 1878 were struck before production on the new Morgan dollars began. Plenty of dies and huge stockpiles of blank planchets were delivered to the coining room behind the Paying Teller's office. Led by Superintendent Crawford, the coiner and his crew excitedly ran the first few coins through the press, very pleased with the finished product. Though not initially content with the design of the eagle, nor the size of the mintmark, the Carson coin staff was not about to utter a peep of dissension; that would be left to the newspapers.

The dies were received in mid-April, and within three weeks more than 300,000 1878-CC Morgan silver dollars had been produced, and almost immediately bags of these new dollars were being shipped to out of state destinations. Hauled on the V&T Railroad to Reno, the coins were transferred to box cars on the Central Pacific and sent to destinations such as St. Louis, Chicago, Cincinnati, and New Orleans, while more than enough were stored on premises to satisfy local demand.

NUMISMATIC NOTES

Most 1878-CC dollars were apparently reserved in Treasury vaults across the country until the 1940s, when thousands were paid out in exchange for silver certificates. This continued through the 1950s and into the early 1960s, at which time payments ceased. Approximately 61,000 pieces were part of the GSA sales which began in the 1970s. Collector interest was minimal until that time, and when the Fed began offering them for a suggested price of $30 each in 1973, coin dealers scoffed, commenting that this price was double the market value. Still there was a virtual overnight sellout, and prices for the 1878-CC dollar have never retreated.

VARIETY CONSIDERATIONS

Reverse of an 1878-CC Morgan silver dollar with 7 tailfeathers and a small mintmark.

All 1878-CC's feature the *Flatbreast* eagle and have *Small* "CC"s, with various positional placements. At least 26 VAM varieties have been discovered for the date, none of which command significant price premiums. Many specimens are seen with various degrees of rotation on the reverse, usually bringing substantial prices above normal for the date.

(Photo courtesy American Numismatic Rarities)

Mintage: 756,000

GSA Population: 4,123

Finest Knowns*:

Normal Mintmark:

PCGS MS-66 (2)

PCGS MS-65 (64)**

NGC MS-65 (29)**

PCGS MS-65PL (3)

PCGS MS-65DMPL (2)

NGC MS-65PL (3)

NGC MS-65DMPL (1)

Capped Die Mintmark:

PCGS MS-65 (4)

NGC MS-65 (6)**

Notable Pedigrees:

Mike Gilley
ex: PCGS Tour

Jack Lee

Survival Estimates in All Grades:	19,000-23,000
Estimated in Uncirculated:	
1879-CC Normal Mintmark:	4,500-5,500
1879-CC *Capped Die* Mintmark:	2,000-3,000
Estimated in XF to AU	
Combined Varieties:	2,200-3,500
Total Certified Examples in All Grades (PCGS and NGC)*:	
1879-CC Normal Mintmark:	3,076
1879-CC *Capped Die* Mintmark:	1,602

(* As of July 2003)

(** Possible resubmissions of one or more of the same coins)

REFLECTIONS:

EARLY HAPPENINGS

In 1867, when the Legislature of Nevada petitioned Congress to appropriate more funds to increase their mint's size and expand its coinage operations they were anticipating a lion's share of deposits from the Comstock mines. In the resolutions sent to Washington, legislators described the miner's burdens of paying high assay fees, coinage fees, transportation fees, and then having to sell their freshly minted coins at a 3% discount to a banker. This was the scenario in 1867 when miners were shipping to San Francisco, and as proposed by Nevada legislators, a local mint in Carson City would lessen those burdens. Unfortunately, this did not prove to be the solution, as by 1879, San Francisco assayers and bankers made it more profitable

for miners to continue shipping to San Francisco, thereby undercutting the Carson Mint. This put Carson City on the Treasury's expendable list, and coinage operations were suspended at the end of February of 1879.

No silver dollars had been minted for months due to a shortage of bullion, and then in August, production resumed. This coining season would be short lived, however, as operations were again suspended in November of 1879, beginning a three year regression of silver dollar production at the Carson City Mint.

NUMISMATIC NOTES

Once considered more common than 1881-CC and 1885-CC dollars, the 1879-CC rose in rarity ranking in the early 1960s when it was discovered that only 4,123 were included in the Treasury's holdings. Prohibitively

COIN WORLD, Wednesday, February 5, 1964   Page Seventy-Two

Collectors' Clearinghouse – Numismatic Answering Service

Readers Respond To 'Odd Mint Mark'

Comments Reveal Coin May Be Legitimate Variety

The 1879-CC BU silver dollar with an odd Mint mark pictured in the January 17 Clearinghouse, and reprinted h e r e, seems to have attracted considerable response from interested readers, but no conclusive results except that it appears to be a legitimate variety.

Capped CC?

Our first inkling of the interest came on the Saturday evening of the week the paper came out, when a reader phoned us from Massachusetts. He said the coin was a variety that had been described in a Hollinbeck-Kagin auction catalogue for October, 1962, and called "rare."

Coin World's library skips that particular catalogue, although it has the one before and the one after. In the same firm's auction for February 4, 1963, under lot 518, we find this:

1879-CC 'Cap on CC,' Brilliant Uncirculated. RARE. (estimated) $150."

In the picture, there seems to be some metal at the tops of the CC's which might well be called a "cap." So, until somebody who knows tells us differently, we assume the coin owned by Weimar White is a "Capped CC" variety. The rarity factor, however, seems to be highly debatable. In the same firm's catalogue for September 18, 1961, we find this:

"Lot 1167. 1879-CC BU, choice. One of the best specimens of this rare date we recall seeing. (estimated) $200."

That leaves us a bit in the dark as to comparative scarcity. If the "normal" coin in choice BU was valued at $200, and the rare "Cap on CC" in BU was valued at $150 one year later, what do we know about rarity? Nothing.

Checking the current issue of Coin World at this writing (January 29 issue), we found a few BU or Unc. 1879-CC dollars advertised at $150-$160, and one ad offering them in BU at $114! So we know less about value than we did before, assuming all those in the ads were "normal" Mint mark coins (which is not a good assumption, seeing that White and his friend ordered just BU dollars and got the variety).

Before we get to the letters that have come in about this coin, we have one more interesting reference to cite, in the M.A.N.A. Convention sale of October 28-29, 1955, catalogued by Associated Coin Auction Co. of New Jersey. Lot 1778 reads in part as follows:

"....pseudo-proof showing t h e usual bag marks. The Mint mark CC appears to be cut over something else; first seen like it."

We wonder if that is the first published mention of this variety. Neither Carmichael nor Wallace in their 1951 and 1959 Scrapbook articles on Morgan dollar varieties m e n t i o n any such coin, nor did Drost or Klaes. Now for the letters.

Three readers reported "perfect" CC's; Mrs. Walker Gunderson of Ohio, Sig Schwartz of Tennessee, and Herbert P. Hicks of Massachusetts.

On the other hand, 10 readers say they have coins to match the picture, with about 20 pieces or more represented. Tom Mason of

Wyoming says he has five or so, and that it is from a "rusted die." He says the only perfect Mint mark type he has seen was on a proof surface coin, presumably first strike, according to him.

Other remarks by several of the letter-writers include t h e statement that they have been told this is "normal" for the 1879-CC. Russell A. Hibbs of West Virginia says he has two pieces left of a roll that popped up in a Federal Reserve Bank in 1956. One of them is identical, the other seems also to have something wrong with the bottom of the right-hand letter.

We can now answer White's original question to the extent that the coin is a legitimate variety, possibly c a l l e d a "Capped CC." Beyond that, we are still in the dark. Which is normal, which is scarcer? Maybe we'll hear from somebody that knows. In addition to Hibbs and Mason, other writers with the oddity include:

Henry Boyce, New Hampshire; Roberta Finklestein, New York; Curtis Brook, Illinois; Jim Robertson, N. J.; F. R. Baughman, Ohio; William Shepard, Florida; Lucien Dube, New Jersey; and William D. Clark, Michigan.

(Copyright 1964 Coin World, Sidney OH 45365 USA.
Reprinted with permission from the February 5, 1964 issue of Coin World.)

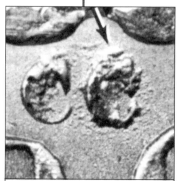

Coin World article from 1964 featuring commentary on Weimar White's inquiry about his "Capped Die" 1879-CC silver dollar. Also shown is a close-up of this popular variety. (*Article courtesy Weimar White*)

---

scarce in DMPL (Deep-Mirror-Prooflike) condition, this date is also the third rarest in the series in MS-64 and above. Choice Uncirculated specimens in the black box GSA holders command premiums as high as 300% over pieces in MS-60 to 62.

Because few 1879-CC dollars were released into local circulation, XF and AU specimens are very scarce, and as a result are on collectors' want lists across the nation. Problem-free AU examples will bring double the listed wholesale prices.

VARIETY CONSIDERATIONS:

Of course, the most well known variety is the *Capped Die,* exhibiting a faint image of the small "CC" from 1878

beneath the large "CC" introduced in 1879. The engraving is a study in slovenly work. There are at least three other VAM varieties for this date, none valued at more than the 1879-CC already commands.

Author and collector Weimar White contacted the editor of *Coin World* in early 1964 seeking information on the strange 1879-CC dollar that he had obtained, and most importantly, desiring to know if the coin was a legitimate variety. In response, *Coin World* published an article about the *Capped "CC"* 1879-CC in their February 5, 1964 edition. At the time, little was known about this variety, but in the 40 or so years since, VAM references and professional grading services have shed much light on it.

1880-CC

(Photo courtesy Bowers and Merena)

Mintage: 591,000

GSA Population: 131,529

Finest Knowns*:

    Normal Mintmark: Reverse of 1879:

        NGC MS-67 (6)**

        PCGS MS-67 (20)

        PCGS MS-66 (304)**

        NGC MS-66 (127)

        PCGS MS-66PL (4)

        NGC MS-66PL (11)**

        PCGS MS-66DMPL (2)

    Flatbreast Reverse of 1878:

        PCGS MS-66 (50)

        PCGS MS-66PL (I)

        NGC MS-66 (8)

Notable Pedigrees:

    Various

Survival Estimates in All Grades:

  Combined Varieties: 170,000-200,000

Estimated in Uncirculated:

  1880-CC Reverse of 1879: 140,000 -150,000

  1880-CC *Flatbreast*: 7,500-10,000

Estimated in XF to AU

  Combined Varieties: 7,500-10,000

Total Certified Examples
in All Grades (PCGS and NGC)*:

  1880-CC Reverse of 1879: 12,613

  1880-CC *Flatbreast*:.. 2,982

(As of July 2003)*

*(** Possible resubmissions of one or more of the same coins)*

REFLECTIONS:

EARLY HAPPENINGS

After the suspension of coinage in November of 1879, Carson Mint employees were put on reduced work schedules for six months. In May 1880 the suspension was lifted on coinage operations, but nothing was produced until the summer. Not even gold coins were minted with any regularity, and no $20 double eagles were struck at all.

In a year with such limited activity, inconsistencies occurred with the appearance and weight of silver dollars; appearances were the responsibility of the Philadelphia Mint, weights on the other hand, were a local matter. Sample dollars from the Carson Mint were examined the following year at the annual Assay Commission meeting, and found to be 3.3 grains short of silver, causing each 1,000 coin bag of 1880-CC dollars to be $8 below the legal standard. It was determined that 96,000 of the low weight coins were struck, all in July of 1880. To complicate matters, the Assayer at the Carson Mint responsible for the oversight had died before being questioned. An order was sent to Superintendent Crawford to melt the 96,000 substandard weight dollars and re-coin them, resulting in a net mintage for 1880 of 495,000.

NUMISMATIC NOTES

By the 1950s this date had lost its *premium* ranking. Apparently thousands of Uncirculated specimens were distributed from the late 1930s for approximately $2 apiece, although prices at one time had been in the $10 range. Even after this release, it was not unusual to see the $10 mark hit at auction sales; for instance, the *Jack Roe*

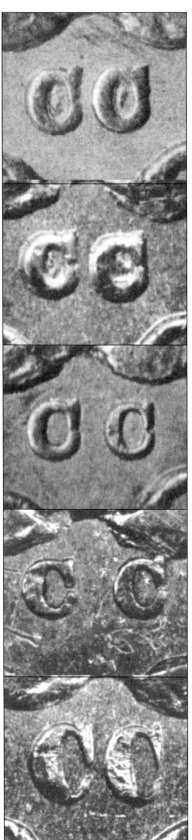

Small "CC"
Closely spaced letters.

Small "CC"
Medium spacing
between letters.

Small "CC"
Widely spaced letters.

Small "CC"
Extremely wide spacing
between letters.

Large "CC"
Medium spacing
between letters.

specimen brought $10.50 in 1945. When the GSA sales were launched in the 1970s, the 1880-CC was recognized as being scarcer than Morgan dollars dated 1882 to 1884.

Many budget conscious collectors in the early years of the 21st century believe that a circulated example is an inexpensive alternative to an Uncirculated piece, however, in most cases, this is not true. Premiums for circulated 1880-CC's are high, due to low supply, often making it a wise decision to pay a little extra and get an MS-60 to 62. There are probably 10 to 15 times more Uncirculated examples than circulated.

VARIETY CONSIDERATION

As it says in the VAM book, "normal dies **without** varieties **do not exist** for this date."[1] [Emphasis added] There are at least 10 varieties, including overdates, *Doubled "CC"*, *Dots in "CC"*s and, of course, the *Flatbreast* Reverse of 1878. There are two mintmark sizes, *Small* and *Large*, the *Small* being the same used in 1878-CC.

Choice to Gem Uncirculated *Flatbreast* specimens are very rare and worth significant premiums.

[1] Leroy Van Allen & George Mallis, *Comprehensive Catalog & Encyclopedia of Morgan & Peace Dollars.*

1881-CC

(Photo courtesy Bowers and Merena)

Mintage: 296,000

GSA Population: 147,485

Finest Knowns*: **

    PCGS MS-68 (3)

    NGC MS-68 (2)

    PCGS MS-67 (71)

    NGC MS-67PL (1)

    NGC MS-67 (35)

    PCGS MS-66DMPL (36)

    NGC MS-66 DMPL (6)

    PCGS MS-66PL (14)

    NGC MS-66PL (8)

Notable Pedigrees:

    Various

Survival Estimates in All Grades: ...	170,000-200,000
Estimated in Uncirculated:	160,000-190,000
Estimated in XF to AU:	3,500-5,000
Total Certified Examples in All Grades (PCGS and NGC)*:	18,816

(* As of July 2003)

(** Possible resubmissions or crossovers throughout this entire list.)

REFLECTIONS:

EARLY HAPPENINGS

For the first three months of 1881 it appeared as if operations at the Carson City Mint would result in a higher output than produced in the suspension-shortened year of 1880. Apparently the Philadelphia Mint believed this was the case, as evidenced by the 25 sets of dies shipped to the struggling Carson facility. However, just as momentum began to build, bullion ran out, and on April 1, 1881, Carson Mint operations were suspended again, this time for the rest of the year. Adding to the disconsolate state of affairs; this occurred while the Nevada branch mint was under fire from the Assay Commission and the Secret Service.

The Assay Commission was appeased without delay, but the allegations of skimming precipitated the visit of a Secret Service agent to investigate the Carson City facility, after which he scorned Carson residents, declaring that their town was no place to have a mint. Without coinage operations, it was as if the town did not have a mint anyway, and as reported by the Director, when the bullion ran out, the Carson Mint was "discontinued, and so remained until the close of the year." But it was not totally out of service, as the Director continued, "The mint was kept open…for the reception of and purchase of bullion."[1]

NUMISMATIC NOTES

With such a low mintage this date should be scarce and valuable, but it is neither. Other than a small quantity released locally, nearly all of the 296,000 1881-CCs remained in the mint vault until 1885. Then, along with nearly 70% of the mintage of silver dollars from 1880 through 1885, they were sent to Treasury facilities in Washington D.C. and San Francisco. Of course, collectors did not know this for decades and the 1881-CC was considered extremely scarce. For example, an Uncirculated specimen in the *Jack Roe Collection* sold for $21 in 1945, while at the same auction, the Gem, semi-Proof 1889-CC fetched $7.25. In today's market (2003-2004), the 1881-CC is on par with the 1880-CC and is readily available in Uncirculated, though it is much scarcer than the 1880-CC in circulated grades.

VARIETY CONSIDERATIONS

There are at least six varieties for this date, all considered common. One of the most interesting is the *Doubled 88.* All varieties come with a *Large* "CC" mintmark.

---

[1] *Annual Report of the Director of the Mint,* 1881.

1882-CC

(Photo courtesy Bowers and Merena)

Mintage: 1,133,000

GSA Population: 605,029

Finest Knowns*:

    PCGS MS-68 (1)

    PCGS MS-67DMPL (1)

    PCGS MS-67 (38)**

    NGC MS-67 (17)**

    PCGS MS-66DMPL (51)**

    NGC MS-66DMPL (4)

Notable Pedigrees:

    Various

Survival Estimates in All Grades: ...	675,000-725,000
Estimated in Uncirculated:	600,000-650,000
Estimated in XF to AU:	10,000-20,000
Total Certified Examples in All Grades (PCGS and NGC)*:	26,424

(* As of July 2003)

(** Possible resubmissions of one or more of the same coin.)

REFLECTIONS:

EARLY HAPPENINGS

Treasury records from 1882 report that coinage operations resumed in October of 1881 at the Carson City Mint, seemingly contradicting the report from 1881. As usual, the confusion stems from *fiscal year* versus *calendar year* reporting. Until the Bureau of the Mint went on a strict *calendar year* accounting system in their annual reports, mintages for each year covered production from July 1 to June 30 of the following year. For instance, in the 1882 *Director's Report*, the mintage for 1881 silver dollars is listed as 539,000. Obviously, the total of 243,000 above the traditional mintage figure of 296,000 for the 1881-CC dollars must be credited to 1882's total; but this still does not synthesize the data for both years because in the same report, 1882's mintage is listed as 763,000. Adding that figure to the 243,000 equals 1,006,000, a number still 127,000 short of the traditional mintage for 1882. But thank goodness, the Treasury conducted a major accounting analysis in 1887 and arrived at solid figures that have been passed on to successive generations.

Carson Mint workers did not care how the Treasury tabulated the coins, as long as they were allowed to keep producing them. It seemed as if 1882 was going to be a good year, as even gold coin production revived from the pitifully low output in 1881. In fact, 1882 was the first year since 1879 that four denominations were struck: three gold and one silver.

NUMISMATIC NOTES

There is no logical explanation why the Treasury preserved more than 50% of the original mintage of 1882-CC silver dollars. In fact, it is a mystery why approximately 23% of Carson City's entire silver dollar production was spared from release and the melting pot. But since this information was unknown to collectors until the 1960s, even common dates like the 1882-CC brought premium prices over dates from other mints. But after the GSA sales in the 1970s, prices reached equilibrium, consistent with supply and demand. Until the early years of the 21st century, Uncirculated 1882-CC's were priced at the same levels as they had been 20 years earlier. For instance in 2000, MS-60 to MS-62 1882-CC dollars were selling for approximately $80 to 100, which is exactly what the prices had been in 1980. During a pulsing rare coin market in 1989, MS-65 specimens sold for $1,200, but in 2003 the same coins brought $400. Home-shopping-television programs as well as the Internet began to heavily promote Carson City dollars in the early years of the 21st century, driving prices higher. Foreign demand also put pressure on existing supplies; and if these trends continue, there will be waiting lists for even the most common dates from the Carson City Mint.

VARIETY CONSIDERATIONS

For such a relatively high mintage, only six varieties have been discovered, all of which are common. Reverse dies left over from 1881 were probably used, as these two dates share commonalities. All 1882-CC's have *Large* "CC" mintmarks.

The Carson City Mint in the 1880s. The man standing with his hands to his side in front of the entrance might be Superintendent James Crawford. (*Courtesy Nevada State Museum*)

1883-CC

(Photo courtesy Bowers and Merena)

Mintage: 1,204,000

GSA Population: 755,518

Finest Knowns*:

> PCGS MS-68 (3)
>
> PCGS MS-67DMPL (2)
>
> PCGS MS-67PL (7)
>
> NGC MS-67PL (1)
>
> PCGS MS-67 (70)
>
> NGC MS-67 (47)

Notable Pedigrees:

> Various

Survival Estimates in All Grades: 825,000-900,000
Estimated in Uncirculated: 795,000-860,000
Estimated in XF to AU: 20,000-25,000
Total Certified Examples in All Grades (PCGS and NGC)*: 37,227

(* As of July 2003)

REFLECTIONS:

EARLY HAPPENINGS

During the two year period encompassing 1882 and 1883, annual coin production at the Carson City Mint averaged 1,275,320 pieces for gold and silver combined. In face value, this equaled approximately $2.5 million per year. According to the annual *Director's Report*, the Treasury was content with operations at their Nevada affiliate. Platitudes such as "This institution is of advantage to the mine owners...," or, "The work performed at the Carson Mint was nearly double that of the preceding year,"[1] added peripheral fluff to the Director's commentary. But if the truth be told, the Mint Director and Treasury Secretary eagerly awaited the day that the Carson City Mint would close.

NUMISMATIC NOTES

This is another date whose original mintage was nearly entirely held back from release. There had been unknown quantities distributed to other regions, and if the percentage for quantities of all "CC" dollars stored at the local mint through 1885 is used, approximately 360,000 1883-CC dollars would have been removed by then. This would have left 843,000 to be included in the mass shipment of dollars after the mint was shut down in 1885. Using this information with the knowledge that there were approximately 755,500 pieces in the GSA hoard during the 1960s and 1970s, it can be estimated that approximately 87,000 1883-CCs were available between 1885 and 1963 to be distributed and/or melted.

By the 1950s the wholesale value for 1883-CC dollars in Uncirculated was $1.25, as collectors paid little attention to them. Gradually, prices rose, but interest continued to lag, even when the coins were priced at $2. In the 1970s, the GSA sold thousands at $30 each, and in the early years of the 21st century, average Uncirculated examples were selling for $125 apiece. On the higher end of the grading scale, a specimen in MS-68 might bring $10,000 or more.

VARIETY CONSIDERATIONS

There are at least seven varieties of this date, including a *Slanted* "CC", a *Doubled Date*, and a *Doubled* "CC", none of which command premiums. All 1883-CC dollars have *Large* "CC"s.

---

[1] *Annual Report of the Director of the Mint*, 1882, 1883.

1884-CC

(Photo courtesy Bowers and Merena)

Mintage: 1,136,000

GSA Population: 962,638

Finest Knowns*:

> PCGS MS-68 (5)
>
> PCGS MS-67DMPL (3)
>
> NGC MS-67DMPL (1)
>
> PCGS MS-67PL (1)
>
> NGC MS-67PL (4)
>
> PCGS MS-67 (48)
>
> NGC MS-67 (30)

Notable Pedigrees:

> Various

Survival Estimates in All Grades: ..	1,020,000-1,060,000
Estimated in Uncirculated:	980,000-1,010,000
Estimated in XF to AU:	25,000-30,000
Total Certified Examples in All Grades (PCGS and NGC)*:	39,165

(* As of July 2003)

REFLECTIONS:

EARLY HAPPENINGS

As the recession in bullion production continued, deposits at the Carson City Mint gradually reached par with yields from the nearby Comstock mines. This was of minor consequence, however, since silver production was but a whisper of what it had been. Nevertheless, the Mint Director was quick to point out that, "A steady supply of silver has been purchased...and the silver coinage [at the Carson Mint] has averaged about $100,000 per month."[1] This sounded encouraging, but in contrast, the San Francisco Mint was purchasing at least 25 times more bullion than Carson City, while averaging close to $2.75 million in monthly coinage production.

By 1884, silver dollar distributions had declined, and stockpiles were building up in the Carson Mint's vaults. Whereas in 1878 and 1879 approximately 90 to 95% of silver dollars were distributed to other regions of the country, it is estimated that 95% of 1884-CC dollars remained on the premises. The majority of these dollars would survive in Uncirculated condition and be sold during the GSA sales in the 1970s. This percentage of extant surviving dollars is the highest of any coin from the pre-1950 era.

NUMISMATIC NOTES

Because nearly the entire population of 1884-CC dollars was stored in Treasury vaults for decades, collectors had difficulty locating them. In the 1950s, 50,000 Uncirculated 1884-CCs were reportedly distributed by the Treasury Department, many of which were spent and account for the bulk of circulated examples in existence. In the early 1960s, before the revelation of vast Treasury holdings, prices were slightly higher for 1884-CC dollars than for 1882-CCs and 1883-CCs. Since that time, the 1884-CC has been the least expensive date in the Carson City dollar series.

VARIETY CONSIDERATIONS

A larger mintage resulted in at least 11 varieties of this date, all very interesting, but none worthy of a premium. One variety in particular is the *Spiked Date* featuring raised die metal. There are the typical assortment of doubled dates and mintmarks as well. All 1884-CC's have *Large* mintmarks.

---

[1] *Annual Report of the Director of the Mint,* 1884.

(Photo courtesy American Numismatic Rarities)

Mintage: 228,000

GSA Population: 148,285

Finest Knowns*:

    PCGS MS-68 (1)

    NGC MS-68 (5)

    PCGS MS-67DMPL (2)

    PCGS MS-67PL (1)

    NGC MS-67PL (3)

    PCGS MS-67 (33)

    NGC MS-67 (12)

Notable Pedigrees:

    Various

Survival Estimates in All Grades: 157,000-165,000
Estimated in Uncirculated: 150,000-155,000
Estimated in XF to AU: 3,000-5,000
Total Certified Examples in All Grades (PCGS and NGC)*: 17,716

(* As of July 2003)

REFLECTIONS:

EARLY HAPPENINGS

Two hundred thousand silver dollars were struck at Carson City in the first two months of 1885, consistent with the 100,000 monthly averages achieved in the final five months of 1884. At some point prior to March 18, another 28,000 dollars were minted which did not show up in log reports until later in the year. This brought the total mintage to 228,000, lowest in the "CC" dollar series and third lowest in the set of Morgan dollars (not counting 1895). Mint Superintendent James Crawford died on March 8, 1885, at the age of 50. Immediately, lightning struck again and business was suspended, once again closing the Carson Mint; but this time it would not be a brief pause, as the shutdown lasted four years.

Throughout 1885 the new superintendent, William Garrard, scorned by locals, supervised transfers of nearly 3.2 million silver dollars to Washington D.C., San Francisco, and other distribution points, nearly all of which were dated 1882, 1883, 1884, and 1885.

NUMISMATIC NOTES

Although significant quantities exist, this date presents a challenge to thousands of silver dollar collectors around the world, especially to builders of circulated sets, since there are probably fewer than 7,000 specimens in grades below Uncirculated. Budget-minded hobbyists are generally surprised to discover how scarce 1885-CC dollars are in lower circulated grades. Price differences between specimens in MS-60 to MS-62 and those in Good through VF are minimal, and even less in XF and AU. Often it is expedient and prudent for collectors searching for circulated pieces to spend the extra 10 to 15% and purchase an Uncirculated piece.

VARIETY CONSIDERATIONS

Only four varieties are known for the 1885-CC, none more valuable than the date itself. All examples have a *Large* "CC" mintmark. The date is often found in dazzling condition, with exceptional detail, and either super frosty or prooflike surfaces. On the other hand, many examples also come very baggy, with some being weakly struck around Ms. Liberty's ear.

1889-CC

(Photo courtesy Bowers and Merena)

Mintage: 350,000

GSA Population: 1

Finest Knowns*:

    PCGS MS-68 (1)

    PCGS MS-65 (1)

    NGC MS-65PL (1)

    NGC MS-65 (4)**

Notable Pedigrees:

    Eliasberg (1997)

    Jack Lee (1999)

      ex: Eliasberg

Survival Estimates in All Grades:	11,000-16,000
Estimated in Uncirculated:	4,000-7,500
Estimated in XF to AU:	4,000-5,000
Total Certified Examples in All Grades (PCGS and NGC)*:	3,223

(* As of July 2003)

(** Possible resubmissions or crossovers of one or more of the same coins.)

REFLECTIONS:

EARLY HAPPENINGS

Carson City Mint employees were eager to get back to work in July of 1889. Four years of dormancy had left the facility in a state of disrepair, but clean up crews re moved the cobwebs, aired out the rooms, and dusted off the machinery in preparation for a resurrection of coinage operations. First on the agenda was the ousting of Superintendent Garrard; his replacement was respected city undertaker, Sam Wright. Then followed the arrival of five sets of 1889 dies from Philadelphia. Newly appointed coiner Charles H. Colburn read the manuals, studied the coin presses and got excited when the silver planchets were ready. Then in October, 100,000 specimens of what was destined to become the scarcest date in the "CC" Morgan dollar series were struck in precision–like succession. A relatively high percentage of these handsome new dollars displayed deep mirrored prooflike surfaces, gradually descending to brilliant prooflike, and tapering off to semi-prooflike. In November, another 100,000 1889-CC dollars were delivered by coiner Colburn, and then in December, the final 150,000 dollars fell into the drop bin beneath the coin press.

NUMISMATIC NOTES

For unknown reasons, approximately 250,000 to 325,000 1889-CC silver dollars were eventually melted, securing this date as one of the keys to a set of Morgan dollars. Until the early 1950s, several dates in the "CC" dollar series were considered rarer than the 1889-CC, but as the Treasury began releasing thousands of other dates in the "CC" series, collectors realized 1889-CC's were not to be included. Prices shot up immediately, and when it was discovered that 1889-CC dollars were not part of the GSA sales, prices soared. Rumors of a 7,000 to 10,000 coin hoard of Uncirculated 1889-CC's kept a loose lid on price jumps for a while, but the sale of MS-65 specimens for $300,000 in the 1990s, and an MS-68 coin for $500,000 dared those hoarded coins to show their faces.

Although there are numerous quantities of low-grade circulated 1889-CC dollars with various levels of damage, there is a shortage of problem-free circulated pieces in the VG to XF range, resulting in many collectors being placed on waiting lists.

VARIETY CONSIDERATIONS

Only three varieties are known for this rarity, and all 1889-CCs have *Large* "CC"s. Many counterfeits and altered mintmark examples exist, which are easy enough to have authenticated.[1]

---
[1] One of the *Top 25.*

(Photo courtesy Bowers and Merena)

Mintage: 2,309,041

GSA Population: 3,949

Finest Knowns*:

> PCGS MS-66 (8)
>
> NGC MS-66 (2)
>
> PCGS MS-65DMPL (16)
>
> NGC MS-65DMPL (6)
>
> PCGS MS-65PL (7)
>
> NGC MS-65PL (2)
>
> PCGS MS-65 (161)
>
> NGC MS-65 (41)

Notable Pedigrees:

> Various

Survival Estimates in All Grades:	100,000-150,000
Estimated in Uncirculated:	25,000-30,000
Estimated in XF to AU:	40,000-75,000
Total Certified Examples in All Grades (PCGS and NGC)*:	8,068

(* As of July 2003)

REFLECTIONS:

EARLY HAPPENINGS

As 1890 began, over 350 million silver dollars had been manufactured following the enactment of the *Bland/Allison* bill in 1878, of which nearly 280 million were being held in storage. Yet still, on July 14, 1890, Congress voted to produce more than ever before. Silver production nationwide continued to surge, and during the three year period between 1890 and 1892 averaged 56.8 million ounces annually. Even Comstock mines had experienced a minor spurt in production in the late 1880s to early 1890s. Deposits at the Carson City Mint more than fulfilled requirements for the silver dollars being produced, even as in January of 1890 the Carson Mint duplicated its silver dollar output of 150,000 from the preceding December and steadily climbed, reaching a peak monthly quota of 200,000 by March. After the *Sherman Act* was enacted in July, surplus silver purchases from the 1878 Coinage Act were used until exhausted, and then in the fall, silver supplied by the new legislation was utilized. In December, Carson Mint employees struck a record 245,000 cartwheels, bringing 1890's total to 2.3 million, also a mint record. Another record was broken, this on a national scale, as all four U.S. mints combined to produce 38 million silver dollars.

NUMISMATIC NOTES

Because of its high mintage, this date has always been easy to locate in most grades up to MS-62. Thousands of 1890-CC's were released in the 1940s and 1950s by the Treasury Department, and a number of bags were shipped back to Nevada and claimed by banks, casinos and residents such as LaVere Redfield. Though abundant in lower grades, this date is quite scarce in MS-64 and above. It is one of only a few dates from the Carson City dollar series with no specimens grading above MS-66. Only 3,949 examples were sold during the GSA sales, establishing the date as one of the keys to a set of *Black Box* dollars.

VARIETY CONSIDERATIONS

To be expected, the date with the highest mintage also features the most varieties, 13 in all. One of the most unusual die varieties in the entire silver dollar series is known as the 1890-CC *Tailbar*, caused by a large gouge made on the reverse die, creating a long raised strip of metal below the eagle's tail. This date also features some spectacular Deep-Mirror-Prooflike specimens.

1891-CC

(Photo courtesy Bowers and Merena)

Mintage: 1,618,000

GSA Population: 5,687

Finest Knowns*:

    PCGS MS-68PL (1)

    PCGS MS-67 (1)

    NGC MS-67 (1)

    PCGS MS-66PL (1)

    PCGS MS-65DMPL (1)

    NGC MS-65DMPL (1)

    PCGS MS-65PL (11)**

    NGC MS-65PL (5)**

    PCGS MS-66 (25)**

    NGC MS-66 (7)**

    PCGS MS-65 (296)**

    NGC MS-65 (93)**

Notable Pedigrees:

    Eliasberg (1997)

Survival Estimates in All Grades:	75,000-105,000
Estimated in Uncirculated:	30,000-40,000
Estimated in XF to AU:	35,000-50,000
Total Certified Examples in All Grades (PCGS and NGC)*:	11,263

(* As of July 2003)

(** Possible resubmissions or crossovers of one or more of the same coins.)

REFLECTIONS:

EARLY HAPPENINGS

Essential provisions of the *Sherman Act* of 1890, stipulated that the Treasury should purchase 4.5 million ounces of silver each month, and produce a minimum of two million silver dollars for 12 consecutive months. Thereafter, the mandatory coinage of silver dollars would cease, and it was left to the discretion of the Secretary to provide for Treasury note redemptions. At the Carson City Mint, silver dollar production proceeded at nearly the same vigorous pace as 1890. From January through March, the monthly average was 180,000, and then in April and May momentum reversed, slowing to 75,000 and 85,000, respectively. June rebounded with a high energy output of 186,000 pieces, and from July through the end of the year, Carson City's monthly average was 120,000. This moderate reduction paralleled that of the other mints around the country in response to the compulsory coinage of silver dollars ceasing in July. During 1890 and 1891, approximately 500,000 Carson City silver dollars were distributed annually. Probably the highest percentage of the distributed coins were 1890-CC's, though it is believed that thousands of 1891-CC's were included.

NUMISMATIC NOTES

Although large quantities of 1891-CC dollars were released in the 1930s, 1940s and 1950s, only a small percentage remained in circulation long enough to produce low grade circulated coins. However, there is a profusion of XF to AU examples, and Uncirculated specimens are easy enough to locate in most grades below MS-63, although finding them above the MS-64 mark presents a challenge. The date is exceedingly scarce in DMPL condition, though frosty white specimens are plentiful. At the top of the Condition Census chart is the famous *Eliasberg* coin, graded MS-68PL by PCGS.

VARIETY CONSIDERATIONS

There are at least five varieties of this date, the most well known being the *Spitting Eagle*, which teams up well with the 1890-CC *Tailbar* to make a very popular two coin variety set.

1892-CC

(Photo courtesy Bowers and Merena)

Mintage: 1,352,000

GSA Population: 1

Finest Knowns*:

> PCGS MS-67 (2)
>
> NGC MS-67 (1)
>
> PCGS MS-65DMPL (2)
>
> NGC MS-65DMPL (1)
>
> PCGS MS-66 (15)
>
> NGC MS-66 (9)
>
> PCGS MS-65PL (8)
>
> NGC MS-65PL (3)

> PCGS MS-65 (173)
>
> NGC MS-65 (95)

Notable Pedigrees:

> Eliasberg (1997)

Survival Estimates in All Grades:	75,000-100,000
Estimated in Uncirculated:	17,000-25,000
Estimated in XF to AU:	15,000-22,000
Total Certified Examples in All Grades (PCGS and NGC)*:	6,675

(* As of July 2003)

REFLECTIONS:

EARLY HAPPENINGS

A consistent production pace averaging 112,600 silver dollars every month, kept Carson City Mint workers busy all year in 1892. Gold coin mintages, though slashed to half of 1891's output, also remained steady throughout 1892.

Distribution of silver dollars being produced at the Carson City Mint had been reduced to a minimal amount by 1892, averaging 75,000 annually for 1892 and 1893, as opposed to an average of nearly 500,000 annually in 1890 and 1891. Carson City had begun stockpiling dollars, and eventually built up an inventory of 5.3 million by the time operations ceased. Very few 1892-CC dollars were released prior to the 20th century.

NUMISMATIC NOTES

Though not widely distributed until the 1940s and 1950s, this date, because of its relatively high mintage for a "CC" dollar, was not considered to be scarce. A small collector base during the first half of the 20th century had sufficient supplies to meet the demand.

Somewhere, it is said, exist thousands of Uncir-

culated examples of 1892-CCs, however, this presumption begs the question, where are they? When it was discovered during the GSA sales that there was only one 1892-CC dollar in the Treasury's holdings prices doubled overnight. By the 1980s, Uncirculated 1892-CCs were valued at more than all other "CC" issues except 1889, 1893, and 1879.

In the early years of the 21st century, specimens of the 1892-CC in MS-65 and above are prized by silver dollar specialists. High grade DMPL specimens are exceedingly scarce, and problem-free XF and AU examples are in relatively short supply as well, although ample supplies of lower grade circulated pieces are available.

VARIETY CONSIDERATIONS

A "Perfect brilliant proof" specimen, attributed to the *Colonel Green Collection,* sold for $67.50 as part of the *Jack Roe* collection at the *Waltman* sale in 1945. This coin has not been certified as yet.

At least nine varieties exist for this date, half of them relating to the mintmark. Several of the interesting selections are the *Slanted* "CC", *Dropped* "CC", *Doubled* "CC", and *Wide Spaced* "CC". None of the varieties are valued at more than the date itself.

1893-CC

(Photo courtesy Bowers and Merena)

Mintage: 677,000

GSA Population: 1

Finest Knowns*:

    NGC MS-65DMPL (1)

    PCGS MS-65PL (2)

    PCGS MS-65 (7)**

    NGC MS-65 (5)**

Notable Pedigrees:

    Jack Lee (1999)

    Mike Gilley (Current)

      ex: Jack Lee

Survival Estimates in All Grades:	12,500-17,500
Estimated in Uncirculated:	6,000-10,000
Estimated in XF to AU:	3,000-4,000
Total Certified Examples in All Grades (PCGS and NGC)*:	3,946

(* As of July 2003)

(** Possible resubmissions or crossovers throughout this entire list)

REFLECTIONS:

EARLY HAPPENINGS

From October of 1889 through December of 1892, the Carson City Mint's monthly silver dollar production averaged 144,000 pieces, sometimes higher. During the first five months of 1893, the mint was on a monthly pace of 135,400 silver dollars, which incidentally would have resulted in the same output as in 1891. But then everything came to an abrupt halt on June 1, 1893 when coinage operations ceased.

Newly elected president Grover Cleveland parleying with a divided Congress, determined that the *Sherman Silver Purchase Act* had failed, and needed to be repealed. Silver dollar production was suspended across the nation, pending the passage of the repeal act in November of 1893. Treasury Secretary John G. Carlisle and Mint Director Robert E. Preston seized the opportunity to deactivate Carson City's coinage operations, reducing it to an Assay Office. And then it was over, with 1893 being the last date ever stamped on a U.S. coin with the "CC" mintmark.

NUMISMATIC NOTES

Since the mintage was not that low in comparison to other Carson City dates like 1881, 1885 and 1889, the 1893-CC dollar was not considered to be particularly scarce during the first 40 years of its existence. Then, as larger quantities of Uncirculated examples of other "CC" dollars were sold at various Treasury locations, it became obvious that there were far fewer 1893-CC's being distributed. By the 1940s, prices for this date had risen above every other date in the "CC" dollar series except the 1889. On occasion, specimens of the 1893-CC would bring more than similarly graded 1889-CC's.

When figures for the Treasury holdings were revealed during the GSA sale era, only one 1893-CC was included. This news quickly established the date as the second scarcest "CC" dollar, trailing only the 1889-CC. In the 30 or so years since the GSA sales, occasional small hoards have appeared, for example, the one in the *Redfield* estate.

Not surprisingly, specimens of the 1893-CC are prohibitively scarce in grades of MS-65 and above, and as of this writing (2003) no 1893-CC dollar has been graded higher than MS-65. Circulated pieces are constantly in demand usually requiring being placed on a waiting list. Most Uncirculated examples are heavily bagmarked, and some come weakly struck, known as *pancake strikes.*

Variety Considerations

At least five die variations exist for this date, one of the more interesting features Liberty's profile lightly doubled. All 1893-CC's have *Large* "CC"s.

For more information concerning this date please see the section on Proof "CC" dollars.

Bags of silver coins stacked in Treasury vaults were a common sight in the 19th century.

Comparison of Morgan Dollar Production at the
Carson City Mint with the
Philadelphia Mint's From 1878 to 1893

MORGAN DOLLAR MINTAGE TOTALS		
Year	Carson City	Philadelphia
1878 All Kinds	2,212,000	10,509,550
1879 All Kinds	756,000	14,807,100
1880 All Kinds	591,000	12,601,355
1881	296,000	9,163,984
1882	1,133,000	11,101,100
1883	1,204,000	12,291,039
1884	1,136,000	14,070,875
1885	228,000	17,787,930
1889	350,000	21,726,811
1890	2,309,041	16,802,590
1891	1,618,000	8,694,206
1892	1,352,000	1,037,245
1893	677,000	378,792
TOTAL	13,862,041	150,972,577
	Carson City	Philadelphia
Silver Coin Cumulative Total From 1870 to 1893	54,762,546	266,535,907

1900-O/CC***

(Photo courtesy Bowers and Merena)

Mintage: Unknown (Estimated 1,150,000-1,500,000)

Finest Knowns*:

    PCGS MS-67 (2)

    NGC MS-67 (1)

    PCGS MS-66 (52)

    NGC MS-66 (9)

    PCGS MS-65 (423)

    NGC MS-65 (101)

Notable Pedigrees:

    Various

Survival Estimates in All Grades:	100,000-150,000
Estimated in Uncirculated:	27,500-49,500
Estimated in XF to AU:	9,500-20,000
Total Certified Examples in All Grades (PCGS and NGC)*:	4,544

(* As of July 2003)

(*** Minted at New Orleans – optional date in "CC" set.)

REFLECTIONS:

EARLY HAPPENINGS

After the Carson Mint's coinage operations were discontinued in June of 1893, all coining machinery and related gear was painted, leaded, or in other ways protected, until a final decision was made about the mint's future. Apparently a half dozen or so reverse dies for Morgan dollars remained, either for the possibility of resumed production or perhaps just an oversight. Regardless, in 1899 when the status of the Carson Mint was officially changed to Assay Office, all coining machinery and gear were sent to other locations as directed, the reverse dies going to Philadelphia.

Then in 1900, silver dollar production was extremely active for the second year in a row at the New Orleans Mint, and Philadelphia sent at least five of the old "CC" reverse dies to New Orleans to facilitate that mint's heavy output. Each of these reverse dies had an "O" mintmark punched over the partially effaced Carson City letters. It is not known how many of the *over-mintmark* coins were struck, however an estimate based on the number of old "CC" reverse dies utilized, arrives at an average of 200,000 to 250,000 per die. If this is nearly accurate, approximately 10% of 1900-O silver dollars are the "O/CC" variety.

NUMISMATIC NOTES

It has been reported that this variety became known to the larger numismatic community in the late 1920s, when it was publicized by Howard R. Newcomb, and then Will W. Neil, in a 1928 article in *The Numismatist*. Price guides did not generally list this variety until the 1970s, at which time interest in it increased. It was no easy task to determine price due to the variety's unknown availability. Rumors abounded of bag quantities but only occasional small hoards surfaced; typically, a roll or two of Uncirculated pieces would constitute a hoard in the early years of the 21st century. This date is moderately priced in grades up through MS-65, but then becomes rather expensive in higher grades. Circulated examples are readily available and it is wise for the collector to select problem-free specimens.

VARIETY CONSIDERATIONS

Being a variety itself, this date is divided into a subset of seven variations. Degrees of definition on the underlying "CC"s vary from faint to heavy, and one variety displays rough die chips, possibly mixed with die rust around the mintmark reminiscent of the 1879-CC *Capped Die*. There are no prooflike examples of the 1900-O/CC known to exist.

NGC:

1882-CC NGC SP-65

1883-CC NGC PR-65

1884-CC NGC PR-66 CAMEO

1884-CC NGC PR-64

(6) 1893-CC NGC PR-60, 62, 63, 65 (2), 67**

PCGS:

(10) 1893-CC PCGS PR-62, 63 (4), 64 (2), 65, 66, 67**

(** Possible resubmissions and crossovers have increased the reported populations.)

REFLECTIONS:

EARLY HAPPENINGS

From the first year of operations at the Carson City Mint, Proof or Deep-Mirror-Prooflike specimens of most silver issues played an integral part in its legacy. Although there are no official Proof or Specimen Strike coins listed in the Treasury's statistics for Carson City, numismatists have long acknowledged the existence of such pieces. In early auction catalogs from the 1890s through the 1940s, it was not uncommon for the cataloguer to describe coins as he saw them, often resulting in Proof descriptions for Carson City silver dollars, especially so with B. Max Mehl. Noted numismatic author and dealer Wayte Raymond listed an original mintage of 12 1893-CC Proof silver dollars in his *Standard Catalogue* during the first half of the 20th century. Raymond stated that these 12 specimens had been coined at the Carson City Mint's closing ceremonies in 1893. He reported that he had seen one of the 12 coins, but until the 1970s, no one from the coin collecting community at large had ever handled a speci-

---

**FINEST KNOWN 1893-CC PROOF DOLLAR
THE DISCOVERY PIECE**

See Color Plate

1099   1893-CC   **BRANCH MINT PROOF!** The specimen from our 1973 FUN Sale (Lot #753) from whose description we quote the following:

1893-CC The issuance of this OUTSTANDING NUMISMATIC RARITY has long been known. Wayte Raymond listed it in his Standard Catalogue as has Don Taxay in his Comprehensive Catalogue. There were supposedly 12 pieces struck during the closing ceremonies of the Carson City Mint in 1893, and distributed to dignitaries present. This is the FIRST SPECIMEN to be located and offered for public sale! Wayte Raymond reportedly had seen one specimen, the location of which remains a mystery, and it is possible that this is the specimen that he saw. This piece is accompanied by a letter of Authentication issued by Walter Breen, dated August 14, 1972. The letter reads in part.

"This certifies that I have examined the accompanying coin, and that I UNHESITATINGLY DECLARE IT A GENUINE 1893-CC PROOF DOLLAR. Were this coin without a mintmark, nobody could question its proof state. It has every earmark of the genuine article: frosty devices brought up more sharply than on normal business strikes; struck at least twice (as normally on proofs) from brilliantly repolished dies on a highly polished blank. Border details are as clear as on many Philadelphia (and

N.O. and S.F.) proofs, clearer than on many uncs., surpassed only by the most carefully minted proofs.

I had heard of the original 12 proof 1893-CC dollars, coined for distribution at the ceremony closing the Carson City mint, from Wayte Raymond (1951) who had seen at least one from that source. This listing was carried in the Standard Catalogue of U.S. Coins through its final edition (1957), though at that time nobody had managed to trace any examples aside from one Wayte Raymond had earlier encountered . . .

The dies, incidentally, differ from the regularly listed 1893-CC varieties in Van Allen's book, largely in faint cracks, peculiar 3 (trace of extra curve at right betwen loops) and position of CC mintmark. At present it is the ONLY ONE I HAVE SEEN, and I cannot exclude the possibility that it is the one Wayte Raymond had seen sometime prior to World War II."

Respectfully submitted,
Walter Breen

This dollar has a Superb Mirror surface with great depth to it, and beautifully frosty devices. The coin is permanently identified by a tiny rim bruise opposite the fourth star on the left . . . and is the RAREST OF ALL MORGAN DOLLARS, and certainly the RAREST OF ALL CARSON CITY COINAGE, surpassing even the 1876-CC Twenty Cent Piece and the 1870-CC Double Eagle . . .

At the time that this description was written, this was the only 1893-CC Dollar that had been verified as a Proof. However, in Breen's book on U.S. Proof coins, he lists three other specimens as now being known, although one of them has not been documented. Of the pieces known, though, this easily has to rank as THE FINEST KNOWN, and as such should realize a price commensurate with its obvious rarity and incomparable quality — far more than the $18,000 it realized over six years ago, before the Silver Dollar market even came close to reaching the level of activity and interest it now enjoys.

Appearing in Auction '79, this stunning Proof 1893-CC silver dollar realized $39,000.

men. Then in 1973, RARCOA auctioned one at its *FUN* (Florida United Numismatists) sale, resulting in an $18,000 price realized, the first time a Morgan dollar cracked the $10,000 barrier. This same specimen sold again in 1979, this time for $39,000, becoming part of the *Wayne Miller* set.

NUMISMATIC NOTES

With the advent of professional grading services, the definition of a Proof or Specimen strike for a coin rests with them. A certificate and grade from PCGS or NGC, confirming a coin's method of striking, can translate into thousands of dollars in additional value. These two services are the accepted standard-bearers in the early years of the 21st century, and without their blessing, no matter how much a coin may look like a Proof, the market will not acknowledge it as such.

So far (2003-2004), NGC has certified four dates from the "CC" Morgan dollar series as Proofs or Specimen strikes, and PCGS has only confirmed the 1893-CCs as Proofs. Other dates in the "CC" Morgan dollar series

allegedly struck as Proofs are: 1878-CC, 1885-CC, 1889-CC, 1890-CC, 1891-CC, and 1892-CC. However, as Q. David Bowers suggests, Proof descriptions for these dates are probably due to overzealous cataloguers drooling over Deep-Mirror-Prooflike specimens.[1]

In the early years of the 21st century, any Proof Carson City Morgan dollar will bring a minimum of $25,000 and for *Finest Knowns,* double or triple that amount.

---

[1] One exception may be B. Max Mehl's description of the 1892-CC in the *Jack Roe* collection from 1945, evidence by the $67.50 price realized which was very high for the time.

COINAGE RECORDS FOR ALL MINTS DURING THE CARSON CITY ERA 1870-1893

MINT MARK	DIMES	20 CENTS	QUARTERS	HALF DOLLARS	TRADE DOLLARS
CARSON CITY	20,901,108	143,290	10,316,792	5,308,627	4,211,400
PHILADELPHIA	130,249,454	556,950	55,450,034	34,893,311	5,107,539
NEW ORLEANS	47,913,116	0	6,104,000	1,779,000	0
SAN FRANCISCO	39,598,614	1,155,000	27,261,314	19,254,028	26,647,000

MINT MARK	DOLLARS*	HALF EAGLES	EAGLES	DOUBLE EAGLES
CARSON CITY	13,881,329	709,617	299,778	864,178
PHILADELPHIA	213,301,815	15,739,161	12,123,186	5,345,670
NEW ORLEANS	115,614,529	120,000	97,693	2,325
SAN FRANCISCO	79,455,074	11,490,900	5,308,350	23,880,400

* Seated Liberty and Morgan

CHAPTER SEVEN

The Gold Coins of the Carson City Mint

Three denominations of gold coins were minted at Carson City between 1870 and 1893, all with the Liberty Head design. There are 19 dates in a set of $5 half eagles, dated 1870 to 1884, then again from 1890 to 1893. In the $10 denomination there are also 19 dates, paralleling the half eagle years. A set of $20 double eagles consists of 19 dates, altering slightly from the eagles and half eagles, running from 1870 to 1885 (no 1880, or 1881) and then from 1889 to 1893. All told, the combined total for all three denominations is 1,873,573 coins. In comparison, the total mintages for these same three denominations during those same years at the Philadelphia Mint, was 34,230,161 coins.

In terms of quantity and face value, $20 double eagles were clearly the most heavily produced gold coins at the Carson City Mint. These larger coins accommodated payments for deposited bullion easier than the smaller denominations.

FORMAT

This section is arranged similar to the chapter on silver coins. Each denomination of gold coin is separated into complete sets, with dates in consecutive order. Included in the data section for individual dates are "Mintages," "Finest Knowns," "Notable Pedigrees," "Survival Estimates in All Grades," "Uncirculated, and XF/AU," and finally, "Total Certified Examples in All Grades."

"Finest Knowns" data is taken from PCGS and NGC population reports. "Notable Pedigrees" include only the most recognizable names associated with each date. In some cases, the generic term "Various" will be used. Survival estimates rely heavily on auction catalogs, population reports, the author's personal experience, and to a degree, the statistics from Douglas Winters' *Gold Coins from the Carson City Mint.* In any exercise, such as estimating survival populations, so much depends on inconclusive evidence, yet researchers use what is available, and do their best. As decades pass, turning into a century and beyond, cumulative data allows more precision in estimates, always moving toward the goal of accuracy. With an aggregate mintage of 1,873,573, Carson City gold coins begin with a quantity less than some of Philadelphia and San Francisco's **annual** outputs. This narrows the playing field in the process of making estimates considerably.

A quick arm's-length calculation based on gold coin survival percentage in general, immediately slashes 95% off the top of Carson City's gold coin production. All of a sudden it becomes clear to the researcher that there is a relatively small quantity of coins to contend with. After that the work intensifies, and numismatists acknowledge that there is much left to be done. As noted in the chapter on silver coins, the "Total Certified Examples" data is taken from the two largest grading services, PCGS and NGC.

In the "Reflections" section, comments will be brief, limited to rudimentary bits of information about "CC" gold coins that might be helpful, and hopefully not too redundant. Readers are encouraged to review Winter's book on "CC" gold coins for a more detailed study on the subject.

Carson City's gold coin production got off to a rather inauspicious start in 1870, minting only 17,372 combined half eagles, eagles, and double eagles with a total face value of $173,235. In comparison, the *Golden State's* San Francisco Mint produced over one million gold coins with an aggregate face value of nearly $20 million. Still, Superintendent Curry, and the town's folk in Carson were thrilled to have a neighborhood branch mint.

Bullion deposits were limited to what local miners brought in as Carson City's only duty was to the residents and mining operators in the region. San Francisco's mint had already been open 16 years when the Carson facility commenced operations, and handily supplied Pacific states with gold coins, as well as providing for export demand. Yet at the time, no one knew the potential that lay buried in the earth around the Comstock, nor how large the population base in that region might grow.

Nevada legislators were optimistic when lobbying Congress on behalf of the Carson Mint, forecasting that production from the Comstock mines would increase if that facility were expanded. In one of their resolutions, lawmakers declared that "the amount of production might be increased to an extent which would seem almost **incredible** to those not familiar with the **vast extent of our mineral ledges.**" [1] [Emphasis added] By the time the mint finally opened in 1870, Congress had not appropriated as much as Nevada legislators had asked for, a precursor of things to come. Still, bullion depositors demonstrated at least perfunctory interest in the new mint, bringing in $124,000 worth of gold ore during 1870.

Deposits increased from 1871 through 1873, though gold coin production did not keep pace. From 1874 through 1877, gold deposits tapered off, but during those years, coin production was nearly on par with the bullion coming in. From 1878 through 1881, gold deposits dropped sharply, with coinage outputs generally keeping pace. At right is a table exhibiting the gold deposits at the Carson Mint and corresponding coinage production from 1870 through 1885.

During this same period it became apparent that local miners' support of the Carson Mint would be lim-

ited, as favorable transportation costs and assay expenses compelled them to send their gold to San Francisco, as well as other destinations. Carson City's share was approximately 33% of the $85.5 million in gold hauled from the mines, of which 60% was minted into coins. Gold coin production would typically be held to a minimum, though on occasion, Carson City would experience upsurts.

In the half eagle series in particular, mintages rose to levels inconsistent with normal production schedules at different times during the 1880s. These heightened coinage yields corresponded with the second phase of the *Specie Resumption Act* of 1879, when greenbacks and other

---

[1] *40th Congress, 1st session, House of Representatives, Misc. Doc #8*, March 11, 1867.

GOLD DEPOSITS AND COINAGE AT THE CARSON CITY MINT BETWEEN 1870 AND 1885		
Year	Deposits By Fiscal Years	Coinage By Calendar Years[*]
1870	$124,155	$173,235
1871	1,003,810	469,440
1872	4,371,573	732,900
1873	5,004,537	530,710
1874	2,213,042	2,575,360,
1875	2,540,058	2,359,310
1876	3,175,047	2,850,215
1877	1,738,298	928,020
1878	737,720	341,310
1879	318,852	318,185
1880	368,174	366,985
1881	517,572	309,580
1882	1,016,966	1,264,525
1883	1,472,802	1,384,030
1884	1,451,820	1,804,040
1885	1,505,665	189,000
Total	$27,560,091	$16,596,845[**]

[*] Face Value
[**] *Annual Report of the Director of the Mint,* 1887

paper currency became redeemable in gold coin. Concurrent with these currency redemptions, an unusually high volume of foreign gold coins and bullion were imported to the New York Assay Office and production of gold coins at the Philadelphia Mint was increased in order to pay these foreign depositors. At first the gold coin of preference was the double eagle, which was the easiest to count. But then the Treasury decided to increase the volume of half eagles and eagles and decrease double eagle production, hoping it would deter withdrawal of the larger gold coins from the country and increase the use of paper money. Mints across the nation escalated the coinage of half eagles and eagles to keep pace with millions of dollars in gold and currency being redeemed, and Carson City received a small share of the pie.

In the early 1890s, half eagles were again needed for redemption payouts, this time for the Treasury notes being used to purchase silver under the *Sherman Act*. In fact, had it not been for the *Specie* and *Sherman* acts in addition to excessive export demand, half eagle and eagle mintages may have been only 40% to 50% of the original outputs. For instance, during 13 of the 19 years that half eagles were produced at the Carson Mint, the annual average was approximately 13,150 pieces; but in the six peak production years the average rose to 90,000 coins.

Hundreds of thousands of half eagles were shipped from Carson City to banks in California and other states, and apparently, large quantities of "CC" gold coins were sent abroad to be returned in small hoards decades later. Heaps of "CC" half eagles were presumably lost to the Presidential Act of 1933, recalling gold coins, although

normal means of attrition and periodic meltdowns also account for the small populations extant.

A low survival rate is common to the three "CC" gold denominations: In the half eagle series for instance, most of the dates are estimated to number as few as $1/2$ to 1% of the original mintages extant. Another characteristic shared by many dates from the pre-1885 era is a weak strike, more noticeable on specimens grading XF and above. Circulated pieces show less of the weakness in strike primarily due to natural wear causing the same effect.

Many "CC" half eagles, especially in lower circulated grades have been cleaned, brushed, wiped, or in other ways abused. Examples in AU to MS-61 are often heavily bagmarked or scuffed, and possess medium to dull luster. Many specimens in these grades, as well as those in lower conditions, appear *dirty,* and early date "CC" half eagles exuding eye appeal are extremely scarce, although there are several notable specimens that stand head and shoulders above all others in the series.

Very few high grade sets with average grades above AU exist, and if there were one consisting of the finest known examples it would be a sight to behold, and would undoubtedly shatter all price records if sold at public auction.

At present (2003-2004), a massive gold coin research project is nearing completion with the goal of updating survival population data, revising Condition Census standings, tracking pedigrees, and compiling price histories. From the perspective of the Carson City gold series, this project should provide valuable insight into the chronological course these coins have traveled since leaving that mint.

Bureau of the Mint Data For Carson City Gold Half Eagle Production

Total Combined Mintage: 709,617

Total Face Value: $3,548,085

Total Ounces of Gold Used: .... 171,638 ozs.

Design Type: .... Coronet or Liberty Head With Motto

Designers: .... Christian Gobrecht

James B. Longacre – Motto Scroll

Metal Composition: .... 900 Gold .100 Copper

Actual Gross Weight: .... 8.359 grams

Actual Fine Gold Content: .... .24187 oz.

Value of Gold in One Half Eagle Between 1870 and 1893: $4.99-5.005

1870-CC

(Photo courtesy Bowers and Merena)

Mintage: 7,675

Finest Known*:

NGC MS-62 (I)

PCGS MS-6I (2)**

NGC MS-6I (I)

PCGS AU-58 (2)***

NGC AU-58 (9)***

Notable Pedigrees:

Harry W. Bass, Jr. (1999)

Henry S. Lang (2002)

Nevada Collection (Current)

Survival Estimates in All Grades:	70-85
Estimated in Uncirculated:	4-6
Estimated in XF to AU:	35-40
Total Certified Examples in All Grades (PCGS and NGC)*:	74

(* As of April 2003)

(**It is possible that one is the NGC MS-62 coin)

(*** Possible resubmissions of one or more coins)

REFLECTIONS:

Key to a set of "CC" half eagles and highly esteemed by gold coin specialists, the 1870-CC $5 is rarely available in grades above XF and practically nonexistent in Uncirculated condition. This date is unknown in Choice Uncirculated, and the few Mint State pieces known to exist, lack eye appeal.

This date often possesses a weak strike on the eagle's neck down to the shield, and most examples are very baggy, with many circulated pieces having been cleaned. Problem-free specimens with sharp strikes are worth considerable premiums in any grade.[1]

---

[1] One of the *Top 25.*

As work on the Carson City Mint progressed in the 1860s, Abraham Curry received many endorsements such as this from Nevada's leading politicians. In this memo Senators Nye and Stewart assure the Treasury Department that, "We are satisfied that Mr. Curry's estimate and judgement is correct in the matter, and that he will be able to perform the work as per statement." *(Courtesy Nevada Historical Society)*

1871-CC

(Photo courtesy Bowers and Merena)

Mintage: 20,770

Finest Known*:

NGC MS-63

NGC MS-61

PCGS AU-58 (2)**

NGC AU-58 (4)**

Notable Pedigrees:

E.A. Carson (1976)

RARCOA Auction '79 (1979)

Paramount Auction '80 (1980)

Louis E. Eliasberg, Sr. (1982)

Harry W. Bass, Jr. (1999)

Stack's 66th Anniversary Sale (2001)

Henry S. Lang (2002)

Nevada Collection (Current)

Survival Estimates in All Grades:...... 140-175
Estimated in Uncirculated: 3-4
Estimated in XF to AU:.............................. 60-90
Total Certified Examples in All Grades (PCGS and NGC)*: ... 137

(* As of April 2003)

(** Possible resubmissions of one or more of the same coins.)

REFLECTIONS:

Though production nearly tripled from the preceding year, the survival estimate for 1871-CC half eagles is less than 1% of the original mintage, establishing the date as one of the scarcest in the series. In Uncirculated condition, for instance, the 1871-CC is nearly as scarce as the 1870-CC; surprisingly an NGC-certified Choice MS-63 specimen exists and is one of the stand-out attractions in the entire series. Despite the date's rarity in Mint State condition, XF examples are not that elusive, and AU specimens, though challenging, are generally available.

In comparison to 1870-CC half eagles, the strike on the 1871-CC is above average, with typical softness at the center of the eagle's neck. A rather high mintmark, at times nearly touching the arrow feather, is similar to the one found on the 1870-CC. Another variety features a slightly lower mintmark, with the letters nearly parallel.

Problem-free circulated specimens are always in demand, but can still be purchased for smaller premiums than might be expected. As the collector base for "CC" gold coins increases, examples of this date will quickly disappear.

(Photo courtesy Bowers and Merena)

Mintage: 16,980

Finest Known*:

    PCGS AU-58 (1)

    NGC AU-58 (1)

    PCGS AU-55 (2)

    NGC AU-55 (2)

    PCGS AU-53 (1)

Notable Pedigrees:

    E.A. Carson (1976)

    Harry W. Bass, Jr. (1999)

    Nevada Collection (Current)

Survival Estimates in All Grades:...... 100-125

Estimated in Uncirculated: 1-3

Estimated in XF to AU:............................ 35-50

Total Certified Examples
    in All Grades (PCGS and NGC)*: 83

(* As of April 2003)

REFLECTIONS:

At the turn of the 21st century, the 1872-CC is the only date in the Carson City half eagle series that has not had a specimen graded in Mint State condition by either PCGS or NGC. At the top of the Condition Census are two AU-58 specimens (possibly the same coin). Survival percentage estimates for the 1872-CC half eagles are lower than any other date in the series, with less than ¹/₂ of 1% extant.

One of the reverse dies used to strike the 1872-CC's features a much lower mintmark than the two preceding years. The letters in it are nearly parallel, with the left "C" slanting slightly above the left stem in the *V* in *FIVE*. Weakness is an issue, as with many of the dates in the "CC" series, but a shortage of specimens above XF puts limitations on a thorough study of strike characteristics for this date.

Prices for XF to AU examples have gradually risen to levels commensurate with this date's rarity, yet lower grade circulated pieces seem undervalued (as of 2003). Problem-free pieces in Fine to Very Fine offered at anywhere near the listed price levels currently offer good value.

1873-CC

(Photo courtesy Bowers and Merena)

Mintage: 7,416

Finest Known*:

    PCGS MS-62 (1)**

    NGC MS-62 (1)**

    PCGS MS-61 (1)

    PCGS AU-55 (2)

    NGC AU-55 (2)

Notable Pedigrees:

    Charles Williams (Menjou) (1950)

    Harold S. Bareford (1978)

    Harry W. Bass, Jr. (1999)

    Henry S. Lang (2002)

    Nevada Collection (Current)

Survival Estimates in All Grades:............ 80-85	
Estimated in Uncirculated: 3	
Estimated in XF to AU:.............................. 35-40	
Total Certified Examples in All Grades (PCGS and NGC)*: 67	

(* As of April 2003)

(** Possibly the same coin graded at both services.)

REFLECTIONS:

Any date that has the second lowest mintage in a series is noteworthy, and when it is in the "CC" gold category there is even more prestige. Though the 1873-CC technically ranks second in terms of rarity behind the 1870-CC, there is a possibility that the two dates are tied for that position. In fact, at present (2003), it is somewhat easier to obtain an 1870-CC half eagle than it is an 1873-CC.

As with many dates in the "CC" half eagle series, the estimated survival percentage for the 1873-CC is near 1%. Because of the limited mintage, this factor is even more significant and it is highly probable that there are fewer than 80 pieces extant.

Somehow, several Uncirculated specimens of this date have survived and are prized numismatic treasures. Circulated pieces graded less than XF tend to be below average in eye appeal for the grades. Most are well worn and have too many nicks and scratches. Problem-free examples in any grade will command much higher premiums above prices listed.

With the interest in 1873 coinage in general, 1873-CC half eagles are popular with type collectors, date collectors, history buffs, and of course "CC" collectors.

1874-CC

(Photo courtesy Bowers and Merena)

Mintage: 21,198

Finest Known*:

> PCGS MS-62 (2)
>
> PCGS AU-58 (3)
>
> NGC AU-58 (7)**
>
> PCGS AU-55 (8) **
>
> NGC AU-55 (6)**

Notable Pedigrees:

> Ellis Robison (1979)
>
> Bowers and Merena *Polis* sale (1991)
>
> Reed Hawn (1993)
> ex: Ellis Robison
>
> Harry W. Bass, Jr. (1999)
>
> Nevada Collection (Current)
> ex: Reed Hawn

Survival Estimates in All Grades:...... 180-215
Estimated in Uncirculated: 3-4
Estimated in XF to AU:....................... 100-125
Total Certified Examples in All Grades (PCGS and NGC)*: ... 161

(* As of April 2003)
(** Possible resubmissions of one or more of the same coins.)

REFLECTIONS:

Easily the most accessible date from the first nine years of half eagle production at the Carson City Mint, the 1874-CC is still considered very scarce by gold coin specialists. Survival percentages are in the 1% range, in conformity with most "CC" half eagles in the 1870s. Barely nudging out the 1871-CC for highest mintage honors at Carson City between 1870 and 1880, the 1874-CC also has the distinction of surpassing Philadelphia and San Francisco's half eagle production in 1874.

Uncirculated examples of this date were once thought to be *Unique*; Walter Breen stated that in the 1970s he had heard of an Uncirculated 1874-CC half eagle, but had never seen one. Then a very special piece appeared in the *Doris and Ellis Robison Collection*, auctioned by Stack's in February of 1979. A record price at the time of $19,000 was achieved, and in 1993 it sold for the same price in the *Reed Hawn* sale. This coin was subsequently placed in the prestigious *Nevada Collection*.

Examples in VF to XF are available without much effort, and even lower end AU pieces are seen with regularity. Above that grade, the date becomes very challenging.

(Photo courtesy Bowers and Merena)

Mintage: 11,828

Finest Known*:

    NGC MS-63 (1)

    PCGS MS-61 (1)

    NGC AU-58 (2)

    PCGS AU-55 (3)

    NGC AU-55 (5)

Notable Pedigrees:

    Harry W. Bass, Jr. (1999)

    Henry S. Lang (2002)

    Nevada Collection (Current)

Survival Estimates in All Grades:......	140-160
Estimated in Uncirculated:	3-4
Estimated in XF to AU:	75-85
Total Certified Examples in All Grades (PCGS and NGC)*: ...	129

(* As of April 2003)

REFLECTIONS:

Mintages for "CC" half eagles began a gradual decline beginning in 1875, as double eagles dominated gold production at the mint. Furthermore, silver coinage took a significant hike in 1875 as the Treasury prepared for specie payment redemptions.

Of the 11,828 half eagles minted at Carson City in 1875 a large majority were shipped out of state in obedience to Treasury orders. Very few have survived in grades approaching Uncirculated, suggesting meltdowns at some point in time.

With workers at the Carson Mint concentrating on other denominations in 1875, it seems as if the quality of the half eagles was often neglected, resulting in many weakly struck specimens. Readers must bear in mind that due to such a small sampling of surviving pieces, it is not entirely fair to judge the entire mintage by those extant. Since only 1% or thereabouts of the original mintage is estimated to exist, there is no way to evaluate the workmanship of the remaining 99%.

Collectors must choose from a limited selection of high grade 1875-CCs, and experience has proven that fully struck specimens are rarely available. One lone example of this date has been graded MS-63 by NGC, with MS-61 being the next highest grade. Even high end AU pieces command high prices in the early years of the 21st century, and most often exhibit typical weakness in Liberty's hair and at the middle of the eagle's breast.

Problem-free circulated pieces in Fine to Very Fine tend not to show much striking weakness because of natural wear, and will generally bring premiums over listed prices. High-end XF examples routinely sell for prices closer to those listed for AU graded coins.

Two varieties of mintmarks offer specialists extra opportunity; one comes with the letters closer together, while the other has wider spaced "CC"s.

1876-CC

(Photo courtesy Bowers and Merena)

Mintage: 6,887

Finest Known*:

    PCGS MS-66 (1)***

    NGC MS-61 (1)

    PCGS AU-58 (2)

    NGC AU-58 (2)

    PCGS AU-55 (5)**

    NGC AU-55 (3)**

Notable Pedigrees:

    Belden E. Roach (1944)

    Louis E. Eliasberg (1982)

    Virgil Brand (1983)

    Harry W. Bass, Jr. (1999)

    Henry S. Lang (2002)

      ex: Eliasberg

    Nevada Collection (Current)

      ex: Lang, Eliasberg

Survival Estimates in All Grades:	**120-135**
Estimated in Uncirculated:	**2-3**
Estimated in XF to AU:	**65-75**
Total Certified Examples in All Grades (PCGS and NGC)*:	**115**

(* As of April 2003)

(** Possible resubmissions of one or more of the same coins)

(*** NGC includes this coin in their census data as an MS-64 and MS-65)

REFLECTIONS:

This date has the distinction of being the lowest mintage half eagle in the Carson City series. Conversely, 1876 proved to be the highest output year for "CC" double eagles, as well as yielding peak quantities of silver coinage.

Possibly due to early collector demand, a higher percentage of 1876-CC half eagles have survived relative to the original mintage. Still, there are probably fewer than 125 pieces extant and most are in grades of XF and below, with AU specimens being in short supply.

There are two Uncirculated examples of this date known as of the early years of the 21st century; one is the celebrated *Eliasberg* specimen, which first came into prominence as a consignment in the auction of that famous collector's gold set in 1982. It is astonishing that a gold coin from the Carson City Mint could possess such a flawless appearance.

After selling for $26,400 in the *Eliasberg* sale, the coin traded hands several times through various auctions, and ultimately received an MS-65 grade. In 2002, after hav-

ing sold several times for over $120,000, this splendid piece was upgraded to MS-66.

With regard to quality, it remains the premier gold coin of any date or denomination to have survived from the Carson City Mint; it is even more mind-boggling that it happens to be the lowest mintage half eagle in that series. Words can simply not express this coin's significance.

At some point after leaving Nevada, this 1876-CC half eagle wound up in Philadelphia, possibly as an assay specimen. Purchased by J.M. Clapp from the Chapman brothers in 1893 for less than $10, it became part of the *Louis E Eliasberg, Sr.* cabinet in 1942. Surprisingly, the grades of the first six half eagles in Mr. Eliasberg's famous collection—1870 to 1875—averaged only VF-30; then came the 1876-CC.

A quick diagnostic note: all known examples of the 1876-CC half eagle have a die lump of metal on Liberty's neck between her jaw line and hair curls.

Eliasberg's 1876-CC gold $5, arguably the rarest and highest quality gold coin surviving from the Carson City Mint.

1877-CC

(*Photo courtesy Bowers and Merena*)

Mintage: 8,680

Finest Known*:

> PCGS MS-62 (1)
>
> PCGS MS-60 (1)
>
> NGC AU-58 (4)***
>
> PCGS AU-58 (2)
>
> PCGS AU-55 (7)
>
> NGC AU-55 (8)**

Notable Pedigrees:

> Harry W. Bass, Jr. (1999)
>
> Henry S. Lang (2002)
>
> Nevada Collection (Current)

Survival Estimates in All Grades:	125-150
Estimated in Uncirculated:	3-4
Estimated in XF to AU:	75-85
Total Certified Examples in All Grades (PCGS and NGC)*:	121

(* As of April 2003)

(** Possible resubmissions of one or more of the same coins)

(*** SEGS (Sovereign Entity Grading Service) has graded one of these coins MS-63 (2003). Two of the other AU-58 specimens are possible resubmissions.)

One of the finest known 1877-CC half eagles, graded by one of the less recognized services, SEGS (Sovereign Entities Grading Services).

REFLECTIONS:

Although the mintage for half eagles rose 26% from 1876's total, output remained low, but still continued to outpace that of the Philadelphia Mint. In fact, from 1870 through 1877, the only time that Carson City did not surpass Philadelphia's half eagle production was in the *Coinage Act* year of 1873. The table below compares half eagle mintages at the three mints for the years 1874 to 1877.

As the Treasury continued to order massive amounts of silver coins from the mints in 1877, banks and merchants exchanged greenbacks for them in the East and gold coins for them in the Pacific states. Half eagles and eagles partially fulfilled this need in California and the surrounding region, with the Carson City Mint supplementing San Francisco's demands for these coins.

Gold deposits, although slacking off at the Carson City Mint by 1877, were still adequate to cover that facility's production quotas. Approximately $1.7 million in gold ore was deposited at Carson City in 1877, almost evenly split between requests for gold coins or gold bars.

Only a small percentage of Carson City's half eagles were used in local commerce; most being sent out of state. As a result, dates like 1877-CC are rarely found in Nevada, and those that do surface are usually heavily abraded. Generally, examples of this date come from sources around San Francisco, the eastern states, or even foreign countries.

This is another date in the "CC" series with a surviving population estimated at between 1 to 1.5%. Currently (2003-2004) only three 1877-CC half eagles have been certified in Uncirculated condition. One of these pieces was originally graded by NGC as AU-58 and subsequently upgraded at the lesser-known SEGS (Sovereign Entities Grading Service) to MS-63. In all fairness, the coin probably deserves an MS-61 grade.

Undoubtedly, the 1877-CC half eagle will remain elusive in Uncirculated condition, and even in AU presents a formidable challenge. Problem free examples in VF to XF are currently undervalued and should be given consideration by collectors.

HALF EAGLE MINTAGES AT PHILADELPHIA, SAN FRANCISCO, AND CARSON CITY FROM 1874 TO 1877	
Year & Mint	**Quantity Minted**
1874	3,508
1874-CC	21,198
1874-S	16,000
1875	220
1875-CC	11,828
1875-S	9,000
1876	1,477
1876-CC	6,887
1876-S	4,000
1877	1,152
1877-CC	8,680
1877-S	26,700

(Photo courtesy Bowers and Merena)

Mintage: 9,054

Finest Known*:

    NGC MS-63 (1)

    PCGS AU-58 (2)

    NGC AU-58 (1)

    NGC AU-55 (1)

    PCGS AU-55 (2)

Notable Pedigrees:

    Wayte Raymond Mail Bid Sale (1941)

    Harry W. Bass, Jr. (1999)

    Henry S. Lang (2002)

    Nevada Collection (Current)

Survival Estimates in All Grades: 75-90
Estimated in Uncirculated: 2
Estimated in XF to AU: 40-50
Total Certified Examples in All Grades (PCGS and NGC)*: 69

(* As of April 2003)

REFLECTIONS:

This was the year of the *Bland/Allison Act* and Morgan silver dollars, and at the Carson City Mint production on all other denominations was significantly cut back. Half eagles were minted in small quantities consistent with the preceding two years. Taking into account the 9,054 pieces minted in 1878 with those delivered in 1876 and 1877, the annual average was approximately 8,200.

Though the mintage for 1878 was slightly above that three year annual average, estimates of surviving pieces extant are 1% or less, easily establishing this date as one of the top three in overall rarity for the "CC" half eagle series. It was virtually unknown in Uncirculated condi-

tion until 2003 when a spectacular MS-63 specimen was graded by NGC. Other than this lone Mint State piece, the highest grades known are three AU-58 examples.

Comparable in overall rarity to the 1870-CC and 1873-CC half eagles, the 1878-CC is nearly deadlocked with the 1872-CC and 1876-CC for rarity in Uncirculated condition.[1]

Prices for the 1878-CC in circulated grades from Fine to XF parallel those of the 1873-CC, though so few pieces change hands, new pricing information is required every time a sale is made.

---

[1] As of the writing of this book (2003) there has not been an 1872-CC graded in Mint State.

(Photo courtesy Bowers and Merena)

Mintage: 17,281

Finest Known*:

    PCGS MS-61 (1)

    NGC MS-61 (2)

    NGC MS-60 (1)

    PCGS AU-58 (6)**

    NGC AU-58 (14)**

Notable Pedigrees:

    Belden E. Roach (1944)

    J.F. Bell (1944)

    R.L. Miles (1968)

    E.A. Carson (1976)

    Norweb Collection (1987)

    Harry W. Bass, Jr. (1999)

      ex: Norweb

    Henry S. Lang (2002)

    Nevada Collection (Current)

Survival Estimates in All Grades:...... 225-275
Estimated in Uncirculated: 4-6
Estimated in XF to AU:........................ 140-150
Total Certified Examples in All Grades (PCGS and NGC)*: ... 204

(* As of April 2003)

(** Possible resubmissions of one or more of the same coin)

REFLECTIONS:

This is the final year from the first decade of half eagle production at the Carson City Mint and the most accessible date from that 10 year run. By 1879 the Philadelphia Mint had greatly increased half eagle production to meet currency redemption demands, and between 1878 and 1879, Philadelphia manufactured over 430,000 $5 gold pieces compared with Carson City's output of 26,335 pieces. San Francisco topped all mints in half eagle production during those two years with an output of 570,900.

Overall, Carson City's gold coin mintages dropped sharply in 1879, reflective of a steep decline in gold ore deposits, and a temporary work stoppage at the facility. But despite double eagle and eagle deliveries being very low at the Carson City Mint that year, half eagle production almost doubled that of 1878, resulting in the third highest mintage of the 1870s.

Several higher grade AU specimens of this date exhibit sharper than average strikes and impressive eye appeal. One appeared in the *Norweb* sale in 1987 and was subsequently graded AU-55 by PCGS. Years later it was upgraded to MS-60 by NGC and is one of four known Uncirculated 1879-CC half eagles. Many lower grade examples are unattractive and less appealing to collectors. Higher available quantities of this date have kept its pricing lower than all other dates from the 1870s.

1880-CC

(Photo courtesy Bowers and Merena)

Mintage: 51,017

Finest Known*:

PCGS MS-62 (1)

NGC MS-62 (6)

PCGS MS-61 (2)

NGC MS-61 (9)**

PCGS MS-60 (1)

NGC MS-60 (1)

PCGS AU-58 (13)**

NGC AU-58 (27)**

Notable Pedigrees:

Belden E. Roach (1944)

J.F. Bell (1944)

W.C. Atwater (1946)

Thomas G. Melish (1956)

R.L. Miles (1968)

Nathan Shapero (1971)

E.A. Carson (1976)

Norweb (1987)
ex: Melish

Harry W. Bass, Jr. (2000)
ex: Norweb, Melish

Henry S. Lang (2002)

Nevada Collection (Current)

Survival Estimates in All Grades:	475-600
Estimated in Uncirculated:	20-30
Estimated in XF to AU:	300-400
Total Certified Examples in All Grades (PCGS and NGC)*:	339

(* As of April 2003)

(** Possible resubmissions of one or more of the same coins.)

REFLECTIONS:

According to Treasury records, gold deposits at all U.S. mint facilities reached an all-time high aggregate total of nearly $99 million in 1880, exceeding by $30 million the previous high achieved in 1861. Over $62 million of that total was deposited by foreign customers.

This sudden increase in gold deposits was precipitated in part by the Treasury's shift in policy away from double eagles and toward lower denomination gold coins. For years, leading European nations such as Great Britain, Germany and France issued gold coins in denominations equivalent to something less than $5. People's needs were better accommodated by smaller gold coins and Treasury officials having observed this, decided it was time to change direction.

Consequently, half eagle production soared in 1880, with the Philadelphia Mint multiplying its output ten-fold and San Francisco by over 300%. Although the Carson City Mint's only gold deposits came from the diminishing production of the Comstock mines, its half eagle output also increased nearly 300%, albeit at the expense of the double eagles.

A large percentage of the 1880-CC half eagles were shipped out of state as depositors chose certificates of deposit from banks in lieu of actual coins. Mass meltings and exportations account for a survival rate of approximately 1% of the original mintage.

There is a generous quantity of Uncirculated and high grade AU specimens of the 1880-CC available, though nothing higher than MS-62. Collectors desiring an attractive example of a pre-1890-CC half eagle can generally choose between the 1880-CC and 1882-CC.

Problem-free circulated examples offer an affordable possibility for ownership of a "CC" gold coin.

1881-CC

(Photo courtesy Bowers and Merena)

Mintage: 13,886

Finest Known*:

    PCGS MS-65 (I)

    NGC MS-63 (I)

    NGC MS-62 (I)

    PCGS MS-61 (I)

    NGC AU-58 (3)

    PCGS AU-55 (2)

    NGC AU-55 (6)

Notable Pedigrees:

    Charles M. Williams (Menjou) (1950)

    Alto Collection (1970)

Nathan Shapero (1971)

E.A. Carson (1976)

Harry W. Bass, Jr. (1999)

Henry S. Lang (2002)

Nevada Collection (Current)

Survival Estimates in All Grades:	120-130
Estimated in Uncirculated:	4-5
Estimated in XF to AU:	80-90
Total Certified Examples in All Grades (PCGS and NGC)*:	108

(* As of April 2003)

REFLECTIONS:

While the Philadelphia and San Francisco mints reached maximum production levels of gold coins in 1881, the coin presses were shut down most of the year at the Carson Mint. Record volumes of gold continued to be deposited at Bureau of the Mint facilities, with foreign imports rising even higher than the previous year. An all-time high number of half eagles were minted at Philadelphia in 1881; the total surpassed 5.7 million coins.

At Carson City during this work-shortened year, half eagle production was slashed by nearly 73%. No double eagles were minted, yet at the same time $10 eagle output curiously doubled.

Of the five dates of half eagles struck at Carson City in the 1880s, the 1881-CC is the rarest, nearly paralleling the 1876-CC in surviving pieces extant; though similar in rarity, 1881-CC half eagles are generally valued at half or less than half the price of 1876-CC's.

Examples of this date are often seen with a lackluster appearance, typically exhibiting evidence of a past cleaning. There are, however, a handful of specimens that possess pleasing eye appeal; one in particular is in near Gem condition, having been graded MS-65 by PCGS.

Beginning with this date, a much larger "CC" was used on all half eagles from this mint except the 1883-CC; with the mintmark being located midway between the *V* in *FIVE* and the eagle's claws.

1882-CC

(Photo courtesy Bowers and Merena)

Mintage: 82,817

Finest Known*:**

    PCGS MS-62 (3)

    NGC MS-62 (3)

    PCGS MS-61 (6)

    NGC MS-61 (13)

    PCGS MS-60 (1)

    NGC MS-60 (2)

    PCGS AU-58 (32)

    NGC AU-58 (72)

Notable Pedigrees:

    J.F. Bell (1944)

    Belden E. Roach (1944)

    R.L. Miles (1968)

    Alto Collection (1970)

    Nathan Shapero (1971)

RARCOA Auction '79 (1979)

Louis E. Eliasberg (1982)

Norweb (1987)

Harry W. Bass, Jr. (1999 & 2000)

Henry S. Lang (2002)

Nevada Collection (Current)

Survival Estimates in All Grades: 515-600
Estimated in Uncirculated: 40-50
Estimated in XF to AU: 400-450
Total Certified Examples in All Grades (PCGS and NGC)*: ... 456

(* As of April 2003)

(** All told, 132 coins on this list. Many entries are probably the same coins being upgraded or crossed over from one grading service to the other.)

Reflections:

This turned out to be a good year for the Carson City Mint as production of silver dollars and gold coins increased sharply from the previous year, and in terms of face value, coinage rose to nearly $2.4 million, compared to 1881's total of $605,000.

Two factors contributed to this upsurge: the first was a full 12-month work schedule, and the second was the beginning of a modest resurgence in mining yields on the Comstock. For several years, the Carson Mint had been returning gold coin for nearly all the bullion being deposited, but at the same time, deposits were at the lowest levels since the mint opened in 1870. Then in the latter half of 1880, new ore discoveries were made on the Comstock and a portion of the residual effect spilled over to the local minting facility.

This proved to be Carson City's most productive year for half eagles in its first 13 years of operation, not to be surpassed until the 17th year in which half eagles were coined. As in previous years, only a small percentage of the 1882-CC $5 gold pieces remained in Nevada. Yet because of the large quantity minted, the number of pieces that circulated locally was substantially greater than any other dates from the 1870s and 1880s; and as a result, there is a plentiful supply of circulated examples in Fine to XF available to collectors.

Even AU coins are not that difficult to locate, and Uncirculated specimens, though existing in lower quantities, are more available than any pre-1890-CC date. In grades above MS-62 the 1882-CC is virtually unique, and a Gem quality piece would be a major event.

1883-CC

(Photo courtesy Bowers and Merena)

Mintage: 12,958

Finest Known*:

    NGC MS-64 (I)

    PCGS MS-62 (I)

    PCGS MS-61 (2)

    NGC MS-61 (I)

    PCGS AU-58 (II)**

    NGC AU-58 (24)**

Notable Pedigrees:

    J.F. Bell (1944)

    Nathan Shapero (1971)

    RARCOA Auction '79 (1979)

Norweb (1987)

Harry W. Bass, Jr. (1999 & 2000)

Henry S. Lang (2002)

Nevada Collection (Current)

| Survival Estimates in All Grades: ...... 185-225 |
| Estimated in Uncirculated: .... 7-8 |
| Estimated in XF to AU: .... 140-160 |
| Total Certified Examples in All Grades (PCGS and NGC)*: ... 162 |

(* As of April 2003)

(** Possible resubmissions of one or more of the same coins.)

REFLECTIONS:

Foreign gold imports had decreased since the peak levels of 1881 and half eagle production at the nation's mints had fallen to its lowest output since the late 1870s. Yet San Francisco's double eagle production remained constant.

In the Comstock region, miners were in the middle of a small post-*Bonanza* rally, and the Carson City Mint was again receiving almost 100% of gold deposits from the area. In exact numbers, gold production on the Comstock in 1883 was reported to be approximately $1.6 million, and gold deposits at the Carson Mint totaled nearly $1.5 million, of which almost $1.4 million in face value was minted into gold coins, with the remainder issued in bars.

Half eagle production dropped closer to traditional quantities, as the mintage of double eagles once again took center stage. Estimated survival percentages for 1883-CC half eagles are slightly higher than those of the other "CC" dates in the 1880s, ranging from 1.25% to 1.7%. Yet because the mintage was small to begin with, quantities extant place the 1883-CC in the middle of the 19 dates in the series in terms of overall rarity.

For a scarce date, there is a relatively generous supply of 1883-CC half eagles available in AU condition, with a few of them being borderline Uncirculated. But in true Mint State condition this date becomes very elusive and new price levels are reached just about every time an Uncirculated specimen appears on the market. At Bowers and Merena's *Rarities Sale* in July of 2002, the *Henry S. Lang* coin, graded MS-61 by PCGS, sold for $29,900, even though current wholesale bids were in the $12,500 to $15,000 range.

As of April of 2003, NGC reported that it had certified an 1883-CC half eagle in MS-64, a coin that will no doubt cause excited bidding when offered at auction.

For unknown reasons the 1883-CC was struck on a reverse die punched with a *Small* "CC" similar to the one used on the pre-1881 half eagles. After 1883 the *Large* "CC" is found on all dates.

1884-CC

(Photo courtesy Bowers and Merena)

Mintage: 16,402

Finest Known*:

PCGS MS-62 (1)

PCGS MS-61 (1)

NGC MS-61 (6)**

PCGS AU-58 (5)**

NGC AU-58 (17)**

PCGS AU-55 (12)**

NGC AU-55 (25)**

Notable Pedigrees:

J.F. Bell (1944)

Nathan Shapero (1971)

E.A. Carson (1976)

Bowers and Merena May Sale (1993)

Harry W. Bass, Jr. (1999)
  ex: Shapero

Henry S. Lang (2002)

Nevada Collection (Current)

Survival Estimates in All Grades:	**190-225**
Estimated in Uncirculated:	**10-12**
Estimated in XF to AU:	**155-165**
Total Certified Examples in All Grades (PCGS and NGC)*:	**174**

(* As of April 2003)

(** Possible resubmissions of one or more of the same coins.)

REFLECTIONS:

Although gold deposits at the Carson City Mint in 1884 were nearly identical to those of 1883, gold coin production was approximately $450,000 higher, an anomaly due in part to fiscal year accounting verses calendar year accounting used in Treasury reports. To be certain, there was no loss of momentum in gold ore production on the Comstock, and in 1884 reported yields were approximately $1.9 million. Evidence that the largest percent of this output was deposited at the Carson Mint is the increased production of double eagles in 1884.

Half eagle production rose 26%, but still totaled only 16,402 coins. Survival percentages are just a nudge over 1% of the original mintage, and the estimated quantity extant is in a virtual dead heat with the 1883-CC. Values for the two dates are identical on paper; however, with any of these rare "CC" dates, prices are practically determined on a piece by piece basis. There are so few of any of these dates in Uncirculated condition that price levels are tested at every auction appearance.

Like the 1883-CC, the 1884-CC is relatively affordable in FINE to XF. Moreover, it must be stressed that problem-free examples in circulated grades will always command premium prices.

As previously mentioned, the reverse die used on this date once again displayed the *Large* "CC" seen on the 1881-CC and 1882-CC.

1890-CC

(Photo courtesy Bowers and Merena)

Mintage: 53,800

Finest Known*:**

    PCGS MS-66 (1)

    PCGS MS-65 (1)

    NGC MS-65 (2)

    PCGS MS-64 (27)

    NGC MS-64 (20)

    PCGS MS-63 (17)

    NGC MS-63 (29)

Notable Pedigrees:

    World's Greatest Collection (1946)

    Thomas G. Melish (1956)

    R.L. Miles (1968)

    E.A. Carson (1976)

Nathan Shapero (1971)

RARCOA Auction '79 (1979)

Louis E. Eliasberg, Sr. (1982)

Harry W. Bass, Jr. (2000)

Henry S. Lang (2002)

Nevada Collection (Current)

Survival Estimates in All Grades: 700-800
Estimated in Uncirculated: 300-330
Estimated in XF to AU: 350-400
Total Certified Examples in All Grades (PCGS and NGC)*: ... 603

(* As of April 2003)

(** At least 280 Uncirculated examples are listed in the population and census reports, many undoubtedly are resubmissions and crossovers.)

REFLECTIONS:

Gold half eagles were minted once again at Carson City in 1890 after a five year gap, during which San Francisco was the primary distributor of $5 gold pieces. But in 1890, that task surprisingly fell on Carson City's shoulders, as the San Francisco Mint was so busy coining dimes, dollars and double eagles that the Nevada facility was commissioned to supplement gold depositors' demands for half eagles, eagles, and double eagles.

Approximately $2 million worth of gold bullion was produced on the Comstock in 1890 as the last semblance of the prosperity the region enjoyed in the 19th century began to tail off. Almost 100% of this output was deposited at the local mint and turned into coins with a face value of $2.28 million.

Large gold deposits received at the nation's mints and assay offices in the early 1880s had been reduced to much lower levels by 1890, and gold supplies had further been drained by substantial transfers to European buyers.

At right is a table exhibiting the slackening gold deposits from 1880 through 1890.

The time had finally come when Carson City's contribution to the coinage supply of the United States was appreciated for the simple reason that during the final four years of this mint's coining operations, the nation welcomed gold coins from any source that could deliver them.

Naturally the higher mintage in 1890 resulted in a higher population extant. When compared to 1880, a year in which a similar amount of half eagles were produced at Carson City, 1890's survival rate is higher. Scores of 1890-CC half eagles have been retrieved from foreign countries, with more likely to follow.

Plentiful supplies of Choice Uncirculated examples of this date are available, and almost without exception, even AU coins come fully struck with pleasing luster. It is actually more difficult to find circulated pieces in grades below XF than it is to locate higher grade specimens. Prices for 1890-CC half eagles in grades below MS-60 currently run 2 ½ to 3 times what generic common dates in this series sell for (in 2003).

VALUE OF THE GOLD RECEIVED AT U.S. MINTS AND ASSAY OFFICES DURING THE FISCAL YEARS 1880-1890	
Fiscal Years	**Gold**
1880	$98,835,096
1881	130,833,102
1882	66,756,652
1883	46,347,106
1884	46,326,678
1885	52,894,075
1886	44,909,749
1887	68,223,072
1888	72,225,497
1889	42,136,436
1890	42,663,095

1891-CC

(Photo courtesy Bowers and Merena)

Mintage: 208,000

Finest Known*:**

    PCGS MS-65 (I)

    NGC MS-65 (5)

    PCGS MS-64 (26)

    NGC MS-64 (34)

    PCGS MS-63 (46)

    NGC MS-63 (90)

Notable Pedigrees:

    Belden E. Roach (1944)

    J.F. Bell (1944)

    R.L. Miles (1968)

    Nathan Shapero (1971)

    E.A. Carson (1976)

Fairfield Collection (1977)

RARCOA Auction '79 (1979)

Superior Auction '88 (1988)

Harry W. Bass, Jr. (1999)

Henry S. Lang (2002)

Nevada Collection (Current)

Survival Estimates in All Grades:	**... 2,800-3,500**
Estimated in Uncirculated:	**.............. 1,100-1,400**
Estimated in XF to AU:	**..................... 1,500-1,800**
Total Certified Examples in All Grades (PCGS and NGC)*:	**.... 1,772**

(* As of April 2003)

(** Multiple resubmissions and crossovers throughout the hundreds of specimens graded AU-58 and above.)

REFLECTIONS:

Without question 1891 was the high water mark in half eagle production at the Carson City Mint. Elsewhere, the nation's mints were concentrating on striking Seated Liberty coins for the final time, as well as silver dollars, gold coins, and minor coinage. If the San Francisco Mint had not been burdened with dimes and quarters, chances are Carson City might have coined fewer half eagles, but as it was, San Francisco employees had their hands full.

Yields from Comstock mines had dropped to $1.38 million by 1891, and since gold coin production reached nearly $2.2 million for the second year in a row at Carson City, it was necessary for bullion to be procured from outside the local area. This may have been the first time that gold from sources other than Comstock mines was used at the Carson Mint.

Because of the double demand resulting from currency redemptions and foreign exportation of U.S. gold, the Treasury was pressured to utilize any mint in its network to increase supplies, benefiting the oft neglected Carson Mint.

Estimates of the surviving population of 1891-CC half eagles clearly establish it as the most common date in the series. Ample supplies of Uncirculated examples are available at lower prices than any "CC" gold coin denomination in this condition, and attractive AU specimens offer collectors an inexpensive alternative for owning a "CC" gold coin.

SMALL HOARD OF 1890'CC' HALF EAGLES

Lot No. 1111

1111 **1890'CC' Brilliant Uncirculated**, full lustre, light toning.

1112 **1890'CC'** Another example as above. **Brilliant Uncirculated**, frosty lustre.

1113 **1890'CC'** A third example as above. **Brilliant Uncirculated**, frosty lustre.

1114 **1890'CC'** A fourth example as above. **Brilliant Uncirculated**, frosty lustre.

1115 **1890'CC'** A fifth example as above. **Brilliant Uncirculated**, frosty lustre.

SMALL HOARD OF 1891'CC' HALF EAGLES

Lot No. 1118

1118 **1891'CC' Brilliant Uncirculated**, prooflike surfaces, light bagmarks.

1119 **1891'CC'** Another example. **Brilliant Uncirculated**, frosty lustre

1120 **1891'CC'** A third example. **Brilliant Uncirculated**, frosty lustre.

1121 **1891'CC'** A fourth example. **Brilliant Uncirculated**, frosty, light coppery toning.

1122 **1891'CC'** A fifth example. **Brilliant Uncirculated** and lustrous, light coppery toning.

Small hoards of Carson City gold coins have surfaced from time to time as discoveries have been made, usually abroad. These $5 half eagles were in the *James A. Stack* sale in November of 1989.

1892-CC

(Photo courtesy Bowers and Merena)

Mintage: 82,968

Finest Known*:**

NGC MS-66 (1)

NGC MS-64 (3)

PCGS MS-63 (8)

NGC MS-63 (3)

PCGS MS-62 (13)

NGC MS-62 (35)

PCGS MS-61 (19)

NGC MS-61 (33)

PCGS MS-60 (12)

NGC MS-60 (8)

Notable Pedigrees:

J.F. Bell (1944)

Dr. Clarence W. Peake (1955)

R.L. Miles (1968)

Alto Collection (1970)

Nathan Shapero (1971)

E.A. Carson (1976)

RARCOA Auction '79 (1979)

Louis E. Eliasberg, Sr. (1982)

Norweb (1987)
  ex: Peake

Harry W. Bass, Jr. (1999)
  ex: Norweb, Peake

Nevada Collection (Current)

Survival Estimates in All Grades:	700-850
Estimated in Uncirculated:	160-190
Estimated in XF to AU:	450-490
Total Certified Examples in All Grades (PCGS and NGC)*:	603

(* As of April 2003)

(** Multiple resubmissions and crossovers in grades AU-58 and above.)

REFLECTIONS:

Production of half eagles decreased by nearly 60% at the Carson City Mint in 1892, but the mintage was still the second highest in the 19 year series. A mere 151 coins separate it from the date in third place, minted 10 years earlier.

An estimated 1% of the original mintage of the 1892-CC is extant, with the possibility of small quantities still remaining in foreign countries.

This date is generally seen with lustrous surfaces in AU and above, typical of "CC" half eagles from the 1890s. Compared to dates from the 1870s, the strike is superior.

Though not as plentiful in Uncirculated as the 1890-CC and 91-CCs, locating a specimen in MS-60 to MS-62 is not too formidable of a challenge. Choice to Gem examples, however, are very scarce, with the *Eliasberg* coin graded MS-66 by NGC the finest known. Only two other dates in the "CC" half eagle series feature a specimen graded that high, the 1876-CC and 1891-CC.

1893-CC

(Photo courtesy Bowers and Merena)

Mintage: 60,000

Finest Known*:**

NGC MS-65 (3)

PCGS MS-64 (4)

NGC MS-64 (8)

PCGS MS-63 (2)

NGC MS-63 (17)

PCGS MS-62 (13)

NGC MS-62 (40)

PCGS MS-61 (21)

NGC MS-61 (31)

PCGS MS-60 (7)

NGC MS-60 (10)

Notable Pedigrees:

J.F. Bell (1944)

Mason Williams (1947)

Jerome D. Kern (1950)

R.L. Miles (1968)

Nathan Shapero (1971)

E.A. Carson (1976)

Harold S. Bareford (1978)
  ex: Mason Williams

RARCOA Auction '79 (1979)

Harry W. Bass, Jr. 1999

Nevada Collection (Current)
  ex: Bass

Survival Estimates in All Grades:	650-900
Estimated in Uncirculated:	175-250
Estimated in XF to AU:	400-550
Total Certified Examples in All Grades (PCGS and NGC)*:	578

(* As of April 2003)

(** Multiple resubmissions and crossovers in grades AU-58 and above.)

REFLECTIONS:

Exports of U.S. gold coins were at an all-time high in 1893 as approximately $105 million in face value was shipped to Europe, Canada, Central and South America, Mexico and the West Indies. Between 1891 and 1893, nearly $215 million in gold coins had been moved from Treasury vaults to foreign nations, causing reserves to fall below panic levels. To keep up with the demand, the Philadelphia and San Francisco mints were working double time, and even New Orleans got into the act.

At Carson City, the year had begun on a pace to equal or surpass 1892's coinage production. By the middle of May, 60,000 half eagles had been struck, but suddenly op-

erations were suspended as of June 1, making this the final mintage figure for the year. Accounts were settled, inventory was taken, and the gold coins stored on premises were shipped to other Bureau of the Mint facilities.

Workmanship on 1893-CC half eagles was as good as or better than on any other year in the series and many quality examples survive today. Perhaps as many as 1.5% of the original mintage survives, offering collectors yet another alternative when acquiring a relatively inexpensive AU to MS-61 "CC" $5 gold piece. In Choice to Gem Uncirculated, prices rise sharply, with an MS-65 specimen in the $25,000 to $30,000 range (as of 2003).

(Photo courtesy Bowers and Merena)

On the whole, coining gold coins was the most important business of the U.S. Mint during the final three decades of the 19th century. In terms of sheer quantity, it would seem that silver coins predominated, yet there was no steady demand for them, and although at various times coin shortages would precipitate accelerated production of silver coins, generally speaking there were far more stored in Treasury vaults than there were in circulation.

Gold coins on the other hand were vital to both domestic and international trade. Gold was considered to possess a much stabler intrinsic value, without the volatility of swinging silver prices. Treasury gold reserves provided security, whereas silver was considered riskier and could potentially result in significant losses. Silver coins seemed to always be entangled in the complexities of *specie redemptions* and silver politics, while gold coin production was unimpeded by such distractions.

Gold coins were the mainstay of America's monetary system and were always in demand; and the free coinage of gold was still a privilege of the public as depositors were allowed to redeem their mineral ore in exchange for coins. Banks would issue certificates for the amount of gold coins issued, and each bank's security was measured by how much gold coinage they held in reserves. In fact, if word got out that a bank's gold reserves were low depositors would make a run on the bank, frantically trying to withdraw the savings in their accounts.

Carson City's minting facility played a minor role in gold coinage production during its years of operation, and for $10 eagle coins this role was nothing but a bit part. Over a 19-year span, slightly fewer than 300,000 gold eagles were minted at Carson City, averaging 15,778 coins per year. If the mintage figure from its peak production year of 1891 is subtracted, the annual average is reduced to 10,891.

Restricted mintages of $10 eagles were uncommon throughout the rest of the Bureau of the Mint's network. Nationwide, $20 double eagles were the dominant gold

coins of course, yet gold eagles were still put to heavy use; substantial volumes of $10 gold pieces were coined at Philadelphia and San Francisco beginning in 1879, corresponding to the Treasury silver purchases under the *Bland/Allison Act*. Coincidentally, 1879 was the lowest production year for $10 eagles at the Carson City Mint, as a mere 1,762 were delivered.

Examining Carson City's $10 eagle output gives one the impression that this denomination was not in as much demand as $5 half eagles. Totals for both illustrate the difference: $10 gold eagles produced from 1870 to 1893 totaled 299,778 pieces, whereas $5 half eagle production totaled 709,617. Yet on a national scale, gold eagles outnumbered half eagles by a wide margin in terms of face value.

Why were $10 eagles not as much in demand as $5 half eagles at Carson City? Apparently, half eagles were used to a greater degree for currency redemptions in the regions around Carson City. This becomes clearer when separating the 19 year mintage histories for both denominations into three periods. In the first nine year period from 1870 to 1878, face value amounts were nearly equal, with a slight edge in favor of the $10 eagles. From 1879 to 1884, half eagles show a 48% advantage over eagles; and finally, in the last four years coins were minted at Carson City, from 1889 to 1893, half eagles again surpassed eagles by just over 15%. The last two periods were both associated with mass silver purchases payable in currency that was redeemable in gold. Though three gold denominations, $5, $10 and $20 were used, Carson City's needs obviously favored half eagles and double eagles. The table on the next page exhibits the figures from the three periods just described.

To put it all into perspective, it is helpful to compare Carson City's gold eagle production with that of Philadelphia and San Francisco.[1] At the bottom of the following page a chart illustrates the disparity in quantities.

---

[1] It is worth noting that the New Orleans Mint also produced gold coins, however, this southern mint was on a more restricted schedule than even Carson City. During the Carson Mint's 19 years of gold production, New Orleans struck eagles in eight of those years.

PRODUCTION OF $5 HALF EAGLES AND $10 EAGLES
AT THE CARSON CITY MINT DIVIDED INTO THREE
PERIODS FROM 1870 THROUGH 1893

PERIOD 1

Years	Denomination	Mintage	Face Value
1870-1878	$5	110,488	$522,440
1870-1878	$10	58,890	$588,900

PERIOD 2

| 1879-1884 | $5 | 194,361 | $971,805 |
| 1879-1884 | $10 | 65,656 | $656,560 |

PERIOD 3

| 1889-1893 | $5 | 404,768 | $2,023,840 |
| 1889-1893 | $10 | 175,232 | $1,752,320 |

If, as it has been suggested, Carson City shipped large percentages of its $10 eagle production east, the impact would have been minimal, bordering on unnecessary. Philadelphia's mintage totals were so large in comparison that it hardly seems as if it would have been worth the effort.

If the eagles ever left Nevada in the first place, a more likely scenario would suggest that Carson City sent their puny output to San Francisco to be absorbed into that mint's holdings. Even this is a tenuous argument, considering that Carson City's entire $10 eagle mintage was only 5.6% of that from San Francisco. Although conclusions on the matter have not been drawn and there is still more research pending to discover what happened to Carson City's scant number of gold eagles, one point chosen from the possible explanations are the small quantities recovered from Europe in the last quarter of the 20th century.

Regardless of what future findings may reveal, the Carson City gold eagle series is firmly established as one of the rarest of any U.S. coin series. Only 2% to 2 ½ % of the original mintage is believed to exist, suggesting that there are only 6,000 to 7,500 pieces extant, one third or more of this number dated 1891, the highest mintage date in the series. Many dates in a set of "CC" gold eagles have estimated surviving populations of 125 or fewer, with a few estimated below 75.

In AU condition and above, 75% of the dates are extremely rare and nearly impossible to locate in Uncirculated condition. Nevertheless, an estimated 30% of the total survivors extant are in Uncirculated grades. This seeming anomaly stems from the disproportionate number of Uncirculated 1891-CC eagles extant, estimated to be as high as 1.5% of the original mintage. This date alone accounts for approximately 85% to 88% of all Uncirculated "CC" gold eagles, or nearly 1,500 pieces. If the estimated extant population of Uncirculated gold eagles from 1890-CC and 1892-CC are added to 1891's total, the trio accounts for 95% of the existing "CC"s in this condition.

Dates from the 1870s are either unknown in Uncirculated condition, or possibly one example exists. Most Uncirculated specimens from the 1870s grade MS-60 to MS-62 at best, with only one very special coin in MS-65 (1874-CC). Excluding this exceptional piece, it is virtually impossible to find an attractive Uncirculated "CC" $10 eagle from the 1870s. There are a handful of pleasing examples in AU condition, but overall, "CC" gold eagles from the 1870s will not win any beauty contests.

Circulated examples from the 1870s are available in VF to XF possessing a fair amount of eye appeal for the grades, an advantage for low budget collectors, who for a fraction of the price of an AU (or Uncirculated) specimen, may be able to own one of these historic coins. Although many collectors concentrate only on Uncirculated pieces in other coin series, a set of Carson City gold eagles in nearly matching grades from VF to XF will surely reward the owner with satisfaction.

When assembling a 10-piece type set of "CC" coins, obtaining Uncirculated specimens of any dates in the gold eagle category other than 1890-CC, 1891-CC, and 1892-CC is not feasible; collectors are most grateful especially for the 1891-CC for this purpose, as pleasing examples of this date with flashy surfaces are available in MS-62 and MS-63. Surprisingly, with its large surviving population, there has not yet been one 1891-CC eagle graded MS-65 (as of 2003).

MINTAGE TOTALS FOR $10 GOLD EAGLES AT
PHILADELPHIA, SAN FRANCISCO AND CARSON
CITY ALL-INCLUSIVE BETWEEN 1870 AND 1893

Mint	Mintage	Face Value
Philadelphia	12,123,186	$121,231,860
San Francisco	5,308,350	53,083,500
Carson City	299,778	2,997,780

BUREAU OF THE MINT DATA FOR CARSON CITY GOLD EAGLE PRODUCTION

Total Combined Mintage: 299,778

Total Face Value: $2,997,780

Total Ounces of Gold Used: .... 145,018 ozs.

Design Type: .... Coronet or Liberty Head

Designers: .... Christian Gobrecht

James B. Longacre – Motto in Scroll

Metal Composition: .... .900 Gold .100 Copper

Actual Gross Weight: .... 16.718 grams

Actual Fine Gold Content: .... .48375 oz.

Value of Gold in One Half Eagle Between 1870 and 1893: $9.98-10.01

Wells Fargo stagecoaches routinely traveled through snowy mountain passes in and out of Carson City. (*Courtesy Wells Fargo Bank*)

(Photo courtesy Bowers and Merena)

Mintage: 5,908

Finest Knowns*:

    PCGS AU-55 (1)

    PCGS AU-53 (1)

    PCGS AU-50 (4)**

    NGC AU-50 (4)**

Notable Pedigrees:

    RARCOA Auction '79 (1979)

    Norweb (1988)

    Nevada Collection (Current)

Survival Estimates in All Grades: 70-80
Estimated in Uncirculated: 1
Estimated in XF to AU: 35-40
Total Certified Examples in All Grades (PCGS and NGC)*: 60

(* As of April 2003)

(**Possible resubmissions of one or more of the same coins.)

REFLECTIONS:

A member of the revered trio of first year gold coins from the Carson City Mint, the 1870-CC eagle is at the top of the list in terms of overall rarity for the series. At one time this date/denomination was considered rarer than the double eagle issued the same year at the Carson City Mint, however, during the last decade of the 20th century handfuls of unknown examples were introduced onto the market.

This did not diminish the respect gold specialists have for the date, but it has had an effect on its value. Whereas in the early years of the 21st century, XF or AU 1870-CC double eagles bring $150,000 or more in public auctions, eagles in the same grade trade in the $30,000 to $35,000 range.

An important note to point out is that the market has never been tested with a superior quality AU specimen of this date, as without exception, even high end XF's, as well as the known AU's, are visually unappealing. If a problem-free 1870-CC eagle in AU-58 ever surfaces a bidding frenzy will generate excitement, and if an Uncirculated specimen is offered, the sky is the limit.

This is not a date for the casual gold coin collector, as even in lower circulated grades, prices tend to be hefty. But for the "CC" specialist attempting to build a 19 piece eagle set, this date is the key to success.[1]

---

[1] One of the *Top 25*.

(Photo courtesy Bowers and Merena)

Mintage: 7,185***

Finest Knowns*:

    PCGS MS-62 (1)

    NGC MS-62 (1)

    NGC MS-60 (1)

    NGC AU-58 (3)**

    PCGS AU-55 (1)

    NGC AU-55 (6)

Notable Pedigrees:

    RARCOA Auction '79 (1979)

    Heritage March ANA (1995)

    Warren Miller (1995)**

Harry W. Bass Jr. (1999)

Nevada Collection (1999)

Henry S. Lang (2002)

    ex: Heritage March ANA (1995)

Nevada Collection (Current)

Survival Estimates in All Grades:	120-150
Estimated in Uncirculated:	3-5
Estimated in XF to AU:	80-90
Total Certified Examples in All Grades (PCGS and NGC)*:	102

(* As of April 2003)

(** Possible resubmissions of one or more of the same coins.)

(***Some sources list 8,085.)

REFLECTIONS:

Gold ore yields on the Comstock were on the rise in 1871, yet the Carson Mint was not receiving the bulk of it. Output from the mines in the region was reported to be over $4 million that year, but only 25% of it was deposited at the local mint. From that amount, nearly $470,000 was turned into gold coins, with eagles accounting for approximately 15% of that total.

In 1871, there was $21 million in gold coinage produced at the nation's mints. It was also in 1871 that the United States began exporting large quantities of gold coins to foreign lands, over $55 million in gold coins in 1871 alone. Though Carson City's gold coin output was consistently lower than Philadelphia's and San Francisco's,

significant quantities of "CC"s left the country, as evidenced by occasional small hoards returning from overseas or South America.

There is no way to ascertain where the 1871-CC eagles wound up after they left Nevada, or for that matter, how many actually left the state, but as with many "CC" issues, apparently few were saved.

This date has a slightly higher survival rate than many "CC" gold issues of the era, but because of the low original mintage still ranks in the top 10 in overall rarity. Though not as difficult to locate in VF to XF, this date becomes increasingly scarcer in AU-55 and above. Uncirculated specimens exist, but are typically being held in "strong hands."

(Photo courtesy Bowers and Merena)

Mintage: 5,500[1]

Finest Knowns*:**

    PCGS AU-55 (2)

    NGC AU-55 (3)

    PCGS AU-53 (2)

    NGC AU-53 (1)

    PCGS AU-50 (5)

    NGC AU-50 (4)

Notable Pedigrees:

    Belden E. Roach (1944)

    J.F. Bell (1944)

    Warren Miller (1995)

    Harry W. Bass, Jr. (2000)

H. Jeff Browning (2001)

Henry S. Lang (2002)
    ex: Warren Miller

Nevada Collection (Current)
    ex: Harry W. Bass, Jr.

Survival Estimates in All Grades:	70-85
Estimated in Uncirculated:	0-1
Estimated in XF to AU:	40-50
Total Certified Examples in All Grades (PCGS and NGC)*:	64

(* As of April 2003)

(**Possible resubmissions of one or more of the same coins in each grade.)

REFLECTIONS:

Although gold coinage output rose at the Carson City Mint in 1872, $10 eagle production dropped to 5,500 pieces, as the bulk of the increase occurred in the double eagle category.

This date is seldom seen in problem-free condition and the highest grade known in the early years of the 21st century is AU-55. One of the most eye appealing specimens was sold in July 2002 as part of the *Henry S. Lang* collection, auctioned by Bowers and Merena. This piece, graded AU-55 by PCGS, realized $41,400 in spite of a wholesale bid of $16,000 in AU, affirming that collectors can expect to pay substantial premiums for problem-free examples of this date.

Circulated examples of 1872-CC gold eagles in VF offer excellent value at anywhere near current retail price levels (2003).

---

[1] Some sources report 4,600.

1873-CC

(Photo courtesy Bowers and Merena)

Mintage: 4,543

Finest Knowns*:

    NGC AU-55 (1)

    PCGS AU-53 (2)

    NGC AU-53 (3)

    PCGS AU-50 (6)

    NGC AU-50 (4)

Notable Pedigrees:

    William C. Atwater (1946)

    RARCOA Auction '79 (1979)

    NERCA ANA (1979)

Harry W. Bass, Jr. (1999 and 2000)

Henry S. Lang (2002)

Nevada Collection (Current)

Survival Estimates in All Grades:	75-85
Estimated in Uncirculated:	0-1
Estimated in XF to AU:	45-55
Total Certified Examples in All Grades (PCGS and NGC)*:	71

(* As of April 2003)

REFLECTIONS:

Production of gold coinage across the nation surged in 1873, yet at the Carson Mint there was barely a flicker. Again the double eagle was the predominant gold denomination at mint facilities across the nation, increasing from one million pieces in 1872 to over 2.7 million. On the other hand, $10 eagles were minted in traditionally low quantities, evidenced by the meager 825 eagles at Philadelphia, and San Francisco continuing its low output trend, delivering only 12,000 pieces.

To no one's surprise, Carson City's gold eagle mintage declined once again, dropping to the lowest quantity of that mint's first four years of service. Apparently these coins were either distributed locally by the depositors who exchanged gold bullion for them or by the Carson Mint itself if certificates were issued to depositors in lieu of coins. Evidence of heavy local circulation around the Comstock region is the inferior quality seen on practically all examples extant. Considering the complexities of ascertaining accurate disbursement information about "CC" gold coins, it is also conceivable that a percentage of the minuscule mintage eventually wound up abroad, as examples of the date have been discovered in Europe, albeit very sparingly.

Currently there are no specimens of this date in Mint State, and chances seem slim that there will be. The choicest piece known came from the *Harry W. Bass, Jr.* collection and is graded AU-55 by NGC. Collectors desiring an example of this date must overcome inferior eye appeal as well as the high price, certainly not a positive combination. But the incentive to own a genuinely rare date usually counters all objections

From 1870 through 1873 the mintmark on the "CC" eagles was small and roundish, centered below the claw and feather tip, directly above the center of *E* and *N* in *TEN*.

(Photo courtesy Bowers and Merena)

Mintage: 16,767

Finest Knowns*:

NGC MS-65 (1)

PCGS MS-63 (1)

NGC AU-58 (1)

PCGS AU-55 (5)

NGC AU-55 (6)

PCGS AU-53 (2)

NGC AU-53 (6)

PCGS AU-50 (8)

NGC AU-50 (8)

Notable Pedigrees:

Belden E. Roach (1944)

NERCA ANA (1979)

Louis E. Eliasberg, Sr. (1982)

RARCOA Auction '84 (1984)

Warren Miller (c. 1995)

Harry W. Bass, Jr. (2000)
ex: Eliasberg

Henry S. Lang (2002)
ex: Warren Miller

Nevada Collection (Current)
ex: Bass, Eliasberg

Survival Estimates in All Grades:	**260-300**
Estimated in Uncirculated:	**2-4**
Estimated in XF to AU:	**170-200**
Total Certified Examples in All Grades (PCGS and NGC)*:	**244**

(* As of April 2003)

REFLECTIONS:

Gold coin production rose nearly 500% at the Carson City Mint in 1874, the bulk of it $20 double eagles. Mintages for $10 eagles grew by nearly 370%, passing the 10,000 mark for the first time.

Survival percentages for the 1874-CC are estimated to be slightly higher than the average for "CC" gold eagles, resulting in the highest population extant for dates in the 1870s. Though not as challenging in grades below AU, this date becomes very scarce in AU-55 and above, with only two Mint State specimens documented.

One of these Uncirculated pieces sold in July of 2002 as part of the *Henry S. Lang* collection auctioned by Bowers and Merena. It is by far the finest known specimen, having been graded MS-64 by NGC; and after the Lang sale it was upgraded to MS-65, reportedly being offered for over $200,000. In terms of rarity and quality it is one of the elite of the Carson City gold series.

Another Uncirculated specimen appeared in the *Louis E. Eliasberg, Sr.* sale in 1982, certified years later by PCGS as MS-63. Prospects of other Uncirculated specimens surfacing are possible, but not likely.

Collectors content with a circulated piece in grades below AU will be pleasantly surprised to discover that this is the lowest priced "CC" eagle from the 1870s.

Beginning in 1874 and continuing through 1876 the mintmark on "CC" gold eagles remained small and roundish, slightly shifted to the right, with the second "C" above the *N* in *TEN*.

(Photo courtesy Bowers and Merena)

Mintage: 7,715

Finest Knowns*:

NGC MS-63 (1)

NGC MS-60 (1)

PCGS AU-58 (1)

PCGS AU-55 (4)

NGC AU-55 (2)

PCGS AU-53 (6)

NGC AU-53 (2)

PCGS AU-50 (4)

NGC AU-50 (2)

Notable Pedigrees:

J.F. Bell (1944)

William C. Atwater (1946)

R.L. Miles (1968)

Harry W. Bass (2000)

Henry S. Lang (2002)

Nevada Collection (Current)

Survival Estimates in All Grades:	95-115
Estimated in Uncirculated:	2-4
Estimated in XF to AU:	55-65
Total Certified Examples in All Grades (PCGS and NGC)*:	86

(* As of April 2003)

REFLECTIONS:

For unknown reasons, there were fewer $10 eagles produced at the nation's mints in 1875 than in any year after the Civil War. For the first time since it opened in 1854, the San Francisco Mint did not strike any gold eagles, and Philadelphia delivered an all time low of 120 pieces, 20 of which were Proofs, leaving Carson City as the leader for the year with a whopping 7,715 eagles minted.

Gold coin exports greatly exceeded production for the year, as nearly $60 million worth of U.S. gold was shipped to foreign countries. San Francisco's chief focus was on double eagles, trade dollars, and the new 20-cent pieces, entrusting the Carson City Mint with the role of auxiliary supplier of $10 eagles for the Pacific states. It is possible that 90% or more of the mintage of 1875-CC eagles left Nevada, destined for use in the western states, or foreign commercial centers.

This date is ranked in the top half of the Carson City eagle series in terms of overall rarity. It is very elusive in Uncirculated condition, with most collectors settling for a low end AU or XF for inclusion in their sets. Because most examples are dirty, bagmarked, and lackluster, problem-free coins are deserving of substantial price premiums.

1876-CC

(Photo courtesy Bowers and Merena)

Mintage: 4,696

Finest Knowns*:**

    PCGS AU-58 (2)

    NGC AU-58 (2)

    PCGS AU-55 (2)

    NGC AU-55 (2)

    PCGS AU-53 (3)

    NGC AU-53 (3)

    PCGS AU-50 (8)

    NGC AU-50 (5)

Notable Pedigrees:

    Belden E. Roach (1944)

    Stack's ANA (1976)

Robert W. Miller, Sr. (1992)

Warren Miller (1995)

Harry W. Bass, Jr. (2000)

Henry S. Lang (2002)

Nevada Collection (Current)

Survival Estimates in All Grades: 135-155
Estimated in Uncirculated: 1-2
Estimated in XF to AU: 80-90
Total Certified Examples **in All Grades (PCGS and NGC)*:** ... 134

(* As of April 2003)

(** Possible resubmissions of one or more of the same coins on this list.)

REFLECTIONS:

To meet heavy export demand, the nation's gold coinage production increased sharply in 1876, fortified by bountiful gold discoveries in Nevada and other mining regions. By then the Carson City Mint was receiving only 25% of the deposits from the Comstock mines, most of it returned in the form of $20 gold pieces.

Meager amounts of $10 eagles were once again delivered by the three coinage mints: San Francisco resumed production, barely beating out Carson City with a total of 5,000 compared to 4,696. Years later, the Treasury would make a concerted effort to fill the void left by a shortfall in gold eagles during these lean production years of the 1870s by substantially increasing outputs.

Though the mintage was sparse, the survival rate for 1876-CC gold eagles is approximately 3%, resulting in a higher population extant than would be expected. One explanation might be the significance of 1876 as the Centennial year, possibly influencing more people to save coins with this date. At the time, though, $10 was two to three days wages for many workers, and saving gold coins would have been confined to wealthier members of society.

From the examples of this date that have survived, it appears as if an effort was made at the Carson City Mint to achieve a higher level of appearance. Luster and strike seem superior to earlier dates, however there are very unattractive 1876-CC's just as with any of the "CC" gold issues.

Currently (2003), the highest grade specimens are in AU-58, with the finest known being the *Henry S. Lang* coin.

1877-CC

(Photo courtesy Bowers and Merena)

Mintage: 3,332

Finest Knowns*:**

> PCGS AU-58 (1)
>
> NGC AU-58 (1)
>
> PCGS AU-55 (2)
>
> NGC AU-55 (2)
>
> PCGS AU-55 (4)
>
> PCGS AU-50 (3)
>
> NGC AU-50 (3)

Notable Pedigrees:

> Samuel W. Wolfson (1962)
>
> R.L. Miles (1968)
>
> Paramount Auction – Feb. (1974)
>
> Fairfield Collection[1] (1977)

Warren Miller (1995)

Harry W. Bass, Jr. (2000)

H. Jeff Browning (2001)

Henry S. Lang (2002)
> ex: Warren Miller (2002)

Nevada Collection (Current)

Survival Estimates in All Grades:............ 70-80

Estimated in Uncirculated: 0-2

Estimated in XF to AU: 45-50

**Total Certified Examples
in All Grades (PCGS and NGC)*:** 61

(* As of April 2003)

(** Possible resubmissions of one or more of the same coins on this list.)

REFLECTIONS:

As the *Big Bonanza* on the Comstock was yielding peak levels of gold bullion, the Carson City Mint's share of the action was shrinking. Whereas during the preceding three years Comstock miners were depositing nearly 25% of their gold at the local mint, by 1877, the percentage had been reduced to 12% or less, and just when it appeared as if Carson City's gold coin production would reach record levels, it actually dropped 68% and would never again equal the gold coin output achieved in 1874 through 1876.

In 1877 gold mintage totals continued a gradual decline, which would not rebound until 1880, and none of the three gold denominations minted at Carson City would be produced in lower quantities than the $10 eagles.

Comparable in rarity to all other scarce "CC" dates from the 1870s, except the 1870-CC and 1879-CC, the 1877-CC is a late bloomer in terms of valuation in wholesale and retail price guides. Astute collectors might take advantage of this oversight until the market adjusts. That this correction has already begun is evidenced by the $24,250 price realized for an AU-55 specimen sold in July 2002 as part of the *Henry S. Lang* collection, although the wholesale bid was $10,000.

On the 1877 gold eagles, the mintmark was similar to the small roundish letters seen on the pre-1874 Carson City dates, and centered above the *E* and *N* in *TEN*.

---

[1] Arthur Lamborn Collection.

1878-CC

(Photo courtesy Bowers and Merena)

Mintage: 3,244

Finest Knowns*:**

    NGC MS-63 (1)

    NGC AU-58 (3)

    PCGS AU-55 (4)

    NGC AU-55 (2)

    PCGS AU-53 (2)

    NGC AU-53 (2)

    PCGS AU-50 (8)

Notable Pedigrees:

    Stack's April Sale (1976)

    Robert W. Miller, Sr. (1992)

    James A. Stack (1995)

    Warren Miller (1995)

    Harry W. Bass, Jr. (1999)

      ex: Warren Miller

    Harry W. Bass, Jr. (2000)

    Henry S. Lang (2002)

    Nevada Collection (Current)

Survival Estimates in All Grades:	70-80
Estimated in Uncirculated:	1-2
Estimated in XF to AU:	45-50
Total Certified Examples in All Grades (PCGS and NGC)*:	71

(* As of April 2003)

(** Possible resubmissions of one or more of the same coins on this list.)

REFLECTIONS:

Carson City continued to buck the national trend of increasing gold coin production in 1878: at Philadelphia, the gold eagle mintage surged from 817 pieces in 1877 to 73,800 in 1878, and San Francisco's output increased from 17,000 to 26,100. At the Carson City Mint gold eagle deliveries actually dropped from the minuscule level of 3,332 to an even skimpier quantity of 3,244.

But this would have been expected, as the Comstock gold bonanza bubble burst, and with it, Carson City's share of the miner's deposits. Gold coin production at the Carson Mint had fallen from $2.85 million in 1876, to $928,020 in 1877, and then $341,310 in 1878. There was no momentum, just a free-fall decline.

Nearly identical to the 1877-CC in its estimated survival population, the 1878-CC gold eagle has the dis-

tinction of being one of only two dates on the top 10 "CC" eagle rarity list with a specimen in MS-63 (1875-CC is the other). After the lone Choice Uncirculated piece, the next highest grade is AU-58.

Collectors must be patient when pursuing an example of this date for their set, since most are uninspiring in appearance. Problem-free 1878-CC gold eagles are worth hefty premiums, and substandard pieces seem to be a little overvalued at the present time (2003). With all due consideration, these "CC" gold coins are not getting any easier to locate, and today's prices will most certainly seem like bargains in the years to come.

Another mintmark modification on the "CC" gold eagles occurred in 1878, as the letters were made taller and were centered more proportionately between the bottom of the eagle and the word *TEN*.

1879-CC

(Photo courtesy Bowers and Merena)

Mintage: 1,762

Finest Knowns*:**

    PCGS AU-58 (1)

    NGC AU-58 (3)

    PCGS AU-55 (2)

    NGC AU-55 (2)

    PCGS AU-53 (3)

    NGC AU-53 (2)

    PCGS AU-50 (7)

    NGC AU-50 (2)

Notable Pedigrees:

    J.F. Bell (1944)

    Samuel W. Wolfson (1962)

    R.L. Miles (1968)

      ex: Wolfson

    Alto Collection (1970)

    E.A. Carson (1976)

      ex: Miles, Wolfson

Fairfield Collection[1] (1977)

Bowers and Merena May Sale (1993)

James A. Stack (1995)

Harry W. Bass, Jr. (1999)

    ex: Alto Collection

Harry W. Bass, Jr. (2000)

    ex: Fairfield Collection

Henry S. Lang (2002)

Nevada Collection (Current)

    ex: James A. Stack

Survival Estimates in All Grades:	65-70
Estimated in Uncirculated:	1
Estimated in XF to AU:	40-45
Total Certified Examples in All Grades (PCGS and NGC)*:	66

(* As of April 2003)

(** Possible resubmissions and crossovers of one or more coins on this list.)

REFLECTIONS:

Just when it seemed that mintages for $10 eagles at the Carson City Mint could not decline any further, 1879 arrived. A work stoppage combined with shrinking bullion deposits resulted in an all time low coinage of 1,762 pieces. Ironically, this occurred at a time when overall gold eagle production across the country reached the highest level since the California gold rush year of 1849.

In a classic example of stating the obvious, the rarity of the 1879-CC gold eagle has been acknowledged since Heaton's *Treatise* of 1893; a study based more on analyzing low mintages than researching the populations extant. It is still a safe bet that as Heaton's observations suggested, dates with the lowest mintages (especially when it is 1,762) are the rarest coins.

Though not as elusive as once estimated, the 1879-CC might tie the 1870-CC for first place on the overall rarity list. In grades above AU-50, however, 1870-CC reigns supreme.

There are currently no Uncirculated specimens of the 1879-CC gold eagle graded by PCGS or NGC (2003), though in 1944 the cataloguer for the *J.F. Bell* sale described one as being in this condition. Its whereabouts are unknown, but if it ever surfaces, a record price is guaranteed.

---

[1] Arthur Lamborn Collection.

1880-CC

(Photo courtesy Bowers and Merena)

Mintage: 11,190

Finest Knowns*:**

NGC MS-62 (2)

PCGS MS-61 (1)

NGC MS-61 (4)

PCGS MS-60 (2)

NGC MS-60 (6)

PCGS AU-58 (8)

NGC AU-58 (17)

Notable Pedigrees:

R.L. Miles (1968)

Nathan Shapero (1971)

Stack's ANA Sale (1976)

Bowers and Merena May Sale (1993)

Harry W. Bass, Jr. (1999)

ex: Miles

Harry W. Bass, Jr. (2000)

Henry S. Lang (2002)

Dr. Nathan Sonnheim (Current)

Nevada Collection (Current)

Survival Estimates in All Grades:	295-325
Estimated in Uncirculated:	17-25
Estimated in XF to AU:	240-260
Total Certified Examples in All Grades (PCGS and NGC)*:	242

(*As of April 2003)

(** Possible resubmissions and crossovers of one or more coins on this list.)

REFLECTIONS:

Because of an unusual increase in imports of foreign gold into the United States in 1880 and taking heed of the demand for lower denomination coins, the Treasury altered its normal policy of maintaining larger inventories of double eagles. As a result, $10 eagle production spiked, rising from 612,032 in 1879 to 2.17 million in 1880.

Carson City's gold eagle mintage accounted for ½ of 1% of the national total, not too impressive in the overall context, but a 635% increase at the local level. This was also the first year since that mint opened that eagles and half eagles were minted in the absence of double eagles.

Possibly because a portion of the "CC" gold eagle output was exported in 1880, many coins were preserved until the next century, accounting for a higher than average survival rate. In addition, there was a noticeable improvement in quality compared to the issues from the 1870s, as sharp strikes, glowing yellow/gold luster, and possibly better prepared planchets enhance the eye appeal. Of course it also helps that there are many more Uncirculated specimens of this date available than there are from those earlier years.

This date is very affordable in grades of AU-55 and below, but becomes rather expensive in grades above AU-58. An attractive specimen graded MS-61 by NGC sold in the *Henry S. Lang* sale for $19,550 in July of 2002.

There was a slight shift in the position of the mintmark on this date, placing the "CCs" closer to the *EN* in *TEN.*

1881-CC

(Photo courtesy Bowers and Merena)

Mintage: 24,015

Finest Knowns*:**

    NGC MS-64 (1)

    PCGS MS-62 (5)

    NGC MS-62 (22)

    PCGS MS-61 (6)

    NGC MS-61 (11)

    PCGS MS-60 (2)

    NGC MS-60 (9)

    PCGS AU-58 (15)

    NGC AU-58 (53)

Notable Pedigrees:

    E.A. Carson (1976)

    NERCA ANA Sale (1979)

Louis E. Eliasberg, Sr. (1982)

Warren Miller (1995)

Harry W. Bass, Jr. (2000)

Henry S. Lang (2002)
    ex: Eliasberg

Nevada Collection (Current)

Survival Estimates in All Grades:...... 455-525

Estimated in Uncirculated: 45-65

Estimated in XF to AU:........................ 370-400

**Total Certified Examples
    in All Grades (PCGS and NGC)*:** ... 433

(* As of April 2003)

(** Possible resubmissions and crossovers of one or more of the coins on this list.)

REFLECTIONS:

In response to increased demand for gold coin denominations less than $20, gold eagle production flew off the chart in 1881. Nearly 4.9 million $10 gold pieces were produced at the nation's mints, an all time record for this denomination. A record was also set for half eagles.

At the Carson City Mint it seemed like it could be one denomination or the other, but not both, and this year gold eagles took center stage. The total mintage of 24,015 for 1881-CC gold eagles was the highest in that mint's first 15 years of operation. Once again, this happened during a year in which no double eagles were coined at Carson City.

In grades below MS-60, the 1881-CC is readily available, and is the least expensive "CC" eagle from the 1880s. There is a relatively generous supply of Uncirculated pieces up to the grade of MS-61, but beyond that this date becomes elusive.

Yet another mintmark modification moved it upward, much closer to the eagle claw and feather tip, with the right "C" lower than the left.

(Photo courtesy Bowers and Merena)

Mintage: 6,764

Finest Knowns*:

    NGC MS-62 (1)

    PCGS AU-58 (6)**

    NGC AU-58 (21)**

    PCGS AU-55 (16)**

    NGC AU-55 (31)**

    PCGS AU-53 (9)**

    NGC AU-53 (11)**

    PCGS AU-50 (21)**

    NGC AU-50 (8)**

Notable Pedigrees:

    J.F. Bell (1944)

    William C. Atwater (1946)

    R.L. Miles (1968)

    Louis Engel (1970)

Nathan Shapero (1971)

George F. Scanlon (1973)

Westchester Collection (1973)

RARCOA Auction '79 (1979)

Louis E. Eliasberg, Sr. (1982)

Warren Miller (1995)

Harry W. Bass, Jr. (1999 & 2000)

Henry S. Lang (2002)

Nevada Collection (Current)

Survival Estimates in All Grades:	200-235
Estimated in Uncirculated:	2-4
Estimated in XF to AU:	175-200
Total Certified Examples in All Grades (PCGS and NGC)*:	202

(*As of April 2003)

(** Possible resubmissions of many of the same coins listed.)

REFLECTIONS:

After five years of declining gold coin production at the Carson City Mint, 1882 brought on a slight resurgence. New mineral ore discoveries had been made on the Comstock, producing yields that previously would have hardly aroused attention, but in these lean times, it helped. Miners realized that lower outputs were not worth negotiating with out of state brokers, making it more expedient to deposit their bullion at the Carson Mint.

As a result, double eagle coinage was resumed and gold coin production increased from $309,580 in 1881 to over $1.26 million in 1882. Gold eagles accounted for only 5 1/3% of this total, as half eagle production reached record levels.

An estimated 3% of the original mintage of 1882-CC eagles is extant today, offering collectors a larger selection of pieces than the sparse output might indicate. A fair quantity of AU specimens is available, yet only one 1882-CC eagle has been certified in Uncirculated condition, although there were at least seven examples of this date listed as being in Mint State in auction catalogs prior to 1981, as well as several others after that.

(Photo courtesy Bowers and Merena)

Mintage: 12,000

Finest Knowns*:**

    NGC MS-61 (2)

    PCGS MS-60 (1)

    NGC MS-60 (2)

    PCGS AU-58 (2)

    NGC AU-58 (11)

    PCGS AU-55 (7)

    NGC AU-55 (12)

    PCGS AU-53 (9)

    NGC AU-53 (7)

    PCGS AU-50 (20)

    NGC AU-50 (18)

Notable Pedigrees:

    R.L. Miles (1968)

    Nathan Shapero (1971)

    E.A. Carson (1976)

    NERCA March Sale (1977)

    Warren Miller (1995)

    James A. Stack (1994)

    Harry W. Bass, Jr. (1999 and 2000)

    Henry S. Lang (2002)

      ex: W. Miller

    Nevada Collection (Current)

Survival Estimates in All Grades:...... 250-280

Estimated in Uncirculated:............................ 6-9

Estimated in XF to AU:....................... 200-230

Total Certified Examples
    in All Grades (PCGS and NGC)*: ... 228

(* As of April 2003)

(** Possible resubmissions and crossovers of coins on this list.)

REFLECTIONS:

Moderate levels of gold flowed into the Carson City Mint as Comstock miners decided to bring nearly all of their deposits to the local facility. More than 86% of the gold coinage being produced at Carson was in the form of double eagles, with 8.66% minted as $10 eagles.

After three years of steady increases in gold eagle production in the United States, quantities were sharply cut back in 1883, plunging from nearly 2.5 million in 1882 to 259,540. It was evident by then that the output at the Carson Mint was defined less by Treasury policies and more by the deposits brought in by local miners.

Of the 12,000 1883-CC gold eagles minted, an estimated 2% have survived with fairly generous quantities of AU specimens. In Uncirculated condition this date becomes difficult to obtain. Of the handful of Mint State pieces in existence, most are in "strong hands," and not expected to be offered for many years. When an Uncirculated example does appear, spirited bidding is a certainty.

Still another mintmark variation was introduced on this date with the two "C"s widely spaced and set at a diagonal angle, with the left "C" higher.

1884-CC

(Photo courtesy Bowers and Merena)

Mintage: 9,925

Finest Knowns*:**

    PCGS MS-63 (1)

    PCGS MS-62 (1)

    PCGS MS-61 (1)

    NGC MS-61 (1)

    PCGS MS-60 (2)

    NGC MS-60 (3)

    PCGS AU-58 (12)

    NGC AU-58 (37)

    PCGS AU-55 (12)

    NGC AU-55 (18)

    PCGS AU-53 (10)

    NGC AU-53 (15)

Notable Pedigrees:

    Paramount ANA Sale (1969)

    Nathan Shapero (1971)

Stack's ANA Sale (1971)

Bowers and Merena May Sale (1993)

Warren Miller (1995)

Harry W. Bass, Jr. (2000)
    ex: Paramount ANA

Henry S. Lang (2002)
    ex: W. Miller

Nevada Collection (Current)

Survival Estimates in All Grades:......	265-300
Estimated in Uncirculated:	10-12
Estimated in XF to AU:	225-250
Total Certified Examples in All Grades (PCGS and NGC)*: ...	239

(* As of April 2003)

(** Possible resubmissions and crossovers of many of the coins on this list.)

REFLECTIONS:

In the 15th year of coinage operations at Carson City, double eagle production increased, as did half eagles, but gold eagle output declined by 17.5%. It has been suggested that there was no intention to even strike gold eagles at this mint in 1884, but a last minute request required coiner Levi Dague to use a partially cancelled obverse die. This is one explanation for the heavy raised-metal lines flowing across Liberty's neck. Another explanation for the imperfection is that a step in the die finishing process was skipped. Most 1884-CC eagles display this rather obtru-

sive defect, although Walter Breen also listed a normal die variety in his *Encyclopedia*.

Whatever the ultimate verdict turns out to be, this date was the final year for gold eagle output at the Carson Mint until production was resumed in 1890. Estimated survival rates are 2.5% of the original mintage, with most extant specimens in XF or above. In Uncirculated condition the 1884-CC is a challenge, though not as much as the low mintage might suggest. Examples in circulated grades from VF to XF are currently priced below $1,000 (as of 2003).

1890-CC

(Photo courtesy Bowers and Merena)

Mintage: 17,500

Finest Knowns*:

    PCGS MS-63 (4)

    NGC MS-63 (9)

    PCGS MS-62 (21)

    NGC MS-62 (25)

    PCGS MS-61 (16)

    NGC MS-61 (28)

    PCGS MS-60 (20)

    NGC MS-60 (19)

    PCGS AU-58 (44)

    NGC AU-58 (67)

Notable Pedigrees:

    World's Greatest Collection (1946)

    Charles M. Williams (Menjou) 1950

    Alto Collection (1970)

Stack's ANA Sale (1971)

Nathan Shapero (1971)

George F. Scanlon (1973)

H. Philip Speir Sale (1974)

E.A. Carson (1976)

Stack's ANA Sale (1976)

RARCOA Auction '79 (1979)

Harry W. Bass, Jr. (2000)

Henry S. Lang (2002)

Nevada Collection (Current)

Survival Estimates in All Grades:...... 525-750

Estimated in Uncirculated:.................. 155-225

Estimated in XF to AU:........................ 335-465

Total Certified Examples
    in All Grades (PCGS and NGC)*: ... 449

(* As of April 2003)

(** Possible resubmissions and crossovers of coins on this list.)

REFLECTIONS:

From 1885 to 1889, when the Carson Mint was dark, certain mine owners from the Comstock region pledged to make deposits at the local facility if the Treasury would revive coining operations there. Yields on gold ore had been moderately consistent throughout the last six years of the 1880s, and by 1890 more than $1.5 million worth of gold had been deposited at Carson City, more than adequate to begin minting coins again.

Double eagle production had gotten off to an early start at Carson City, having begun in 1889, and proved once again to be the predominant gold coin in 1890. Gold eagle production resumed that year, and though never approaching the mintage levels of the double eagles, ended 1890 with a respectable total of 17,500, second highest up to that time.

A large percentage of these gold eagles were exported in response to huge orders for U.S. gold from foreign countries during the 1890s. Small hoards of these coins returned to the United States in the 20th century.

This date is the third most common in the "CC" gold eagle series in terms of overall rarity, and second in the Uncirculated category. Currently (2003), Choice AU examples are available for approximately $1,000. In Choice Uncirculated condition, however, prices rise dramatically as evidenced by the $18,400 realized for the *Henry S. Lang* specimen in July of 2002.

1891-CC

(Photo courtesy Bowers and Merena)

Mintage: 103,732

Finest Knowns*:**

    PCGS MS-64 (1)

    NGC MS-64 (7)

    PCGS MS-63 (23)

    NGC MS-63 (55)

    PCGS MS-62 (148)

    NGC MS-62 (235)

    PCGS MS-61 (169)

    NGC MS-61 (270)

    PCGS MS-60 (271)

    NGC MS-60 (179)

Notable Pedigrees:

    J.F. Bell (1944)

    Jerome D. Kern (1950)

    R.L. Miles (1968)

    Louis Engel (1970)

    Alto Collection (1970)

    Nathan Shapero (1971)

Yale University Sale (1971)

George F. Scanlon (1973)

E.A. Carson (1976)

RARCOA Auction '79 (1979)

NERCA ANA Sale (1979)

Louis E. Eliasberg, Sr. (1982)

Norweb Collection (1988)

Heritage June Sale (1998)

Harry W. Bass, Jr. (2000)

Henry S. Lang (2002)

Nevada Collection (Current)

Survival Estimates in All Grades:	**3,200-4,500**
Estimated in Uncirculated:	**1,500-1,700**
Estimated in XF to AU:	**1,500-2,500**
Total Certified Examples in All Grades (PCGS and NGC)*:	**2,564**

(* As of April 2003)

(** Because of the large quantities of coins listed, many resubmission/crossover possibilities exist.)

REFLECTIONS:

Treasury officials were faced with distress in 1891, as foreign demand for U.S. gold coins threatened to deplete reserves to critically low levels, a crisis which grew worse during the next few years before beginning to improve.

At the same time, the Philadelphia Mint was burdened with the task of providing millions of minor coins. San Francisco was called upon to fill the insatiable demand for double eagles and the Carson City Mint was given the responsibility of restocking diminishing reserves of gold eagles and half eagles.

At no time in the history of this small Nevada coining facility were such quantities of these lower denomination gold coins delivered. The table at right exhibits the mintages of the two mints that produced gold eagles and half eagles in 1891.

As a result of unprecedented mintages of gold eagles at the Carson Mint in 1891, more examples of this date are extant than all of the other 18 years of "CC" gold eagles combined. Estimated survival rates range from 3% to 4% with nearly half in Uncirculated condition. Like the 1884-CC silver dollar, the 1891-CC gold eagle is Carson City's gift to the coin collecting community.

COINAGE OF HALF EAGLES AND EAGLES AT CARSON CITY AND PHILADELPHIA IN 1891		
Denomination	Philadelphia	Carson City
$5 Half Eagle	61,413	208,000
$10 Eagle	91,868	103,732

1892-CC

(Photo courtesy Bowers and Merena)

Mintage: 40,000

Finest Knowns*:**

    PCGS MS-64 (2)

    NGC MS-64 (1)

    PCGS MS-63 (1)

    PCGS MS-62 (5)

    NGC MS-62 (6)

    PCGS MS-61 (3)

    NGC MS-61 (8)

    PCGS MS-60 (5)

    NGC MS-60 (4)

Notable Pedigrees:

    R.L. Miles (1968)

    George F. Scanlon (1973)

    E.A. Carson (1976)

RARCOA Auction '79 (1979)

NERCA FUN Sale (1980)

Louis E. Eliasberg, Sr. (1982)

Bowers and Merena May (1993)

Superior May Long Beach (1999)

Far Rockaway Collection (1999)

H. Jeff Browning Collection (2001)

Nevada Collection (Current)

Survival Estimates in All Grades:.. 800-1,200
Estimated in Uncirculated: 39-50
Estimated in XF to AU: 600-900
Total Certified Examples in All Grades (PCGS and NGC)*: ... 519

(* As of April 2003)

(** Possible resubmissions and crossovers of several of the coins on this list.)

REFLECTIONS:

Demand for gold coins smaller than $20 remained strong throughout 1892. The Philadelphia Mint, already juggling a hectic schedule of supplying the nation with cents and five-cent coins, was now challenged to add the new Barber silver coinage to its strenuous workload. At the same time, the urgent need for gold eagles could not be ignored, and the Philadelphia Mint was compelled to increase its output by 870%. To facilitate this, silver dollar production was slashed 88% from 1891's totals.

At the Carson City Mint, gold eagle production dropped sharply from the record level of 1891, yet still checked in as the second highest mintage in this branch's history. Mining reserves from the Comstock were dissipating, requiring every last ounce of gold to meet coinage quotas.

Possibly 95% of the 40,000 1892-CC gold eagles were exported as huge transfers to foreign countries

Millions of dollars in gold were stored in the form of bars in Treasury vaults.

continued. Estimated survival rates for this date are lower than those of the 1890-CC and 91-CC, resulting in a higher rarity ranking than the mintage might suggest.

Values for 1892-CC gold eagles in AU and below are comparable to those for the 1890-CC and 1891-CC, but in Mint State the 1892-CC tends to be a bit pricier. There are several specimens of this date in near Gem Uncirculated condition, the finest of which is the impressive *Eliasberg* coin, now in a PCGS MS-64 holder.

Surprisingly, the *Harry W. Bass, Jr. Collection*, one of the most renowned collections of Carson City gold coins, did not include an Uncirculated example of this date; and neither did one other notable collection, owned by *Henry S. Lang*, which oddly did not include an example in any grade.

(Photo courtesy Bowers and Merena)

Mintage: 14,000

Finest Knowns*:*

NGC MS-62 (1)

PCGS MS-62 (2)

PCGS MS-61 (2)

NGC MS-61 (3)

NGC MS-60 (3)

PCGS AU-58 (12)

NGC AU-58 (22)

Notable Pedigrees:

World's Greatest Collection (1946)

William C. Atwater (1946)

Golden Sale of the Century II (1963)

R.L. Miles (1968)

Nathan Shapero (1971)

NERCA ANA Sale (1979)

Bowers and Merena May Sale (1993)

Far Rockaway Collection (1998)

Nevada Collection (1999)

Harry W. Bass, Jr. (2000)

Henry S. Lang (2002)

Survival Estimates in All Grades:	**300-330**
Estimated in Uncirculated:	**12-15**
Estimated in XF to AU:	**230-260**
Total Certified Examples in All Grades (PCGS and NGC)*:	**252**

(* As of April 2003)

(** Possible resubmissions and crossovers of several of the same coins on this list.)

REFLECTIONS:

Before the Carson Mint was shut down at the end of May 1893, production was on pace to equal or exceed 1892's level. Enough deposits were still being made to sustain coinage operations, but it was only a matter of time until those Comstock mines would be virtually exhausted.

But the Treasury no longer had patience for the often maligned Nevada branch of their Bureau of the Mint network, and likely influenced by the new administration of Grover Cleveland, shut it down.

At the time operations were suspended in 1893, the Carson Mint had already produced $808,040 worth of gold coins, and probably had at least that much still stored on the premises. As a result of the work shortened year, gold eagle output was the lowest of the four years in the 1890s, but still the sixth highest from the 19 year run.

Surprisingly, there are no exceptional specimens of this date known to exist given the Carson City mint worker's predilection for prooflike coins and other novelties. It seems plausible that at least a few specially prepared specimens might have been struck to commemorate the closing.

Currently the highest grade known for this date is MS-62, and the luster on these is typically frosty with slightly textured surfaces. There are far fewer Uncirculated examples of this date available than any of the four years in the 1890s.

Values for the 1893-CC gold eagles in XF and below are comparable to the other three "CC" dates from the 1890s, but as might be expected, in grades above AU this date becomes much more expensive.

(Photo courtesy Bowers and Merena)

Silver was in the spotlight during the years that coins were being manufactured at the Carson City Mint, but without question gold reigned supreme. Silverite politicians could pontificate until they were blue in the face about the value of the white metal to the nation's economic system, yet at the end of the day, gold was preferred by bankers, international financiers and hard money people. The strength of the Treasury was not assessed by how much silver it held, but how much gold was in reserve. Gold was the foundation upon which the United States stood.

Owners of gold bullion could deposit it at Treasury facilities and receive gold coins in return as there were no debates over the *free coinage* of gold; instead this privilege was tantamount to an unalienable right and consequently, gold coins were produced without constraint at the nation's mints.

Shortages of silver and gold had contrasting effects upon the country; when subsidiary silver coin supplies proved inadequate, retailers panicked due to the effects on everyday commerce. Yet if gold holdings dwindled, na-tionwide financial panics set in, as banks closed, businesses failed, foreign countries grew restless, and depressions ensued. Gold was the international standard, and demonetization of gold coins was not an option.

In terms of total mass, double eagle production towered above that of half eagles and eagles during the Carson City era, as more than 46 million $20 gold pieces were coined at the nation's mints between 1870 and 1893, compared to 26 million eagles, and 37 million half eagles. Considering that double eagles were the highest denomination of the three, their face value resulted in even larger margin spreads between the other two, with nearly $925 million, compared to $260 million in eagles, and $186 million in half eagles. The table below exhibits these figures.

Since the output of double eagles was so much higher, the extant population is greater. Nevertheless, the survival rate is harmonious. Generally speaking, the percentage of Uncirculated double eagles extant is higher than the other two denominations in this grade compared to original mintages. A major factor contributing to this is the use of double eagles in intrabank trading, and signifi-

GOLD COINS PRODUCED AT THE MINTS OF THE UNITED STATES BETWEEN 1870 AND 1893		
Denomination	Mintage	Face Value
$5	37,271,065	$186,355,325
$10	26,049,237	260,493,370
$20	46,243,645	924,873,900

cant transfers abroad. These big coins were more suited to remaining in vaults, rather than being circulated like their smaller counterparts.

At the Carson City Mint, double eagle production, compared to half eagles and eagles, approximated the ratios for the entire nation's coinage. This was the predominant denomination at the Nevada branch, and except for a few low output years, was delivered on a consistent basis, even during slow times.

Approximately $30 million in gold bullion was deposited at the Carson Mint from 1870 through 1893, and well over half of that was redeemed in $20 gold pieces. Many were sent to San Francisco to be held as reserves for the certificates of deposit mine operators received upon dropping off their mineral ore. At least a small percentage of the original mintages circulated in and around Carson City, attested to by stories of large stacks of double eagles in bank vaults and occasionally on poker tables. This use in commerce would have been more likely in the first half of Carson City's tenure as a mint, as the area was much more prosperous during the *Big Bonanza* period. However, during the second and final stage of the Carson City Mint's coinage years, economic conditions probably would not have necessitated widespread local distribution of gold coins, and as a result, large percentages of the mint's output were shipped out of state.

Survival rates for "CC" double eagles range between 2% and 4% of the original mintages, and it is estimated that there are fewer than 25,000 Carson City double eagles extant, with the highest surviving quantities concentrated in four dates: 1875-CC, 1876-CC, 1884-CC, and 1890-CC. It is possible that 45% or more of all surviving "CC" double eagles are included in this quartette.

Less than $1/3$ of 1% of the aggregate original mintages of double eagles with the "CC" mintmark survive in Uncirculated condition, and of these, only three specimens have been graded as high as MS-64 by either PCGS or NGC (as of 2003).

A mere 90 or so have been graded MS-63, with 96% of all certified Uncirculated specimens in the MS-60 to MS-62 condition rating. Most are heavily bagmarked, and although some exhibit bright sparkling luster, the majority are dirty looking.

Of course, the highest percentage of Uncirculated specimens are from the more common years, and the first five years, 1870 to 1874, account for only 40 examples in this condition range. Just two specimens dated in the first five years, an 1871-CC and an 1873-CC, have been graded as high as MS-63, and 1870-CC, the first date in the set, lacks an Uncirculated specimen.

Pedigree information for "CC" gold coins was not tracked for much of the first century after this series began, and as late as the 1930s, premiums for any "CC" double eagles were minimal, usually not much more than 15% above the bullion value in the coin.

As with most mintmarked gold, numismatists relied on original mintages to determine rarity, so naturally Augustus Heaton declared that, "The first date only should be rare, and 1885, 1879, 1878, and 1891 rather scarce."[1] This of course was a safe prognostication, and if Heaton had included the 1871-CC and 1872-CC he would have been right on the mark 110 years later.

Beyond question, the 1870-CC is the scarcest of the scarce, and considered a classic rarity in the pantheon of numismatic elite coins. Though survival estimates have doubled from 25 in 1990 to nearly 50 pieces in 2003, demand continues to increase, and rising prices have placed the coin in the automatic six figure category. Within two years of the publication of this book (2003-2004), the 1870-CC double eagle will break the $200,000 barrier, and continue to soar.[2] If an Uncirculated specimen is discovered, $1 million mark here it comes!

Two significant types of the Carson City double eagle are: the Type II TWENTY D. reverse, used 1870 through 1876, and the Type III TWENTY DOLLARS reverse completing the series from 1877 through 1893. There were other minor die changes between the two types providing the specialist with much fascinating study.

No one in the collector community knew how large the population base for "CC" $20 gold pieces was throughout much of the 20th century. Small hoards began surfacing in Europe in the 1950s, but as prices began to appreciate for U.S. gold coins in general (specifically mintmarked gold coins) in the 1970s, several large rare coin firms set up offices in Europe, South America, and other foreign destinations, in search of exported holdings. Company representatives contacted banks and foreign exchanges soliciting reserves of U.S. gold coins. In time, hoards were discovered and transferred back to the United States, resulting in many "CC" gold coins being recovered.

---

[1] Augustus G. Heaton, Mint Marks, A Treatise, 1893.
[2] An 1870-CC double eagle graded AU-53 by PCGS sold for a record $368,000 in January 2004 at a Heritage auction, just as this book was being released.

Though these rare coin firms suggest that supplies are drying up, it will probably be many years before anything close to a final tally can be taken. In all likelihood, populations of "CC" double eagles will not change drastically in the years to come, especially for lower mintage dates. As with all Carson City coins, it must always be kept in mind how few coins were actually produced there—for double eagles, a total of 864,178 pieces over a 19 year period, less than just about any single year's output at the San Francisco Mint during that same span.

Just like half eagles and eagles, a set of "CC" double eagles consists of 19 dates, differing slightly in the run of years. Excluding the 1870-CC, a set of double eagles is generally easier to assemble than the other two denominations, but a complete 19 piece set is much more of a challenge because of the 1870-CC.

BUREAU OF THE MINT DATA FOR CARSON CITY GOLD DOUBLE EAGLE PRODUCTION

Total Combined Mintage: 864,178

Total Face Value: $17,283,560

Total Ounces of Gold Used: .... 836,092 ozs.

Design Type: .... Coronet or Liberty head

Designers: .... James B. Longacre
(With William Barber from 1877-1893)

Metal Composition: .... .900 Gold .100 Copper

Actual Gross Weight: .... 33.436 grams

Actual Fine Content: .... .9675 oz.

Value of Gold in One Double Eagle

Between 1870 and 1893: .... $19.96-$20.01

1870-CC

(Photo courtesy Bowers and Merena)

Mintage: 3,789

Finest Knowns*:

    PCGS AU-50 (4)

    NGC AU-50 (2)

    PCGS XF-45 (7)**

    NGC XF-45 (5)**

    PCGS XF-40 (5)**

    NGC XF-40 (5)**

Notable Pedigrees:

    J.F. Bell (1944)

    William C. Atwater (1946)

    Stack's ANA Sale (1971)

    Stack's Brant, Mathey, Long (1973)

    Paramount ANA Sale (1974)

    Superior ANA Sale (1975)

    Stack's T. Henry Allen Sale (1977)

    Ellis Robison (1979)

    Louis E. Eliasberg, Sr. (1982)

      ex: Possibly W.C. Atwater

    RARCOA Auction '89 (1989)

    Bowers and Merena August Sale (1998)

    Harry W. Bass, Jr. (1999)

    Nevada Collection (1999)

    H. Jeff Browning (2001)

    Eagle Collection January (2002)

    Henry S. Lang (2002)

Survival Estimates in All Grades: 45-50
Estimated in Uncirculated: 0-1
Estimated in XF to AU: 28-33
Total Certified Examples in All Grades (PCGS and NGC):* 38

(* As of April 2003)

(** Possible resubmissions of several of the same coins.)

REFLECTIONS:

To get things off to a much anticipated start, Comstock miners deposited approximately $125,000 worth of gold ore at the new local mint in the first half of 1870. In February, $16,440 worth of the gold bullion was minted into $10 eagles, followed by $2,000 worth of $5 half eagles, and in March, $26,640 in new 1870-CC double eagles.

Superintendent and town founder Abe Curry was proud of every coin being minted, but especially the $20 double eagles. As he held these heavy gold coins in his hand he could not help but admire every detail of them. In November of 1868, during construction of the mint, Curry had promised to send the first double eagle produced to newly elected President Ulysses S. Grant. Curry had hoped to fulfill this promise in 1869, but because of delays, coinage operations were postponed until 1870. Although there is no documentation to verify if Curry ever sent a new double eagle to the President, it is known that he did indeed send Grant a new 1870-CC silver dollar.

A 20th-century rumor alleged that Curry was not satisfied with the quality of the first double eagles struck; ordered them to be melted, and then had his crew start all over again. As the story unfolds, Curry is said to have surreptitiously stashed 3,600 inferior quality 1870-CC double eagles, sealing them in a box made for Winchester rifles and then storing them in one of the mint's vaults, thus rescuing them from the melting pot. If true, Curry would have to have falsified accounting records and covered up $72,000 in gold. No one will ever know for sure.[1]

Regardless of what really happened, it is certain that at least a percentage of the double eagles from 1870 circulated with the other "CC" gold coins around the Comstock region. Mine workers' wagers were paid in gold coins; banks held gold coins in reserve, and depositors of gold ore at the mint had the option of receiving gold coins in exchange. Throughout the 20th century discoveries of small quantities of these rare double eagles around northern Nevada also validate local circulation of these coins.

This date's low mintage automatically qualifies it as very scarce, and the small estimated survival rate of 1 to 1.3% accentuates the fact. At one time, the survival rate was estimated to be half of what it is today, and surprisingly, when it was thought that there were fewer examples extant, the value of 1870-CC double eagles relative to the prevailing coin market was lower than it is today (2003).

Granted, this date has always been the most expensive in the Liberty double eagle series, but even as late as the 1950s, examples sold for $250 to $300, and for a date missing from many famous collections, with an estimated extant population at the time of 10 to 15 pieces, this price seemed on the low side. By the early 1960s, the value of 1870-CC double eagles had increased by 1000%, as had the value of many other rare coins. An old timer from Reno remembers when he sold three examples of this date in one month in the early 1960s for $2,500 apiece.

In 1963, the *Wolfson* specimen brought $4,000 at auction. Then in 1976 the *E.A. Carson* specimen realized $12,500 in a Bowers and Ruddy sale. At the landmark *Louis E. Eliasberg, Sr.* gold sale in 1982, the famous 1870-CC double eagle, reportedly purchased at the *William C. Atwater* sale in 1946 for $275, sold for $22,000.

By the 1990s, survival estimates had increased from 10 to 15 pieces, to 20 to 25, and prices had risen to the $25,000 to $60,000 range. As the decade came to an end, the $75,000 price barrier had been broken, preparing the ground for the $100,000 mark to be reached in the early years of the 21st century.

At Bowers and Merena's *Rarities* sale in July of 2002, the *Henry S. Lang* 1870-CC double eagle went to the winning bidder for $149,500, despite survival estimates having been adjusted again, placing the number of pieces extant in the 45 to 50 range. Even so, after the *Lang* sale, several other specimens were offered in the $160,000 to $225,000 range. Another curious point is that there are no 1870-CC double eagles graded higher than AU, so the quality of coins with dazzling eye appeal plays no part in the price inflation. Although no Uncirculated 1870-CC double eagles are known to exist, Q. David Bowers once reported that he had handled one in Mint State condition. If this piece were ever to hit the market, the sky would be the limit as far as price was concerned.

Most known examples are fairly banged up and lackluster in appearance, and several pieces have severe rim dings. Many XF to AU specimens have lost their originality due to cleanings, and many lower grade circulated pieces are rather scruffy looking.

More often than not all of these deficiencies are excused due to the date and mintmark combination, by "CC" gold specialists who are able to pay the hefty price tag to own an 1870-CC double eagle, as there is no equal as far as they are concerned.[2]

---

[1] For more information about this story, please see *Alleged Cover-Up of 3,600 1870-CC Double Eagles* in the Appendix.

[2] One of the *Top 25*.

(Photo courtesy Bowers and Merena)

Mintage: 14,687***

Finest Knowns*:

NGC MS-63 (I)

NGC MS-61 (I)

PCGS AU-58 (I)

NGC AU-58 (7)**

PCGS AU-55 (8)**

NGC AU-55 (14)**

PCGS AU-53 (9)**

NGC AU-53 (9)**

PCGS AU-50 (14)**

NGC AU-50 (18)**

Notable Pedigrees:

Donald Groves (1974)

E.A. Carson (1976)

NERCA Prudential Sale (1978)

Akers Auction '88 (1988)

Bowers and Merena January Sale (1994)

Stack's October Sale (1994)

Superior January Sale (1995)

Bowers and Merena May Sale (1995)

Heritage ANA Sale (1999)

Bowers and Merena January Sale (1999)

Nevada Collection (2000)

Heritage February Sale (2001)

Heritage ANA Sale (2001)

Eagle Collection January (2002)

Henry S. Lang (2002)

Survival Estimates in All Grades:	**200-235**
Estimated in Uncirculated:	**3-4**
Estimated in XF to AU:	**150-175**
Total Certified Examples in All Grades (PCGS and NGC)*:	**187**

(* As of April 2003)

(** Possible resubmissions of several of the same coins.)

(*** Some sources report 17,387)

REFLECTIONS:

Gold deposits had increased more than 800% at the Carson Mint between 1870 and 1871, though less than half of the gold bullion was returned in coin form, as miners requested equal amounts in the form of bars. This kept mintages lower, although double eagle production rose by nearly 390%.[1]

It is believed that the largest percentage of double eagles minted in Carson City during the first few years of operations remained in Nevada, at least for a while. Years later, quantities of "CC" $20 gold pieces made their way to for-eign lands as export demand increased. The early "CC" issues that did indeed circulate locally acquired heavy bagmarks and surface damage, greatly marring their appearance.

Of the surviving 1871-CCs extant, few are inspiring, although there are several AU-55 and AU-58 examples which possess higher than average eye appeal, and two Uncirculated specimens in particular stand head and shoulders above the rest, especially one that is graded by NGC as an MS-63.

---

[1] Some references list the mintage for 1871-CC double eagles as 17,387, although official U.S. mint records have reported it as 14,687 since 1887.

1872-CC

(Photo courtesy Bowers and Merena)

Mintage: 29,650***

Finest Knowns*:**

NGC MS-61 (4)

PCGS MS-60 (1)

NGC MS-60 (3)

PCGS AU-58 (10)

NGC AU-58 (32)

PCGS AU-55 (15)

NGC AU-55 (21)

PCGS AU-53 (20)

NGC AU-53 (24)

PCGS AU-50 (36)

NGC AU-50 (34)

Notable Pedigrees:

R.L. Miles (1968)

Pine Tree-Breen II Sale (1975)

Steve Ivy – July Sale (1979)

Bowers and Merena January Sale (1994)

Bowers and Merena H. Halpern Sale (1995)

Bowers and Merena - Shababian, M.D. Sale (1996)

Bowers and Merena August Sale (1998)

Heritage ANA Sale (1999)

Heritage – Santa Clara Sale (1999)

Harry W. Bass, Jr. (2000)

H. Jeff Browning (2001)

Eagle Collection January (2002)

Henry S. Lang (2002)

Nevada Collection (Current)

Survival Estimates in All Grades:	**450-500**
Estimated in Uncirculated:	**8-10**
Estimated in XF to AU:	**375-400**
Total Certified Examples in All Grades (PCGS and NGC)*:	**425**

(* As of April 2003)

(** Possible resubmissions of several of the same coins.)

(*** Some sources report 26,900)

REFLECTIONS:

As gold deposits at the Carson City Mint increased, the quantity of gold coins produced also rose, yet the percentage of deposits to gold coins requested further declined, as in 1872, miners requested just 16% of their deposits to be paid in gold coins, with the balance being returned as gold bars or certificates drawn on San Francisco banks.

Approximately 1.5% of the original mintage of the 1872-CC double eagle is estimated to survive, moving this date lower on the overall rarity scale than it was at one time. Uncirculated specimens, though very rare, are more available than one might think, and there is a generous supply of AU examples available, although the challenge is to find one with original color and without the typical heavily bagmarked surfaces.

Because of the higher quantities of 1872-CC double eagles in AU, prices are currently (2003) favorable to collectors, especially considering that this date is from the third year of Carson City's operations. A pleasing AU specimen, for example, can be purchased for $6,500 or less, much less than a comparable 1872-CC half eagle or eagle.

(Photo courtesy Bowers and Merena)

Mintage: 22,410

Finest Knowns*:**

    PCGS MS-63 (1)

    PCGS MS-62 (1)

    NGC MS-62 (1)

    NGC MS-61 (1)

    PCGS MS-60 (2)

    NGC MS-60 (11)

    PCGS AU-58 (27)

    NGC AU-58 (52)

    PCGS AU-55 (17)

    NGC AU-55 (29)

Notable Pedigrees:

    William C. Atwater (1946)

    Milton A. Holmes (1960)

    R.L. Miles (1968)

    E.A. Carson (1976)

    Numisco Suburban Sale (1980)

    Paramount – Auction '80 (1980)

    Raymond J. Wayman (1981)

    Bowers and Merena Stetson University (1993)

    Bowers and Merena January Sale (1995)

    Heritage ANA Sale (1995)

    Sotheby's June Sale (1996)

    Kingswood Coin Auctions June (1998)

    Bowers and Merena August Sale (1998)

    Harry W. Bass, Jr. (1999 and 2000)

    H. Jeff Browning (2001)

    Eagle Collection January (2002)

    Henry S. Lang (2002)

    Nevada Collection (Current)

Survival Estimates in All Grades:	425-475
Estimated in Uncirculated:	10-17
Estimated in XF to AU:	360-400
Total Certified Examples in All Grades (PCGS and NGC)*:	382

(* As of April 2003)

(** Possible resubmissions of several of the same coins.)

REFLECTIONS:

Gold deposits reached a peak of approximately $5 million at the Carson Mint in 1873. Although gold coin mintages were barely 10% of that total in 1873, large portions of the deposits would not be processed until 1874, when coin production increased by 500%.

Double eagle mintages at Carson City during the first half of 1873 lagged far behind the monthly average from 1872, but in the second half of the year production nearly tripled, and output finished just 7,240 short of 1872's.

Across the nation in this *Coinage Act* year, double eagle production increased by more than 260%. It was a very opportune time for America's connection to Comstock gold, as yields from that region more than doubled from the year before, and continued to surge for six more years. Although the Carson Mint received only a small share of the gold bullion from the Comstock, massive volumes of it were shipped to the San Francisco Mint as that facility became known for its heavy double eagle production, and some was also shipped to the Philadelphia Mint.

The estimated survival rate for the 1873-CC double eagle is a virtual mirror of that of the 1872-CC. A noticeable difference is seen in the Uncirculated category, mostly attributable to the 11 examples graded MS-60 by NGC, though some may be resubmissions. A simply beautiful specimen of this date is currently in a PCGS MS-63 holder.

(Photo courtesy Bowers and Merena)

Mintage: 115,085

Finest Knowns*:

    PCGS MS-62 (1)

    NGC MS-62 (1)

    PCGS MS-61 (3)

    NGC MS-61 (3)

    PCGS MS-60 (4)

    NGC MS-60 (7)**

    PCGS AU-58 (18)**

    NGC AU-58 (161)**

Notable Pedigrees:

    Paramount NENA Sale (1966)

    George F. Scanlon (1973)

    RARCOA CSNS Sale (1975)

    Stack's ANA Sale (1976)

    E.A. Carson (1976)

    T. Henry Allen (1977)

    Stack's M.F. Kortjohn Sale (1979)

    Bowers and Merena January Sale (1994)

    Bowers and Merena September Sale (1994)

    Bowers and Merena January Sale (1995)

    Stacks June Sale (1995)
      ex: Stack's ANA (1976)

    Heritage ANA (1995)

    Bowers and Merena January Sale (1996)

    Kingswood Coin Auctions June (1998)

    Henry S. Lang (2002)

    Eagle Collection January (2002)

    Nevada Collection (Current)

Survival Estimates in All Grades: 2,000-2,500

Estimated in Uncirculated: 18-30

Estimated in XF to AU: 1,600-2,000

Total Certified Examples in All Grades (PCGS and NGC)*: 1,390

(* As of April 2003)
(** Possible resubmissions of several of the same coins.)

REFLECTIONS:

In 1874, it was time for the Carson City Mint to reload and kick gold coin production up a notch. Double eagle output reached the 100,000 coin mark for the first time since the facility opened, with much of the bullion coming from deposits made the previous year. In comparison, San Francisco's double eagle mintage increased by 173,400, representing a 16 ½% rise.

With Carson City's multiplying $20 gold piece production, larger quantities were being shipped out of state, though sufficient reserves were required locally to meet depositors' redemptions.

As a result of the higher mintages, an even higher survival rate prevails. Many 1874-CC double eagles extant today have returned from lands outside of the United States where hundreds of thousands of all denominations of gold coins were exported between 1871 and 1936.

Along with increased production, the quality improved on the double eagles at Carson City, as luster, color, and strike on most high grade 1874-CC double eagles is more appealing than that seen on examples from earlier years.

There is a tendency toward roughness in areas on the surfaces of many 1874-CC double eagles, often thought to be the result of a slightly different type of gold bullion ore from the Comstock mines.

(Photo courtesy Bowers and Merena)

Mintage: III,I5I

Finest Knowns*:**

    PCGS MS-64 (I)

    PCGS MS-63 (I2)

    NGC MS-63 (I9)

    PCGS MS-62 (I09)

    NGC MS-62 (I22)

    PCGS MS-6I (80)

    NGC MS-6I (II5)

    PCGS MS-60 (70)

    NGC MS-60 (70)

Notable Pedigrees:***

    J.F. Bell (1944)

    Belden E. Roach (1944)

    R.L. Miles (1968)

    Clark E. Gilhousen (1973)

    E.A. Carson (1976)

    RARCOA Auction '79 (1979)

    NERCA ANA Sale (1979)

    Paramount Auction '80 (1980)

    Steve Ivy ANA Sale (1980)

    Earl Victor Tuttle (1981)

    Raymond J. Wayman (1981)

Stack's Auction '81 (1981)

Bowers and Merena January Sale (1993)

Stack's October Sale (1994)

Heritage June Sale (1998)

Bowers and Merena August Sale (1998)

Heritage February Sale (1999)

Harry W. Bass, Jr. (1999 & 2000)

Heritage February Sale (2000)

H. Jeff Browning (2001)

Bowers and Merena August Sale (2001)

Eagle Collection January (2002)

Henry S. Lang (2002)

Nevada Collection (Current)

Survival Estimates in All Grades: .. 2,800-3,600

Estimated in Uncirculated: 650-800

Estimated in XF to AU: 1,900-2,500

Total Certified Examples in All Grades (PCGS and NGC)*: 2,0I5

(* As of April 2003)

(** Because of the large quantities numerous resubmissions and crossovers possible.)

(*** There were nearly 100 auction appearances of this date in Uncirculated condition during the century ending in 1981. Since then, the pace has remained steady. This list is an abridgement of those numerous appearances.)

REFLECTIONS:

Bonanza times kept gold flowing from Comstock mines during the mid-1870s and yields gradually increased to four to five times the levels of when the Carson Mint opened in 1870. But as mining production boomed, the local mint's percentage of deposits grew increasingly slimmer. Still there were sufficient amounts of gold bullion on hand and being deposited to keep the mint's gold coinage department busy. Silver coin production of course, began to escalate in 1875.

Mintage totals for $20 double eagles at Carson City were practically equal to those of the previous year, though survival rates are estimated to be 35 to 40% higher. Once again, the quality of double eagles struck in 1875 was of a very high caliber. This aside, it is a little surprising that the highest grade known for this date is one lone MS-64 coin, but at the same time, many examples exist in MS-63.

One point to consider is that although the estimated extant populations of these mid-1870s "CC" double eagles are much higher than others in the series, it does not mean that they are common coins. For example, another "CC" issue, the 1879-CC silver dollar is considered a key date in Uncirculated condition, even though 4,100 Mint State pieces were distributed in the GSA sales. In comparison, estimates for the extant population of Uncirculated 1875-CC double eagles is $1/6$ that amount.

(Photo courtesy Bowers and Merena)

Mintage: 138,441

Finest Knowns*:**

    NGC MS-64 (1)

    NGC MS-63 (4)

    PCGS MS-62 (45)

    NGC MS-62 (57)

    PCGS MS-61 (28)

    NGC MS-61 (73)

    PCGS MS-60 (44)

    NGC MS-60 (49)

Notable Pedigrees:

    Numis. Gall. *Memorable Collection* (1948)

    Samuel W. Wolfson (1962)

    Stack's June Sale (1973)

    RARCOA CSNS Sale (1975)

    Bowers & Ruddy *Kensington* Sale (1975)

    E.A. Carson (1976)

    NERCA FUN Sale (1980)

    NASCA April Sale (1981)

    Robert W. Miller, Sr. (1992)

    Bowers and Merena May Sale (1993)

    Bowers and Merena January Sale (1994)

    Bowers and Merena September Sale (1994)

    Bowers and Merena November Sale (1995)

    Bowers and Merena August Sale (1998)

    Heritage ANA Sale (1998)

    Superior June Sale (1999)

    Harry W. Bass, Jr. (2000)

    Eagle Collection January (2002)

    Nevada Collection (Current)

Survival Estimates in All Grades:	**3,500-4,500**
Estimated in Uncirculated:	**325-375**
Estimated in XF to AU:	**2,750-3,500**
Total Certified Examples in All Grades (PCGS and NGC)*:	**2,308**

(* As of April 2003)

(** Large quantities equate to numerous resubmissions and crossovers.)

REFLECTIONS

This was the final year of the Type II design on $20 double eagles, featuring *TWENTY D.* on the reverse, and also the Carson City Mint's peak year of coinage production. A record number of 138,441 1876-CC double eagles were delivered during this year when national production of this denomination reached its highest level since 1873. Silver coin production at the Carson Mint also rose to record proportions in this centennial year.

From a technical standpoint, the quality of workmanship on 1876-CC double eagles receives high marks, yet because of repeated shipping and handling, eye appeal, at least from a collector's viewpoint, is often less than desirable. There are, however, several very attractive examples in Choice Uncirculated, one in particular having been graded by NGC as an MS-64.

Several hoards of 1876-CC double eagles entered the market during the 1990s, greatly expanding the population base of Uncirculated examples, with more than 100 Mint State coins being added. Although the value of 1876-CCs declined relative to other dates in the series, at the same time, interest in "CC" gold coins was on the rise, causing prices for 1876-CC double eagles to rebound. Through it all, values for MS-62 to MS-63 specimens remained steady. The table at right shows the wholesale prices for 1876-CC double eagles in 1993, 1996 and 2003.

PRICES FOR 1876-CC DOUBLE EAGLES FROM 1993 TO 2003					
YEAR	VF	XF	AU	MS-60	MS-63
1993	$450	$525	$725	$7,000	$24,000
1996	490	530	725	2,400	24,000
2003	785	910	1,100	2,800	24,000

Gold $20 double eagles were produced in greater quantities than all other gold coins at the Carson City Mint. Both the "Type II" and "Type III" varieties were minted there.

1877-CC

(Photo courtesy Bowers and Merena)

Mintage: 42,565

Finest Knowns*:**

    PCGS MS-62 (1)

    NGC MS-62 (4)

    PCGS MS-61 (7)

    NGC MS-61 (3)

    PCGS MS-60 (9)

    NGC MS-60 (8)

    PCGS AU-58 (24)

    NGC AU-58 (71)

Notable Pedigrees:

    J.F. Bell (1944)

    R.L. Miles (1968)

    Donald Groves (1974)

    Bowers & Ruddy January Sale (1975)

    RARCOA CSNS Sale (1975)

    E.A. Carson (1976)

    Paramount NASC Sale (1977)

    Bowers & Ruddy ANA Sale (1978)

    RARCOA Auction '79 (1979)

Stack's December Sale (1979)

Stack's Auction '80 (1980)

Bowers and Merena May Sale (1993)

Bowers and Merena January Sale (1994)

Stack's May Sale (1995)

Bowers and Merena August Sale (1998)

Bowers and Merena October Sale (2000)

Harry W. Bass, Jr. (2000)

Heritage ANA Sale (2001)

H. Jeff Browning (2001)

Eagle Collection January (2002)

Henry S. Lang (2002)

Nevada Collection (Current)

Survival Estimates in All Grades: ...	**1,000-1,300**
Estimated in Uncirculated:	**35-40**
Estimated in XF to AU:	**800-1,000**
Total Certified Examples in All Grades (PCGS and NGC)*:	**916**

(* As of April 2003)

(** Possible resubmissions of several or more of the same coins.)

Reflections:

A new design for double eagles debuted in 1877 that included several notable changes: on the obverse, a trimmer portrait of Ms. Liberty is well positioned within the diameter of the coin, causing a greater distance between her neck and the date; on the reverse, the scrolls surrounding the eagle were widened, causing the curves to nearly touch the letters in the newly designed *TWENTY DOLLARS*.

Yields from the Comstock mines were the highest in the history of that legendary region, but since a progressively smaller percentage of the gold ore was being deposited at the Carson City Mint, that facility seemingly lost a great opportunity when its gold coin production suddenly took a sharp drop in 1877. Double eagle mintages fell nearly 70% from the previous year's total, and overall gold coin output declined from $2.85 million in 1876 to $928,020 in 1877.

Higher than average survival rates for the 1877-CC double eagles provide collectors with an adequate supply to choose from in grades below MS-61, but above that, the population is rather diminutive. Only a handful of examples of this date grade as high as MS-62, with none better.

1878-CC

(Photo courtesy Bowers and Merena)

Mintage: 13,180

Finest Knowns*:**

    PCGS MS-62 (2)

    PCGS MS-61 (2)

    NGC MS-61 (2)

    NGC MS-60 (2)

    PCGS AU-58 (7)

    NGC AU-58 (21)

    PCGS AU-55 (21)

    NGC AU-55 (22)

    PCGS AU-53 (18)

    NGC AU-53 (14)

Notable Pedigrees:

    World's Greatest Collection (1946)

    R.L. Miles (1968)

    Stack's Bryant, Mathey, Long (1973)

    RARCOA Auction '80 (1980)

    Raymond J. Wayman (1981)

    RARCOA Auction '88 (1988)

Akers Auction '90 (1990)

Bowers and Merena May Sale (1993)

Bowers and Merena November MHS Sale (1994)

Superior September Sale (1996)

Heritage Mid-Winter ANA (1998)

Harry W. Bass, Jr. (1999)

H. Jeff Browning (2001)

Eagle Collection January (2002)

Henry S. Lang (2002)

Nevada Collection (Current)

Survival Estimates in All Grades: 390-450

Estimated in Uncirculated: 10-12

Estimated in XF to AU: 310-360

Total Certified Examples in All Grades (PCGS and NGC)*: 368

(* As of April 2003)

(** Possible resubmissions and crossovers of several of the coins on this list.)

REFLECTIONS:

From the collector's viewpoint, just when it seemed as if "CC" double eagles had become less of a challenge, the 1878-CC appeared and brought everyone back to reality. This is true, in spite of a higher than average survival rate for the date. Considering that the original mintage was only 13,180, even a relatively high 3% survival rate results in a much smaller extant population than the Carson City issues of 1874 through 1877.

On the West Coast, the San Francisco Mint reached its highest double eagle output of the 1870s, while the Carson City Mint only managed to score its third lowest of that decade. Gold deposits fell below the $1 million mark for the first time since the Carson Mint had opened in 1870, and gold coin production was slashed by nearly two thirds.

For a date with such a low mintage, there are more Uncirculated specimens of the 1878-CC than might be expected, and a relatively generous supply of AU examples is also available.

Prices for choice AU-58 pieces typically run 60 to 80% of MS-60 wholesale bids, and in AU-50 through AU-55, prices are generally about half of this amount. Problem-free examples in XF currently offer good value at anywhere near listed retail prices (2003).

As a point of reference, in the 1960s, an 1878-CC double eagle pedigreed to Milton Kaufman was reportedly assigned a grade of MS-65 or thereabouts. This specimen is unknown today, but if it ever surfaces and proves to be anywhere near this condition it will definitely be the finest known.

(Photo courtesy Bowers and Merena)

Mintage: 10,708

Finest Knowns*;**

NGC MS-62 (1)

PCGS MS-61 (6)

NGC MS-61 (15)

PCGS MS-60 (1)

NGC MS-60 (2)

PCGS AU-58 (4)

NGC AU-58 (22)

PCGS AU-55 (8)

NGC AU-55 (15)

PCGS AU-53 (15)

NGC AU-53 (13)

Notable Pedigrees:

Milton A. Holmes (1960)

Clark E. Gilhousen (1973)

George F. Scanlon (1973)

RARCOA CSNS Sale (1975)

E.A. Carson (1976)

NERCA MNY Sale (1978)

RARCOA Auction '79 (1979)

NERCA ANA Sale (1979)

Richard J. Wayman (1981)

Amon G. Carter, Jr. (1984)

Stack's Auction '86 (1986)

    ex: R.J. Wayman

Bowers and Merena May Sale (1993)

Bowers and Merena January Sale (1994)

Stack's October Sale (1994)

Bowers and Merena August Sale (1998)

Heritage ANA Sale (1998)

Heritage February Sale (1999)

Superior June Sale (1999)

Nevada Collection (2000)

Harry W. Bass, Jr. (2000)

Richard Genaitis (2001)***

Heritage ANA Sale (2001)***

H. Jeff Browning (2001)

Eagle Collection January (2002)

Henry S. Lang (2002)

Nevada Collection (Current)

Survival Estimates in All Grades:	390-435
Estimated in Uncirculated:	25-30
Estimated in XF to AU:	340-360
Total Certified Examples in All Grades (PCGS and NGC)*:	358

(* As of April 2003)

(** Possible resubmissions and crossovers of several or more coins of the coins on this list.)

(*** Two different Uncirculated specimens in the same sale.)

REFLECTIONS:

New Director of the Mint Horatio C. Burchard, and Secretary of the Treasury John Sherman pondered the immediate future of the Carson City Mint in the first few months of 1879; they made a decision to place it on a reduced work schedule and await further developments. Gold deposits had diminished to the point where less than $325,000 worth of gold coins could be manufactured in a year, while everyone knew that the San Francisco Mint could do that much in a day.

It was also during the last half of 1879 that the Treasury decided to make a concerted effort to produce more $5 and $10 gold pieces, which would for a while, decrease the demand for $20 double eagles. For the Carson

City Mint, the net result of these decisions and events was the lowest $10 eagle mintage in its history, and the second lowest double eagle mintage of its first 10 years of operations.

Despite the low mintage of double eagles in 1879 at Carson City, the estimated surviving population is remarkably high, with perhaps as many as 3% to 4% of the original mintage extant today. PCGS and NGC alone have certified over 350 examples, a total probably inflated somewhat due to resubmissions.

At one time this date was thought to be much scarcer than it actually is, especially in Mint State. In fact, in David Akers' monumental book on double eagles, it is stated that "mint state specimens..., are for all practical purposes non-existent."[1] Today there are approximately 25 1879-CC double eagles grading Uncirculated, due in part to an unexpected hoard of 10 or so Mint State specimens entering the market in late 2002.

Collectors may also find relief in knowing that specimens of 1879-CC double eagles in AU are relatively easy to locate; but of course, price is always a factor, and because of this date's low mintage, examples will tend to cost a bit more than the higher population might suggest.

---

[1] *Double Eagles, An Analysis of Auction Records,* David W. Akers, 1982.

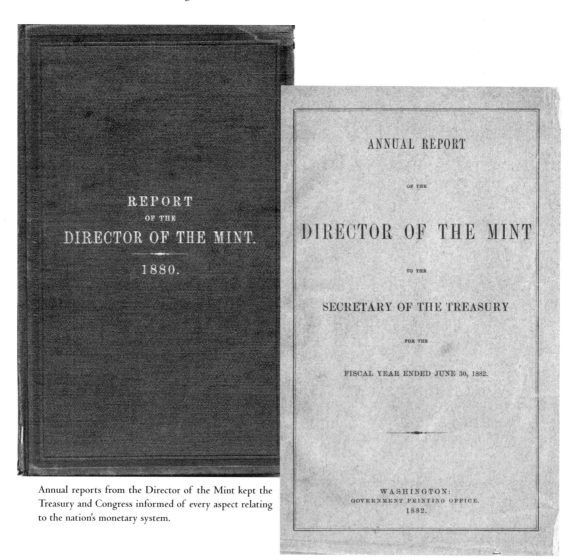

Annual reports from the Director of the Mint kept the Treasury and Congress informed of every aspect relating to the nation's monetary system.

(Photo courtesy Bowers and Merena)

Mintage: 39,140

Finest Knowns*:**

    PCGS MS-62 (9)

    NGC MS-62 (17)

    PCGS MS-61 (17)

    NGC MS-61 (14)

    PCGS MS-60 (5)

    NGC MS-60 (19)

Notable Pedigrees:

    J.F. Bell (1944)

    World's Greatest Collection (1946)

    R.L. Miles (1968)

    Bowers and Merena May Sale (1972)

    George F. Scanlon (1973)

    Stack's Auction '79 (1979)

    Stack's Kortjohn Sale (1979)

    Bowers and Merena June Sale (1991)

    Stack's March Sale (1992)

    Bowers & Merena May Sale (1993)

    Bowers and Merena January Sale (1994)

    Superior January/February Sale (1994)

    Stack's October Sale (1994)

    Bowers and Merena August Sale (1998)

    Heritage CSNS Sale (1999)

    Heritage ANA Sale (1999)

    Harry W. Bass, Jr. (1999 & 2000)

    H. Jeff Browning (2001)

    Heritage October Sale (2001)

    Henry S. Lang (2002)

    Nevada Collection (Current)

Survival Estimates in All Grades:	1,200-1,500
Estimated in Uncirculated:	70-90
Estimated in XF to AU:	1,000-1,250
Total Certified Examples in All Grades (PCGS and NGC)*:	1,031

(* As of April 2003)

(** Possible resubmissions and crossovers of several of the coins on this list.)

REFLECTIONS:

Double eagle production at the Carson City Mint was divided into three time periods: 1870 through 1879, 1882 to 1885, and 1889 through 1893. The gap of two years in the mintage of $20 gold pieces at Carson City from 1880 to 1881 was the result of unconnected circumstances: deposits from Comstock miners diminished to stunted levels as mineral ore yields were all but expended, which in turn caused temporary coinage suspensions, limiting the Carson City Mint to no more than five months of production annually during those two years. In addition to these local events, double eagle output was decreased on a national scale as the Treasury implemented its new policy of expanding the distribution of $5 and $10 gold pieces.

It was the Treasury's conviction that if more gold coins in denominations less than twenty dollars were in reserve at Mint offices around the country, depositors would accept these coins in payment in lieu of waiting for additional double eagles to be struck. As stated in the Director of the Mint's *Annual Report*, "while the law gives the depositor the option into what denominations his bullion shall be coined, if in lieu of waiting for such coins to be struck he asserts his right to be paid the value out of the bullion funds kept by the Treasury at the Mint...he must take such funds and denominations as are lawfully provided."[1]

With Carson City's ever diminishing bullion transactions, this was of course less significant than at the other

[1] *Annual Report of the Director of the Mint*, 1880.

mints, but nonetheless, if there had been occasion to coin double eagles at Carson City in 1880 and 1881, the Treasury's adopted policy would have squelched it.

But finally in 1882, double eagles were once again being minted at Carson City to the tune of $782,800 in face value, a respectable figure considering that none had been produced there for two years, and the last time any had been, in 1879, the face value had only totaled $214,160.

This date is readily available in XF to AU, and though not as accessible in Mint State as the 1875-CC or 1876-CC, is still much more available than any of the other dates from the 1870s; however, in spite of a rather generous population of Uncirculated examples, to date none have been graded above MS-62.

In the Mint State category, prices start at $5,000, with Choice AU specimens currently priced at less than $2,700 and representing good value (2003).

1883-CC

(Photo courtesy Bowers and Merena)

Mintage: 59,962

Finest Knowns*:**

    PCGS MS-63 (2)

    NGC MS-63 (3)

    PCGS MS-62 (9)

    NGC MS-62 (12)

    PCGS MS-61 (25)

    NGC MS-61 (35)

    PCGS MS-60 (12)

    NGC MS-60 (27)

    PCGS AU-58 (40)

    NGC AU-58 (172)

Notable Pedigrees:

    J.F. Bell (1944)

    George H. Hall (1945)

    William C. Atwater (1946)

    Abe Kosoff ANA Sale (1968)

    R.L. Miles (1968)

    George F. Scanlon (1973)

    Stack's *Westchester* Sale (1973)

    Donald Groves (1974)

    RARCOA CSNS Sale (1975)

    Superior ANA Sale (1975)

    E.A. Carson (1976)

    Stack's ANA Sale (1976)

NERCA MNY Sale (1978)

Stack's Auction '79 (1979)

Kagin's MANA Sale (1979)

Stack's Kortjohn Sale (1979)

NERCA July Sale (1980)

RARCOA Auction '80 (1980)

Robert W. Miller, Sr. (1992)

Bowers and Merena November Sale (1992)

Bowers and Merena May Sale (1993)

Bowers and Merena January Sale (1994)

Bowers and Merena August Sale (1998)

Harry W. Bass, Jr. (2000)

H. Jeff Browning (2001)

Eagle Collection January (2002)

Henry S. Lang (2002)

Nevada Collection (Current)

Survival Estimates in All Grades: 1,500-1,800
Estimated in Uncirculated: 130-160
Estimated in XF to AU: 1,200-1,450
Total Certified Examples in All Grades (PCGS and NGC)*: 1,321

(* As of April 2003)

(** Possible resubmissions and crossovers of several of the coins on this list.)

REFLECTIONS:

By 1883, yields from the Comstock mines were staging a minor comeback, and nearly all of the output was being deposited at the Carson City Mint for processing. This fueled resuscitated coinage operations at the local minting facility, which had begun in 1882. Gold coin production at Carson City had climbed back over the $1 million mark in 1882, and rose another 9 1/2% in 1883.

Double eagle production once again led the way in gold coin output for this mint, with nearly 60,000 pieces, representing $1.2 million in coin value. Exports of U.S. gold coinage had rebounded sharply from 1882 through 1883 and it is plausible that local Comstock depositors were enticed to ship large percentages of their double eagles to San Francisco for this purpose.

Many 1883-CC $20 gold pieces remained in the western states, mostly as backup reserves in bank vaults, where they did not circulate, but instead were sealed in canvas bags in quantities of 250 or 500. Though not acquiring the wear associated with circulation, these big gold coins were subject to heavy contact marks and friction, explaining why on a date as readily available as the 1883-CC, Choice Uncirculated specimens are in such short supply.

Estimated survival rates for this date are in the 2 1/2 to 3% range, placing it near the top of the list of most common dates in the "CC" double eagle series. Currently, prices in AU and below are very reasonable (2003). For Uncirculated specimens, collectors should be very selective and patient since there are sufficient supplies to choose from, though because of the appeal of "CC" gold coins in Mint State condition there will not be much relief price-wise.

(Photo courtesy Bowers and Merena)

Mintage: 81,139

Finest Knowns*:**

    PCGS MS-63 (3)

    NGC MS-63 (4)

    PCGS MS-62 (21)

    NGC MS-62 (43)

    PCGS MS-61 (33)

    NGC MS-61 (94)

    PCGS MS-60 (59)

    NGC MS-60 (72)

Notable Pedigrees:

    George H. Hall (1945)

    World's Greatest Collection (1946)

    Farish Baldenhofer (1955)

    R.L. Miles (1968)

    George F. Scanlon (1973)

    RARCOA CSNS Sale (1975)

    E.A. Carson (1976)

    Reed Hawn (1977)

    Stack's Kortjohn Sale (1979)

    Stack's Auction '81 (1981)

      ex: Reed Hawn

Richard J. Wayman (1981)

Amon G. Carter, Jr. (1984)

Stack's Auction '84 (1984)

Bowers and Merena May Sale (1993)

Superior January/February Sale (1994)

Bowers and Merena May Sale (1995)

Kingswood Coin Auctions January (1996)

Kingswood Coin Auctions June (1998)

Bowers and Merena August Sale (1998)

Bowers and Merena June Sale (2000)

Superior June Sale (2000)

H. Jeff Browning (2001)

Henry S. Lang (Not Sold) (2002)

Nevada Collection (Current)

Survival Estimates in All Grades: 2,200-2,600

Estimated in Uncirculated: 340-390

Estimated in XF to AU: 1,600-1,900

Total Certified Examples in All Grades (PCGS and NGC)*: 1,906

(* As of April 2003)

(** Possible resubmissions and crossovers of several of the coins on this list. Over 300 listings for AU-58 coins were reported. No one will ever know how many of these are resubmissions, or how many will eventually upgrade to the Mint State category.)

REFLECTIONS:

In 1884, the Carson City Mint reached a creditable level of gold coinage, producing $1.8 million in face value, the fourth highest total between 1870 and 1889. This, of course, occurred during the third consecutive year of steady silver dollar production at the Carson Mint, as throughout 1884, monthly averages for silver dollar mintages ran about 95,000 pieces, added to the approximately 6,500 double eagles struck each month. These quotas combined with the much smaller $10 eagle and $5 half eagle outputs, kept a full crew busy all year.

The estimated survival rate for 1884-CC double eagles is consistent with the two preceding years, and because of the higher original mintage, it is the most common date "CC" double eagle from the 1880s. In fact, it is probably the fourth most common date in the series, possibly tied with the 1874-CC.

Occasionally, small groups of Uncirculated examples will appear all at once, as in Superior's January 1994 sale when three Mint State pieces were offered. Previously unknown hoards of 1884-CC double eagles continue to enter the market from time to time, yet the likelihood of any considerable change in the number extant seems slim.

Current values seem very reasonable in all grades up to AU-58, yet caution should be exercised when purchasing examples in MS-60 to MS-62 because of the effect that even small population increases will have on future values.

The highest graded examples of this date available today are a limited selection of MS-63s, with the finest among that small group predictably bringing justifiable premiums.

1885-CC

(Photo courtesy Bowers and Merena)

Mintage: 9,450

Finest Knowns*:

    PCGS MS-63 (1)

    PCGS MS-62 (9)**

    NGC MS-62 (6)

    PCGS MS-61 (8)**

    NGC MS-61 (3)**

    PCGS MS-60 (5)**

    NGC MS-60 (6)**

    PCGS AU-58 (20)**

    NGC AU-58 (29)**

Notable Pedigrees:

    World's Greatest Collection (1946)

    William C. Atwater (1946)

    Charles M. Williams (Menjou) (1950)

    R.L. Miles (1968)

    Clark E. Gilhousen (1973)

    Superior October Sale (1974)

    Donald Groves (1974)

    Superior ANA Sale (1975)

    E.A. Carson (1976)

    NERCA MNY Sale (1978)

    NERCA FUN Sale (1980)

    Bowers and Ruddy August Sale (1980)

    Richard J. Wayman (1981)

    Amon G. Carter, Jr. (1984)

    Stack's Auction '85 (1985)

    Stack's Auction '86 (1986)

    Bowers and Merena January Sale (1994)

    Stack's June Sale (1994)

    Bowers and Merena January Sale (1997)

    Bowers and Merena August Sale (1998)

    Heritage September Sale (1999)

    Harry W. Bass, Jr. (2000)

    Stack's June Sale (2001)

    H. Jeff Browning (2001)

    Eagle Collection January (2002)

    Henry S. Lang (2002)

    Nevada Collection (Current)

Survival Estimates in All Grades:	375-435
Estimated in Uncirculated:	40-50
Estimated in XF to AU:	290-325
Total Certified Examples in All Grades (PCGS and NGC)*:	354

(* As of April 2003)

(** Possible resubmissions and crossovers of several of the coins on this list.)

REFLECTIONS:

During the first two months of 1885, operations proceeded much as they had throughout 1884 at the Carson Mint. Then on March 8, Superintendent James Crawford died, and a series of events unrelated to Crawford's death spelled short term deprivation for this Nevada landmark. As a requiem for the eminent suspending of operations only silver dollars and double eagles were struck at the Carson City Mint in 1885, one of only two years that annual output was limited to just two denominations.

In contrast to the high quality generally seen on the 1885-CC silver dollars, double eagles from that year tend to be substandard; as a result of the low mintage and slightly inferior workmanship, the number of eye appealing examples of the 1885-CC double eagle is sparse. Uncirculated specimens, though occasionally seen with a lustrous golden yellow color, are mostly silhouetted by a sooty effect, making them appear dirty. Excessive contact marks and friction are also detracting.

All negatives aside, this date, when available, is very desirable in accurately graded Mint State condition, and specimens possessing above average eye appeal will command very strong premiums.

If it had not been for a small hoard of 1885-CC double eagles that entered the market in the early years of the 21st century, the population of Uncirculated specimens would be much lower. At one time it was estimated that only 10 to 15 Uncirculated examples existed, but now the figure is closer to 40 to 50. This date's low mintage will, similar to the 1879-CC, most assuredly sustain its value in spite of a gradually increasing population base.

1889-CC

(Photo courtesy Bowers and Merena)

Mintage: 30,945

Finest Knowns*:*

    PCGS MS-64 (1)

    PCGS MS-63 (3)**

    PCGS MS-62 (60)**

    NGC MS-62 (17)**

    PCGS MS-61 (29)**

    NGC MS-61 (13)**

    PCGS MS-60 (29)**

    NGC MS-60 (17)**

Notable Pedigrees:

    R.L. Miles (1968)

    Stack's ANA Sale (1971)

    George F. Scanlon (1973)

    Stack's MNY Sale (1974)

    RARCOA CSNS Sale (1975)

    E.A. Carson (1976)

    T. Henry Allen (1977)

    Stack's Kortjohn Sale (1979)

    Stack's Auction '79 (1979)

    Stack's Auction '81 (1981)

Richard J. Wayman (1981)

Norweb Collection (1988)

Bowers and Merena ANA Sale (1991)

Bowers and Merena May Sale (1993)

Bowers and Merena January Sale (1994)

Bowers and Merena September Sale (1994)

Heritage ANA Sale (1998)

Heritage ANA (1999)

Nevada Collection (2000)

H. Jeff Browning (2001)

Eagle Collection January (2002)

Henry S. Lang (2002)

Survival Estimates in All Grades: 1,100-1,250

Estimated in Uncirculated: 175-195

Estimated in XF to AU: 835-1,000

Total Certified Examples in All Grades (PCGS and NGC)*: 976

(* As of April 2003)

(** Possible resubmissions and crossovers of several of the coins on this list.)

REFLECTIONS:

Coinage operations, suspended since March of 1885 at Carson City, resumed on October 1, 1889, when after five months of renovations, silver dollars and double eagles were once again minted. Promises had been made to the Bureau of the Mint every year the Carson facility was closed, "of the readiness on the part of certain producers of bullion to deposit the same at the Mint at Carson instead of sending it to private refineries."[1]

It was unfortunate that the local mint was not operating from 1886 through most of 1889, since Comstock mines experienced a profitable rally during that period. In any event, by the time gold coins were ready to be struck, sufficient supplies of bullion were on hand and nearly 31,000 1889-CC double eagles were struck in the relatively short time before the year ended.

Of this amount it is estimated that 3 1/2 to 4% are extant today, establishing the 1889-CC as one of the more common dates in the "CC" double eagle series. The population base for this date increased substantially between 1993 and 2003, with more continuing to be added on an annual basis.

There is an unusually large quantity of Uncirculated 1889-CC double eagles, but still this date becomes very elusive above MS-62. It is one of only three dates in the CC double eagle series represented by an example in MS-64 condition.

---

[1] *Annual Report of the Director of the Mint, 1886.*

1890-CC

(Photo courtesy Bowers and Merena)

Mintage: 91,209

Finest Knowns*:

    PCGS MS-63 (1)

    PCGS MS-62 (23)**

    NGC MS-62 (15)**

    PCGS MS-61 (45)**

    NGC MS-61 (44)**

    PCGS MS-60 (41)**

    NGC MS-60 (51)**

Notable Pedigrees:

    J.F. Bell (1944)

    World's Greatest Collection (1946)

    William C. Atwater (1946)

    Golden Sale of the Century (1962)

    R.L. Miles (1968)

    Paramount ANA Sale (1969)

    Donald Groves (1974)

    RARCOA CSNS Sale (1975)

    Stack's ANA Sale (1976)

    Reed Hawn (1977)

    RARCOA Auction '79 (1979)

    Stack's Kortjohn Sale (1979)

    Paramount Auction '80 (1980)

    Stack's Auction '81(1981)

    Raymond J. Wayman (1981)

    Louis E. Eliasberg (1982)

    RARCOA Auction '89 (1989)

    Heritage ANA Sale (1990)

    Bowers and Merena May Sale (1993)

    Bowers and Merena January Sale (1994)

    Superior January/February Sale (1994)

    Bowers and Merena May Sale (1994)

    Heritage March Sale (1999)

    Bowers and Merena August Sale (1999)

    Stack's October Sale (1999)

    Heritage ANA Sale (2001)

    Henry S. Lang (2002)

    Nevada Collection (Current)

Survival Estimates in All Grades: 2,600-3,100

Estimated in Uncirculated: 225-300

Estimated in XF to AU: 2,150-2,550

Total Certified Examples in All
    Grades (PCGS and NGC)*: 2,303

(* As of April 2003)

(** Possible resubmissions and crossovers of several of the coins on this list.)

REFLECTIONS:

Thanks to a new silver purchase act and increased gold deposits in 1890, the Carson City Mint experienced one of the most productive years in its volatile history. In fact, in terms of the face value of all coins produced, 1890 was the third highest out of 21 years of coinage operations. This year was also the fourth highest for gold coin production, as well as the fourth highest annual mintage of double eagles, cover-ing the entire span of time the facility struck coins.

Hundreds of thousands of U.S. $20 double eagles were exported during the first few years of the 1890s, the bulk from the San Francisco Mint, but also large percentages of the relatively small mintages from Carson City. Large scale meltdowns of millions of these gold coins from the nation's mints have drastically reduced the extant populations of U.S. double eagles.

Survival estimates for the 1890-CC double eagles range from 2.8% to 3.3%, positioning the date as one of the three most common in the "CC" series. Uncirculated examples are plentiful and there are generous quantities of Choice AU pieces. As of 2003, PCGS and NGC had certified over 400 AU-58 1890-CC's, and even factoring in multiple resubmissions, some of these will probably upgrade to the Mint State level in the future.

Sketch of a Comstock miner meeting up with the V&T Railroad.

(Photo courtesy Bowers and Merena)

Mintage: 5,000

Finest Knowns*:**

    PCGS MS-63 (1)

    PCGS MS-62 (2)

    NGC MS-62 (14)**

    PCGS MS-61 (4)**

    NGC MS-61 (9)**

    PCGS MS-60 (5)**

    NGC MS-60 (6)**

    PCGS AU-58 (15)**

    NGC AU-58 (30)**

Notable Pedigrees:

    Belden E. Roach (1944)

    J.F. Bell (1944)

    Samuel W. Wolfson (1962)

    R.L. Miles (1968)

    Alto Collection (1970)

    Clark E. Gilhousen (1973)

    Stack's MNY Sale June (1974)

    RARCOA CSNS Sale (1975)

    Superior ANA Sale (1975)

    E.A. Carson (1976)

    NERCA MNY Sale March/April (1978)

Superior January Sale (1980)

NERCA MNY Sale April (1980)

Raymond J. Wayman (1981)

Amon G. Carter, Jr. (1984)

Robert W. Miller, Sr. (1992)

Bowers and Merena May Sale (1993)

Bowers and Merena January Sale (1994)

Bowers and Merena August Sale (1998)

Heritage February Sale (1999)

Nevada Collection (2000)

Harry W. Bass, Jr. (2000)

Bowers and Merena June Sale (2000)

H. Jeff Browning (2001)

Bowers and Merena March Sale (2001)

Eagle Collection January (2002)

Henry S. Lang (2002)

Survival Estimates in All Grades:	270-325
Estimated in Uncirculated:	42-50
Estimated in XF to AU:	205-250
Total Certified Examples in All Grades (PCGS and NGC)*:	261

(* As of April 2003)

(** Possible resubmissions and crossovers of several of the coins on this list.)

Reflections:

Because the San Francisco Mint's services were in much greater demand in other areas of coinage production in 1891, the Carson City Mint shared the duty of supplying the nation with gold eagles and half eagles with the Philadelphia Mint. As a result, the approximate $2 million in gold that was used to strike the eagles and half eagles left only $100,000 from bullion deposits to produce $20 double eagles at Carson City. This scant mintage of 5,000 pieces is the second lowest in the "CC" double eagle series, with only the 1870-CC recording a smaller quantity.

Yet small mintages and a common mintmark are the only traits shared by the 1870-CC and 1891-CC as these two dates are miles apart in terms of rarity and price. An estimated survival rate of 5% to 6% for the 1891-CC is inordinately high for this series; consequently, what should be an extremely scarce date is only moderately so, especially in Mint State grades. A telltale sign of why this is so can be observed in the relatively large quantities of 1891-CC double eagles that have been imported in recent years. Apparently a significant percentage of these were exported along with the multitudes of other U.S. gold coins during the 1890s.

Discoveries of these coins on foreign soil are still being made: for example a rather large group of Uncirculated 1891-CC double eagles entered the market in the early years of the 21st century. As a result of a rather swollen population of Mint State examples for such a low mintage date, the 1891-CC appears to be currently overvalued in Uncirculated condition. (2003).

PRICE COMPARISON BETWEEN 1870-CC AND 1891-CC DOUBLE EAGLES[*]			
DATE	VF	XF	AU
1870-CC	$85,000	$115,000	$160,000
1891-CC	3,500	5,500	8,500

[*]As of 2003

1892-CC

(Photo courtesy Bowers and Merena)

Mintage: 27,265

Finest Knowns*:**

    PCGS MS-63 (4)

    NGC MS-63 (4)

    PCGS MS-62 (24)

    NGC MS-62 (25)

    PCGS MS-61 (28)

    NGC MS-61 (41)

    PCGS MS-60 (23)

    NGC MS-60 (27)

Notable Pedigrees:

    William C. Atwater (1946)

    Federal Coin Ex. FUN Sale (1963)

    R.L. Miles (1968)

    Clark E. Gilhousen (1973)

    George F. Scanlon (1973)

    Stack's MNY Sale June (1974)

    Donald Groves (1974)

    RARCOA CSNS Sale (1973)

    E.A. Carson (1976)

    Stack's ANA Sale (1976)

    Kagin's ANA Sale (1977)

    NERCA MNY Sale March/April (1978)

    NERCA MNY Sale March/April (1979)

    NERCA ANA Sale (1979)

    Stack's Kortjohn Sale (1979)

    RARCOA Auction '79

    NERCA MNY Sale April (1980)

    RARCOA Auction '80 (1980)

    Steve Ivy ANA Sale (1980)

    Raymond J. Wayman (1981)

    Bowers and Merena November Sale (1992)

    Bowers and Merena May Sale (1993)

    Heritage April Sale (1999)

    Heritage ANA Sale (1999)

    Harry W. Bass, Jr. (1999)

    Heritage February Sale (2000)

    Heritage ANA Sale (2001)

    H. Jeff Browning (2001)

    Eagle Collection January (2002)

    Henry S. Lang (2002)

    Nevada Collection (Current)

Survival Estimates in All Grades: 975-1,150

Estimated in Uncirculated: 180-200

Estimated in XF to AU: 745-880

Total Certified Examples in All Grades (PCGS and NGC)*: 925

(* As of April 2003)

(** Possible resubmissions and crossovers of several of the coins on this list.)

REFLECTIONS:

In the Carson City Mint's penultimate season, it was abundantly clear that miners on the Comstock were beginning to scrape bottom in their search for more gold ore deposits. Yet in 1892 there was sufficient gold and silver on hand to manage another respectable year of coinage production at the local facility. Workers at the Carson Mint would continue to make coins until the bullion ran out, the machinery broke down, the Treasury shut down operations, or any combination of these or other circumstances prevented them from doing so.

A positive factor in Carson City's quest for survival was the continued heavy export demand for gold coins facing the Treasury. Though the Carson Mint's 1892 output of gold coins was only 3% of the total exported from the U.S. that year, Treasury officials would take as much as they could get from whatever source could supply it.

Just like other "CC" dates from the 1890s, the 1892-CC has a relatively high survival rate of 3 $\frac{1}{2}$% to 4%, suggesting that a percentage of the original mintage was included in the exported gold coins sent out from San Francisco's harbor. It was also around this time that the seeds were planted for collectors' interest in mintmarks; perhaps a few choice examples of this date were put away in this respect.

Because of a rather large extant population, examples of the 1892-CC in grades below MS-60 are currently priced at what appear to be reasonable levels. There are a fair amount of MS-63 specimens and though a bit pricey, they still represent good value at current levels (2003), especially if exhibiting above average eye appeal.

1893-CC

(Photo courtesy Bowers and Merena)

Mintage: 18,402

Finest Knowns*:

> NGC MS-64 (1)
>
> PCGS MS-63 (14)
>
> NGC MS-63 (18)**
>
> PCGS MS-62 (94)**
>
> NGC MS-62 (83)**
>
> PCGS MS-61 (53)**
>
> NGC MS-61 (73)**
>
> PCGS MS-60 (36)**
>
> NGC MS-60 (38)**

Notable Pedigrees:

> Belden E. Roach (1944)
>
> J.F. Bell (1944)
>
> Jerome Kern (1950)
>
> R.L. Miles (1968)
>
> Clark E. Gilhousen (1973)
>
> George F. Scanlon (1973)
>
> RARCOA CSNS Sale (1975)
>
> E.A. Carson (1976)
>
> Fairfield Collection (1977)
>
> NERCA MNY Sale March/April (1978)
>
> RARCOA Auction '79 (1979)
>
> Paramount Auction '79 (1979)
>
> NERCA ANA Sale (1979)
>
> Stack's Kortjohn Sale (1979)
>
> NERCA MNY Sale April (1980)
>
> RARCOA Auction '80 (1980)
>
> Steve Ivy ANA Sale (1980)
>
> Richard J. Wayman (1981)
>
> Amon G. Carter, Jr. (1984)
>
> RARCOA Auction '88 (1988)
>
> RARCOA Auction '89 (1989)
>
> Robert W. Miller, Sr. (1992)
>
> Bowers and Merena May Sale (1993)
>
> Heritage March Sale (1998)
>
> Heritage June Sale (1998)
>
> Bowers and Merena August Sale (1998)
>
> Heritage ANA Sale (1998)
>
> Stack's December Sale (1998)
>
> Heritage June Sale (1999)
>
> Harry W. Bass, Jr. (2000)
>
> Heritage ANA Sale (2001)
>
> Stack's June Sale (2001)
>
> Henry S. Lang (2002)
>
> Nevada Collection (Current)

Survival Estimates in All Grades:	1,000-1,250
Estimated in Uncirculated:	450-500
Estimated in XF to AU:	500-650
Total Certified Examples in All Grades (PCGS and NGC)*:	886

(* As of April 2003)

(** Possible resubmissions and crossovers of several of the coins on this list.)

REFLECTIONS:

Whether or not the coiner and his staff at the Carson Mint knew that 1893 would be the finale is debatable. What is evident from the surviving population of 1893-CC double eagles is that the workers put forth extra effort to produce the highest quality coins possible and collectors today can thank them for this. When beholding just about any problem free 1893-CC in AU or above, one can see the superiority of the strike, luster and color.

Additionally, this date is estimated to have a survival rate of between 5 to 7% of its original mintage, and as a result, there is a larger extant population than the low mintage would suggest. This date also boasts one of the most generous populations of Uncirculated specimens, not to mention, a large number of high quality AU pieces, as well as very reasonable prices in grades below MS-63 (as of 2003).

There is a single MS-64 specimen of this date, placing it in the special category of being one of only three "CC" double eagles that have been graded that high.

Since very few collectors will have an opportunity to own an example of the first year in the "CC" double eagle series, the 1893-CC provides a rewarding opportunity to own an eye appealing example from the final year of operations.

COMPARISON OF TOTAL GOLD COIN PRODUCTION AT THE CARSON CITY MINT WITH THE PHILADELPHIA MINT'S FROM 1870 TO 1893

$5 GOLD MINTAGE TOTALS			$10 GOLD MINTAGE TOTALS			$20 GOLD MINTAGE TOTALS		
YEAR	CARSON CITY	PHILADELPHIA	YEAR	CARSON CITY	PHILADELPHIA	YEAR	CARSON CITY	PHILADELPHIA
1870	7,675	4,035	1870	5,908	4,025	1870	3,789	155,185
1871	20,770	3,230	1871	7,185	1,820	1871	14,687	80,150
1872	16,980	1,690	1872	5,500	1,650	1872	29,650	251,880
1873	7,416	112,505	1873	4,543	825	1873	22,410	1,709,825
1874	21,198	3,508	1874	16,767	53,160	1874	115,085	366,800
1875	11,828	220	1875	7,715	120	1875	111,151	295,740
1876	6,887	1,477	1876	4,696	732	1876	138,441	583,905
1877	8,680	1,152	1877	3,332	817	1877	42,565	397,670
1878	9,054	131,740	1878	3,244	73,800	1878	13,180	543,645
1879	17,281	301,950	1879	1,762	384,770	1879	10,708	207,630
1880	51,017	3,166,436	1880	11,190	1,644,876	1882	39,140	630
1881	13,886	5,708,802	1881	24,015	3,877,260	1883	59,962	92
1882	82,817	2,514,568	1882	6,764	2,324,480	1884	81,139	71
1883	12,958	233,461	1883	12,000	208,740	1885	9,450	828
1884	16,402	191,078	1884	9,925	76,905	1889	30,945	44,111
1890	53,800	4,328	1890	17,500	58,043	1890	91,209	75,995
1891	208,000	61,413	1891	103,732	91,868	1891	5,000	1,442
1892	82,968	753,572	1892	40,000	797,552	1892	27,265	4,523
1893	60,000	4,528,197	1893	14,000	1,840,895	1893	18,402	344,339
TOTAL	709,617	17,723,362	TOTAL	299,778	11,442,338	TOTAL	864,178	5,064,461

CHAPTER EIGHT

Early Collector Interest

I have personally written hundreds of letters to dealers and collectors all over the United States regarding Carson City coins for sale. More than 75% answer that they have no Carson City coins of any kind.
-Harold M. Budd, article in *The Numismatist*, August, 1945

During the years the Carson City Mint operated as a coinage facility, collectors were generally unimpressed with "CC" mintmarked coins. In fact, collecting coins issued by any of the branch mints was not much of a priority, as at the time the focus was on pre-1808 coins, patterns, and Proof strikes. In the absence of price guides similar to the *Red Book* introduced in the 20th century, collectors had no way of comparing mintages between various dates, as well as no way of ascertaining relative rarities or values.

As a result, mintmarked coins were ignored in favor of those with established rarities and values. Gradually, as more literature became available on the subject, the learning curve began moving upward. Since knowledge is power and provides confidence and security when making purchasing decisions, collectors began looking for opportunities in the mintmarked coin category during the 1890s, thanks in large part to articles in the fledgling *Numismatist* magazine, distributed by the American Numismatic Association. A feature contributor to this newsletter was Augustus G. Heaton, who had been an ardent collector of mintmarked coins for some time. In 1893, Heaton published a compilation of his essays on the subject in a small pamphlet titled, *A Treatise on the Coinage of the United States Branch Mints.*

Information in Heaton's pamphlet awakened an interest in collecting coins by mintmark that has proliferated in this segment of the hobby up to the present day (2003). One of the most revealing findings from Heaton's study was the relative rarity of Carson City coins in comparison to those from the other mints, which triggered a sudden fixation with "CC" mintmarked coins among collectors.

As mintage figures became more readily available, the low quantities for many of the Carson City dates became obvious to collectors. Of course, a low original mintage does not necessarily equate to extreme rarity, but it is a place to start. Heaton's entire analysis of the relative rarity of dates was based on original mintages. This was in the days before population reports as well as travel limitations. Heaton lived on the East Coast and was not able to search out mintmarked coins in other states; one advantage Heaton did have was his proximity to official U.S. Mint records and to the *Annual Reports of the Director of the Mint*, which provided mintage figures, as well as scores of other pertinent information.

Auction companies in the 1890s did not think twice about the blanket use of adjectives such as "very rare" and "extremely scarce" for any coin with a "CC" mintmark. For instance, in Ed Frossard's June 7, 1894 sale of the *W.M. Friesner Collection*, half the "CC" coins are described as rare or scarce, even the 1883-CC silver dollar.

By the end of the 19th century, auction companies had become well aware of the paucity of "CC" coins in their sales. Certain dates, like the 1873-CC *Without Arrows* dime and quarter, were conspicuously missing from collections; and gold coins from the Carson City Mint also made infrequent appearances. Yet, surprisingly, collector demand still had not reached a level that would dramatically increase prices for these coins.

Part of this incongruity was due to the fact that, notwithstanding lower mintages for many dates in the "CC" series, no one knew for sure what the surviving populations were. But as time passed, it became evident that Carson City coins were in short supply, and prices gradually edged higher. For example, in the 1907 *Matthew Adams Stickney* sale, cataloged by Henry Chapman, an 1870-CC dollar described as Uncirculated, sold for $7, as compared to an 1865 dollar in the same condition that brought $1.75. Likewise, an 1873-CC Seated dollar in VG was purchased for $6.50, compared to an 1859-S dollar in Fine that sold for $2.20. Even the 1875-CC 20-cent piece in Uncirculated at $1, exceeded the price realized of 35 cents for an 1875 Philadelphia 20 cents in similar condition.

Then in May of 1915, the most famous Carson City coin of all time appeared in the *Collection of a Prominent American* sale, featuring the consignments of H.O. Granberg and William Woodin conducted by the U.S. Coin Company (Wayte Raymond). No one knew at the time whether the 1873-CC *Without Arrows* dime in this sale was *Unique*, meaning only one specimen known; but according to previous auction sales, the only other offering of this date appears to have occurred 37 years earlier in the 1878 *John Swan Randall* sale cataloged by Edward Cogan. It is uncertain whether the piece in the Randall sale was in fact the *Without Arrows* variety, but Cogan's description of, "1873 **Old Style** C.C. Mint. Fine impression," [Emphasis added][1] suggests that it was. A lowly price realized of just 17 cents at the *Randall* sale provided no indication of the coin's potential greatness.

Things had changed by the time of the *Granberg* sale in 1915 and the rare dime brought a very impressive price of $170. In the decades since, numismatic researchers have pondered the question of what happened to the *Randall* specimen, all predicated of course upon Cogan's description being accurate. It seems improbable that the two coins are one and the same, based on long standing tradition that the *Woodin* specimen was part of the U.S. Mint's collection from 1874 through 1909, and could not have been for sale at the 1878 auction.

After the 1873-CC *Without Arrows* dime sold in 1915, Carson City coins in general seemed to gain more respect among dealers, collectors, and consequently, prices advanced. Confirmation of this can be seen in the prices realized from another U.S. Coin Company auction held on June 15, 1916, where dealers were buying most of the "CC" coins, no doubt on behalf of their clients. For example, Lyman Low, who counted notable collector Virgil Brand on his client list, bought the following Carson City specialties:

1873-CC Half, Uncirculated - $30

1873-CC Half *Without Arrows*, Uncirculated - $32

1871-CC Quarter, Uncirculated - $24

1871-CC Dime, Uncirculated - $31.50

Another famous dealer from that period, Henry Chapman, outbid all competitors to win the 1873-CC *With Arrows* dime described as "Uncirculated, with mint luster."[2] He paid a record price of $82.50 for this dime that the cataloger declared was, "a splendid companion to the specimen *Without Arrows* which sold in our sale last May for $170."[3] One more notable coin from this auction was an 1872-CC dime, described as being "Uncirculated, proof surface,"[4]

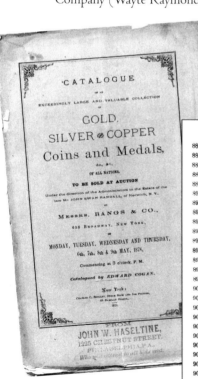

This auction from 1878 with consignments from John Swan Randall featured an 1873-CC *Without Arrows* dime. Note the description for lot #902, "Old style." The price realized was 17 cents. (*Price realized courtesy of Karl Moulton*)

	AMERICAN SILVER.	37
885	1857 O. Mint. Nearly as good. Scarce	
886	1858 Fine impression	
887	1858 O. Mint. Barely fair impression. Scarce	
888	1859 Very fine impression	
889	1859 S. Mint. Poor impression. Scarce	
890	1860 Fine impression	
891	1861 Fine impression	
892	1862 Fine impression	
893	1865 Fine impression	
894	1866 Fine impression. Proof polish	
895	1869 S. Mint. Good impression	
896	1870 Very fair impression	
897	1871 C. C. Mint. Fine impression. Almost proof	
898	1871 S. Mint. Uncirculated	
899	1872 C. C. Mint. Good impression	
900	1872 S. Mint. Fine impression	
901	1873 Old style. Fair impression	
902	1873 Old style. C. C. Mint. Fine impression	
903	1873 New style. Fine impression	
904	1873 New style. S. Mint. Fine impression	
905	1874 C. C. Mint. Very fine impression	
906	1874 Very fine impression	
907	1875 Fine impression	
908	1875 C. C. Mint. Fine impression	
909	1875 S. Mint. Uncirculated	
910	1876 Very fine, nearly proof impression	
911	1876 S. Mint. Fair impression	
912	1877 Very good impression	
913	1877 C. C. Mint. Almost proof impression	
914	1877 C. C. Mint. A variety	
915	1877 S. Mint. Fine impression	
	HALF DIMES.	
916	1794 A fair impression, and scarce	
917	1795 A fair impression, and scarce	
918	1796 Very good for date. Scarce	

[1] *John Swan Randall Sale*, Edward Cogan, May 6-9, 1878.

[2] U.S. Coin Company, *June 15, 1916 Auction.*

[3] Ibid.

[4] Ibid.

for which prominent numismatist and author Howard R. Newcomb paid $47.50.

Today (2003), these prices turn collectors green with envy, but in 1916 new barriers were being broken. It was becoming clear that many Carson City issues were very elusive, especially in Mint State condition. Most collectors in the first half of the 20th century were more concerned with acquiring the "CC" issues in any grade, rather than waiting for Uncirculated pieces to appear. Many of the finest collections of that period included lower grade examples of "CC" dates, even though the average condition for most coins in the collection was much higher.

In the *Louis E. Eliasberg, Sr.* collection for instance, the 1872-CC dime was graded VF, the 1873-CC *With Arrows* dime was only VG, as was the 1874-CC dime. To cite one more example, we mention a collection of such breadth and grandeur that in 1945 auctioneers Abe Kosoff and Abner Kriesberg, dubbed it the *World's Greatest Collection.* Later on it became common knowledge that the consignor was F.C.C. Boyd, who had a reputation for being a rare coin connoisseur. Mr. Boyd was only content with obtaining the finest quality available, and with a bankroll to afford it, his collection was known for the many Condition Census specimens it contained. In spite of this, he had to settle for many of the "CC" coins in his collection being in subpar condition according to his standards. A few examples are:

> 1872-CC Dime in VF
>
> 1870-CC Quarter in VF
>
> 1872-CC Quarter in Fine
>
> 1870-CC Half in Fine
>
> 1871-CC Half in Fine
>
> 1870-CC $20 Double eagle – Missing

By the time the *World's Greatest Collection* was auctioned, the two most recognized rarities from the Carson City Mint were the 1876-CC 20-cent piece and the 1873-CC *Without Arrows* quarter. A verdict had not yet been reached on the 1873-CC *Without Arrows* dime, though its recognition was not far off. In the *World's Greatest Collection* sale, the 1876-CC 20 cents in Uncirculated condition sold for $1,500, and the 1873-CC *Without Arrows* quarter realized $725. Collectors acknowledged that building complete sets of the Carson City series was for people with deep pockets.

In 1950, the status of the 1873-CC *Without Arrows* dime was settled, at least in most people's minds. Against a pre-sale estimate of $1,000 in Numismatic Gallery's *Adolphe Menjou* sale, the only known specimen of this date brought $3,650. For the rest of the 20th century, and into the next, this coin has been listed as *Unique*. It was a defining moment for Carson City coins as a series, because now this mint had a representative in the *ultra rarity* class. The popularity of "CC" coins grew as each new decade gave way to the next.

Early Collectors of Carson City Coins

Late 19th Century to Mid 20th Century

JOHN SWAN RANDALL

Though much more known for his hoard of Uncirculated large cents dated 1817, 1818, 1819, 1820, and 1825, John Swan Randall also had an impressive collection of Carson City coins. Mr. Randall lived in central New York about 40 miles north of the Pennsylvania border and his collecting endeavors extended from the 1860s to the time of his death in 1878. Randall apparently had a working relationship with the most prominent dealer of the day, Edward Cogan, whose office was on State Street in Brooklyn.

It remains a mystery how Randall acquired his Carson City coins, but beyond question he owned the first significant collection of dates from that mint. He has the distinction of being one of the few men in history to have owned an 1873-CC *Without Arrows* dime and quarter at the same time. Obviously his connection with Edward Cogan provided Randall with opportunities most coin collectors only dream about. Five months after Randall died, Edward Cogan, through the agency of Bangs and Company of New York City, auctioned Randall's collection, which included the following among the "CC" coins:

> 1871-CC Dime, Fine impression. Almost Proof.
>
> 1872-CC Dime, Good impression.
>
> 1873-CC Dime *Old Style*, Fine impression.
>
> 1874-CC Dime, Very Fine impression
>
> 1871-CC Quarter, Uncirculated impression.
>
> 1872-CC Quarter, Uncirculated impression.
>
> 1873-CC Quarter, *Old Style*, Nearly Uncirculated.
>
> 1875-CC Twenty cent, Uncirculated.
>
> (2) 1870-CC Half dollars, Both Uncirculated.
>
> 1871-CC Half dollar, Uncirculated.

1872-CC Half dollar, Uncirculated.

(2) 1873-CC Half dollars, *Old Style*, Both Uncirculated

1874-CC Half dollar, Uncirculated

Also included in the consignment was every date of Carson City Seated dollars except 1873, every "CC" trade dollar from 1873 through 1877, and all the other dates of dimes, quarters, and halves through the 1877-CC. For a collector from a small town in central New York, this was no small accomplishment. It is obvious that Randall was acquiring examples of every "CC" silver coin for each year; the only thing keeping him from the 1878 issues was his untimely death.

It is a sure bet that Edward Cogan was Randall's source for these Carson City coins, and might possibly have owned some for his personal account. There is no doubt that Philadelphia dealer John W. Haseltine, whose office was close to the U.S. Mint, supplied at least some of the coins, if not all. Haseltine, known as the *Numismatic Refrigerator*, is included in the pedigree to all three known Uncirculated specimens of the 1873-CC *Without Arrows* quarter, and apparently was able to obtain assay coins from the Mint at will. (His nickname refers to his ability to keep so many delectable numismatic rarities on ice.) Regardless of how this group of coins wound up in the 1878 *Randall* auction, it remains the single finest known set of "CC" coins from the pre-Heaton era.

WILLIAM M. FRIESNER

On June 7 and 8, 1894, the *William M. Friesner Collection* was auctioned by prominent dealer Edouard Frossard. Numismatists of the day were enthusiastic about the wide spectrum of material being offered. Showcased in this sale was a stunning example of the first branch mint half dollar dated 1838-O, of which only 20 were minted, all in Proof condition, and destined to become classic American rarities. Other notable pieces in this famous auction included a complete run of Proof Seated dollars from 1850 to 1858, and an ultra rare 1802 half dime.

Mr. Friesner, recognized as one of the earliest collectors of mintmarked coins, had also assembled an extraordinary

Prominent 19th-century coin dealer and auctioneer Edouard Frossard handled many notable Carson City coins.

selection of Carson City coins. In the shadows of so many landmark rarities, the "CC" coins did not attract as much attention. But to today's Carson City enthusiast, this group would excite the senses, as it included a complete set of "CC" half dollars with both varieties of the 1873. One of the stand outs from this set was an 1878-CC half described as being "Brilliant, sharp, Uncirculated."[1] All told, there were 40 different "CC" coins in this consignment, at the time one of the largest assortments ever offered.

Taking place just one year after the publication of Heaton's *Treatise on Mint Marks*, this sale gave numismatists a great opportunity to fill in their collections.

JOHN MARTIN CLAPP AND JOHN HENRY CLAPP

By the age of 35, John Martin Clapp had accumulated great wealth through his endeavors in Pennsylvania's booming oil industry during the late 1860s and early 1870s. Sometime after the birth of Clapp's last child, John H. Clapp in 1880, he developed an interest in coin collecting. His first three children had been born before he turned 38 and the first, a son named Ralph M. Clapp died at the age of 12 in 1878.

In any event, with millions in the bank, John Martin Clapp spent the last two decades of his life pursuing his numismatic pastime, while at the same time building a strong financial foundation for his children. His fascination with coins inspired him to study everything he could get his hands on; he soon became involved in a coin club, and began corresponding with collectors and dealers in the east. Curiously, although the American Numismatic Association was founded in 1891, J.M. Clapp did not become a member until 1901. He did, however, maintain close relationships with the founder, Dr. George F. Heath, and members such as Augustus G. Heaton and Virgil Brand.

It was Clapp's camaraderie with Heaton that influenced his aggressive pursuit of mintmarked coins. Clapp had been a customer of the Philadelphia Mint for many years, ordering new Proof sets annually, as well as any other interesting coins that might be available. He then gradually began ordering coins from the other mints around the country, usually through agents. Clapp, along with Heaton and several other noted specialists, became known for complete sets of dates and mintmarks for the various series that they had assembled.

[1] Edouard Frossard, *William M. Friesner Collection*, June 7, 8, 1894.

Before he died in 1906, J.M. Clapp had formed one of the most extensive coin collections ever seen. His Carson City collection is recognized for its completeness and high quality. In the "CC" quarter section alone, Clapp managed to acquire the first three years in Uncirculated condition. Only Louis E. Eliasberg, Sr. (who purchased Clapp's 1870-CC and 1872-CC), and then one other collector in the late 1990s (who bought the *Eliasberg* specimens) accomplished this feat.

Two very rare dates in the half dollar series, an 1874-CC and an 1878-CC, were included in Clapp's holdings, both in Gem Uncirculated condition. Clapp obtained one of the highlights of his collection, an 1876-CC 20-cent piece in Gem quality, at the *Dr. S.L. Lee* sale in 1899. He was able to purchase two half eagles directly from the Carson City Mint, an 1892-CC and an 1893-CC. Clapp often took advantage of his connections with banks in his area to acquire coins on his want list. One in particular was a dazzling 1892-CC $10 eagle, purchased at the teller window of a local Pennsylvania bank at face value. That coin, like the majority of coins in the Clapp family treasure chest, wound up in the *Eliasberg* collection where it remained until 1982. At that time it was auctioned by Bowers and Ruddy as part of Eliasberg's gold coin holdings, cataloged as Gem Uncirculated and considered to be the finest example of the date in existence. Years later, this 1892-CC eagle was graded MS-64 by PCGS and remains number one on the Condition Census.

After J.M. Clapp passed away in 1906, his only surviving son, John Henry Clapp, inherited the duties of curator of the family's coin collection. Thanks to his father's meticulous record keeping, the younger Clapp was able to take a thorough inventory and note which dates were missing. He carried on his family's tradition of connoisseurship and purchased many classic rarities during the next three decades, including an 1854-S $2 1/2 gold piece and a remarkable 1825/4 gold half eagle.

Early in his role as the family's numismatic buyer, young J.H. Clapp inquired if specimens existed of the 1873-CC *Without Arrows* dime and quarter. He later discovered that the two dates did in fact exist, but was never able to obtain either for the family's collection. Clapp was also unsuccessful in his efforts to obtain examples of several dates in the "CC" gold series, including the elusive 1870-CC double eagle.

When John H. Clapp died in 1940 at the age of 60, having never married, he had no progeny of his own

to take up the mantle of family numismatist. Consequently, within two years the collection was sold by Stack's in New York to Louis E. Eliasberg, Sr. for $100,000. This extensive assortment of numismatic delights became the foundation of Eliasberg's fabulous set of coins and has continued to be meted out to many appreciative collectors through the years.

RICHARD B. WINSOR AND HARLAN PAGE SMITH

A collection of U.S. coins was assembled by Richard B. Winsor from Rhode Island in the final quarter of the 19th century. The quality of many of the pieces led catalogers Samuel and Henry Chapman to comment that, "These grand and perfect coins are far more rare…than even the advanced numismatists imagine."[1] Winsor was described as being, "a fastidious buyer, and if the specimen offered did not meet his views of superior preservation it was most surely to be rejected."[2]

Though Mr. Winsor did not specialize in Carson City coins, three have survived the test of time, validating his reputation as having a sharp eye for quality. All three coins are considered common dates in the "CC" series, one being an 1876-CC half dollar, described in the 1895 catalog as "Uncirculated…Brilliant mint luster."[3] With a price realized of only 95 cents, the piece was certainly not a head turner, but 102 years later this 1876-CC half sold for $25,300 in the Eliasberg sale and is currently encased in an NGC MS-68 holder. Both of the other coins were grouped as a two piece lot, listed in the quarter category as "1875, 1876 Carson City Mint…Uncirculated."[4] Bidders were obviously not too enthused, as the price realized for the two was only 35 cents. Yet once again, more than a century later, collectors acknowledged that Winsor's standards were timeless, as the 1875-CC was bid to $5,720 and the 1876-CC quarter sold for $6,380 at the 1997 *Eliasberg* sale.

A contemporary of Richard Winsor's was Harlan Page Smith, who outlived Winsor by approximately seven years. From the time Smith was a young man until he turned 42 in 1880, he was an amateur coin collector, becoming zealous about the hobby after the Civil War. From 1880, until the time of his death in 1902, Smith

[1] H. and S.H Chapman, *Richard B. Winsor Collection*, 1895.
[2] Ibid.
[3] Ibid.
[4] Ibid.

was a professional coin dealer, forming several partnerships along the way which he generally bankrolled.

Smith's most successful partnership was formed in 1888 when he teamed with numismatist David U. Proskey, doing business as the New York Coin and Stamp Company. During the 14 years before Smith died their company handled just about every important U.S. coin, as well as a wide variety of foreign material. Many significant collections were consigned to the company's auction sales including the *R. Coulton Davis Sale* in January of 1890, the *Lorin G. Parmlelee Sale* in June of 1890, and the *Edward Goldschmidt Sale* held on April 27, 1895. All told, Smith and Proskey conducted 19 auctions together and had the privilege of cataloging scores of classic rarities.

Through it all, Smith never lost his passion for collecting, and independent of the company's inventory, assembled an impressive collection of his own. He was another 19th century numismatist attracted to Carson City coins and in his position as the owner of a coin store and auctioneer, he witnessed firsthand how infrequently many dates in the "CC" series appeared. It was indeed a special occasion at the *Davis* sale in 1890, when an 1876-CC 20-cent piece was offered right alongside a Brasher doubloon. At the time, it was estimated that there were no more than four specimens of the scarce 20-cent piece extant. At the *Goldschmidt* sale in 1895, a desirable trio of high grade "CC" Seated dollars were offered, which included an 1870-CC, 1872-CC, and 1873-CC.

Harlan P. Smith was a distinguished member of the numismatic community, and counted among his many friends and clients men like Augustus G. Heaton and John M. Clapp. He was said to have sold an 1873-CC *Without Arrows* quarter to Heaton, and is frequently mentioned as a source for many of J.M. Clapp's Carson City coins. When Smith's collection was sold in two separate auctions by the Chapman brothers in 1906, a commendable assortment of "CC" pieces were part of the consignment, including an 1893-CC silver dollar that the Chapman's described as being a "Proof." There is one important comment that should be made concerning the "CC" coins in the *Harlan Page Smith* sales. Although the following dates are pedigreed to Smith in the *Eliasberg* catalog of 1997, they are not listed in the Smith catalogs: 1870-CC quarter, and 1871-CC, 1872-CC, 1873-CC *With Arrows* and 1874-CC halves. These pedigrees originated in the Clapp family inventory ledger books and perhaps Smith was indeed the source, only under different circumstances. Notwithstand-

ing, there is no question that Smith handled many Carson City coins during his collecting and coin dealer days.

HONORABLE MENTIONS

As the 20th century approached, interest in Carson City coins increased. Dealers who had handled more coins than the average collector, of course had an edge in their knowledge of the relative rarity of most categories of coins. In the years immediately after the Carson Mint closed, it became clear that many dates from that facility were very elusive. Coin dealers knew how futile it would be for collectors to attempt to obtain complete sets of any "CC" series and only a few brave clients even pondered the idea.

Some were fortunate enough to have connections in banks, regional offices out west, or even within the Treasury Department, providing access to obscure pieces now and again. It is not unusual to look through catalogs from 100 years ago and see complete runs of Proof sets from the post Civil War years, as well as nearly complete sets of scarce early copper and silver coins, but only a smattering of common date "CC" silver coins. This does not, however, appear to have resulted from a lack of interest, especially after Heaton's *Treatise on Mint Marks* had become a popular topic.

A major hurdle these early collectors had to overcome was a lack of mintage data, making it difficult to ascertain how available an example would be. Information exchanged within the collecting community helped to uncover some of the mysteries, but often, especially in the case of Carson City coins, estimating original mintages or extant populations was more of a *shoot from the hip* process. For example, in the *R. Coulton Davis* sale in 1890, the catalogers commented regarding the 1876-CC 20-cent piece, "We know of no duplicate of this mintage."[1] In other words, the piece being offered in this sale was considered *Unique,* in their opinion.

Dealers were well aware that if they sold one example of any number of dates from the Carson City Mint, it might be a long time—if ever—before they saw another. But for their adventuresome clients, the pursuit of the unobtainable was a rewarding pastime.

One dealer who was up for the task was J. Colvin Randall from Philadelphia, who began his career as a professional numismatist before the Carson City Mint opened and was active almost until his death, circa 1901. He had a

---

[1] New York Coin and Stamp Company. *Robert Coulton Davis Collection,* January 20-24, 1890.

close working relationship with John Haseltine and became well known for his *Type Table* used to categorize U.S. coins.

Randall was financially secure throughout his mature adult years, and apparently was as much of a collector as he was a dealer. His personal collection included many duplicates and even triplicates of some very desirable dates. Randall obviously had an interest in "CC" coins, though he would not be considered a specialist in the field.

One of Randall's friends and clients was John M. Clapp, who reportedly purchased several Choice Uncirculated Carson City silver dollars from him, including an 1890-CC, 1892-CC and a possible Proof 1893-CC. Randall seems to have enjoyed coin collecting immensely and was one of the few who had the privilege of being involved in the hobby from the time the Carson City Mint opened through the time it closed.

Two other late 19th century collectors with a fondness for Carson City coins were Edward Goldschmidt and John G. Mills. At the *Edward Goldschmidt* sale conducted by the New York Coin Company in April of 1895, three out of four of the "CC" Seated Liberty dollar dates were sold, including an 1870-CC and the 1872-CC and 1873-CC; the latter two were purchased by John M. Clapp, and eventually became part of Eliasberg's collection.

John G. Mills also seemed to favor Carson City silver dollars, as reflected in the auction of his collection held by the Chapman brothers in April of 1904. According to J.M. Clapp's notebook, as well as the 1997 Eliasberg catalog, Mills at one time owned the finest known 1889-CC dollar. Clapp of course purchased that 1889-CC, and it too was eventually owned by Louis E. Eliasberg, Sr. Several other "CC" Morgan dollars can be pedigreed to the Mills collection, including an 1885-CC, which in 1904 was actually considered scarcer than the 1889-CC. In 1997, the 1885-CC realized $1,760 at the *Eliasberg* sale, while the 1889-CC set a record at $462,000. Early collectors like Mills have made it possible for treasures such as these to be passed down to later generations.

DR. SIMEON L. LEE

There is no one more deserving of inclusion in a list of men representing early interest in collecting Carson City coins than Dr. Simeon Lemuel Lee. Born in Vandalia,

Dr. Simeon L. Lee, a veteran Union officer from the Civil War, would often wear his full dress uniform in public. He was one of Carson City's more prominent citizens. (*Courtesy Nevada State Museum*)

Illinois on September 4, 1844, Lee served in the Union army during the Civil War rising to the rank of Lt. Colonel at the age of 21, after serving under General Grant in the 8th Illinois Volunteer Infantry. As soon as the war ended, the young Lee, pursuing a career in medicine, attended an unorthodox school in Cincinnati called Physio-Medical Institute, which specialized in botanical remedies. Graduating in 1870 with an M.D. degree Dr. Lee, fascinated with the tales he had heard of the western United States, moved to of all places, Carson City, Nevada. After establishing his roots in the capital city for two years, Lee was offered a position in the burgeoning mining camp at Pioche, Nevada, and for the next 6 1/2 years Dr. Lee experienced the rigors of being a doctor in the frontier mining towns of Pioche and Eureka.

In 1879, he was ready to return to Carson City where he spent the last 48 years of his life. Always an avid reader, Dr. Lee constantly challenged himself to further his education in medicine, as well as countless other subjects. In an article in the *Carson Daily Appeal* eulogizing his death, Dr. Lee is remembered for "the tremendous amount of reading that he followed through life…He burned midnight oil so many years that the familiar light in his room will be missed with his passing."[1]

To the residents of Carson City, Dr. Lee was one of the leaders in town who could be called upon in times of need. He had an overpowering presence, being a large and robust man in perfect health, and on occasion he would don his military dress blues, with medals on his chest and a sword at his side. Dr. Lee had a full crop of hair, and wore prominent sideburns connected by a bushy mustache most of his life.

In his profession as a medical doctor, Lee was the one people would call in times of emergency. Sometimes he would burrow his way through snow to reach someone on the outskirts of town in need of medical attention, and often he would trek up to Lake Tahoe by wagon or horse-

---

[1] *Carson Daily Appeal*, January 12, 1927.

back to deliver a baby or set a broken leg. During his 48 years in Carson City, Dr. Lee served as the head physician at the Nevada Hospital, a surgeon for the two main railroads connecting to Carson, and as the Secretary of the State Board of Health, all while maintaining his personal practice.

Dr. Lee is remembered for many things, but his affinity for the underdog earned him much respect and gratitude. He had a tender spot in his heart for the oppressed and those who were down-and-out, and it may have been this very trait that caused him to turn a blind eye to the criminal acts of former mint employee James Heney during the stolen gold scandal of 1895 in Carson City. Dr. Lee and several other prominent men posted bail for the runaway fugitive before his trial. Dr. Lee was also sensitive to the plight of Native Americans and some historians have suggested that famed Washoe Indian basket maker Dat-so-la-lee, was supported in her work by Dr. Lee, and that her name is an Indian derivative of his.

Good friends of Dr. Lee's would admit that at times the typically gracious doctor would curse up a blue streak but somehow not seem profane, and those who opposed him sometimes witnessed a fiery temper and thought twice about challenging him a second time. For the most part though, Dr. Lee led a peaceful life and believed that his duty was to serve his community.

One of Dr. Lee's diversions was collecting things and from his leading position in town, he was able to seize opportunities and was financially rewarded for many of them. In that same article in the *Carson Daily Appeal* at the time of his death, a reflective comment reminded readers that, "From the time he arrived in this state he has been busy collecting the various fine minerals, gems and Indian relics, until today his collection remains the most complete and valuable in the state."[1]

An inventory was taken upon his passing and included the following:

2,500 - Indian relics such as arrows, arrowheads, wampum, beads, tomahawks, etc.

230 – Indian baskets

600 – Polished stones

3,200 – Mineral specimens

200 – Ceramics

150 – Shells

400 – Metal badges, souvenirs, and coins

That last item, coins, is of course of most interest in this present writing, for Dr. Lee seems like the archetypal collector representing early interest in Carson City coins. But surprisingly, he is one of the only known residents from the area who actually collected his city's coins during the years the local mint was producing them. The lack of Carsonites who found the coins of their fair city fascinating has remained a baffling question for decades. Even the connection between Dr. Lee and the coins from the Carson City Mint is not widely known.

For years, auction catalogers have pedigreed one of the finest known specimens of the 1876-CC 20-cent piece to the *Dr. S.L. Lee collection,* but without reference to Dr. Lee being one of the leading citizens in Carson City during the era the Mint was active. Dr. Lee's 1876-CC 20-cent piece was purchased by John M. Clapp out of the J.W.

---

[1] *Carson Daily Appeal,* January 12, 1927.

CATALOGUE
OF
A DESIRABLE COLLECTION
OF
U. S. AND FOREIGN COINS,

Including a complete set of Cents in very fine condition, and many curious and interesting Gold, Silver and Copper Coins from all parts of the world, representing all ages and nations.

THE PROPERTY OF DR. S. L. LEE.

CATALOGUED BY
The J. W. Scott Co., L'd, - 36 John St., New York City.

SOLD BY
HENRY C. MERRY, Auctioneer,
351 FOURTH AVENUE.

MONDAY, JUNE 12, 1899,
Commencing at 2 P. M.

344

178 1850, O mint, uncirculated.
179 1851, very fine.
180 1852, fine, rare.
181 1852, O mint, good, rare.
182 1853, barely circulated.
183 1854, O mint, fine.
184 1855, O mint, fine.
185 1856, O mint, uncirculated.
186 1857, fine.
187 1859, uncirculated.
188 1859, uncirculated.
189 1860, O mint, uncirculated.
190 1861, uncirculated.
191 1862, uncirculated.
192 1863, brilliant proof.
193 1864, fine.
194 1865, fine.
195 1866, barely circulated.
196 1867, barely circulated.
197 1868, proof.
198 1869, fine.
199 1870, uncirculated.
200 1871, uncirculated.
201 1872, uncirculated.
202 1872, CC mint, uncirculated.
202a 1872, barely circulated.
203 1874, uncirculated.
204 1875, brilliant proof.
205 1876, brilliant proof.
206 1877, brilliant proof.
207 1878, brilliant proof.
208 1879, brilliant proof.
209 1880, brilliant proof.
210 1881, proof.
211 1882, proof.
212 1892 Columbian half dollar.
213 1832 quarter dollar, proof.
214 1852 quarter dollar, barely circulated.
215 1853 quarter dollar, without arrow points or rays, uncirculated, very rare, especially in this condition.
216 1876 20c., fine, CC mint, proof surface, very rare.

This auction from 1899 featured the coins of Dr. Simeon L. Lee from Carson City. Note the price realized of $26.25 for lot #216, an 1876-CC 20-cent piece.

Scott Company's auction of *The Property of Dr. S.L. Lee* on June 12, 1899, and remained in the Clapp family estate until 1942 when Louis E. Eliasberg, Sr. bought the entire collection. It then remained in Eliasberg's set until it was sold on April 6, 1997 for $148,500 after a spirited bidding war, at the time, the first example of this date to break the $100,000 barrier.

One bothersome question—no two bothersome questions, linger. Where did Dr. Lee get the 1876-CC 20-cent piece and why did he sell it in 1899? Question number one opens up all kinds of doors. For instance, in 1876 Dr. Lee was in Pioche far away from Carson City, limiting the likelihood that someone would send one to him, and he did not return to Carson City until 1879, two years after all of the 1876-CC 20-cent pieces were supposedly melted. This begs the question: did someone at the mint save some of the fabled 20-centers, and if so, was Dr. Lee the only one who received one? Is it remotely possible that a connection can be made between the Baltimore hoard of 1876-CC 20-cent pieces that suddenly appeared in the 1950s and the rest of the Dr. Lee story?

Another possible explanation of Dr. Lee's acquisition is that he simply ordered the 1876-CC 20-cent piece through the mail because he was interested in its significance to the city he lived in. It seems more plausible that Dr. Lee's source was local; but no one knows and it will probably remain an unsolved mystery.

As for question number two—why did Dr. Lee sell his 1876-CC in 1899? He certainly did not need the money, for he was a wealthy man by then. He may have been aware that the *R. Coulton Davis* specimen had sold for $7 in 1890, and since then one other specimen had surfaced. Pre-sale price estimates for this date in 1899 were in the $20 to 25 range, which considering Dr. Lee's wealth was not going to have much impact. There were also other coins in the sale, including an 1872-CC half dollar in Uncirculated condition, and many foreign and ancient coins. Perhaps Dr. Lee was simply downsizing his collection, preparing to concentrate more on Indian relics and baskets, and there is the possibility that the rare 20-cent

This picture of Dr. Lee, taken in his office, shows him in his later years, long past the time his famous 1876-CC 20-cent piece had been auctioned. (*Courtesy Nevada State Museum*)

piece was a duplicate in Dr. Lee's collection.

In any event, his 1876-CC 20-cent piece brought $26.25 in the auction and his 1872-CC half realized $6.60. He did in fact, continue his endeavors in baskets and Indian relics, and in 1906 bought a piece of property at the corner of Minnesota and Telegraph streets where he built an impressive 11 room multi–gabled house, with plenty of room to display all of his artifacts. Years later in 1934, after his passing, Mrs. Lee donated his entire collection to the State of Nevada. She died one month later at the age of 86.

Dr. Lee's collection was transferred to the Nevada Museum and Art Institute in 1941 when the State Museum housed in the old mint officially opened. For over six decades, visitors to the Nevada Museum have been captivated by the enormity of the displays of relics and artifacts native to Nevada. Some of the baskets in Dr. Lee's collection are worth thousands of dollars, and overall the collection is now worth a fortune. All that said, there still seems to be a gaping hole in the collection Dr. Lee left behind—just the size of an 1876-CC 20-cent piece.

A New Century of Collector Interest

As the 20th century dawned, increased numbers of coin collectors became fascinated with the Carson City series, as gradually, it became a symbol of status and fulfillment to include rare dates from the Nevada mint in one's collection. Notable numismatists with widely diversified collecting preferences from early type coins, patterns, classic rarities, and set building, would often include a rare date Carson City issue in their holdings. Some would even attempt to assemble complete sets of the individual series from the Carson Mint.

Prominent collectors such as William Woodin, Virgil Brand, S. Benton Emery, Albert Holden, Elmer Sears, Robert Garrett, John Work Garrett, William F. Dunham, and H.O. Granberg were among those who respected and owned coins from the Carson City Mint.

William Woodin, through his strong political connections, once owned the 1873-CC *Without Arrows* dime, yet his collecting interests leaned more toward pattern coins and classic rarities in general. One of the three known Uncirculated 1873-CC *Without Arrows* quarters is pedigreed to H.O. Granberg from the 1919 auction featuring a consignment from his collection. As for the 1876-CC 20-cent piece, one example was purchased by S. Benton Emery in 1900, and another by H.O. Granberg at a later date. Eccentric heir to the Hetty Green fortune, Colonel E.H.R. Green, also owned an 1876-CC 20-center, along with his five 1913 Liberty nickels.

A very impressive selection of Carson City silver coins from the collection of an unidentified consignor was auctioned by the United States Coin Company in 1916, with several of the more noteworthy dates going directly into Virgil Brand's cabinet. This period is considered to be a time of foundational development for interest in "CC" coins. In the years leading up to the Great Depression, and continuing past World War II, this popular series attracted increasing numbers of collectors.

New blood competing for the relatively small population base of "CC" coins, included well-known collectors such as, F.C.C. Boyd, William C. Atwater, William W. Neil, Dr. Charles W. Green, Charles Williams, Jack Roe, Belden E. Roach, J.F. Bell, and Louis E. Eliasberg, Sr. As interest escalated, prices rose dramatically for many of the scarcer Carson City issues and circulated examples of some dates were bringing more than Uncirculated specimens did several decades earlier. For example, at the 1916 U.S. Coin Company auction, an Uncirculated specimen of the 1873-CC *With Arrows* dime sold for $82.50, whereas at the *William D. Waltman* sale in 1945, an example in Fine condition brought $205. This was true even for common date "CC" coins, as illustrated by an 1876-CC quarter in Uncirculated condition selling for 50 cents at the 1916 auction, and the same date in Almost Uncirculated bringing $2.75 at the *Belden E. Roach* sale in 1944.

After the *World's Greatest Collection* (F.C.C. Boyd) sale in 1945, a new era in the pricing and popularity of Carson City coins had arrived. Gone were the days when 1876-CC 20-cent pieces could be purchased for $26.25, reflected by the $1,500 price realized from the *WGC* sale. And the 1916 price of $31.50 for an Uncirculated 1871-CC dime was ancient history compared to the $185 paid for the *Boyd* specimen in similar condition.

Years later a new generation of numismatists would be green with envy at how fortunate collectors from the 1940s were to buy coins like these at such low prices, a sentiment expressed by collectors from every preceding generation. When looking backward, current prices seem high, but it is only the strong at heart that can see prices in the context of looking forward.

HAROLD M. BUDD

Picture if you will a man who lived and breathed the subject and experience of collecting Carson City coins; a man so devoted to the "CC" mintmark and its legacy that he would talk about it to strangers, write about it incessantly, gaze at his coins from this mint in awe and think of ways he could return the favor to Carson City for being home to this special series. If there was ever an honorary spokesman for Carson City coins in the first half of the 20th century it was Harold M. Budd.

Harold Budd did not include Carson City coins in the framework of a diversified collection; these were all he pursued and his passion for the topic was contagious. It was his commitment to the task that ultimately led to the completion of a set of every date and denomination of silver coins issued by the Carson Mint, except one, the 1873-CC *Without Arrows* dime, which he did not believe existed until two months before his death.

A frequent contributor to numismatic publications, Budd once sent a letter to the *Numismatist* explaining why he believed that there were no 1873-CC *Without Arrows* dimes. It was his "contention that as to the new silver act that went into effect…in the year 1873, that by the time the Carson City Mint got ready to make dimes, [no] without arrows was ever made."[1] Budd did not think he was alone in his theory, for "a great deal of research had been given on this by many over a period of the past 15 years, and up to the present…, I have been unable to find anyone who had one, or knew of anyone having one."[2] More than a year would pass before Budd, and the whole world would learn the truth about this date.

In the same letter, Budd expounded on the highlight of his collection, "the 1873 Carson City 25¢ piece *Without Arrows* [that] auction records and other records will show that this has only been offered once in the past 25 years (*WGC* sale) and, outside of myself, I have been un-

---

[1] *Numismatist*, ANA, January, 1949.
[2] Ibid.

A postcard sent by Harold Budd from Carson City to a friend in Los Angeles in March of 1945. Budd reports to his friend: "Snowing up here and cold. I know you would enjoy going through this building–very interesting city–No CC coins up here –Budd." Friends described Budd as "the finest little guy who ever lived." (*Courtesy Hal V. Dunn*)

able to find anyone that has one."[1] The provenance of the *Budd* specimen of this rare date has never been verified, but it is clear that Budd was unaware of the *James A. Stack* specimen.

If he was uninformed on any topic regarding the Carson City Mint it was not due to lack of research on his part, as he spent his life studying every reference he could get his hands on about Carson City coins, and he wrote letters to dealers and collectors around the country seeking answers to satisfy his inquisitive mind. Never one to be stingy with his findings, Budd was always willing to share information with anyone who was interested.

In an article he submitted to *The Numismatist* in 1945, Budd provided readers with a brief overview of the history and coinage from the Carson City Mint. First, he gave an introduction of how he became interested in the subject. Growing up in Connecticut and then educated at Yale University, Budd described how he used to dream of the Wild West as a boy; and with reference to his move to California in 1910 at the age of 24, Budd said, "Once I moved west, I immediately became attached to its legends and determined to relive those days of America's wonderful growth."[2] Out of all the regions he visited in the west, "in first place... is Carson City Nevada ... there, history was made..., there, for the rich numismatic world flourished the fabulous Carson City Mint, whose output... has now almost vanished to a very few coins, most of which are collector's items."[3] Budd related how the history of the old west became more real when he began collecting Carson City coins. In light of his numismatic accomplishments he was able to attest that, "I am very proud of my collection because it began in an amateur sort of way and has helped me to grasp more fully the history of our great West."[4]

It is understandable why Budd's collecting activities started out slow, as he first needed to launch a career and raise a family. By the 1930s he was firmly established in the wholesale textile industry, a good provider for his wife and two sons. Throughout the 1940s his income was sufficient to channel discretionary funds into his collecting pursuits. Budd became a valuable client of the Numismatic Gallery, owned by Abe Kosoff and Abner Kriesberg and was an active bidder at the *World's Greatest Collection* sale in 1945, losing the 1873-CC *Without Arrows* quarter to Louis E. Eliasberg, Sr. Budd's memory must have failed him four years later when he wrote that letter to the *Numismatist* relating how he was unaware of anyone other than himself having an 1873-CC *Without Arrows* quarter.

Finally, in June of 1950 Harold M. Budd "completed his lifelong desire of possessing a specimen of each and every silver coin minted at Carson City when he purchased an 1876-CC 20-cent piece at the famous *Menjou* sale in Beverly Hills,"[5] the same auction which included the unique 1873-CC *Without Arrows* dime that eventually wound up in Eliasberg's collection. Harold Budd must have been surprised to discover that the dime existed, since it had been 15 months earlier that he had written the letter declaring that it did not. Apparently he was

---

[1] Ibid.

[2] *The Numismatist*, August 1945.

[3] Ibid

[4] Ibid.

[5] *The Numismatist*, October, 1950.

Home of America's   *Finest Coin Sales*

UNITED STATES HALF DOLLARS

PART III OF ONE OF THE

WORLD'S GREATEST COLLECTIONS

OF

UNITED STATES SILVER COINS

AUCTION CATALOGUE NO. 31

Featuring 13 varieties of 1794 Half Dollars;
45 varieties of 1795; an uncirculated gem of
1796; a splendid 1797, and the EXCESSIVE-
LY RARE 1838-O, with attributions accord-
ing to the standard work on the series, "A
REGISTER OF HALF DOLLAR DIE VA-
RIETIES," by M. L. Beistle, (available at
your dealer's at $7.50, postpaid)
CATALOGUE FREE TO PURCHASERS OF THE
PRICE LIST AT $1.00

SALE OF PART III APRIL 7, 1945, AT 1:30 P. M.

NUMISMATIC GALLERY

A. KOSOFF   ABNER KREISBERG

42 East 50th Street   New York 22, N. Y.

Advertisement for the April 1945 session of the *World's Greatest Collection*. From January 1945 to January 1946, five sessions were held to auction this incredible set of coins.

more preoccupied with his success in obtaining the coveted 1876-CC 20-cent piece, as evidenced by this note he sent to Abe Kosoff after the sale: "I cannot express to you how very happy I am to receive the 1876-CC 20-cent piece. It is a great joy to me as I have waited several years to obtain the same. Many of my friends will be happy to know that it has helped me to complete my Carson City Mint silver series. If you don't remember this, I would like to freshen your memory that at least 95% of the really rare coins in this series were bought through you...Thanks again for your many favors."[1]

After this marvelous achievement, Harold Budd proceeded with his plans to have a custom plaque made containing the first issue coins from the Carson City Mint to deliver to the museum there. When it was complete, Budd placed it in the trunk of his car beside the rest of his collection that he wished to show the museum staff. Eventually, he wanted to not only donate the first year of issue plaque, but to loan his complete collection to the museum to put on display.

Budd was accompanied on his trip from Los Angeles to Carson City by a friend and as the two approached the small town of Bridgeport, California, about 75 miles south of Carson City, they stopped abruptly when they sighted an overturned vehicle. A man's body was lying in the street, Budd and his friend got out of their car to provide care, and almost at once, a thug came out of hiding and held them at gunpoint as he drove away in Budd's car. It was a terrible predicament that only got worse, for when the police arrived, it was revealed that the overturned vehicle had also been stolen and the passenger who died in the wreck had been a hitchhiker.

Tragically, Mr. Budd, who at 63 had been suffering from ill health for over a year, had a coronary attack when he realized that his prized coin collection was in the trunk of his car. Police rushed him to a hospital in Carson City, but he never recovered. This incident occurred less than two months after the *Menjou* sale, just two months before Budd's 64th birthday.

One day later, Budd's car was recovered with all the coins still stored in the trunk. No one knew better how tragic the whole event was than his wife Dorothy. She knew how much her husband had looked forward to enjoying his beloved "CC" collection during his retirement years and his plans to become involved with the museum in Carson City, further spreading his message about the coins that meant so much to him. Budd's message was clear, "Collecting Carson City coins has been a delight, not only for the joy of collecting, but because it has enabled me to drink deep of that glorious fountain of American history, right here in the West, where history was made by giants."[2] Harold M. Budd was truly a giant in the corridors of the history of the coins he specialized in.

Kosoff's
COIN BULLETIN

Published by A. KOSOFF, P. O. Box 456, Encino, California, for Interested Collectors.
Phone STate 4-5005

NUMBER 1   SEPTEMBER   1954

WE HOPE YOU LIKE US

IT'S been just about a year and a half since I last edited such a periodical. Since the same mailing list is being used, most of you will remember the Numismatic Gallery Monthly. Your letters indicated that you liked it—many offered to subscribe to it, and we enjoyed putting it out.

Unfortunately the pressure of other affairs prevented a regular release and it was with regret that it was discontinued in April, 1953. Now I hope to take up the regular periodic release of KOSOFF'S COIN BULLETIN.

You are invited to criticize, suggest, buy, sell, trade, or what have you. Interesting articles, news items, etc., pertaining to numismatics or numismatic personalities are welcome and will be published as space permits. We hope you like us.

CARSON CITY COINAGE

A splendid collection of the silver coins of the Carson City Mint is being marketed by the Numismatic Gallery. If your wants include CC coins—send us your list.

Ad from *Abe Kosoff's Bulletin* in 1954, highlighting a "Splendid collection" of Carson City coins.

[1] Q. David Bowers. *Abe Kosoff: Dean of Numismatics.*

[2] *The Numismatist*, August, 1945

Famous 1873-CC Without Arrows Quarter

One of Three Known to Exist

1847 **1873-CC Without Arrows. MS-63 to 64.** Sharply struck and well defined in all areas. Deep mint frost is overlaid on the obverse and reverse by mottled light lilac toning.

Just three examples of the 1873-CC Without Arrows quarter are believed to exist. A detailed article on the 1873-CC Without Arrows quarter and dime appeared in our *Rare Coin Review,* issue No. 66, pages 90 and 91. The author, P. Scott Rubin, detailed the pedigrees of the three known examples:

1. Uncirculated
   A. U.S. Mint
   B. A.L. Snowden
   C. J.W. Haseltine
   D. J.K. Nagy
   E. W.H. Woodin
   F. H.O. Granberg
   G. 1919 B. Max Mehl's 54th sale, Lot 358
   H. F.C.C. Boyd
   I. 1945 World's Greatest Collection sale, Lot 378 (realized 725)
   J. Louis Eliasberg
   K. Louis Eliasberg family
2. Uncirculated
   A. John Swan Randall
   B. 1878 Cogan's 5/6 sale, Lot 795 (realized
   C. Browning Collection
   D. James A. Stack

   E. 1975 James A. Stack Collection sale, Lot 136 (realized $80,000)
   F. William Grayson (B & B Coins)
   G. 1979 NASCA's London sale, the coin had a reserve bid that was not met and did not sell
   H. 1980 Metropolitan New York sale, Lot 519 (was said to have realized $205,000)
   I. Bob Riethe and Greg Holloway
3. Uncirculated
   A. H.M. Budd
   B. Numismatic Gallery
   C. Imperial Coins, 1954
   D. **Norweb Collection**

Famous 1873-CC *Without Arrows* quarter pedigreed to the Norwebs and featured on the page shown above from Bowers and Merena's *Norweb Collection.* This lovely piece was also owned by Harold M. Budd.

I CAN SEE YOU

OAKLAND-SAN FRANCISCO—April 26-27-28
Hotel Claremont, Oakland, California

DETROIT, MICHIGAN—April 29-30, May 1-2
Hotel Statler, Detroit

NEW YORK CITY—May 3rd to 10th
Park Sheraton Hotel, N. Y. C.

*If you want to discuss a numismatic problem, write to me and
we can arrange a meeting*

I WANT TO BUY

- Gem Large Cents
  I will not quote any fabulous buying prices I'll pay them
- 1864 L proof cent — I'll pay $225.00
- 1864 2 cents small motto proof — I'll pay $175.00
- 1867 nickel with rays, proof — I'll pay $300.00
- 1876-CC 20 cent piece — I'll pay $2,500.00
- 1873-CC 25 cents, either type, uncirculated. Name your price.
- 1901-S 25 cents uncirculated — I'll pay $475.00
- 1914-S 25 cents (lists at $22.50) — I'll pay $50.00

I could go on—and on. I'll quote on your coins—only if you send them.
If you send a list, then I'll have to have your price.

A. KOSOFF
Phone STate 4-5005

P. O. Box 456   Encino, Calif.

Abe Kosoff's success with Carson City coinage through the 1950s led him to place "Buy" ads like this one from 1955.

Sadly, Budd's name has become obscure in the pages of numismatics through the years and no one has ever revealed what became of his prized coin collection, for it surely did not wind up on display at the Nevada State Museum. Surely, because of the quality of the coins belonging to Harold Budd, anyone purchasing them would have certainly questioned their pedigree. One of Budd's acquaintances described the collection in flattering terms by relating that, "Most of the specimens are not only Brilliant Uncirculated but have a semi-proof surface."[1]

Within a couple years after Budd's death, Carson City coins lit up the market and the publicity from the sale of the 1873-CC *Without Arrows* dime in 1950 contributed to their heightened popularity. Several subsequent incidents may shed light on the whereabouts of Harold M. Budd's collection. Abe Kosoff, who was Budd's primary source for "CC" coins, might have been called upon by Mrs. Budd to liquidate her husband's collection; there is little doubt that Kosoff stocked an impressive inventory of Carson City coins during the years following Budd's death. His success in selling them led Kosoff to mount an aggressive advertising campaign establishing himself as a key player in this specialized market. Moreover, in one of

his company newsletters from September of 1954, he made special mention that, "A splendid collection of silver coins of the Carson City Mint is being marketed by the Numismatic Gallery…"[2]

At this same time, the Imperial Coin Company, owned by Ben Stack in Las Vegas, Nevada, marketed many significant specimens from the Carson City Mint. Kosoff and Ben Stack patronized one another frequently, due to the close proximity between Southern California and Las Vegas. One of Ben Stack's biggest retail clients was the Norweb family who are on record as purchasing many "CC" coins during this period, one in particular being a beautiful 1873-CC *Without Arrows* quarter. In the catalog featuring this coin in the *Norweb* sale, Bowers and Merena list "H.M. Budd, Numismatic Gallery and Imperial Coins, 1954,"[3] in the pedigree information. Throughout the rest of the *Norweb* catalogs numerous "CC" coins are pedigreed to both Imperial Coin and Numismatic Gallery, but there is no other mention of H.M. Budd. For some unknown reason, only the 1873-CC *Without Arrows* quarter was pedigreed to H.M. Budd, although the Imperial Coin/Numismatic Gallery connection dominates the Norweb's "CC" listings.

It is practically unmistakable that a majority of Harold Budd's Carson City coins became part of the famous *Norweb Collection,* and it will be fitting justice if this is confirmed at some point in the future and Budd's name is included in the roster of pedigrees for the coins he once owned. At the same time, it would also be appropriate to have a picture of Mr. Budd hung in the Nevada State Museum as a tribute to the most enthusiastic Carson City coin collector of all time.

---

[1] *The Numismatist,* October, 1950

[2] *Numismatic Gallery Monthly,* September, 1954

[3] Bowers and Merena, *Norweb Collection,* March 24, 25, 1988

CHAPTER NINE

Three Special Collections

There have been many noteworthy numismatists who have included coins from the Carson City Mint in their collections and in the chapter on *Early Collector Interest*, some of the more well known individuals from the pre-1950 era were profiled. After the early 1950s, as interest in "CC" coins blossomed to an unprecedented dimension, a cavalcade of new collectors grabbed the torch from the preceding generation and enthusiastically continued the tradition.

Such prominent numismatists as the Norwebs, James A. Stack, Charles Cass, R.L. Miles, Samuel Wolfson, Milton Holmes, Reed Hawn, Waldo Bolen, Donald Groves, Amon G. Carter, Jr., and Harold S. Bareford are counted among the ranks of the quintessential admirers of Carson City coins. Most of the collections assembled by these pacesetters covered the wide spectrum of American coinage, from early colonial issues to territorial gold. Often the classic regular (or irregular) mint issues, such as 1804 and 1870-S silver dollars, 1885 trade dollars, and 1894-S dimes overshadowed Carson City coins, yet the presence of "CC" mintmarked dates was never ignored.

One of the lesser known Carson City coin enthusiasts entered the world of numismatics by accident in 1958. In his own words, E.A. Carson describes how it happened: "My business associate and I were standing on a corner waiting for a taxi, when a young man burst out of a shop carrying several coin holders, with the proprietor in hot pursuit yelling, 'Stop, thief!' An off-duty policeman made a flying tackle and quite a struggle ensued…While waiting… I wandered into the coin shop and browsed around."[1] And it was at this time that E.A. Carson was bitten by the collecting bug, and in his own words, "Since my name is Carson, it didn't take long to discover that there had been a Carson City Mint…what better reason could there have been for starting to collect Carson City dollars, and ultimately extending into all coins minted [at] Carson City?"[2]

Mr. Carson's collection of "CC" coins was sold at public auction in June of 1976 by Bowers and Ruddy, and represented one of the finest sets of its kind ever assembled. In the descriptions, cataloger Q. David Bowers posed the question, "Are coins a good investment?"[3] Bowers then went on to list some of the prices that E.A. Carson paid for his "CC" coins in comparison with prices realized after the sale. The table on the following page exhibits a few selected lots for reference.

Impressive gains to be sure, but numismatists in the early years of the 21st century now acknowledge that these prices from 1976 were only the tip of the iceberg.

Louis E. Eliasberg, Sr., probably the most celebrated coin collector of all time, passed to his final resting place on February 10, 1976 at the age of 80. His legacy and the coins he left behind have been discussed as much as any topic in the field of numismatics. A portion of this chapter will present a brief profile of Eliasberg, especially with regard to the Carson City coins from his collection.

In a second section of this chapter, readers will be given an introductory glimpse into the life of another collector with strong ties to the coins from the Carson City Mint. By request, the identity of

---

[1] Bowers and Ruddy, *Dr. Edward B. Willing Collection*, June 25-26, 1976.

[2] Ibid.

[3] Ibid.

Coin	Grade	Date Purchased	Purchase Price	Price Realized	Gain/Loss	%
1871-CC 10¢	VF	4-30-65	$ 425	$ 600	+175	41%
1872-CC 10¢	UNC	2-6-65	568	1,000	+432	76%
1873-CC AR 10¢	VF	3-26-64	675	1,000	+325	48%
1874-CC 10¢	VF	4-30-65	450	1,300	+850	288%
1875-CC 20¢	UNC	3-10-64	100	660	+560	660%
1876-CC 20¢	XF	Circa 1965	3,300	16,000	+12,700	485%
1870-CC 25¢	VF	4-30-65	500	1,600	+1,100	320%
1871-CC 25¢	AU	4-10-69	1,100	1,050	-50	-4.5%
1872-CC 25¢	VF	3-18-64	465	1,000	+535	215%
1873-CC AR 25¢	XF	3-6-64	900	1,350	+450	150%
1870-CC 50¢	UNC	6-27-64	675	3,100	+2,425	459%
1872-CC 50¢	UNC	2-1-66	350	700	+350	200%
1873-CC NA 50¢	XF	6-29-66	174	400	+226	230%
1873-CC AR 50¢	UNC	3-24-62	275	2,100	+1,825	764%
TOTALS			$9,957	$31,860	+$21,903	320%

PRICES REALIZED VERSUS COST TO CONSIGNOR FROM THE *E.A. CARSON* COLLECTION, JUNE, 1976[1]

this individual will remain anonymous, yet his experience with "CC" coins could be used as a composite sketch of an assortment of collectors with similar interests. This person was alive at the time Eliasberg died, but had no recollection of the towering numismatic giant and it would not be until 15 years after Eliasberg's passing that this collector became seriously involved in the hobby.

Finally, in the last third of this chapter, a portrait of Norman H. Biltz will be presented. Though virtually unknown in numismatic circles, Biltz deserves recognition for his contributions in fostering the image of Nevada being the *last frontier*, and for preserving the legacy of the Carson City Mint by the collection he left behind. Visionaries from Nevada like Norman Biltz are responsible for the old west theme associated with the state, and it is this theme, so often used in promotions for "CC" coins, that has contributed to their immense popularity with collectors and non-collectors alike.

LOUIS E. ELIASBERG, SR.

In the world of coin collecting there is much emphasis placed on pedigrees. Auction catalogs are filled with references about who once owned specific coins and when. For example, in Bowers and Merena's *Rarities Sale* in July of 2002, lot 613, an 1876-CC $5 half eagle, provided bidders with the following:

"From the collection of Henry S. Lang. Purchased from Bowers and Merena…, June 1991; earlier from the Chapman brothers, 1893; John H. Clapp, 1942; Our sale of the *Louis E. Eliasberg, Sr. Collection*, October 1982…."[2]

Though numerous collectors owned this coin through the years, once it became part of Eliasberg's collection, the pedigree was established for life, as Eliasberg's name is ranked number one on the roll call of numismatic pedigrees.

At the young age of 23, Louis E. Eliasberg, Sr. became a partner in The Finance Company of America in Baltimore, Maryland. From this beginning in 1919 until the stock market crash of 1929, Eliasberg shrewdly managed the business and saw its revenues soar. Intuitive foresight and conservative decisions resulted in continued growth during the depression of the 1930s.

Parlaying his success in the finance business, Eliasberg formed partnerships in several other profitable ventures, including an insurance company, a mortgage company, a brewery, a distillery and various real estate investments. By 1933 he had achieved much status in the Baltimore area and became a director in the National Bank there. Years later, he even became a part-owner of the Baltimore Orioles baseball team.

After the birth of his two sons in 1929 and 1931, Eliasberg devoted much time to building a solid financial foundation for his family. He was the consummate mentor to his sons and took an interest in all of their educational and extracurricular activities.

Several years before his children were born, Eliasberg acquired an interest in coin collecting, starting off slow at first but then accelerating in the early 1930s. One of the factors contributing to his growing fervency was the loophole coin collecting provided for people to own gold coins in spite of the Presidential Gold Recall Act.

[1] Ibid.

[2] Bowers and Merena, *Rarities Sale*, July 2002.

Eliasberg foresaw the weakening of America's financial strength when F.D.R. decided to take the country off the gold standard. Owning gold coins, in his opinion, provided insurance against the declining value of currency.

Never one to pursue his undertakings halfheartedly, Eliasberg took to the study of numismatics with a passion. He was fascinated with the history of coinage, and immediately saw the tie-in with monetary history. His sharp, calculating banker's mind enabled him to keep track of mintages, rarity ratings, price movements, coin types and varieties.

In 1942 at the age of 46, Eliasberg consummated one of the greatest numismatic transactions of all-time. His success in business had placed him in an enviable position of having untapped financial resources which enabled him to make aggressive offers for whatever in his mind represented good value. This had worked to his advantage so often in real estate and business investments, and now he was presented with an opportunity in his favorite pastime. He had been collecting for nearly 16 years and had assembled an award winning cabinet of coins. Dealers across the eastern seaboard respected Eliasberg and many would give him first shot at new purchases.

One of the coin companies Eliasberg conducted business with on a frequent basis was Stack's of New York,

Louis E. Eliasberg, Sr., in his office studying his favorite subject. (*Courtesy Bowers and Merena*)

and Stack's had been retained by the Clapp family to liquidate their collection after the death of John H. Clapp. Morton and Joseph Stack had the option of auctioning the family's coins or selling it by private treaty. Because of the size and value of the collection, few numismatists in the country were in a position to entertain the idea of purchasing it in its entirety. But knowing Eliasberg as they did, the Stack's approached him with the opportunity.

As he studied the inventory sheets compiling the collection, Eliasberg jotted down what he thought each coin was worth. After tallying his figures he came up with a nice round number of $100,000 that he was willing to pay the Clapp family. With apparently no negotiation, the Clapps accepted the offer and after Eliasberg inspected the coins personally the deal was done. Stack's received a 1% commission on the transaction and ultimately an immeasurable amount of publicity, plus a substantial portion of Eliasberg's future business.

It is difficult for collectors in the early years of the 21st century to comprehend the magnitude of this transaction. To gain partial insight into the financial significance of the sale, it might be helpful to imagine a single buyer purchasing everything included in all three Eliasberg catalogs. Aggregate prices realized for the 1982, 1996, and 1997 sales totaled $45 million, and if the three auctions were held today (2003 to 2004), it is safe to presume that the total would be much higher.

Immediately following his triumphal purchase, Eliasberg and his secretary began the arduous task of cataloging the collection. Using the *Mint Record and Type Table of United States Coins*, the equivalent of today's *Red Book*, Eliasberg checked off every date he owned, leaving the unchecked dates as his want list, providing the incentive to put a check next to every entry in the book. For the next eight years, Eliasberg was consumed with accomplishing this goal.

As his want list grew shorter, upgrading some of the coins already in the collection evolved into a rewarding task. By the end of World War II, most of the dates Eliasberg needed were key rarities missing from all but the most prestigious collections. He commented years later that: "Acquisition of the rarities presented quite a problem as they were very seldom offered...I flew to Los Angeles, Texas and other places in quest of these rare items"[1]

Always a shrewd negotiator, with a mind for value, Eliasberg loosened his strict standards during the final years

[1] Q. David Bowers. *Louis E. Eliasberg, Sr. King of Coins.*

of the mission. By this time, even though his trusted numismatic consultants would advise him that a price for a certain piece might be too high, Eliasberg recalled: "My own feelings were different. I felt that any premium that I paid for coins that I didn't have was insignificant in the overall value of the collection."[1] This was wise reasoning indeed, too often rejected by many modern collectors.

In 1947, Eliasberg paused long enough to gather a considerable quantity of duplicates for consignment to a Stack's auction. Requesting anonymity, the sale was billed as the *H.R. Lee Collection*; with the initials H.R. standing for his mother's first and middle name, and the Lee, standing for Louis E. Eliasberg. It was a clever attempt, but most numismatists knew who the consignor was. Prices realized for the sale of just his duplicates totaled $93,000, nearly as much as he had paid for the Clapp collection five years earlier.

By 1949, Eliasberg needed only an 1841 quarter eagle to finish the gold section of his extraordinary collection. One of his favorite dealers Abe Kosoff negotiated a deal with another client Jacob Shapiro (nee J.F. Bell) to acquire an 1841 gold quarter eagle for him at a price of $4,200 in February of 1949. Another friend and trusted dealer sent Eliasberg the message, "Everything comes to him who waits."[2] The end was now in sight, but over a year and a half would pass before it was time to break out the champagne.

In June of 1950, Abe Kosoff and Abner Kreisberg conducted the *Adolph Menjou* sale from their offices at the Numismatic Gallery in Beverly Hills. There were two coins in this auction Eliasberg needed to complete his goal. One was a circulated 1853-O half dollar *Without Arrows* or *Rays*, one of the classic rarities in the Seated Liberty coin series. With an estimated extant population of only three pieces, this date was obviously missing from most collections. But still, it was the second of the two coins that posed the greatest challenge for Eliasberg, the famous 1873-CC *Without Arrows* dime, with an unknown extant population. Only a year earlier, Carson City coin specialist Harold M. Budd had written a letter to *The Numismatist* declaring that this date did not exist. When publicizing the auction, Abe Kosoff stated that he could not remember hearing of another example of this date.

Eliasberg was not so concerned with how many 1873-CC *Without Arrows* dimes survived; he was determined to own the one being offered at the sale. He made pre-auction attempts to buy the piece from Kosoff, offering

Every U.S. Coin

Louis E. Eliasberg with part of his collection, the only one in the world containing a specimen of every regularly minted American coin. He is pointing to a unique $2.50 goldpiece of 1875. Story inside.

Eliasberg was featured in many magazine articles and other publications, and was always willing to share his collection with all who were interested. (*Courtesy Bowers and Merena*)

more than double the pre-sale estimate of $1,000 for it. Kosoff told Eliasberg that he was not at liberty to sell it before the auction, thus setting up one of the most contentious bidding wars in numismatic history.

Everyone knew that Eliasberg needed the 1873-CC *Without Arrows* dime, making it seem only a formality for him to attend the auction, raise his hand, and triumphantly walk out with the coin. To the surprise of those in attendance, Eliasberg's plans were foiled by two dealers with whom he had previously maintained an amiable business relationship. There were other dealers and collectors in the crowd who would have purchased the rarity, and Harold M. Budd was in attendance and probably raised his bidding paddle a couple of times. And then there was the successful bidder for the 1894-S dime, who most certainly entertained the thought of owning both of these rare dimes. He was fortunate to win the 1894-S for $1,850, against a pre-sale estimate of $2,500. At the time, this date was considered scarcer than the 1873-CC *Without Arrows*, though there were estimated to be six specimens known compared to only one of the Carson City dime.

---

[1] Ibid.
[2] Ibid.

After the bidding for the *Without Arrows* dime passed the $2,000 mark, just about everyone had dropped out except Eliasberg and the two dealers, James Kelly and Sol Kaplan who teamed up against Eliasberg. Past the $2,000 level these two dealers would have had no one else to sell the coin to except Eliasberg, so they obviously were not buying it for inventory. But they remained steadfast and finally bid it up to over $3,300. Eliasberg had not planned to exceed $2,500, let alone $3,000, but almost in anger he retaliated and raised his hand one last time at around $3,550. Kelly and Kaplan trumped him, and the hammer fell at $3,650.

No one knows for sure what the two dealers' motives were, but in a move that required much courage, they offered the coin to Eliasberg after the sale, an offer that was rejected, as Eliasberg chose to allow them some time to contemplate their actions. Five months passed and Kaplan finally called Eliasberg, asking what he would offer for the dime. At that point, Eliasberg could have forced Kaplan and Kelly to take a loss, but he graciously of-fered them a $350 profit, purchasing the piece for $4,000. Numismatic history was made that day, November 7, 1950, as Eliasberg became the only man ever to own an example of every coin produced in the United States from colonial times through 1950. His want list finally had a check mark next to every entry.

Years later his son, Richard A. Eliasberg summa-rized his father's achievement: "Over the years, with the assistance of a number of coin dealers, he upgraded the quality of the coins in his collection, replacing the lesser quality coins with better condition ones. In addition to the U.S. coin collection, my father also collected U.S. pa-per money, colonial pieces, private and pioneer coins, pat-terns, commemoratives, and some foreign gold and minor coins. The total collection exceeded 10,000 coins."[1]

From the time the set was completed in 1950 until his death 26 years later, Eliasberg displayed his mammoth collection, wrote articles, gave speeches, consented to in-terviews and corresponded with interested parties across the nation. Newspapers and feature magazines like *Life* and *Look* ran headline stories about him. He literally became, *The King of Coins.*

HIGHLIGHTS OF ELIASBERG'S CARSON CITY COINS

Louis E. Eliasberg, Sr. is not remembered exclusively for his Carson City coins, although he is the only man who ever had a complete collection from that mint. There have been a small number of collectors who have come

[1] Ibid.

A REPORT ON THE MENJOU SALE

With a crowded room of collectors and dealers, the big sale got under way at 8:00 P.M. on Thursday, June 15th. Among those in attendance were Jim Kelly of Day-ton, Ohio; Joe Stack of N.Y.C.; Sol Kaplan of Cincinnati; Bob Schermerhorn of Dallas; Louis Eliosberg of Baltimore; John Pittman of Rochester, N. Y.; Earl Parker and Brant Eubanks of San Francisco, and of course many from the California area.

The elite among the collecting fraternity was represented either by their Bid Sheets or by the dealers who had traveled thou-sands of miles to attend the greatest public auction sale of rare coins ever held—and it turned out to be a really great sale.

It was not long before the rarities came up for sale—Lot 97—the 1802 half dime was sold cheaply at $425.00. Before long the famous 1894-S dime was up and down at $1850.00; the 1895-O sold at $155.00 and the auctioneer announced that a bid of $270.00 had been received for this item.

Now we arrive at the point destined to provide the most sensational bidding in many a year: the unique uncirculated 1873 Carson City dime without arrows. Cataloguing at $350.00 in the standard lists this rarity was estimated at $1000.00, although it was really expected to go to $2000.00—and that bid was received. Opening at $1100.00 bidding was brisk and soon the $2000.00 mark was passed. James Kell-topped it. The foremost collector of Amer-ican Coins, Mr. Louis Eliasberg, then en-tered the field. Mr. Eliasberg made the flight from Baltimore in order to obtain only two coins he needed to complete an **entire collection** of U.S. coins of every date and every mint in every metal. This 1873 dime was one of them. Bidding soon reached $3000.00 and was still continuing. Ap-parently the cataloguer had something when he stated: "Among the rarest of all U.S. coins not excluding the 1804 dollar or the 1913 nickel." Apparently Mr. Eliasberg was determined to win but so was Kelly and he did—at $3650.00. In our opinion it took "guts" for Mr. Eliasberg to drop out—it certainly wasn't the money but his con-viction that the coin—at that moment—wasn't worth the price. Kelly, on the other hand, feels that it is the greatest rarity among the U.S. coins. We are inclined to agree.

A full report will be included in our List of Prices realized—($1.00) ready soon. The other highlights: 1876-CC 20 cents, $1325.00; 1827 quarter, $2725.00; 1838-O

Numismatic Gallery's monthly newsletter reporting on the *Menjou* sale, highlighting the story of the 1873-CC *Without Arrows* dime.

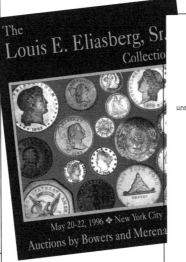

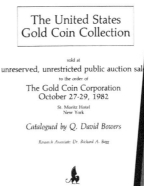

The United States Gold Coin Collection

sold at unreserved, unrestricted public auction sale to the order of The Gold Coin Corporation October 27-29, 1982

St. Moritz Hotel New York

Catalogued by Q. David Bowers

Research Associate: Dr. Richard A. Bagg

Bowers & Ruddy Galleries, Inc. Los Angeles, California

In three unforgettable auctions, Eliasberg's remarkable collection was sold for a cumulative price realized of nearly $45 million.

Sixteen Stand-Out "CC" Coins from the Eliasberg Collection

Date	Denomination	Grade	Pedigree	Price Realized	Year of Sale
1873-CC	*Without Arrows* 10¢	NGC MS-65	*Menjou* Sale (Chas. Williams) 1950	$550,000	1996
1870-CC	25¢	NGC MS-64	Clapp Family 1942	187,000	1997
1889-CC	$1	PCGS MS-68	Clapp Family 1942	462,000	1997
1873-CC	*Without Arrows* 25¢	PCGS MS-64	*World's Greatest Collection* 1945	187,000	1997
1876-CC	$5	PCGS MS-66	Clapp Family 1942	26,400	1982
1872-CC	25¢	NGC MS-66	Clapp Family 1942	99,000	1997
1871-CC	25¢	PCGS MS-65	*World's Greatest Collection* 1945	165,000	1997
1876-CC	20¢	PCGS MS-65	Clapp Family 1942	148,500	1997
1873-CC	*With Arrows* 25¢	PCGS MS-64	Unlisted	88,000	1997
1876-CC	Trade $1	PCGS MS-65	Clapp Family 1942	63,800	1997
1874-CC	50¢	PCGS MS-66	Clapp Family 1942	60,500	1997
1878-CC	50¢	PCGS MS-66	Clapp Family 1942	77,000	1997
1870-CC	$20	NGC XF-40*	William C. Atwater 1946	22,000	1982
1874-CC	$10	PCGS MS-63	Clapp Family 1942	17,600	1982
1891-CC	$1	PCGS MS-68 PL	Possibly Clapp Family 1942	121,000	1997
1873-CC	*With Arrows* 50¢	NGC MS-66**	Clapp Family 1942	35,200	1997

(* Possibly NGC XF-45, or PCGS XF-40 or 45) (** Possibly PCGS MS-65)

close, usually winding up two coins short, and on a handful of occasions lacking only the 1873-CC *Without Arrows* dime.

Eliasberg belongs to every category of U.S. coin specialists, for the scope of his collection was too broad and extensive for any one group to claim him as their poster boy. But because of his accomplishments in the Carson City series, especially the publicity that elevated the status of the 1873-CC *Without Arrows* dime to the *Unique* classification, he receives honorary membership in the Carson City Mint hall of fame.

From his unparalleled collection of "CC" coins, 16 in particular stand out. The above table features these 16 coins with grade, price and pedigree information, ranked according to overall rarity factors combined with condition ratings. Some of the position rankings may be interchangeable with others; what is most important is the overarching superiority of the group.

The Battle Born Collection

One of the hallmarks of the rich heritage of the Carson City Mint is the institution's deep-rooted ties to *Nevadaism*. From cowboys on the range, to Basque farmers, to silver miners, to ranchers, to politicians stumping in the town square, to newspaper editors, to mill operators, to railroad men, to reclamationists, and all other inhabit-

ants of the *Sagebrush State,* a sense of territorial and cultural pride is second nature.

Though not always knowing what they find so appealing about their state, Nevadans are proud that it is a little different than the rest of the country. There is a collective perception of being freer than citizens of other states, having fewer restrictions, and perhaps a more untamed environment. It is this very image, however, that has resulted in derisive remarks being cast at it from outsiders. But, in truth, Nevadans are proud of this too.

Nevadaism is an ideology rooted in the state's fight for survival in the late 19th century, blossoming to fruition in the early part of the 20th century. Reacting to opportunists, who like predators, set foot in the state, stripped it of its natural resources, and then abandoned it, Nevadans, "were determined to free themselves from carpetbag rule and assert their sovereignty."[1]

Elected officials began governing the state from the inside out, rather than the opposite. Laws were passed which benefited residents of the state, with an emphasis on fewer restrictions and lower taxes. In general, Nevada's edict to the national political scene was *you mind your business, and we will mind ours.* This bodes well in theory, but the fact that the federal government owned approximately 90%

---

[1] Gilman M. Ostrander, *Nevada, The Great Rotten Borough.*

of Nevada's land would always lead to ramifications. Despite this, Nevada has remained one of the most progressive states in America.

NEVADANS BEAM WITH PRIDE
OVER POPULARITY OF "CC" COINS

After four decades of a strengthening sense of *Nevadaism*, residents of the state were delighted when the old Carson City Mint building was converted into the Nevada State Museum. Ten years later in 1950, the sale of a dime from the Carson Mint for $4,000 gave Nevadans a further excuse to strut their stuff, as it seemed with the passing of time the popularity of "CC" coins increased.

Suddenly, every collector in the country wanted coins from the Nevada mint, and state residents were no exception. Already instilled with pride and respect for their state's heritage, coins from the local mint were natural expressions enabling them to hold a snapshot of this picturesque history in their hands.

Great Seal of the State of Nevada since the 1860s.

By the time the GSA sales in the 1970s sparkled the nation with "CC" silver dollars, locals residing in the Carson City/Reno area were actively participating in the collecting craze. The region became a good source for many "CC" dates to the delight of those collectors living there, most of whom would start with a collection of the 13 dates in the "CC" Morgan dollar series, as all but the 1889-CC were in plentiful supply, especially in circulated grades. Collecting gold coins from the Carson City series presented too great a financial challenge for most people, and though hundreds of examples of Seated Liberty silver coins circulated in this area of Nevada, the majority were common dates from the mid-1870s. Only in their dreams could collectors hope to acquire dates from the early 1870s, or a coin like the legendary 1876-CC 20-cent piece.

There was a young man, bred in the traditions of *Nevadaism*, hard at work building up his own business during the "CC" silver dollar mania of the 1970s. He was well acquainted with the legacy of the Carson City Mint and greatly appreciated the coins produced there, but as his capital was tied up in his business and raising a family, the time was not right for him to get heavily involved in the hobby. He knew LaVere Redfield on a casual basis and had even done yard-work at the old coin-hoarder's

mansion. When Redfield died and his massive silver dollar holdings were revealed, this young man, like everyone else in the country, read about it with amazement.

A succession of propitious events, including timely real estate investments, booming local development, and increased profitability in his business, secured this person's financial future by the end of the 1980s and as the 1990s approached, he was in a position to use more of his discretionary income for the pursuit of leisure activities. During the years leading up to the 1990s, this person, who has requested anonymity, dabbled in coin collecting, building multiple sets of "CC" Morgan dollars, mostly in circulated grades except for the common dates. He had also acquired examples from some of the other Carson City denominations, none being of much consequence.

With a healthy bankroll, this casual hobbyist evolved first into an apprentice, and then into a journeyman coin collector during the 1990s. Several factors attracted him to the gold coins from Carson City at first, one being the uniformity of three distinct 19 piece denominational sets. He had already completed several sets of "CC" Morgan dollars, and found this pursuit lacked the challenge to motivate him. Also contributing to his interest in Carson City gold coins was the publication of a book on the subject during the early stages of his collecting pursuits.[1] Lastly, like just about everyone else, he liked the glitter of gold, and he was now at the place where he could afford it.

This collector, born and raised in Nevada, experienced all the trials and errors associated with the hobby as he diligently assembled his gold sets. His protective net was certified grading, though at times even certification does not guarantee consistency. Pricing was always a challenge, since evaluating Carson City gold was (and still is) a work in progress. Until the 1990s, no one really knew what the extant populations were for this series. For instance, the 1870-CC double eagle, which at one time was estimated to have a surviving population of fewer than 20 pieces, a figure adjusted many times between 1988 and 2003, and eventually raised to between 45 and 50 pieces.

Unknown hoards of Carson City gold coins also remained to be discovered, periodically entering the mar-

---

[1] Douglas Winter and Lawrence E. Cutler, M.D., *Gold Coins of the Old West*.

ket and causing further price adjustments. For example, at Stack's November 1989 sale, a group of five Uncirculated 1890-CC, and five Uncirculated 1891-CC half eagles were offered. Other than such auction appearances of many of the common date "CC" gold coins, appearances of key and semi key dates were minimal, making it difficult for editors of dealer and retail price guides to compile comprehensive track records for dates that were only being offered every three to ten years. A case in point is the Eliasberg 1876-CC half eagle, which sold at the prestigious 1982 auction for $26,400. In subsequent years it was graded by PCGS as MS-65, and in 1990 sold at a Superior auction for $121,000, representing a 458% increase. But what would the listed price be for this coin in 2002? Surely in 12 years its value would have appreciated at a steady rate. Yet at the July 2002 sale of the *Henry S. Lang* collection, the price realized was $138,000, a strong figure indeed, but still only a 14% increase over the 1990 sale price.

This *Battle Born* collector came to realize that occasional variations in grading standards and a volatile pricing structure were all part of the Carson City gold market. As long as he understood the rules he could play the game. Besides, inconsistencies in grading could work both ways, and occasionally his coins were upgraded when resubmitted, resulting in substantial price gains. As the years passed and he was able to view many coins, his eye for quality became sharper, strengthening his confidence when making purchasing decisions.

At some point in his collecting odyssey, Mr. *Battle Born* decided to add silver type coins from the Carson City Mint to his want list. He quickly learned that this was a totally different ball game, as instead of neat, well-defined 19 piece sets, the "CC" silver series included such varieties as *With* or *Without* arrows, and mintmarks *Above* and *Below* wreaths. And though some of the dates in the "CC" gold series were very scarce, many of the dates in the silver series were virtually nonexistent. Early, on, he ruled out the possibility of including the 1873-CC *Without Arrows* dime in his collection, figuring that the chances of acquiring the one and only specimen were equivalent to catching a comet.

Even with that one date eliminated there were formidable challenges, but his growing appreciation for the mint from his native state and the thrill of the hunt kept him in pursuit. One of his most exciting experiences as a coin collector was when he purchased an Uncirculated example of an 1876-CC 20-cent piece. He had heard about

this date since he was a boy and remembered back in the 1970s when specimens were offered in the $20,000 to $60,000 range—more than he paid for his first house. Then, almost as being struck by double lightning, he purchased one of the only three known Uncirculated 1873-CC *Without Arrows* quarters. He was walking on air, though at the same time reminding himself that this was the most money he had ever spent on a single coin. If someone had told him eight years earlier that he would someday be buying six-figure coins he probably would have scoffed.

But now he had done it. Between his 1870-CC double eagle and a few other gold rarities he was in the big leagues of coin collecting. He had crossed every major hurdle as it came, and was now standing near the summit, ready to accomplish something that no other native Nevadan, and very few outside the state, had ever achieved. There was no stopping him as he picked off dates right and left, and then, he was done. His set of coins from the Carson City Mint included one example from every date produced there except the *Unique* 1873 *Without Arrows* dime, a total of 110 pieces, with a few extra varieties for good measure.

Without a doubt, this *Battle Born* collection is the finest and most complete set of Carson City coins ever assembled by a native born Nevadan, as well as being one of the finest and most complete sets regardless of the owner's state of origin.

In the years following the completion of this set the collector has continued to upgrade it when possible, and thoroughly enjoy the privilege of ownership. In his opinion there is no other individual coin or series of coins that can compete with those from the Carson City Mint; perhaps there is a trace of *Nevadaism* in that sentiment, but you cannot blame the man for being proud, not only of his coin collection, but also of his state and his life's achievements as a businessman.

Nevada State Museum Collection

A Wells Fargo stagecoach pulled by four horses rumbles south down Carson Street with the agent cracking his whip yelling *Yaaahh!* Suddenly the driver pulls on the reins, bringing the cradle on wheels to a halt in front of the old mint building. A robust guard pulls a heavy strongbox off the coach as the driver opens the door, allowing the Governor of Nevada and a Wells Fargo Bank executive to step down. At that point, the bank executive hands the strongbox to Nevada's Governor, symbolic of a gift.

This recreation of a scene from the classic days of the old west is part of a ceremony celebrating a historic donation of a nearly complete collection of Carson City coins by the Wells Fargo Bank to the Nevada State Museum. Actually, the collection had been on display at the museum for 10 years prior to this December 1999 event; since May 1989 it had been on loan to the State of Nevada from Wells Fargo's predecessor First Interstate Bank. First Interstate had taken possession of the collection when it had absorbed the assets of the collection's previous owner, First National Bank of Nevada. First National's ownership dated back to February of 1971 when it purchased it from the man who had assembled the collection, Norman H. Biltz.

In a letter sent to Norman Biltz's stepson John F. Nash from a Wells Fargo executive vice president six days before the 1999 donation, the bank's intentions were expressed, "Wells Fargo Bank is pleased to inform you that we are donating the Bank's collection of Carson City minted coins to the State of Nevada for permanent display at the State Museum in Carson City... By donating this fine collection to the State of Nevada it will be shared with all citizens of the state and provide a permanent attraction for visitors to the State Museum."[1]

These words from the bank executive in 1999 echoed the sentiments of Norman Biltz from 28 years earlier when Biltz was nearing the end of his life and putting his affairs in order. On February 21, 1971, he was sitting in First National Bank president Art Smith's office in Reno where he told Smith about his coin collection and offered to sell it to the bank. Though he had been offered upwards of $100,000 for his prized set of Carson City coins,

Biltz asked Smith for $50,000 to do the deal. There were three stipulations that Biltz spelled out to Smith:

1)   The bank would never sell the collection.

2)   The collection would never leave Nevada.

3)   The collection would be displayed on a regular basis.

Without hesitation, Smith reached his hand across his desk and the two men shook on the deal.

Later on it was reported that Biltz hired local attorney Jack Barry to draw up a contract for the transaction, but no one seems to know what became of that contract. Biltz's stepson John F. Nash insisted that he saw a copy of the contract many years ago and has written numerous letters to the different banks who had taken possession of the collection through mergers requesting a copy, yet no one has been able to produce the document.

Rumors abounded as to why Biltz sold the collection in the first place. There were suggestions that he needed the money, yet according to his stepson, Biltz was worth over $4 million at the time, not including his wife's fortune. According to John F. Nash, his stepfather sold the collection for two reasons: the primary was that Biltz's home had been broken into around that time, with the burglar stealing one of his prized collector guns and leaving Biltz, who also kept his coin collection in a drawer at home, fearful of another break-in. He said that if he could not show his collection to his friends, he did not want to keep it. Furthermore, Biltz's health was failing him and he had recently begun putting all of his affairs in order. This was certainly not the way Biltz had planned on spending the twilight years of his colorful life.

A COLORFUL LIFE

And a colorful life it had been. Born on July 6, 1902 in Bridgeport, Connecticut, Biltz spent his childhood and teenage years traveling back and forth between Connecticut, Massachusetts and New York. At 18, he married the first of his three wives, but almost at once became estranged from her. Seeking more adventure than New England could offer, Biltz joined the incessant migration of easterners to California, and as a 20 year old go-getter went through job after job until he found his niche as a salesman. Forming his first company with a partner, he achieved immediate success, but his partner's weakness for gambling resulted in substantial losses of company assets and it was time for Biltz to start over.

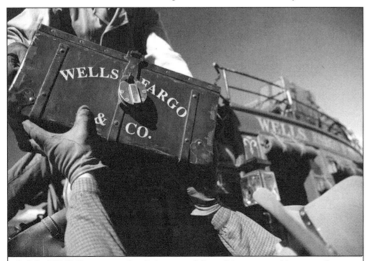

Original Wells Fargo strongbox being passed from driver to guard in a staged event in the 1990s. (*Courtesy Wells Fargo*)

[1] Letter from Wells Fargo to John F. Nash, December 3, 1999.

At 25 years old Biltz, having already experienced enough for a man 10 years his senior, traveled from San Francisco to Lake Tahoe located on the California/Nevada border. This is where he discovered the destiny that set him on track for all his eventual successes. Lake Tahoe was a dreamland for the young visionary, with its crystal clear waters, pine trees growing to maturity just 50 years after being deforested to build Comstock mines, scintillating fragrances in the air, and the matchless beauty of the Sierra Nevada mountain range surrounding this natural wonder of environmental beauty. It was also basically virgin territory in terms of real estate development.

Biltz could see the potential of it all in 1927 and determined that his life's ambition would be to place himself right in the middle of the development of it. His personal affairs took precedence at first, as he divorced his first wife, from whom he had been separated for years. Almost before the ink was dry on the certificate, he married his second wife, which again proved to be a premature attempt by Biltz to become a husband and ended in divorce within a year.

Marital failures aside, Biltz had become involved in the first of many successful business relationships, which would assist him in achieving his dreams. Crucial to a young man starting out with no capital was the financial support of a backer, a role fulfilled in Biltz's life during the early years by Robert Sherman, a successful real estate developer from Southern California. Sherman already owned property in Lake Tahoe by way of an inheritance from his father, and saw in the young and enthusiastic Biltz the agent he needed to develop and eventually sell it.

At first, Biltz lived at the Riverside Hotel in Reno and commuted between Robert Sherman's different real estate holdings. For a young man in his late 20s this was an exciting road indeed, as one day he would be in San Francisco, the next in Lake Tahoe, then on to Los Angeles, and back again to Reno. During several of his trips to Southern California, Biltz sold two of Sherman's major real estate holdings: the lot where the MGM Movie production company was located and for good measure, Santa Monica Beach. This was around 1929, and though

these were big deals at the time, either one of these would be a career-defining event for a realtor today (2003).

BILTZ FOCUSES ON NEVADA

Gradually, Biltz began to focus all of his attention on Nevada, as he quickly identified the advantages in Nevada's tax laws he could use as selling points to lure wealthy investors into the state. In his promotional literature Biltz informed prospects that "Nevada is an easy state to live in. It has a genial climate, a pleasure-loving people, and liberal laws."[1] Among these liberal laws, Biltz elaborated, "Nevada collects no income tax, no inheritance tax, no sales tax, no gift tax, and no tax on intangibles."[2] This is why, as Biltz stated, "Nevada has been excellently named, the *Cyclone Cellar* for the tax weary."[3]

Armed with what he considered a sales strategy guaranteed to succeed, Biltz targeted prospective clients, by researching tax rolls and corporate files from other states across the nation. From this study he was able to prepare a list of the top 200 or so wealthiest individuals in America. He found out everything he could about them, including their preferences in food, alcohol, entertainment and politics, as well as any temperamental characteristics that might help him get to know them better. Then he began calling on them, presenting his sales pitch as he went.

Young Norman Biltz posing in his office in the 1930s. His casual dress suited him throughout his career.

One of Biltz's first successful solicitations was to a Chicago advertising man named James L. Stack (apparently not related to the famous coin collector). Stack's fortune had come to him early in life, not from his profession, but from his successful investment in the burgeoning Quaker Oats Company. Although Mr. Stack had recently suffered a stroke leaving him paralyzed on one side of his body, Biltz's persistence persuaded him to spend a couple days in Lake Tahoe. In Biltz's own words, "...we brought Jim up to Lake Tahoe...it was early June... So what happens? We get a snowstorm... and we can't move. And we needed this sale so bad... So I looked at that terrain [and] I thought, 'Well by God, I can carry him

---

[1] *Nevada, the Last Frontier*, Norman Biltz and Associates, 1939.
[2] Ibid.
[3] Ibid.

over there…I said 'Jim get on my back, by God, we've come all this way… to see this property!'…So I packed him over there and packed him back… I know he was awful heavy on the way back."[1] Biltz's efforts paid off, because James L. Stack bought the property for between $35,000 and $50,000 in cash. This was only a precursor of things to come, as Biltz cultivated his business of importing millionaires into Nevada during the next 30 years.

THE THIRD TIME IS THE CHARM

With this landmark sale under his belt, Biltz felt it was time to get serious about starting a family and as he later reminisced: "In 1929 at the Cal Neva, I ran into a gal who rented one of our houses, and became enamored [with her, and] decided we might get married."[2] And this was not just any *gal*, she happened to be Mrs. Esther Auchincloss Nash, granddaughter of one of the founders of Standard Oil. There has been some speculation as to whether Mrs. Nash just happened to be on Biltz's list of prospects, yet there is overwhelming evidence that he became infatuated with her before knowing anything of her family relations. It appears as if their meeting was one of those divinely appointed moments bringing two lives together that would not have otherwise met. Esther Nash was staying at the Cal Neva in Lake Tahoe awaiting her divorce to be finalized. Biltz was part owner of the Lodge through his partnership with Sherman, and at the age of 27 was walking on clouds after his success in the James L. Stack deal.

Apparently the couple wanted to get married right away, but reality set in when Esther's family insisted on meeting Biltz first, and furthermore demanded that marriage plans be delayed for one year. Love won out, the pair waited through the required engagement period and finally wed in 1930. By then, Biltz had learned all about his wife's background. She was not only an heir to the Standard Oil fortune; she was also the aunt of a baby girl named Jacqueline Bouvier Auchincloss through her brother Hugh Auchincloss's second marriage. Although of little consequence at the time, in 1953 when Jacqueline married Senator John F. Kennedy, Biltz's political connections would grow even stronger. Another of Esther's family connections was famous poet Ogden Nash, the brother of her first husband and uncle to her three children.

Biltz was in for the ride of his life as he took Esther Auchincloss Nash to be his dearly beloved wife. Though she was extremely wealthy and would become more so through continuance inheritances, Biltz vowed to never

touch his wife's money. As a rule, he made good on that vow throughout his life, yet he could not help taking advantage of her family ties when the need arose.

Norman and Esther Biltz at a celebration at the Cal Neva Lodge.

He was determined to become a good stepfather to her children Edmund (Ted), John, and Anita. He admitted that family life brought about big changes in him, saying years later that, "I really had to work myself over pretty well, and change faces and hats, and this staying up until two or three o'clock in the morning had to stop."[3] Biltz was concerned about taking care of Esther in a fashion she was accustomed to and later reflected, "Just think back how we spent our honeymoon. My wife was used to a great deal more than I could give her…She had never worked in her life; she didn't know how to boil water."[4] But she was obviously very committed to him and appreciated his intentions to take care of everything, nevertheless, she told her husband, "Here's the way we'll run it. I have the three children, so I'm going to pay $2/3$ of the bills, and you pay $1/3$, and we'll live on it." [5]

Biltz accepted the generous offer but became even more determined to make his own fortune. He worked twice as hard, and reformed in many ways: "I quit gambling and greatly retarded my drinking… plus keeping myself away from past associates, or least some of them."[6] Most of the time, as he related: "I worked my tail off… The days were long; my wife was very cooperative, although she felt that it wasn't worth it…well, to her it wasn't, but to me it was…she didn't interfere."[7]

In their first few years of marriage the newlyweds spent half their time in Reno and half in New York and

[1] *Memoirs of "The Duke of Nevada," Norman H. Biltz,* Oral History Program University of Nevada Reno.
[2] Ibid.
[3] Ibid.
[4] Ibid.
[5] Ibid.
[6] Ibid.
[7] Ibid.

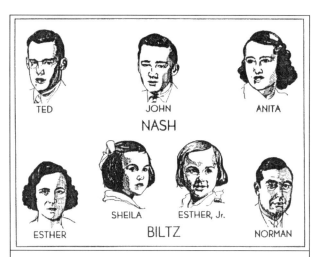

Special Christmas card sketched by a local Reno artist for the Biltz family in the 1930s.

Connecticut visiting Esther's family. Two daughters, Sheila and Esther, were born in 1932 and 1934, adding the final touches to the couple's blended family. Biltz was naturally very fond of his daughters, but was also devoted to his three stepchildren. He often felt inadequate in his role as a stepfather and found it discouraging that he could never provide financial aid to his step kids comparable to the trust funds set up for them on his wife's side. He lamented: "Not being able to, at that time, give them any social advantages, about the only thing I could see that I could do would be…to make them love me, and to make connections everywhere and anywhere I could that…would be advantageous to their business or married lives later on."[1]

Biltz scored high on both points, his step kids, as well as his two daughters grew to love him immensely, and he made more connections than anyone in the history of Nevada. A myriad of people became associated with Biltz throughout his long career in Nevada, none of whom influenced him more than John Mueller (pronounced Muller).

A SUCCESSFUL PARTNERSHIP

Mueller had arrived in Nevada in the early 1920s and soon began traveling from one end of the state to the other in his position as Assistant State Engineer. The population of Nevada was very small in those years so Mueller practically knew everyone and spent many days in Carson City discussing the development of the state with legislators. Because of his obliging manner, Mueller posed no threat to them and quickly became a man who could be trusted. He had an attentive mind and knew how to interview people without appearing to be prying into their business, thus becoming a walking information machine.

At the early stages of Biltz's rise to power, the information Mueller provided was one of his most valuable assets. In 1931, when Nevada was faced with a depression-era stagnant economy, Biltz and Mueller teamed with other lobbyists to persuade lawmakers to legalize gambling, reduce residency requirements for divorces from three months to six weeks, and permit liquor to be sold 24/7. This was all part of Biltz's grand design to attract more people to Nevada and stimulate growth.

Biltz was also concerned about the calamitous effects that the severe drought of 1930 and 1931 were having on the state. Mueller knew every inch of ranchland in Nevada, including who owned it, how many acres there were, what the mortgage balance was, and whether the water rights were transferable. With this information in hand, Biltz and Mueller could appraise the ranches that were being forced into bankruptcy. Biltz's goal was to bail out the ranch owners, spare the banks the burden of taking the ranches into receivership, and at the same time induce more of the millionaires on his list to invest in Nevada. At 30 years of age, Biltz was taking on projects well beyond his level of experience, but what he lacked in background and maturity he made up for with exuberance and vision.

In no time the team of Biltz and Mueller had sold bankrupt ranches to wealthy individuals from out of state. A list of these men includes such recognizable names as gin and yeast magnate Max C. Fleischman, Wall Street broker Dean Witter, singer and movie star Bing Crosby, automobile and aviation pioneer E.L. Cord, and even Biltz's brother-in-law, Hugh Auchincloss II. As the years passed, other notable men, such as Wilbur D. May of the May Company department stores, and Charles S. Howard, owner of the legendary racehorse, Seabiscuit, were lured to Nevada. A solid foundation had been laid during these early years for Biltz to build on, and his name was already being mentioned as one to be reckoned with.

With no formal education, not even a high school diploma, Biltz's vocabulary would have been considered unrefined back in New England, but out west he fit right in. He spoke in the vernacular of movie cowboys, calling his associates "pardner," and his female friends "ma'am." He even called Esther, his cultured wife, "Mammy." But it was not his vocabulary that made him successful; Biltz had a home-on-the-range kind of charm that set people at ease. He was the Will Rogers of real estate salesmen, always promoting but never in bad taste.

---

[1] Ibid.

One of the next "pardners" on Biltz's team was Henry Trevor, a San Francisco real estate investor who with Biltz sold a 27 mile stretch of land around the shore of Lake Tahoe to eccentric millionaire George Whittell. In the original agreement, Whittell was to buy the property and Biltz and Trevor were to parcel it out and sell it. During the first two months sales were brisk, but then without warning, Whittell reneged on his part of the agreement. He told Biltz that he did not want to sell any more property and the deal was off, cutting out Biltz and Trevor completely and they never made a dime on the sale. A short time later, Biltz realizing he was no match for the wealthy Whittell, lost his temper and together with Trevor went to Whittell's house, tore up the contract, threw the pieces at him and then spit in his face. Years later, after Biltz had achieved great success, he was still bitter over this whole affair, and when Whittell's name was mentioned, would get a scowl on his face. As for Whittell, he made millions of dollars on his Lake Tahoe property and his mansion there is a tourist attraction today.

Some Mythical Stories

When chronicling the life of Norman Biltz the boundaries between historical fact and myth sometimes collide making it difficult to separate one from the other. Yet even if certain anecdotes lean toward the mythical side, there is probably enough fact incorporated to lend credibility to them. For instance, Biltz describes how he sold the Cal Neva Lodge to Bill Graham and Jim McKay for $65,000 after gambling was legalized in 1931. Supposedly the two men gave Biltz a $6,500 down payment, with the balance due at the end of the year. According to Biltz, "in those days I had some bad habits and one of them was gambling."[1] Apparently another bad habit was drinking, because Biltz attended the grand opening of the casino at the Cal Neva, had too much to drink, and passed out. "I got up about noon and went in to see Jim McKay. I said, 'well, you had a good night.' He said, 'Well you don't owe me anything Norm.' I said, 'Thank God for that.' Then [McKay] said: 'I got news for you, we don't owe you anything either.' I'd lost $58,000. But they were good to me. They loaned me $500 to get out of town."[2]

If this incident really occurred, it means that Biltz attended Graham and McKay's grand opening, got drunk, lost the $58,000 that they owed him, passed out, and then woke up the next morning not remembering what he had done. Based on recounts of his reckless years in the 1920s, this story sounds plausible, but there is one significant detail that is puzzling: Biltz had been married to Esther for over one year when this supposedly took place and he had vowed to reform his ways. What could he have possibly told his wife when she asked him where the money went from the sale of the Lodge? Of course, this does not mean that it did not happen; it just puts a new slant on his commitment to be a good family man.

Another story Biltz told often was how he met the *King of Nevada*, George Wingfield, once again with gambling as the backdrop. Biltz was staying at Wingfield's Riverside Hotel in Reno and losing at the gaming tables, presumably after gambling was legalized in Nevada in 1931, unless, of course, Wingfield was running an underground casino. If it was 1931 or later, why was Biltz staying at the Riverside and why was he not at home with his family? There again, maybe this was one of those times when his wife was back east, but in any event, Biltz was $1,600 in debt, and Wingfield ordered him into his office, and told Biltz to move out of the Riverside and go to the Golden Hotel because rooms were much cheaper. Offering no explanation, Biltz tells how Wingfield gave him free meals and laundry service and how one day he walked into Wingfield's office and insisted that they take a trip to Lake Tahoe. For some reason, the powerful Wingfield agreed and after they arrived at the lake, Biltz showed him some property, asking Wingfield for a $50,000 loan to buy the parcel, and promising to pay him back at 8% interest, plus the $1,600 gambling debt. On the trip back to Reno, Wingfield told Biltz: "You know, you've got guts enough to ask me to do that. I'm going to do it." Supposedly that is how Biltz purchased one of his most valuable pieces of Lake Tahoe property, and became closely associated with the most powerful man in Nevada at the time.

Truth or myth, fact or fiction, it really does not affect the Biltz legacy either way. He was the kind of person who loved everything about Nevada and wanted to be involved in every part of it. His life was right out of a Hollywood movie. A screenwriter could not have written a more glamorous story. Throughout the 1930s Biltz's influence grew in leaps and bounds, a fact illustrated by his accomplishments between 1927 and 1932 alone. In those five short years he had owned and sold the Cal Neva Lodge in Lake Tahoe, persuaded James L. Stack to establish his residency in Nevada, married the heir to part of the Standard Oil fortune, formed a political and business alliance

---

[1] Ibid.

[2] Ibid.

with Johnny Mueller, successfully lobbied to legalize gambling and reduce divorce residency requirements, sold at least a dozen multimillionaires on the idea of buying ranches and establishing residency in Nevada, and become closely associated with George Wingfield. Impressive as all this seems, it was only the beginning, because Biltz was on the verge of connecting with arguably the most powerful political figure in the history of Nevada.

THE 1933 INAUGURATION AND A NEW SENATOR

At the inauguration ceremony for Franklin Delano Roosevelt in 1933, Biltz, his wife, and a small group of Biltz's fellow Nevadans were sitting in a prime section overlooking the Presidential platform. For a young man from humble beginnings, not yet 31 years old, this was indeed an honor and a privilege. It is not clear how Biltz had received such a prestigious invitation at this early stage in his career, but the possibilities are numerous. After all, his client list included some of the wealthiest men in the United States who had undoubtedly acquired political influence. Correspondingly, his new pardner, Johnny Mueller, as well as his newly formed alliance with George Wingfield provided immediate links to legislators in Washington, D.C., and not insignificant was Biltz's own elevated social status via his marriage to a Standard Oil girl.

His attendance at his first Presidential inauguration may have been orchestrated by any one or a number of these new relationships, but within a few years, he would be the one pulling the strings to afford others special perks such as this. Throughout the rest of his life he would be welcomed by every U.S. President into the White House, and his phone calls would be put through to them without hesitation.

A new Nevada U.S. Senator was also being sworn in while Biltz and company were in Washington D.C., as Patrick A. McCarran finally achieved his life's goal at the age of 56 when he beat Wingfield's man Tasker L. Oddie in the Senate race. Some attributed McCarran's victory to the collapse of Wingfield's power base after his banks failed in the election year of 1932, while others surmised that Oddie lost because voters were frightened and frustrated over the devastating effects of the depression and wanted new blood to step in and help them. Though Biltz had become closely associated with Wingfield during the two years leading up to the election he was not yet as involved in the political process as he would be in the years to come. Still, anyone linked to Wingfield was considered to be a member of his gang, and Biltz was definitely a member.

Apparently Biltz was more familiar with McCarran than the latter was with Biltz. As a native born Nevadan, McCarran was, of course, conscious of all developments within the state, and was certainly aware of Biltz's millionaire-importing enterprise, as well as many of his real estate deals, but by 1933 the two men had not become closely acquainted. Then, at the 1933 inauguration ceremony, Biltz and McCarran crossed paths in a brief but career defining moment. "I'm getting in the elevator," Biltz remembered, "and here is Senator Pat and he's got his top hat on, you know, and his swallowtail coat. I went up and I said, 'Senator McCarran, let me congratulate you. You did a fantastic race.' [McCarran] said, 'I fooled you and the rest of your gang on the corner, didn't I?' I said, 'You certainly did Senator.' "[1] That was all there was to it, brief, but still an introduction.

During the next six years, McCarran would prove to be a powerful leader in spite of his status as a junior senator. Unlike many younger men who went to Washington, D.C. for the first time, in need of orientation to get their feet wet, McCarran, at 57 years old entered the scene as if he had been made for the part. He had been raised in Nevada, and since his teenage years, had witnessed the political maneuverings of the *silver senators*, the bank crowd and the railroad men and he was familiar with the tactics employed by power brokers like C. "Black" Wallace and George Wingfield. From his seat on the Chief Justice bench in Nevada, McCarran knew who was insincere and who was legitimate, and having been exposed to all the games people play, he could see right through a smokescreen. By the time he entered the halls of Congress in 1933 he was not about to be a passive spectator; he did not have any time to waste.

BILTZ'S CONTINUING SUCCESS

Meanwhile, Norman Biltz traversed from one real estate deal to another, as his empire grew and his sphere of influence expanded. Subdividing became his specialty, using his innate sense of what a raw piece of land would look like once it was fully developed with houses, office buildings, streets, and other improvements. During the mid-1930s he contracted the first residential tract in modern Reno's history and each additional subdivision project would exceed the size of the one preceding it. Biltz was a pioneer of real estate development, blazing trails not only in Reno and Lake Tahoe, but extending out to north-central Nevada and also in nearby Truckee, California.

---

[1] Ibid.

With the success of each undertaking as his reputation ripened for putting the right people together to achieve outstanding results, Biltz attracted new investors and deals would be dropped on his doorstep, ever expanding his purchasing power. If there had been 10 men operating like him in the state, competition would have cut into his territory. But that was the essence of his good fortune; Biltz was one of only a handful of men taking advantage of Nevada's untapped natural resources, and no one had honed it to a science as he had.

It was all there for the taking and Biltz did not hesitate in grabbing his share. He and his partners developed much of the north shore of Lake Tahoe, including Crystal Bay, Brockway and Kings Beach. Thanks to the information furnished by confidant Johnny Mueller about government irrigation plans in the Lovelock and Winnemucca areas, Biltz and company developed huge ranching operations. Biltz and Mueller were also benefactors of a lucrative oil lease deal involving over 100,000 acres of Nevada soil, and he let his friend E.L. Cord in on a big payoff from the largest uranium deposit in Nevada.

Biltz learned the value of political influence through the 1930s, and by the end of Senator McCarran's first term had formed a strong bond with him. From 1938 until McCarran died in 1954 their allegiance to one another was like that of father and son. Biltz had an empty spot in his life for a father figure, since his own dad had committed suicide years before, and McCarran, though well versed in politics and the law, had not had much success in business. Biltz was always there to provide McCarran with a tip on a good deal, or perhaps a donation to his campaign fund; and Johnny Mueller was always available to ensure that everything was kept squeaky clean.

Before long, the McCarran/Biltz/Mueller alliance controlled most of northern Nevada and parts of the south as well. Decisions about government contracts in Nevada crossed Biltz's desk for review, and new jobs were always being created for his pardners. There is no doubt that Biltz and his friends reaped bountiful profits from their endeavors, but in hindsight, the men's motives seem to have been pure and it genuinely appears as if one of their priorities was Nevada's future. It was imperative to Biltz that the laws in the state continued to favor tax advantages, describing Nevada as the, "State where you get the most for your tax dollar."[1]

He believed that the millionaires taking up residency in Nevada would ensure a sound economic base and add to the state's political influence, thus strengthening its credibility in the eyes of the nation. But he knew that wealthy individuals alone were not enough; reclamation of barren land, small business development, a healthy mining industry, and small to medium sized factories would also be required.

BILTZ'S VISION OF NEVADA

Biltz's vision of an ideal Nevada consisted of several key fundamentals. First, was maintaining the integrity of the state's environment and natural resources. Biltz was an outdoorsman at heart and saw the beauty in Nevada's lakes, mountains, rivers, deserts, plant life, animals and climate—a giant natural park for residents to enjoy. He also believed that real estate, when developed properly, would provide adequate housing for the population, whereas overbuilding and a rapidly expanding population base would lead to congestion, traffic problems, and threats to the environment. At the time Biltz was forming his vision for an ideal Nevada, the population in the entire state was only around 100,000 people and therefore it is impossible to estimate what he believed a safe limit for population growth should be. Biltz was primarily interested in northern Nevada, and no one could have predicted the unstoppable growth that would occur in southern Nevada during the last quarter of the 20th century. Suffice it to say, Biltz was concerned with comfortable living conditions for everyone in the state.

The third fundamental of Biltz's visionary plan centered on the economy: Everyone living in the state would need jobs; jobs would require business; and businessmen, according to Biltz, could be lured by low taxes. Biltz believed that if everyone cooperated, Nevada would be a wonderful place to live, and the two cornerstones in his plan were a significant group of wealthy investors to bankroll the venture, and a capable team of politicians to govern over the state and ensure that the laws remained conservative.

It was all very simple as far as Biltz was concerned, but prior to his emergence in the 1930s and 1940s, there had been no one in the history of the state that had come forward with such conceptual farsightedness. Every prominent leader before Biltz had been either too self-serving or too narrow-minded. The Comstock millionaires had not seen Nevada in this light, nor had men like Wingfield and Nixon, who in the early decades of the 20th century gave rise to *Nevadaism*, but never looked much beyond their own riches.

---

[1] W.K. Bixler, *A Dozen Sierra Success Stories.*

If there is one man from Nevada's past who parallels Biltz to any degree, it might be the founder of Carson City, Abe Curry. Obviously, things were much different in 1858 than they were 75 to 85 years later, but there are similarities between Curry and Biltz. Both had come west from the east, and were salesmen at heart, developers, and visionaries. In addition, these two men seemed to care about the welfare of their neighbors and fellow citizens and beyond question, each of these men in his own way helped put Nevada on the map. Curry had his partners just like Biltz, although it appears as if Biltz's partners probably possessed much more in resources, and put much more faith in his vision. One wonders what Curry could have accomplished if there had been a Robert Sherman or a Johnny Mueller in his life. Notwithstanding, Biltz and Curry rank high on Nevada's list of all-time most influential men, but surprisingly, it is difficult to find any mention of either of them in this context.

A FORCE TO BE RECKONED WITH

Within a decade after Biltz's arrival in Nevada he had become a force to be reckoned with, sporting a reputation for getting things done. There was no delaying or stalling with Biltz; procrastination was not a part of his game plan. Whether it was the financing of a real estate deal, the construction of a building, the irrigation of ranchland, or the passage of a favorable tax law, he knew who to contact and how to remove impeding obstacles. When his friends were in trouble he would rally in support, providing whatever was necessary to facilitate a speedy recovery. For example, on May 16, 1937, when the Cal Neva Lodge burned to the ground, Biltz brought an unprecedented crew of 500 construction workers to the secluded site in Lake Tahoe to rebuild the casino in a seemingly impossible 31 days. Biltz had promised it would be ready for the 4th of July weekend, and as usual he kept his word.

It was the same in politics. In 1944 when his friend and ally Pat McCarran faced strong opposition in the senate race from Key Pittman's brother Vail, Biltz came out in full force. Through his fundraising efforts he was able to supply a desperate McCarran with needed capital. Biltz called upon his many contacts throughout the state, many of whom he had gifted with past favors, to support McCarran and influence their neighbors. Employing the power of the press, Biltz was also able to entreat his connections at the newspapers to offer editorial support for his candidate and in the end, McCarran won the election

by a slim margin of 1,500 votes. Without Biltz he would have surely lost.

By the mid 1940s the McCarran/Biltz political machine was nearly invincible. Many names were added to the list of influential people Biltz was acquainted with during this time, as Fred Fisher of General Motors, as well as the head of the Simmons Bed Company, and Arthur Bourne, CEO of the Singer Sewing Machine Company were recruited to Nevada by

LaVere Redfield, another Nevadan with immense real estate holdings. He became more famous for his huge hoard of silver dollars than anything else in his life.

Biltz. One of Biltz's political heroes, Ed Flynn from New York, became a confidant and partner on several business deals. Biltz admired the way Flynn ran the Bronx, and always encouraged his associates to read Flynn's book *You're the Boss*. Another political boss and entrepreneur Biltz became acquainted with was Joseph Kennedy. These were in the days when John Fitzgerald Kennedy was still wet behind the ears and attending Harvard. Little did Biltz know that in 1953 he would become the younger Kennedy's uncle by way of his marriage to Esther, Kennedy's wife's aunt.

In an ironic twist, Biltz became a business partner of Stanley Dollar of the Dollar Steamship Company for whom Biltz had worked as a stevedore less than 20 years earlier. Things had changed, and now Biltz was using his political clout to assist Dollar in an attempt to get his company back, years after the depression had stripped it from him. Dollar had called upon Biltz in the years immediately following World War II when the government was planning on selling whatever Dollar still owned of the company to the Ambassador of Norway. As Biltz recalled, Dollar asked: "Norm, do you think you could get hold of a friend of McCarran's or some of your friends, and block this sale?"[1] In typical style, Biltz went to work, eventually beseeching another acquaintance, President Harry S. Truman, and ultimately taking it to the Supreme Court of the United States. Dollar did not get his company back, but he did manage to retrieve a payment of $13.7 million from the deal. Later

---

[1] *Memoirs of Norman H. Biltz*, Oral History Program, University of Nevada Reno.

on, Biltz found a beautiful piece of property for him at Lake Tahoe, which became known as *Dollar Hill.*

Biltz was a contemporary and loosely acquainted with famous silver dollar hoarder, LaVere Redfield. During the time Biltz was building a real estate empire, Redfield was purchasing large parcels of property himself. Always a shrewd buyer, Redfield searched for the most opportune deals and snatched them up. Biltz recalled that at one time Redfield had purchased over 42,000 acres of what is now southwestern Reno for $1 an acre. One of the big differences between Biltz and Redfield (and there are many) is that Biltz purchased real estate to develop it, and Redfield bought his properties on speculation with no intention of making improvements.

Nothing underscores Biltz's long-range game plan of acquiring and developing real estate more than what became known as the *Nile of Nevada* on the Humboldt River. By 1950, Biltz owned over 43,000 acres of fertile ranchland in this region and between his two ranching partnerships, claimed 14,000 head of cattle. In an article in *Time Magazine* in June of 1953, it was said of Biltz that, "he collects ranches much as other rich men collect securities or old masters."[1]

Seizing another opportunity in the 1940s, Biltz convinced partners Stanley Dollar and Ed Waltz to purchase what amounted to nearly the entire shoreline of Donner Lake in northern California, near Lake Tahoe. As Biltz proceeded in his accomplished style of subdividing, building, and sales, hundreds of new landowners bought properties at Donner Lake, turning it into a popular residential and recreational area. Today (2003), Donner Lake just outside of Truckee, California is a symbol of Biltz's visionary foresight.

The Family Ranch

When Norman and Esther Biltz were first married in 1930, Esther had been gracious to her 28 year old husband, offering to pay $2/3$ of the family's expenses. Before long, Biltz had no need for his wife's contributions and for the remainder of their long marriage always made sure his family was well provided for. Never extravagant, but certainly affluent and upper class, the Biltz family's lifestyle granted the children a pleasurable experience while growing up. One of Biltz's greatest gifts to his family was the 165 acre mini-ranch he developed in southwest Reno. Referred to as the *Gentleman's Ranch,* the compound featured three New England style mansions, surrounded by lush trees and shrubs, a duck pond, rolling hills with manicured lawns, horse facilities, and outdoor recreation areas for barbecues, picnics and sports. This lovely retreat complemented Biltz's penchant to entertain people, as evidenced by the scores of friends, politicians, movie stars, sports celebrities and artists from many fields who were his guests over the years. Among those whom he welcomed were future President and First Lady, John and Jacqueline Kennedy, investor Bernard Baruch, movie star Rex Bell and heir to the Vanderbilt fortune, Cornelius Vanderbilt, Jr., as well as all of his close friends and associates such as Johnny Mueller, Senator Pat McCarran, bankers Eddie Questa and Carl Wente, and investment partner Stanley Dollar. Biltz sold this luxurious landmark property in 1955 and within two years it was purchased by another Reno icon, casino owner Bill Harrah. After demolishing the mansion Biltz lived in and then building his own, the gaming mogul renamed the property *Rancharrah.*

At different times Biltz also owned homes in Lake Tahoe as well as other locations in Reno. Of the four or five residential subdivisions Biltz developed in Reno, he owned a beautiful home in the Greenfield section in southwestern Reno. In Tahoe, Mr. and Mrs. Biltz owned *his* and *her* lakefront homes, on different sides of the main road running through Crystal Bay. Beginning in 1939 and continuing through the 1940s, Biltz developed a getaway for family and friends in a secluded mountain spot above Lake Tahoe, which became known, as Little Lake, an outdoorsmen's paradise, replete with fish and beautiful scenery. Biltz sold shares in this private resort to his closest friends.

Politics and Controversies in the 1950s

In the early 1950s, Biltz flexed his political muscles as never before, and began to take more flack than he had ever experienced. As the decade began, Biltz assembled a handpicked team to put his group's man in the Governor's mansion. Although a Republican, party affiliations never bothered Biltz and it was bipartisan all the way, especially since their gubernatorial candidate Charles Russell was a Republican and Biltz's chief political ally, Senator McCarran was a Democrat. Biltz was only concerned with getting the job done. When Russell was inaugurated in 1951, Biltz, Mueller and McCarran virtually owned the state of Nevada.

---

[1] *Time Magazine,* June 15, 1953.

Granting favors was a commitment that incoming political leaders realized they owed their supporters, and in those days, favors might consist of issuing a gaming or liquor license, or perhaps giving a job to the friend of a supporter. Biltz estimated that there were at least 1,800 members of the team he rallied to ensure Governor Russell a victory, each of whom had family and friends, friends of friends, and so on. Biltz began calling Russell's note due immediately after the Governor moved into the official mansion in Carson City.

But for some reason, Governor Russell did not understand the rules of the game, and denied a request from Bill McKay, one of the prior owners of the Cal Neva Casino, upsetting Biltz, who realized that the man he helped put into office was not going to cooperate. It was a bitter blow, and Biltz recalled years later that he withdrew his support of Governor Russell, reflecting, "I never understood why he did it… You have to put out some favors… You have to say, 'Well you know, I scratched your back, now scratch mine.' "[1] From then on, Biltz did not have anything to do with the Governor.

In 1952, Biltz became entangled in a controversy with a nonresident of Nevada, Tom Mechling, who entered the U.S. Senate race from within the state. Initially, Mechling approached Biltz offering to give him half of his power as a Senator if Biltz would help him get elected. Fortunately for Biltz he had a tape recorder running when Mechling made his offer, because Mechling reported to the press that Biltz and his partner Johnny Mueller had attempted to buy his services. Biltz played the tape for reporters, and Mechling looked like a fool, and lost the election.

By this time Biltz had learned valuable lessons about the political system, realizing that those who lived by the sword could also die by the sword. One of his favorite sayings was a quote from Harry S. Truman, "If you can't stand the heat, stay out of the kitchen." At times, his dearest friend, Senator McCarran, who Biltz adoringly called Patsy, would grow weary due to the vicious attacks against him, including those by Hank Greenspun, editor of the *Las Vegas Sun*, who was relentless in his accusations of McCarran's connections to organized crime in Nevada. The alleged power-grip that the McCarran/Biltz political machine had on Nevada was also an easy target for adversarial journalists like Greenspun and as Greenpun's railings against McCarran grew more vociferous, the Senator's backers retaliated by suddenly pulling all casino advertising from the *Las Vegas Sun*. Greenspun filed a lawsuit against the casino owners and McCarran, a deal was

eventually negotiated and Greenspun received approximately $85,000 from the gamblers. Not everyone in the state sympathized with Greenspun, but the publicity helped boost his newspaper's circulation.

Biltz's professional and personal standing in Nevada suffered little damage because of the controversies. He had been affiliated with McCarran for at least 15 years by now, and for over 20 years with Johnny Mueller and together they had made valuable contributions toward the promotion and development of Nevada, yet at the same time, their success stimulated criticism. But Biltz had too many friends to worry about the small army of faultfinders and he had confidence in the direction he and his pardners had taken the state, and for most observers, the evidence spoke for itself.

MR. BIG IN NEVADA

Concurrent with the muckraking and political setbacks in the early 1950s, Biltz was gaining notoriety in a more positive manner. Prominent national magazines such as *Time* and *Fortune* viewed Biltz as a pioneer and a mover and a shaker, as each ran flattering feature articles, with *Time* magazine labeling Biltz *Mr. Big in Nevada.* His style was compared more to a benevolent baron, than a strong-armed political boss, as *Time* stated: "His political grip is neither Gestapo-like nor especially sinister, but he quietly exercises a kind of all-embracing, behinds the scenes influence…"[2] There was no hesitation in this article where Biltz's relationship with McCarran was concerned, stating matter of factly that, "McCarran communes with him almost daily."[3] Furthermore, "The legislature…seldom disappoints Biltz."[4] If anything, this article saw Biltz's efforts as a godsend, since: "Nevada got back on the high road to prosperity…and with the formation of the Biltz-McCarran axis, [Biltz] became the state's dominant political force…As such he is seldom challenged. For one thing, the state's citizens have no feeling of being bossed… For another, even Norman Biltz's critics find him hard to resist, particularly if he woos them amid squads of millionaires at one of his mountaintop barbecues."[5] In summation, the article contrasts Biltz with his accuser Tom Mechling, quoting Biltz, "Mechling is bad inside…He wants to knock down everything. He criticizes the state

---

[1] Ibid.
[2] Ibid.
[3] Ibid.
[4] Ibid.
[5] Ibid.

and the government and all the things we believe in here in America. 'I love this state,' [says Biltz] 'and I'll do any damn thing I can to keep it the way it is.' "[1]

George Wingfield was once called the *King of Nevada*, and *Fortune Magazine* crowned Biltz the *Duke of Nevada*[2] in their 1956 article, a laudatory tribute to Biltz's nearly 30 years as a trailblazing promoter in the state. After a lengthy profile of his accomplishments, the article ended by asking the distinguished *Duke of Nevada* if his critics bother him. "Biltz is not worried about his unfavorable publicity. 'I can look myself in the eye when I shave in the mornings, pardner', he says with disarming earnestness, 'and pardner, that's what counts'."[3]

CHANGING TIMES

While Biltz still possessed the charm, which had helped him close so many sales and win countless friends and associates, he was in his 50s and beginning to show the effects of his busy and stressful life. His hair had been silvery gray for some time, and his once smooth face was becoming rougher as each day passed. Grief over the death of one of his closest friends added more gray hairs and puffiness under his eyes.

He knew it was coming in 1954, because at 78, Senator Pat McCarran was 26 years older than Biltz. But still, when he heard that his beloved Patsy had dropped dead while campaigning in Hawthorne, Nevada on September 28, his eyes filled with tears. They were closer than blood relatives and for over 16 years had experienced a phenomenal run, but now it was time to arrange funeral plans and bury his adopted father. He somehow knew that he would not only be burying McCarran, he would also be laying much of his own political zeal to rest.

With Nevada's surging population growth in the 1950s, especially in the Las Vegas area, the *good old boy* politics of the past had all but faded and while a politician might be able to control the sparsely populated northern regions of the state, the concerns in southern Nevada could differ greatly. Biltz's counsel would still be sought in specific matters; on certain occasions he could marshal forces from his many contacts and pull strings, and Johnny Mueller was still a much respected lobbyist in Washington D.C. Yet for the most part, Biltz distanced himself from the political scene after McCarran's death, and would often cast a suspicious eye on new candidates.

With a gradual shift in focus away from political activism, Biltz consolidated his efforts into real estate, financ-

ing, and promoting Nevada. It was time to strengthen long-time relationships, both in the state and outside it. Many of the wealthy individuals whom Biltz had imported to Nevada were solidly committed to the *Silver State*, and gratefully paid homage to him for selling them on the idea.

William Lear, of Motorola and Learjet fame, kept in close touch with Biltz after being invited to Nevada by him. Lear made valuable contributions to the state and with Biltz's counsel developed prime land around what is now Stead Air Force Base.

Biltz again teamed up with Stanley Dollar, a business partner in many projects, to build the Holiday Hotel on the Truckee River in Reno. Their original plan was for the Holiday to be a non-gaming establishment, because according to Biltz, if it was successful, others in the hospitality business might be induced to build hotels in Reno. This idea was short lived, however, and in Biltz's words, "You could shoot a cannon through the place. I think on a good night we might have had a 5% occupancy."[4] But once again, Biltz had the solution, calling on one of his pardners, Newt Crumley from Elko, to take over with his gaming license, and as soon as gambling was added, the Holiday Hotel was successful.

Biltz always had strong ties to Reno's First National Bank and knew every president of that organization from the 1930s on. One of his closest friends going back to the 1930s was Carle Wente, who shared Biltz's vision of bringing wealthy individuals to Nevada to give the state credibility. Wente had been president of FNB between 1934 and 1937, a critical period in Biltz's career. Wente saw potential in this young man in his 30s and after one of Biltz's financial setbacks, arranged a bank loan for $5,000 to finance Biltz's first residential tract project in Reno.

One of the most popular bank presidents in the history of northern Nevada was Eddie Questa, who served in that position at FNB from 1952 to 1962, was a frequent guest at Biltz gatherings and next to Johnny Mueller, was probably Biltz's closest friend. Questa, in his position at the bank, was at the forefront of Nevada's first significant expansion in the casino industry. When he became the president of FNB in 1952, there were six casinos in Las Vegas on the highway that would become known as the Strip; by the end of the 1950s, at least six more casi-

---

[1] Ibid.

[2] *The Art of Success, The Duke of Nevada*, Freeman Lincoln, 1956.

[3] Ibid.

[4] *Memoirs of Norman Biltz*, Oral History Program, UNR.

nos were built on the Strip, as well as new ones in the old downtown area, known as *Glitter Gulch*. In Reno, William Harrah's gaming empire rose to prominence. Eddie Questa, acting on behalf of the First National Bank of Nevada financed much of this expansion; during this same period, Biltz was at the center of the growth and development in Reno and northern Nevada, with Questa always willing to supply his friend with needed capital.

Throughout much of Biltz's career he operated out of a corner in the Riverside Hotel where a phone had been conveniently connected at one of the tables across from the bar. All day long clients would come in and discuss business with Biltz, and often the phone would ring constantly. Employees at that hotel told stories for years following about the many notable individuals who met Biltz at his table across from the bar. In the 1950s, Biltz opened an office in one of the buildings he had constructed at 19 North Sierra Street, and his client traffic was transferred across from the Riverside.

BILTZ IN THE 1960S

In 1959, Biltz and his wife sailed on a cruise ship for a vacation in Hawaii, where stepson John F. Nash was living, overseeing properties owned by the family. Biltz looked forward to this extended period of rest, because deep down inside he knew that 1960 was going to be a very busy year.

The relationship between Norman Biltz and Joseph Kennedy could be traced to the early days at the Cal Neva Lodge in Lake Tahoe where Kennedy had been a frequent guest. Of course Biltz was not in Kennedy's league when Biltz first arrived at the Cal Neva in 1927, but many of the millionaires whom Biltz began recruiting to take up residency in Nevada were acquainted with the senior Kennedy. When Biltz became the owner of the Cal Neva during the 1928/1929 season he became familiar with Joe Kennedy and for the rest of their lives the two men would stay in touch, especially during Kennedy's frequent visits to the Lake Tahoe resort.

Almost as if it had been scripted, Biltz married Esther Auchincloss Nash in 1930 who of course was the aunt of Joseph Kennedy's son's future wife; when John F. Kennedy and Jackie Bouvier Auchincloss were married in 1953, the bond between the two families was strengthened. In 1960, when Joseph Kennedy's son and Esther Biltz's niece were in the race to become the President and First Lady of the United States, past favors, family rela-

tions and unquestionable loyalty would draw Norman Biltz into the election with as much intensity as he had exercised back in 1944 when he stood by Patrick McCarran in one of the most knockdown drag-out political contests in Nevada's history. Biltz was ready to summon up the accumulated wisdom from the lessons he had learned about politics over the years and put them to use to ensure his relative by marriage would be victorious.

From the start, the Presidential election in 1960 was a rough and tumble affair with *Tricky Dick* Nixon from California seeking to thwart John F. Kennedy's plans of becoming the first Catholic president. Nixon, of sweaty lips fame, was the incumbent vice-president from the popular Republican White House of Dwight D. "Ike" Eisenhower. Slowly, JFK's momentum began to build, and it became obvious that this election would be decided not necessarily by platforms, but by the size of campaign war chests, subterfuges at all levels, and favors being returned from patronages dating back 30 years.

Nixon was practically assured of winning the Pacific states surrounding California, plus he carried the strength of Eisenhower's two-term political machine. Kennedy had his father's deep rooted political ties which reportedly dovetailed into organized crime syndicates, as well as his father's access to enormous sums of cash, reportedly both clean and dirty. The one burr in Nixon's western saddle was the State of Nevada, which was California's neighbor and the native state of Nixon's wife Pat, but also home to JFK's aunt and uncle by marriage. Not incidentally, some of Joseph Kennedy's longest standing business partners operated casinos there. If John F. Kennedy could carry Nevada in the voting, it might just provide him with the margin needed to win the election.

Immediately, Biltz and Joseph Kennedy formed a strategic plan which would not only ensure JFK's victory in Nevada, but also raise millions of dollars for the campaign. This was old hat to Biltz, although there was a big difference in getting candidates elected at the state level as opposed to on a national scale. Years earlier, Biltz had declared that a senator could win a seat in Nevada for only $30,000, but in this 1960 election, that amount would not even pay for a fund raising banquet at the Cal Neva. All parties involved knew that the tab on this contest would be excessive, without doubt, the most expensive in the history of the United States.

All year long, Biltz toiled at his task with dauntless energy, supported by his friends and pardners from one end of the state to the other who pledged funds and votes. This event provided Biltz with an opportunity to call in markers from scores of favors he had extended over the years. In Biltz's mind, John F. Kennedy "was a man of destiny,"[1] groomed for the presidency by his father for 20 years, and now it was his time.

Joe Kennedy kept in constant contact with Biltz throughout the campaign, well pleased with Biltz's successful efforts. Several times through the year, Biltz was able to host the Kennedy patriarch, in Reno, as well as Lake Tahoe, and the candidate and his wife were also guests of their hospitable uncle. On one occasion, Joseph Kennedy and Biltz discussed the merits of a proposed debate between JFK and Nixon. Joe Kennedy was reluctant to allow his son to spar off against the more experienced debater, Nixon, in a nationally televised event, but in the end, the younger Kennedy scored high marks against Nixon who was seemingly caught off guard by his opponent's more relaxed style. As Biltz commented later: "It probably was the deciding factor in the election... ."[2]

Of course, other important factors included Kennedy choosing Lyndon Johnson as a running mate, the bountiful cash balance in their war chest, and the crucial votes won in Nevada, all of which proved to be the difference between victory and defeat when John F. Kennedy emerged the winner by the smallest margin in a Presidential election in the 20th century. Nixon had been defeated by fewer than 115,000 votes nationwide, less than 2% of the total.

Cries of fraud, voting irregularities, secret ballot counts, and illegal campaign funds, echoed across the nation. Nixon claimed he had been cheated and immediately called for a vote recount and an investigation. It has been described by political historians as one of the most corrupt elections in the history of the United States, and the fact that it was for the highest office broadens the impact. But in the end, Nixon withdrew his complaints and JFK was inaugurated in 1961.

Back in Nevada, the Biltz clan was exhausted, but elated. Though later accused of numerous infractions connected to the election, Biltz had a clean conscience. He knew that nothing more had been done to aid in winning this election than had been done in countless other elections and in his mind, unless a man was without sin he should not go about throwing stones.

With John and Jackie Kennedy securely in the White House, it was time for Biltz to experience some of the

Director of the Mint Eva Adams addressing a crowd in front of the old Carson City Mint in the 1960s. Adams was a native Nevadan and former secretary to Senator Pat McCarran.

privileges of political patronage. One of the Biltz family's closest friends was Senator McCarran's former assistant, Eva Adams. She was a frequent guest at the Biltz home, often for holiday gatherings and years earlier, Biltz had made Eva Adams a partner in one of his ranches. Through the urging of Norman Biltz, Eva Adams was appointed by President Kennedy to the position of Director of the Mint in 1961, the second woman to fill this position after Nellie Taylor Ross's appointment during the FDR administration. It was indeed a proud moment for Biltz when the assistant of his dear friend Patsy was sworn into this prestigious office.

Even Hank Greenspun, one of Biltz's former enemies, received a good deed from the White House due to Biltz's influence. For years, the Las Vegas newspaper editor had pleaded with representatives in Washington D.C. to pardon the felony conviction he received for transporting weapons into Israel during that country's war for freedom in 1948, an offense that caused Greenspun to be stripped of his rights as a U.S. citizen. After Kennedy became President, Greenspun was fearful that Biltz would thwart his pardon seeking efforts. But Biltz contacted Greenspun, and in spite of the journalist's vicious smear campaigns against Senator McCarran, received Biltz's assurance that he would put in a good word for him. In a letter dated November 8, 1961, Greenspun acknowledged Biltz's generosity after receiving word that he would be granted a pardon.

---

[1] *Memoirs of Norman Biltz*, Oral History Program, UNR.
[2] Ibid.

Johnny Mueller keeping an eye on Norman Biltz during a phone conversation.

Dear Norm,

Thanks for the good wishes. I'm not unmindful that it was your nephew that rewarded me thusly, and I can think of no greater gift, as you know how much I have looked forward to it. Also, it is your niece who was so keenly aware of our relationship. I know these things didn't hurt. Thanks again for everything Norm.

Sincerely,
Hank[1]

POWER AND TRAGEDY

With JFK in the White House, Biltz probably had more power than ever, yet he was determined not to abuse it. Besides, he had achieved practically all of his goals, and was looking forward to slowing down a bit and enjoying the fruits of his labors, as well as the company of many of the good friends he had made through the years.

All of a sudden, tragedy struck on February 10, 1962 when a friend he considered as close as a brother was killed with another of his friends when a small aircraft crashed outside of Tonopah. News of Eddie Questa's death sent shock waves throughout the banking and gaming industries in Nevada. Questa was one of the most beloved and respected banking figures in the state's history. Another respected Nevada businessman Newt Crumley piloted the plane and also died in the crash. Norman Biltz was grief-stricken and could not stop sobbing for days. All of the joy and jubilation of President Kennedy's inauguration just three weeks earlier, abruptly turned into sorrow and mourning and even years later, Biltz found it difficult to talk about Questa's death.

From this point until his own death, a dark cloud seemed to hang over Norman Biltz as one heartbreaking

event after another tested his threshold for pain and mental resolve.

Less than six months after Questa and Crumley died, celebrated movie actress Marilyn Monroe spent a weekend at the Cal Neva Lodge in Lake Tahoe, reportedly suffering from depression. Frank Sinatra was one of the owners of the Cal Neva at the time and was said to have kept a chalet vacant for the actress at all times. Though nobody knows what happened at the Lodge that weekend, it is reported that several of Monroe's Hollywood friends were there to cheer her up and one rumor even suggested that her ex-husband Joe DiMaggio was a guest that weekend offering his encouragement. There is certainly no immediate connection between Norman Biltz and this event, however, northern Nevada was his territory, and Lake Tahoe, and especially the Cal Neva was his stomping ground. He was well acquainted with all parties involved and his nephew, John F. Kennedy, was reportedly one of Monroe's lovers. Conjecture has it, that the cause of Monroe's depression was a result of being informed that she needed to end her relationship with JFK and there have even been rumors that Kennedy called Monroe at the Cal Neva that weekend to end their affair. A week later, newspapers reported that on August 5, 1962, Marilyn Monroe had committed suicide at the age of 36 in her Los Angeles home, news that struck Biltz, along with Monroe's fans, to the bone.

A year later, Biltz lost his closest friend and partner of 30 years when Johnny Mueller died on August 1, 1963, causing Biltz himself to be treated for depression. Within a year and a half, he had lost his two closest friends, Johnny

[1] *Memoirs of Norman Biltz*, Oral History Program, UNR.

Two best friends, Norman Biltz (left) and First National Bank president Eddie Questa.

Mueller and Eddie Questa and those around him saw the anguish he was experiencing, but could do nothing but let time take its course.

Just 113 days after Johnny Mueller died, Norman and Esther Biltz watched in horror with the rest of the nation, as John F. Kennedy was assassinated on November 22, 1963. No one, it seemed, was immune from the terrible arrow of death. This time, the Biltz's would cast aside their own grief, and lend their support to the Kennedy family, especially Jackie Kennedy. Biltz would have given his own life to return his niece's husband to her, but Biltz had learned that he had no control over death. Despite being a fixer and problem solver his whole life, he realized that death was the ultimate foe, against which he had no strategy.

In the mid 1960s, Biltz's health began to deteriorate. Though only in his early 60s, his body organs were like those of a much older man. Like many American men of his generation, Biltz smoked cigarettes and consumed alcoholic beverages, and showed little concern for his diet, eating just about anything he desired. For most of his life this active outdoorsman burned off enough calories to maintain an ideal weight, but sadly it all began to catch up with him as he grew older.

A condition known as shingles was reactivated in Biltz, causing him severe pain from the rash-like virus and varicose veins developed in his legs, adding to his misery. His physician of many years treated him for these medical problems, but gave Biltz no hope for recovery. Later on, surgery was performed removing a good portion of his stomach. By then he was drinking heavily to help kill the pain, but at times even alcohol could not deaden the torment. Another local physician prescribed a drug laced with arsenic as a measure of last resort. He was groggy most of the time in his final years, but his close friends could still see the Biltz trademark charm emanate through his suffering, despite a nerve disease in his mouth which made it difficult for him to talk.

During Biltz's decline he kept his hand in selected real estate projects, always ready to share with one of his pardners. His company, Reno Properties, was involved in several projects in the last half of the 1960s, though Biltz was finding it more difficult to secure capital as even the First National Bank of Nevada was reluctant to finance his deals. According to his stepson John F. Nash, bank president Art Smith turned his stepfather down on a loan request in the late 1960s.[1] A decision like that would have been unheard of in Eddie Questa's day, or even back in the 1930s after Biltz had gone broke when Carl Wente came through for him. But the bloom was off the Biltz rose toward the end of his life, and the man many of the young bankers were seeing in no way resembled the *Duke of Nevada*.

A PROPOSITION

On February 24, 1971, Norman Biltz walked into the President of FNB's office and made him a proposition. President Art Smith, 20 years his junior listened as Biltz described the collection of Carson City coins he owned, 109 coins in the set, including one example of every date and denomination produced at the Nevada mint except two. Of these two dates that were missing, there was only one known specimen of one of them, and three known of the other. All the coins were housed in custom made acrylic plastic display cases, with separate cases for each denomination. Biltz told Smith that it had taken him a number of years to complete the set and one of the last pieces he had acquired, an 1876-CC 20-cent piece, was the most valuable. Then Biltz presented the terms of his proposal beginning with the price. He would sell it to the bank for $50,000 despite having received offers of nearly $100,000, with the sale contingent upon the following three conditions:

1.   The set would never be broken up.
2.   The set would never leave the state of Nevada.
3.   The set would be displayed on a regular basis.

At the conclusion of Biltz's presentation Smith extended his hand saying, "Norm you've got a deal." As the two men shook hands there must have been a tinge of sadness in Biltz's already disconsolate heart.

After the sale was finalized and the collection was transferred to the main office of the First National Bank of Nevada in downtown Reno, preparations were made to put it on display. Bank employees interested in coin collecting, were given the assignment of upgrading any of the coins from the bank's own inventory of old Carson City silver dollars and miscellaneous denominations. An effort was also made to locate the two missing dates. However, it soon became apparent that Biltz had been correct when he told Smith that these dates were virtually impossible to obtain. On one occasion, a Reno coin dealer of questionable integrity, attempted to pass off an altered 1878-CC quarter to the bank claiming it was an 1873-CC *Without Arrows* variety.

[1] Personal interview with John F. Nash, August 9, 2002.

The unveiling of the Carson City coin collection sold by Norman Biltz to the First National Bank in Reno: (clockwise from top left) Front cover of a brochure handed out at the 1971 unveiling (*Courtesy of Peter Plath*); Norman Biltz unveiling the coins when the set was first displayed; the lobby of the bank was crowded with guests on the day of the unveiling; Norman Biltz talking to FNB president Art Smith in front of the display.

Finally on November 18, 1971, the bank formally unveiled the collection in the lobby of their main office. Dozens of invited guests, including prominent businessmen and women, state and city officials, attended the ceremony. Biltz himself pulled the curtain, revealing his proud set of coins. Special brochures describing the coins and the history of the Carson City Mint were distributed. Local newspapers and television stations covered the event, which gave Biltz one last opportunity to be seen at a public gathering. Although the collection was left on display for the remainder of the year, it would later be taken down and stored in a bank vault, only to appear periodically over the next several years, until it was put away for a lengthy period.

In the informational brochure about the collection, it was indicated that Biltz spent 35 years assembling the set, dating the starting point sometime back in the 1930s, and while possible, according to Biltz's stepson as well as a coin dealer from northern California, it is not likely. John F. Nash does not have any recollection of his stepfather having a serious interest in coins until the early 1960s, surely no earlier than the late 1950s, which coincides with an old San Francisco coin dealer's memories of Biltz and his collection.[1]

There is no doubt that Biltz was a collector at heart, evidenced by the wide variety of items he collected, including guns, art, and wood carvings. In fact some of the woodcarvings still in the Biltz family collection are priceless. Norman Biltz paid a character nicknamed *Stuttering Pete* $10 for his hand-carved wood images of cowboys, horses, Indians, and other Old West themed objects, exceptionally detailed with lifelike features. In turn, *Stuttering Pete* would go back to the gambling tables, or perhaps buy himself a meal.

Biltz always appreciated silver dollars, but more in a generic sense as he thought they made wonderful gifts. Often, he would have special acrylic holders made for them with the inscription "Greetings from Norm Biltz." On other occasions he would have old silver dollars dipped in gold paint to pass out to friends, telling them, "Here you go pardner, it's just a little memento to my friends."[2]

But when did he decide to build a complete set of coins from the Carson City Mint? This question will probably never be answered, but it is entirely possible that his

[1] Personal Interviews with John F. Nash and San Francisco dealer R. Johnson, August 2002.
[2] *Reno Evening Gazette*, July 5, 1973.

interest in the project evolved over a period of many years. One of his good friends was Judge Clark J. Guild who had a deep fascination for Carson City, and especially the mint there. Guild helped found the Nevada Museum and Art Institute and of course spearheaded the effort to purchase the old mint and convert it into a museum, a plan in which Biltz's close friend, Senator Pat McCarran, had played a significant role. In 1947 and 1948, Biltz actually served on the Nevada Museum's board, offering a strong possibility that he was aware of Harold M. Budd's intentions to donate a display of the coins from the Carson Mint's first year. And though there is no evidence to corroborate it, Budd might have told Biltz about the complete set of "CC" coins he was assembling, and his intentions of loaning it to the Museum to put on display.

Another link to Biltz's coin collecting pursuits may have been Eva Adams, who was the Director of the Mint in the 1960s, and introduced Biltz to Robert Bridges, the Superintendent of the San Francisco Mint, who may have possibly introduced Biltz to a coin dealer in the Bay Area. Bridges may have also shared what he knew about Carson City coins, further stimulating Biltz's interest.

Though these possible scenarios explaining how, why and when Biltz became interested in building a collection of his own do not provide categorical answers, one thing is certain, Biltz owned his magnificent set in 1971 when he sold it to the bank, and he had been working on it for at least six to ten years.

According to one source, Biltz purchased the crown jewel in his collection, an Uncirculated example of the 1876-CC 20-cent piece, from Abner Kreisberg through an intermediary sometime around 1966.[1] When reviewing auction records from that era, the author found an Uncirculated 1876-CC 20-cent piece in an Abner Kreisberg/Hans Schulman sale held on May 20 and 21, 1966. The price realized for the piece was $12,750, which concurs perfectly with the information provided by Biltz's stepson John F. Nash, as well as the coin dealer from the Bay Area.

Nash believes that his stepfather began seriously building his collection of Carson City coins after the deaths of Eddie Questa and Johnny Mueller, which makes

One of the most recognizable men in Nevada for over 45 years, Norman H. Biltz was called the *Duke of Nevada*. (*Courtesy John F. Nash*)

sense, considering that Biltz needed an activity to divert his heartbreak toward something more positive. His stepson also added that Biltz was always in competition with the stepson's mother, as for many years Esther had been assembling a very impressive stamp collection. Years later, Esther Biltz's stamp collection sold for over $100,000 and was considered one of the most complete of its kind.

At the time Norman Biltz sold his coin collection to the First National Bank of Nevada, he still had the shell of his real estate company set up, although activities were limited to the maintenance of his many holdings and staying in touch with his many friends. In a throwback to the old days, Biltz produced a two page brochure in partnership with FNB and two law firms, entitled "Why Not Nevada?"; and a similar theme that Biltz had been promoting for 44 years was printed in bold ink, "All that's required to take advantage of the remarkably favorable taxation in Nevada is that a person establish residence in that state…"[2] A chart compared the income taxes, inheritance taxes, and gift taxes in Nevada with those in five other western states, with Nevada, of course, the only state on that chart exhibiting zero taxes in all three categories. This brochure was a last hurrah for Biltz as he became more confined to home with each passing day.

Tributes to Norman Biltz

As the Fourth of July approached in 1973, Americans were glued to their television sets watching the Watergate hearings, but it is doubtful that Norman Biltz was coherent enough at this time to follow the proceedings. Just 13 years earlier, he had valiantly supported his nephew's bid to beat the formidable Richard M. Nixon in the presidential election. Now Nixon was suffering a worse humiliation than his loss to JFK, but Biltz was probably not able to comment on it. He was heavily medicated every day and consuming large quantities of alcohol. His stepson John F. Nash had moved back to Reno from Hawaii with his wife Mary to assist his mother in taking care of her afflicted husband.

[1] Personal telephone interview with San Francisco coin dealer R. Johnson August 14, 2002.

[2] *Why Not Nevada?* Brochure, Reno Properties, 1971.

On July 3, 1973, a loud gunshot startled everyone in the Biltz residence and when Esther Biltz ran to her husband's room she saw him lying dead with a self inflicted wound.

The following day, the Fourth of July, local newspapers briefly mentioned Biltz's death; they needed an extra day to gather all the facts. Then on July 5, newspapers throughout Nevada ran headline stories, "Noted Nevada Financier Norman Biltz, 71, Dead."[1] Most new residents in the *Silver State* were surprised by how much press coverage this man, unfamiliar to them was receiving. It was as if a prominent dignitary or a well known celebrity had died and many Nevadans asked one another: "Who was Norman Biltz?" To answer this question, reporters interviewed dozens of old-time residents who had known the *Duke of Nevada,* and comprehensive profiles elaborated on all of Biltz's achievements. People were amazed to hear about everything the man had done for the State of Nevada. But how could he have accomplished as much as he did, yet remain relatively obscure? Usually only governors, senators and wealthy mine operators in Nevada received as much attention as Biltz was receiving. Reporters brought out the old articles from *Time* and *Fortune* magazines from 20 years earlier to show all curious souls that Biltz had been well known at one time. Then people began asking if there were any streets or parks or buildings named after him. No one could find any, although Biltz had named streets after friends of his like Eva Adams, Tom Dant, and Johnny Mueller. This was all so incredible, a man who made as much of a contribution to the growth, development, and preservation of Nevada as any in the history of the state, yet very few people knew who he was.

Accolades had certainly come late, but upon Biltz's death tributes were given which probably should have come

years sooner. An editorial writer attempted to answer the question of why, if Biltz had done so much, was he so unknown: "There are two major reasons for the unfamiliarity of the average present-day Nevadan with the name of Norman Biltz. The most immediate one is that the growth of the state population-wise, has accelerated so fast in late years that Biltz's activities in finance, real estate and politics had virtually ceased by the time they arrived, mainly because he had achieved all his goals. The second reason is that Biltz was never very obvious, as a true public figure…He never held public office or served on public boards. He shunned the limelight, [and] although he was cordial and helpful to most reporters, he didn't like being quoted…He preferred to work behind the scenes."[2]

Some reporters surmised that Biltz's obscurity resulted from a growing criticism about the way he stifled growth in northern Nevada while at the same time southern Nevada was thriving. In answer to that argument, the writer of the above editorial pointed out that, "the argument on the other side is that this is exactly the way it ought to be… Perhaps most who live [in northern Nevada] go along with the belief that the restraint of Norman Biltz was also a vision of a growing need to preserve a very special environment. If that is true, the most remarkable fact…is for good or bad, he was able to carry out that vision…"[3]

Probably no more fitting tribute was paid to Biltz than this one by Nevada's State Attorney General Robert List: "Nobody has contributed more to Nevada since statehood, to its progress, its prosperity, than Norman Biltz. It's the end of an era and we are going to miss him very much."[4]

---

[1] *Nevada State Journal,* July 5, 1973.
[2] *Nevada Appeal,* July 8, 1973 view from the Nevada Capitol.
[3] Ibid.
[4] *Nevada State Journal,* July 5, 1973.

THREE SPECIAL COLLECTIONS
THE SILVER COINS

DIMES

Date	Eliasberg	Nevada Museum	Battle Born
1871	AU-50	G/VG	AU-55 PCGS
1872	VF-20	F/VF	AU-58 PCGS
1873 *Without Arrows*	MS-65	Missing	Missing
1873 *With Arrows*	VG-8	VG/F	MS-65 NGC
1874 *With Arrows*	VG-8	Uncirculated	XF-45 PCGS
1875 MM Below	MS-64	F/VF	MS-65 PCGS
1875 MM Above	MS-65	Uncirculated	MS-67 NGC
1876	MS-66	Uncirculated	MS-66 NGC
1877	MS-66	Uncirculated	MS-66 NGC
1878	MS-66	Uncirculated	MS-66 NGC

20 CENT PIECES

Date	Eliasberg	Nevada Museum	Battle Born
1875	MS-64	EF	MS-65 NGC
1876	MS-65	Uncirculated	MS-64 NGC

QUARTERS

Date	Eliasberg	Nevada Museum	Battle Born
1870	MS-64	VF	AU-53 NGC
1871	MS-65	EF	MS-65 PCGS
1872	MS-66	F/VF	MS-62 PCGS
1873 *Without Arrows*	MS-63	Missing	MS-64 PCGS
1873 *With Arrows*	MS-63	VF	MS-64 PCGS
1875	MS-64	AU	MS-64 NGC
1876	MS-65	AU	MS-67 NGC
1877	MS-66	VF/EF	MS-67 NGC
1878	MS-61	Uncirculated	MS-66 PCGS

HALF DOLLARS

Date	Eliasberg	Nevada Museum	Battle Born
1870	VF-20	EF/AU	AU-50 PCGS
1871	MS-61PL	Uncirculated	MS-64 PCGS
1872	MS-63	AU	MS-63 PCGS
1873 *Without Arrows*	AU-50	VF	MS-64 PCGS
1873 *With Arrows*	MS-65	VF	MS-64 PCGS
1874	MS-64	Uncirculated	MS-64 PCGS
1875	MS-64	Uncirculated	MS-65 PCGS
1876	MS-66	EF	MS-65 NGC
1877	MS-66	Uncirculated	MS-65 PCGS
1878	MS-65	VF	MS-63 NGC

SEATED LIBERTY $1'S

Date	Eliasberg	Nevada Museum	Battle Born
1870	MS-62 PL	VF	MS-63 PCGS
1871	AU-58 PL	EF	MS-61 NGC
1872	MS-62 PL	VF	MS-64 NGC
1873	AU-58 PL	EF	G-06 PCGS

TRADE $1'S

Date	Eliasberg	Nevada Museum	Battle Born
1873	AU-50	VF	MS-64 NGC
1874	VF-30	AU	MS-63 NGC
1875 Type I/I	MS-63	AU	MS-64 NGC
1876	MS-66	XF	MS-64 NGC
1877	MS-61	AU	MS-64 NGC
1878	EF-40	VF	MS-63 NGC

MORGAN $1'S

Date	Eliasberg	Nevada Museum	Battle Born
1878	MS-63	Uncirculated	MS-66 PCGS
1879	MS-63	Uncirculated	MS-65 PCGS
1880	AU-50	Uncirculated	MS-66 PCGS
1881	MS-66	Uncirculated	MS-66 PCGS
1882	MS-62	Uncirculated	MS-66 PCGS
1883	MS-63	Uncirculated	MS-66 PCGS
1884	MS-65 PL	Uncirculated	MS-67 PCGS
1885	MS-64 DMP	Uncirculated	MS-66 PCGS
1889	MS-66 PL	Uncirculated	MS-63 PCGS
1890	MS-65	Uncirculated	MS-65 PCGS
1891	MS-66 DMP	Uncirculated	MS-65 PCGS
1892	MS-65 PL	Uncirculated	MS-65 PCGS
1893	MS-64DMP	Uncirculated	MS-64 PCGS

THREE SPECIAL COLLECTIONS
THE GOLD COINS

HALF EAGLES

Date	Eliasberg	Nevada Museum	Battle Born
1870-CC	VF-30	F/VF	PCGS MS-61
1871-CC	XF-40	VF	NGC MS-63
1872-CC	VF-20	VF	PCGS AU-58
1873-CC	VF-20	VF	PCGS MS-61
1874-CC	XF-40	EF	PCGS MS-62
1875-CC	VF-30	VF/EF	PCGS MS-61
1876-CC	MS-65	VF	PCGS MS-66
1877-CC	VF-30	EF	PCGS AU-58

HALF EAGLES (*cont.*)

Date	Eliasberg	Nevada Museum	Battle Born
1878-CC	XF-45	VF	PCGS AU-55
1879-CC	VF-30	EF	PCGS MS-61
1880-CC	AU-50	VF	PCGS MS-62
1881-CC	XF-40	VF	PCGS MS-61
1882-CC	AU-55	EF	PCGS MS-61
1883-CC	XF-45	EF	PCGS MS-62
1884-CC	XF-45	EF	PCGS AU-58
1890-CC	MS-65	VF/EF	PCGS MS-65
1891-CC	AU-55	Unc.	PCGS MS-65
1892-CC	MS-65	EF/AU	NGC MS-64
1893-CC	AU-55	VF/EF	NGC MS-65

EAGLES

Date	Eliasberg	Nevada Museum	Battle Born
1870-CC	VF-20	VF	PCGS AU-50
1871-CC	XF-40	VF	PCGS MS-62
1872-CC	VF-30	VF	PCGS AU-55
1873-CC	VF-30	VF	PCGS AU-50
1874-CC	MS-60	VF	PCGS MS-63
1875-CC	XF-40	EF	PCGS AU-58
1876-CC	VF-30	VF	PCGS AU-58
1877-CC	VF-30	VF/EF	PCGS AU-53
1878-CC	VF-20	VF/EF	NGC AU-58
1879-CC	VF-30	EF	NGC AU-58
1880-CC	XF-40	VF/EF	NGC MS-61
1881-CC	MS-63	Unc.	PCGS MS-62
1882-CC	AU-55	VF	PCGS AU-58
1883-CC	XF-45	AU	NGC MS-61
1884-CC	XF-40	AU	NGC MS-62
1890-CC	VF-30	Unc.	PCGS MS-62
1891-CC	MS-60	Unc.	NGC MS-64
1892-CC	MS-65	VF	PCGS MS-62
1893-CC	XF-40	EF	PCGS MS-61

DOUBLE EAGLES

Date	Eliasberg	Nevada Museum	Battle Born
1870-CC	VF-20	VF/EF	PCGS AU-50
1871-CC	VF-20	EF	PCGS AU-55
1872-CC	XF-40	EF	PCGS AU-58
1873-CC	XF-40	EF/AU	NGC MS-61
1874-CC	XF-40	Fine	PCGS MS-62
1875-CC	XF-45	EF/AU	NGC MS-62
1876-CC	AU-50	EF/AU	PCGS MS-62
1877-CC	XF-40	VF	NGC MS-62
1878-CC	VF-30	EF	PCGS MS-61
1879-CC	VF-30	VF/EF	PCGS MS-61
1882-CC	VF-30	EF	PCGS MS-62
1883-CC	AU-55	VF	PCGS MS-63
1884-CC	AU-55	EF	PCGS MS-63
1885-CC	AU-50	AU	PCGS MS-62
1889-CC	XF-45	AU	PCGS MS-62
1890-CC	MS-63	Unc.	PCGS MS-62
1891-CC	VF-30	Unc.	PCGS MS-62
1892-CC	XF-40	AU	PCGS MS-62
1893-CC	AU-50	AU	NGC MS-63

Reno's Morning and Sunday Newspaper

Nevada State Journal

104th Year—No. 222   Thursday, July 5, 1973   ★   15c Daily—35c Sunday

Noted Nevada Financier Norman Biltz, 71, Dead

Norman H. Biltz, a financier and real estate man who played a vital role in the development of Nevada, particularly Lake Tahoe and the Reno area, died Tuesday at his Reno home.

The death by shooting was "an apparent suicide," Sparks Coroner Jack Lamberti said. Biltz, 71, had been "in ill health," his doctor said Wednesday.

A native of Bridgeport, Conn., Biltz came to Nevada in 1927. Recognizing Nevada's tax advantages for the wealthy, he became a quiet, but successful salesman of Nevada as a real estate man and financier.

His clients were mostly millionaires. Included among them were Max C. Fleischmann, E. L. Cord, Bing Crosby, Dean

Witter, George Whittell and more than 40 others.

Those men became known as the "Biltz' immigrants."

He retired from active business in 1947 and sold his interest in the real estate firm of Bennett & Biltz to Henry F. Bennett and Ben Edwards. Biltz also retired as president of the Nevada Packing Co.

He continued to operate his personal businesses, including real estate activities which included a 12,000-acre ranch development in the Lovelock area and the Donner Lake project.

In his real estate activities Biltz was associated in the development of Kings Beach, Brockway Vista, the Cal Neva District, Crystal Bay and the Incline beach areas at Lake Tahoe.

In Reno, he developed the Reno Lake ranch on South Virginia Road and opened the Greenridge and Greenfield residential subdivisions next to the Washoe County Golf Course, and the Plumb Lane subdivision.

The west side of Sierra Street from the river to First Street was built up through his efforts. The Gray-Reid-Wright Building on the east side of Sierra Street damaged in the Sierra Street explosion in later years, was one of his projects.

Construction projects at Lake Tahoe included the Cal-Neva Lodge and a number of smaller properties.

He was featured in Time Magazine in 1953 under the title

NORMAN BILTZ

apparent suicide

(See RENO Page 2, Col. 5)

Headlines appeared on the front pages of every newspaper in Nevada when Biltz died. Many residents of the state wondered who this notable man was.

After Norman Biltz died, his properties and business interests were distributed between family members and business associates. His stepson estimates that his stepfather's estate was worth approximately $4 million when he died. Certainly commendable, but considering that his net worth in 1952 at the time of the magazine articles was estimated to be between $8 to $10 million, it was nowhere what it could have been. In fact, some financial historians have estimated that from the level where Biltz was at in the early 1950s, his fortune could have easily reached $100 million by the time of his death. Even LaVere Redfield, who was not a developer and had practically no political connections, amassed real estate holdings that were worth over $250 million to his heirs in the years following his death.

But Biltz was not as concerned with multiplying his assets as he was with making Nevada a better place to live. He made no secret about the fact that he had made considerable profits from his numerous contacts, but he also gave away many times over his share of lucrative investments to his friends.

His wife Esther was worth far more than Biltz thanks to her inheritances and the trust funds set up for her children. But in the 43 years they were married, Biltz tried to remain faithful to his commitment not to touch his wife's money. Esther outlived her husband by 14 years, spending time between Nevada and the family's out of state residences. Tragically, the two daughters born to

her and Biltz died before her, both while in their 40s, as Sheila choked to death on food stuck in her throat, and Esther, Jr. died of a brain tumor.

Throughout the rest of her life, Esther Biltz attempted to keep track of the coin collection her husband sold to the bank. When long periods of time would pass without the set being displayed, she and her son John F. Nash would make inquiries to the bank. Sometimes their efforts would produce results, but most often not. Then in 1986, a year before Mrs. Biltz died, plans were made for the successor to the old FNB, First Interstate Bank, to loan the collection to the Nevada State Museum in Carson City. This effort was still in process when Esther Biltz died, but in 1989, it became a reality, and the set has been on display at the facility ever since, first on loan, then by acquisition through Wells Fargo Bank's donation.

Fittingly, the set is called the Nevada State Museum Collection, but occasionally Norman Biltz's name is mentioned as the collector who assembled it. Generally, when people hear his name they become curious to find out who he was. Just as people were surprised to find out about the real Norman Biltz when he died in 1973, many have the same reaction today (2003). Surprisingly, there has never been a book written about him, and there are still no streets or public landmarks named after him. But for visitors to the Nevada State Museum, his wonderful coin collection serves as a perpetual memorial to him.

Norman Biltz's coin collection on display inside the old mint building that Abraham Curry brought to life is a match made in historical heaven. These are two of the most forgotten pioneers and promoters in the history of Nevada and deserve much more recognition for the contributions they made to the state. They died 100 years apart and their legacies are now preserved together in the same building— indeed the perfect pardners.

CHAPTER TEN

Collecting Opportunities

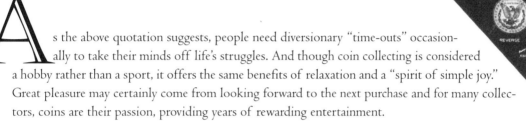

In a world of life and death conflicts, spectator sports give us a "time out"; an opportunity to relax and celebrate human skill, dedication, and success in a spirit of simple joy.

From *The Lure of Baseball* by Thomas A. Bowden

As the above quotation suggests, people need diversionary "time-outs" occasionally to take their minds off life's struggles. And though coin collecting is considered a hobby rather than a sport, it offers the same benefits of relaxation and a "spirit of simple joy." Great pleasure may certainly come from looking forward to the next purchase and for many collectors, coins are their passion, providing years of rewarding entertainment.

Many doors of exciting activities open when people begin acquiring coins, not least of which is the camaraderie experienced with other collectors. Exchanging facts and research findings about interesting varieties, grading standards, and "finest knowns" provides inexhaustible learning opportunities; discovering new historical information and population figures can cause collectors to appreciate the coins they own even more. Rare coins allow collectors to look back to the past when they have a desire to forget the present.

Many people are able to use coin collecting to return to a time in their childhood, for instance, of which they have fond memories, perhaps when they started building their first set of Lincoln pennies in a blue cardboard album or when their grandfather gave them a few old silver dollars.

Often after high school, those early collecting interests are set aside in lieu of military service, college, marriage, business pursuits, or all of the above; but years later, after fulfilling other commitments, they are able to find the time, as well as sufficient discretionary income, to rekindle their love for collecting.

A person's coin collection often provides a sense of identity and they become known for what they collect: VAMs, early American coppers, Full Head Standing Liberty quarters, error coins, or DMPL dollars for example.

Reasons for getting involved in numismatics are numerous, just as are the number of available categories: some people collect for the challenge, while others collect for sheer profit. But whatever a person's motives are for collecting coins, it is inescapable that it is by far the most popular nonathletic pastime in the United States. Eventually, every family in the nation is touched by it one way or the other.

CHOOSING CARSON CITY COINS

Although it is not physically possible to go back and experience the tradition, romance, ambiance, and nostalgia that attract you to bygone eras, you can evoke imagery of it by owning symbols of those times. Collectors of Carson City coins have discovered the meaning of this. As Q. David Bowers reflected, "Whenever I see a . . . silver dollar with a 'CC' mintmark minted in the 1880s, I can conjure up in my imagination a vision of Carson City, Nevada in the rough and ready days of the Wild West; of miners working underground to take precious silver ore from the Comstock Lode, and the main street of nearby Virginia City with its saloons, gambling parlors, red light district and perhaps . . . a shoot-out. . . ."[1]

General Services Administration (GSA) staff used this imagery when marketing the nearly three million Carson City silver dollars still remaining in Treasury vaults during the 1970s. References to these silver dollars being "relics of the Old West" and part of the "Big Bonanza" flowered government advertising literature.[2] Embellishing the connection between "CC" silver dollars and nostalgic times for maximum effect, GSA brochures captivated potential customers' imaginations with such fanciful prose as "Six-guns and overnight millionaires were commonplace in the era of the Carson City silver dollars. . . . These were some of the greatest and most memorable days in American history."[3]

In a classic case of promotional innuendo, these ads suggested that the legendary "CC" silver dollars would take a person back in time to: "Days that will never be seen again!"[4] This strategy obviously worked, as thousands of orders flooded GSA offices for seven successive years until all the dollars were gone.

America is not the only country enamored with the lore of the "Old West" era, as enthusiasts around the globe are mesmerized by cowboys, stagecoaches, gunfights, and bank robbers. Citizens in Japan, for instance, are infatuated with American baseball and the "Old West," and every year Japanese special interests groups sponsor "Western Days" where people with last names like Shimimota and Nakatani dress up like Wyatt Earp and Wild Bill Hickock. Events like this in the United States are celebrated every weekend in one location or another, and can be traced back to Buffalo Bill's Wild West Shows in the 19th century, showing the undeniable yearning that many people have to find a link with this period in America's past.

A familiar phrase once expressed by men riding horseback across the wide open spaces in the western half of America was "Don't sell your saddle," in response to the innovation of the automobile and more advanced modes of transportation. At the same time, the ranching industry was consolidating as large corporations were absorbing many independent ranches, and railroads were buying spacious parcels of this once-undisturbed land. Jobs for cowboys, ranch hands, and other saddle-sore workers became scarce as the "Old West" era faded into the sunset, but still, there was a heartfelt desire deep within many of the

Six-guns and overnight millionaires . . .

. . . were commonplace in the era of the Carson City Silver Dollars. These were the times when men toiled night and day taking silver and gold ore by the ton out of subterranean deposits discovered almost daily. When they came out of the mines, it was off to the 24-hour-a-day saloons and gambling halls for whiskey straight up, roulette, blackjack and five-card stud where fortunes changed hands nightly. These were America's late-1800s in the Old West of Nevada, California and Colorado . . . the days of the Comstock Lode when shanty towns became shanty cities overnight. Magic names like Virginia City . . . Silver City . . . Cripple Creek, laden with silver, suddenly screamed riches and rowdyism.

Elsewhere, America was sanely trying to enter the 20th Century. Horse-drawn trains gave way to trolleys in the Nation's great cities . . . Sarah Bernhardt was making her first appearances on the American stage and the game of basketball was being invented. It was during these times that the Statue of Liberty was being erected . . . the first telephones were installed and Edison was developing the electric light.

These were some of the greatest and most memorable days in America's history. Days that will never be seen again!

It was in those wild days of the Old West that the Carson City Mint was organized to convert the precious metal of the Big Bonanza into the only coins in our history to carry the unique "CC" double-letter mint mark.

Never circulated — and found in the original sealed mint bags — these 90% silver dollars, all of the Morgan type, are truly the last of a legacy left to us from a by-gone era. A unique treasure from these exciting years, the Carson City Silver Dollars should be among your most prized possessions.

Mixed CC Dollars

These coins have never before been circulated by the U.S. Government. The years 1879 through 1885 plus 1890 and 1891 are included. These are the coins that have been culled out of the entire Government holding of CC dollars since they did not meet the numismatic standards for "uncirculated" classification.

Approximate number available: 517,569

Minimum Bid: $15.00

1882-CC

1st Major League Doubleheader

Total CC Silver Dollars Minted: 591,000
Total CC Silver Dollars Available: 35,700

Minimum Bid: $30.00

1883-CC

Northern Pacific Railroad completed.
Total CC Silver Dollars Minted: 1,204,000
Total CC Silver Dollars Available: 226,052

Minimum Bid: $30.00

1884-CC

Trolleys replace horse-drawn trains on East and West coasts.

Total CC Silver Dollars Minted: 1,136,000
Total CC Silver Dollars Available: 456,520

Minimum Bid: $30.00

1880-CC

Sarah Bernhardt makes American acting debut.

Total CC Silver Dollars Minted: 591,000
Total CC Silver Dollars Available: 40,847

Minimum Bid: $60.00

1881-CC

Clara Barton organizes the American Red Cross.

Total CC Silver Dollars Minted: 296,000
Total CC Silver Dollars Available: 51,587

Minimum Bid: $60.00

1885-CC

Washington Monument dedicated.

Total CC Silver Dollars Minted: 228,000
Total CC Silver Dollars Available: 62,781

Minimum Bid: $60.00

GSA brochure advertising Carson City silver dollars.

[1] Q. David Bowers, *Buyers Guide to the Rare Coin Market*, 1990.

[2] *GSA Promotional Brochures*, 1973, 1974.

[3] Ibid.

[4] Ibid.

men from the open ranges that the lifestyle from the old days might be restored. This longing to return to seemingly more innocent and nostalgic times has continued into the early years of the 21st century.

Rare coins, of course, offer an excellent opportunity for people to collect and preserve the past. Carson City coins in particular are quintessential reminders of not only the "Old West" era, but also the "Gilded Age," the various coinage acts of 1873, 1878, and 1890, and one of the prolific ages of invention in history. When caught up into the specialized field of Carson City coins, a collector can fall in love with the series. Doors will be opened to the history of one of the most exciting and critical periods America has ever known, and the background of the coins with the "CC" mintmark is the stuff movie scripts are inspired by.

First Considerations for Starting a Collection

Collectors choose Carson City coins for many of the reasons mentioned above, but in a numismatic sense, the series offers just the right combination of challenge, variety, price levels, and pride of ownership. Beginning Carson City coin collectors, although eager to start, are often in a quandary when trying to decide how to proceed. Much of the decision rests upon budget, but the exhortation given by Augustus Heaton in 1893 as he urged collectors to consider mintmarked coins in general might be helpful: "In a final word, we urge upon all American numismatists the giving of their attention to the Branch Mint coinage of our country without delay. If not to all, certainly to the silver series."[1] Furthermore, Heaton advised anyone with the means that: "They should without fail save the rarest dates of any series if chancing upon them, for with the decline of Mint Mark coinage, such pieces will attain great value."[2] His words have proven to be truly prophetic.

Though not all collectors have the luxury of starting out with the rarest dates, the silver series as a whole does indeed provide many opportunities in a broad budgetary range. Two considerations should be addressed before decisions are made about which Carson City coins to collect. With regard to budget, three basic levels of pricing structure afford collectors in varying financial brackets options to assist in the creation of want lists. The first level is the *budget-conscious* collectors with strict financial limitations. Their discretionary purchasing decisions will have a significant impact on their ability to make their

rent or house payments and cover all other cost-of-living expenses. Naturally, the quality and rarity of coins available at this level will be a decisive factor. Fortunately in the Carson City series there are many opportunities within the different silver coin denominations. If a rare date that exceeds budgetary allotments is desired, the old-fashioned method of saving money over a period of time can prove to be a viable solution and often, the longer a person waits for something, the more it is appreciated.

At the middle level are the *advanced* collectors, who through professional accomplishments, success in business, or inheritances have comfortable financial cushions. Their discretionary funds, though not unlimited, afford them a wide variety of collecting options. At this level, many of the rarities in the Carson City series are within reach, and a higher standard for quality is an available luxury. Several obstacles facing collectors at this level might be low populations, limited choices in quality for selected dates, and a few select pieces that might be prohibitively expensive. Patience, as in any endeavor, is a virtue and will be required of anyone seriously committed to "CC" coins.

Even collectors at the third level will need to be patient and tenacious in their pursuit of their Carson City coinage goals. This is the *ultimate* collector category, a person for whom price is no object. Those favored and fortunate enough to be at this level are not restricted by financial limitations of any kind, purchasing coins for their collections is like other people buying the ordinary things in life. Without blinking an eye, they are able to write checks for whatever price tag is on a coin; and if inclined, these wealthy individuals could assemble complete sets of Carson City coins in the highest condition possible—with limitations, of course, for even all the money in the world cannot produce coins out of thin air. Several dates in the "CC" series needed to build complete sets are either "Unique" (only one specimen known) or virtually unobtainable. Nothing underscores the formidableness of assembling a complete 111-piece set of Carson City coins better than the fact that only one individual in history has accomplished the feat.

Laying the Groundwork

After a collector's level of financial participation has been established, the second factor to consider is a breakdown of the different grade categories to choose from.

[1] Augustus G. Heaton, A *Treatise on Mint Marks*, 1893.
[2] Ibid.

This, of course, is subordinate to the collector's financial level, and is plainly subject to available quantities. Grades, or the condition ratings of coins, may be divided into the following four sections:

Grade Category

> Good to Very Fine
>
> Extra Fine to AU
>
> MS-60 to MS-62
>
> MS-63 and above

Using a combination of price guides and population reports, collectors can map out a game plan for assembling their sets of Carson City coins which can help focus collecting strategy, especially as the universe of the Carson City series is juxtaposed alongside price ranges.

Often in a burst of ignorant exuberance collectors rush head first into purchasing Carson City coins, usually well intentioned, but unprepared. After wasting time and money on bad deals, they finally learn to cut their losses and do things the right way. Just as in any field, it is helpful to seek counsel and advice from those with experience.

Questions collectors need to ask themselves before becoming too independent are:

1. Do I realize that there are three levels of quality within each point rating on the numeric grading scale? (This is essential in grades above MS-63).

2. Can I tell the difference between cleaned (or doctored) coins and original coins?

3. Do I know the rudimentary basics of toning, and what effect it has on a coin's appearance, appeal, and value?

4. Do I know the acceptable characteristics for DMPL (Deep Mirror Prooflike) coins?

5. Do I know about the predominant grading services and do I realize that there may be substantial price differences between coins with the same date and grade, but different services?

6. Do I know how coin prices are derived? Do I think prices are all based on the "Greysheet" or the "Bluesheet"? (Both are coin dealer wholesale price indicators.)

7. Am I familiar with the buy/sell margins for the dates I wish to purchase?

8. Have I ever researched auction prices realized?

9. Do I realize how incongruous it is to believe that I can buy all of my coins for below-market prices and yet expect to get way above market price when I sell them?

10. Have I checked out population figures and other valuable reference resources?

Unfortunately, many collectors bypass the learning stage and begin buying coins from the most visible sources, which are usually Ebay, "home shopping" channels on TV, other high-profile Internet sites, or mail-order companies blanketing the nation with advertising. If this describes you, put your student cap on, swallow some pride, and seek out a reputable coin dealer or veteran collector. They will be happy to assist you, and collecting Carson City coins is much too pleasurable of an experience to waste on bad decisions and lack of knowledge.

As with any field of participation, there is a learning curve that coin collectors must traverse on their way to becoming seasoned veterans. Novices begin with very little knowledge about coins in general. Usually, within one year, if they are under the proper tutelage and are observant, they will have heard many terms and gained experience which will prove vital to their advancement for years to come. After five or so years, if diligent, the collector will be able to converse on a variety of related topics, as his numismatic experience and vocabulary have greatly expanded. As time passes and the collector reaches the 10-year mark and beyond, he may have a sense that coin collecting has always been a part of his life. His vast knowledge on a diversity of numismatic subjects will impress fellow collectors and non-collectors alike. Countless numbers of collectors will have followed this path throughout the history of the United States, laying a foundation for future generations. If you are not yet headed in this direction but have been attempting to build a coin collection, now is the time to get back on track and walk in the footprints of successful collectors from the past.

SOURCES FOR CARSON CITY COINS

Practically every weekend, somewhere in the United States, there is a coin show being held. These shows vary in size, from small coin club-sponsored shows to major events with thousands of people in attendance. A list of the most prominent shows includes the Mid-Winter and Summer ANA Conventions, the FUN show (Florida United Numismatists), three separate Long Beach shows in California, and the Central States Numismatic Society Convention held at various locations throughout the Midwest. Schedules for all of these shows are provided in various numismatic publications. A major advantage to collectors attending coin shows—especially the major ones—is the huge selection of items on display. Unless you have been a collector for many years, it is possible that you will see more coins at large shows than you would normally see in a lifetime. This does not necessarily mean that there will be an abundance of Carson City coins, but chances are there will be many more than you possess. As a word of advice: when attending coin shows, learn proper etiquette, take your time, and absorb all that you can.

Often held in conjunction with coin shows are auctions. Typically, there is at least one major rare coin auction per month, sometimes two or more. These auctions feature anywhere from 500 to 5,000 lots to bid on. You are welcome to attend the auction viewing in advance of the event, at which time you will be required to establish credit with the company. Many auction companies have begun to offer simultaneous Internet bidding for those who are unable to attend the live sales in person. You will still need to arrange to inspect the coins for yourself, as the Internet images are no substitute for live viewing. Some people may object to this last statement, declaring that as long as the coins are graded by a major service there is nothing to worry about, but before you succumb to that belief, read the ten questions listed above one more time. Ask yourself: If the experts and professionals refuse to bid without first viewing the coins in person, why should you act to the contrary? Just as at coin shows, there is no guarantee of a large assortment of Carson City coins, but there is usually at least a small representative group for sale. Not incidentally, the rarest and most prestigious "CC" coins are generally sold at public auction.

Other sources for rare coins are the numismatic publications circulating weekly and monthly across the country, although in spite of the pages of ads, offerings of Carson City coins are typically minimal, and as a rule, with the exception of Morgan silver dollars, there are more "CC" gold coins offered in these ads than silver issues. Also, growing in leaps and bounds in the early years of the 21st century is the popularity of Internet websites featuring rare coins. One of the most innovative websites in recent times (2003) is the auction place of the world, Ebay. Everything from gold crowns from teeth to airplanes is sold on Ebay, and rare coins quickly became one of the most popular categories.

For collectors of Carson City coins it is simple to do a search with the entries "CC" or Carson City, and anything related suddenly appears. There are no apparent advantages to buying "CC" coins off of Ebay, though occasionally a small bargain might slip through, but people seem fascinated with the site, almost as an alternative form of entertainment. Collectors should exercise caution when purchasing coins on Ebay, guarding against overgrading and counterfeits, making sure there are return privileges provided by sellers. Again, there is no substitute for proper education and preparation before making coin purchases.

One of the best sources for these vital fundamentals of coin collecting are veteran coin dealers located in retail stores around the country. At your local coin shop you can gain valuable experience as you continue to expand your numismatic education, see coins up close on a regular basis and ask questions. It goes without saying that all coin shops are not equal; some are numismatic showcases offering large selections of delightful coins, while others have only meager inventories of items on display. Some collectors are fortunate to have helpful and knowledgeable coin dealers at their local shop, yet others become turned off by the rude behavior of their local dealer. One thing to keep in mind is that the fraternity of coin dealers throughout history has done more to preserve the hobby than tear it down and there is a long-established tradition of coin dealer commitment and loyalty to their customers. There will always be bad apples, just as in any other business, but overall, the profession of coin dealer is an honorable one, and for collectors it is imperative to establish a relationship with one. You will need him or her, and when you find the dealer that suits you best, you will gain far more than you anticipated.

PRICE CONSIDERATIONS FOR CARSON CITY COINS

Prices are necessary as a means of keeping score and providing the thrill of competition and also for collectors to see the value of their coins increase. Without prices there are no markets, and without markets there is no exchange of goods. Buyers and sellers "dance" around prices until one is agreed upon, or a no-sale is declared. Often, though, collectors view prices as evil, hastily putting up their guards without analyzing the factors involved in the sale. For this, and other reasons, you as a collector must not allow prices to be your enemies, because, when it comes time for you to sell, prices hopefully will become your best friends. As a buyer of Carson City coins, prices will either lead you to rewarding satisfaction or turn you into a sourpuss who misses opportunities to enjoy the pastime.

Now this is not to say that you should place a big "kick me" sign on your back or draw the word "sucker" across your forehead. You do not want to get ripped off, and most certainly you will look for values. But if you are buying accurately graded "CC" coins at prices relatively close to what other collectors or dealers have paid—or are paying—you can feel safe. Just realize that Carson City coins are very popular and not overly abundant, and collectors are lined up waiting whenever they hit the market. Does this mean that they are overvalued, and you should consider a different series of coins? Not at all; prices for Carson City coins were suppressed for the first 75 years of the 20th century, and when they began their run in the 1970s there was a lot of ground to make up for.

For many collectors, prices get in the way of fulfilling their goals. For instance, a "CC" coin priced at $1,500 when listed in a book or guide for $1,000 poses a dilemma. But if the collector has done his homework and prepared himself, he will know what to do. Assume, for instance, that this collector realizes the price is close enough, and purchases the coin, pursuing his goals with availability of the coins his motivating factor, not price. Sometimes buying coins for your collection requires a little "sweat on the palms," and often, this stretching a little to get just the coin you have been looking for, adds to the thrill of the pursuit.

One of the greatest coin collectors of all time was Harry W. Bass, Jr., who assembled such a massive collection of incredible coins during his time in the hobby that today his coins are held up as references by which to judge others of similar dates and grades. Throughout his coin-collecting career, Bass followed an acquisition strategy that allowed him to assemble his magnificent assortment of numismatic riches, summarized by Q. David Bowers in one of Bowers and Merena's auction catalogues featuring the Bass collection: "Harry also realized at an early time that a listed price for a rarity represented either what such a piece had sold for sometime in the past, or was a ballpark estimate put down by a catalog compiler who had to come up with some figure, but who could find no market data."[1] Bass knew "that if a particular gold coin . . . was listed at . . . $1,000, but during the past 100 years only three or four had come on the market—none recently—he could bid $2,000, or $5,000, or even $10,000 to acquire [it] at auction; and then own it, while everyone else was waiting to buy one at the catalog price!"[2] There was a flipside, of course, for the more common dates. Bass was well aware that there would be some coins listed at $1,000, "that each year a half dozen . . . were sold at auction, and even more were held in the private stocks of dealers."[3] He knew that, "he could bide his time and wait for a piece that was just right. . . ."[4]

In the Carson City silver coin series, and less so for the gold coins, there are common date issues that will be offered at low to moderate premiums over listed prices. Prime examples are the Morgan dollars dated 1882-CC, 1883-CC, 1884-CC, and the Seated Liberty dimes, quarters, and halves dated 1876-CC and 1877-CC. Exceptions, even for these common dates, however, are specimens in superior condition, as collectors usually cast aside monetary inhibitions whenever any high quality Carson City coins with unbelievable eye appeal are offered.

For most of the semi-key to key dates in the Carson City series, collectors must be prepared to follow Harry W. Bass, Jr.'s acquisition philosophy. A recent example of this occurred in 2002, when an 1871-CC quarter graded F-15 by PCGS sold at a public auction for $10,250. Coin dealer price guides listed the bid/ask spread for this coin at $3,100 to $4,200, but this is a date that seldom appears on the market. No doubt there were many discouraged collectors who were prepared to pay close to, or even a slight premium over, the listed price; but in the end, the market determined the coin's true value. Does it mean that the buyer paid too much? Not necessarily. On the contrary, it could very well indicate that the price guide listing was out of sync with reality.

Greysheet BUYERS

During the past decade (1994-2003), there has been a proliferation of retail coin customers known as *Greysheet Buyers*. Originally, this so-called *Greysheet*, officially named *The Coin Dealer Newsletter*, was a resource made available to professional numismatists to aid them in monitoring the wholesale coin market. It does not contain any secret or inside information to speak of, just a report of "the national Dealer to Dealer wholesale coin market, monitoring all possible transactions and offers to buy and sell coins sight-seen."[5] This newsletter is a resource tool for coin dealers, especially in the categories of bulk generic coins and government-issue items such as Proof sets. On the front page of the *Greysheet* is a chart with the estimated Bid/Asks for generic U.S. gold coins, as well as the spreads for bullion-related products such as gold Krugerrands and bulk quantities of 90% silver coins. Dealers are also welcome to place ads that inform their peers of various business activities.

[1] Bowers and Merena, *Harry W. Bass, Jr. Collection, Part 1*, May 7-9, 1999.
[2] Ibid.
[3] Ibid.
[4] Ibid.
[5] *The Coin Dealer Newsletter*, CDN, Inc.

For over 30 years, the *Greysheet* remained, for the most part, an in-house publication reserved for the dealer community. Then, in the 1990s, the editors of the newsletter decided to expand their horizons and market it to the coin collecting hobby at large. As more nonprofessional coin enthusiasts subscribed, the editors at the *Greysheet* were compelled to add more descriptive disclaimers to alert retail customers that: "The prices in this newsletter are from Dealer to Dealer transactions; you should expect to pay a premium above 'Ask' when purchasing coins in a retail transaction; you may also [pay a commission to] a Dealer for your purchases."[1]

New retail subscribers were not provided with instructions how to use the *Greysheet* (or its cousin, the *Bluesheet*) and mistakenly believed that the prices listed therein represented dealer cost for every coin in inventory and customers should be entitled to pay just a small percentage markup over *Greysheet* to purchase coins at the retail level. Occasionally, this is the way it works, yet beneath the surface is an elaborate pricing structure that would require a lengthy discussion to explain.

As complex as the subject of dealer-cost versus selling price relative to the *Greysheet* is for common-issue coins, scarcer dates present an even greater challenge. Statisticians at the *Coin Dealer Newsletter* work tirelessly to monitor activity in the coin market for every U.S. coin in every condition rating. However, there are too many categories with infrequently traded coins, making it nearly impossible to provide accurate pricing information for all.

There is also the matter of grading criteria. Unfortunately, despite the loud cries from diehards, grading is not a science; it is subjective, and certification does not guarantee market acceptance. Therefore, dealers may pay less than *Greysheet* for one example of a given issue, yet a percentage over *Greysheet* for another example of the same date and grade. Subsequent sales of the two coins will result in the first example seeming like a good deal to the so-called *Greysheet Buyer*, yet the second piece would probably be considered overpriced. An old adage might seem fitting in this instance, for it is well-acknowledged that, generally, "you get what you pay for."

Editors at the *Greysheet* found it necessary to further inform their readership—especially the retail segment—"that the 'Bid' prices listed within represent what individual dealers are willing to pay for coins that **meet their particular grading criteria** [Emphasis added]."[2] Emphatically disclosing that this might not be a universally accepted set of criteria, transcending even the criteria of the professional grading services, the editors continued, "Coins graded by other dealers or grading services, such as PCGS . . . ANACS, NGC, and any other services, may not conform to the grading standards interpreted by the dealer . . . whose bid is represented."[3] Next came the most important statement, which should be required reading for all *Greysheet Buyers*: "**Therefore, a specific coin could be worth more or less than the listed bid price.**" [Emphasis added][4]

One caveat to those in the beginning stages of their coin collecting pursuits seems appropriate: A *Greysheet Buyer* who does not know how to grade coins is looking for failure. Many times, novice *Greysheet Buyers* show their new purchases to professionals, and much too often, the quality of the coins speaks louder than words. A glance through a recent copy of *Krause's Auction Prices Realized* can be an enlightening experience concerning the disparity in price between coins of the same date and grade. When one example of a certain date graded MS-65 by PCGS sells for $1,700 and another with the same date, grade, and service realizes $985, it is clear that a *Greysheet Buyer* would have a difficult time explaining how this happened when the *Greysheet* price was $1,100.

Contrary to the notion embraced by many budding *Greysheet Buyers*, this newsletter is not an equalizer, placing retail customers on a level playing field with dealers. Sadly, the *Greysheet* becomes a hindrance to collectors, sometimes preventing them from truly enjoying the hobby, despite attempts by the editors of this publication to inform readers what their newsletter is and what it is not. Even coin dealers, at times, have been known to be dogmatic in their adherence to *Greysheet* prices, often wondering why they never seem to obtain the more desirable specimens.

Used in the proper way, the *Greysheet* is a wonderful resource for many items; however, in the hands of the uninformed, it often proves to be detrimental. If you are a retail customer and plan on using a *Greysheet* when purchasing Carson City coins, make sure to supplement it with other pricing references, such as auction prices realized and retail price guides. Your coin dealer, if you confide in one, should also be able to offer valuable information. For over 40 years, *Greysheet* prices have served as footprints left from past purchases made by collectors

---

1 Ibid.
2 Ibid.
3 Ibid.
4 Ibid.

and dealers along the way, and as such, they are useful tools. But flashing your *Greysheet* in the face of a seller is tantamount to standing at the checkout counter at Big 5 Sporting Goods using a copy of the store's cost of goods report to negotiate the price of a set of golf clubs you want to buy. Even in this case, the sporting goods store's report accurately reflects the wholesale price for the golf clubs, whereas the *Greysheet* may have no relevance to the cost of the dealer's inventory.

INVESTMENT POTENTIAL OF CARSON CITY COINS

Closely related to the topic of the pricing of coins is the investment potential they provide. In the past 100 or so years, Carson City coins have proven to be excellent investments. Whether they will continue to be is, of course, dependent upon many unpredictable factors, yet all indications point toward a steady pace of appreciation for years to come. Whether key dates will mirror the returns from past decades seems questionable, though not impossible. Consider, for instance, the 1876-CC 20-cent piece in Uncirculated condition. In order for this date to match its rate of appreciation from 1950 to 2003 over the next 50 years, it would need to reach the $17 million mark. The rarest "CC" coin of all, the 1873-CC *Without Arrows* dime, would be worth in the neighborhood of $100 million by 2053. Even if the rate of appreciation from the first half of the 20th century for these two dates is equaled 50 years from now, the 1876-CC 20-center will be worth approximately $9 million; and the 1873-CC *Without Arrows* dime will approach the $15 million level.

These values are incomprehensible to the modern collector, just as prices of $1,500 for an 1876-CC 20-center and $4,000 for an 1873-CC *Without Arrows* dime would have been to those living in 1900. One important point to consider when making such prognostications, regardless of the era, is the effect such skyrocketing price increases have on the cost of living in general. For instance, what will it mean in terms of the value of cars, food, clothing, electronics, health care, travel, real estate, and the like 50 years from now if coins like this appreciate at these rates? Will starter homes for a new family be in the $1 million price range? Additionally, the value of the U.S. dollar would have inflated to unthinkable proportions, and minimum wages for workers 50 years into the future could be what high-paid mid-level corporate managers earn now.

Of course, if these coins appreciate, independent of a corresponding inflationary rise in the CPI, GDP, and other leading economic indicators, only billionaires will be able to afford them, and that would be no fun.

Professional athletes signing $250 million contracts and small houses in California selling in the $600,000 to $1 million range would not even have crossed the mind of a person living in the United States during the first 50 to 60 years of the 20th century, but now, it's old news. Groundwork has been laid for soaring increases in the prices of collectibles, not only in rare coins, but also in the field of art, in which paintings selling for $10 to $20 million barely rouse the auction attendees. Even numismatics has experienced its first $7 million coin, with several waiting on the sidelines ready to blow past the $10 million mark.

Carson City coins will veritably reap their share of any future appreciation in the rare coin market, and not just the high-profile dates. So many "CC" issues have been undervalued and just the slightest increase in demand will advance prices accordingly. Many of the scarcest dates remain off the market for years and as a result become springloaded, as if packed with tons of gunpowder. When the time comes, they are ready to explode out of the owner's collection with a force usually reserved for ballistic missiles. A new owner pays a record price, and the coin goes into hibernation for another extended period of time. Collectors seeking coins like this must make the most of every fleeting opportunity.

Not all Carson City coins are reserved for the wealthy, which is good news to the majority of collectors, who are the foundation of the "CC" market, strengthening the market with their buying power and enthusiasm. Whether the collector is a Harry W. Bass, Jr., said to have had "a generous purchase budget,"[1] or one of the thousands of anonymous "CC" enthusiasts who save their money for several months to make a purchase, the anticipation and excitement is similar. When you finally obtain the coin you have been waiting for, you want to go off by yourself somewhere and study and admire it.

This is where sound rare coin investing begins, with the pure heart of a collector. If you will collect your coins and catalog them, compare them with others, weigh them, measure them, learn how to grade them, research them, study their designs, write about them, and talk to others about them, you will possess the ultimate investment. Begin with

---

[1] Bowers and Merena, *Harry W. Bass, Jr. Collection, Part 1*, May 1999.

a desire to collect, not even entertaining the thought of investing, and you will be rewarded in both categories.

Augustus G. Heaton, writing in 1905, aptly interposed a noble side-benefit, interlacing the collecting and investing aspects of rare coins, attesting that, "those persons who hold their Uncirculated pieces now, will not only profit in time, but will have the benediction of future generations of collectors."[1] Today's collectors serve as custodians of the coins they own, helping to connect one generation to the next, often earning generous profits in the process.

MULTIPLE CHOICES FOR THE CARSON CITY COLLECTOR

Where does a person begin? Is there any right or wrong way to collect Carson City coins? These are questions asked practically every day by collectors bitten by the "CC" bug. In answer to the second question, no, there is no right or wrong way to collect these popular coins; however, a thorough consideration of the first question will almost guarantee a successful and rewarding experience.

Armed with the preparatory rudiments briefly outlined earlier in this chapter, you already know what financial level fits your profile and possibly have had an opportunity to peruse a price list of "CC" coins, including a breakdown of grade categories. Presumably, you have come to grips with the issue of pricing and will not let it detract from your joy of collecting. Grab a *Greysheet* if you must, but try not to think of it as a holy scroll. And, hopefully you will have the heart of a collector, even if you would like to see your collection increase in value in the years to come.

13-PIECE SET OF MORGAN DOLLARS

It is an inescapable fact that Carson City silver dollars rank high in popularity. Even collectors with no intentions of assembling sets of "CC" dollars will spice up their collections with at least a few examples. Depending on the condition rating you choose for this set, it could be a relatively simple task—or a wallet-bursting experience.

Three of the dates, 1882-CC, 1883-CC, and 1884-CC present very little challenge regardless of the grade category chosen. One of the most popular dates is the first year of issue, 1878-CC, and thanks to a relatively large mintage, there are ample supplies in all grades up to MS-63. Above this grade, supplies begin to diminish rapidly, and the date is very scarce above MS-65.

Five dates—1880-CC, 1881-CC, 1885-CC, 1890-CC, and 1891-CC—are comparable in availability in Uncirculated grades; however, in circulated condition, you should probably give up hope of finding an 1885-CC, and pay the extra $50 to $100 for an Uncirculated example (In 2004). Two of the other dates, 1880-CC and 1881-CC, are available in circulated grades, though not nearly as plentiful as the 1890-CC and 1891-CC.

Of the remaining four dates in the "CC" Morgan dollar series, the 1892-CC is the easiest to locate, though not as available as the nine dates previously described. In grades above MS-64, the 1892-CC is on par with the 1890-CC, yet there are fewer examples with stunning eye appeal.

Surprisingly, the 1893-CC, with a mintage of 677,000, is one of the keys to the set, as circulated pieces are always in demand, and there is a dearth of XF to AU specimens. In Uncirculated grades up through MS-63, this date is comparable to the 1879-CC (both varieties combined), but in MS-64 and above, the 1893-CC becomes much more elusive. Examples in Gem condition are among the rarest in the entire Morgan dollar series, and DMPL specimens are coveted by specialists.

When surviving populations of both varieties of 1879-CC dollars are combined, the mintage is slightly higher than that of the 1893-CC. Yet, excluding the "Capped Die" variety, the 1879-CC becomes scarcer than the 1893-CC. However, there is a generous supply of 1879-CCs in Gem condition, and circulated examples of this date do not present much of a challenge, except in the AU category.

Of course, the key date in the series is the 1889-CC, well known for its extreme scarcity in grades above MS-64. Many numismatically aesthetic specimens of this date exist with Deep-Mirror-Prooflike surfaces, always commanding hefty price tags. For collectors assembling Uncirculated sets the starting price in 2003 for an 1889-CC in lower Mint State grades is approximately $11,000. Because of the paucity of examples in grades above MS-63, the number of collections including one at this level will be limited to fewer than 25 at any one time. And for grades above MS-64, the number of sets possible could be counted on one hand.

In 2003, the starting price for one of the elusive MS-65 specimens is in the $250,000 range; but for collectors not interested in the high-rent district of Uncirculated 1889-CC silver dollars, there is relief, since there are

[1] Augustus G. Heaton, article in *The Numismatist*, November 1905, quoted from Q. David Bowers, *Silver Dollars and Trade Dollars of the United States.*

13-PIECE SET OF CARSON CITY MORGAN DOLLARS RATING OF ACHIEVEMENT LEVEL IN DIFFERENT GRADE CATEGORIES	
Grade Range	**Achievement Level**
Good to Very Fine	Sand lot
Extra Fine to AU	Semi-pro
MS-60 to MS-62	Triple AAA
MS-63 and Above	Major League
MS-65 and Above	Hall of Fame

enough circulated examples to keep prices moderately reasonable for enthusiasts with limited budgets. Of course, there is always the possibility that the collector base for "CC" Morgan dollars will double or more in size in the upcoming years, causing today's prices for even circulated pieces to seem like bargains in comparison.

GSA CARSON CITY DOLLARS - SETS AND SUBSETS

Responsible for introducing more people to Carson City coins than any other source, GSA "Black Box" silver dollars are as popular as ever despite it being more than 30 years since they first appeared. Collectors and non-collectors alike have owned and enjoyed these historic symbols of the American West. Probably one of the most influential factors leading to the success of the GSA's sales promotion was the large quantity involved. Nearly three million coins guaranteed widespread distribution.

The table at center lists the quantity allocation of the different dates represented in this landmark event.

These silver dollars were placed in complementary plastic display cases, imitated to varying degrees by professional grading services years later. A certificate briefly profiling the Carson City Mint with a serial number preceded by the coin's date was enclosed with the plastic display case in a stylish black box with light-velvet lining. Overall, it made for an attractive presentation piece.

Almost without exception, the public loved these GSA dollars. As

ORIGINAL HOLDINGS OF CARSON CITY SILVER DOLLARS AVAILABLE IN GSA SALE	
Date	**Quantity**
1878-CC	60,993
1879-CC	4,123
1880-CC	131,529
1881-CC	147,485
1882-CC	605,029
1883-CC	755,518
1884-CC	962,638
1885-CC	148,285
1889-CC	1
1890-CC	3,949
1891-CC	5,687
1892-CC	1
1893-CC	1

time passed, growing numbers of collectors broke the dollars out of the display cases for a number of reasons, the foremost being a desire to see the coins without having to remove them from the boxes all the time as well as to insert these "CC" dollars into Morgan dollar albums. With the advent of grading services, many more GSA dollars were broken out of their holders to be submitted to grading services and in turn encased in new plastic slabs.

As a result of this proliferation of GSA breakouts, thousands, possibly millions, of these "CC" dollars are no longer in the presentation cases first issued in the 1970s. No one seemed to notice this deficiency at first, but eventually, as in many collectible categories, preservation of original packaging took on primary importance. Eventually, premiums were offered for Carson City dollars with original GSA boxes and certificates, and breakouts for the most part came to an abrupt halt.

Naturally, prices for the dates with low original GSA quantities have been influenced the most. For instance, in 2003 the 1890-CC and 1891-CC in Uncirculated grades below MS-64 are available for $400 to $600, yet in GSA original packaging the price jumps to $1,500 or more. Another example is the 1879-CC dollar, available for less than $1,900 in MS-60 to MS-61; yet if encased in a GSA holder in similar condition, be prepared to pay close to $4,000 (again, in 2003).

Of course, the three dates with only a single GSA offering, 1889-CC, 1892-CC, and 1893-CC, are unmentionables regarding the premiums that would be commanded; these three dates are not included on the want lists of collectors desiring to build sets of GSA dollars.

With this background aside, it is time to consider the options available in the GSA category. Start with the basic number of three, comprising the most common dates, 1882-CC, 1883-CC, and 1884-CC, one of the most popular trios of coins ever marketed. Even with the attrition rate of the original GSA-holdered dollars, substantial quantities of these three dates are available, though with the

CARSON CITY SILVER DOLLAR GSA SETS RATING OF ACHIEVEMENT LEVEL FOR COMPLETION	
Number of Pieces	**Achievement Level**
3-piece set	Sandlot
7-piece set	Semi-pro
10-piece set	Major League
13-piece set	Immortal

spread of Internet marketing and shop-at-home television, a larger audience is being exposed to such coins all the time, practically guaranteeing that existing inventories will be absorbed in a short time.

A natural progression for collectors who already own the three-piece set would be to expand it to seven pieces, adding the 1878-CC, 1880-CC, 1881-CC, and 1885-CC. Though much more of a challenge than the three common dates, these additional mid-level "CC" issues are relatively easy to locate (at least through 2003). Currently, average prices for any of these four dates in grades below MS-64 are in the $450 to $600 range.

Upon completion of a seven-piece set, a collector now possesses a solid nucleus from which to advance to the next level. There are only three other collectable dates in this series, the 1879-CC, 1890-CC, and 1891-CC,

bringing the set total available to mortals to 10. Anyone completing this set has accomplished no small feat. With the diminishing supply of all GSA dollars, and these three tough dates in particular, collectors will be placed on long waiting lists to experience the privilege of owning a 10-piece set.

Beyond that, of course, invariably only one individual could own a 13-piece set at a time. Currently, no one has ever publicly revealed ownership of a set of this stature. In fact, it has only been in the past decade (through 2003) that the existence of an 1889-CC in a GSA holder was reported.

In addition to these traditional alternatives to collecting GSA dollars, recent trends have provided more options for collectors. One emerging offshoot to the customary way of building sets of GSA dollars has been to collect by grade. Naturally, anyone assembling a set desires the finest quality available, yet it is obvious that examples of some dates in MS-65 or higher are extremely scarce. As a result, a scant number of collectors have seen the mountain and have decided to climb it. A complete 10-piece set of GSA dollars averaging MS-65 will up the ante considerably; and even assembling a set averaging MS-64 is a formidable task. Price premiums for high-quality "CC" silver dollars in GSA holders have been skyrocketing in recent years and this trend will likely continue as the competition heats up.

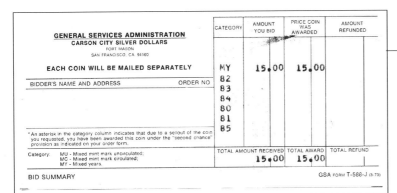

During the 1970s, thousands of people received notices like this from the GSA informing them of their successful bids for Carson City silver dollars. On this particular order, the customer's winning bid was $15 for the dates listed. (*Author's personal collection*)

Although "Johnny-come-latelys" in the GSA game, the two major grading services, PCGS and NGC, have begun offering their clientele the option of having their GSAs graded without requiring the coins to be removed from the original holders. As populations increase for these GSA "graded-in-the-holder" dollars, another set-building option will be available to collectors.

VARIETIES OF CARSON CITY MORGAN DOLLARS

A wide selection of die varieties in the "CC" series awaits collectors interested in the unusual. As PCGS states concerning the entire universe of rare coins in general, it "recognizes all major varieties; there are thousands of minor varieties, most of which have significance only to specialists in the particular series."[1] Of course, there are not thousands of varieties of Carson City coins, but there are a significant number within the silver and gold series combined.

Five of the most recognized varieties available to collectors in the Morgan dollar series, including their ratings based on acquisition achievement levels are shown in the table at right. Without a doubt, a set of all five of these varieties would provide a collector with enjoyment and pride of ownership. And while hunting for these coins, curiosity might also be aroused to explore many of the other numerous VAM varieties attributed to the Carson City Morgan dollar series.

YEAR SETS OF CARSON CITY COINS

From the first year coins were issued at the Carson City Mint in 1870 through the last year of coinage operations in 1893, many interesting themes for year sets developed. Beyond question, the most noteworthy year was 1873 and completing a set of one example of every coin struck at Carson City in that year is one of the most elite accomplishments in the numismatic world.

This set comprises 11 extraordinary coins. One in particular, the 1873-CC *Without Arrows* dime, stands tall and formidable, daring anyone to surmount the odds and achieve their goal. Before anyone contemplates acquiring this "Unique" classic rarity, they must first hurdle the obstacle of locating an example of the 1873-CC *Without Arrows* quarter. After these two indomitable challenges have

CARSON CITY MORGAN DOLLAR VARIETIES AND RATING OF ACHIEVEMENT LEVEL FOR ACQUISITION		
Date and Variety	Grade Range	Achievement Level
1880-CC (Reverse of 1878)	Good to MS-64	Sand lot
1880-CC (Reverse of 1878)	MS-65 and above	Triple AAA
1879-CC (Capped Die)	Good to AU	Sand lot
1879-CC (Capped Die)	MS-60 to MS-64	Semi-pro
1879-CC (Capped Die)	MS-65 and above	Major League
1890-CC (Tail Bar)	Good to MS-62	Sand lot
1890-CC (Tail Bar)	MS-63 to MS-64	Triple AAA
189)-CC (Tail Bar)	MS-65 and above	Major League
1891-CC (Spitting Eagle)	Good to MS-64	Sand lot
1891-CC (Spitting Eagle)	MS-65 and above	Triple AAA
1900-O/CC	Good to MS-65	Sand lot
1900-O/CC	MS-66 and above	Triple AAA

been conquered, acquiring the rest of the coins in the set will seem like child's play, though each of them in its own way elicits respect from veteran numismatists.

Besides the *With Arrows* and *Without Arrows* variations, 1873 is also acknowledged as one of the years two different silver dollars were issued, one a Seated Liberty design and the other a trade dollar type; both issues with the "CC" mintmark are considered to be very scarce, especially the Seated Liberty. Each of the three gold coins from 1873 is among the rarest dates in its respective denomination. Rounding out the 11-piece set are the 1873-CC *With Arrows* dime—a significant rarity in its own right—the 1873-CC *With Arrows* quarter, and the two varieties of the 1873-CC half dollar.

Usually a person stands at the bottom of a coin-collecting mountain and works upward and rarely is this attempted in reverse. Yet noted collector Waldo E. Bolen, Jr. assembled his 11-piece 1873-CC set from the vantage point of standing on the mountain and looking down. He had collected many different series of coins over the years, enjoying much success, but unable to complete a set of U.S. dimes, thwarted, like so many collectors, by the 1873-CC *Without Arrows*. Partly in frustration and partly looking for new challenges, Bolen sold his dime collection. Shortly thereafter, the *Eliasberg* 1873-CC *Without Arrows* dime appeared in the famous auction in 1996. Although Bolen no longer owned a dime collection, he pur-

---

[1] *Official Guide to Coin Grading and Counterfeit Detection,* PCGS.

WALDO BOLEN'S 11-PIECE 1873-CC TYPE SET SOLD APRIL 23, 1999		
Date	Denomination	Grade
1873-CC *Without Arrows*	Dime	PCGS MS-64
1873-CC *With Arrows*	Dime	PCGS MS-64
1873-CC *Without Arrows*	Quarter	PCGS MS-62
1873-CC *With Arrows*	Quarter	PCGS MS-63
1873-CC *Without Arrows*	Half dollar	PCGS MS-66
1873-CC *With Arrows*	Half dollar	NGC MS-63
1873-CC Seated Liberty	Dollar	NGC AU-58
1873-CC Trade	Dollar	PCGS MS-63
1873-CC	$5 Half eagle	PCGS XF-40
1873-CC	$10 Eagle	NGC XF-45
1873-CC	$20 Double eagle	PCGS MS-60

picked off the other ten coins and became one of the only people in history to accomplish this monumental goal. Within a short time after completion, he decided that there were other mountains to climb, and he sold his fabulous 11-piece 1873-CC type set. At left is a list of the coins in his collection.

The total price realized for the set was $1,056,275, with the 1873-CC *Without Arrows* dime accounting for $632,500 of that amount.

Not everyone will choose a set of this proportion to satisfy a desire for Carson City coins, but that is the beauty of the series. There are 20 other years available to collectors to ponder, from the two-piece sets of 1885 and 1889 to the eight-piece sets of 1875, 1876, and 1878. A first-year six-piece set from 1870 would provide a few anxious moments, not to mention tremendous pressure on the checkbook. On the other hand, a final-year set from 1893 would be a nice memento to remember the Carson City Mint by, without taking food off your table.

Year sets offer collectors many options to get involved in the Carson City series. Ratings for achievement

chased the elusive 1873-CC *Without Arrows* anyway, for $550,000. Before the ink was dry on his auction payment check, Bolen decided to complete a set, not of dimes this time, but the 1873-CC type collection. One by one, he

Assembling an eight-piece set of coins minted at Carson City in 1875 provides a rewarding challenge.

AVERAGE PRICES FOR CARSON CITY GOLD COINS
FROM *LUSK AND LEONARD* SALE, 1930

Denomination	# of Pieces Offered	Average Price
$5 Half eagle	9	$17.67
$10 Eagle	9	$31.20
$20 Double eagle	8	$35.13

and acquisition levels vary depending upon the years chosen and the grade quality selected, and although there are a few year sets available for sand-lotters, most will require semipro experience and higher. Obviously the Waldo Bolen 1873-CC 11-piece set belongs in the Hall of Fame.

COMPLETE SETS OF CARSON CITY GOLD COINS

Focusing briefly on the gold coinage from the Carson City Mint requires an acknowledgment that there will be few options for low-budget collectors in this category. However, a "CC" gold coin or two may still be included in a person's type set of one example of each denomination from this legendary mint.

For early collectors dating back to the late 19th century and early 20th century, the intrinsic value of bullion presented an additional challenge on top of the rarity factor when considering gold coins as an option. There was also a lack of availability of gold coins in general due to massive exports, especially in the 1930s. As a result, sets of Carson City gold coins were not standard fare for collectors until well into the 1940s, at which point the recognized scarcity of many of the dates was established.

Attempts were made to estimate the value of the gold coins from the Carson Mint by notable numismatic dealers and authors, one of the most respected being Wayte Raymond. In 1928 Raymond published his *United States Gold Coins of the Philadelphia and Branch Mints* listing estimated retail prices for many gold issues. Under the Carson City series, $5 half eagles averaged $21.50 each; $10 eagles, $40.50; and $20 double eagles, $46. In 1930, B. Max Mehl offered the *Lusk and Leonard* sale, the average prices shown above were realized for an impressive offering of "CC" gold coins.

Included in both the half eagle and eagle categories were circulated pieces dated 1870-CC.

On the other hand, in the double eagle section none of the dates prior to 1876 were offered. Most, if not all, of the coins in all three denominations were in circulated condition.

Though Carson City gold coins commanded premiums above their common-date counterparts from the other mints, no one really knew at this time just how rare the series was. Consider, for example, the prices listed in the 1943 *Handbook of United States Coins* for Carson City gold: on the half eagle page, the total price suggested for a complete 19-piece set in XF was $140, or an average of $7.40 per coin. Of course, the most expensive date in the set was the 1870-CC, topping out at $8.75. In the gold eagle section, the editors estimated that a complete 19-piece set in XF was worth roughly $266, or $14 individually. Finally, a full 19-piece collection of $20 double eagles in XF was valued at approximately $532, for an average of $28 each. Surprisingly, not even the 1870-CC double eagle was afforded premium status by the renowned numismatic luminaries who compiled the data.

As always, rare coin auctions are where price estimates come to terms with market reality. One in particular was the *Belden E. Roach* sale held by B. Max Mehl in 1944. All three denominations in the Carson City gold series were well represented, with the double eagle set including 17 of the 19 pieces, and both the half eagles and eagles comprising 14 out of the possible 19 dates in each set. Overall, the quality of the "CC" gold in this collection was higher than that in the *Lusk and Leonard* sale 14 years earlier, yet the majority of coins were in average circulated condition. Not much had changed since the 1930 sale in the half eagle and eagle categories; however, the prices for double eagles showed substantial gains, being somewhat influenced by the Gold Act of 1933, which raised the bullion price of the metal. Below is a breakdown of the prices realized from the *Roach* sale.

When *A Guide Book of United States Coins* (the *Red Book*) premiered in 1947, progress had been made in the evaluation of Carson City gold coins, yet the true rarity of this

AVERAGE PRICES FOR CARSON CITY GOLD COINS
FROM THE *BELDEN E. ROACH* COLLECTION, 1944

Denomination	# of Pieces Offered	Average Price
$5 Half eagle	14 (No 70-CC, 71-CC, 73-CC, 75-CC, 77-CC)	$17.80
$10 Eagle	14 (No 70-CC, 75-CC, 79-CC, 83-CC, 84-CC)	$29.66
$20 Double eagle	17 (No 70-CC, 85-CC)	$70.50

series had not become fully appreciated. At least the editors of the *Red Book* had access to the prices realized from a number of landmark auctions, including the *Belden E. Roach* and *World's Greatest Collection* sales. In a brave and significant gesture, the *Red Book* staff even listed values for Carson City gold in Uncirculated condition, revealing an "it does not hurt to try" or "nothing ventured, nothing gained" attitude. Notwithstanding this precarious attempt, there simply were no Uncirculated examples of most of the "CC" gold coins appearing on the market, especially dates between 1870 and 1873.

Consequently, a price of $300 was listed for the 1870-CC double eagle in Uncirculated and $175 for an 1871-CC in the same condition. Values were also provided for the "CC" gold series in Fine condition, offering collectors a more economical alternative. Below is a table exhibiting 1947 *Red Book* prices for the three denominations in the Carson City gold coin series.

Throughout the 1950s and proceeding virtually nonstop to the end of the 20th century, significant quantities of many dates in the Carson City gold series were imported back into the United States. And as the price of gold continued to rise, pushing the value of Carson City gold coins higher, domestic hoards began appearing on the market. Rather than having the effect of depressing prices, the larger populations stimulated unprecedented collector interest in Carson City gold that has continued to the present day (2003). Moreover, after thousands of these coins had surfaced through international and domestic intermediaries, relative rarity scales for all three denominations became more apparent.

It became obvious which were the scarcest dates, not only by mintage figures but by populations extant. Subsequently, Condition Census data were updated with greater precision and accuracy. Therefore, collectors in the early years of the 21st century are light-years ahead of their predecessors from 50 to 100 years ago in terms of the knowledge available to them concerning this series. The flip side, of course, is the accelerated appreciation in prices. Yet this is that very same thing which preceding generations of collectors have always pondered: can today's high prices possibly go any higher? Evidence in decades past, as well as in the present (2003), points to an affirmative answer to that question.

As you have seen, each of the three denominations in the Carson City gold coin series consists of 19 dates, bringing the total number for a complete set to 57 pieces. Regardless of which of the three denominational sets a collector chooses, or perhaps deciding to go all the way and start on a 57-piece set, a minimum of semipro experience will be required, and depending on the grade levels, possibly Triple AAA. To reach the degree of achievement associated with contemporary all-star sets such as the *Henry S. Lang* or *Nevada* collections, a Major League performance is mandatory.

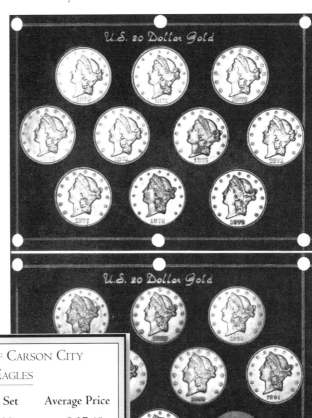

Display frame for $20 gold double eagles. Frames such as these were very popular for several decades.

| 1947 *RED BOOK* PRICES FOR COMPLETE SETS OF CARSON CITY HALF EAGLES, EAGLES, AND DOUBLE EAGLES ||||||
Denomination	Quantity in Set	Grade	Price Per Set	Average Price
$5 Half eagle	19	Fine	$ 330.00	$ 17.40
$5 Half eagle	19	Uncirculated	675.00	35.50
$10 Eagle	19	Fine	610.00	32.00
$10 Eagle	19	Uncirculated	1,062.50	56.00
$20 Double eagle	19	Fine	1,375.00	72.40
$20 Double eagle	19	Uncirculated	2,150.00	113.00

For those collectors not wishing to spend as much money on coins as they paid for their homes, a couple of options are available. One of the more popular routes to take is a three-piece type set of the different gold denominations from the Carson City Mint. Naturally, price will vary depending upon the dates chosen and the condition rating desired, but sufficient supplies of common date "CC" half eagles, eagles, and double eagles are available in circulated grades for very affordable prices (in 2003).

Another alternative to owning representative examples of gold coins with the "CC" mintmark is a two-piece set of the "Type II" and "Type III" $20 double eagles. Fortunately, for collectors with limited discretionary funds, dates are available from the "Type II" years, 1870-1876, for moderately low prices, especially in grades below AU (in 2003). Likewise, several dates in the "Type III" series are comfortably affordable. Together, the two varieties will provide a collector with opportunities for research, sharing, and personal satisfaction.

10-PIECE TYPE SET OF CARSON CITY COINS

Often when collectors ask dealers for ideas how to break into the Carson City coin series, they are introduced to 10-piece type sets. Typically, a light flashes in a collector's mind when informed about this option. Because of the orderly arrangement and made-to-order design, a set like this offers the opportunity to learn about the Carson City

CHECKLIST FOR TEN-PIECE TYPE SET OF CARSON CITY COINS

Denomination	Years Minted
Dime	1871-1878
Twenty cent	1875-1876
Quarter	1870-1878
Half dollar	1870-1878
Seated Liberty dollar	1870-1873
Trade dollar	1873-1878
Morgan dollar	1878-1893
Half eagle	1870-1893
Eagle	1870-1893
Double eagle	1870-1893
*Dime *Mintmark Below Bow*	1875
*Double eagle "Type II"	1870-1876
	*Optional

series, to experience the diversity of the gold and silver coins, and possess a visually appealing collection which will hold the attention of all who examine it.

Beginning with a dime and finishing with a $20 double eagle, this set is comprised of seven silver coins and three gold coins. While in the process of building it, or upon completion, some collectors become motivated to branch off into the other varieties, thus expanding from 10 pieces to 11, 12, or more. An obvious variety to include is the "Type II" double eagle mentioned above. Another popular type to add is the *Mintmark Below Bow* dime, to place alongside the *Above Bow* variety. There are also options in the *With Arrow* and *Without Arrow* categories, though budget concerns must be thoughtfully considered before proceeding, especially with the dime and quarter.

At bottom left is a checklist for a 10-piece type set of "CC" coins, with two optional selections for either 11 or 12-piece sets.

This set is achievable even at the sandlot level, at least if most of the coins are in circulated condition; there have been sets assembled that, because of the high quality of the individual coins, deserved a Major League designation. Keep in mind that no matter at what level you would feel comfortable participating; the experience will be a rewarding one.

COMPLETE SET OF ALL COINS FROM THE CARSON CITY MINT

There is no grander way to end this chapter than with the 111-piece complete set of coins from the "people's choice" for U.S. mints. Anyone who considers this adventurous task must possess an awareness of the cost and commitment essential to succeeding, or else a childlike faith incapable of acknowledging defeat as an option.

If a feasibility study were administered to determine if the project were achievable, results would indicate that 98 to 99% success was practically guaranteed, conditioned, of course, upon the person being well-financed, patient, and possessing a fortitudinous spirit. To achieve 100% completion, the intrepid collector would need all of the above, plus perfect timing and a shot of good luck.

Of course, there is the inevitable question of the quality that would be desired. Naturally, the lower the standard for condition ratings, the more achievable, not to mention less expensive, the project becomes. For some of the dates it would need to be resolved that grading requirements were restricted to what was available.

Carson City Mint in the 1960s.

In the early years of the 21st century, the *Battle Born* collector has nudged a nose in front of those courageous competitors who reached the 109-coin mark but were ultimately forced to concede; yet with 110 in the collection, he is still a great distance from Eliasberg's 111-piece set. There again, this distance is measured by the magnitude of the 1873-CC *Without Arrows* dime. Besides the *Battle Born* collection, one other 110-piece set was reportedly assembled in the 1970s through the 1990s and subsequently broken up. There is no pedigree information or name associated with this reported collection, making it difficult to trace or confirm; and it is entirely possible that more collectors have reached the 110-piece level. However, without corroboration, the accomplishment will not be recorded in numismatic pedigree accounts.

Once the preliminary analysis was conducted and a decision had been made to build the set, where would the collector begin? Like Eliasberg, one might search for a nearly complete collection and buy it all at once, as he did the *Clapp Family* collection in 1942. Or, possibly the collector is attracted to one particular series from the Carson City Mint or leans toward one of the two bullion metals used to produce the coins. Of equal importance is to simply get started, for as the old saying goes, "a long journey begins with the first step."

When the set nears completion, the collector's level of exhilaration will increase with each new acquisition. Of strategic consequence at this point would be whether the collection included any or all of three of the Carson City classics: the 1873-CC *Without Arrows* dime and quarter, and the 1876-CC 20-cent piece. Possession of this trio determines if the collector experiences the thrill of victory in achieving what only one other person in history accomplished.

Time after time, collectors have hit the wall after obtaining one of the coins from this heralded numismatic trinity. With the 1876-CC 20-center added, there are 109 in the collection; however, those final two *Without Arrows* dates have been the stumbling blocks standing in the way of ultimate glory for many determined collectors through the years. Norman Biltz was unable to obtain these two, and Harold M. Budd almost made it, (at least in the silver category) finishing with all but one, the 1873-CC *Without Arrows* dime.

Beyond 2003, any collector up for the challenge of building a complete 111-piece set of Carson City coins will be able to publicly enter the competition by submitting the collection to the PCGS Registry Set program. This will be a milestone event for Carson City enthusiasts, who have already been invited by PCGS to register their sets of 13-piece "CC" Morgan dollars, and "CC"

Visitors at the Nevada State Museum in the late 1970s viewing a special display of the 1870-CC coins found in the cornerstone of the Capitol building. (*Courtesy Nevada State Museum*)

Beautiful scene of the front of the old Carson City Mint with snow-capped mountains in the background. On the side is one of the old engines from the V&T Railroad.

half eagles, eagles, and double eagles. Now these individual sets will be brought together collectively with the Seated Liberty coinage and trade dollars from the Carson Mint to form an unrivaled collecting opportunity. Though most collectors will be spectators to the competition, observing the brave souls attempting to scale this towering summit will be a joy to watch. Many individuals, as well, may be inspired to find a segment within the Carson City series in which to get involved.

Without a doubt, the 111-piece complete set of "CC" coins is in a class by itself. There is only one choice for rating the achievement level of the one person who accomplished the goal: Louis E. Eliasberg, Sr. is enshrined as a Hall of Famer. Any of the noble collectors who have reached the 109-piece mark are Major League stars in their own rights and certainly candidates for the Hall of Fame. The *Battle Born* collector and any others with 110-piece sets have already been inducted.

In conclusion, whatever you decide to collect in the Carson City series, can bring incalculable gratification.

There are other options to choose from, but I hope the ones mentioned briefly in this chapter will provide you with direction and inspire you to action if you are not already involved. Carson City enthusiasts speak often about getting "bitten by the bug," and truly it is a passion that grips a person, heart and soul.

Of course, it is possible that "CC" coins may never become your cup of tea, but at least having read this book you will have a chance to observe from a distance what goes on in this segment of the hobby. Be careful, though, about getting too close—you just might get bit.

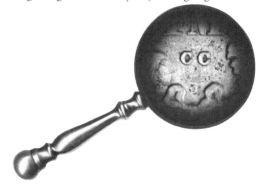

CHECKLIST FOR "CC" COINS BY DATE

DIMES			
Series	Year	Grade	Value[1]
Seated Liberty Dimes	1871	VF-20	$6,500
Seated Liberty Dimes	1872	VF-20	$3,500
Seated Liberty Dimes	1873 *Without Arrows*	VF-20	———
Seated Liberty Dimes	1873 *With Arrows*	VF-20	$10,000
Seated Liberty Dimes	1874	VF-20	$16,750
Seated Liberty Dimes	1875 MM Above	VF-20	$35
Seated Liberty Dimes	1875 MM Below	VF-20	$24
Seated Liberty Dimes	1876	VF-20	$20
Seated Liberty Dimes	1877	VF-20	$20
Seated Liberty Dimes	1878	VF-20	$200

TWENTY-CENT PIECES			
Series	Year	Grade	Value
Seated Liberty Twenty Cents	1875	VF-20	$200
Seated Liberty Twenty Cents	1876	VF-20	$75,000

QUARTERS			
Series	Year	Grade	Value
Seated Liberty Quarters	1870	VF-20	$13,500
Seated Liberty Quarters	1871	VF-20	$12,000
Seated Liberty Quarters	1872	VF-20	$4,500
Seated Liberty Quarters	1873 *Without Arrows*	VF-20	———
Seated Liberty Quarters	1873 *With Arrows*	VF-20	$13,500
Seated Liberty Quarters	1875	VF-20	$350
Seated Liberty Quarters	1876	VF-20	$60
Seated Liberty Quarters	1877	VF-20	$55
Seated Liberty Quarters	1878	VF-20	$100

HALF DOLLARS			
Series	Year	Grade	Value
Seated Half Dollar	1870	VF-20	$4,500
Seated Half Dollar	1871	VF-20	$900
Seated Half Dollar	1872	VF-20	$450
Seated Half Dollar	1873 *Without Arrows*	VF-20	$1,000
Seated Half Dollar	1873 *With Arrows*	VF-20	$900
Seated Half Dollar	1874	VF-20	$1,700
Seated Half Dollar	1875	VF-20	$120

HALF DOLLARS (CONT.)			
Series	Year	Grade	Value
Seated Half Dollar	1876	VF-20	$100
Seated Half Dollar	1877	VF-20	$100
Seated Half Dollar	1878	VF-20	$1,500

DOLLARS			
Series	Year	Grade	Value
Trade Dollar	1873	VF-20	$450
Trade Dollar	1874	VF-20	$250
Trade Dollar	1875	VF-20	$250
Trade Dollar	1875 S/CC*	VF-20	$500
Trade Dollar	1876	VF-20	$300
Trade Dollar	1877	VF-20	$300
Trade Dollar	1878	VF-20	$1,000
Series	Year	Grade	Value
Seated Liberty Dollar	1870	VF-20	$950
Seated Liberty Dollar	1871	VF-20	$5,000
Seated Liberty Dollar	1872	VF-20	$3,250
Seated Liberty Dollar	1873	VF-20	$9,500
Series	Year	Grade	Value
Morgan Dollar	1878	VF-20	$90
Morgan Dollar	1879 Normal	VF-20	$200
Morgan Dollar	1879 Capped Die*	VF-20	$175
Morgan Dollar	1880 RV78*	VF-20	$150
Morgan Dollar	1880 RV79	VF-20	$150
Morgan Dollar	1881	VF-20	$270
Morgan Dollar	1882	VF-20	$90
Morgan Dollar	1883	VF-20	$90
Morgan Dollar	1884	VF-20	$90
Morgan Dollar	1885	VF-20	$310
Morgan Dollar	1889	VF-20	$1,100
Morgan Dollar	1890	VF-20	$100
Morgan Dollar	1891	VF-20	$100
Morgan Dollar	1892	VF-20	$125
Morgan Dollar	1893	VF-20	$375
Morgan Dollar	1900 O/CC*	VF-20	$100

[1] For accurately graded coins. Prices as of November 2003.

* Optional to a complete 111 piece set of Carson City coins.

GOLD HALF EAGLES

Series	Year	Grade	Value
Coronet Head	1870	VF-20	$5,000
Coronet Head	1871	VF-20	$1,700
Coronet Head	1872	VF-20	$1,500
Coronet Head	1873	VF-20	$3,000
Coronet Head	1874	VF-20	$1,000
Coronet Head	1875	VF-20	$1,700
Coronet Head	1876	VF-20	$1,700
Coronet Head	1877	VF-20	$1,700
Coronet Head	1878	VF-20	$4,000
Coronet Head	1879	VF-20	$900
Coronet Head	1880	VF-20	$475
Coronet Head	1881	VF-20	$475
Coronet Head	1882	VF-20	$400
Coronet Head	1883	VF-20	$450
Coronet Head	1884	VF-20	$575
Coronet Head	1890	VF-20	$350
Coronet Head	1891	VF-20	$350
Coronet Head	1892	VF-20	$350
Coronet Head	1893	VF-20	$350

GOLD EAGLES

Series	Year	Grade	Value
Coronet Head	1870	VF-20	$12,000
Coronet Head	1871	VF-20	$2,500
Coronet Head	1872	VF-20	$3,500
Coronet Head	1873	VF-20	$5,000
Coronet Head	1874	VF-20	$1,000
Coronet Head	1875	VF-20	$4,500
Coronet Head	1876	VF-20	$3,500
Coronet Head	1877	VF-20	$2,500
Coronet Head	1878	VF-20	$4,000
Coronet Head	1879	VF-20	$7,000

GOLD EAGLES (CONT.)

Series	Year	Grade	Value
Coronet Head	1880	VF-20	$500
Coronet Head	1881	VF-20	$500
Coronet Head	1882	VF-20	$800
Coronet Head	1883	VF-20	$550
Coronet Head	1884	VF-20	$600
Coronet Head	1890	VF-20	$500
Coronet Head	1891	VF-20	$500
Coronet Head	1892	VF-20	$525
Coronet Head	1893	VF-20	$525

GOLD DOUBLE EAGLES "TWENTY D."

Series	Year	Grade	Value
Coronet Head	1870	VF-20	$95,000
Coronet Head.	1871	VF-20	$4,500
Coronet Head.	1872	VF-20	$2,500
Coronet Head	1873	VF-20	$1,800
Coronet Head	1874	VF-20	$1,100
Coronet Head	1875	VF-20	$1,100
Coronet Head.	1876	VF-20	$1,100

GOLD DOUBLE EAGLES "TWENTY DOLLARS"

Series	Year	Grade	Value
Coronet Head	1877	VF-20	$1,500
Coronet Head	1878	VF-20	$1,950
Coronet Head	1879	VF-20	$2,000
Coronet Head	1882	VF-20	$1,100
Coronet Head	1883	VF-20	$1,150
Coronet Head	1884	VF-20	$1,100
Coronet Head	1885	VF-20	$1,950
Coronet Head	1889	VF-20	$1,400
Coronet Head	1890	VF-20	$1,100
Coronet Head	1891	VF-20	$3,300
Coronet Head	1892	VF-20	$1,300
Coronet Head	1893	VF-20	$1,500

Epilogue

I will set down a tale as it was told to me by one who had it of his father, which later had it of his father, this last having in like manner had it of his father — and so on, back and still back, three hundred years and more, the fathers transmitting it to the sons and so preserving it.

From *The Prince and the Pauper* by Mark Twain, 1881

Until events occurring in the 20th century established Carson City coins as major contenders in the world of numismatics, the legacy of the small Nevada mint seemed locked in a time warp waiting to be unveiled.

Where at one point it appeared as if destiny was slipping through the empty rooms at the Carson City Mint, it rushed forward bringing an astonishing resurgence of popularity and fame. Collectors began speaking fervently about coins with the "CC" mintmark and history itself shined brightly on the grand epic of the era and region from whence the coins came.

Indeed, these were remarkable times: the 1870s, 1880s, and 1890s, never to be repeated, but often relived in the minds and imaginations of countless numbers of people seeking links to the past.

So much more than metal went into the production of coins from the Carson City Mint; witness for instance, the political drama that unfolded behind the scenes affecting decisions concerning the continued minting of coins there and even whether or not the State of Nevada would survive economically and most importantly, as a member of the Union. Consider for example the battles fought in the 1860s to ensure there would even be a mint in Carson City and then after it opened, voices in Washington called for it to be shut down.

Politicians such as Thomas Fitch and H.H. Bartine campaigned tirelessly on behalf of their state and the Carson City Mint, yet are often overlooked when Nevada's early history is recounted. Then there were the celebrated *Silver Senators* William M. Stewart and John P. Jones, who at times appeared as self-sacrificing public servants assiduously defending Nevada and its chief product, but at other times resembled shameless self-promoters. But all contradictions aside, Stewart and Jones' political careers meshed together with the Carson City Mint's years of service as a coinage facility and undoubtedly influenced fateful events occurring there.

Mint Directors, Treasury Secretaries, and even U. S. Presidents played pivotal roles at various times in factors relating to the eventual course the Carson City Mint would take. And influential forces were not just confined to the American continent, as ramifications from circumstances in Great Britain and other foreign nations sailed back to Nevada altering its path at times. There were the political calculations inherent in corporate power, especially manifest in the banking and railroad industries that filtered down to ground level right up to the doorstep of the Carson City Mint.

In spite of the oftentimes maddening political environment with its *Silverites, Goldbugs, Populists, Bimetallists,* and *Bank Crowd,* business pressed on at the Carson Mint with stifled regularity; it is the coins that have survived that showcase this venerable institution, providing a vivid testimony of its significance both in American history and in the field of numismatics. Without those coins and the popularity engendered by them there would be less incentive to dig up their past. In truth, there is little known about what took place at the Carson City Mint on a daily or monthly basis, and compared to other historical topics such as the Civil War, only a stingy amount of reference material is available pertaining to it. If, for instance, a person wanted to study any detail of the Civil War, there would be vast resources available; but for the Carson Mint, there is virtually nothing. In fact, there is more available on one minor battle or one lesser known general of the Civil War than for all that has ever been written about the Carson City Mint.

But it is because of the interest in the coins that numismatic researchers continue to explore, ready to tap even the most superfluous references just to uncover the smallest pittance of information. In spite of the shortage of information, anyone attempting to delve into the study of the Carson City Mint immediately becomes aware of how broad the subject is, as there are seemingly countless side-paths one can journey down which branch off from the category of coins, and wind their way toward biographies, local and national events, and politics.

Making brief reference to biographies, there are of course, the men and women who worked at the Carson City Mint, including such names as Henry F. Rice, Frank D. Hetrich, Theodore R. Hofer, and Annie Martin, all of whom would be interesting subjects. Then there are the collectors of "CC" coins such as Dr. Simeon L. Lee, Harold M. Budd, and Norman H. Biltz, none having ever had a biography written about them.

Inextricably linked to the biographies are histories of the communities surrounding Carson City, such as Gold Hill, Silver City, Empire, and of course the granddaddy of them all, Virginia City. This region in northwestern Nevada pulsed with stories of miners, raucous living, and newspaper reporters who became more celebrated than the beat they covered, like Mark Twain and Dan DeQuille. Any one of these subjects, and many more, open the doors to boundless opportunities for enchanting studies.

In telling the story of the Carson City Mint there are practically no primary sources available—no memoirs from ex-mint superintendents, no 19th century histories of the "CC" Mint, and not even the foremost books on

The author in front of the Nevada State Museum on North Carson Street.

the history of Nevada provide more than a paragraph or two on the state's famous minting facility.

In fact, all that is really available are newspaper clippings and a sparse assortment of archived documents, with the most informative reference sources being the *Annual Reports from the Director of the Mint.* How enlightening it would be if journals had been kept by figures such as Mint Superintendent James Crawford during his 10 years in office; but there is scarcely anything even written about Crawford, let alone by him and most surprisingly, not even a picture of the man is available.

Even Mary Curry, wife of city founder and man most responsible for the existence of a mint there apparently

The Carson City Mint in modern times, now home to the Nevada State Museum. (*Author's collection*)

left no diary behind. If she had, it would have quenched the inquisitiveness of many thirsty researchers. Thanks to author Doris Cerveri there is at least a biography of Abraham Curry, though its focus is not on his involvement with the mint he helped create, but it does a wonderful job of summarizing his 15 years in Carson City.

Apparently in the early years of the 20th century much more information was available about the Carson City Mint, but sometime around 1925 most of the records were destroyed, either by accident or willfully, the explanation not being clear. With those lost records went details of the controversial mintage figures, as well as information about the meltdowns that created many of today's rarities. Also lost was correspondence between superintendents at the Carson Mint and officials in Philadelphia and Washington D.C. Perhaps if these records were still available more light would be shed on the life of Superintendent James Crawford, who by all reports was deserving of honor for his 10 years of distinguished service. Possibly questions which persist about rumors of illegal mintages, alleged employee embezzling and many other scandals that have fomented through the decades would be answered.

If only the walls inside the old mint could talk, many secrets might be revealed; but it has been resolved by historians and researchers that much will remain shrouded in mystery. In a way, the Carson City Mint is like a person who suddenly became famous and everyone beckoned to

hear the "Behind the scenes details" or "True story." Perhaps this is an apt metaphor, but sometimes it is just as alluring when all the facts are not known, adding more intrigue to the subject.

Lingering questions or not, coins with the "CC" mintmark have attracted the attention of multitudes of collectors and will invariably do so into the future. Although there is not a club devoted solely to Carson City coinage (an inevitable possibility?), many numismatic groups provide full coverage to the subject within the broad context of their overall theme. One in particular is the "Seated Liberty Collectors Club", whose emphasis is the study and enjoyment of Seated Liberty coins. While perusing the index of this club's quarterly magazine, *The Gobrecht Journal,* titles with "CC" or Carson City coins are abundant.

These captivating coins which have inspired enthusiasm and brought thrills and gratification to so many people will continue to bear silent witness to the history and grandeur of the era in which they originated.

CONCLUSION

This book began with references made to Abraham Curry and fittingly should end in similar fashion. One of his friends and admirers, Alf Doten, was asked to write a few words for his newspaper when Curry died:

> Col. Curry was a type of the frontier, of that hearty manhood and open generous nature which scorns both effeminacy and hypocrisy; and finds its counterpart only in the free air and unbounded liberty of our western wilderness.
>
> Carson City will miss 'Uncle Abe'. To him more then any man is that beautiful village indebted for its existence and success. Through difficulties which would have deterred a less sanguine and persevering man, he not only built the United States Mint, but placed it in operating condition![1]

And operate it did, from 1870 through 1893 as a coinage facility, then later as an assay office, and since 1941 as the Nevada State Museum. It has provided an extraordinary subject to study, and the most exciting assortment of coins to collect and enjoy. To those enam-

---

[1] *Gold Hill News,* October 23, 1873.

ored with the Carson City Mint and its coins there is nothing else like it.

Explorer John C. Frémont, senior officer to Kit Carson, led an expedition through the region near the site of what became Carson City, and when departing reflected that, "It is such a fascinating land. For all its hardship, I shall hate to leave it."[1]

And so it is difficult to leave the subject of the Carson City Mint, but hopefully, the end of this book does not signal an impulse to leave it, but rather to continue exploring it over and over again; like the land surrounding it, it is indeed fascinating.

[1] Quote from John C. Frémont in 1844: taken from, Grant H. Smith, *The History of the Comstock Lode*

Alleged Cover-Up of 3,600 1870-CC Double Eagles

On or around March 29, 1870, Carson City Mint Superintendent Abe Curry reportedly stored 3600 inferior quality 1870-CC $20 double eagles in a wooden Winchester rifle box and hid it in one of the vaults. This box containing $72,000 in gold coins remained in this location even after Curry resigned his office in September of 1870 to make a bid for Lieutenant Governor of Nevada.

Curry's replacement at the mint, Henry F. Rice, discovered the box lying on the floor of the vault covered with a canvas blanket in October of 1870, and being understandably curious, came back later in the evening to investigate after everyone except a night watchman had gone home. It was customary whenever anyone entered a mint vault that a watchman would log him in and then record when he left and that the vault was locked. Rice was accompanied on this occasion by Curry's former son-in-law William J. Cowan, and instructed Cowan to leave him alone for about 20 minutes while he conducted an inventory.

After Cowan wandered off, Rice knelt down, and lit a candle to melt the red wax off the padlock on the rifle box that had been sealed by Abe Curry in the traditional manner used by mint superintendents to ensure no one would tamper with locks only they possessed keys to. Noticing a message attached to the top of the box from Abe Curry ordering no one to open it without his approval, Rice lifted the lid and was startled to see 72 burlap covered rolls approximately six to seven inches long and 1 1/2 inches wide stacked inside. He quickly lifted a roll and sliced it open on one end and suddenly a $20 double eagle dated 1870 dropped out. Rice spilled a few more into his hand, and realizing the night watchman was due back, put the rest back and sealed the box, melting his own red wax across the lock, covering everything back up with the blanket.

Upon returning to his office, Rice examined the four double eagles, finding them to be flawed in many ways, especially on the obverses where it was clear that the portrait of Liberty was covered with unsightly laminations and planchet flakes, usually caused by impurities in the metal. His immediate assessment was that Curry had been ashamed of these impaired coins and stored them until he could figure what to do with them.

But that had been over six months ago and now Curry was gone, and it was in Rice's hands. He decided to steal the coins, perhaps assuming Curry had forgotten about them. Rice devised a plan to have five custom-crafted wooden boxes built by a local wood-maker, three with false bottoms, and then announced that an order had been received for 5,000 1870-CC half dollars, with 1,000 pieces to be placed in each box. He took precautions to ensure that it would be difficult to detect the additional weight of the gold coins he planned on loading into the wooden boxes by ordering them to be built weighing 114 lbs. each.

Lock and key similar to those involved when Henry F. Rice opened the vault and discovered 3,600 1870-CC double eagles stacked in a Winchester rifle box in October 1870.

A closed vault door inside the Carson City Mint, perhaps where Abe Curry stashed the box of 1870-CC double eagles (*Courtesy of National Archives*)

On the day Rice implemented his devious plan he instructed his assistants to load the boxes that he had already filled with double eagles with half dollars and sent them to the man's house who supposedly ordered them. But before the wagon transporting them was out of sight, Rice ordered it back, informing employees that the customer had changed his mind and wanted silver dollars instead. All of the half dollars were removed from the three boxes with false bottoms and consolidated into the other two boxes which were returned to the mint. Rice ordered the drivers to go ahead and deliver the three boxes that were now supposedly empty to the customer's house, and as soon as the other two boxes were returned to the mint and the 5000 half dollars were replaced with 5,000 silver dollars they would be sent along to complete the customer's order.

Another scheme Rice deployed was to falsify an order to melt 3,600 inferior quality double eagles, an order that he would shuffle into the stacks of paperwork piled up in the accounting office. Believing that he had committed the perfect crime, Rice waited at the customer's house (who happened to be in Europe at the time), for the two boxes containing the 5,000 silver dollars and the three boxes with false bottoms containing the 3,600 double eagles. Unbeknownst to anyone, Rice was house-sitting for the man who was in Europe, and figured he would have sufficient time to remove the double eagles, replace them with the 5,000 silver dollars, and ship the boxes to another location, winding up $72,000 richer, minus the cost of the boxes. He would have the option to either keep the 5,000 silver dollars which he would be obligated to pay for, resulting in a wash, or he could simply return them to the mint, saying the customer changed his mind.

It all seemed so easy.

But Rice's plan began to unravel when the two drivers hauling the three boxes of gold coins stopped at a local saloon, got drunk and in their inebriated state decided to steal the three boxes themselves, not having any idea what the boxes contained since they were locked. They reckoned that something valuable must be inside, based on nothing more than the ornate design and their weight. First they needed to get the boxes buried somewhere on the outskirts of town and then lie to Rice about being robbed by thieves.

It was late at night by the time the two-bit scoundrels buried the boxes near the railroad tracks and then ran the horses and wagon off. When they arrived at the house where Rice was waiting for them he was beside himself with anger. Not believing their story for one minute, Rice had the two men arrested, and although they spent a year in prison, and were incessantly questioned by Rice, they never confessed, and the location of the buried treasure was never revealed.

After their release, "Dumb" and "Dumber" attempted to find their hidden booty, but by then new railroad tracks had been laid covering the ground and altering the landscape making it virtually impossible to remember where they had buried it. Nothing was ever heard about this anonymous duo again.

If this tale is true, there are still 3,600 1870-CC double eagles buried somewhere within five miles of Carson City near the old route of the V&T Railroad. For all his efforts, Rice certainly received nothing in return; in fact, his two and a half years as a superintendent at the Carson City Mint were tumultuous times for him, as he was under suspicion on several occasions, eventually being forced to resign in 1873. As a side note, William J. Cowan, the night watchman who had accompanied Rice the night the superintendent took his first peek at the box of gold, died approximately one month later.

There are so many incongruities in this story that in truth it is unfathomable, if for no other reason than how the amount of gold supposedly involved compares to how few gold coins were minted that first year at Carson City. With only 3,789 1870-CC $20 double eagles reportedly minted, it begs the question: how could Curry have covered up 3,600 pieces not being delivered, especially since at the time, the only gold coins being produced were for depositors of gold bullion? If $75,780 in gold was deposited to be exchanged for double eagles, but only $3,580 was delivered, someone would have spoken up.

And if that is not reason enough to poke a hole in this fanciful account, what about Abe Curry's memory? Would he have forgotten that he stored a box of gold coins worth $72,000 with his instructions on the lid and not attempted to do something about it before he resigned? It certainly would have been interesting to hear the exchange between Curry and Rice when they bumped into each other in town during the autumn of 1870: Picture if you will, Curry asking Rice: "How's it going on your new job, have you experienced anything interesting yet?"

But like so many of the mysteries relating to the Carson City Mint, no one will ever know the truth about this seemingly spurious account of the cover-up of 3,600 1870-CC double eagles. That is, unless a lucky treasure seeker hits it big with his metal detector somewhere near the north line of the V&T Railroad heading out of town.[1]

---

[1] Acknowledgement for much of this account is credited to an article appearing in a PCGS essay contest written by Michele Elizabeth Frazer in November of 2000. Frazer cites her source being her grandfather who was reportedly a distant relative of H.F. Rice.

Top 25 Dates in the Carson City Series

Out of 111 different dates in the series it is indeed a challenge to narrow it down to 25 to be placed above the other 86; the challenge is not that there are too few to choose from, but in limiting the list to only 25. It would be a snap if the list included just three dates: the 1873-CC *Without Arrows* dime and quarter, and the 1876-CC 20-cent piece. But it begins getting tougher even when extending the list to ten dates, as this requires choosing only seven of the remaining 108 dates and involves much more brain-twisting, leading to a concession that the list needs to include at least 15 dates. This again proves to be too restrictive, at which time the list becomes a *Top 20,* which is still not enough because there are other deserving dates and excluding them leaves a void. But the count must stop somewhere, so 25 it is, still producing a cringe when other dates miss the cut.

And then there is always the Condition Census factor to consider, since some of the dates left out would qualify in a heartbeat if the highest graded specimen were considered, the first one coming to mind being the 1876-CC gold half eagle grading PCGS MS-66. This is unquestionably the pre-eminent gold coin surviving from the Carson City Mint, surpassing even the dates that are included in the *Top 25* list. Next is possibly the second finest gold coin extant; the 1874-CC eagle graded NGC MS-65, which in this state of preservation would not only qualify for a top position on an elite list of Carson City coins, but would easily find a spot among any category of first-class rare coins. The also-eligible list for inclusion in the Carson City *Top 25* is not confined to gold coins, as the finest known example of an 1876-CC trade dollar, graded MS-65 by PCGS, towers above many silver coins in its class.

If these three specific examples are considered for qualification in the *Top 25* they most surely will knock other dates off the list. The following table provides prices for the three coins mentioned above showcasing their significance in the grand array of Carson City coinage:

Coin	Price in VF	Estimated Value in Highest Grade
1876-CC Half eagle	$ 2,000	$ 275,000
1874-CC Eagle	1,700	200,000
1876-CC Trade dollar	250	125,000

As evident by the values for the highest graded specimens, the *Top 25* list could easily become the *Top 28,* and it does not end there because there are more dates that could be considered if Condition Census were factored in.

Each of the dates on the *Top 25* list is considered a key in its respective series, some obviously being much more elusive than others, but all being the coveted coins that want lists are made of. Any collector fortunate enough to acquire the entire group is virtually guaranteed of completing the 111 piece set, always giving due honor to the 1873-CC *Without Arrows* dime.

TOP 25 DATES IN THE CARSON CITY SERIES

Coin	Price in VF[*]	Estimated Value in Highest Grade[*]
DIMES		
1871-CC	$ 5,000	$150,000 (NGC MS-65)
1872-CC	3,000	50,000 (PCGS MS-61)
1873-CC *Without Arrows*	——	750,000 (NGC MS-65)
1873-CC *With Arrows*	10,000	150,000 (NGC MS-65)
1874-CC	15,000	165,000 (PCGS MS-63)
TWENTY CENT PIECES		
1876-CC	70,000	250,000 (PCGS MS-66)
QUARTERS		
1870-CC	12,000	375,000 (NGC MS-64)
1871-CC	11,000	200,000 (PCGS MS-65)
1872-CC	6,000	250,000 (NGC MS-66)
1873-CC *Without Arrows*	85,000	500,000 (NGC MS-66)
1873-CC *With Arrows*	10,000	200,000 (NGC MS-65)
HALF DOLLARS		
1870-CC	5,000	175,000 (PCGS MS-62)
1871-CC	1,200	90,000 (PCGS MS-64)
1872-CC	600	35,000 (PCGS MS-63)
1873-CC *Without Arrows*	1,000	90,000 (PCGS MS-67)
1874-CC	2,500	200,000 (PCGS MS-66)
1878-CC	1,600	175,000 (NGC MS-66)
SEATED LIBERTY DOLLARS		
1871-CC	6,500	300,000 (PCGS MS-64)
1873-CC	10,000	350,000 (NGC MS-65)
TRADE DOLLARS		
1873-CC	600	135,000 (NGC MS-65)
1878-CC	1,500	185,000 (NGC MS-66)
MORGAN DOLLARS		
1889-CC	1,500	650,000 (PCGS MS-68)
GOLD HALF EAGLES		
1870-CC	6,500	115,000 (NGC MS-62)
GOLD EAGLES		
1870-CC	10,000	55,000 (PCGS AU-55)
GOLD DOUBLE EAGLES		
1870-CC	95,000	175,000 (PCGS AU-53)

* As of November 2003.

APPENDIX THREE

Aggregate Value of Certified Carson City Coins

In case readers are curious to know what it would cost to purchase every Carson City coin that has been certified by PCGS and NGC the following "Aggregate Totals" have been compiled.

The first step in the process of compiling this data was to isolate and create a separate population report for all "CC" coins certified by the two grading services—only business strike issues were included with the exception of the four 1876-CC dimes in Proof condition. Once the reports were completed it was then necessary to audit the population figures as much as was practical to eliminate duplicate listings of the more expensive high profile coins, such as the 1873-CC *Without Arrows* dime which has been encased in an NGC MS-65 holder for more than several years, but still appeared in PCGS' data file as an MS-64 until July 2003. Another example is the Eliasberg 1889-CC Morgan dollar, graded MS-67 by NGC and also MS-68 by PCGS: these two coins alone would skew the bottom-line by $1 to $1.5 million to the plus side if duplicate listings were not removed.

Of course, without spending inexhaustible hours it would be impossible to eliminate all duplicates, which even the grading services are not aware of because of the preponderance of resubmissions, not to mention the innumerable mechanical errors that occur at the data entry level. But dates in the "CC" Morgan dollar series, for instance, with relatively high populations do not affect the bottom-line to any significant degree if multiple listings of the same coins remain.

After the populations were gathered and audited, the next step was to assign values to every coin. This was accomplished using a host of pricing information, including wholesale pricelists, auction prices realized, retail price guides, and the author's personal experience. Although not pushed to a scientific level of accuracy, judgment was applied to pricing the coins to ensure a "ballpark" level of consistency. That was the ultimate goal: to arrive at a "ballpark" estimate of what the aggregate value of all Carson City coins certified by the two major grading services amounted to.

As the project began, no one on staff had the slightest clue what the total would be. One of the first guesses was approximately $100 million, but it soon became apparent that this would be much too low. During the course of the project, more coins would surface necessitating revisions, and at the same time, prices for Carson City coins began to heat up, as new records were set for such dates as the 1870-CC half dollar, 1871-CC silver dollar, 1876-CC 20-cent piece and 1874-CC dime. A cutoff date was set, after which no new pricing information would be accepted to ensure that this book would make it to the publisher on time.

The end result has been a very rewarding experience, for now at least at this one point in time, a "close-as-can-be" estimation of value has been established for the bulk of all certified Carson City coinage on the planet, and 10, 20, 30 or more years into the future similar exercises can be conducted for comparison studies.

Readers must not forget that there are still a relatively large quantity of Carson City coins not yet certified by PCGS and NGC and thus unaccounted for. These coins will ultimately affect the bottom line in the years to come, but it seems safe to assume that there are no quantities of unknown 1889-CC silver dollars in grades above MS-65 out there, or 1873-CC *Without Arrows* dimes and quarters, and other high profile dates.

So until evidence surfaces to the contrary, if a person were inclined to purchase every "CC" coin certified by PCGS and NGC as of the spring of 2003, here is the amount to write the check for:

$259,183,667*

How accurate is this figure? Obviously a categorical answer is impossible; however, there is enough evidence to conclude that no more than a 10% variance in either direction is applicable, and probably no more than 5%. This translates into a precise range of at least $200 million, but not more than $300 million. And like the National Debt scoreboard in Times Square, the numbers are in a constant state of revision, not in gigantic upward surges, but rather in a consistent rhythmic movement.

---

*Word was received just as this book went to press that talks were in progress to have the 109 piece set of Carson City coins on display at the Nevada State Museum submitted to one of the major grading services; if this is completed, an additional $1 million can be added to the "Aggregate Total".

AGGREGATE MARKET VALUE OF ALL CARSON CITY COINS
CERTIFIED BY PCGS & NGC AS OF APRIL 1, 2003

PCGS *Population Report* totals for Carson City coins 173,260

NGC *Census Report* totals for Carson City coins 75,674

Total number of "CC" coins graded by PCGS and NGC 248,934

Grading Service:	Total Coins:	Total Market Value
PCGS:		
Dimes, 20-Cent Pieces, Quarters, Halves	2,589	$ 8,254,037
Seated Liberty Silver Dollars	500	4,544,290
Trade Dollars	849	3,351,031
Morgan Silver Dollars	153,545	90,936,155
Total Silver Coins	**157,483**	**$107,085,513**
Half Eagles	2,970	$8,005,205
Eagles	3,214	8,671,930
Double Eagles	9,593	26,055,600
Total Gold Coins	**15,777**	**$ 42,732,735**
Total PCGS Certified "CC" Coins	**173,260**	**$149,818,248**
NGC:		
Dimes, 20-Cent Pieces, Quarters, Halves	2,058	$ 10,091,022
Seated Liberty Silver Dollars	184	2,593,143
Trade Dollars	535	3,227,777
Morgan Silver Dollars	58,216	42,626,880
Total Silver Coins	**60,993**	**$ 58,538,822**
Half Eagles	3,004	$9,446,188
Eagles	2,907	9,447,619
Double Eagles	8,770	31,932,790
Total Gold Coins	**14,681**	**$ 50,826,597**
Total NGC Certified "CC" Coins	**75,674**	**$ 109,365,419**

Aggregate Market Value of all PCGS certified "CC" coins $149,818,248

Aggregate Market Value of all NGC certified "CC" coins... $109,365,419

Aggregate Market Value of PCGS and NGC certified "CC" coins **$259,183,667**

As a comparison, here are the prices realized for the following auctions:

Eliasberg .... $45 million

Harry W. Bass, Jr. .... $38 million

Garrett Collection .... $25 million

Norweb Collection .... $20 million

John J. Pittman .... $28 million

TOTAL .... **$156 million**

APPENDIX FOUR

NGC and PCGS Population Totals[1]

NGC Census Report

Carson City Silver Coins

DIMES SEATED LIBERTY LEGEND OBVERSE (NGC)

Date	Total Graded	G/VG	F	VF	40	45	50	53	55	58	60	61	62	63	64	65	66	67	68
1871	8	1	2	1	0	1	1	0	0	0	0	1	0	0	0	1	0	0	0
1871 J. Stack	1	0	0	0	0	0	0	0	0	0	0	0	0	0	0	1	0	0	0
1872	15	2	3	5	3	1	0	0	1	0	0	0	0	0	0	0	0	0	0
1873 No Arrows Eliasberg	1	0	0	0	0	0	0	0	0	0	0	0	0	0	0	1	0	0	0
1873 Arrows	13	5	6	1	0	0	0	0	0	0	0	0	0	0	0	1	0	0	0
1873 Arrows Norweb	1	0	0	0	0	0	0	0	0	0	0	0	0	0	0	1	0	0	0
1874 Arrows	5	0	1	0	0	0	2	0	0	0	0	0	2	0	0	0	0	0	0
1875	128	0	0	0	0	0	1	0	1	7	0	9	16	30	37	21	3	3	0
1875 Eliasberg	1	0	0	0	0	0	0	0	0	0	0	0	0	0	0	1	0	0	0
1875 Pittman	1	0	0	0	0	0	0	0	0	0	0	0	0	0	0	0	1	0	0
1875 CC Below Bow	11	0	0	0	0	0	0	0	0	0	0	0	1	2	1	6	1	0	0
1875 CC Above Bow	36	0	0	0	0	0	0	0	0	2	0	0	3	9	10	4	7	1	0
1876	191	0	0	0	0	0	1	1	2	10	1	4	14	39	70	29	16	3	0
1876 Eliasberg	1	0	0	0	0	0	0	0	0	0	0	0	0	0	0	0	1	0	0
1876 CC DDO FS-004	7	0	0	3	0	1	0	0	0	1	0	0	1	0	1	0	0	0	0
1876 Proof	4	0	0	0	0	0	0	0	0	0	0	0	0	0	0	3	1	0	0
1877	238	0	0	0	0	1	0	1	2	11	0	3	15	40	67	63	27	5	3
1877 Eliasberg	1	0	0	0	0	0	0	0	0	0	0	0	0	0	0	0	1	0	0
1877 Pittman	1	0	0	0	0	0	0	0	0	0	0	0	0	0	1	0	0	0	0
1878	41	0	0	1	1	0	0	1	0	1	0	0	0	5	17	6	7	1	0
1878 Eliasberg	1	0	0	0	0	0	0	0	0	0	0	0	0	0	0	0	0	1	0
1878 Knoxville	1	0	0	0	0	0	0	0	0	0	0	0	0	0	0	0	0	0	1

TWENTY-CENT PIECES

Date	Total Graded	G/VG	F	VF	40	45	50	53	55	58	60	61	62	63	64	65	66	67	68
1875	279	3	1	3	2	9	7	2	11	43	5	15	32	41	76	25	4	0	0
1875 Pittman	1	0	0	0	0	0	0	0	0	0	0	0	0	0	0	1	0	0	0
1876	5	0	0	0	0	0	0	0	0	0	0	0	0	0	2	3	0	0	0

[1] As of April 2003.

QUARTERS, SEATED LIBERTY, MOTTO

Date		Total Graded	G/VG	F	VF	40	45	50	53	55	58	60	61	62	63	64	65	66	67	68
1870		12	I	I	6	2	I	0	I	0	0	0	0	0	0	0	0	0	0	0
1870	Eliasberg	I	0	0	0	0	0	0	0	0	0	0	0	0	0	0	I	0	0	0
1870	Pittman	I	0	I	0	0	0	0	0	0	0	0	0	0	0	0	0	0	0	0
1871		9	3	2	2	0	0	2	0	0	0	0	0	0	0	0	0	0	0	0
1871	Eliasberg	I	0	0	0	0	0	0	0	0	0	0	0	0	0	0	I	0	0	0
1872		13	6	2	2	I	I	0	0	0	0	0	0	0	0	0	0	0	0	0
1872	Eliasberg	I	0	0	0	0	0	0	0	0	0	0	0	0	0	0	0	I	0	0
1872	Pittman	I	0	0	0	0	0	I	0	0	0	0	0	0	0	0	0	0	0	0
1873 No Arrows		3	0	0	0	I	0	0	0	0	0	0	0	0	0	I	0	I	0	0
1873	Arrows	11	3	2	4	0	0	I	0	0	0	0	0	0	0	0	I	0	0	0
1875		28	0	0	I	0	I	0	2	4	8	0	I	0	3	5	3	0	0	0
1875	Pittman	I	0	0	0	0	0	0	0	0	0	0	0	0	0	0	I	0	0	0
1876		152	0	I	0	2	3	2	2	4	13	3	9	16	26	45	14	9	3	0
1876	Eliasberg	2	0	0	0	0	0	0	0	0	0	0	0	0	I	0	I	0	0	0
1876 Fine Reeding		I	0	0	0	0	0	0	0	0	0	0	0	0	I	0	0	0	0	0
1877		257	0	0	I	0	I	5	2	6	18	I	10	42	66	73	22	5	4	0
1877	Garrett	I	0	0	0	0	0	0	0	0	0	0	0	0	0	0	I	0	0	0
1877	Eliasberg	I	0	0	0	0	0	0	0	0	0	0	0	0	0	0	I	0	0	0
1878		157	0	0	0	I	2	I	0	4	19	2	11	18	34	44	16	4	I	0
1878	Pittman	I	0	0	0	0	0	0	0	0	0	0	0	0	0	I	0	0	0	0

HALF DOLLARS SEATED LIBERTY, MOTTO

Date		Total Graded	G/VG	F	VF	40	45	50	53	55	58	60	61	62	63	64	65	66	67	68
1870		17	5	3	3	2	3	0	0	0	0	0	0	0	0	0	0	0	0	0
1871		19	2	0	9	2	2	0	1	0	0	0	1	1	0	0	0	0	0	0
1872		27	2	1	6	4	4	2	2	2	1	0	0	0	3	0	0	0	0	0
1873 No Arrows		19	0	0	3	2	2	2	1	1	2	0	1	2	1	0	0	1	1	0
1873 Arrows		40	2	0	4	6	4	2	3	7	3	0	2	0	2	3	1	1	0	0
1873 Arrows Eliasberg		1	0	0	0	0	0	0	0	0	0	0	0	0	1	0	0	0	0	0
1873 Arrows Pittman		1	0	0	0	0	0	0	0	0	0	0	0	0	0	0	1	0	0	0
1874		27	4	0	3	4	2	1	0	2	2	0	0	1	5	3	0	0	0	0
1875		60	0	0	0	0	2	0	2	2	5	1	5	8	16	17	1	1	0	0
1876		69	1	0	1	0	2	1	1	3	7	0	5	8	12	19	6	2	1	0
1876	Eliasberg	1	0	0	0	0	0	0	0	0	0	0	0	0	0	0	0	0	0	1
1876	Pittman	1	0	0	0	0	0	0	0	0	0	0	0	0	0	0	1	0	0	0
1877		112	0	0	1	0	3	0	1	0	2	2	5	8	34	31	19	4	2	0
1877	Eliasberg	1	0	0	0	0	0	0	0	0	0	0	0	0	0	0	0	0	0	1
1878		16	4	2	2	1	1	2	0	1	0	0	0	1	1	0	1	0	0	0
1878	Eliasberg	1	0	0	0	0	0	0	0	0	0	0	0	0	0	0	0	1	0	0

SILVER DOLLARS SEATED LIBERTY, MOTTO

Date		Total Graded	G/VG	F	VF	40	45	50	53	55	58	60	61	62	63	64	65	66	67	68
1870		91	1	4	20	10	6	5	9	14	16	0	3	1	2	0	0	0	0	0
1870	Eliasberg	1	0	0	0	0	0	0	0	0	0	0	0	0	0	1	0	0	0	0
1870	Pittman	1	0	0	0	0	0	0	0	0	1	0	0	0	0	0	0	0	0	0
1871		27	1	2	7	3	5	1	2	2	2	0	1	0	1	0	0	0	0	0
1872		41	6	1	5	6	2	6	2	2	3	2	3	0	0	2	1	0	0	0
1872	Eliasberg	1	0	0	0	0	0	0	0	0	0	0	1	0	0	0	0	0	0	0
1872	Pittman	1	0	0	1	0	0	0	0	0	0	0	0	0	0	0	0	0	0	0
1873		20	0	0	8	0	4	0	2	2	1	0	1	0	0	1	1	0	0	0
1873	Eliasberg	1	0	0	0	0	0	0	0	0	0	0	1	0	0	0	0	0	0	0

SILVER DOLLARS MORGAN LIBERTY HEAD

Date		Total Graded	G/VG	F	VF	40	45	50	53	55	58	60	61	62	63	64	65	66	67	68
1878	MS	5021	4	5	3	5	10	13	10	11	28	32	92	377	1424	2328	583	89	1	0
1878	MSPL	633	0	0	0	0	0	0	0	0	1	4	24	85	248	204	62	4	0	0
1878	MSDPL	298	0	0	0	0	0	0	0	0	0	0	8	39	116	102	32	0	0	0
1878	Eliasberg	1	0	0	0	0	0	0	0	0	0	0	0	0	0	1	0	0	0	0
1879	MS	809	4	16	38	22	31	16	8	10	9	22	37	148	223	196	29	0	0	0
1879	MSPL	112	0	0	0	0	0	0	0	0	0	6	14	26	42	21	3	0	0	0
1879	MSDPL	65	0	0	0	0	0	0	0	0	1	2	8	17	26	10	1	0	0	0
1879	Capped MS	469	2	1	22	12	13	17	6	6	16	41	37	84	117	89	6	0	0	0
1879	Capped MSPL	18	0	0	0	0	0	0	1	0	0	0	2	2	6	7	0	0	0	0
1879	Capped MSDPL	25	0	0	0	0	0	0	0	0	0	0	3	6	9	7	0	0	0	0
1880 Rev of 78 MSDPL		30	0	0	0	0	0	0	0	0	0	2	1	5	10	9	3	0	0	0
1880	Rev of 78 MS	741	0	1	1	0	0	0	0	0	0	3	15	63	208	371	71	8	0	0
1880	Rev " Ted Clark	1	0	0	0	0	0	0	0	0	0	0	0	0	1	0	0	0	0	0
1880	Rev of 78 MSPL	29	0	0	0	0	0	0	0	0	0	1	3	3	8	10	4	0	0	0
1880	Rev " Eliasberg	1	0	0	0	0	0	0	0	1	0	0	0	0	0	0	0	0	0	0
1880	MS	2921	1	2	0	0	0	1	1	1	0	11	41	140	548	1357	694	118	6	0
1880	MSPL	437	0	0	0	0	0	0	0	0	0	0	4	22	111	202	82	11	0	0
1880	MSDPL	283	0	0	0	0	0	0	0	0	0	1	4	27	59	163	29	0	0	0
1881	MS	4231	2	0	1	0	0	0	0	1	0	5	31	164	648	1730	1256	359	32	2
1881 ANA Grading Set MS		1	0	0	0	0	0	0	0	0	0	0	0	0	1	0	0	0	0	0
1881	MSPL	297	0	0	0	0	0	0	0	0	0	1	2	25	83	135	42	8	1	0
1881	MSDPL	336	0	0	0	0	0	0	0	0	0	1	8	24	77	174	46	6	0	0
1882	MS	5406	0	2	2	0	0	1	0	0	3	15	53	265	1016	2214	1574	244	17	0
1882	Eliasberg	1	0	0	0	0	0	0	0	0	0	0	0	0	1	0	0	0	0	0
1882	ANA Grading Set	1	0	0	0	0	0	0	0	0	0	0	0	0	1	0	0	0	0	0
1882	MSPL	624	0	0	0	0	0	0	0	0	0	1	5	36	164	279	119	20	0	0
1882	MSDPL	528	0	0	0	0	0	0	0	0	0	0	2	41	168	243	70	4	0	0
1883	MS	7537	3	0	0	0	0	0	0	0	3	7	35	238	1118	3107	2533	448	45	0
1883	MSPL	897	0	0	0	0	0	0	0	0	2	2	7	44	176	413	218	33	1	0
1883	Eliasberg	1	0	0	0	0	0	0	0	0	0	0	1	0	0	0	0	0	0	0
1883	MSDPL	876	0	0	0	0	0	0	0	0	0	3	5	45	209	421	171	22	0	0
1884	MS	8519	0	0	1	0	0	0	0	0	1	10	69	358	1617	3677	2403	344	29	0
1884	MSPL	927	0	0	0	0	0	0	0	0	0	2	9	58	223	442	161	29	3	0
1884	Eliasberg	1	0	0	0	0	0	0	0	0	0	0	0	0	0	0	1	0	0	0
1884	MSDPL	888	0	0	0	0	0	0	0	0	0	0	3	41	225	445	153	20	1	0

SILVER DOLLARS MORGAN LIBERTY HEAD (Continued)

Date		Total Graded	G/VG	F	VF	40	45	50	53	55	58	60	61	62	63	64	65	66	67	68
1885	MS	3746	0	0	0	I	0	0	0	0	0	9	35	168	701	1558	1049	207	12	5
1885	MSPL	339	0	0	0	0	0	0	0	0	0	I	9	34	85	127	69	II	3	0
1885	MSDPL	350	0	0	0	0	0	0	0	0	0	I	5	32	93	149	57	13	0	0
1885	Double Dash	I	0	0	0	0	0	0	0	0	0	0	0	0	0	0	I	0	0	0
1889	MS	927	36	59	141	74	140	70	63	80	82	10	35	68	40	26	3	0	0	0
1889	MSPL	95	0	0	0	0	0	4	0	4	20	5	12	12	33	4	I	0	0	0
1889	MSDPL	79	0	0	0	0	0	0	0	I	2	5	12	20	26	13	0	0	0	0
1890	MS	1809	5	2	5	5	8	7	8	5	39	34	100	347	701	502	38	2	0	0
1890	Eliasberg	I	0	0	0	0	0	0	0	0	0	0	0	0	0	0	I	0	0	0
1890	MSPL	125	0	0	0	0	0	0	0	0	I	5	10	23	54	30	2	0	0	0
1890	MSDPL	303	0	0	0	0	0	0	0	0	I	2	13	58	123	100	6	0	0	0
1891	MS	2619	2	4	0	I	2	5	2	12	45	39	123	369	1025	892	89	6	I	0
1891	Redfield	15	0	0	0	0	0	0	0	0	0	0	I	4	8	I	I	0	0	0
1891	MSPL	166	0	0	0	0	0	0	0	0	0	3	7	23	80	48	5	0	0	0
1891	MSDPL	122	0	0	0	0	0	0	0	0	I	2	6	34	59	19	I	0	0	0
1891 Spitting Eagle MS		148	0	I	0	0	0	I	0	I	2	4	12	56	47	22	I	0	0	0
1891 Spitting Eagle MSPL		3	0	0	0	0	0	0	0	0	0	0	0	I	I	I	0	0	0	0
1892	MS	1870	I	0	I	3	11	0	5	6	27	42	125	364	625	556	94	8	I	0
1892	Eliasberg	I	0	0	0	0	0	0	0	0	0	0	0	0	0	0	0	I	0	0
1892	Redfield	I	0	0	0	0	0	0	0	0	0	0	0	0	I	0	0	0	0	0
1892	MSPL	207	0	0	0	0	0	0	I	I	2	7	28	53	66	46	3	0	0	0
1892	MSDPL	71	0	0	0	0	0	0	0	I	0	I	4	21	20	23	I	0	0	0
1893	MS	1010	9	15	78	26	28	14	8	8	13	47	134	244	286	95	5	0	0	0
1893	MSPL	92	0	0	0	0	0	0	0	0	2	9	26	38	16	I	0	0	0	0
1893 Eliasberg MSPL		I	0	0	0	0	0	0	0	0	0	0	0	0	I	0	0	0	0	0
1893	MSDPL	7	0	0	0	0	0	0	0	0	0	0	0	4	2	0	I	0	0	0
1900-O/CC MS		1143	2	2	9	8	12	6	4	7	18	7	32	116	342	466	101	8	I	0

TRADE DOLLARS

Date	Total Graded	G/VG	F	VF	40	45	50	53	55	58	60	61	62	63	64	65	66	67	68
1873	57	0	2	2	0	3	0	4	6	13	5	4	6	7	4	1	0	0	0
1874	119	0	0	2	0	1	2	2	7	11	9	20	23	25	13	4	0	0	0
1875	140	1	0	1	4	6	3	1	6	20	9	22	28	19	17	2	0	0	0
1875 S/CC FS-012.5	33	0	0	0	0	0	0	1	2	8	4	6	5	3	3	1	0	0	0
1876	66	0	0	1	1	2	2	1	7	14	7	14	6	7	4	0	0	0	0
1876 CC DDR FS-014	7	0	0	0	0	0	2	0	2	1	0	2	0	0	0	0	0	0	0
1877	62	0	1	4	2	1	0	2	4	13	3	11	8	5	7	1	0	0	0
1877 Eliasberg	1	0	0	0	0	0	0	0	0	0	0	0	0	1	0	0	0	0	0
1878	50	1	1	4	3	4	1	3	2	8	1	6	1	6	7	1	1	0	0

Carson City Gold Coins

HALF EAGLES CORONET, MOTTO (NGC)

Date	Total Graded	G/VG	F	VF	40	45	50	53	55	58	60	61	62	63	64	65	66	67	68
1870	29	2	2	4	0	4	1	2	3	9	0	1	1	0	0	0	0	0	0
1871	65	3	4	14	10	14	1	6	7	4	0	1	0	1	0	0	0	0	0
1871 Bass	1	0	0	0	1	0	0	0	0	0	0	0	0	0	0	0	0	0	0
1872	31	3	3	5	4	10	0	3	2	1	0	0	0	0	0	0	0	0	0
1873	19	0	1	7	3	3	2	0	2	0	0	0	1	0	0	0	0	0	0
1874	75	3	6	14	6	17	6	6	10	7	0	0	0	0	0	0	0	0	0
1874 Bass	1	0	0	1	0	0	0	0	0	0	0	0	0	0	0	0	0	0	0
1875	59	1	1	16	3	19	4	7	5	2	0	0	0	1	0	0	0	0	0
1875 Bass	1	0	0	0	0	0	0	0	0	1	0	0	0	0	0	0	0	0	0
1875 Ashland City	1	0	0	0	0	0	0	0	1	0	0	0	0	0	0	0	0	0	0
1876	48	3	3	9	5	15	3	2	3	2	0	1	0	0	1	1	0	0	0
1877	51	0	4	6	9	14	3	3	8	4	0	0	0	0	0	0	0	0	0
1877 Ashland City	1	0	0	0	0	0	0	1	0	0	0	0	0	0	0	0	0	0	0
1878	26	0	1	5	6	4	5	2	1	1	0	0	0	1	0	0	0	0	0
1878 Ashland City	1	0	0	0	1	0	0	0	0	0	0	0	0	0	0	0	0	0	0
1879	95	0	4	10	13	23	13	9	6	14	1	2	0	0	0	0	0	0	0
1880	173	2	1	22	10	35	21	14	24	27	1	9	6	0	0	0	0	0	0
1881	45	0	1	5	5	13	7	3	6	3	0	0	1	1	0	0	0	0	0
1881 Ashland City	1	0	0	0	0	0	0	0	0	1	0	0	0	0	0	0	0	0	0
1882	244	0	2	17	12	31	26	37	29	72	2	13	3	0	0	0	0	0	0
1882 Ashland City	1	0	0	0	0	0	0	0	0	1	0	0	0	0	0	0	0	0	0
1883	94	0	0	6	4	20	9	12	17	24	0	1	0	0	1	0	0	0	0
1884	98	1	2	3	7	16	14	7	25	17	0	6	0	0	0	0	0	0	0
1884 Bass	2	0	0	0	0	0	0	0	0	1	1	0	0	0	0	0	0	0	0

HALF EAGLES CORONET, MOTTO (Continued)

Date		Total Graded	G/VG	F	VF	40	45	50	53	55	58	60	61	62	63	64	65	66	67	68
1884	Ashland City	I	0	0	0	0	0	0	0	0	I	0	0	0	0	0	0	0	0	0
1890		305	0	0	3	7	18	16	11	23	66	10	42	58	29	20	2	0	0	0
1890	Ashland City	I	0	0	0	0	0	0	0	0	0	0	0	I	0	0	0	0	0	0
1891		884	0	0	8	10	29	32	29	68	180	57	154	188	90	34	5	0	0	0
1891	Bass	I	0	0	0	0	0	0	0	0	0	0	0	0	I	0	0	0	0	0
1891	Ashland City	I	0	0	0	0	0	0	0	0	0	0	0	0	I	0	0	0	0	0
1892		331	0	3	7	13	44	27	22	53	79	8	33	35	3	3	0	I	0	0
1892	Bass	I	0	0	0	0	0	0	0	0	0	I	0	0	0	0	0	0	0	0
1892	Ashland City	I	0	0	0	0	0	0	0	0	0	0	0	I	0	0	0	0	0	0
1893		315	0	0	6	4	25	19	30	37	85	10	31	40	17	8	3	0	0	0
1893	Ashland City	I	0	0	0	0	0	0	0	0	0	0	0	0	I	0	0	0	0	0

EAGLES CORONET, MOTTO

Date		Total Graded	G/VG	F	VF	40	45	50	53	55	58	60	61	62	63	64	65	66	67	68
1870		20	0	0	5	5	6	4	0	0	0	0	0	0	0	0	0	0	0	0
1870	Browning	I	0	0	0	I	0	0	0	0	0	0	0	0	0	0	0	0	0	0
1870	Ashland City	I	0	0	0	I	0	0	0	0	0	0	0	0	0	0	0	0	0	0
1871		46	2	0	5	6	16	3	3	6	3	I	0	I	0	0	0	0	0	0
1871	Ashland City	I	0	0	0	0	0	I	0	0	0	0	0	0	0	0	0	0	0	0
1872		27	I	I	6	5	6	4	I	3	0	0	0	0	0	0	0	0	0	0
1872	Browning	I	0	0	0	0	0	I	0	0	0	0	0	0	0	0	0	0	0	0
1872	Ashland City	I	0	0	0	0	I	0	0	0	0	0	0	0	0	0	0	0	0	0
1873		31	2	I	5	5	10	4	3	I	0	0	0	0	0	0	0	0	0	0
1873	Bass	I	0	0	0	0	0	0	0	0	I	0	0	0	0	0	0	0	0	0
1874		121	2	3	23	31	40	8	6	6	I	0	0	0	0	0	I	0	0	0
1875		28	I	I	10	6	2	2	2	2	0	I	0	0	I	0	0	0	0	0
1876		60	I	4	16	5	22	5	3	2	2	0	0	0	0	0	0	0	0	0
1876	Browning	I	0	0	0	0	I	0	0	0	0	0	0	0	0	0	0	0	0	0
1877		26	0	2	6	5	7	3	0	2	I	0	0	0	0	0	0	0	0	0
1878		21	0	2	3	3	5	0	2	2	3	0	0	0	I	0	0	0	0	0
1878	Ashland City	I	0	0	0	0	0	0	0	I	0	0	0	0	0	0	0	0	0	0
1879		31	0	I	7	6	8	2	2	2	3	0	0	0	0	0	0	0	0	0
1879	Ashland City	I	0	0	0	0	0	0	0	0	I	0	0	0	0	0	0	0	0	0
1880		123	0	0	2	11	21	22	10	28	17	6	4	2	0	0	0	0	0	0
1880	Bass	I	0	0	0	0	0	0	0	I	0	0	0	0	0	0	0	0	0	0
1880	Ashland City	I	0	0	0	0	0	0	0	I	0	0	0	0	0	0	0	0	0	0

EAGLES CORONET, MOTTO

Date		Total Graded	G/VG	F	VF	40	45	50	53	55	58	60	61	62	63	64	65	66	67	68
1881		219	0	0	4	13	41	26	18	22	53	9	11	22	0	0	0	0	0	0
1881	Eliasberg	1	0	0	0	0	0	0	0	0	0	0	0	0	0	1	0	0	0	0
1881	Pittman	1	0	0	0	0	0	0	0	1	0	0	0	0	0	0	0	0	0	0
1881	Bass	1	0	0	0	0	0	0	0	0	1	0	0	0	0	0	0	0	0	0
1881	Ashland City	1	0	0	0	0	0	0	0	0	0	0	1	0	0	0	0	0	0	0
1882		97	0	0	4	3	18	8	11	31	21	0	0	1	0	0	0	0	0	0
1882	Browning	1	0	0	0	0	0	0	1	0	0	0	0	0	0	0	0	0	0	0
1882	Bass	1	0	0	0	0	0	0	0	0	1	0	0	0	0	0	0	0	0	0
1882	Ashland City	1	0	0	0	0	0	0	0	1	0	0	0	0	0	0	0	0	0	0
1883		124	0	2	8	20	42	18	7	12	11	2	2	0	0	0	0	0	0	0
1883	Browning	1	0	0	0	0	1	0	0	0	0	0	0	0	0	0	0	0	0	0
1883	Bass	3	0	1	0	0	1	0	0	1	0	0	0	0	0	0	0	0	0	0
1883	Ashland City	1	0	0	0	0	0	0	0	1	0	0	0	0	0	0	0	0	0	0
1884		132	0	0	7	11	21	18	15	18	37	3	1	0	0	0	0	0	0	0
1884	Bass	1	0	0	0	0	0	0	0	0	1	0	0	0	0	0	0	0	0	0
1884	Ashland City	1	0	0	0	0	0	0	1	0	0	0	0	0	0	0	0	0	0	0
1890		198	0	0	0	4	6	9	8	23	67	19	28	25	9	0	0	0	0	0
1890	Ashland City	2	0	0	0	0	0	0	0	0	0	1	0	1	0	0	0	0	0	0
1891		1209	0	0	4	9	45	34	31	84	256	179	270	235	55	7	0	0	0	0
1891	Bass	3	0	0	0	0	0	0	0	1	1	0	1	0	0	0	0	0	0	0
1891	Ashland City	2	0	0	0	0	0	0	0	1	0	0	0	0	0	1	0	0	0	0
1892		231	0	1	5	16	39	45	28	30	47	5	8	6	0	1	0	0	0	0
1892	Bass	1	0	0	0	0	0	0	0	0	0	0	1	0	0	0	0	0	0	0
1892	Ashland City	1	0	0	0	0	0	0	0	0	1	0	0	0	0	0	0	0	0	0
1893		127	0	0	6	6	30	23	21	12	22	3	3	1	0	0	0	0	0	0
1893	Bass	1	0	0	0	0	0	0	0	1	0	0	0	0	0	0	0	0	0	0
1893	Ashland City	1	0	0	0	0	0	0	0	0	1	1	0	0	0	0	0	0	0	0

DOUBLE EAGLES CORONET, TYPE 2

Date		Total Graded	G/VG	F	VF	40	45	50	53	55	58	60	61	62	63	64	65	66	67	68
1870		17	0	0	5	5	5	2	0	0	0	0	0	0	0	0	0	0	0	0
1871		90	0	0	7	15	18	18	9	14	7	0	1	0	1	0	0	0	0	0
1872		223	0	0	13	24	68	34	24	21	32	3	4	0	0	0	0	0	0	0
1873		201	0	1	5	23	33	22	22	29	52	11	1	1	0	0	0	0	0	0
1873	Browning	1	0	0	0	0	0	0	0	0	1	0	0	0	0	0	0	0	0	0
1874		694	0	2	44	87	128	83	73	103	161	7	3	1	0	0	0	0	0	0
1874	Bass	3	0	0	0	0	0	0	0	1	2	0	0	0	0	0	0	0	0	0
1875		949	0	0	36	41	122	60	66	91	206	70	115	122	19	0	0	0	0	0
1875	Bass	2	0	0	0	0	0	0	0	0	0	1	0	1	0	0	0	0	0	0
1876		1050	0	0	33	74	156	92	80	137	293	49	73	57	4	1	0	0	0	0
1876	Bass	2	0	0	0	0	0	0	0	0	2	0	0	0	0	0	0	0	0	0

DOUBLE EAGLES CORONET, TYPE 3

Date		Total Graded	G/VG	F	VF	40	45	50	53	55	58	60	61	62	63	64	65	66	67	68
1877		463	0	1	34	57	97	52	59	76	71	8	3	4	0	0	0	0	0	0
1878		170	0	2	26	20	42	19	14	22	21	2	2	0	0	0	0	0	0	0
1879		172	0	2	8	23	46	25	13	15	22	2	15	1	0	0	0	0	0	0
1882		484	0	0	7	33	64	55	37	75	163	19	14	17	0	0	0	0	0	0
1882	Browning	1	0	0	0	0	0	0	0	0	0	0	1	0	0	0	0	0	0	0
1882	Bass	1	0	0	0	0	0	0	0	0	1	0	0	0	0	0	0	0	0	0
1883		635	0	0	23	55	91	59	54	105	172	27	35	11	3	0	0	0	0	0
1884		902	0	0	13	49	128	78	65	127	229	72	94	43	4	0	0	0	0	0
1884	Browning	1	0	0	0	0	0	0	0	0	0	0	0	1	0	0	0	0	0	0
1885		153	0	0	8	21	30	16	20	14	29	6	3	6	0	0	0	0	0	0
1889		466	0	2	17	27	68	37	36	84	148	17	13	17	0	0	0	0	0	0
1890		1134	0	0	37	74	162	110	108	197	336	51	44	15	0	0	0	0	0	0
1891		122	0	0	5	3	12	17	11	15	30	6	9	14	0	0	0	0	0	0
1892		429	0	0	12	21	61	39	27	52	120	27	41	25	4	0	0	0	0	0
1892	Browning	1	0	0	0	0	0	0	0	0	0	0	1	0	0	0	0	0	0	0
1892	Bass	1	0	0	0	0	0	0	0	0	0	0	0	1	0	0	0	0	0	0
1893		403	0	0	7	17	13	9	11	29	104	38	73	83	16	1	0	0	0	0

PCGS Population Report

Carson City Silver Coins

LIBERTY SEATED DIMES, LEGEND (PCGS)

Date	Total Graded	VG/VF	40	45	50	53	55	58	60	61	62	63	64	65	66	67	68
1871	18	8	1	1	1	0	1	0	0	0	1	0	1	0	0	0	0
1872	29	19	2	4	0	0	0	1	0	1	0	0	0	0	0	0	0
1873 No Arrows	0	0	0	0	0	0	0	0	0	0	0	0	0	0	0	0	0
1873 Arrows	24	24	0	0	0	0	0	0	0	0	0	0	0	0	0	0	0
1874 Arrows	18	8	3	1	0	0	0	0	0	0	0	1	0	0	0	0	0
1875 MM Above	156	1	1	1	3	3	5	11	1	6	26	37	34	16	10	0	0
1875 MM Below	24	2	0	1	2	0	4	2	0	0	2	4	5	2	0	0	0
1876	176	6	0	1	0	2	8	7	3	4	17	50	40	29	7	2	0
1877	207	0	0	3	0	3	8	11	0	6	40	38	49	30	17	3	0
1878	43	5	1	0	2	0	4	4	0	1	4	8	6	7	1	0	0

TWENTY CENT PIECES

Date	Total Graded	VG/VF	40	45	50	53	55	58	60	61	62	63	64	65	66	67	68
1875	419	24	13	15	19	14	44	61	14	9	43	47	94	13	4	0	0
1876	12	0	0	0	0	0	0	0	0	1	2	1	4	2	2	0	0

LIBERTY SEATED QUARTER, WITH MOTTO

Date	Total Graded	VG/VF	40	45	50	53	55	58	60	61	62	63	64	65	66	67	68
1870	18	9	2	1	0	0	1	0	0	0	0	0	0	0	0	0	0
1871	13	9	1	0	0	0	0	0	0	0	0	0	1	1	0	0	0
1872	28	21	1	1	0	0	1	0	0	0	1	0	0	0	0	0	0
1873 No Arrows	2	0	0	0	0	0	0	0	0	0	1	0	1	0	0	0	0
1873 Arrows	14	9	1	0	0	0	1	0	0	0	0	0	1	0	0	0	0
1875	37	10	2	3	2	0	4	1	0	1	4	3	5	1	0	0	0
1876	144	2	0	1	2	3	9	15	3	15	20	31	30	7	4	1	0
1877	328	3	1	1	2	1	15	18	2	16	66	88	74	26	8	6	0
1878	158	3	0	2	2	2	5	25	4	6	24	29	39	13	4	0	0

LIBERTY SEATED HALF DOLLAR, MOTTO

Date	Total Graded	VG/VF	40	45	50	53	55	58	60	61	62	63	64	65	66	67	68
1870	49	30	3	3	I	2	I	0	0	0	I	0	0	0	0	0	0
1871	47	19	6	5	3	I	3	5	I	0	I	0	I	0	0	0	0
1872	59	2I	8	9	2	2	5	5	I	0	0	5	0	0	0	0	0
1873 No Arrows	47	19	5	2	I	0	7	3	0	I	3	0	3	I	I	I	0
1873 Arrows	99	42	10	8	8	2	8	5	I	2	2	2	5	I	0	0	0
1874 Arrows	35	12	3	3	I	2	4	I	0	I	3	I	I	I	I	0	0
1875	9I	3	5	3	9	I	6	7	I	3	13	16	2I	2	I	0	0
1876	120	3	3	6	7	8	12	11	7	6	20	14	12	7	4	0	0
1877	148	0	5	3	5	I	4	5	I	8	18	44	32	17	2	0	0
1878	26	11	I	2	0	I	2	0	I	0	I	I	I	4	0	0	0

LIBERTY SEATED DOLLAR, WITH MOTTO

Date	Total Graded	VG/VF	40	45	50	53	55	58	60	61	62	63	64	65	66	67	68
1870	239	78	28	3I	32	20	26	9	0	I	3	8	0	0	0	0	0
1871	74	30	16	7	4	6	6	3	0	0	0	I	I	0	0	0	0
1872	123	57	13	6	II	4	10	9	2	2	3	2	0	0	0	0	0
1873 Seated	64	26	7	10	7	4	3	2	I	0	0	0	0	0	0	0	0

TRADE DOLLAR

Date	Total Graded	VG/VF	40	45	50	53	55	58	60	61	62	63	64	65	66	67	68
1873	125	II	15	19	14	9	16	15	I	4	12	6	2	0	0	0	0
1874	18I	3	4	7	II	8	30	15	12	20	24	36	10	0	I	0	0
1875	214	12	4	9	17	10	24	12	13	27	33	34	18	0	I	0	0
1875 S/CC	50	3	2	2	5	4	7	7	I	3	8	4	3	I	0	0	0
1876	88	5	7	8	9	4	12	12	2	7	19	2	0	I	0	0	0
1876 Dbld Die	6	I	0	2	0	0	I	2	0	0	0	0	0	0	0	0	0
1877	88	9	9	4	I	3	7	14	0	I	18	14	7	0	I	0	0
1878	97	30	10	4	7	5	9	4	3	5	7	3	9	I	0	0	0

MORGAN DOLLAR

Date		Total Graded	VG/VF	40	45	50	53	55	58	60	61	62	63	64	65	66	67	68
1878	MS	10783	21	12	13	12	20	47	52	189	410	1670	3991	3304	881	155	4	0
1878	MSPL	940	0	0	0	0	0	0	0	23	66	218	339	232	53	9	0	0
1878	MSDM	361	0	0	0	0	0	0	0	6	14	65	130	111	32	3	0	0
1879	MS	1787	114	32	35	22	18	14	15	65	131	343	481	443	64	2	0	0
1879	MSPL	191	0	0	0	0	0	0	0	12	23	51	64	38	3	0	0	0
1879	MSDM	67	0	0	0	0	0	0	0	2	0	17	26	20	2	0	0	0
1879	Capped Die MS	973	64	15	21	13	12	21	34	120	129	195	168	172	4	0	0	0
1879	Capped Die MSPL	56	0	0	0	0	0	0	0	5	6	10	11	24	0	0	0	0
1879	Capped Die MSDM	15	0	0	0	0	0	0	0	2	2	2	5	4	0	0	0	0
1880	MS	7266	13	1	1	1	0	1	2	43	202	737	2009	2739	1228	266	20	0
1880	MSPL	604	0	0	0	0	0	0	0	6	23	98	196	204	73	4	0	0
1880	MSDM	231	0	0	0	0	0	0	0	1	12	28	86	75	27	2	0	0
1880 8/ HIGH 7	MS	262	0	0	0	0	0	0	0	0	0	14	36	112	76	20	4	0
1880 8/ HIGH 7	MSPL	22	0	0	0	0	0	0	0	0	0	4	5	9	4	0	0	0
1880 8/ HIGH 7	MSDM	24	0	0	0	0	0	0	0	0	0	2	2	8	12	0	0	0
1880 8/ LOW 7	MS	204	0	0	0	0	0	0	0	0	0	7	19	94	75	9	0	0
1880 8/ LOW 7	MSPL	36	0	0	0	0	0	0	0	0	0	1	8	20	6	1	0	0
1880 8/ LOW 7	MSDM	23	0	0	0	0	0	0	0	0	0	0	5	15	2	1	0	0
1880/79 Rev 1878	MS	1728	1	1	0	0	0	1	0	20	44	199	501	712	221	27	0	0
1880/79 Rev 1878	MSPL	41	0	0	0	0	0	0	0	0	2	11	13	10	4	1	0	0
1880/79 Rev 1878	MSDM	32	0	0	0	0	0	0	0	0	5	7	10	8	2	0	0	0
1880 8/ 7 Rev 78	MS	233	0	0	0	0	0	0	0	0	0	15	44	104	55	14	0	0
1881	MS	12066	10	0	2	0	0	0	2	28	134	753	2676	4710	2820	858	67	3
1881	MSPL	685	0	0	0	0	0	0	0	7	18	78	245	237	85	14	0	0
1881	MSDM	869	0	0	0	0	0	0	0	11	10	89	258	337	128	36	0	0
1882	MS	16355	4	0	1	0	0	2	5	59	302	1412	4664	6420	2985	460	37	1
1882	MSPL	1517	0	0	0	0	0	0	0	3	22	159	503	571	218	41	0	0
1882	MSDM	1536	0	0	0	0	0	0	0	7	29	195	457	587	211	49	1	0
1883	MS	22589	3	0	0	0	0	2	1	87	350	1719	5637	8845	4907	963	69	3
1883	MSPL	2333	0	0	0	0	0	0	0	6	41	260	739	827	381	72	7	0
1883	MSDM	2465	0	0	0	0	0	0	0	8	40	212	722	933	479	69	2	0
1884	MS	23865	6	0	0	0	0	2	2	91	415	2145	6481	9321	4604	743	46	5
1884	MSPL	2035	0	0	0	0	0	0	0	9	35	203	643	812	277	55	1	0
1884	MSDM	2294	0	0	0	0	0	0	0	11	38	199	620	961	381	81	3	0
1885	MS	11137	6	0	0	0	0	2	3	42	169	862	2841	4438	2257	484	30	1

MORGAN DOLLAR (Continued)

Date		Total Graded	VG/VF	40	45	50	53	55	58	60	61	62	63	64	65	66	67	68
1885	MSPL	771	0	0	0	0	0	0	0	8	30	103	239	278	98	14	1	0
1885	MSDM	1018	0	0	0	0	0	0	0	9	36	142	280	346	162	41	2	0
1889	MS	1809	597	206	259	134	93	137	139	16	42	66	70	17	1	0	0	1
1889	MSPL	53	0	0	0	0	0	0	0	6	8	20	16	3	0	0	0	0
1889	MSDM	171	0	0	0	0	0	0	0	9	26	61	55	20	0	0	0	0
1890	MS	4807	17	6	20	26	28	73	91	149	432	1118	1660	1028	146	8	0	0
1890	MSPL	203	0	0	0	0	0	0	0	5	29	65	62	35	7	0	0	0
1890	MSDM	572	0	0	0	0	0	0	0	28	49	132	222	125	16	0	0	0
1890	Tail Bar MS	66	5	2	2	1	1	3	4	0	3	12	22	8	0	0	0	0
1890	Tail Bar MSDM	4	0	0	0	0	0	0	0	0	0	0	3	1	0	0	0	0
1891	MS	7387	15	3	9	15	27	67	88	307	674	1685	2574	1608	289	23	1	0
1891	MSPL	335	0	0	0	0	0	0	0	3	38	98	111	72	11	1	0	1
1891	MSDM	241	0	0	0	0	0	0	0	15	25	72	90	38	1	0	0	0
1892	MS	3930	24	10	21	15	24	53	79	131	343	1030	1198	815	167	15	2	0
1892	MSPL	303	0	0	0	0	0	0	0	26	38	97	82	52	8	0	0	0
1892	MSDM	173	0	0	0	0	0	0	0	13	27	60	39	32	2	0	0	0
1893	MS	2521	187	50	48	27	17	26	36	215	393	660	568	268	7	0	0	0
1893	MSPL	213	0	0	0	0	0	0	0	63	61	63	22	1	2	0	0	0
1893	MSDM	7	0	0	0	0	0	0	0	0	0	3	2	2	0	0	0	0
1900	O/ CC	3336	6	4	7	3	4	10	28	21	82	433	1108	1157	423	48	2	0

Carson City Gold Coins

LIBERTY $5, WITH MOTTO (PCGS)

Date	Total Graded	VG/VF	40	45	50	53	55	58	60	61	62	63	64	65	66	67	68
1870	45	19	2	9	4	2	3	2	0	2	0	0	0	0	0	0	0
1871	72	48	6	7	4	1	3	2	0	0	0	0	0	0	0	0	0
1872	52	30	2	10	2	1	2	1	0	0	0	0	0	0	0	0	0
1873	48	26	4	9	0	1	2	0	0	1	1	0	0	0	0	0	0
1874	86	43	9	8	3	7	8	3	0	0	2	0	0	0	0	0	0
1875	70	28	13	11	7	5	3	0	0	1	0	0	0	0	0	0	0
1876	67	30	8	11	2	4	5	2	0	0	0	0	0	0	1	0	0
1877	72	27	11	15	5	1	7	2	1	0	1	0	0	0	0	0	0
1878	43	19	5	8	5	1	2	2	0	0	0	0	0	0	0	0	0
1879	109	46	13	14	10	7	11	6	0	1	0	0	0	0	0	0	0
1880	166	42	16	30	31	13	17	13	1	2	1	0	0	0	0	0	0
1881	63	24	11	8	9	5	2	0	0	1	0	0	0	1	0	0	0
1882	212	31	15	27	39	22	35	32	1	6	3	0	0	0	0	0	0
1883	68	10	6	16	6	7	8	11	0	2	1	0	0	0	0	0	0
1884	76	13	9	14	16	4	12	5	0	1	1	0	0	0	0	0	0
1890	298	11	14	20	21	19	46	48	21	18	34	17	27	1	1	0	0
1891	888	19	19	56	75	47	128	137	83	111	140	46	26	1	0	0	0
1892	272	20	24	34	31	32	43	35	12	19	13	8	0	0	0	0	0
1893	263	16	17	29	42	24	48	39	7	21	13	2	4	0	0	0	0

LIBERTY $10, WITH MOTTO

Date	Total Graded	VG/VF	40	45	50	53	55	58	60	61	62	63	64	65	66	67	68
1870	40	20	9	5	4	1	1	0	0	0	0	0	0	0	0	0	0
1871	56	16	13	15	7	3	1	0	0	0	1	0	0	0	0	0	0
1872	37	17	6	5	5	2	2	0	0	0	0	0	0	0	0	0	0
1873	40	16	5	11	6	2	0	0	0	0	0	0	0	0	0	0	0
1874	123	52	30	25	8	2	5	0	0	0	0	1	0	0	0	0	0
1875	58	23	12	7	4	6	4	1	0	0	0	0	0	0	0	0	0
1876	74	33	14	12	8	3	2	2	0	0	0	0	0	0	0	0	0
1877	35	13	7	5	3	4	2	1	0	0	0	0	0	0	0	0	0
1878	50	18	9	9	8	2	4	0	0	0	0	0	0	0	0	0	0
1879	35	13	5	4	7	3	2	1	0	0	0	0	0	0	0	0	0
1880	119	15	16	25	30	10	12	8	2	1	0	0	0	0	0	0	0
1881	212	27	40	44	34	15	24	15	2	6	5	0	0	0	0	0	0
1882	105	10	12	31	21	9	16	6	0	0	0	0	0	0	0	0	0
1883	104	23	17	25	20	9	7	2	1	0	0	0	0	0	0	0	0

LIBERTY $10, WITH MOTTO (Continued)

Date	Total Graded	VG/VF	40	45	50	53	55	58	60	61	62	63	64	65	66	67	68
1884	107	12	22	19	15	10	12	12	2	1	1	1	0	0	0	0	0
1890	251	4	15	32	30	25	40	44	20	16	21	4	0	0	0	0	0
1891	1355	13	35	67	105	81	212	230	271	169	148	23	1	0	0	0	0
1892	288	23	39	71	55	47	24	14	4	3	5	1	2	0	0	0	0
1893	125	10	25	20	26	10	18	12	0	2	2	0	0	0	0	0	0

LIBERTY $20 "TWENTY D."

Date	Total Graded	VG/VF	40	45	50	53	55	58	60	61	62	63	64	65	66	67	68
1870	21	5	5	7	4	0	0	0	0	0	0	0	0	0	0	0	0
1871	97	19	15	31	14	9	8	1	0	0	0	0	0	0	0	0	0
1872	202	26	37	57	36	20	15	10	1	0	0	0	0	0	0	0	0
1873	181	11	30	32	37	23	17	27	2	0	1	1	0	0	0	0	0
1874	696	128	105	192	106	90	49	18	4	3	1	0	0	0	0	0	0
1875	1066	106	125	194	134	62	111	62	70	80	109	12	1	0	0	0	0
1876	1258	103	191	255	225	116	167	85	44	28	44	0	0	0	0	0	0

LIBERTY $20 "TWENTY DOLLARS"

Date	Total Graded	VG/VF	40	45	50	53	55	58	60	61	62	63	64	65	66	67	68
1877	453	84	104	115	48	32	29	24	9	7	1	0	0	0	0	0	0
1878	198	38	32	51	27	18	21	7	0	2	2	0	0	0	0	0	0
1879	186	21	39	56	35	15	8	4	1	6	0	0	0	0	0	0	0
1882	547	64	58	139	98	44	62	51	5	17	9	0	0	0	0	0	0
1883	686	90	102	151	121	53	81	40	12	25	9	2	0	0	0	0	0
1884	1004	117	146	195	172	70	105	83	59	33	21	3	0	0	0	0	0
1885	201	29	20	38	26	21	24	20	5	8	9	1	0	0	0	0	0
1889	510	35	51	89	62	48	48	55	29	29	60	3	1	0	0	0	0
1890	1169	125	140	256	187	91	171	89	41	45	23	1	0	0	0	0	0
1891	139	15	14	17	30	15	21	15	5	4	2	1	0	0	0	0	0
1892	496	35	47	58	69	50	100	58	23	28	24	4	0	0	0	0	0
1893	483	18	17	36	29	33	55	98	36	53	94	14	0	0	0	0	0

Price History for "CC" Coins 1932-2002

70-Year Price Summary

BRIEF OVERVIEW

Prices for coins are established by thousands of collectors and dealers who have bought and sold them through the years, with transactions being recorded and catalogued in such publications as *Auction Prices Realized* and the *Red Book*. Plateaus are achieved and stabilized from decade to decade bringing some declines, with the majority trending upward. Numismatists view these price trends as yardsticks measuring performance, revealing anticipated as well as surprising movements in direction. Purchasing decisions are made by observing price histories, and over the course of time there are selected series of coins that seem to be perpetual gainers, while others are perennial laggards.

For the purpose of this book, a 70 year price history on coins from the Carson City Mint was compiled, vividly illustrating the ever-increasing demand and popularity they have achieved through the years.

This study is divided into five specific decades, providing a panoramic snapshot of price movements during the 70 years it chronicles. It begins with the year 1932, since this is the year that Wayte Raymond published his *Price Guide for U.S. Coins*. Although there had been auction and private sales of "CC" coins in the five decades prior to 1932, it is difficult to find anything resembling a standard price guide until the 1930s.

From 1932 this price study skips ahead 40 years to 1972 corresponding with the reliable and invaluable *Auction Prices Realized* series introduced that year. This 40 year span also provides sufficient time for significant price changes to have occurred, as the 1950s and 1960s proved to be decades of exuberant activity in the rare coin market.

On the strength of a powerful uptrend in the 1970s, prices for rare coins in general advanced in leaps and bounds from the 1980s to the present (2003), with one prolonged pause from 1991 to 1997. As a result of this accelerated appreciation from the 1970s forward it became expedient to follow price movements in shorter intervals; consequently, after 1972, this current price history proceeds a decade at a time until the year 2001, which is the year the 2002 *Auction Prices Realized* covers, and also the closest edition available before the current book went to press.

CONSIDERATIONS

Of course the issue of coin grading will always be a source of debate, argument and conjecture, but for this study the condition rating of Uncirculated was used whenever possible, and if there were no prices for Uncirculated coins, the highest circulated grade available was chosen, with these circulated grades being placed in parentheses. In the years prior to professional coin grading services, standards tended to be much looser, especially in the decades leading up to the 1960s. Nothing resembling the modern emergence of "gradeflation" existed, as there were no wide margins between grades as there is today. As the major grading services such as PCGS and NGC began to define market grading standards beginning in 1986, a noticeable emphasis on more precise point ratings can be observed, and these have also been placed in parentheses.

Most issues from the Carson City Mint are unlike many of the more common generic coins in the field of numismatics which lend themselves to exact grade comparisons from year to year. For instance, there are frequencies of auction appearances for common coins such as 1881-S Morgan dollars in Gem Uncirculated (later designated MS-65), and it is easy to do a decade-by-decade price analysis of them, or a 1924 $20 Saint Gaudens in Choice Brilliant Uncirculated (later MS-63). Massive quantities of such coins are sold year after year, and although changes in grading standards could be debated from time to time in reference to them, arguing that there could be a big difference in price of what would have been considered an accurately graded Gem 1881-S dollar in 1972, and a PCGS graded MS-65 version in 2002, is tantamount to the "number of angels dancing on a pin head" argument. Carson City coins, on the other hand, especially the scarcer dates, do not appear as frequently; many of them are never available in Uncirculated condition.

With that being said, readers are encouraged to glean the positive revelations from this study and not be overly concerned with the grading issue, because it is virtually impossible to compare descriptions of the condition rating of coins from past decades to those of today. One must never forget that with "CC" coins the important thing to consider when using a price study such as this is the increase in values over long periods of time regardless of grade. For example, the 1875-CC 20-cent piece in 1932 was listed at $3.00 in Uncirculated condition, and although it is unknown whether that was the price for what is considered an MS-63, MS-65, or MS-66 today, it is safe to assume that the $3.00 would have been within a dollar or two of the market price for any Uncirculated specimen back then. But no one in 1932 could have fathomed that this date would increase15,000% by 1972, and the appreciation did not end there, for this date increased another 1,278% from 1972 to 2001.

Another fact that becomes apparent is that none of the coins in the Carson City series have decreased in value from their 1932 price levels; but have steadily risen from one decade to the next. As a point of reference, there were declines for a few of the more common dates in the "CC" Morgan silver dollar series from the late 1980s to the present; but that was more attributable to the over-promotion of

any coin resembling a common date in the reckless period of the late 1980s than to the loss of support in the "CC" dollar market. Notwithstanding, Carson City dollars have experienced steady appreciation since then, whereas many other dates of common silver dollars will probably never again approach their highs of the late 1980s.

In conducting this 70 year price history there were many different grade categories that could have been used for comparison, and there were many different examples of certain dates which could have chosen. But this study was designed as a simple reference tool to provide enthusiasts with a guideline to conduct further studies, and in the process demonstrate the upward trend of prices for Carson City coins from decades past, to the present.

In some cases, such as the 1873-CC *Without Arrows* dime, dates appear so infrequently that a decade is not long enough to track their price history; for these dates the format of specific years within a decade has been modified to provide readers with at least some price information.

PRICES REALIZED FOR "CC" COINS 1932-2001*

All prices are for Uncirculated Coins Unless Otherwise Noted

The Silver Coins

CARSON CITY DIMES						
YEAR			**YEAR**			
1871			1875 MM Above Bow			
	1932	$20.00		1932	$1.25	
	1972	$925.00 (XF)		1972	$57.00	
	1982	$1,900.00 (XF)		1982	$58.00	
	1992	$2,300.00 (XF)		1992	$1,000.00 (MS-63 PCGS)	
	2001	$1,668.00 (2000) (VG)		2001	$1,840.00 (MS-65 PCGS)	
1872			1875 MM Below Bow			
	1932	$15.00		1932	$1.25	
	1972	$150.00 (F)		1972	N/A	
	1982	$825.00 (XF)		1982	N/A	
	1992	$850.00 (VF)		1992	N/A	
	2001	$4,830.00 (XF)		2001	$1,610.00 (MS-64 NGC)	
1873 *Without Arrows*			1876			
	1932	N/A		1932	$1.25	
	1952	$4,000.00 - (1950) (Eliasberg)		1972	$75.00	
	1972	N/A		1982	$450.00	
	1982	N/A		1992	$2,800.00 (MS-65 NGC)	
	1992	N/A		2001	$345.00 (MS-64 ICG)	
	2001	$632,500.00 (1999) (MS-64 PCGS)				
1873 *With Arrows*			1877			
	1932	$25.00 (F)		1932	$1.50	
	1972	$27,000.00		1972	$70.00	
	1982	$600.00 (VF)		1982	$900.00	
	1992	N/A		1992	$1,430.00 (MS-65 PCGS)	
	2001	$3,105.00 (2000) (VF)		2001	$2,300.00 (MS-66 NGC)	
1874			1878			
	1932	$25.00 (F)		1932	$10.00	
	1972	$1,450.00 (1973) (XF)		1972	$400.00 (1973) (Gem UNC)	
	1982	$7,000.00		1982	$675.00	
	1992	$2,310.00 (F)		1992	$170.00 (VF)	
	2001	$12,075.00 (XF)		2001	$1,955.00 (MS-65 PCGS)	

*Prices are for Uncirculated coins except where noted. Auction catalogs were not always consistent in grading descriptions, especially in the first seven decades of the 20th century.

CARSON CITY TWENTY CENT PIECES

YEAR			YEAR		
1875			1876		
	1932	$3.00		1932	$350.00
	1972	$455.00		1972	$24,000.00
	1982	$2,400.00		1982	$25,000.00 (XF)
	1992	$12,650.00 (MS-65 PCGS)		1992	$55,000.00 (MS-60 PCGS)
	2001	$5,750.00 (MS-65 NGC)		2001	$161,000.00 (MS-66 NGC)

CARSON CITY QUARTERS

YEAR			YEAR		
1870			1875		
	1932	$12.50		1932	$3.50
	1972	$455.00 (1973) (F)		1972	$310.00
	1982	$2,500.00 (F)		1982	$1,525.00
	1992	$3,800.00 (1991) (F)		1992	$190.00 (VF)
	2001	$27,600.00 (AU-53 NGC)		2001	$322.00 (2000) (VF)
1871			1876		
	1932	$12.50		1932	$1.25
	1972	$14,000.00 (1973) (XF)		1972	$110.00
	1982	N/A		1982	$1,815.00
	1992	$420.00 (1991) (F)		1992	$1,551.00
	2001	$4,140.00 (F-15 NGC)		2001	$3,680.00 (MS-65 PCGS)
1872			1877		
	1932	$12.50		1932	$1.25
	1972	N/A		1972	$115.00
	1982	$1,400.00 (VF)		1982	$2,500.00
	1992	$2,530.00 (XF)		1992	$990.00 (MS-63 PCGS)
	2001	$1,983.00 (VF-25 NGC)		2001	$977.00 (MS-64 PCGS)
1873 *Without Arrows*			1878		
	1932	N/A		1932	$2.50
	1972	$88,000.00 (1975 Gem UNC)		1972	$90.00
	1982	N/A		1982	$2,200.00
	1992	$286,000.00 (1991 MS-65 PCGS)		1992	$2,750.00 (MS-65 NGC)
	2001	$106,375 (1999 MS-62 PCGS)		2001	$1,782.00
1873 *With Arrows*					
	1932	$25.00			
	1972	$900.00 (VF)			
	1982	$1,600.00 (VF)			
	1992	$2,200.00 (1991) (F)			
	2001	$13,800.00 (XF-45 PCGS)			

CARSON CITY HALF DOLLARS

YEAR			YEAR		
1870			1874		
	1932	$15.00		1932	$15.00
	1972	$13,500.00 (1973)		1972	$150.00
	1982	$21,000.00		1982	$1,400.00
	1992	$16,000.00 (VF)		1992	$600.00 (XF)
	2001	$16,675.00 (AU-50 PCGS)		2001	1437.00 (VF)
1871			1875		
	1932	$15.00		1932	$5.00
	1972	$4,000.00 (1973)		1972	$90.00
	1982	$800.00		1982	$800.00
	1992	$325.00 (XF/F)		1992	$450.00
	2001	$14,300.00 (AU-55 PCGS)		2001	$1,955.00 (MS-64 NGC)
1872			1876		
	1932	$15.00		1932	$5.00
	1972	$750.00 (1973)		1972	$175.00
	1982	700.00 (VF)		1982	$1,800.00
	1992	$130.00 (VF)		1992	$1,815.00 (MS-63 NGC)
	2001	$632.00 (XF)		2001	$4,140.00 (MS-65 PCGS)
1873 *Without Arrows*			1877		
	1932	$20.00		1932	$5.00
	1972	$2,100.00		1972	$150.00
	1982	$8,500.00		1982	$2,000.00
	1992	$1,430.00 (1991) (XF)		1992	$900.00 (MS-63 PCGS)
	2001	$23,000.00 (MS-64 PCGS)		2001	$1,783.00 (MS-64 PCGS)
1873 *With Arrows*			1878		
	1932	$12.50		1932	$10.00
	1972	$725.00		1972	$14,000.00
	1982	$350.00 (XF)		1982	$2,000.00
	1992	$2,200.00		1992	$1,980.00 (XF PCGS)
	2001	$21,850.00 (MS-65 NGC)		2001	$18,400.00 (MS-63 NGC)

CARSON CITY SEATED LIBERTY DOLLARS

YEAR			YEAR		
1870			1872		
	1932	$15.00		1932	$20.00
	1972	$750.00		1972	$1,500.00
	1982	$1,500.00		1982	$3,750.00
	1992	$1,850.00		1992	$13,750.00
	2001	$36,800.00 (MS-63 PCGS)		2001	$17,250.00 (MS-60 PCGS)
1871			1873		
	1932	$50.00		1932	$50.00
	1972	$650.00 (VF)		1972	N/A
	1982	$6,500.00		1982	$3,750.00
	1992	$10,725.00		1992	$7,150.00 (VF PCGS)
	2001	$19,550.00 (AU-55 PCGS)		2001	$13,512.00 (AU-50 ANACS)

CARSON CITY TRADE DOLLARS

YEAR			YEAR		
1873			1876		
	1932	$7.50		1932	$5.00
	1972	$575.00		1972	$270.00
	1982	$1,950.00		1982	$1,200.00
	1992	$12,500.00		1992	$10,500.00
	2001	$74,750.00		2001	$18,400.00 (MS-64 NGC)
1874			1877		
	1932	$7.50		1932	$5.00 (VF)
	1972	$220.00		1972	$250.00
	1982	$950.00		1982	$1,900.00
	1992	$4,400.00 (MS-63 ANACS)		1992	$13,000.00
	2001	$54,625.00		2001	$7,590.00 (MS-63 PCGS)
1875			1878		
	1932	$3.50		1932	$5.00 (VF)
	1972	$325.00		1972	$1,150.00
	1982	$1,000.00		1982	$14,500.00
	1992	$3,600.00		1992	$21,000.00
	2001	$8,740.00 (MS-64 PCGS)		2001	$17,250.00 (MS-63 NGC)
1875 S/CC					
	1932	N/A			
	1972	$1,400.00			
	1982	$1,430.00			
	1992	$6,250.00			
	2001	$2,300.00 (2000) (MS-61 PCGS)			

CARSON CITY MORGAN DOLLARS

YEAR			YEAR		
1878			**1880 Third reverse**		
	1932	$4.00		1932	$6.00
	1972	$20.00		1972	$75.00
	1982	$300.00		1982	$525.00
	1992	$3,025.00 (MS-66 PCGS)		1992	$2,200.00
	2001	$2,127.00 (MS-65 ANACS)		2001	$20,700.00 (MS-67 PCGS)
1878 Prooflike			**1880 80/ 79**		
	1932	$4.00		1932	$6.00
	1972	N/A		1972	$200.00 (1973)
	1982	$385.00		1982	$310.00
	1992	$2,200.00		1992	$1,050.00
	2001	N/A		2001	$5,520.00 (MS-66 PCGS)
1879			**1880 80/ 79 Prooflike**		
	1932	$4.00		1932	$6.00
	1972	$240.00		1972	N/A
	1982	$1,875.00		1982	$600.00
	1992	$3,190.00(MS-64 PCGS)		1992	$412.00
	2001	$14,950.00 (MS-65 PCGS)		2001	$632.00 (MS-64 PCGS)
1879 Prooflike			**1880 8/ 7**		
	1932	$4.00		1932	$6.00
	1972	N/A		1972	$150.00
	1982	$2,200.00		1982	$190.00
	1992	$2,500.00		1992	$90.00
	2001	$18,400.00 (MS-64 PCGS)		2001	$287.00 (MS-64 ANACS)
1879 Capped mintmark			**1880 8/7 Third reverse**		
	1932	N/A		1932	$6.00
	1972	N/A		1972	$160.00
	1982	N/A		1982	$270.00
	1992	N/A		1992	$130.00
	2001	$13,800.00		2001	$1,898.00 (MS-66 PCGS)
1879 Capped mintmark prooflike, reverse prooflike			**1880 8/ High 7 Third reverse, prooflike**		
	1932	N/A		1932	$6.00
	1972	N/A		1972	N/A
	1982	N/A		1982	$350.00
	1992	N/A		1992	N/A
	2001	$8,625.00		2001	$368.00 (MS-64 ANACS)
1880 Prooflike			**1880 8/ Low 7 third reverse**		
	1932	$6.00		1932	$6.00
	1972	N/A		1972	$160.00
	1982	$525.00		1982	$210.00
	1992	$270.00 (MS-64 NGC)		1992	N/A
	2001	$2,990.00 (MS-65 PCGS)		2001	$661.00 (MS-65 NGC)
1880 Second reverse (Rev. of '78)			**1881**		
	1932	$6.00		1932	$10.00
	1972	N/A		1972	$76.00
	1982	$300.00		1982	$495.00
	1992	$460.00 (MS-64 PCGS)		1992	$1,870.00 (MS-66 PCGS)
	2001	$966.00 (MS-65 PCGS)		2001	$26,450.00 (MS-68 PCGS)

CARSON CITY MORGAN DOLLARS *continued*

YEAR			YEAR		
1881 Prooflike			**1885**		
	1932	$10.00		1932	$20.00
	1972	N/A		1972	$64.00
	1982	$550.00		1982	$550.00
	1992	$1,430.00		1992	$5,280.00 (MS-67 PCGS)
	2001	$2,645.00 (MS-66 PCGS)		2001	$4,945.00 (MS-67 PCGS)
1881 8/7			**1885 Prooflike**		
	1932	$10.00		1932	$20.00
	1972	N/A		1972	N/A
	1982	N/A		1982	$900.00
	1992	$360.00		1992	$3,520.00 (MS-66 PCGS)
	2001	N/A		2001	$3,910.00 (MS-66 PCGS)
1882			**1889**		
	1932	$3.00		1932	$5.00
	1972	$38.00		1972	$1,500.00
	1982	$350.00		1982	$17,500.00
	1992	$1,265.00 (MS-66 PCGS)		1992	$5,775.00 (MS-60 PCGS)
	2001	$46,000.00 (SP-65 NGC)		2001	$529,000.00(MS-68 PCGS)
1882 Prooflike			**1889 Prooflike**		
	1932	$3.00		1932	$5.00
	1972	N/A		1972	N/A
	1982	$600.00		1982	$10,250.00
	1992	$1,320.00 (MS-65 PCGS)		1992	$15,950.0 (MS-63 NGC)
	2001	$2,875.00 (MS-66 PCGS)		2001	$60,950.00 (MS-64 PCGS)
1883			**1890**		
	1932	$3.50		1932	$3.00
	1972	$40.00		1972	$55.00
	1982	$200.00		1982	$680.00
	1992	$1,850.00		1992	$4,290.00 (MS-65 PCGS)
	2001	$4,140.00 (MS-67 PCGS)		2001	$16,100.00 (MS-66 PCGS)
1883 Prooflike			**1890 Prooflike**		
	1932	$3.50		1932	$3.00
	1972	N/A		1972	N/A
	1982	$375.00		1982	$850.00
	1992	$226.00 (MS-65 NGC)		1992	$1,650.00
	2001	$1,955.00 (MS-66 PCGS)		2001	$1,552.00 (MS-64 PCGS)
1884			**1891**		
	1932	$10.00		1932	$3.00
	1972	$44.00		1972	$42.00
	1982	$240.00		1982	$600.00
	1992	$1,050.00 (MS-66 PCGS)		1992	$5,775.00 (MS-66 PCGS)
	2001	$4,945.00 (MS-67 PCGS)		2001	$7,935.00 (MS-66 PCGS)
1884 Prooflike			**1891 Prooflike**		
	1932	$10.00		1932	$3.00
	1972	N/A		1972	N/A
	1982	$475.00		1982	$700.00
	1992	$2,200.00		1992	$660.00
	2001	$3,220.00 (MS-67 ANACS)		2001	$1,552.00 (MS-64 ANACS)

CARSON CITY MORGAN DOLLARS *continued*

YEAR			YEAR		
1892			1893		
	1932	$5.00		1932	$5.00
	1972	$72.00		1972	$410.00
	1982	$1,000.00		1982	$1,600.00
	1992	$7,150.00 (MS-66 PCGS)		1992	$6,800.00 (MS-64 PCGS)
	2001	$21,850.00 (MS-66 PCGS)		2001	$34,500.00 (MS-65 PCGS)
1892 Prooflike			1893 Prooflike		
	1932	$5.00		1932	$5.00
	1972	N/A		1972	N/A
	1982	$1,600.00		1982	N/A
	1992	$7,700.00 (MS-64 PCGS)		1992	$10,450.00 (MS-64 PCGS)
	2001	$4,025.00 (MS-65 ANACS)		2001	$2,012.00 (MS-62 PCGS)

The Gold Coins

CARSON CITY $5.00 GOLD PIECES

YEAR			YEAR		
1870			1877		
	1932	$25.00 (XF)		1932	$22.00 (VF)
	1972	$385.00 (VG)		1972	$1,100 (1973) (XF)
	1982	$2,360.00		1982	$1,210.00 (VF)
	1992	$11,000.00 (XF PCGS)		1992	$2,640.00 (XF NGC)
	2001	$13,800.00 (XF)		2001	$2,990.00 (2000) (XF)
1871			1878		
	1932	$25.00 (XF)		1932	$23.00 (XF)
	1972	$150.00 (VG)		1972	$825.00 (VF)
	1982	$1,210.00 (XF)		1982	$2,200.00 (XF)
	1992	$2,970.00 (XF NGC)		1992	$1,700.00 (VF)
	2001	$23,000.00		2001	$2,415.00 (VF-25 ANACS)
1872			1879		
	1932	$20.00 (VF)		1932	$25.00 (VF)
	1972	$975.00 (1973) (XF)		1972	$300.00
	1982	$715.00 (VF)		1982	$660.00 (VF)
	1992	$687.00 (VF PCGS)		1992	$1,375.00 (XF PCGS)
	2001	$12,075 (AU-50 PCGS)		2001	$3,680.00 (AU-55 PCGS)
1873			1880		
	1932	$21.00 (VF)		1932	$12.00 (XF)
	1972	$310.00 (XF)		1972	$180.00
	1982	$495.00 (VF)		1982	$825.00
	1992	$5,000.00 (XF)		1992	$1,760.00 (NGC AU)
	2001	$12,075.00 (XF-45 PCGS)		2001	$9,200.00 (MS-61 NGC)
1874			1881		
	1932	$21.00 (VF)		1932	$24.00 (AU)
	1972	$200.00 (VF)		1972	$250.00
	1982	$605.00 (XF)		1982	$495.00 (XF)
	1992	$525.00 (VF)		1992	$1,155 (XF ANACS)
	2001	$10,637.00 (AU-58 PCGS)		2001	$4,600.00 (AU-53 ICG)
1875			1882		
	1932	$22.00 (XF)		1932	$15.00 (VF)
	1972	$120.00 (F)		1972	$120.00
	1982	$522.00 (VF)		1982	$1,815.00
	1992	$3,500.00 (XF NGC)		1992	$660.00 (PCGS AU)
	2001	$8,625.00 (AU-55 NGC)		2001	$2,760.00
1876			1883		
	1932	$25.00 (XF)		1932	$15.00 (XF)
	1972	$325.00 (VF)		1972	$210.00
	1982	$26,400.00		1982	$605.00 (XF)
	1992	$4,620.00 (XF PCGS)		1992	$9,817.00 (MS-60 PCGS)
	2001	$1,150.00 (VF)		2001	$6,900.00 (AU-58 PCGS)

CARSON CITY $5.00 GOLD PIECES *continued*

YEAR						
1884						
	1932	$17.00 (VF)				
	1972	$190 (XF)				
	1982	$935.00 (XF)				
	1992	$5,060.00 (AU-58 PCGS)				
	2001	$6,037.00 (AU-58 NGC)				
1890			1892			
	1932	$11.00 (XF)		1932	$10.00 (AU)	
	1972	$97.00		1972	$77.00 (XF)	
	1982	$1,980.00		1982	$4,400.00	
	1992	$1,200.00		1992	$1,100.00	
	2001	$6,900.00 (MS-64 PCGS)		2001	$1,870.00	
1891			1893			
	1932	$10.00 (AU)		1932	$12.00 (AU)	
	1972	$125.00		1972	$100.00	
	1982	$347.00		1982	$1,210.00	
	1992	$1,155.00		1992	$1,900.00 (MS-60 NGC)	
	2001	$4,600.00 (MS-64 PCGS)		2001	$2,875.00 (MS-62 PCGS)	

CARSON CITY $10.00 GOLD PIECES

YEAR			YEAR		
1870			1875		
	1932	$45.00 (VF)		1932	$37.00 (XF)
	1972	$750.00 (VF)		1972	$325.00 (1973 VF)
	1982	$3,575.00 (VF)		1982	$1,980.00 (XF)
	1992	$4,100.00 (VF)		1992	$4,400.00 (XF ANACS)
	2001	$21,850.00 (AU-50 NGC)		2001	$12,650.00 (AU-50 NGC)
1871			1876		
	1932	$35.00 (VF)		1932	$35.00 (XF)
	1972	$450.00 (XF)		1972	$600.00 (1973 VF)
	1982	$2,420 (XF)		1982	$1,540.00 (VF)
	1992	$6,325.00 (XF PCGS)		1992	$7,975.00 (XF PCGS)
	2001	$9,200.00 (AU-50 ANACS)		2001	$10,925.00 (AU-53 PCGS)
1872			1877		
	1932	$30.00 (VF)		1932	$35.00 (AU)
	1972	$955.00 (1973) (XF)		1972	$1,000.00 (1973)
	1982	$935.00 (VF)		1982	$2,000.00
	1992	$9,075 (XF NGC)		1992	$5,775.00 (XF PCGS)
	2001	$20,125.00 (AU-50 PCGS)		2001	$1,782.00 (VF-25 PCGS)
1873			1878		
	1932	$36.00 (XF)		1932	$40.00 (AU)
	1972	$390.00 (VF)		1972	$1,000.000 (1973) (XF)
	1982	$1,600.00 (XF)		1982	$1,760.00 (VF)
	1992	$7,150.00 (XF)		1992	$20,350.00 (AU PCGS)
	2001	$2,990.00 (VF-20 NGC)		2001	$5,635.00 (EF-40 NGC)
1874			1879		
	1932	$32.00 (VF)		1932	$38.00 (VF)
	1972	$175.00 (VF)		1972	$2,900.00 (1973) (VF)
	1982	$17,600.00		1982	$3575.00 (VF)
	1992	$8,140.00 (AU PCGS)		1992	$4,400.00 (XF)
	2001	$1,840.00 (XF-40 PCGS)		2001	$14,375.00 (AU-50 PCGS)

CARSON CITY $10.00 GOLD PIECES *continued*

YEAR			YEAR		
1880			1890		
	1932	$30.00 (XF)		1932	$38.00 (XF)
	1972	$220.00		1972	$160.00
	1982	$600.00		1982	$925.00
	1992	$1,155.00		1992	$1,150.00 (MS-60 PCGS)
	2001	$2,875.00 (AU-55 NGC)		2001	$3,105.00 (MS-62 NGC)
1881			1891		
	1932	$35.00 (XF)		1932	$15.00 (AU)
	1972	$100.00 (XF)		1972	$130.00
	1982	$3,850.00		1982	$1,155.00
	1992	$5,750.00 (MS-60 ANACS)		1992	$1,800.00 (MS-60 NGC)
	2001	$4,370.00 (MS-61 PCGS)		2001	$1,150.00 (MS-62 PCGS)
1882			1892		
	1932	$35.00 (AU)		1932	$30.00 (VF)
	1972	$482.00		1972	$75.00 (XF)
	1982	$3,080.00		1982	$9,900.00
	1992	$5,060.00 (PCGS UNC)		1992	$715.00 (PCGS AU)
	2001	$2,875.00 (AU-50 PCGS)		2001	$2,070.00 (AU-58 PCGS)
1883			1893		
	1932	$20.00 (VF)		1932	$35.00 (XF)
	1972	$140.00 (XF)		1972	$85.00 (XF)
	1982	$825.00 (XF)		1982	$605.00 (XF)
	1992	$1,760.00		1992	$2,420.00 (PCGS UNC)
	2001	$9,545.00 (MS-60 NGC)		2001	$1,288.00 (AU-55 ANACS)
1884					
	1932	$40.00 (AU)			
	1972	$200.00			
	1982	$800.00			
	1992	$5,775.00 (NGC UNC)			
	2001	$5,520.00 (AU-58 PCGS)			

CARSON CITY $20.00 GOLD PIECES

YEAR			YEAR		
1870			1872		
	1932	$60.00 (VF)		1932	$36.00 (VF)
	1972	$24,000.00 (1973)(AU)		1972	$180.00 (VF)
	1982	$22,000.00 (VF)		1982	$1,100.00 (XF)
	1992	N/A		1992	$3,740.00 (AU)
	2001	$89,125.00 (VF-25 NGC)		2001	$6,210.00 (AU-55 PCGS)
1871			1873		
	1932	$45.00 (VF)		1932	$35.00 (VF)
	1972	$1,250.00 (1973)(VF)		1972	$475.00
	1982	$1,650.00 (VF)		1982	$500.00 (VF)
	1992	$3,960.00 (XF PCGS)		1992	$5,060.00 (AU PCGS)
	2001	$13,225.00 (XF-40 PCGS)		2001	$3,737.00 (AU-53 NGC)

CARSON CITY $20.00 GOLD PIECES

YEAR			YEAR		
			1883		
	1932	$35.00 (VF)		1932	$35.00 (VF)
	1972	$250.00 (XF)		1972	$250.00 (XF)
	1982	$1,320.00		1982	$1,320.00
	1992	$6,325.00 (MS-60 PCGS)		1992	$6,325.00 (MS-60 PCGS)
	2001	$4,255.00 (MS-61 NGC)		2001	$4,255.00 (MS-61 NGC)
1874			1884		
	1932	$35.00 (XF)		1932	$32.00 (VF)
	1972	$380.00 (AU)		1972	$300.00
	1982	$1,045.00 (XF)		1982	$1,320.00
	1992	$1,650.00 (NGC AU)		1992	$2,255.00 (MS-60 PCGS)
	2001	$2,846.00 (AU-58 NGC)		2001	$2,760.00 (MS-61 PCGS)
1875			1885		
	1932	$45.00 (AU)		1932	$47.00 (XF)
	1972	$270.00		1972	$950.00
	1982	$950.00		1982	$3,080.00
	1992	$13,000.00 (NGC MS-63)		1992	$3,190.00 (PCGS UNC)
	2001	$6,210.00 (MS-62 PCGS)		2001	$9,200.00
1876			1889		
	1932	$35.00 (AU)		1932	$45.00 (XF)
	1972	$230.00		1972	$475.00
	1982	$1,100.00		1982	$1,350.00
	1992	$13,750.00 (MS-60 PCGS)		1992	$2,970.00 (MS-60 ANACS)
	2001	$4,140.00		2001	$2,185.00 (AU)
1877			1890		
	1932	$40.00 (XF)		1932	$40.00 (XF)
	1972	$120.00 (VF)		1972	$290.00
	1982	$935.00 (XF)		1982	$2,970.00
	1992	$2,700.00 (AU)		1992	$3,080.00
	2001	$13,225.00 (MS-61 NGC)		2001	$5,175.00 (MS-62 NGC)
1878			1891		
	1932	$35.00 (AU)		1932	$40.00 (XF)
	1972	$285.00 (AU)		1972	$1,900.00
	1982	$1,300.00 (AU)		1982	$3,100.00
	1992	$3,520.00 (AU NGC)		1992	$11,000.00 (XF)
	2001	$8,337.00 (AU-50 PCGS)		2001	$12,650.00 (MS-61 PCGS)
1879			1892		
	1932	$45.00 (VF)		1932	$32.00 (VF)
	1972	$420.00 (XF)		1972	$310.00
	1982	$1,500.00 (AU)		1982	$1,150.00
	1992	$7,975.00 (AU)		1992	$5,940.00 (MS-60 HLMRK)
	2001	$26,450.00 (MS-62 NGC)		2001	$5,347.00 (MS-62 PCGS)
1882			1893		
	1932	$40.00 (XF)		1932	$37.00 (AU)
	1972	$365.00		1972	$420.00
	1982	$700.00 (AU)		1982	$1,650.00
	1992	$5,060.00 (PCGS MS-62)		1992	$1,980.00 (MS-60 NGC)
	2001	$4,025.00 (MS-60 NGC)		2001	$5,290.00

Afterword

Though this book's breadth is impressive, it is not intended to be a comprehensive history of the Carson City Mint, the Comstock era, the nation's monetary system, or the political landscape of the late 19th century. Rather the author sought to open up these subjects to readers illustrating how it was all interrelated. Nor does this book intend to present comprehensive biographies of the vast number of individuals briefly profiled; rather it was the author's earnest desire to introduce readers to these fascinating people hoping to spark supplementary interest.

Readers must also keep in mind that comprehensive coverage has not been provided for every date and denomination issued at the Carson City Mint; rather the author attempted to present a fundamental preview of the complete set, showing every date in its historical context, and showcasing the most significant ones. There are encyclopedias covering each series of coins produced at the Carson City Mint that delve into much greater detail than presented within the scope of this book and at the same time still not exhausting their subjects.

In truth, there are individuals or subjects mentioned only in fleeting sentences throughout the pages of this book that deserve full chapters, and in a fair number of cases entire books. It is axiomatic of many of the subjects covered that they are inexhaustible, indeed some already having volumes written on them. Yet other subjects captured only in passing glimpses are ripe for further authorship. There are ineffable delights awaiting all who get caught up in the sweeping topic of the life and times of the Carson City Mint.

Selected Bibliography

Ahwash, Kamal M. *Encyclopedia of United States Liberty Seated Dimes 1837-1891.* Kamal Press, 1977.

Akers, David W. *Double Eagles, An Analysis of Auction Records.* Paramount Publications, 1982.

_____*John Jay Pittman Collection,* auction, May 1998.

American Heritage Dictionary. Maynard, Mass.: Houghton Mifflin, 1976.

American Park Network. *Unveiling of the Statue of Liberty,* October 28, 1886.

Annual Reports of the Director of the Mint. 1870-1901.

_____Upon the Production of Precious Metals. 1886.

_____Report on the Production of Gold and Silver in the United States.

Aquinas, St, Thomas. *St. Thomas Aquinas Summa Theologica (translated by Fathers of the English Dominican Provinco) (5 Volume Set).* Thomas More Publishing, Complete English Translation from Latin edition, June 1, 1981.

Arrington, Leonard J. "Coin and Currency in Early Utah," *Utah Historical Quarterly* 20, January, 1952.

Auction Prices Realized. Krause Publications, Inc., Iola, WI. Various years.

Auctions by Bowers and Merena, Inc. Wolfeboro, NH

_____*1993 Stetson Sale, Auction Catalog,* May 1993.

_____*1997 Louis Eliasberg Sr. Collection,* Auction Catalog. April 1997

_____*1996 Louis Eliasberg Sr. Collection,* Auction Catalog, May 1996

_____ Various catalogs

Bass, Louis. *A Treatise on Monetary Reform.* 1789.

Benjamin Harrison Papers. Library of Congress; February 18 1889.

Bible, The. Acts 3:6, Isaiah 22:13, I Samuel 4:21.

Bixler, W.K. *A Dozen Sierra Success Stories.* A Sierra Publication, 1964.

Bowen, Thomas M. *Speech to Congress,* February 1885.

Bowers, Q. David. *Silver Dollars and Trade Dollars of The United States, A Complete Encyclopedia.* New Hampshire: Bowers & Merena Galleries, August 1993.

_____*Abe Kosoff, Dean of Numismatics.* Bowers and Merena Galleries, 1985.

_____*Louis E. Eliasberg Sr. - King of Coins.* New Hampshire: Bowers and Merena Galleries, 1996.

_____*United States Dimes, Quarters, and Half Dollars.* New Hampshire: Bowers and Merena Galleries, 1986.

_____*United States Gold Coins, An Illustrated History.* New Hampshire: Bowers & Merena Galleries, December 1982.

Bowers and Ruddy, various catalogs.

Breen, Walter. *Walter Breen's Complete Encyclopedia of U.S. and Colonial Coins.* Doubleday, November, 1987.

Briggs, Larry. *Comprehensive Encyclopedia of U.S. Liberty Seated Quarter.* LBRC,1991.

Brown, George, ed. *Reminiscences of Senator William M. Stewart of Nevada.* New York: Neale Publishing Co., 1908.

Bryan, Willam J. *The Cross of Gold Speech,* 1896.

Budziszewski, J. *Revenge of The Conscience.* Spence Pub 1 Ed edition, October, 1999.

Carothers, Neil. *Fractional Money: A History of Small Coins and Fractional Paper Currency of the United States.* New Hampshire: Bowers and Merena Galleries, Inc. 1988.

Carruth, Gorton. *What Happened When: Chronology of Life and Events in America.* Harper& Row, 1989.

Carson Daily Appeal, 1865-1913,

Cartwright, A.P. *The Gold Miners.* Cape Town: Purnell, 1962.

Cerveri, Doris. *With Curry's Compliments: The Story of Abraham Curry.* Dexter Michigan: Thompson-Shore, Inc., 1990.

Chapman, H and S.H. *Richard B. Winsor Collection, Auction,* 1895.

Cogan, Cogan. *Randall, John Swan Sale, Auction,* May,1878.

Coinage Laws of the United States 1792-1894. Fourth Edition. Washington, D.C.: Government Printing Office, 1894.

Coin Dealer Newsletter, CDN, Inc.

Coin World, Sidney, Ohio; Amos Press Inc., Feb., 1964.

Coin World Almanac. Sidney, Ohio: Amos Press Inc., 1978.

Davis, Samuel P. ed. *History of Nevada.* Nevada Publications; August 1984.

Delong, Charles. Speech at Nevada Constitutional Convention in 1864, from *Desert Challenge: An interpretation of Nevada.* By Richard Lillard, Greenwood Publishing Group, August 1979.

DeQuille, Dan (William Wright). *History of the Comstock Silver Lode & Mines, Nevada & the Great Basin Region, Lake Tahoe & the High Sierras (The Far Western Frontier).* Ayer Co. Pub., June 1973.

_____ *The Big Bonanza.* Alfred A. Knopf, 1947 Reprint, Original 1876.

_____History of the Comstock Mines. F. Boegle, Virginia City, NV, 1889.

Doten, Alfred, Clark, Walter Van Tilburg, editor. *The Journals of Alfred Doten*. University of Nevada Press, February 1975.

Edmunds, Senator George F. (VT) in Congressional Globe, interview 1893.

Edwards, Jerome. *Nevada's Readings and Perspectives, "Nevada's Power Broker," "Pat McCarran and his Political Machine."*

Elliot, Gary E. and Michael S. Green. Nevada: Readings and Perspectives.

Ellis, Elmer. *Henry Moore Teller, Defender of The West*. Idaho: Caxton Printers, 1941.

Fields, Dorothy. *Sunny Side of the Street*. Song 1951.

Frandkin, Philip. *Stagecoach: Wells Fargo and the American West*. New York: Simon and Schuster source, 2002.

Freeman, Lincoln. *The Art of Success, The Duke of Nevada*. J.B. Lippincott Company, 1956.

Frossard, Edouard. *William M. Friesner Collection*. June 1894.

Galaxy Magazine, 1876.

Ghent, W.J. *Our Benevolent Feudalism*. MacMillan Company, 1902.

Gibbon Edward. *The History of the Decline And Fall of The Roman Empire*. New York: Harper, 1829,

Glass, Mary Ellen. "The Silver Governors." *Nevada Historical Society Quarterly*. 1978.

Gobrecht Journal Collective Volumes #1-4. LSCC, 1996.

Green, Michael. *Interview. Nevada Historian. Nevada, Michael S. Green and Gary S. Elliott editorials*. Nevada Readings and Perspective, Reno, Nevada Historical Society, 1997.

Greer, Brian. T*he Complete Guide to Liberty Seated Dimes*. DLRC Press, December 1992.

Groseclose, Elgin. *Money and Man: A Survey of Monetary Experience*. University of Oklahoma Press, June 1977.

GSA Promotional Brochures, 1973, 1974.

Harold, Kirk, and Donald Bruce Johnson. *National Party Platforms, 1840-1968*. University of Illinois Press, January 1990.

Harper's Weekly. Article, July 1893.

Hay, John. Letters and Diaries 1838-1905. Brown University.

Heaton, Augustus G. *A Treatise on the Coinage of the United States Branch Mints*. 1893. Reprint. New Hampshire: Bowers and Merena Galleries, Inc., 1987.

Heritage Numismatic Auctions, various catalogs.

Hetrich, Frank D. Superintendent of Carson City Mint, letter to Director of the Philadephia Mint, 1873.

Hickson, Howard. *Mint mark: "CC": The Story of the United States Mint at Carson City, Nevada. Popular Series*. No.4 ed. Guy Shipler, Carson City , NV, 1972.

House of Representatives. 49ᵗʰ Congress. Executive Document #267, U.S. Mint, Carson City, NV., Washington, D.C.: Government Printing Office, 1886.

James, Ronald M. *The Roar and the Silence: A History of Virginia City and the Comstock Lode (Wilbur S. Shepperson Series in History and Humanities)*. University of Nevada Press, September 1998.

Johnson, Donald Bruce, Harold, Kirk. *National Party Platforms, 1840-1968*. University of Illinois Press, January 1990.

Jones, John P. *Speech. Congress Senate of the United States*. Government Printing Office, 1894.

Julian, R.W., *Numismatic News*, article October 2002.

_____*Coins Magazine*, article, May 1977

Karsner, David. *Silver Dollar the Story of the Tabors*. Random House, No publishing date listed.

Kittredge, Herman. *A Biographical Appreciation of Robert G. Ingersoll*. 1911. Speech by Robert Ingersoll, Washington, D.C., 1882.

Laxalt, Robert. *Sweet Promised Land (Basque Series)*. Reno, NV: University of Nevada Press, Reprint edition October 1988.

Letter from Hill. "*Yerington to Senator Stewart, 1890.*" William M. Stewart Papers, Nevada Historical Society.

Lewis, Oscar. *The Big Four*. Comstock Book Distributors, November 1988.

Lillard, Richard G. *Desert Challenge: An Interpretation of Nevada*. Greenwood Publishing Group, August 1979. "The Desert Challenge." The *Chicago Tribune*. 1989.

Lyon County Times. May —August 1890.

Mehl, Max B, various catalogs.

Miller, Wayne. *Morgan and Peace Dollar Textbook*. Metairie, Louisiana: Adam Smith Publishing Company, 1982.

Morgan-Webb, Sir Charles. *The Money Revolution*. Committee for the Nations, 1935.

Nevada State Journal. May 8, 1890: September 5 1894:

Nevada, the Last Frontier. Norman Biltz and Associates, 1939.

New York Coin and Stamp Company. *Robert Coulton Davis Collection*, January 1890.

Numismatic Galleries, various catalogs.

Numismatic Gallery Monthly, September 1954.

Numismatic Guaranty Corporation of America Census Report. Sarasota FL: NGC, April 2003 and various editions.

Numismatist, The. ANA, various issues as noted.

Oral History Program, University of Nevada Reno,

_____Norman H. Biltz

_____Clark J. Guild

_____Claire H. Hewes

_____various interviews.

Ostrander, Gilman M. *The Great Rotten Borough.* New York: Alfred A. Knopf, 1966.

Overton, A.C. *Early Half Dollar, Die Varieties.* Donald L. Parsley, California, 1970.

Paine, Albert Bigelow. *Mark Twain, A Biography.* Harper and Brothers, 1912.

PCGS Population Report. Newport Beach, CA: PCGS, April 2003 and various editions.

Phillips, Kevin. *Wealth and Democracy: A Political History of the American Rich.* Broadway Books, May 2002.

Populists. *The Omaha Platform,* July 4, 1892.

Porter, Cole, *Don't Fence me in,* Song, 1944.

Reno Evening Gazette, July 1973.

Reno Properties. *Why Not Nevada?* Brochure, 1971.

Ritter, Gretchen. *Goldbugs and Greenbacks : The Antimonopoly Tradition and the Politics of Finance in America, 1865-1896.* Cambridge University Press, March 1997.

Rocha, Guy. "Wanted: The Real Reno." Nevada State Library and Archives. Article, *Reno Gazette Journal.* February 17, 2003.

Rockoff, H. Acknowledgement to "The Wizard of Oz as a Monetary Allegory." *Journal of Political Economy 98.* August, 1990.

Rowley, William. Interview. KNPB The Nevada Experience. Nevada.

San Francisco Chronicle. May 15, 1890.

Schlup, Leonard. "Nevada's Doctrinaire Senator: John P. Jones and the Politics of Silver in the Gilded Age." *Nevada Historical Society Quarterly. Winter 1993.*

Sherman, Senator John. *The Sherman Letters, Recollections of Forty Years in the House, Senate and Cabinet.* ed. by R.S. Thorndike 1894,1895.

Silver Institute. September 2002. www.silverinstitute.org.

Smith, Grant H. *The History of the Comstock Lode, 1850-1920.* Nevada Bureau of Mines and Geology in Association with the University of Nevada Press, revised edition 1943.

Stacks, various catalogs.

_____*2002 Queller Family Auction Catalog,* 2002.

Stevenson, Robert Louis. *Across the Plains,* London: Chattus and Windus, 1892.

Stewart, William M. Papers, Nevada Historical Society, Reno, NV.

Stone, Irving. *Men to Match My Mountains: The Opening of the Far West, 1840-1900.* Doubleday and Co., 1956.

Superior Galleries, various catalogs.

Swinton, John. *Striking for Life: Labor's Side of the Labor Question; The Right of the Workingman to a Fair Living.* Greenwood Publishing Group, January 1971.

Taxay, Don. *The United States Mint and Coinage.* Arco Pub, January 1966.

_____*Rayner, Isidor. Speech to Congress, 1893,* from *The United States Mint and Coinage.* Arco Pub, January 1966.

Territorial Enterprise, 1859-1915.

Thayer, Ernest L. *Casey at the Bat: A Ballad of the Republic Sung in the Year 1888.* Simon & Schuster (Juv), March 2003.

Time Magazine, article, June 15, 1953.

Twain, Mark. *Prince and the Pauper.* Bantam Books, November 1983.

_____*Roughing It.* Signet Book, November 1985.

U.S Coin Company, June 15, 1916 Auction.

Van Allen, Leroy C, Mallis, George. *Comprehensive Catalog and Encyclopedia Of Morgan and Peace Dollars.* Virginia Beach, VA: Worldwide Ventures Inc; 4 edition, May 1998.

Van Ryzin, Robert. *Crime of 1873: The Comstock Connection.* Iola, WI: Krause Publications, February 2001.

Virginia Chronicle, July 13, 1880.

Walbert, M.W. *The Coming Battle: A Complete History of the National Banking Money Power in the United States.* Walter Publishing, 3rd edition March 25, 1997.

White, Weimer. *The Seated Liberty Dollar 1840-1873.* New York: Sanford J. Durst, 1985..

Wiley, Randy and Bill Bugert. *The Complete Guide to Liberty Seated Half Dollars.* Virginia Beach, VA: DLRC Press, 1993.

Willem, John M. *The United States Trade Dollar.* Long Island City, NY: Western Publishing Company, 1983.

Winter, Douglas. *Gold Coins of the Carson City Mint.* Dallas, TX: DWN Publishing/Ivy Press Books, 2001.

Yeoman, R.S. *Guide Book of U.S. Coins.* edited by Kenneth Bressett, Whitman Coin Publishing, Aug 2002.

Zanjani, Sally Springmeyer. *The Unspiked Rail, Sally Springmeyer Zanjani.* University of Nevada Press, December 1981.

Index